RORTY

AND HIS CRITICS

PHILOSOPHERS AND THEIR CRITICS

General Editor: Ernest Lepore

Philosophy is an interactive enterprise. Much of it is carried out in dialogue as theories and ideas are presented and subsequently refined in the crucible of close scrutiny. The purpose of this series is to reconstruct this vital interplay among thinkers. Each book consists of a temporary assessment of an important living philosopher's work. The body of the work consists of a collection of essays written by a group of critics addressing the substantial theses of the philosopher's corpus. Each is followed by an essay in which the philosopher responds to his or her critics, clarifies crucial points of the discussion, or updates his or her doctrines.

RORTY

AND HIS CRITICS

Edited by

Robert B. Brandom

First published 2000

2 4 6 8 10 9 7 5 3 1

Blackwell Publishers Inc.
350 Main Street
Malden, Massachusetts 02148
USA

Blackwell Publishers Ltd
108 Cowley Road
Oxford OX4 1JF
UK

Library of Congress Cataloging-in-Publication Data
Rorty and his critics / edited by Robert B. Brandom.
    p. cm. — (Philosophers and their critics ; 9)
    Includes bibliographical references and index.
    ISBN 0-631-20981-6 (alk. paper) — ISBN 0-631-20982-4 (pbk. : alk. paper)
    1. Rorty, Richard. I. Brandom, Robert. II. Series.
B945.R524 R673 2000
191—dc21
                                                                            99-086000

British Library Cataloguing in Publication Data
A CIP catalogue record for this book is available from the British Library.

Typeset in 10pt Ehrhardt
by SetSystems Ltd, Saffron Walden, Essex
Printed in Great Britain by
T.J. International, Padstow, Cornwall

This book is printed on acid-free paper.

Contents

Notes on Contributors

BARRY ALLEN is Professor of Philosophy at McMaster University. He is the author of *Truth in Philosophy* (Harvard University Press, 1993).

AKEEL BILGRAMI is Johnsonian Professor of Philosophy, and Department Chair at Columbia University. He is the author of *Belief and Meaning* (Blackwell, 1992), and has two books forthcoming from Harvard University Press: *Self-Knowledge and Intentionality* and *Politics and The Moral Psychology of Identity*.

JACQUES BOUVERESSE is Professor at the Collège de France. Among his books is *Wittgenstein Reads Freud: The Myth of the Unconscious* (Princeton University Press, 1996).

ROBERT BRANDOM is Distinguished Service Professor of Philosophy at the University of Pittsburgh. He is the author of *Making It Explicit* (Harvard University Press, 1994), and *Articulating Reasons* (Harvard University Press, 2000).

JAMES CONANT is Professor of Philosophy at the University of Chicago. He works and teaches principally in German idealism, aesthetics, continental philosophy, Wittgenstein, early analytic philosophy, and the history of American philosophy.

DONALD DAVIDSON is Willis S. and Marion Slusser Professor of Philosophy at the University of California at Berkeley. Among his books are *Essays on Actions and Events* (Oxford University Press, 1980), *Inquiries into Truth and Interpretation* (Oxford University Press, 1984).

DANIEL DENNETT is Distinguished Arts and Sciences Professor and Director of the Center for Cognitive Studies at Tufts University. His books include *Content and Consciousness* (Routledge, 1969), *Elbow Room* (M.I.T. Press, 1984), *The International Stance* (M.I.T. Press, 1987), *Consciousness Explained* (Little, Brown, 1992), and *Darwin's Dangerous Idea* (Touchstone, 1996).

JÜRGEN HABERMAS is Emeritus Professor of Philosophy at the University of Frankfurt. Among his books are *Knowledge and Human Interests* (Beacon Press, 1971), *Theory and*

Practice (Beacon Press, 1973), *The Theory of Communicative Action*, vol. 1 (Beacon Press, 1984), *The Theory of Communicative Action*, vol. 2 (Beacon Press, 1987), and *Between Facts and Norms* (M.I.T. Press, 1996).

JOHN MCDOWELL is University Professor of Philosophy at the University of Pittsburgh. He is the author of *Mind and World* (Harvard University Press, 1994), and two volumes of collected papers: *Mind, Value, and Reality* (Harvard University Press, 1998) and *Meaning, Knowledge and Reality* (Harvard University Press, 1998).

HILARY PUTNAM is Cogan University Professor at Harvard University. His books include three volumes of *Collected Papers* (Cambridge University Press), *Meaning and the Moral Sciences* (Routledge, 1978), *Reason, Truth and History* (Cambridge University Press, 1981), *Realism with a Human Face* (Harvard University Press, 1990), *Words and Life* (Harvard University Press, 1995), and *Pragmatism* (Blackwell, 1995).

MICHAEL WILLIAMS is Charles and Emma Morrison Professor in the Humanities at Northwestern University. He is the author of *Groundless Belief* (Blackwell, 1997) and *Unnatural Doubts* (Blackwell, 1992).

Introduction

Richard Rorty is one of the most original and important philosophers writing today. He is also one of the most influential beyond the confines of professional academic philosophy. But the views that have made him famous as a public intellectual arise out of his specifically philosophical reflections on topics that remain central to the Anglo-American tradition of analytic philosophy: the nature and significance of objective reality and truth, and of our knowledge of them. In this volume, twelve philosophers – including some of the most eminent and interesting writing today – expound, assess, and critically engage with the arguments that stand behind Rorty's neopragmatism. All of them have been concerned with these topics, and with Rorty's understanding of them, for the bulk of their careers. What we are offered here are the latest, most developed stages of many-sided, intricately interwoven conversations that have been pursued fruitfully now for decades.

This volume also contains a book's worth of Rorty's most recent philosophical thinking. It provides a perspective on his work that is particularly interesting and valuable because it is focused on the topics and claims central to his thought that his most philosophically knowledgeable and sophisticated critics find most objectionable. Every serious criticism of Rorty's approach that has surfaced over the last three decades – and some are serious indeed – finds an able advocate here. The debate is sharp and vigorous throughout, with even Rorty's most sympathetic critics pressing him on points where, as it seems to them, he has "gone too far." Each interlocutor is concerned to hold Rorty's feet to the fire, to pin him down and make him say just why he should not be convicted of one or another confusion or excess. Rorty's replies are patient and complete, pointed and vigorous. It is impossible to read these exchanges without vicariously participating, taking sides, thinking things through with the authors.

The book begins with a long new essay by Rorty, "Universality and Truth," which continues a long-standing dialogue with Jürgen Habermas. It presents Rorty's arguments against the necessity of understanding ordinary empirical assertions as universal validity claims, which implicitly involve undertaking a commitment to justify them rationally to any and all potential challengers. It is followed by Habermas' complementary assessment of Rorty's arguments for the intelligibility and adequacy of construing knowledge claims in terms of a more particularistic justificatory responsibility – one tied indexically to *our* community – and then by a substantial response from Rorty in turn. In the next essay, Donald Davidson argues, on the basis of considerations that are common to his approach and to Rorty's, that a notion of truth more robust than Rorty will admit is required to make sense of our interpretations of others as engaged in *meaningful* discourse. Besides Rorty's reply, Davidsonian themes are pursued in detail by both McDowell and Ramberg. Rorty's characteristically trenchant responses bring discussions in this area to a new level. This sort of Socratic dialogue, which characterizes the whole book, is philosophy at its best; it allows a much deeper understanding of the issues than is possible from reading an article, or even a book, presenting just one point of view.

Rorty holds some distinctive and distinctively philosophical views. In his essay in this volume, Bjørn Ramberg summarizes some of the more important ones this way:

> For thirty years or more, Rorty has worked to break the grip on analytic philosophy of two problem-defining assumptions. The first is the Kantian idea that knowledge, or thinking generally, must be understood in terms of some relation between what the world offers up to the thinker, on one side, and on the other the active subjective capacities by which the thinker structures for cognitive use what the world thus provides. The second is the Platonic conviction that there must be some particular form of description of things, which, by virtue of its ability to accurately map, reflect, or otherwise latch on to just those kinds through which the world presents itself to would-be knowers, is the form in which any literally true – or cognitively significant, or ontologically ingenuous – statement must be couched. Together, these comprise what Rorty calls representationalism.

As we'll see, the primary focus of this volume is a set of core arguments concerning the notions of truth, objectivity, and reality. But we can ask a more general question about Rorty's metaphilosophical views: what is his attitude toward this corner of the high culture? The answer may seem obvious. In his classic work, *Philosophy and the Mirror of Nature*, he notoriously prophesized approvingly the "death of philosophy." Although he now regrets this bit of rhetoric – he certainly never meant to deny that we would always need professors to help students read the great books that make up the philosophical tradition, for instance – he has never relinquished his commitment to the dissolution of a certain sort of philosophy: philosophy as a discipline with epistemology at its heart, a sort of super-science, limning the limits of the knowable, explaining the nature of the relationship between reality and our representations of it. Philosophy so conceived he presents as a literary genre that arose in response to particular historical demands and conditions, and which has outlived its usefulness. His subsequent willingness to engage and converse with post-modern literary theorists gave some (I would say: those who were not paying close attention to what he was actually saying in those conversations) the impression that he considered philosophy itself *vieux jeux*. As is clear from the discussion in this volume, this impression is about as far from the truth as it well could be. In fact Rorty sees philosophy as having an absolutely crucial cultural role to play in the current situation – a role far more significant than that envisaged by most analytic philosophers.

Jacques Bouveresse, in his contribution to this volume, summarizes what is perhaps Rorty's master idea like this:

> For Rorty, the idea that matter, spirit, the self or other such things have an intrinsic nature that in principle is in no way dependent upon our activities of knowing and that we attempt to represent in increasingly better ways, represents the secular descendent of a conception which should not have survived the era of the theological world-view from which it emerged.

John McDowell offers a fuller version:

> An illuminating context for Rorty's campaign against epistemology is a Deweyan narrative of Western culture's coming to maturity.
>
> In simple outline, the story goes like this. The sense of sin from which Dewey freed himself was a reflection of a religious outlook according to which human beings were called on to humble themselves before a non-human authority. Such a posture is infantile in its submissiveness to something other than ourselves. If human beings are to achieve maturity, they need to follow Dewey in liberating themselves from this sort of religion, a religion of abasement before the divine Other. But a humanism that goes no further than that is still incomplete. We need a counterpart secular emancipation as well. In the period in the development of Western culture during which the God who figures in that sort of religion was stricken, so to speak, with his mortal illness, the illness that was going to lead to the demise famously announced by Nietzsche, some European intellectuals found themselves conceiving the secular world, the putative object of everyday and scientific knowledge, in ways that paralleled that humanly immature conception of the divine. This is a secular analogue to a religion of abasement, and human maturity requires that we liberate ourselves from it as well as from its religious counterpart.
>
> What Rorty takes to parallel authoritarian religion is the very idea that in everyday and scientific investigation we submit to standards constituted by the things themselves, the reality that is supposed to be the topic of the investigation. Accepting that idea, Rorty suggests, is casting the world in the role of the non-human Other before which we are to humble ourselves. Full human maturity would require us to acknowledge authority only if the acknowledgement does not involve abasing ourselves before something non-human. The only authority that meets this requirement is that of human consensus. If we conceive inquiry and judgment in terms of making ourselves answerable to the world, as opposed to being answerable to our fellows, we are merely postponing the completion of the humanism whose achievement begins with discarding authoritarian religion.
>
> The idea of answerability to the world is central to the discourse of objectivity. So Rorty's call is to abandon the discourse, the vocabulary, of objectivity, and work instead towards expanding human solidarity. Viewed in the context I have just sketched, this invitation has a world-historical character. As Rorty sees things, participating in the discourse of objectivity merely prolongs a cultural and intellectual infantilism, and persuading people to renounce the vocabulary of objectivity should facilitate the achievement of full human maturity. This would be a contribution to world history that is, perhaps surprisingly, within the power of mere intellectuals.

In fact, it is not just intellectuals in general who have this world-historical task; it is *philosophers* in particular. That undertaking is nothing less than to complete the project of the Enlightenment, as Kant codifies it in "Was ist Aufklärung?": to bring humanity out of its adolescence into full maturity, by taking *responsibility* for ourselves, where before we had been able only to acknowledge the dictates of an alien *authority*. Rorty's biggest idea is that the next progressive step in the development of our understanding of things and ourselves is to do for epistemology what the first phase of the Enlightenment did for religion. Before the first transformation, it was widely believed that essential practices of assessing actions as good or bad, better or worse, worthy or unworthy depended for their very intelligibility on being grounded in the authority of a special kind of thing: God. In advance of the second transformation, it is widely believed that essential practices of assessing empirical claims as true or false, more or less justified, rationally credible or not, depend for their very intelligibility on being grounded in the authority of a special kind of thing: objective reality. Rorty thinks that just as we have learned to understand moral assessments in terms of relations among humans, without needing to appeal to any sort of authority apart from that manifested in social practices, so we should learn to understand cognitive assessments in terms of relations among humans, without needing to appeal to any sort of authority apart from that manifested in social practices. From his point of view, the howls of outrage that his claim tends to elicit – the accusations of inviting cognitive irresponsibility, severing our connections to the world, undercutting the distinction between true claims and merely fashionable ones, and so on – are to be compared to the analogous responses of the pious during the first round of Enlightenment. Pragmatist views of cognition are to show us how to do without ontologically grounded extra-social authority on the theoretical side, as secular views of morality showed us how to do without ontologically grounded extra-social authority on the practical side.

This idea is deservedly controversial. In what ways are the two cases analogous and disanalogous? Is the idea of an external *cognitive* authority (the idea that we are responsible for the correctness and rational justifiability of our beliefs to an objective reality construed as prior to and independent of our practices) really objectionable in the same ways and for the same reasons that the idea of an external *moral* authority (the idea that we are responsible for the correctness and rational justifiability of our actions to the commands of a God construed as prior to and independent of our practices) is objectionable? Is it necessary, desirable, or even possible to come to understand our practices of assessing claims to truth and justification – the practices that provide the cash for our talk of being concerned to get things right – in terms that don't appeal to the notion of an objective world whose authority we are acknowledging by making those assessments? These are evidently real and important questions. Every essay in this volume pursues these sorts of questions raised by Rorty's master idea. But whatever verdict one might come to upon considering those critical arguments and Rorty's responses, it is clear that one criticism that can*not* be directed at this thought is that it lacks philosophical ambition. Rorty's claim is that philosophy now has a desperately important mission: liberating humanity from the most deeply rooted form of superstition, mystification, and disavowal of our responsibilities that we are now in a position to bring into view, one that, if he is right, keeps us from understanding the real lessons we ought to learn from the rise of modern science – the most spectacularly successful social institution of the last three hundred years.

In his response to Michael Williams, Rorty summarizes a number of the themes that structure his attitude toward philosophy:

> I shall conclude by using another handle to pick up the question "Where would we be if epistemology fell apart?" . . . This handle is the realism-vs.-antirealism debate. That debate is a downmarket version of the nineteenth-century debate between those who did not want to let go of religion and those who thought that, now that we knew how things worked, we could forget God . . . Nowadays the role once played by defenders of religious belief is played by defenders of realism. These people are the defenders of what they call "sound common sense" against radical innovation. They think they know the answer to the demarcation problem: the natural sciences are in touch with The Intrinsic Nature of Reality, and perhaps no other portion of culture is. In their view, people who do not accept this answer are undermining civilization as we know it (the same view that Wilberforce took of T. H. Huxley). Such people lack humility; they lack respect for non-human Reality. To have this humility is to grant the knowledge-claims of the natural scientist a special character – "objectivity", or "objective truth." (As I say in my "Response to Daniel Dennett," many contemporary calls to resist the subversive power of 'post-modernism' are expressions of scientistic cultural chauvinism.) . . . If we ever did lose this

sense of pathos, then the question I suggested was definatory of philosophy would be answered. The answer would be "No, there is nothing non-human out there with which we need to get in touch, because human beings have always been in causal touch with the rest of the universe, and that is the only kind of touch there is." Would that be the end of philosophy? Certainly not. There would still be the need to reconcile the old and the new – to reshape old metaphors and vocabularies so as to accommodate them to new insights. That is why philosophy will last as long cultural change does. But philosophy may eventually cease to be thought of as a super-science, or as supplying a foundation for science, or as a substitute for religion, or as supplying weapons to be used to defend either religion or science against their cultured despisers. Philosophy would be a matter of conciliating the human present with the human past. If this comes to pass, the science–religion debate and the realism–antirealism debate will seem equally quaint.

Understanding Rorty's views about *philosophy*, then, requires keeping firmly in view both the critical and the positive sides: both what he thinks philosophy ought not and cannot continue to do, and what he thinks philosophy ought and must do. A similar caution is in order concerning his views towards *science*. Like Arthur Fine (in his discussion of the "natural ontological attitude"), Rorty wants to distinguish between the attitudes that are implicit in the pursuit of scientific inquiry and a certain theoretical overinterpretation of those attitudes: between scientific practice and scientistic theories of those practices. His criticisms of scientistic views of the ontological privilege and unique authority of science – of the view that, in Sellars' formulation, "Science is the measure of all things, of those that are, that they are, and of those that are not, that they are not" – have been mistaken for expressions of an antiscientific cultural bias. (This note is struck, in various ways, in Bilgrami's essay, by Dennett, and by Putnam.) Here is a representative sample of the sort of passages in which Rorty assaults the way modern philosophy has sought to understand modern science:[1]

> Galileo and his followers discovered, and subsequent centuries have amply confirmed, that you get much better predictions by thinking of things as masses of particles blindly bumping into each other than by thinking of them as Aristotle thought of them – animistically, teleologically, and anthropomorphically. They also discovered that you get a better handle on the universe by thinking of it as infinite and cold and comfortless than by thinking of it as finite, homey, planned, and relevant to human concerns. Finally, they discovered that if you view planets or missiles or corpuscles as point-masses, you can get nice, simple, predictive laws by looking for nice simple mathematical ratios. These discoveries are the basis of modern technological civilization. We can hardly be too grateful to them. But they do not, *pace* Descartes and Kant, point [to] any epistemological moral. They do not tell us anything about the nature of science or rationality. In particular, they did not result from the use of, nor do they exemplify, something called "the scientific method."
>
> [A] host of philosophers ... have spent the last hundred years trying to use notions like 'objectivity', 'rigor', and 'method' to isolate science from nonscience. They have done this because they thought that the idea that we can explain scientific success in terms of discovering Nature's Own Language must, *somehow*, be right ... Very few thinkers have suggested that maybe science doesn't *have* a secret of success – that there is *no* metaphysical or epistemological or transcendental explanation of why Galileo's vocabulary has worked so well so far, any more than there is an explanation of why the vocabulary of liberal democracy has worked so well so far ...

By contrast, Rorty's view is that:

'Method' and 'rationality' are names for a suitable balance between respect for the opinions of one's fellows and respect for the stubbornness of sensation.

He sees science "as one more human activity, rather than as the place at which human beings encounter a 'hard', nonhuman reality."[2] The vocabularies of the natural sciences are very successful tools for pursuing certain sorts of important purposes, including prediction and control. But for Rorty those purposes have no unique significance in virtue of which the vocabularies best suited to their pursuit deserve to be taken to put us in touch with how things *really* are, in a way that contrasts invidiously with the sort of "contact with reality" provided by other vocabularies. He is taking issue, not with their pre-eminence within their own practical domain, but with conclusions drawn from that fact about the pre-eminence of these vocabularies and how we ought theoretically to understand the relations among the various vocabularies and their domains. Again, Rorty is making a large, hugely controversial philosophical claim (one that, once again, grows out of a reading of the history of philosophy in its relation to other parts of the culture). But the target his criticism aims at is scientism – the philosophical credentials of taking the practical success of science as reason to understand its vocabulary as putting us in closer touch with reality than others – not science itself.

Indeed, Rorty's pragmatism is, like its classical antecedents, itself a form of *naturalism*. The background for the positive alternative he suggests to a picture of vocabularies as representing how things really are (a task some do better than others) is of vocabularies as *tools*, employed by natural creatures in a natural world. "The world can, once we have programmed ourselves with a language, cause us to hold beliefs."[3] Different vocabularies equip us with beliefs that are of more or less use in coping with the environment in various respects. And to understand the sense in which we are "in touch with reality" *all* we need to understand is that *causal* contact with the world, the sort of contact describable in the language of afferent and efferent physiology (underlying perception and action), in the context of an account of how we are (naturally) wired up and (socially) trained. Rorty agrees with Davidson that "only a belief can justify another belief." Once beliefs have been causally occasioned in us, they can stand in evidential and other rational relations to one another. But notions of *authority* and *responsibility* don't get a grip until we are already in the conceptual space opened up by the applicability of a vocabulary. Our relations to our environment are for Rorty purely causal ones, not relations of being *responsible* for the correctness of our claims to how things really are, or how things really are having *authority* over the correctness of our beliefs. To confuse these is to endorse what Sellars calls "the Myth of the Given."[4]

In taking this line, Rorty insists that he is being more resolutely naturalistic than the fans of natural science among analytic philosophers. From his point of view, they have been taken in by the tradition in modern philosophy he adverts to in the quotation above, and have allowed normative notions of authority and responsibility, correctness and incorrectness, evidence and justification to intrude into what should be a purely naturalistic story about our causal transactions with our environment. The Trojan horse that allows the enemy within the gates of naturalism is nothing other than the concept of *representation*. That is to say, at least one of the outermost vocabularies in which Rorty conducts his own philosophical discourse, the one in which he couches and motivates his version of pragmatism, is a naturalistic one.[5] Here, a certain sort of privilege is accorded to the language of natural science – as the best tool for Rorty's purposes in pushing his pragmatism. (The ultimate purpose being, as we have already seen, using philosophical arguments to bring about the next phase of the Enlightenment project for the transformation of human culture.) Like his mentors James and Dewey, Rorty is trying rigorously to think through the consequences of a naturalistic approach to human beings. And from his point of view, contemporary philosophers who pursue a naturalistic explanatory agenda suffer from a failure of nerve that prevents them from pushing it to its logical conclusion. Inheriting from the Descartes-to-Kant tradition the idea that thinking and believing should be understood in terms of representing reality, they resist the thought that the picture of reality as authoritative for the correctness of our representations is incompatible with that naturalism. For Rorty, that picture is a quasi-religious remnant that a thoroughgoing naturalism should sweep away. The fear that *cognitive* relativism must be the result of such a thoroughgoing naturalism is just the analogue of the earlier fear that *moral* relativism would result from it.

Rorty may well be wrong about what the consequences of naturalism are, but it is to say the least ironic that he should be criticized for not taking natural science sufficiently seriously. From where he stands, the issue just is what doing that requires, and what form it should take (religious awe and respect, or empirical problem solving). But the irony in the situation does not just arise from the consequences of overlooking the complexity of Rorty's views about science. For the principal *philosophical* tool that he employs to extract the pragmatist consequences he does from an overarching commitment to naturalism are due precisely to his philosophical nemesis, Kant. Rorty's naturalism leads him where it does because he follows Kant in sharply distinguishing issues of *causation* from issues of *justification*. Enforcing this distinction between the natural and the normative (according to the lessons he learned from Sellars' "Empiricism and the Philosophy of Mind") is what leads Rorty to insist that our environment can at most *cause* us to form beliefs, not *justify* them. In his reliance on this fundamental distinction, Rorty is a Kantian, even as he deploys this tool to criticize the epistemological tradition Kant represents.

If Rorty's intellectual relationship to Kant is complex, the same can be said even for his relation to religion. Most obviously, what I have characterized as his master idea turns on the good reasons the Enlightenment found to reject both the necessity and the possibility of grounding ethical judgments ontologically – on the facts about something outside of the human community. But on the other hand, his ultimate *modest* account of *progress* depends on his (secular) answer to the question he takes to be definitive of *religious* concerns: "What should we be afraid of?"[6] In his response to Habermas, for instance, he counsels the "substitution of fear for hope" in our thinking about the future. "[W]e should be retrospective rather than prospective: inquiry should be driven by concrete fears of regression rather than by abstract hopes of universality." We should think about the mistakes that we can see our ancestors made, the ways in which and the reasons for which they were parochial, cruel, and misguided. And we should examine our own practices to see in what ways we might still be committing analogous follies. For Rorty the central form of a critical argument addressed to our current practice is such an analogy to a past abuse – as, for example, when an incipient vegetarian worries about whether the fact that they are not human really justifies our treatment of animals on farms and dinner tables, thinking of what was taken to be justified by some even a generation ago on the basis of the 'sub-human' character of those to whom it was done. (The problem might be as much to do with the consequences of application associated with classification as 'sub-human', rather than just with its circumstances of application.) Or, to revert to the genuinely Rortyan example, one might worry whether the realistic fighting faith that won the day for science over religious superstition during the Enlightenment might not itself contain a subtler, harder to discern form of the same generic sort of authoritarianism and abdication of responsibility the Enlightenment diagnosed, only on the cognitive rather than the practical side. This historically grounded modest fear of making new versions of old mistakes (modeled well by the process and arguments by which the electoral franchise has been gradually extended over the centuries – and are we sure we're right in denying it to, say, fifteen-year-olds?) is Rorty's meliorist substitute for the supposed need to orient and motivate criticism by a universalist vision of how things always already in the end ought to be for creatures such as ourselves. It is somewhat ironic, but also fitting, that this substitution of concrete fear for abstract hope involves taking sides on (a contemporary version of) what Rorty himself sees as a distinctively religious set of concerns. (See his "Pragmatism as Romantic Polytheism."[7])

But this line of thought highlights another central idea animating Rorty's philosophical project: that liberal politics, too, does not need or admit a metaphysical justification, a grounding in terms of our supposed nature as, say, rational social creatures. As he says in his response to Dennett: "Part of my ambition, to paraphrase Freud, is to help it come to pass that where epistemology and metaphysics were, sociology and history shall be." He rejects the notion of transhistorical problems to which some particular set of social practices could provide the permanent ideal solution. All we should or can do is think through the problems with which a particular historical situation presents us, tinkering with and tweaking the sorts of tools that have been of use in confronting analogous difficulties in the past. Rorty thinks any fair-minded such appraisal will lead us to endorse a version of liberal democracy, improved along dimensions made visible by the trajectories of previous progress. Undertaking such a commitment while eschewing the hope of or need for a grounding in the nature of things yields the position he calls, tongue in cheek, "postmodern bourgeois liberalism." The pragmatist philosopher teaches that concrete, historically situated arguments for the advisability of some particular alteration of political practice don't need to appeal for their authority to a background of religious commandments from outside that history of practice, and they ought not to be understood as overrideable by any appeal of such a kind. Indeed, I think Rorty's concern to argue for the intelligibility of an analogous approach to scientific and epistemic practice more generally – to urge the dispensability for understanding practical cognitive progress, assessments of better and worse moves and methods of framing tropes of "getting in better touch with objective reality" – falls into place as part of the argumentative background he sees as useful and necessary for making the point he wants to make about political practice and theory. As Rorty insists more than once in these pages, in his view, "freedom is more important than truth."

Insofar as there is something to this way of thinking about Rorty's priorities, we must count as quite wrongheaded those who have pictured him as an analytic philosopher unfortunately seduced by the fashionable but unsound ideas of postmodern literary theorists. Rorty is sometimes taken to demean science by his denial that scientific uses of language hook up with reality in a way that is privileged as more *ontologically revealing* than artistic uses of language. But he is not attempting to displace science in order somehow to replace it in its cultural niche with art. (It is instructive on this score to read his critical discussion of what he takes to be two forms of romanticism – opposed to his project of completing the Enlightenment – in "Nineteenth Century Idealism and Twentieth Century Textualism."[8]) One of the dominant themes of *Contingency, Irony, and Solidarity* is that *art* should be reserved for the private sphere, that it is *politics* that is the serious business of the public sphere. As Bouveresse says in his essay in this volume:

> Generally one might say that Rorty's favorite technique, when reading authors like Derrida or Foucault, is to move into the sphere of private self-expression and self-determination, and, on this level, to redeem and recuperate everything which, when judged from the point of view of philosophical discourse destined for public use (as one is in principle meant to do), risks immediately appearing excessive, unacceptable or absurd. He has indisputably found a possible use for Derrida, one which involves reading him as one reads Proust rather than as one reads any philosopher of the tradition (authors such as Nietzsche, Wittgenstein or Heidegger included).

By relegating the postmodern literary figures he discusses to having significance in the *private* sphere, Rorty precisely denies their deployment of vocabularies the *political* significance they seem to crave. *Achieving Our Country* presents an extended argument for the conclusion that mistaking this sort of literary theorizing for genuine political discourse has deleterious political effects.

This issue points to one of the lessons that I think becomes visible when reading the essays and responses that make up this book: one will miss many of the crucial complexities of Rorty's thought if one does not take into account its *development*. In some places, Rorty himself discusses defining episodes in his philosophical career – as in this portion of his response to Jacques Bouveresse, where he addresses the point we have just been considering:

> Fifteen years ago, when I found that almost the only other American academics who were reading the Hegel-Nietzsche-Heidegger-Derrida sequence were people who taught literature rather than philosophy, I optimistically assumed that this European cultural tradition would now, at last, be represented in American universities, to everyone's benefit. I foresaw a happy and harmonious division of labor between philosophy departments (which would stay analytic, and continue to neglect both the history of philosophy and Continental philosophy) and other departments (which would take up the resulting curricular slack). That was one of the reasons I switched jobs, moving from the Princeton philosophy department to a nondepartmental job at the University of Virginia (a university that has distinguished departments of literature, and that I thought might be filled with students who would want to learn about the Hegel-Derrida sequence).
>
> I did not foresee what has actually happened: that the popularity of philosophy (under the sobriquet 'theory') in our literature departments was merely a transitional stage on the way to the development of what we in America are coming to call "the Academic Left." This new sort of 'left' has been called, by Harold Bloom, "the School of Resentment," and the name fits. Its members are typically no more interested in the romance of the Nietzsche-to-Derrida tradition than in that of the Shakespeare-Milton-Wordsworth tradition or the Jefferson-Jackson-Teddy Roosevelt-John F. Kennedy tradition. They prefer resentment to romance. They view themselves as 'subverting' such things as "the humanist subject" or "Western technocentrism" or "masculist binary oppositions." They have convinced themselves that by chanting various Derridean or Foucauldian slogans they are fighting for human freedom. They see the study of literature and philosophy *simply* as a means to political ends.
>
> The political uselessness, relative illiteracy, and tiresomely self-congratulatory enthusiasm of this new Academic Left, together with its continual invocation of the names of Derrida and Foucault, have conspired to give these latter thinkers a bad name in the United States. This complicates my own situation, since I have to keep insisting that my admiration for these two men does not extend to an admiration for their disciples, the

resentful specialists in subversion. Nevertheless, philosophical colleagues who have remained resolutely analytic often say to me: "See what you've done! You helped smooth the way for these creeps! Aren't you ashamed of yourself?"

I am, I must admit, chastened. But I am not ashamed. I can only repeat once again: *Habent sua fata libelli.* One cannot judge an author or a book by what a particular set of readers do with it. That would be like judging Pasteur by the development of germ warfare, or Aristotle by the Inquisition. There are other things to do with Foucault and Derrida than are currently being done with them by the School of Resentment, just as there are other things to be done with Nietzsche than to use him as the Nazis used him. There is no need to solemnly expel Derrida and Foucault from a temple labeled 'philosophy' in order to show one's dislike for the uses to which their work has been put by others. The question of whether they are 'really' philosophers is, for all the reasons I have offered above, without interest. The question of whether they provide a 'model' for philosophy should be answered by saying: of course they do, and so do Plato, Hobbes, Kierkegaard, Nietzsche, Wittgenstein, and Davidson. There are as many models for participation in the conversation that Plato began as there are past participants. But there is no way to simplify one's life and one's philosophical activity by ascertaining, in *advance* of such participation, who the best models are.

The philosophical issues raised by this development arise in a number of places in this volume. The whole exchange with Bouveresse is a discussion of the attitude one ought to have toward such contemporary continental thinkers. Bouveresse approves of Rorty's characteristically deflationary attitude toward some of the most self-important claims, for instance Rorty's remark that "Heideggerese is only Heidegger's gift to us, not Being's gift to Heidegger." And Rorty acknowledges that "the effect of taking science as the model which philosophy should imitate has produced, among the analytic philosophers, a civilized and tolerant community," – close to the highest praise Rorty's lexicon admits. But he is no less deflationary about the postures and pretensions to which analytic philosophers have often been tempted, and has no patience for attempts to identify intellectual seriousness with a particular set of metaphysical commitments (paradigmatically, scientistic ones). As he says in his response to Dennett (as part of a marvelous peroration on the topic that is one of the highlights of his contribution to this volume):

> I have no wish to cast doubt on the distinction between the frivolous and the serious. That is a serious and important distinction. It is well exemplified in the contrast between the silliest, least literate, members of academic departments of literature and honest, hard-working, intellectually curious, laboratory scientists – just as the distinction between self-righteous priggery and tolerant conversability is well exemplified by the contrast between the sulkiest, least literate, members of analytic philosophy departments and honest, hard-working, intellectually curious, literary critics. Neither of these distinctions, however, has any connection with the difference of philosophical opinion between those who do and those who do not believe that truth consists in accurate representation of the intrinsic nature of reality.

Widening the focus somewhat, Dennett begins his essay with this remark about Rorty's intellectual development:

> It may be hard to see the connecting threads between the Princeton professor whose tightly argued "Incorrigibility as the Mark of the Mental" (1970) and "Functionalism, Machines, and Incorrigibility" (1972) were aimed specifically at the smallish clan of analytic philosophers of mind, and the international man of letters described by Harold

Bloom as the most interesting philosopher in the world. Can we see the stirrings of Rorty's later ideas in between the lines of his early papers in the philosophy of mind? Perhaps, but that will not be my topic.

It is, however, explicitly the topic of my contribution to the body of this volume, which appeals to the various uses Rorty makes of the concept of a *vocabulary* to forge the required link. Taking a still longer view, Habermas summarizes another take on Rorty's earliest motivations:

> In "Trotsky and the Wild Orchids" Richard Rorty casts a romantic eye back over his development as a philosopher. Using the form of a "narrative of maturation," he presents his intellectual development as a progressive distancing of himself from his adolescent dream; this was the dream of fusing in a single image the extraordinary beauty of wild orchids and the liberation from profane suffering of an exploited society: the desire "to hold reality and justice in a single vision" (Yeats). The existential background to Rorty's neopragmatism is his rebellion against the false promises of philosophy: a philosophy that pretends to be able to satisfy aesthetic and moral needs in satisfying theoretical ones. Once upon a time, metaphysics wanted to instruct its pupils in spiritual exercises involving a purifying contemplation of the good in the beautiful. But the youthful Rorty, who had allowed himself to be filled with enthusiasm by Plato, Aristotle, and Thomas Aquinas, painfully comes to realize that the prospect of contact with the reality of the extraordinary held out by theory – a contact at once *desirable* and *reconciliatory* – although possibly attainable in the more definite forms of prayer, cannot be achieved along the path of philosophy. As a result, Rorty remembers Dewey – scorned by McKeon, Leo Strauss, and Mortimer Adler – who had not yet been completely forgotten in the Chicago of the 1940s. The realization that everyday reality conceals no higher reality, no realm of being-in-itself to be disclosed ecstatically, and that everyday practices leave no room for a *redemptory* vision, cures the sobered Rorty of his Platonic sickness.

(Think back to the passage I quoted above from Rorty's response to Williams, about philosophy and the need to get in touch with something nonhuman.) Taken together, the writings that make up this book offer an invaluable picture of the complex constellation of concerns that structure and motivate Rorty's thought, and of the fascinating process by which he has arrived at and elaborated them.

It would be wrong, however, to give the impression that the discussions presented here address primarily metaphilosophical issues of grand strategy and world historical significance. All of the authors are analytically minded philosophers. Although they see the larger frame in which Rorty has put the questions that he asks and the claims that he makes, their primary concern here is the argumentative core of Rorty's systematic philosophical vision: the treatment of truth, objectivity, and *reality*. Six of the essays – Rorty's "Universality and Truth", which leads off the volume, and the contributions by Habermas, Davidson, Putnam, McDowell, and Bilgrami – look in detail at the extent to which ordinary assessments of empirical claims as meaningful or not, true or false, and more or less justified involve commitment to various notions of objective reality. Brandom, Williams, Allen, and Ramberg all deal with that same topic, although not always as their central concern. None of these critics is fully satisfied with Rorty's arguments for his claims. Even those most sympathetic to his motivations take issue with some of his formulations and justifications, typically arguing that a less radical departure from traditional ways of talking is required by the considerations he advances. Rorty's responses are pointed, spirited, and cumulatively powerful. Williams and Allen examine the way Rorty has grounded his diagnosis and recommended therapy for our current intellectual ills in an account of the history of epistemology and metaphysics. Their accounts are patient, detailed, sympathetic, and yet also critical. They lead Rorty to some reformulations, and in at least one case (see the opening of his response to Williams) a retraction of views he has long defended. Looking downstream to consequences of his views, rather than upstream to their antecedents, Bouveresse and to some extent Conant press Rorty on the political consequences of his views about truth, objectivity, and reality. Conant's essay is unique in addressing itself at length to Rorty's reading of a particular literary text – Orwell's *Nineteen Eighty Four*. Ramberg's essay on Rorty's objections to central features of Davidson's philosophy of mind (which is usefully read in conjunction with Dennett's treatment of Rorty's earlier views on the philosophy of mind) prompts Rorty to change his mind on matters of some substance. His response ends by totting up which of his previous claims he does and does not feel obliged to relinquish or adjust in the light of the considerations Ramberg advances. The intensive, extended conversation retailed here does not leave Rorty just where he was when it began. We can see throughout that he practices the conversability that he preaches.[9]

Rorty's intellectual vision and sensibility, no less than his prose, are thoroughly Jamesean: equal parts of William, Henry, and Jesse. Dazzled, as one cannot help but be, by the boldness of his conjectures and recommendations, the breathtaking scope of his generalizations, the erudite innovativeness of the connections he discerns between disparate aspects of the culture, and the sheer stylistic brilliance of his prose, it is easy to lose sight of the subtlety and complexity of Rorty's views. The essays and replies in this volume collectively should serve as a corrective to this danger.

Bob Brandom
July 12, 1999

Notes

1 From "Method, Social Science, and Social Hope," in *Consequences of Pragmatism* (University of Minnesota, 1982), pp. 191–194.
2 *Contingency, Irony, and Solidarity*, p. 4.
3 Ibid. p. 6.
4 For an account of this, see Sellars' *Empiricism and the Philosophy of Mind* (reprinted by Harvard University Press, 1997, with an Introduction by Richard Rorty, and a Study Guide by Robert Brandom).
5 In my contribution to this volume, "Vocabularies of Pragmatism: Synthesizing Naturalism and Historicism", I offer a more nuanced account of the relations between Rorty's naturalism and his historicism.
6 So characterized in his response to Williams.
7 In *Philosophy and Social Hope*.
8 In *Consequences of Pragmatism*.
9 See especially the end of his response to Dennett.

1
Universality and Truth[1]

RICHARD RORTY

I. Is the Topic of Truth Relevant to Democratic Politics?

The question of whether there are any beliefs or desires common to all human beings is of little interest apart from the vision of a utopian, inclusivist, human community – one which prides itself on the different sorts of people it welcomes, rather than on the firmness with which it keeps strangers out. Most human communities remain exclusivist: their sense of identity, and the self-images of their members, depend on pride in not being certain other sorts of people: people who worship the wrong god, eat the wrong foods, or have some other perverse, repellent, beliefs or desires. Philosophers would not bother trying to show that certain beliefs and desires are found in every society, or are implicit in some ineliminable human practice, unless they hoped to show that the existence of these beliefs demonstrates the possibility of, or the obligation to construct, a planet-wide inclusivist community. In this paper, I shall use "democratic politics" as a name for the attempt to bring such a community into existence.

One of the desires said to be universal by philosophers interested in democratic politics is the desire for truth. In the past, such philosophers have typically conjoined the claim that there is universal human agreement on the supreme desirability of truth with two further premises: that truth is correspondence to reality, and that reality has an intrinsic nature (that there is, in Nelson Goodman's terms, a Way the World Is). Given these three premises, they proceed to argue that Truth is One, and that the universal human interest in truth provides motive for creating an inclusivist community. The more of that truth we uncover, the more common ground we shall share, and the more tolerant and inclusivist we shall therefore become. The rise of relatively democratic, relatively tolerant, societies in the last few hundred years is said to be due to the increased rationality of modern times, where 'rationality' denotes the employment of an innate a truth-oriented faculty.

The three premises I have listed are sometimes said to be "necessitated by reason." But this claim is usually tautologous, for philosophers typically explain their use of the word 'reason' by listing those same three premises as "constitutive of the very idea of rationality." They view colleagues who have doubts about one or another of these three premises, as 'irrationalists.' Degrees of irrationality are attributed according to how many of these premises the distrusted philosopher denies, and also according to how much or little interest he or she shows in democratic politics.[2]

In this essay I shall consider the prospects for defending democratic politics while denying all three of the premises I have listed. I shall be arguing that what philosophers have described as the universal desire for truth is better described as the universal desire for justification.[3] The grounding premise of my argument is that you cannot aim at something, cannot work to get it, unless you can recognize it once you have got it. One difference between truth and justification is that between the unrecognizable and the recognizable. We shall never know for sure whether a given belief is true, but we can be sure that nobody is presently able to summon up any residual objections to it, that everybody agrees that it ought to be held.

There are, to be sure, what Lacanians call impossible, indefinable, sublime objects of desire. But a desire for such an object cannot be made relevant to democratic politics.[4] On my view, truth is just such an object. It is too sublime, so to speak, to be either recognized or aimed at. Justification is merely beautiful, but it is recognizable, and therefore capable of being systematically worked for. Sometimes, with luck, justification is even achieved. But that achievement is usually only temporary, since sooner or later some new objections to the temporarily justified belief will be developed. As I see it, the yearning for unconditionality – the yearning which leads philosophers to insist that we need to avoid "contextualism" and "relativism" – is, indeed, satisfied by the notion of truth. But this yearning is unhealthy, because the price of unconditionality is irrelevance to practice. So I think the topic of truth cannot be made relevant to democratic politics, and that philosophers devoted to such politics should stick to that of justification.

II.   Habermas on Communicative Reason

In order to place my view within the context of contemporary philosophical controversies, I shall begin with some comments on Habermas. Habermas draws his well-known distinction between subject-centered reason and communicative reason in connection with his attempt to separate out what is useful to democratic politics in the traditional philosophical notion of rationality from what is useless. I think that he makes a tactical error when he tries to preserve the notion of unconditionality. Although I think Habermas is absolutely right that we need to *socialize* and *linguistify* the notion of 'reason' by viewing it as communicative,[5] I also think that we should go further: we need to *naturalize* reason by dropping his claim that "a moment of *unconditionality* is built into *factual processes* of mutual understanding."[6]

Habermas, like Putnam, believes that "reason cannot be naturalized".[7] Both philosophers think it important to insist on this point in order to avoid the 'relativism' which seems to them to put democratic politics on a par with totalitarian politics. Both think it important to say that the former sort of politics is more *rational* than the latter. I do not think that we should say this, because I do not think that the notion of 'rationality' can be stretched this far.

We should instead admit that we have no neutral ground to stand on when we defend such politics against its opponents. If we do not admit this, I think we can rightly be accused of attempting to smuggle our own social practices into the definition of something universal and ineluctable, because presupposed by the practices of any and every language-user. It would be franker, and therefore better, to say that democratic politics can no more appeal to such presuppositions than can anti-democratic politics, but is none the worse for that.

Habermas agrees with the criticism which post-Nietzschean writers have made of 'logocentrism,' and specifically with their denial that "the linguistic function of representing states of affairs is the sole human monopoly."[8] So do I, but I would extend this criticism as follows: only over-attention to fact-stating would make one think that there was an aim of inquiry called "truth" in addition to that of justification. More generally, only over-attention to fact-stating would make one think that a claim to universal validity is important for democratic politics. Still more generally, abandoning the logocentric idea that *knowledge* is the distinctively human capacity would leave room for the idea that *democratic citizenship* is better suited for that role. The latter is what we human beings should take most pride in, should make central to our self-image.

As I see it, Habermas' attempt to redefine 'reason' after deciding that "the paradigm of the philosophy of consciousness is exhausted"[9] – his attempt to redescribe reason as 'communicative' through and through – is insufficiently radical. It is a half-way house between thinking in terms of validity-claims and thinking in terms of justificatory practices. It comes down half way – between the Greek idea that human beings are special because they can *know* (whereas other animals can merely cope) and Dewey's idea that we are special because we can take charge of our own evolution, take ourselves in directions which have neither precedent nor justification in either biology or history.[10]

This latter idea can be made to sound unattractive by dubbing it "Nietzschean" and construing it as a form of the ruthless will to power which was incarnate in the Nazis. I should like to make it sound attractive by dubbing it 'American' and construing it as the idea common to Emerson and Whitman, the idea of a new self-creating community, united not by knowledge of the same truths but by sharing the same generous, inclusivist, democratic hopes. The idea of communal self-creation, of realizing a dream which has no justification in unconditional claims to universal validity, sounds suspicious to Habermas and Apel because they naturally associate it with Hitler. It sounds better to Americans, because they naturally associate it with Jefferson, Whitman and Dewey.[11] The moral to be drawn, I think, is that this suggestion is neutral between Hitler and Jefferson.

If one wants neutral principles on the basis of which to decide between Hitler and Jefferson, one will have to find a way of replacing Jefferson's occasional references to natural law, and self-evident political truths, by a more up-to-date version of Enlightenment rationalism. This is the role in which Apel and Habermas cast "discourse ethics." Only if one has given up hope for such neutrality will the alternative I have suggested seem attractive. Whether one gives up that hope should, I think, be decided – at least in part – by evaluating the argument from performative self-contradiction which is at the heart of that ethics.

I see that argument as weak and unconvincing, but I have no substitute to offer. So I am inclined to reject both discourse ethics and the very idea of neutral principles, and to ask myself what philosophers might do for democratic politics other than trying to ground this politics on principles. My answer is: they can get to work substituting hope for knowledge, substituting the idea that the ability to be citizens of the full-fledged democracy which is yet to come, rather than the ability to grasp truth, is what is important about being human. This is not a matter of *Letztbegründung*, but of redescribing humanity and history in terms which makes democracy seem desirable. If doing that is said to be mere 'rhetoric' rather than 'argument,' I should rejoin that it is no more rhetorical than my opponents' attempt to describe discourse and communication in terms that make democracy seem linked to the intrinsic nature of humanity.

III.   Truth and Justification

There are many uses for the word 'true,' but the only one which could not be eliminated from our linguistic practice with relative ease is the cautionary use.[12] That is the use we make of the word when we contrast justification and truth, and say that a belief may be justified but not true. Outside of philosophy, this cautionary use is used to contrast less-informed with better-informed audiences, past audiences with future audiences. In non-philosophical contexts, the point of contrasting truth and justification is simply to remind oneself that there may be objections (arising from newly discovered data, or more ingenious explanatory hypotheses, or a shift in the vocabulary used for describing the objects under discussion) which have not yet occurred to anyone. This sort of gesture toward an unpredictable future is made, for example, when we say that our present moral and scientific beliefs may look as primitive to our remote descendants as those of the ancient Greeks look to us.

My grounding premise, that you can only work for what you could recognize, is a corollary of James' principle that a difference has to make a difference to practice before it is worth discussing. The only difference between truth and justification which makes such a difference is, as far as I can see, the difference between old audiences and new audiences. So I take the appropriate pragmatist attitude toward truth to be: it is no more necessary to have a philosophical theory about the nature of truth, or the meaning of the word 'true,' than it is to have one about the nature of danger, or the meaning of the word 'danger.' The principal reason we have a word like 'danger' in the language is to caution people: to warn them that they may not have envisaged all the consequences of their proposed action. We pragmatists, who think that beliefs are habits of action rather than attempts to correspond to reality, see the cautionary use of the word 'true' as flagging a special sort of danger. We use it to remind ourselves that people in different circumstances – people facing future audiences – may not be able to justify the belief which we have triumphantly justified to all the audiences we have encountered.

Given this pragmatist view of the truth–justification distinction, what about the claim that all human beings desire truth? This claim is ambiguous between the claim that all of them desire to justify their beliefs to some, though not necessarily all, other human beings, and the claim that they all want their beliefs to be true. The first claim is unobjectionable, and the second dubious. For the only other interpretation which we pragmatists can give to the second claim is that all human beings are concerned about the danger that some day an audience will come into being before which one of their presently justified beliefs cannot be justified.

But, in the first place, mere fallibilism is not what philosophers who hope to make the notion of truth relevant to democratic politics want. In the second place, such fallibilism is not, in fact, a feature of all human beings. It is much more prevalent among inhabitants of wealthy, secure, tolerant, inclusivist societies than elsewhere. Those are the people who are brought up to bethink themselves that they might be mistaken: that there are people out there who might disagree with them, and whose disagreements need to be taken into account. If you favor democratic politics, you will of course want to encourage fallibilism. But there are other ways to do so beside harping on the difference between the conditional character of justification and the unconditional character of truth. One might, for example, harp on the sad fact that many previous communities have betrayed their own interests by being too sure of themselves, and so failing to attend to objections raised by outsiders.

Furthermore, we should distinguish between fallibilism and philosophical skepticism. Fallibilism has nothing in particular to do with the quest for universality and unconditionality. Skepticism does. One will usually not go into philosophy unless one is impressed by the sort of skepticism found in Descartes' *Meditations*, the sort of skepticism which says that the mere possibility of error defeats knowledge-claims. Not many people find this sort of skepticism interesting, but those who do ask themselves: is there any way in which we can insure ourselves against having beliefs which may be unjustifiable to some future audience? Is there any way in which we can insure that we have beliefs which are justifiable to any and every audience?

The tiny minority which finds this question interesting consists almost entirely of philosophy professors, and divides into three groups.

(1) Skeptics like Stroud say that Descartes' argument from dreams is unanswerable; for the skeptics, there is always an audience, the future self who has awoken from the dream, which will not be satisfied by any justification offered by our present, possibly dreaming, self.

(2) Foundationalists like Chisholm say that, even if we are now dreaming, we cannot be wrong about *certain* beliefs.

(3) Coherentists like Sellars say that "all our beliefs are up for grabs, though not all at once."

We pragmatists, who have been impressed by Peirce's criticisms of Descartes, think that both skeptics and foundationalists are led astray by the picture of beliefs as attempts to represent reality, and by the associated idea that truth is a matter of correspondence to reality. So we become coherentists.[13] But we coherentists remain divided about what, if anything, needs to be said about truth. I think that, once one has explicated the distinction between justification and truth by that between present and future justifiability, there is little more to be said. My fellow-coherentists – Apel, Habermas, and Putnam – think, as Peirce also did, that there is a lot more to be said, and that saying it is important for democratic politics.[14]

IV. "Universal Validity" and "Context-Transcendence"

Putnam, Apel and Habermas all take over from Peirce an idea which I reject: the idea of convergence upon the One Truth.[15] Instead of arguing that because reality is One, and truth correspondence to that One Reality, Peircians argue that the idea of convergence is built into the presuppositions of discourse. They all agree that the principal reason why reason cannot be naturalized is that reason is normative and norms cannot be naturalized. But, they say, we can make room for the normative without going back to the traditional idea of a duty to correspond to the intrinsic nature of One Reality. We do this by attending to the universalistic character of the idealizing presuppositions of discourse. This strategy has the advantage of setting aside metaethical questions about whether there is a moral reality to which our moral judgments might hope to correspond, as our physical science supposedly corresponds to physical reality.[16]

Habermas says that every validity claim has "a transcendent moment of universal validity [which] bursts every provinciality asunder" in addition to its strategic role in some context-bound discussion. As I see it, the only truth in this idea is that many claims to validity are made by people who would be willing to defend their claims before audiences other than the one which they are currently addressing. (Not all assertions, obviously, are of this sort; lawyers, for example, are quite aware that they tailor their claims to suit the quaint context of a highly local jurisprudence.) But willingness to take on new and unfamiliar audiences is one thing; bursting provinciality asunder is another.

Habermas' doctrine of a "transcendent moment" seems to me to run together a commendable willingness to try something new with an empty boast. To say "I'll try to defend this against all comers" is often, depending upon the circumstances, a commendable attitude. But to say "I can successfully defend this against all comers" is silly. Maybe you can, but you are no more in a position to claim that you can than the village champion is to claim that he can beat the world champion. The only sort of situation in which you would be in a position to say the latter is one in which the rules of the argumentative game are agreed upon in advance – as in 'normal' (as opposed to 'revolutionary') mathematics, for example. But in most cases, including the moral and political claims in which Habermas is most interested, there are no such rules. The notion of context-dependence has a clear sense in the sorts of cases I have just mentioned – in provincial law courts and in language-games, such as normal mathematics, which are regulated by clear and explicit conventions. For most assertions, however, neither it nor that of 'universal validity' has such a sense. For assertions such as "Clinton is the better candidate," "Alexander came before Caesar," "Gold is insoluble in hydrochloric acid," it is hard to see why I should ask myself "is my claim context-dependent or universal?" No difference to practice is made by coming down in favor of one alternative rather than the other.

Habermas puts forward an analogue of this distinction between the context-dependent and the universal which might seem more relevant to practice. This analogue is what he calls "the tension between facticity and validity." He views this tension as a central philosophical problem, and says that this tension is responsible for many of the difficulties encountered in theorizing democratic politics.[17] He thinks it a distinctive and valuable feature of his theory of communicative action that it "already absorbs the tension between facticity and validity into its fundamental concepts."[18] It does so by distinguishing between the 'strategic' use of discourse and the "use of language oriented to reaching understanding."[19] This latter distinction might seem the one we are looking for: the one which lets us interpret the distinction between context-dependence and universality in a way that makes a difference to practice.

As I see it, however, the distinction between the strategic and non-strategic use of language is just the distinction between cases in which all we care about is convincing others and cases in which we hope to learn something. In the latter set of cases, we are quite willing to give up our present views if we hear something better. These cases are two ends of a spectrum, at one end of which we shall use any dirty trick we can (lying, *omissio veri*, *suggestio falsi*, etc.) to convince. At the other end we talk to others as we talk to ourselves when we are most at ease, most reflective, and most curious. Most of the time we are somewhere in the middle between these two extremes.

My problem is that I do not see that the two extremes have anything in particular to do with the distinction between context-dependence and universality. "The pure pursuit of truth" is a traditional name for the sort of conversation which takes place at one end of this spectrum. But I do not see what that sort of conversation has to do with universality or with unconditionality. It is "non-strategic" in the sense that in such conversations we let the wind blow where it listeth, but it is hard to see that the assertions we make in such conversations presuppose something which is not presupposed in the assertions I make when I am at the other end of the spectrum.

Habermas, however, thinks that unless we recognize that "the validity claims raised *hic et nunc* and aimed at intersubjective recognition or acceptance can at the same time overshoot local standards for taking yes/no positions," we shall not see that "this transcendent moment alone distinguishes the practices of justification oriented to truth claims from other practices that are regulated merely by social convention."[20] This passage is a good example of what seems to me Habermas' undesirable commitment to the logocentric distinction between opinion and knowledge – a distinction between mere obedience to *nomoi*, even the sort of *nomoi* which would be found in a utopian democratic society, and the kind of *phusei* relation to reality which is provided by the grasp of truth. Both the opinion–knowledge and the *nomos–physis* distinction appear to Deweyans like myself as remnants of Plato's obsession with the kind of certainty found in mathematics, and, more generally, with the idea that the universal, being somehow eternal and unconditional, somehow provides an escape from what is particular, temporal, and conditioned.

In this passage Habermas is, I take it, using the term "practices of justification oriented to truth claims" to refer to the nicer end of the spectrum I described above. But from my point of view, truth has nothing to do with it. These practices do not transcend social convention. Rather, they are regulated by certain *particular* social conventions: those of a society even more democratic, tolerant, leisured, wealthy and diverse than our own – one in which inclusivism is built into everybody's sense of moral identity. In this society, everybody always welcomes strange opinions on all sorts of topics. These are also the conventions of certain lucky parts of contemporary society: for example, of university seminars, of summer camps for intellectuals, and so on.[21]

Perhaps the most far-reaching difference between Habermas and me is that pragmatists like myself sympathize with the anti-metaphysical, 'postmodern,' thinkers he criticizes when they suggest that the idea of a distinction between social practice and what transcends such practice is an undesirable remnant of logocentrism. Foucault and Dewey can agree that, whether or not inquiry is always a matter of 'power,' it never transcends social practice. Both would say that the only thing that can transcend a social practice is another social practice, just as the only thing that can transcend a present audience is a future audience. Similarly, the only thing that can transcend a discursive strategy is another discursive strategy – one aimed at other, better, goals. But, because I do not know how to aim at it, I do not think that 'truth' names such a goal. I know how to aim at greater honesty, greater charity, greater patience, greater inclusiveness, and so on. I see democratic politics as serving such concrete, describable goals. But I do not see that it helps things to add 'truth' or 'universality' or 'unconditionality' to our list of goals, for I do not see what we shall do differently if such additions are made.

It may sound at this point as if the difference between me and Habermas is one that makes no difference to practice: we both have the same utopias in mind, and we both engage in the same sort of democratic politics. So why quibble about whether to call utopian communication practices "oriented to truth" or not? The answer is that Habermas thinks that it does make a difference to practice, because he gets to make an argumentative move which is not open to me: he gets to accuse his opponents of performative self-contradiction. Habermas thinks that "the universal discourse of an unbounded community of interpretation" is "unavoidably assumed" by anybody, even me, who gets into an argument. He says that "Even if these presuppositions have an *ideal* content that can only be approximately satisfied, all participants must *de facto* accept them [the presuppositions of communication] whenever they assert or deny the truth of a statement in any way and would like to enter into argumentation aimed at justifying this validity claim."[22]

But what about somebody who is outraged (as are many trustees of American universities) by the social conventions of the better parts of the better universities – places where even the most paradoxical and unpromising claims are seriously discussed, and in which feminists, atheists, homosexuals, blacks, etc. are taken seriously as moral equals and conversational partners. I take it that in Habermas' view such a person will be *contradicting* themselves if they offer *arguments* to the effect that these conventions should be replaced with other, more exclusivist, conventions. By contrast, I cannot tell the narrow-minded trustee that he is contradicting himself. I can only try to wheedle him into greater tolerance by the usual indirect means: giving examples of present platitudes which were once paradoxes, of the contributions to culture made by black lesbian atheists, and so on.[23]

The big question is whether anybody has ever been convinced by the charge of performative self-contradiction. I do not think that there are many clear examples of such a charge being taken to heart. If you tell a bigot of the sort I've sketched that he is committed to making context-surpassing validity claims, to aiming at truth, he will probably agree that that is exactly what he is doing. If you tell him that he cannot make such claims and still balk at the paradoxes or the people at whom he balks, he will probably not get the point. He will say that people who advance such paradoxes are too crazy to argue with or about, that women have a distorted view of reality, and the like. He will think it irrational or immoral, or both, to take such paradoxes and people seriously.[24]

I cannot see much difference between the bigot's reaction to me and Habermas and Habermas' and my reactions to him. I cannot see that anything like "communicative reason" favors our reactions rather than his. This is because I do not know see why the term 'reason' is not as much up for grabs as the term 'academic freedom' or 'morality' or 'pervert,' nor how the anti-foundationalist coherentism which Habermas and I share can make room for a non-recontextualizable, non-relativizable, conversation-stopper called "performative self-contradiction." What the bigot and I do, and I think should do, when told that we have violated a presupposition of communication is to haggle about the meanings of the terms used in stating the purported presupposition – terms like 'true,' 'argument,' 'reason,' 'communication,' 'domination,' etc.[25]

This haggling will, with luck, eventually turn into a mutually profitable conversation about our respective utopias – our respective ideas about what an ideal society, empowering an ideally competent audience, would look like. But this conversation is not going to end with the bigot's reluctant admission that he has entangled himself in a contradiction. Even if, *mirabile dictu*, we succeed in convincing him of the worth of our utopia, his reaction will be to regret his own previous lack of curiosity and imagination, rather than to regret his failure to spot his own presuppositions.

V. Context-Independence Without Convergence: Albrecht Wellmer's View

I agree with Apel and Habermas that Peirce was right in telling us to talk about discourse rather than about consciousness, but I think that the *only* ideal presupposed by discourse is that of being able to justify your beliefs to a *competent* audience. As a coherentist, I think that if you can get agreement from other members of such an audience about what is to be done, then you do not have to worry about your relation to reality. But everything depends upon what constitutes a competent audience. Unlike Apel and Habermas, the moral I draw from Peirce is that we philosophers who are concerned with democratic politics should leave truth alone, as a sublimely undiscuss-able topic, and instead turn to the question of how to persuade people to broaden the size of the audience they take to be competent, to increase the size of the relevant community of justification. The latter project is not only relevant to democratic politics, it pretty much *is* democratic politics.

Apel and Habermas think that the demand to maximize the size of this community is already, so to speak, built into communicative action. This is the cash value of their claim that every assertion claims universal validity.[26] Albrecht Wellmer, who, like me, rejects the convergentism Habermas and Apel share with Putnam, nevertheless accepts their claim that our truth claims "transcend the context – the local or cultural context – in which they are raised."[27] He opposes this claim to my own ethnocentrism, and interprets the latter as denying some things he thinks it important to affirm: in particular, that "the arguments for supporting and critically developing democratic-liberal principles and institutions" are 'good arguments',[28] even though they do not convince everybody.

My problem with Wellmer, Apel, and Habermas is that I do not see what the pragmatic force of saying that an argument which, like most other arguments, con-vinces certain people and not others is a "good argument." This seems like saying that a tool which, like all tools, is useful for certain purposes but not others, is a good tool. Imagine the surgeon saying, after unsuccessfully attempting to dig a tunnel out of his prison cell with his scalpel, "Still, it's a good tool." Then picture him saying, after unsuccessfully trying to argue his guards into letting him escape so that he may resume his position as leader of the resistance, "Still, they were good arguments."

My problem is intensified when I ask myself whether my truth claims "transcend my local cultural context." I have no clear idea whether they do or not, because I cannot see what "transcendence" means here. I cannot even see what the point of taking my assertion as "making a truth claim" is. When I believe that p, and express this belief by asserting it in the course of a conversation, am I making a *claim*? What is the force of saying that I am? What does saying so add to saying that I am (to speak with Peirce) informing my interlocutor about my habits of action, giving her hints about how to predict and control my future conversational and non-conversational behavior? Depending on the situation at hand, I may also be inviting her to disagree with me by telling me about her different habits of action, suggesting that I am prepared to give reasons for my belief, trying to make a good impression on her, and a thousand other things. As Austin reminded us, there are lots of things I do when I make an assertion. All of them together make up the give and take between me and my interlocutor. This give and take is a matter of, roughly, the reciprocal adjustment of our behavior, the strategic coordination of that behavior in ways which may prove to be mutually profitable.

Of course if somebody asks me, after I have asserted p, whether I believe p to be true, I shall say "yes." But I shall wonder, with Wittgenstein, what the point of his question is. Is he questioning my sincerity? Is he expressing incredulity about my ability to offer reasons for my belief? I can try to straighten things out by asking him to spell out why he asks. But if he replies: "I just wanted to be sure you were making a context-transcendent truth claim," I shall be baffled. What does he want to be reassured about, exactly? What would it be like for me to make a context-*dependent* assertion? Of course in the trivial sense that an assertion may not always be apropos, all assertions are context-dependent. But what would it mean for the proposition asserted to be context-dependent, as opposed to the speech-act being context-dependent?

I am not sure how people like Habermas and Wellmer, who have given up on correspondence theories of truth and consequently cannot distinguish between a claim to report a habit of action and a claim to represent reality, can draw this distinction between context-dependence and context-independence. My best guess is that they believe that, in Wellmer's words, "Whenever we raise a truth claim on the basis of what we take to be good arguments or compelling evidence we take the epistemic conditions prevailing here and now to be ideal in the sense that we presuppose that no arguments or evidence that would put our own truth claim into doubt will come up in the future." Or, as Wellmer also puts it, "relying upon reasons or evidences as compelling means excluding the possibility of being proven wrong as time goes on."[29]

If that is what it takes to make a context-transcendent truth claim, then I have never made one. I would not know how to exclude the possibility Wellmer describes. Nor would I know how to presuppose that no arguments or evidence will turn up in the future which will cast doubt on my belief. Relying once again on the fundamental pragmatist principle that any difference has to make a difference to practice, I want to know whether this 'excluding' and 'presupposing' are things I can decide to do or not to do. If they are, I want to know more about how to go about doing them. If they are not, they seem to me empty.

I can make my point in another way by asking: what is the difference between a metaphysician, committed to a correspondence theory of truth, telling me that, whether I know it or will admit it or not, my assertions automatically, willy-nilly, amount to a claim to represent reality accurately, and my fellow Peircians telling me that they automatically, willy-nilly, amount to an exclusion of possibilities, or a presupposition about what the future holds? In both cases I am being told that I presuppose something which, even after considerable reflection, I do not think I believe. But the notion of 'presupposition,' when it is extended to beliefs which the purported presupposer stoutly denies, becomes hard to distinguish from the notion of "redescription of person A in person B's terms." If A can explain what she is doing and why she is doing it in her own terms, what right has B got to keep on saying "No, what A is *really* doing is . . ."? In the case at hand, we Deweyans think we have a perfectly good way of describing our own behavior – behavior of which Habermas approves – in ways which eschew terms like 'universal' and 'unconditional' and 'transcendence.'

It seems to me in the spirit of Peirce's criticism of Descartes' "make-believe doubt" to raise the question of whether we are not dealing here with "make-believe transcendence" – a sort of make-believe response to an equally unreal doubt. Real doubt, Peirce said, comes when some concrete difficulty is envisaged in acting according to the habit which is the belief. (Such a difficulty might be, for example, having to cease believing some relevant but conflicting proposition.) Real transcendence, I should say, occurs when I say "I am prepared to justify this belief not just to people who share the following premises with me, but to lots of other people who do not share those premises but with whom I share certain others."[30] The question of whether I am so prepared is a concrete practical question, whose answer I determine by, for example, imaginatively previewing various other audiences' responses to my assertion that p, and my subsequent behavior.

But such experiments in imagination obviously have limits. I cannot imagine myself defending my assertion to *any possible* audience. In the first place, I can usually think of audiences to whom it would be pointless to try to justify my belief. (Try defending beliefs about justice to Attila, or about trigonometry to three-year-olds.) In the second place, no good pragmatist should ever use the term "all possible . . .". Pragmatists do not know how to imagine or to discover the bounds of possibility. Indeed, we cannot figure out what the point of attempting such feats could be. Under what concrete circumstances would it be important to consider the difference between "all the Xs I can think of" and "all possible Xs"?[31] How could this difference make a difference to practice?

I conclude that Wellmer's way of distinguishing between context-dependent and context-independent claims-cannot be made plausible, at least to pragmatists. Since I can think of no better way, I think that we should ask why Wellmer, Apel and Habermas think this distinction worth drawing. The obvious answer is that they want to avoid the 'relativism' which contextualism purportedly entails. So I turn now to what Wellmer calls "the antinomy of truth"[32] – the clash between relativist and absolutist intuitions.

VI. Must Pragmatists be Relativists?

Toward the beginning of his "Truth, Contingency and Modernity" Wellmer writes as follows:

> If there is irresolvable disagreement about the possibility of justifying truth claims, about standards of argumentation or evidential support, for example, between members of different linguistic, scientific or cultural communities, may I still suppose that there *are* – somewhere – the *correct* standards, the *right* criteria, in short that there is an *objective* truth of the matter? Or should I rather think that truth is 'relative' to cultures, languages, communities or even persons? While relativism (the second alternative) appears to be inconsistent, absolutism (the first alternative) seems to imply metaphysical assumptions. I would call this the antinomy of truth. Much important philosophical work has been done in recent decades to resolve this antinomy of truth; either by trying to show that absolutism need not be metaphysical or by trying to show that the critique of absolutism need not lead to relativism.[33]

My problem with Wellmer's antinomy is that I do not think that denying that there are "the *correct* standards" should lead anybody to say that *truth* (as opposed to justification) is 'relative' to something. As far as I can see, nobody would think that the critique of absolutism leads to relativism unless she thought that the only reason for justifying our beliefs to each other is that such justification makes it more likely that our beliefs are true.

I have argued elsewhere that there is no reason to think such justification makes this more likely.[34] But I do not think this is a cause for concern, for I do not think our practice of justifying our beliefs needs justification. If I am right that the only indispensable function of the word 'true' (or any other indefinable normative term, such as 'good' or 'right') is to caution, to warn against danger by making gestures toward unpredictable situations (future audiences, future moral dilemmas, etc.), then it does not make much sense to ask whether or not justification leads to truth. Justification to more and more audiences leads to less and less danger of rebuttal, and thus to less and less need for caution. ("If I convinced *them*," we often say to ourselves, "I should be able to convince *anybody*.") But one would only say that it leads to *truth* if one could somehow project from the conditioned to the unconditioned – from all imaginable to all possible audiences.

Such a projection makes sense if one believes in convergence. For such a belief sees the space of reasons as finite and structured, so that as more and more audiences are satisfied more and more members of a finite set of possible objections are eliminated. One will be encouraged to see the space of reasons in this way if one is a representationalist, because one will see reality (or at least the spatio-temporal hunk of it relevant to most human concerns) as finite and as constantly shoving us out of error and toward truth, discouraging inaccurate representations of itself and thereby producing increasingly accurate ones.[35] But if one does not take knowledge to be accurate representation of reality, nor truth as correspondence to reality, then it is harder to be a convergentist, and harder to think of the space of reasons as finite and structured.

Wellmer, it seems to me, wants to project from the conditioned (our various experiences of success in justifying our beliefs) to the unconditioned (truth). The big difference between me and Wellmer is that I think that the answer to his question "do our democratic and liberal principles define just *one* possible political language game among others" is an unqualified "yes." Wellmer, however, says that "a *qualified* 'no' can be justified, and by justification I now mean not justification *for us*, but justification, *period*."[36]

As I see it, the very idea of "justification *period*" commits Wellmer to the thesis that the logical space of reason-giving is finite and structured. So I should urge him to abandon the latter thesis for the same reasons that he abandoned Apel's and Habermas' convergentism. But, oddly enough, these reasons are pretty much the reasons he gives for giving his "qualified 'no'." His central point in defense of this answer is one which I whole-heartedly accept: viz., that the very idea of incompatible, and perhaps reciprocally unintelligible, language-games is a pointless fiction, and that in real cases representatives of different traditions and cultures can always find a way to talk over their differences.[37] I entirely agree with Wellmer that "rationality – in any relevant sense of the word – cannot end at the borderline of closed language games (since there is no such thing)."[38]

Our disagreement starts when, after a semi-colon, Wellmer finishes his sentence with "but then the ethnocentric contextuality of all argumentation is quite well compatible with the raising of truth claims which transcend the context – the local or cultural context – *in* which they are raised and in which they can be justified." I should have finished that same sentence by saying "but then the ethnocentric contextuality of all argumentation is quite well compatible with the claim that a liberal and democratic society can bring together, include, all sorts of diverse *ethnoi*." I see no way to get from the premise that there are no such things as mutually unintelligible standards of argument to the conclusion that the claims of democratic societies are "context-transcendent."

Here is a way of summing up the difference between Wellmer and myself: we agree that one reason to prefer democracies is that they enable us to construct ever bigger and better contexts of discussion. But I stop there, and Wellmer goes on. He adds that this reason is not just a justification of democracy *for us*, but "a justification, *period*." He thinks that "the democratic and liberal principles of modernity" should "*pace* Rorty" be "understood in a universalistic sense."[39]

My problem, of course, is that I do not have the option of understanding them that way. Pragmatists like me can't figure out how to tell whether we are understanding a justification as just a "justification for us" or as a "justification, *period*." This strikes me as like trying to tell whether I think of my scalpel or my computer as "a good tool for this task" or as "a good tool, *period*."

At this point, however, one could imagine Wellmer rejoining, "Then so much the worse for pragmatism. Any view which makes you unable to understand a distinction everybody else understands must have something wrong with it." My rebuttal would be: you are only entitled to that distinction as long as you can back it up with a distinction between what seem good reasons to us and what seem good reasons to something like an ahistorical Kantian tribunal of reason. But you deprived yourself of *that* possibility when you gave up on convergentism, and thus gave up the non-metaphysical substitute for such a tribunal – viz., the idealization called the "undistorted communication situation."

I agree with Wellmer in regarding "democratic and liberal institutions as the only ones in which the recognition of contingency could possibly coexist with the reproduction of their own legitimacy,"[40] at least if one takes "reproduce their own legitimacy" to mean something like "make its view of the situation of human beings in the universe hang together with its political practice." But I do not think that the recognition of contingency serves as a "justification, *period*" for democratic politics because I don't think that it does what Wellmer says: namely, "destroys the intellectual bases of dogmatism, foundationalism, authoritarianism and of moral and legal inequality."[41]

This is because I don't think that dogmatism or moral inequality *have* "intellectual bases". If I am a bigoted proponent of the inequality of blacks, women and homosexuals to straight white males, I need not necessarily appeal to the denial of contingency by invoking a metaphysical theory about the true nature of human beings. I could, but I might also, when it came to philosophy, be a pragmatist. A bigot and I can say the same Foucauldian/Nietzschean thing: that the only real question is one of power, the question of which community is going to inherit the earth, mine or my opponent's. One's choice of a community for that role is intertwined with one's sense of what counts as a competent audience.[42]

The fact that there are no mutually unintelligible language games does not, in itself, do much to show that disputes between racists and anti-racists, democrats and fascists, can be decided without resort to force. Both sides may agree that, although they understand what each other says perfectly well, and share common views on most topics (including, perhaps, the recognition of contingency), there seems no prospect of reaching agreement on the particular issue at hand. So, both sides say as they reach for their guns, it looks as if we'll have to fight it out.

My answer to Wellmer's question about whether our "democratic and liberal principles define just *one* possible political language game among others" is "yes, if the force of the question is to ask whether there is something in the nature of discourse which singles this game out." I cannot see what other force the question could have, and I think we have to rest content with saying that no philosophical thesis, either about contingency or about truth, does anything *decisive* for democratic politics.

By 'decisive' I mean doing what Apel and Habermas want to do: convicting the anti-democrat of a performative self-contradiction. The most that an insistence on contingency can do for democracy is to supply one more debating point on the democratic side of the argument, just as the insistence that (for example) only the Aryan race is in tune with the intrinsic, necessary, nature of things supplies one more debating point on the other side. I cannot take the latter point seriously, but I do not think that there is anything self-contradictory in the Nazi's refusal to take me seriously. We may both have to reach for our guns.

VII.   Is Reason Unified by Universalistic Presuppositions?

Unlike Habermas, I do not think that disciplines like philosophy, linguistics, and developmental psychology can do much for democratic politics. I see the development of the social conventions in which Habermas and I both rejoice as a lucky accident. Still, I should be happy to think that I was wrong about this. Maybe the gradual development of those conventions *does*, as Habermas thinks, illustrate a universal pattern of phylo- or onto-genetic development, a pattern captured by the rational reconstruction of competences offered by various human sciences and illustrated by the transition from 'traditional' to modern, 'rationalized' societies.[43]

But, unlike Habermas, I should be unperturbed if the offers currently made by the human sciences were withdrawn: if Chomsky's universalistic ideas about communicative competence were repudiated by a connectionist revolution in artificial intelligence,[44] if Piaget's and Kohlberg's empirical results proved to be unduplicatable, and so on. I do not see that it matters much whether there is a universal pattern here. I do not much care whether democratic politics are an expression of something deep, or whether they express nothing better than some hopes which popped from nowhere into the brains of a few remarkable people (Socrates, Christ, Jefferson, etc.) and which, for unknown reasons, became popular.

Habermas and Apel think that one way to help create a cosmopolitan community is to study the nature of something called 'rationality' which all human beings share, something already present within them but insufficiently acknowledged. That is why they would be depressed if the support for univeralism apparently offered by such empirical studies as those of Chomsky and Kohlberg were, in the course of time, withdrawn. But suppose we say that all that rationality amounts to – all that marks human beings off from other species of animals – is the ability to use language and thus to have beliefs and desires. It seems plausible to add that there is no more reason to expect all the organisms which share this ability to form a single community of justification than to expect all the organisms able to walk long distances, or to remain monogamous, or to digest vegetables, to form such a community. One will not expect such a single community of justification to be created by the ability to communicate. For the ability to use language is, like the prehensile thumb, just one more gimmick which organisms have developed to increase their chances of survival.

If we combine this Darwinian point of view with the holistic attitude toward intentionality and language-use found in Wittgenstein and Davidson, we can say that there is no language-use without justification, no ability to believe without an ability to argue about what beliefs to have. But this is not to say that the ability to use language, to have beliefs and desires, entails a desire to justify one's belief to *every* language-using organism one encounters. Not any language-user who comes down the road will be treated as a member of a competent audience. On the contrary, human beings usually divide up into mutually suspicious (*not* mutually unintelligible) communities of justification – mutually exclusive groups – depending upon the presence or absence of sufficient overlap in belief and desire. This is because the principal source of conflict between human communities is the belief that I have no reason to justify my beliefs to you, and none in finding out what alternative beliefs you may have, because you are, for example, an infidel, a foreigner, a woman, a child, a slave, a pervert, or an untouchable. In short, you are not "one of us," not one of the *real* human beings, the *paradigm* human beings, the ones whose persons and opinions are to be treated with respect.

The philosophical tradition has tried to stitch exclusivist communities together by saying: there is more overlap between infidels and true believers, masters and slaves, men and women, than one might think. For, as Aristotle said, all human beings by nature desire to know. This desire brings them together in a universal community of justification. To a pragmatist, however, this Aristotelian dictum seems thoroughly misleading. It runs together three different things: the need to make one's beliefs coherent, the need for the respect of one's peers, and curiosity. We pragmatists think that the reason people try to make their beliefs coherent is not that they love truth but because they cannot help doing so. Our minds can no more stand incoherence than our brains can stand whatever neuro-chemical imbalance is the physiological correlate of such incoherence. Just as our neural networks are, presumably, both constrained and in part constructed by something like the algorithms used in parallel distributed processing of information by computer programmers, so our minds are constrained (and in part constructed) by the need to tie our beliefs and desires together into a reasonably perspicuous whole.[45] That is why we cannot "will to believe" – believe what we like, regardless of what else we believe. It is why, for example, we have such a hard time keeping our religious beliefs in a separate compartment from our scientific ones, and in isolating our respect for democratic institutions from our contempt for many (even most) of our fellow-voters.

The need to make one's beliefs coherent is, for reasons familiar from Hegel, Mead and Davidson, not separable from the need for the respect of our peers. We have as hard a time tolerating the thought that everybody but ourselves is out of step as we do the thought that we believe both p and not-p. We need the respect of our peers because we cannot trust our own beliefs, nor maintain our self-respect, unless we are fairly sure that our conversational interlocutors agree among themselves on such propositions as "He's not crazy," "He's one of us," "He may have strange beliefs on certain topics, but he's basically sound," and so on.

This interpenetration of the need to make one's beliefs coherent among themselves and the need to make one's own beliefs coherent with the beliefs of one's peers results from the fact that, as Wittgenstein said, to imagine a form of human life we have to imagine agreement in judgments as well as in meanings. Davidson brings out the considerations which support Wittgenstein's dictum when he says: "The ultimate source of both objectivity and communication is the triangle that, by relating speaker, interpreter and the world, determines the contents of thought and speech."[46] You would not know what you believed, nor have any beliefs, unless your belief had a place in a network of beliefs and desires. But that network would not exist unless you and others could pair off features of your non-human environment with assent to your utterances by other language-users, utterances caused (as are yours) by those very features.

The difference between the use which Davidson (and I) would like to make of Hegel's and Mead's realization that our selves are dialogical all the way down – that there is no private core on which to build – and the use which Apel and Habermas make of this realization can be exhibited by looking at the sentence immediately following the one I just quoted from Davidson: "Given this source," Davidson says, "there is no room for a relativized concept of truth."

Davidson's point is that the only sort of philosopher who would take seriously the idea that truth is relative to a context, and particularly to a choice between human communities, is one who thinks that he or she can contrast "being in touch with a human community" with "being in touch with reality." But Davidson's point about there being no language without triangulation means that you cannot have any language, or any beliefs, without being in touch with both a human community *and* non-human reality. There is no possibility of agreement without truth, nor of truth without agreement.

Most of our beliefs must be true, Davidson says, because an ascription to a person of mostly false beliefs would mean either that we had mistranslated the person's marks and noises or that she did not in fact have any beliefs, was not in fact speaking a language. Most of our beliefs must be justified in the eyes of our peers for a similar reason: if they were not justified – if our peers could not attribute to us a largely *coherent* web of beliefs and desires – they would have to conclude that they had either misunderstood us or that we did not speak their language. Coherence, truth, and community go together, not because truth is to be defined in terms of coherence rather than correspondence, in terms of social practice rather than in terms of coping with non-human forces, but simply because to ascribe a belief is automatically to ascribe a place in a largely coherent set of mostly true beliefs.

But to say that there is no contact, via belief and desire, with reality unless there is a community of speakers is as yet to say nothing about what sort of community is in question. A radically exclusivist community – made up only of the priests, or the nobles, or the males, or the whites – is quite as good as any other sort of community for Davidsonian purposes. This is the difference between what Davidson thinks you can get out of reflection on the nature of discourse and what Apel and Habermas think you can get out of it. The latter philosophers think you can get an argument in favor of the inclusivist project – an argument which says that people who resist this project involve themselves in performative self-contradictions.

By contrast, Davidson thinks that any community of justification will do to make you a language-user and a believer, no matter how 'distorted' Apel and Habermas may judge communication within that community to be. From Davidson's point of view, philosophy of language runs out before we reach the moral imperatives which make up Apel's and Habermas' "discourse ethics."

Apel and Habermas run together the need for coherence and for justification which is required if one is to use language at all, and a commitment to what they call "universal validity," a commitment which can only be consistently acted upon by aiming at the sort of domination-free communication which is impossible as long as there are human communities which remain exclusivist. Davidson and I have no use for the claim that any communicative action contains a claim to universal validity, because this so-called 'presupposition' seems to us to have no role to play in the explanation of linguistic behavior.

It does, to be sure, play a part in the explanation of the behavior, linguistic and other, of a small minority of human beings – those who belong to the liberal, universalistic, inclusivist tradition of the European Enlightenment. But this tradition, to which Davidson and I are as much attached as Apel and Habermas, derives no support from reflection on discourse as such. We language-users who belong to this minority tradition are morally superior to those who do not, but those who do not are no less coherent in their use of language.

Apel and Habermas invoke the presupposition of universal validity to get from a commitment to justification to a willingness to submit one's beliefs to the inspection of any and every language-user – even a slave, even a black, even a woman. They see the desire for truth, construed as the desire to claim universal validity, as the desire for universal justification. But as I see it, they are inferring invalidly from "You cannot use language without invoking a consensus within a community of other language-users" to "You cannot use language consistently without enlarging that community to include all users of language."

Because I see this inference as invalid, I think that the only thing which can play the role in which Aristotle, Peirce, Apel, and Habermas have cast the desire for knowledge (and thus for truth) is *curiosity*. I use this term to mean the urge to expand one's horizons of inquiry – in all areas, ethical as well as logical and physical – so as to encompass new data, new hypotheses, new terminologies, and the like. This urge brings cosmopolitanism, and democratic politics, in its train. The more curiosity you have, the more interest you will have in talking to foreigners, infidels, and anybody else who claims to know something you do not know, to have some ideas you have not yet had.

VIII.   Communicating or Educating?

If one sees the desire and possession of both truth and justification as inseparable from using language, while still resisting the thought that this desire can be used to convict members of exclusivist human communities of performative self-contradiction, then one will see inclusivist communities as based on contingent human developments such as the twitchy curiosity of the sort of eccentrics we call 'intellectuals,' the desire for intermarriage beyond tribal or caste boundaries produced by erotic obsession, the need to trade across such boundaries produced by lack of (for example) salt or gold within one's own territory, the possession of enough wealth, security, education, and independence so that one's self-respect no longer depends upon membership in an exclusivist community (on, for instance, *not* being an infidel or a slave or a woman), and the like. The increased communication between previously exclusivist communities produced by such contingent human developments may gradually *create* universality, but I cannot see any sense in which it recognizes a previously existent universality.

Philosophers like Habermas worry about the anti-Enlightenment overtones of the views they call 'contextualist.' They recognize that justification is an obviously context-relative notion – one justifies to a given audience, and the same justification will not work for all audiences. They then infer that putting truth aside in favor of justification will endanger the ideal of human fraternity. Habermas regards contextualism as "only the flipside of logocentrism."[47] He sees contextualists as negative metaphysicians infatuated by diversity, and says that "The metaphysical priority of unity above plurality and the contextualistic priority of plurality above unity are secret accomplices."[48]

I agree with Habermas that it is as pointless to prize diversity as to prize unity, but I disagree with his claim that we can use the pragmatics of communication to do the job which metaphysicians hoped to achieve by appealing to the Plotinian One or to the transcendental structure of self-consciousness. My reasons for disagreement are those offered by Walzer, McCarthy, Ben-Habib, Wellmer and others – reasons nicely summed up in an article by Michael Kelly.[49] Habermas argues for the thesis that

> the unity of reason only remains perceptible in the plurality of its voices – as the possibility in principle of passing from one language to another – a passage that, no matter how occasional, is still comprehensible. This possibility of mutual understanding, which is now guaranteed only procedurally and is realized only transitorily, forms the background for the existing diversity of those who encounter one another – even when they fail to understand one another.[50]

I agree with Habermas – against Lyotard, Foucault, and others – that there are no incommensurable languages, that any language can be learned by one who is able to use any other languages, and that Davidson is right in denouncing the very idea of a conceptual scheme. But I disagree with him about the relevance of this point to the utility of the ideas of "universal validity" and "objective truth."

Habermas says that "what the speaker, here and now in a given context, asserts as valid transcends, *according to the sense of his claim*, all context-dependent, merely local standards of validity.[51] As I said above, I cannot see what 'transcends' means here. If it means that he is claiming to say something true, then the question is whether it makes any difference whether you say that a sentence S is true or whether you simply offer a justification for it by saying "here are my reasons for believing S." Habermas thinks there is a difference because he thinks that when you assert S you claim truth, you claim to represent the real, and that reality transcends context. "With the concept of reality, to which every representation necessarily refers, we presuppose something transcendent."[52]

Habermas tends to take for granted that truth-claims are claims to represent accurately, and to be suspicious of those who, like Davidson and myself, give up on the notion of linguistic representation. He follows Sellars in being a coherentist rather than a skeptic or a foundationalist, but he is dubious about the move I want to make from coherentism to anti-representationalism. He commends Peirce over Saussure because Peirce examines "expressions from the point of view of their possible truth *and*, at the same time, from that of their communicability." He goes on to say that

> from the perspective of its capacity for being true, an assertoric sentence stands in an epistemic relation to something in the world – it represents a state of affairs. At the same time, for the perspective of its employment in a communicative act, it stands in a relation to a possible interpretation by a language-user – it is suitable for the transmission of information.[53]

My own view, which I take from Davidson, is that you can give up the notion of an "epistemic relation to something in the world," and just rely on the ordinary causal relations which bind utterances together with the utterers' environments. The idea of representation, on this view, adds nothing to the notion of "taking part in the discursive practice of justifying one's assertions."

Habermas sees Putnam as, like himself, defending a third position against the metaphysics of unity on the one hand and the enthusiasts for incommensurability on the other. He defines this third position as "the humanism of those who continue the Kantian tradition by seeking to use the philosophy of language to save a concept of reason that is skeptical and postmetaphysical."[54] Putnam and Habermas have offered similar criticisms of my attempt to get rid of a specifically epistemic concept of reason – the concept according to which one is rational only if one tries to represent reality accurately – and to replace it by the purely moral ideal of solidarity. My central disagreement with both Habermas and Putnam is over the question of whether the regulative ideas of "undistorted communication," or "accurate representation of reality" can do any more for the ideals of the French Revolution than the bare, context-dependent, notion of 'justification.'

Some people care about defending their assertions only to a few people, and some care, or say they care, about defending their assertions to everyone. I am not thinking here of the distinction between specialized, technical discourse and non-technical discourse. Rather, the distinction I want is the one between people who would be glad to try to defend their views to all people who share certain attributes – for example, devotion to the ideals of the French Revolution, or membership in the Aryan race – and those who say they want to justify their view to every actual and possible language-user.

There are certainly people who say that the latter is what they want. But I am not sure that they really mean it. Do they want to justify their views to language-users who are four years old? Well, perhaps they do in the sense that they would like to educate four-year-olds to the point at which they could appreciate the arguments for and against the views in question. Do they want to justify them to intelligent but convinced Nazis, people who believe that the first thing to find out is whether the view under discussion is tainted by the Jewish ancestry of its inventors or propounders? Well, perhaps they do in the sense that they would like to convert these Nazis into people who have doubts about the advisability of a Jew-free Europe and infallibility of Hitler, and therefore are more or less willing to listen to arguments for positions associated with Jewish thinkers. But in both of these cases what they want seems to me best described not as wanting to justify their view to everybody, but as wanting to create an audience to whom they would have a sporting chance of justifying their view.

Let me use the distinction between *arguing* with people and *educating* people to abbreviate the distinction I have just drawn: the distinction between proceeding on the assumption that people will follow your arguments and knowing that they cannot but hoping to alter them so that they can. If all education were a matter of argument, this distinction would collapse. But, unless one broadens the term 'argument' beyond recognition, a lot of education is not. In particular, a lot of it is simple appeal to sentiment. The distinction between such appeal and argument is fuzzy, but I take it nobody would say that making an unregenerate Nazi watch films of the opening of the concentration camps, or making her read *The Diary of Anne Frank*, counts as *arguing* with her.

People like Habermas and myself cherish both the ideal of human fraternity and the goal of universal availability of education. When asked what sort of education we have in mind, we often say that it is an education in critical thinking, in the ability to talk over the pros and cons of any view. We oppose critical thinking to ideology, and say that we oppose ideological education of the sort which the Nazis inflicted on German youth. But we thereby leave ourselves wide open to Nietzsche's scornful suggestion that we are simply inculcating our own ideology: the ideology of what he called 'Socratism.' The issue between me and Habermas boils down to a disagreement about what to say to Nietzsche at this point.

I should reply to Nietzsche by conceding that there is no non-local, non-contextual, way to draw the distinction between ideological education and non-ideological education, because there is nothing to my use of the term 'reason' that could not be replaced by "the way we wet Western liberals, the heirs of Socrates and the French Revolution conduct ourselves." I agree with MacIntyre and Michael Kelly that all reasoning, both in physics and ethics, is tradition-bound.

Habermas thinks that this is an unnecessary concession, and more generally that my cheerful ethnocentrism can be avoided by thinking through what he calls "the symmetrical structure of perspectives built into every speech situation."[55] The issue between Habermas and myself thus comes to a head when he takes up my suggestion that we drop the notions of rationality and objectivity, and instead just discuss the kind of community we want to create. He paraphrases this suggestion by saying that I want to treat "the aspiration for objectivity" as "simply the desire for as much intersubjective agreement as possible, namely, the desire to expand the referent of 'for us' to the greatest possible extent." He then paraphrases one of Putnam's objections to me by asking: "can we explain the possibility of the critique and self-critique of established practices of justification if we do not take the idea of the expansion of our interpreted horizon seriously *as an idea*, and if we do not connect this idea with the intersubjectivity of an agreement that allows precisely for the distinction between what is current "for us" and what is current "for them"?[56]

Habermas enlarges on this point by saying

> The merging of interpretive horizons . . . does not signify an assimilation to 'us'; rather, it must mean a convergence, steered through learning, of 'our' perspective and 'their' perspective – no matter whether 'they' or 'we' or both sides have to reformulate established practices of justification to a greater or lesser extent. For learning itself belongs neither to us nor to them; both sides are caught up in it in the same way. Even in the most difficult processes of reaching understanding, all parties appeal to the common reference point of a possible consensus, even if this reference point is projected in each case from within their own contexts. For, although they may be interpreted in various ways and applied according to different criteria, concepts like truth, rationality or justification play the *same* grammatical role in *every* linguistic community.[57]

The nub of the argument between Habermas and myself in this area is a disagreement about how much help for democratic politics can be gotten out of what Habermas here calls 'grammar.' As I said earlier, I think that all that we can get out of the grammar of 'true' and 'rational' is what we can get out of the grammar of a rather thin idea of 'justification.' This thin idea amounts to little more than that of using non-violent means to change people's minds.

Unlike Foucault and some others, I think that it is both possible and important to preserve intact the commonsense distinction between violent and non-violent means. I do not think it helpful to extend the term 'violence' as widely as Foucault extended it. Whatever we are doing when we make Nazis look at pictures of concentration camp survivors, it is not violence, any more than it was violence to educate the Hitler Youth to believe that Jews were worthless vermin.

The inevitable fuzziness of the line between persuasion and violence causes problems, however, when we come to the question of education. We are reluctant to say that the Nazis used *persuasion* on the Hitler Youth, since we have two criteria of persuasion. One is simply using words rather than blows or other forms of physical pressure. One can imagine, with a bit of distortion of history, that, in this sense, only persuasion was employed on the Hitler Youth. The second criterion of persuasion includes abstention from words like "Stop asking these stupid questions about whether there aren't some good Jews, questions which make me doubt your Aryan consciousness and ancestry, or the Reich will find another use for you!" and not assigning *Der Stürmer* to one's students.

Unsocratic methods of this latter sort are the kind which Habermas would say do not respect the symmetrical relationships of participants in discourse. Habermas clearly thinks that there is something in the grammar of "concepts like truth, rationality and justification" which tells us not to use methods of the latter sort. He would presumably grant that use of such words is language-use, but he must then go on to say that it can be seen to be misuse simply by thinking about what language is. This is pretty much what he does. Immediately after the passage I quoted about grammar, he says

> All languages offer the possibility of distinguishing between what is true and what we hold to be true. The *supposition* of a common objective world is built into the pragmatics of every single linguistic usage. And the dialogue roles of every speech situation enforce a symmetry in participant perspectives.

A bit later he says, "From the possibility of reaching understanding linguistically, we can read off a concept of situated reason that is given voice in validity claims that are both context-dependent and transcendent." He then approvingly quotes Putnam as saying "Reason is, in this sense, both immanent (not to be found outside of concrete language games and institutions) and transcendent (a regulative idea that we use to criticize the conduct of all activities and institutions."[58]

It seems to me that the regulative idea that we – we wet liberals, we heirs of the Enlightenment, we Socratists – most frequently use to criticize the conduct of various conversational partners is that of "needing education in order to outgrow their primitive fears, hatreds, and superstitions." This is the concept the victorious Allied armies used when they set about re-educating the citizens of occupied Germany and Japan. It is also the one which was used by American schoolteachers who had read Dewey and were concerned to get students to think 'scientifically' and 'rationally' about such matters as the origin of the species and sexual behavor (that is, to get them to read Darwin and Freud without disgust and incredulity). It is a concept which I, like most Americans who teach humanities or social science in colleges and universities, invoke when we try to arrange things so that students who enter as bigoted, homophobic, religious fundamentalists will leave college with views more like our own.

What is the relation of this idea to the regulative idea of 'reason' which Putnam believes to be transcendent and which Habermas believes to be discoverable within the grammar of concepts ineliminable from our description of the making of assertions? The answer to that question depends upon how much the re-education of Nazis and fundamentalists has to do with merging interpretive horizons and how much with replacing such horizons. The fundamentalist parents of our fundamentalist students think that the entire "American liberal Establishment" is engaged in a conspiracy. Had they read Habermas, these people would say that the typical communication situation in American college classrooms is no more *herrschafisfrei* than that in the Hitler Youth camps.

These parents have a point. Their point is that we liberal teachers no more feel in a symmetrical communication situation when we talk with bigots than do kindergarten teachers talking with their students. In both college classrooms and kindergartens it is equally difficult for the teachers to feel that what is going on is what Habmermas calls a "convergence, steered through learning, of 'our' perspective *and* 'their' perspective – no matter whether 'they' or 'we' or both sides have to reformulate established practices of justification to a greater or lesser extent."[59] When we American college teachers encounter religious fundamentalists, we do not consider the possiblity of reformulating our own practices of justification so as to give more weight to the authority of the Christian scriptures. Instead, we do our best to convince these students of the benefits of secularization. We assign first-person accounts of growing up homosexual to our homophobic students for the same reasons that German schoolteachers in the postwar period assigned *The Diary of Anne Frank*.

Putnam and Habermas can rejoin that we teachers do our best to be Socratic, to get our job of re-education, secularization, and liberalization done by conversational exchange. That is true up to a point, but what about assigning books like *Black Boy*, *The Diary of Anne Frank*, and *Becoming a Man*? The racist or fundamentalist parents of our students say that in a truly democratic society the students should not be forced to read books by such people – black people, Jewish people, homosexual people. They will protest that these books are being jammed down their children's throats. I cannot see how to reply to this charge without saying something like "There are credentials for admission to our democratic society, credentials which we liberals have been making more stringent by doing our best to excommunicate racists, male chauvinists, homo-phobes, and the like. You have to be *educated* in order to be a citizen of our society, a participant in our conversation, someone with whom we can envisage merging our horizons. So we are going to go right on trying to discredit you in the eyes of your children, trying to strip your fundamentalist religious community of dignity, trying to make your views seem silly rather than discussable. We are not so inclusivist as to tolerate intolerance such as yours."

I have no trouble offering this reply, since I do not claim to make the distinction between education and conversation on the basis of anything except my loyalty to a particular community, a community whose interests required re-educating the Hitler Youth in 1945 and required re-educating the bigoted students of Virginia in 1993. I don't see anything *herrschafisfrei* about my handling of my fundamentalist students. Rather, I think those students are lucky to find themselves under the benevolent *Herrschaft* of people like me, and to have escaped the grip of their frightening, vicious, dangerous parents. But I think that the handling of such students is a problem for Putnam and Habermas. It seems to me that I am just as provincial and contextualist as the Nazi teachers who made their students read *Der Stürmer*; the only difference is that I serve a better cause. I come from a better province.

I recognize, of course, that domination-free communication is only a regulative ideal, never to be attained in practice. But unless a regulative ideal makes a difference to practice, it is not good for much. So I ask: is there an ethics of discourse which lets me assign the books I want to assign but makes no reference to the local and ethnocentric considerations which I should cite to justify my pedagogic practices? Can you get such an ethics out of the notions of "reason, truth, and justification," or do you have to load the dice? Can I invoke universalistic notions in defense of my action, as well as local ones?

Like MacIntyre, Ben-Habib, Kelly, and others, I think that you have to smuggle some provinciality into your universals before they do you any good. We think this for the same sorts of reasons as Hegel thought that you had to smuggle in some provinciality – some ethical substance – before you could get any use out of Kant's notion of "unconditional moral obligation." In particular, you have to smuggle in some rule like "no putative contribution to a conversation can be rejected simply because it comes from somebody who has some attribute which can vary independently of his or her opinions – an attribute like being Jewish, or black, or homosexual." I call this rule 'provincial' because it violates the intuitions of a lot of people outside the province in which we heirs of the Enlightenment run the educational institutions.[60] It violates what they would describe as their *moral* intuitions. I am reluctant to admit that these are moral intuitions, and should prefer to call them revolting prejudices. But I do not think that anything in the grammar of the terms 'moral intuition' and 'prejudice' helps us reach agreement on this point. Nor will a theory of rationality do so.

IX.   Do We Need a Theory of Rationality?

As I remarked earlier, Habermas thinks that "the paradigm of the philosophy of consciousness is exhausted" and also that "the symptoms of exhaustion should dissolve with the transition to the paradigm of mutual understanding?"[61] My own view is that that the fruitfulness of the topics Weber suggested – modernity and rationality – have also been exhausted. I think that the symptoms of this exhaustion might dissolve if we stopped talking about the transition from tradition to rationality, stopped worrying about falling back from rationality by becoming relativistic or ethnocentric, and stopped contrasting the context-dependent with the universal.

This would mean explicitly abandoning the hope that philosophy can stand above politics, abandoning the hopeless question "How can philosophy find politically neutral premises, premises which can be justified to anybody, from which to infer an obligation to pursue democratic politics?" Dropping that question would let us admit that, in Wellmer's formula, "democratic and liberal principles define just *one* possible language game among others." Such an admission would be in line with the Darwinian idea that the inclusivist project is no more rooted in something larger than itself than, say, the project of replacing ideographic by alphabetic writing, or of representing three spatial dimensions on a two-dimensional surface. All three of these were good, immensely fruitful, ideas, but none of them need universalistic backup. They can stand on their own feet.[62]

If we abandoned the idea that philosophy can be both politically neutral and politically relevant, we could start asking the question: "Given that we want to be ever more inclusivist, what should the public rhetoric of our society be like? How different should it be from the public rhetoric of previous societies?" Habermas' implicit answer to this question is that we should hang on to a good many Kantian ideas about the connection between universality and moral obligation. Dewey, however, was willing to move much further away from Kant. Though he would have heartily agreed with Habermas that Aristotle's political vocabulary was unable to capture the spirit of democratic politics, he did not like the distinction between morality and prudence which Habermas thinks essential, and on this point he would have thought Aristotle preferable.[63] Dewey thought that the Kantian notion of "unconditional obligation," like the notion of unconditionality itself (and of universality, insofar as that idea is implicitly accompanied by that of unconditional necessity),[64] could not survive Darwin.

Whereas Habermas thinks that we need "the reconstructive sciences designed to grasp universal competences" in order to break out of "the hermeneutic circle in which the *Geisteswissenschaften*, as well as the interpretive social sciences, are trapped,"[65] Dewey did not feel trapped. This was because he saw no need to resolve a tension between facticity and validity. He saw that tension as a philosopher's fiction, a result of separating two parts of a situation for no good (that is, no practical) reason, and then complaining that you cannot put them back together again. For him, all obligations were situational and conditional.

This refusal to be unconditional led Dewey to be charged with 'relativism.' If 'relativism' just means failure to find a use for the notion of 'context-independent validity,' then this charge was entirely justified. But no roads lead from this failure to an inability to engage in democratic politics, unless one thinks that such politics require us to deny that, "democratic and liberal principles define just *one* possible language game among others." The question about universality is, for Dewey, just the question of whether democratic politics can start from an affirmation, rather than a denial, of that claim.

I do not think that we can get much further in debating this question by talking about either modernity or reason. The question of whether Hegel should have developed a theory of communicative reason, or should instead have dropped the topic of reason altogether in the interest of a more thorough-going variety of historicism, is not going to be settled by looking more closely at the grammar of words like 'true' and 'rational', and 'argument.' Neither is the question of whether philosophers like Annette Baier are right in suggesting that we set Kant aside and go back to Hume's attempt to describe reason in terms of conditioned sentiment rather than unconditional obligation.[66]

But although we do not, if I am right, need a theory of rationality, we do need a narrative of maturation. The deepest disagreement between Habermas and myself may be over whether the distinction beween the unconditional and the conditional in general, and the distinction between morality and prudence in particular, is a mark of maturity or a transitional stage on the way to maturity. One of the many points on which Dewey agreed with Nietzsche was that it was the latter. Dewey thought that the desire for universality, unconditionality, and necessity was undesirable, because it led one away from the practical problems of democratic politics into a never–never land of theory. Kant and Habermas think that it is a desirable desire, one which one shares only when one reaches the highest level of moral development.[67]

I have been trying to show how things look when one puts democratic politics in the context of Dewey's narrative of maturation. I cannot offer anything remotely approaching a knock–down argument, based on commonly accepted premises, for this narrative. The best I could do by way of further defense of my view would be to tell a fuller story, encompassing more topics, in order to show how post-Nietzschean European philosophy looks from a Deweyan angle, rather than a universalistic one. (This is something I have tried to do, in bits and pieces, elsewhere.) I think that narratives are a perfectly fair means of persuasion, and that Habermas's *Philosophical Discourse of Modernity* and Dewey's *The Quest for Certainty* are both admirable illustrations of the power of narratives of maturation.

My reasons for preferring Dewey's are not that I think that Dewey got truth and rationality right, and that Habermas gets them wrong. I think that there is nothing to be gotten right or wrong here. At this level of abstraction, concepts like truth, rationality, and maturity are up for grabs. The only thing that matters is which way of reshaping them will, in the long run, make them more useful for democratic politics. Concepts are, as Wittgenstein taught us, uses of words. Philosophers have long wanted to understand concepts, but the point is to change them so as to make them serve our purposes better. Habermas', Apel's, Putnam's and Wellmer's linguistification of Kantian concepts is one suggestion about how to make these concepts more useful. Dewey's and Davidson's thoroughgoing anti-Kantian naturalism is an alternative suggestion.

Notes

1 This paper was prepared for presentation to a colloquium held at Cerisy-la-Salle in 1993, and a revised version was read at the University of Girona in 1996. A shortened version was published in French as "Les assertions expriment-elles une prétention à une validité universelle?" in *La Modernité en Question: de Richard Rorty á Jürgen Habermas*, ed. Françoise Gaillard, Jacques Poulain, and Richard Shusterman (Paris: Editions de Cerf, 1993). Another, also shortened, version, appeared as "Sind Aussagen universelle Geltungsansprüche?" in *Deutsche Zeitschrift für Philosophie* (Band 42, Heft 6 (1994), pp. 975–988). This is the first appearance of the English original of the paper, of its full text.

2 Nietzsche is the paradigm irrationalist because he had no interest whatever in democracy, and because he stoutly resisted all three premises. James is thought to be more confused than vicious, because, although committed to democracy, he was not willing to affirm two of the premises: he admitted that all human beings desire truth, but he thought the claim that truth is correspondence to reality unintelligible, and he toyed with the claim that, since reality is malleable, truth is Many. Habermas sets his face firmly against the latter idea, even though he agrees with James that we have to give up the correspondence theory of truth. So Habermas is condemned as an irrationalist only by die-hards who claim that doubts about truth as correspondence are doubts about the existence, or at least the unity, of Truth. Straussians, and analytic philosophers such as Searle, claim that you need all three premises: to give up any of them is to put yourself on a slippery slope, to risk ending up agreeing with Nietzsche.

3 Readers of my paper "Solidarity or Objectivity?" will recognize this line of argument as a variant on my earlier claim that we need to restate our intellectual ambitions in terms of our relations to other human beings, rather than in terms of our relation to non-human reality. As I say below, that claim is one with which Apel and Habermas are inclined to agree, even though they think my way of carrying through on this project goes too far.

4 The relevance of the sublime to the political is, of course, a point of dispute between Lacanians like Zizek and their opponents. It would take more than a note to deal with their arguments. I have tried to offer some preliminary backup for my claim of irrelevance in the pages of *Contingency, Irony and Solidarity* in which I discuss the difference between the private pursuit of sublimity and the public search for a beautiful reconciliation of conflicting interests. In the present context, perhaps it is enough to remark that I agree with Habermas that Foucault's exaltation of a 'sublime', inexpressible, impossible, kind of freedom – a kind which was somehow *not* constituted by power – made it impossible for him to recognize the achievements of liberal reformers and thus to engage in serious political reflection on the possibilities open to welfare-state democracies. (See *The Philosophical Discourse of Modernity*, pp. 290–291).

5 If you linguistify reason by saying, with Sellars and Davidson, that there are no non-linguistic beliefs and desires, you automatically socialize it. Sellars and Davidson would

heartily agree with Habermas that "[T]here is no pure reason that might don linguistic clothing only in the second place. Reason is by its very nature incarnated in contexts of communicative action and in structures of the lifeworld." (*Philosophical Discourse of Modernity*, p. 322).

6   *Philosophical Discourse of Modernity*, pp. 322–23.

7   I replied to Putnam's criticism of my view (in his essay of 1983 called "Why Reason Can't be Naturalized") in my "Solidarity or Objectivity" (reprinted in my *Objectivity, Relativism and Truth*). I have replied to Putnam's further criticisms of this view (in his *Realism with a Human Face*) in "Putnam and the Relativist Menace" (*Journal of Philosophy*, September 1993).

8   *Philosophical Discourse*, p. 311. At p. 312 Habermas claims that most philosophy of language outside the Austin-Searle "speech-act" tradition, and in particular Donald Davidson's "truth-condition semantics," embodies the typically logocentric "fixation on the fact-mirroring function of language." I think that there is an important strain in recent philosophy of language which is not guilty of this charge, and that Davidson's later work is a good example of freedom from this fixation. See, for example, Davidson's doctrine of 'triangulation' in his "The Structure and Content of Truth," a doctrine which helps explain why fact-stating and communicating cannot be separated. I discuss this doctrine below. (In my view, accepting Davidson's point makes it unnecessary to postulate what Habermas calls "'worlds' analogous to the world of facts ... for legitimately regulated interpersonal relationships and for attributable subjective experiences" (ibid., p. 313). But this disagreement is a side-issue which does not need to be explored further in the present context.)

9   *Philosophical Discourse*, p. 296.

10 As I read Dewey, he would sympathize with Castoriadis' emphasis on imagination, rather than reason, as the engine of moral progress.

11 Consider Habermas' criticism of Castoriadis: "one cannot see how this *demiurgic setting-in-action* of historical truths could be transposed into the *revolutionary project* proper to the practice of consciously acting, autonomous, self-realizing individuals." (*Philosophical Discourse*, p. 318) The history of the United States of America shows how this transposition can be achieved. Apel and Habermas tend to think of the American Revolution as firmly grounded in the sort of universal-validity-claiming principles of which they approve, and which Jefferson spelled out in the Declaration of Independence. (See Apel, "Zurück zur Normalität?" in *Zerstörung des moralischen Selbstbewusstseins*, p. 117). I should rejoin that the Founding Fathers were just the sort of demiurges whom Castoriadis has in mind when he talks about "the institution of the social imaginary." What we now think of as "the American people," a community of "consciously acting, autonomous, self-realizing individuals" devoted to those principles, slowly came into existence in the course of the (very gradual – ask any African-American) process of living up to the Founders' imaginations. So when Habermas goes on to criticize Castoriadis for acknowledging "no reason for revolutionizing reified society except the existentialist resolve 'because we will it'," and asks "who this 'we' of the radical willing might be," I think it would be fair to answer that in 1776 the relevant 'we' was not the American people but Jefferson and some of his equally imaginative friends.

12 See, on this point, the opening pages of my "Pragmatism, Davidson and Truth" in *Objectivity, Relativism and Truth*. What I there call the 'endorsing' and the 'disquotational' uses of the 'true' can easily be paraphrased in terms which do not include 'true.'

13 Being a coherentist in this sense does not necessarily mean having a coherence theory of truth. Davidson's repudiation of the latter label for his view, a label he had previously accepted, is a corollary of his claim that there can be no definition of the term "true-in-L" for variable L. Davidson's present view, with which I have come to agree, is that "[W]e should not say that truth is correspondence, coherence, warranted assertability, ideally justified assertability, what is accepted in the conversation of the right people, what science will end up maintaining, what explains the convergence on single theories in science, or the success of our ordinary beliefs. To the extent that realism and antirealism depend on one or

another of these views of truth we should refuse to endorse either." ("The Structure and Content of Truth", *Journal of Philosophy* vol. 87 (1990), p. 309).

14   Davidson too thinks that there is more to be said, but the sort of thing he wants to say is, as far as I can see, irrelevant to politics. In what follows I draw upon Davidson, but I postpone discussion of the claim, at p. 326 of "The Structure and Content of Truth," that "the conceptual underpinning of understanding is a theory of truth," in a sense of "theory of truth" in which there is one such theory per language. This claim seems to me distinct from the claim, which I invoke below, that "the ultimate source of both objectivity and communication" is what Davidson calls 'triangulation.' I am not sure why, apart from respect for the memory of Tarski, a theory that codifies the results of such triangulation should be described as a theory of *truth*, rather than of the behavior of a certain group of human beings.

15   Putnam has sometimes repudiated this thesis of convergence (see *Realism with a Human Face*, p. 171, on Bernard Williams), but (as I argue in my "Putnam and the Relativist Menace"), I do not think that he can reconcile this repudiation with his notion of "ideal assertibility". As I see it, the only sense in which Truth is One is that, if the process of developing new theories and new vocabularies is choked off, and there is agreement on the aims to be fulfilled by a belief – that is, on the needs to be fulfilled by the actions dictated by that belief – then a consensus will develop about which of a finite list of candidates is to be adopted. This sociological generalization, which is subject to lots of obvious qualifications, should not be confused with a metaphysical principle. The trouble with the idea of convergence at the end of inquiry, as many critics (notably Michael Williams) have pointed out, is that it is hard to imagine a time at which it would seem desirable to cease developing new theories and new vocabularies. As Davidson has remarked, Putnam's "naturalistic fallacy" argument applies as much to his "ideal acceptability" theory of truth as to any other theory of truth.

16   "Communicative reason stretches across the entire spectrum of validity claims: the claims to propositional truth, sincerity and normative rightness." (Habermas, *Between Facts And Norms* (Cambridge Mass: M.I.T. Press, 1996), p. 5).

17   Habermas, *Between Facts And Norms*, p. 6.

18   Habermas, *Between Facts And Norms*, p. 8.

19   Habermas, *Between Facts And Norms*, p. 8.

20   Habermas, *Between Facts And Norms*, p. 15.

21   For Davidsonian reasons, I should prefer the term 'practices' to 'conventions,' but I shall treat the two as synonomous here.

22   Habermas, *Between Facts And Norms*, p. 16.

23   I am not sure whether, when I do this, Apel and Habermas would still view me as *arguing*, or as having abandoned argument and fallen back on strategic sensitivity training.

24   Duellists used to say that some people were not *satisfaktionsfähig: one did not have to accept if challenged by such people.* We need some analogous notion – to describe *people whose requests for justification we are entitled to reject.* The sort of exclusivist bigot I have in mind does not see his or her claim as requiring justification to the wrong sort of people. But the bigot is not the only person who needs to invoke some such notion as *Rechtfertigungsempfäng-lichkeit.* None of us take all audiences seriously; we all reject requests for justification from some audiences as a waste of time. (Consider the surgeon refusing to justify her procedure to Christian Scientists, or to Chinese physicians who suggest relying on acupuncture and moxibustion.) The big difference between us and the bigot, as I say below, is that he thinks such non-discursive matters as racial descent matter in this context, whereas we think only beliefs and desires matter.

25   The bigot may not know how to do this, but then the local conventions which Habermas and I share suggest that we philosophers should step in and help him out – help him construct meanings for these terms which will build in his exclusivist view, just as Habermas' and my inclusivist view is built into our use of those terms.

26   The point of talking about universal validity rather than about truth seems to be to avoid the question of whether ethical and aesthetic judgments have a truth-value. Doubt that they do arises only among representationalists, people who think that there has to be an object to 'make' true judgments true. Non-representationalists like Davidson and me, and even quasi-representationalists like Putnam, are perfectly content to think of "Love is better than hate" as as good a candidate for truth-value as "Energy always equals mass times the square of the speed of light."

27   Albrecht Wellmer's *Endgames: the irreconcilable nature of modernity* (Cambridge, Mass: M.I.T. Press, 1998), p. 150.

28   *Endgames*, p. 151.

29   *Endgames*, p. 142.

30   Consider a lawyer saying to his clients, the officers of a multinational corporation, "My brief relies, I'm afraid, on a funny little kink in the *Code Napoléon*. So though we clearly have a winning case in France, the Ivory Coast, and Louisiana, I can't do anything for you in the courts of, for example, Britain, Germany, Ghana, or Massachusetts." His clients consult another, better, lawyer who says "I can transcend *that*; I've got an argument that will work in the courts of every country except Japan and Brunei."

31   This rhetorical question might be answered by saying: it is important in mathematics. There we say not only that all the Euclidean triangles so far drawn have interior angles which sum to 180 degrees, but that this is the case for all possible triangles. But, as Wittgenstein reminds us in *Remarks on the Foundations of Mathematics*, the cash-value of this claim to have surveyed the realm of possiblity is just that one will not try to justify certain claims to certain people: you don't discuss Euclidean geometry with people who keep on trying to square the circle and double the cube. Once, with Quine and the later Wittgenstein, we drop the analytic-synthetic and language-fact distinctions, we cannot be as comfortable with the distinction between "all possible Xs" and "all Xs envisaged so far" as we once were.

32   *Endgames*, p. 138.

33   *Endgames*, pp. 137–8.

34   See "Is truth a goal of inquiry?: Donald Davidson vs. Crispin Wright," reprinted in my *Truth and Progress*.

35   This metaphor of being nudged toward truths by objects sounds less plausible in ethics and aesthetics than in physics. That is why representationalists are often 'anti-realists' in respect to the former, and why they often reserve the notion of truth-making for elementary particles, which seem more plausible nudgers than do moral or aesthetic values.

36   *Endgames*, p. 148.

37   This is the point made in Davidson's "The Very Idea of a Conceptual Scheme."

38   *Endgames*, p. 150.

39   *Endgames*, p. 152.

40   *Endgames*, p. 152.

41   *Endgames*, p. 152.

42   I develop this point at some length in "Putnam and the Relativist Menace," *Journal of Philosophy* vol. 90 (September, 1993). There I argue that Putnam and I both have the same idea of what counts as a good argument – namely, one which satisfies an audience of wet liberals like ourselves – and that my view, though unlike his in being explicitly ethnocentric, is no more 'relativistic' than his.

43   I tend to agree with Vincent Descombes (in the final chapter of his *The Barometer of Modern Reason*) that Weber's distinction is an invidious and self-serving use of the term 'rational.' But I should admit that if Chomsky, Kohlberg, and the rest survive current criticism, their claims would suggest that Weber had a point.

44   It is perhaps worth remarking that one of the presuppositions of communication which Habermas mentions – the ascription of identical meanings to expressions – is endangered by Davidson's argument in "A Nice Derangement of Epitaphs" that linguistic competence can be had without such ascription, that holistic strategies of interpretation dictated by the

principle of charity render this ascription unnecessary. Davidson's argument that there is no such thing as language-mastery in the sense of the internalization of a set of conventions about what means what chimes with recent 'connectionist' criticism of MIT 'cognitivism' and thus of Chomsky's universalism. Perhaps what Habermas means by "ascription of identical meanings" is simply what Davidson means by "being charitable," but if so then, since charity is not optional, neither is such ascription. It is automatic, and nobody could be convicted of failing to abide by it. So it cannot form the basis for a charge of performative self-contradiction.

45 The 'MIT' notion, associated with Chomsky and Fodor, of 'communicative competence' is gradually being displaced, within the field of artificial intelligence, by the 'connectionist' view favored by those who see the brain as containing no hard-wired flow-charts of the sort constructed by 'cognitivist' programmers. Connectionists urge that the only biologically universal structures to be found in the brain are ones which cannot be described in terms of flow-charts labeled with the names of "natural kinds" of things and words. So the notion of 'communicative competence,' as something common to all human linguistic communities, drops out in favor of the notion of "enough neural connections to permit the organism to be made into a language-user."

46 Donald Davidson, "The Structure and Content of Truth", *Journal of Philosophy* vol. 87 (1990), p. 325.

47 Habermas, *Postmetaphysical Thinking*, p. 50.

48 *Postmetaphysical Thinking*, pp. 116–7.

49 "MacIntyre, Habermas and Philosophical Ethics" in *Hermeneutics and Critical Theory in Ethics and Politics* ed. Michael Kelly (Cambridge, MA: MIT Press, 1990).

50 *Postmetaphysical Thinking*, p. 117.

51 *Postmetaphysical Thinking*, p. 47.

52 *Postmetaphysical Thinking*, p. 103.

53 *Postmetaphysical Thinking*, pp. 89–90.

54 *Postmetaphysical Thinking*, p. 116.

55 *Postmetaphysical Thinking*, p. 117.

56 *Postmetaphysical Thinking*, p. 138.

57 *Postmetaphysical Thinking*, p. 138.

58 These last three quotations are from *Postmetaphysical Thinking*, pp. 138–139. The passage from Putnam is from p. 228 of Putnam's *Reason, Truth and History*.

59 *Postmetaphysical Thinking*, p. 138.

60 One might try to justify this rule by deriving it from the rule that reason alone should have force. If that means "argument alone should have force," then you have to find some sense in which arguments based on the authority of the Christian scriptures are not really arguments. But does the grammar of concepts like 'reason' really tell you that reason gets distorted when you invoke the authority of the Bible? If so, does it also get distorted by a *Bildungsroman* which arouses the reader's pity and sympathy by telling her what it's like to find out, to your horror, that you can only love members of your own sex?

61 *The Philosophical Discourse of Modernity*, p. 296.

62 Consider Vasari on the artistic movement that began with Giotto as an analogue of Hegel on the inclusivist movements which started when Greek philosophy joined up with Christian egalitarianism. Modern art has trained us to see the former movement as optional, but not something we should want to give up now that we have got it. I take post-Nietzschean philosophy to have helped us see that the latter movement was optional, even though not something we have any reason to give up. 'Optional' here contrasts with 'destined,' in a wide sense of 'destined' which covers Habermas' notion about the universalistic tendency of phylogenetic development.

63 See Habermas, *Moral Consciousness and Communicative Action*, p. 206: "In contrast to the neo–Aristotelian position, discourse ethics is emphatically opposed to going back to a stage of philosophical thought before Kant." The context makes clear that Habermas means that

it would be wrong to give up on the morality–prudence distinction which Kant made and Aristotle did not.

64   Dewey could of course have accepted Goodman's distinction between nomological necessity and universal generalizations which are merely accidental, but that is because Goodman makes nomologicality not a feature of the universe but of the coherence of our descriptive vocabulary. (See, on this point, Davidson's comment on Goodman: "Emeroses by Other Names".) Nomological necessity holds of things under descriptions, not, as for Kripke and Aristotle of things *kath' auto*.

65   Habermas, *Moral Consciousness and Communicative Action*, p. 118.

66   Baier describes Hume as "the woman's moral philosopher" because his treatment of morals facilitates her suggestion that we replace 'obligation' by 'appropriate trust' as the basic moral notion. In "Human Rights, Rationality and Sentimentality" (reprinted in my *Truth and Progress*) I discuss Baier's suggestion in connection with my claim (reiterated in this paper) that we should try to create, rather than to presuppose, universality.

67   Another aspect of these two differing stories about maturation is the different attitudes they encourage to the quarrel between Socrates and the Sophists, and more generally to the distinction between *argument* and the modes of persuasion which I have described as 'educative' in the previous section. Apel (*Diskurs und Verantwortung*, p. 353n.) says that one of the many things wrong with the sort of view common to Gadamer, Rorty, and Derrida is these men's insouciance about the "Unterschied zwischen dem *argumentativen Diskurs* und, anderseits, dem '*Diskurs*' im Sinne von *Verhandlungen, Propaganda*, oder auch von *poetischer Fiktion* nicht mehr zu erkennen bzw. anzuerkennen vermögen." Apel goes on to say that that attitude marks "the end of philosophy." It seems to me that it marks a stage in the further maturation of philosophy – a step away from the power-worship involved in the idea that there is a power called 'reason' which will come to your aid if you follow Socrates' example and make your definitions and premises explicit. As a Deweyan tells the story, the idea of philosophy as a *strenge Wissenschaft*, as a search for knowledge, is itself a symptom of immaturity; the Sophists were not wholly in the wrong. The reciprocal accusations of immaturity to which Apel and I tempt one another can easily seem cheap and empty, but they do express heartfelt convictions on both sides, convictions about what utopia looks like, and hence about what progress toward utopia requires.

2

Richard Rorty's Pragmatic Turn

JÜRGEN HABERMAS

In "Trotsky and the Wild Orchids" Richard Rorty casts a romantic eye back over his development as a philosopher.[1] Using the form of a "narrative of maturation," he presents his intellectual development as a progressive distancing of himself from his adolescent dream; this was the dream of fusing in a single image the extraordinary beauty of wild orchids and the liberation from profane suffering of an exploited society: the desire "to hold reality and justice in a single vision" (Yeats). The existential background to Rorty's neopragmatism is his rebellion against the false promises of philosophy: a philosophy that pretends to be able to satisfy aesthetic and moral needs in satisfying theoretical ones. Once upon a time, metaphysics wanted to instruct its pupils in spiritual exercises involving a purifying contemplation of the good in the beautiful. But the youthful Rorty, who had allowed himself to be filled with enthusiasm by Plato, Aristotle, and Thomas Aquinas, painfully comes to realize that the prospect of contact with the reality of the extraordinary held out by theory – a contact at once *desirable* and *reconciliatory* – although possibly attainable in the more definite forms of prayer, cannot be achieved along the path of philosophy. As a result, Rorty remembers Dewey – scorned by McKeon, Leo Strauss, and Mortimer Adler – who had not yet been completely forgotten in the Chicago of the 1940s. The realization that everyday reality conceals no higher reality, no realm of being-in-itself to be disclosed ecstatically, and that everyday practices leave no room for a *redemptory* vision, cures the sobered Rorty of his Platonic sickness. To be sure, the memory of the exotic sight and the overpowering smell of the wild orchids in the mountains of his childhood in the northwest of New Jersey cannot be extinguished completely.

It is roughly thus in terms of his own life-history that Rorty today explains to us the motives for his view of the dual dominance of Dewey and Heidegger developed in *Contingency, Irony, and Solidarity.* Strangely enough, this self-presentation contains no reference to the paramount role played by Wittgenstein, the third party in the alliance. Rorty's report on the experiences of his own philosophical development breaks off with his reading of Hegel as his student days in Yale draw to a close and his work as a professional philosopher is only about to begin. His training in analytic philosophy with his real teacher, Wilfrid Sellars, his basic conviction of the truth of physicalism, his successful career as a young analytic philosopher – these steps in his development are not mentioned at all. However, it is solely his ambivalence toward the tradition of analytic philosophy – the only tradition in whose language Rorty has learned to argue and using which he continues to expound his exciting teachings brilliantly – that can explain why he attributes a culturally critical significance to his anti-Platonic turn, a significance that is supposed to extend far beyond his own person and his private switch of philosophical allegiance.

I will deal briefly with this motivation for a kind of philosophizing that wants to bid farewell to itself as such before confining myself to discussion of the justification for the neopragmatic conception itself. From the pragmatic radicalization of the linguistic turn Rorty obtains a nonrealist understanding of knowledge. In order to test whether he radicalizes the linguistic turn in the right way, I will then compare the contextualist approach with the epistemological doubt of the modern skeptic. In doing so I will recall a problem that was always connected with coherence conceptions of truth: the problem of how truth is to be distinguished from rational acceptability. In responding to this question, there is a parting of philosophical ways. Whereas Rorty assimilates truth to justification at the expense of everyday realist intuitions, others attempt to take account of intuitions even within the linguistic paradigm, whether with the help of a deflationary strategy as regards the problem of truth or through an idealization of the process of justification itself. On the one hand, I will take issue with the deflationary strategy that relies on a semantic conception of truth, emphasizing instead the advantages of a pragmatic viewpoint. On the other hand, again from a pragmatic perspective, I will criticize a kind of epistemization of the idea of truth that I myself once proposed. In doing so I will develop an alternative to the liquidation of unconditional claims to truth. It is this liquidation that has ultimately compelled Rorty to effect a problematic naturalization of linguistified reason – or, at any rate, one that leads to further problems.

A Platonically Motivated Anti-Platonist

Richard Rorty is one of the most outstanding analytic philosophers, consistently arguing in an informed and astute way. But his program for a philosophy that is to do away with all philosophy seems to spring more from the melancholy of a disappointed metaphysician, driven on by nominalist spurs, than from the self-criticism of an enlightened analytic philosopher who wishes to complete the linguistic turn in a pragmatist way. In 1967, when analytic philosophy (in both its versions) had achieved widespread recognition comparable to that enjoyed by neo-Kantianism in the period before the First World War, Rorty edited a reader with the demandingly laconic title *The Linguistic Turn*. This reader, as we can see in retrospect, marks a break in the history of analytic thought. The texts collected in the reader are meant to serve a double purpose. In summing up a triumphant progression, they are intended at the same time to signal its end. At any rate, notwithstanding his laudatory gesture, the metaphilosophical distance from which the editor comments on the texts betrays the Hegelian message that every manifestation of Spirit that achieves maturity is condemned to decline. At that time Rorty gave the starting signal to a discourse that has since given itself the name "postanalytic." In his introduction to the reader, he speculates on the "future" of analytic philosophy – a future that relegates it to the past tense. In the face of a still intact orthodoxy, Rorty points to three approaches that concur in their contradiction of the general basic assumption that "there are philosophical truths still waiting to be discovered that can be justified on the basis of arguments." Rorty links these anti-Platonic approaches with the names Heidegger, Wittgenstein, and Waismann (whose philosophical program Rorty even then described in terms similar to his later description of Dewey's pragmatism).

This distanced gaze on analytic philosophy in no way conceals the immense respect of the initiate who here steps outside of his own tradition: "Linguistic philosophy, over the last thirty years, has succeeded in putting the entire philosophical tradition, from Parmenides through Descartes and Hume to Bradley and Whitehead, on the defensive. It has done so by careful and thorough scrutiny of the ways in which traditional philosophers have used language in the formulation of their problems. This achievement is sufficient to place this period among the great ages of the history of philosophy."[2] Only the irresistibility of analytic philosophy's arguments explains Rorty's real grief. This irresistibility leads him to bid farewell to the alluring promises of metaphysics so irrevocably that, even post analytic philosophy, there can be no alternative to postmetaphysical thinking. Nonetheless, Rorty, then as now, is in search of some mode of thinking that, as Adorno puts it at the end of *Negative Dialectics*, shows solidarity with metaphysics at the moment of its fall.[3] There is melancholy in the strained irony propagated today by Rorty: "Rorty's post-philosophical intellectual is ironic because he realizes that truth is not all he would like it to be. Irony depends essentially on a kind of *nostalgie de la verité*."[4] Even the romantic division of labor between irony and seriousness, Heidegger and Dewey, cannot ease the pain. Because metaphysics has command only over the language of knowledge, the aestheticization of its claim to truth amounts to an anaestheticization of the philosophical tradition as mere cultural heritage. The reality of the ideas with which Platonic theory promised to bring us into contact is not the same as the extraordinary appeal of aesthetic experience. What once aspired to be 'true' in an emphatic sense cannot be preserved in the mode of the 'edifying.' In forfeiting the binding power of its judgments, metaphysics also loses its substance.[5]

When one is faced with this dilemma it is possible to understand the move Rorty finally makes in order to give back to philosophy, even today, something of a 'doctrine,' something of that inimitable combination of wild orchids and Trotsky: his imitation of the gesture, at least, of insight that is at once *stimulating* and *rich in practical consequence*. However, the metaphysical need to liberate philosophy from the sterility of a pusillanimous postmetaphysical thinking can now be satisfied only postmetaphysically. The farewell to analytic philosophy cannot lead back to a devalued metaphysics. For this reason, the only remaining option is to dramatize the farewell to philosophy in general. Only if the act of leave-taking itself were to release a shock and intervene into everyday life would philosophy "at the moment of its fall" be able to acquire a more than purely academic significance. But how is a separation from analytic philosophy carried out with analytic means supposed to achieve significance of a kind that would allow analytic thought to be illuminated one last time in the brilliance of its great tradition? As I understand his naturalistically refracted impulse toward great philosophy, Rorty wants to give an answer to this question.

Rorty begins by showing that analytic philosophy shares a fundamental premise with the tradition it has devalued. This is the conviction that "there are philosophical truths still waiting to be discovered." Thanks to a very German idea that he borrows from Heidegger, Rorty then attributes a dramatic weightiness to this *proton pseudos* of Western metaphysics. According to this Heideggerian thesis, the profane destinies of the West are supposed to have been fulfilled only within the scope of an epochal understanding of being; moreover, one governed by metaphysics. Of course, unlike Heidegger, Rorty can no longer stylize postmetaphysical thinking post analytic philosophy as a sacral "Commemoration of Being" (*Andenken des Seins*). Rorty understands the deconstruction of the history of metaphysics as a deflationary diagnosis in Wittgenstein's sense. Anti-Platonism draws its eminently practical significance only from the severity of the sickness that it is supposed to cure. The unmasking of Platonism is aimed, beyond scholasticism, at a culture that is alienated from itself platonistically. If, finally, the act of leave-taking is not to exhaust itself in negation, Rorty has to open a perspective that will enable a new self-understanding that can take the place of the old, deflated one. With this end in view, he adapts Dewey's Hegelianism for his own purposes in such a way that a perspective is opened on everyday practices that are no longer distorted by Platonist prejudices. In this way, like Hegel, even the 'last' philosophers capture their own time once more in thought.

Rorty knows, of course, that such metaphilosophical reflections cannot transform the self-understanding of philosophy on their own.[6] He cannot get outside of philosophy without using philosophy to claim validity for his thoughts. Rorty would not be the scrupulous and sensitive, suggestive, and stimulating philosopher that he is were he to insist solely on the rhetorical role of the re-educator. The diagnosis of a false self-understanding, too, remains a matter for theory. Rorty has to provide arguments if he is to convince his colleagues that the 'Platonic' distinction between 'convincing' and 'persuading' makes no sense. He has to prove that even analytic philosophy remains captivated by the spell of the metaphysics against which it is battling.

The Pragmatic Turn

Rorty's important book *Philosophy and the Mirror of Nature* (1979) pursues a number of aims. By carrying through to its conclusion the deconstruction of the philosophy of consciousness, he wants to complete a not yet completed linguistic turn in such a way that the Platonist self-misunderstanding deeply rooted in our culture becomes obvious. My doubts relate to the second step. Does the pragmatic turn, which Rorty rightly demands in the face of semantically fixated approaches, require an anti-realist understanding of knowledge?

(a)   The basic conceptual framework of the philosophy of the subject has, from Peirce to Wittgenstein and Heidegger, been subjected to a relentless critique. Rorty draws on contemporary arguments (among others those of Sellars, Quine, and Davidson) in order to expose the basic assumptions of mentalist epistemology with a view to a critique of reason. The ideas of 'self-consciousness' and 'subjectivity' imply that the knowing subject can disclose for itself a privileged sphere of immediately accessible and absolutely certain experiences (*Erlebnisse*) when it does not focus directly on objects but rather reflexively on its own representations (*Vorstellungen*) of objects. For classical epistemology, there is a constitutive separation between inner and outer – a dualism of mind and body – that appeals to the privileged access of the first person to her own experiences. The epistemic authority of the first person is sustained by the wellsprings of three paradigm-constituting assumptions:

1   that we know our own mental states better than anything else;
2   that knowing takes place essentially in the mode of representing objects; and

3   that the truth of judgments rests on evidence that vouches for their certainty.

Analysis of the linguistic form of our experiences and thoughts discovers in these assumptions three corresponding myths – the myth of the given, the myth of thought as representation, and the myth of truth as certainty. It is shown that we cannot circumvent the linguistic expression as the medium for the representation and communication of knowledge. There are no uninterpreted experiences (*Erfahrungen*) that are accessible only privately and elude public assessment and correction. Moreover, knowledge of objects is not an adequate model for the knowledge of propositionally structured states of affairs. Finally, truth is a property of criticizable propositions that cannot be lost; it can be justified only on the basis of reasons – it cannot be authenticated on the basis of the genesis of representations.

Rorty, of course, connects this critique of mentalism with the more far-reaching aim of radicalizing the linguistic turn. He wants to show "what philosophy of language comes to when purified of attempts to imitate either Kant or Hume."[7] So long as the subject–object relation is projected merely onto the sentence–fact relation, the resulting semantic answers remain tied to the mentalist mode of questioning. So long as the representation (*Darstellung*) of states of affairs – like the representation (*Vorstellung*) of objects[8] – is conceived as a two–place relation, the linguistic turn leaves the "mirror of nature" – as metaphor for knowledge of the world – intact.

Rorty wants to make full use of the conceptual scope that has been opened up by the philosophy of language. With Peirce he replaces the two–place relation between representing subject and represented object with a three–place relation: the symbolic expression, which accords validity to a state of affairs, for an interpretive community. The objective world is no longer something to be reflected but is simply the common reference point for a process of communication (*Verständigung*) between members of a communication community who come to an understanding with one another with regard to something. The communicated facts can no more be separated from the process of communication than the *supposition* of an objective world can be separated from the intersubjectively shared interpretive horizon within which the participants in communication always already operate. Knowledge no longer coincides with the correspondence of sentences and facts. For this reason, only a linguistic turn that is rigorously carried to its conclusion can, in overcoming mentalism, also overcome the epistemological model of the Mirror of Nature.

(b)   I am interested in the question of whether Rorty performs this plausible pragmatic radicalization of the linguistic turn in the right way. If we no longer refer epistemological questions only to language as the grammatical form of representation (*Darstellung*), relating them instead to language as it is used communicatively, an additional dimension is opened up. This is the dimension of interactions and traditions – the public space of a lifeworld shared intersubjectively by the language users. This expanded perspective allows the entwining of the epistemological accomplishments of the socialized individuals with their processes of cooperation and communication to become visible: "Once conversation replaces confrontation [of persons with states of affairs], the notion of the mind as Mirror

of Nature can be discarded."[9] The "communication model" of knowledge highlights the point that we have no unfiltered access to entities in the world,
independent of our practices of reaching understanding and the linguistically
constituted context of our lifeworld: "Elements of what we call 'language' or
'mind' penetrate so deeply into what we call 'reality' that the very project of
representing ourselves as being 'mappers' of something 'language-independent' is
fatally compromised from the start."[10]

This is a quotation from Hilary Putnam with which Rorty agrees. Nonetheless,
Rorty has something other than Putnam's "internal realism" in mind. Putnam's
"internal realism" stresses that the conditions for the objectivity of knowledge can
be analyzed only *in connection with* the conditions for the intersubjectivity of a
mutual understanding with regard to what is said. On Rorty's view, "being in
touch with reality" has to be translated into the jargon of "being in touch with a
human community" in such a way that the realist intuition, to which mentalism
wanted to do justice with its Mirror of Nature and its correspondence between
representation and represented object, disappears completely. For Rorty, every
kind of representation of something in the objective world is a dangerous illusion.
Now, it is certainly the case that with the pragmatic turn the epistemic authority
of the first person singular, who inspects her inner self, is displaced by the first
person plural, by the 'we' of a communication community in front of which every
person justifies her views. However, it is only the empiricist interpretation of this
new authority that leads Rorty to equate 'knowledge' with what is accepted as
'rational' according to the standards of our respective communities.

Just as Locke and Hume referred their mentalist reflections to the consciousness
of empirical persons, Kant referred his to the consciousness of subjects "in
general." Linguistic reflections, too, can be referred to communication communities "in general." But Rorty, the nominalist, stands in the empiricist tradition and
refers epistemic authority to the received social practices of 'our' respective
communities. He regards the urge "to see social practices of justification as more
than just such practices"[11] as nonsensical. Rorty himself makes the connection
between, on the one hand, the contextualist interpretation of the pragmatic turn
and the anti-realist understanding of knowledge and, on the other hand, the
rejection of a Kantian strategy of analysis:[12] "If we see knowledge as a matter of
conversation and of social practice, rather than as an attempt to mirror nature, we
will not be likely to envisage a metapractice which will be the critique of all
possible forms of social practice."[13] For Rorty, such a formal-pragmatic attempt
would be a relapse into foundationalism. In the seventeenth century the basic
concepts of subjectivity and self-consciousness had, with "the mental" and
"introspection," respectively, secured for philosophy – which at that time had to
find a new place *alongside* the new physics – an object domain and a method of its
own. As a result, philosophy was able to understand itself as a foundational
discipline that checked and justified the foundations of all other disciplines. Rorty
now holds the view that this same foundationalist self-understanding takes
possession of the philosophy of language when it stops short of a contextualist
understanding of knowledge and justification. Universalist approaches within the
philosophy of language – such as Rorty discerns in Dummett and others – come
under suspicion here.

Contextualism and Skepticism as Problems Specific to Particular Paradigms

When Rorty regards contextualism as the necessary consequence of a fully executed linguistic turn, he is right in one respect: contextualism designates a problem that can occur only when we reckon on a reason embodied in linguistic practices. But he is wrong to see contextualism at the same time as the solution to the problem. This view has its roots, if I am correct, in a problematic understanding of philosophical paradigms.

Like, for example, Apel and Tugendhat, Rorty regards the history of philosophy as a succession of three paradigms. He speaks of metaphysics, epistemology, and the philosophy of language.[14] Of course, the philosophy of language has detached itself only halfheartedly from mentalism. Rorty believes that the linguistic turn can be carried through consistently to its conclusion only in the form of a critique of reason that takes its leave of philosophy as such.[15] It is not just the problems but the way of posing problems that changes with the leap from one paradigm to the next:

> This picture of ancient and medieval philosophy as concerned with *things*, the philosophy of the seventeenth through the nineteenth centuries with *ideas*, and the enlightened contemporary philosophical scene with *words* has considerable plausibility. But this sequence should not be thought of as offering three contrasting views about what is primary, or what is foundational. It is not that Aristotle thought that one could best explain ideas and words in terms of things, whereas Descartes and Russell rearranged the order of explanation. It would be more correct to say that Aristotle did not have – did not feel the need of – a theory of knowledge, and that Descartes and Locke did not have a theory of meaning. Aristotle's remarks about knowing do not offer answers, good or bad, to Locke's questions, any more than Locke's remarks about language offer answers to Frege's.[16]

This *discontinuity* means that philosophical questions are not settled through finding the right answers; rather, they fall into disuse once they have lost their market value. This also holds for the question of the objectivity of knowledge.

On the mentalist view, objectivity is ensured when the representing subject refers to his objects in the right way. He checks the subjectivity of his representations against the objective world: "'subjective' contrasts with 'corresponding to what is out there,' and thus means something like 'a product only of what is in here.'"[17] On the linguistic view, the subjectivity of beliefs is no longer checked directly through confrontation with the world but rather through public agreement achieved in the communication community: "a 'subjective' consideration is one which has been, or would be, or should be, set aside by rational discussants."[18] With this, the intersubjectivity of reaching understanding replaces the objectivity of experience. The language–world relation becomes dependent on communication between speakers and hearers. The vertical world-relation of representations of something, or of propositions about something, is bent back, as it were, into the horizontal line of the cooperation of participants in communication. The intersubjectivity of the lifeworld, which subjects inhabit in common, *displaces* the objectivity of a world that a solitary subject confronts: "For pragmatists, the desire for objectivity is not the desire to escape the limitations of one's community, but simply the desire for as much intersubjective agreement as possible."[19] Rorty wants to say: the paradigm shift transforms perspectives in such a way that epistemological questions as such are passé.

The contextualist understanding of the linguistic turn from which this anti-realism emerges goes back to a conception of the rise and fall of paradigms that excludes continuity of theme between paradigms as well as learning processes that extend across paradigms. In fact, the terms, in which we undertake a comparison of paradigms reflect our hermeneutic starting point – and, thus, our own paradigm. That Rorty selects for his comparison the frame of reference of objectivity, subjectivity, and intersubjectivity results from the basic conceptual perspective from which we now describe the linguistic turn of mentalism. On the other hand the picture of a contingent succession of incommensurable paradigms does not in any way fit with this description. Rather, from the perspective of that frame of reference, a subsequent paradigm appears as an answer to a problem bequeathed to us by the devaluation of a preceding paradigm. Contrary to what Rorty supposes, paradigms do not form an arbitrary sequence but a dialectical relationship.

Nominalism robbed things of their inner nature or essence and declared general concepts to be constructions of a finite mind. Since then, comprehending that which is (*das Seiende*) in thought has lacked a foundation in the conceptual constitution of beings themselves. The correspondence of mind with nature could no longer be conceived as an ontological relation, the rules of logic no longer reflected the laws of reality. *Pace* Rorty, mentalism responded to this challenge by reversing the order of explanation. If the knowing subject can no longer derive the standards for knowledge from a disqualified nature, it has to supply these standards from a reflexively disclosed subjectivity itself. Reason, once embodied objectively in the order of nature, retreats to subjective spirit. With this, the being-in-itself (*das Ansich*) of the world is transformed into the objectivity of a world that is given for us, the subjects – a world of represented objects or *phenomena*. Whereas up to then, the constitution of the world of being-in-itself had enabled a correspondence of thought with reality – true judgments – the truth of judgments is now supposed to be measured against the certainty of evident subjective experiences (*Erlebnisse*). Representational thought leads to objective knowledge insofar as it comprehends the phenomenal world.

The concept of subjectivity introduced a dualism between inner and outer that seemed to confront the human mind with the precarious task of bridging a chasm. With this, the way was cleared for skepticism in its modern form. The private character of my particular subjective experiences, on which my absolute certainty is based, simultaneously provides reason to doubt whether the world as it appears to us is not in fact an illusion. This skepticism is anchored in the constitutive concepts of the mentalist paradigm. At the same time it conjures up memories of the comforting intuition that sustained the ontological paradigm: the idea that the truth of judgments is guaranteed by a correspondence with reality that is grounded in reality itself. This 'residual' intuition, as it were, which had lost none of its suggestive power with the switch of paradigm, joined forces with the new skeptical question of whether – and if so, how – the agreement between representation and represented object is to be grounded on the basis of the evidence of our subjective experiences. It is this question that first provokes the epistemological quarrel between Idealism and Empiricism.[20] However, in light of this genealogy it becomes apparent – and this is my main point here – that contextualism is built into the basic concepts of the linguistic paradigm just as skepticism is built into mentalism. And once again, the intuitions regarding truth that carry over or stick with us from the preceding paradigms lead to an intensification of these problems.

Just as the dispute about universals at the end of the Middle Ages contributed to the devaluation of objective reason, the critique of introspection and psychologism at the end of the nineteenth century contributed to the shaking up of subjective reason. With the displacement of reason from the consciousness of the knowing subject to language as the medium by means of which acting subjects communicate with one another, the order of explanation changes once more. Epistemic authority passes over from the knowing subject, which supplies from within herself the standards for the objectivity of experience, to the justificatory practices of a linguistic community. Up to then the intersubjective validity of beliefs had resulted from the subsequent convergence of thoughts or representations. Interpersonal agreement had been explained by the ontological anchoring of true judgments or by the shared psychological or transcendental endowments of knowing subjects. Following the linguistic turn, however, all explanations take the primacy of a common language as their starting point. Description of states and events in the objective world, like the self-representation of experiences to which the subject has privileged access, is dependent on the interpreting use of a common language. For this reason, the term 'intersubjective' no longer refers to the result of an *observed* convergence of the thoughts or representations of various persons, but to the prior commonality of a linguistic pre-understanding or horizon of the lifeworld – which, from the perspective of the participants themselves, is presupposed – within which the members of a communication community find themselves before they reach understanding with one another about something in the world. Finally, the contextualist question, which should not be confused with the epistemological doubt of skepticism, results from this primacy of the intersubjectivity of shared beliefs over confrontation with reality (a reality that is always already interpreted).

The pragmatic turn leaves no room for doubt as to the existence of a world independent of our descriptions. Rather, from Peirce to Wittgenstein, the idle Cartesian doubt has been rejected as a performative contradiction – "If you tried to doubt everything you would not get as far as doubting anything. The game of doubting itself presupposes certainty."[21] On the other hand, all knowledge is fallible and, when it is problematized, dependent on justification. As soon as the standard for the objectivity of knowledge passes from private certainty to public practices of justification, 'truth' becomes a three-place concept of validity. The validity of propositions that are fallible in principle is shown to be validity that is justified *for* a public.[22] Moreover, because in the linguistic paradigm truths are accessible only in the form of rational acceptability, the question now arises of how in that case the truth of a proposition can still be isolated from the context in which it is justified. Unease with regard to this problem brings older intuitions about truth onto the scene. It awakens memory of a correspondence between thought and reality or of a contact with reality that is sensorially certain. These images, which are still suggestive despite having lost their bearings, are behind the question of how the fact that we cannot transcend the linguistic horizon of justified beliefs is compatible with the intuition that true propositions fit the facts. It is no accident that the contemporary rationality debates circle around the concepts of truth and reference.[23] Just as skepticism does not simply assimilate being to appearance but rather gives expression to the uneasy feeling that we *might* be unable to separate the one from the other convincingly, neither does contextualism, properly understood, equate truth with justified assertibility. Contextualism is rather an expression of the embarrassrnent that would ensue if we did have to assimilate the one to the other. It makes us aware of a problem to which cultural relativism presents a solution that is false because it contains a performative self-contradiction.

Truth and justification

Even in the comprehension of elementary propositions about states or events in the world, language and reality interpenetrate in a manner that for us is *indissoluble*. There is no natural possibility of isolating the constraints of reality that make a statement true from the semantic rules that lay down these truth conditions. We can explain what a fact is only with the help of the truth of a statement of fact, and we can explain what is real only in terms of what is true. Being, as Tugendhat says, is veritative being.[24] Since the truth of beliefs or sentences can in turn be justified only with the help of other beliefs and sentences, we cannot break free from the magic circle of our language. This fact suggests an anti-foundationalist conception of knowledge and a holistic conception of justification. Because we cannot confront our sentences with anything that is not itself already saturated linguistically, no basic propositions can be distinguished that would be privileged in being able to legitimate themselves, thereby serving as the basis for a linear chain of justification. Rorty rightly emphasizes "that nothing counts as justification unless by reference to what we already accept," concluding from this "that there is no way to get outside our beliefs and our language so as to find some test other than coherence."[25]

This does not mean, of course, that the coherence of our beliefs is sufficient to clarify the meaning of the concept of truth – which has now become central. Certainly, within the linguistic paradigm, the truth of a proposition can no longer be conceived as correspondence with something in the world, for otherwise we would have to be able to "get outside of language" while using language. Obviously, we cannot compare linguistic expressions with a piece of uninterpreted or "naked" reality – that is, with a reference that eludes our linguistically bound inspection.[26] None the less, the correspondence idea of truth was able to take account of a fundamental aspect of the meaning of the truth predicate. This aspect – the notion of unconditional validity – is swept under the carpet if the truth of a proposition is conceived as coherence with other propositions or as justified assertibility within an interconnected system of assertions. Whereas well-justified assertions can turn out to be false, we understand truth as a property of propositions "that cannot be lost." Coherence depends on practices of justification that let themselves be guided by standards that change from time to time. This accounts for the question: "Why does the fact that our beliefs hang together, supposing they do, give the least indication that they are true?"[27]

The "cautionary" use of the truth predicates[28] shows that, with the truth of propositions, we connect an unconditional claim that points beyond all the evidence available to us; on the other hand, the evidence that we bring to bear in our contexts of justification has to be sufficient to entitle us to raise truth claims. Although truth cannot be reduced to coherence and justified assertibility, there has to be an internal relation between truth and justification. How, otherwise, would it be possible to explain that a justification of "*p*," successful according to our standards, points in favor of the truth of "*p*," although truth is not an achievement term and does not depend on how well a proposition can be justified. Michael Williams describes the problem as a dispute between two equally reasonable ideas: "First, that if we are to have knowledge of an objective world, the truth of what we believe about the world must be independent of our believing it; and second, that justification is inevitably a matter of supporting beliefs by other beliefs, hence in this minimal sense a matter of coherence."[29] This leads to the contextualist question: "Given only knowledge of what we believe about the world, and how our beliefs fit together, how can we show that these beliefs are likely to be true?"[30]

This question should not, however, be understood in a skeptical sense, for the conception according to which we, as socialized individuals, always already find ourselves within the linguistically disclosed horizon of our lifeworld implies an unquestioned background of intersubjectively shared convictions, proven true in practice, which makes nonsense of total doubt as to the accessibility of the world. Language, which we cannot "get outside of" should not be understood in analogy to the inwardness of a representing subject who is as if cut off from the external world of representable objects. The relationship between justifiability and truth, although in need of clarification, signals no gulf between inner and outer, no dualism that would have to be *bridged* and that could give rise to the skeptical doubt as to whether our world *as a whole* is an illusion. The pragmatic turn pulls the rug from under this skepticism. There is a simple reason for this. In everyday practices, we cannot use language without *acting*. Speech itself is effected in the mode of speech acts that for their part are embedded in contexts of interaction and entwined with instrumental actions. As actors, that is, as interacting and intervening subjects, we are always already in contact with things about which we can make statements. Language games and practices are *interwoven*. "At some point . . . we have to leave the realm of sentences (and texts) and draw upon agreement in action and experience (for instance, in using a predicate)."[31] From the point of view of the philosophy of language, Husserl's pheno-menological conclusion that we "are always already in contact with things" is confirmed.

For this reason, the question as to the internal connection between justification and truth – a connection that explains why we may, in light of the evidence available to us, raise an unconditional truth claim that aims beyond what is justified – is not an epistemological question. It is not a matter of being or appearance. What is at stake is not the correct representation of reality but everyday practices that must not fall apart. The contextualist unease betrays a worry about the smooth functioning of language games and practices. Reaching understanding cannot function unless the participants refer to a single objective world, thereby stabilizing the intersubjectively shared public space with which everything that is merely subjective can be contrasted.[32] This supposition of an objective world that is independent of our descriptions fulfills a functional requirement of our processes of cooperation and communication. Without this supposition, everyday practices, which rest on the (in a certain sense) Platonic distinction between believing and knowing unreservedly, would come apart at the seams.[33] If it were to turn out that we cannot in any way make *this* distinction, the result would be more of a pathological self-misunderstanding than an illusionary understanding of the world. Whereas skepticism suspects an epistemological mistake, contextualism supposes a faulty construction in the way we live.

Contextualism thus raises the question of whether and, as the case may be, how the intuition that we can in principle distinguish between what-is-true and what-is-held-to-be-true can be brought into the linguistic paradigm. This intuition is not 'realist' in an epistemological sense. Even within pragmatism there is a parting of ways with regard to this question. Some are pragmatist enough to take seriously realist everyday intuitions and the internal relation between coherence and truth to which they attest. Others regard the attempt to clarify this internal relation as hopeless, treating everyday realism as an illusion. Rorty wants to combat this illusion by rhetorical means and pleads for *reeducation*. We ought to get used to replacing the desire for objectivity with the desire for solidarity and, with William James, to understanding 'truth' as no more than that in which it is good for "us" – the liberal members of Western culture or Western societies – to believe.

> [Pragmatists) should see themselves as working at the interface between the common sense of their community, a common sense much influenced by Greek metaphysics and by patriarchal monotheism ... They should see themselves as involved in a long-term attempt to change the rhetoric, the common sense, and self-image of their community.[34]

Before I deal with this proposal, I would like to examine whether the alternatives are as hopeless as Rorty assumes. Are there not plausible explanations for the fact that a justification successful in our justificatory context points in favor of the context-independent truth of the justified proposition? I am interested above all in two attempts at explanation: a deflationary one, which disputes that 'truth' has any nature at all that could be explicated; and epistemic one, which inflates the idea of a justified assertion to such an extent that truth becomes the limit concept of the justificatory process. Of course, deflationism is permitted to de-thematize the concept of truth only to the extent that this concept can continue to sustain realist intuitions, while the epistemic conception is allowed to idealize the justificatory conditions only to the extent that its idea of argumentation removed from everyday practices remains within the reach of 'our' practices.[35]

The Semantic Conception of Truth and the Pragmatic Perspective

Tarski's Convention T – "'p' is true if and only if p" – relies on a disquotational use of the truth-predicate that can be illustrated, for instance, by the example of confirming another person's statements: "Everything that the witness said yesterday is true." With this, the speaker makes his own "everything that was said," in such a way that he could repeat the corresponding assertions in the stance of the first person. This use of the truth-predicate is noteworthy in two respects. For one thing, it permits a generalizing reference to subject matter that is mentioned but not explicitly reproduced. Tarski uses this property in order to construct a theory of truth that generalizes about all instances of 'T.' For another, the truth-predicate when used in this way establishes a relation of equivalence between two linguistic expressions – the whole point of the Tarskian strategy of explanation depends on this. For, through exploiting the disquotational function, the inaccessible "relation of correspondence" between language and world or sentence and fact can, it appears, be reflected onto the tangible semantic relation between the expressions of an object language and those of a metalanguage. No matter how one conceives of the representational function of statements, whether as 'satisfaction' of truth conditions or as 'fitting' the facts to the sentences, what is envisaged in every case are pictures of relations that extend beyond language. It now seems possible to clarify these pictures with the help of interrelations that are *internal to language*. This initial idea allows us to understand why weak realist connotations are connected with the semantic conception of truth even if it is clear that this conception cannot sustain a strong epistemological realism in the manner of Popper.[36]

Now, it was already noticed at an early stage that the semantic conception of truth cannot vindicate its claim to be an explication of the full meaning of the truth-predicate.[37] The reason for this is that the disquotational function is not sufficiently informative because it already presupposes the representational function. One understands the meaning of Convention T when one knows what is *meant* (*gemeint*) with the right-hand side of the biconditional. The meaning of the truth-predicate in the sentence "Everything that the witness said yesterday is true" is parasitic on the assertoric mode of the witness's assertions. Before an assertion can be quoted it must be "put forward." This presupposed assertoric meaning can be analyzed in an exemplary way by looking at the 'yes' and 'no' positions of participants in argumentation who raise or refute objections; it can also be seen in the 'cautionary' use of the truth-predicate, which recalls the experience of participants in argumentation that even propositions that have been justified convincingly can turn out to be false.

The truth-predicate belongs – though not exclusively – to the language game of argumentation. For this reason its meaning can be elucidated (at least partly) according to its functions in this language game, that is, in the *pragmatic dimension* of a particular employment of the predicate. Whoever confines herself to the semantic dimension of sentences and of metalinguistic commentaries on sentences comprehends only the reflection of a prior linguistic practice that, as remains to be shown, extends even into everyday practices. However, the deflationary treatment of the concept of truth, through its semantic dimming of the pragmatic meaning of truth, has the advantage of avoiding discussions about the 'nature' of truth without having to forfeit a minimal orientation toward the distinction between knowing and believing, between being-true and being-held-to-be-true. This strategy aims at uncoupling these elementary distinctions from the dispute about substantial epistemological views. If it can be shown that the semantic conception of truth is sufficient to explain the usual methods of inquiry and theory selection – that is, sufficient also to explain what counts as 'success' or 'growth in knowledge' in the scientific enterprise – we can rescue the weak realist supposition of a world independent of our descriptions without boosting up the concept of truth in an epistemological–realist way.[38]

On the other hand, science is not the only sphere – and not even the primary one – in which the truth-predicate has a use. Even if a deflationary concept of truth were sufficient for elucidating the fact of science, for rendering the functioning of our practices of inquiry transparent, this would still not dissipate the contextualist doubt. For this doubt extends not only to the construction and selection of theories, indeed, not only to practices of argumentation in general: with respect to the pretheoretical orientation toward truth inherent in everyday practices, a semantic conception of truth simply does not help us at all.

What is at issue in the lifeworld is the pragmatic role of a Janus-faced notion of truth that mediates between behavioral certainty and discursively justified assertibility. In the network of established practices, implicitly raised validity claims that have been accepted against a broad background of intersubjectively shared convictions constitute the rails along which behavioral certainties run. However, as soon as these certainties lose their hold in the corset of self-evident beliefs, they are jolted out of tranquility and transformed into a corresponding number of questionable topics that thereby become subject to debate. In moving from action to rational discourse,[39] what is initially naively held-to-be-true is released from the mode of behavioral certainty and assumes the form of a hypothetical proposition whose validity is left open for the duration of the discourse. The argumentation takes the form of a competition for the better arguments in favor of, or against, controversial validity claims, and serves the cooperative search for truth.[40]

With this description of justificatory practices guided by the idea of truth, however, the problem is posed anew of how the systematic mobilization of good reasons, which at best lead to justified beliefs, is supposed nonetheless to be adequate for the purpose of discriminating between justified and unjustified truth claims. To begin with, I simply want to keep hold of the picture of a circular process that presents itself to us from a perspective expanded by means of the theory of action: shaken-up behavioral certainties are transformed on the level of argumentation into controversial validity claims raised for hypothetical propositions; these claims are tested discursively – and, as the case may be, vindicated – with the result that the discursively accepted truths can return to the realm of action; with this, behavioral certainties (as the case may be, new ones), which rely on beliefs unproblematically held to be true, are produced once more. What still remains to be explained is the mysterious power of the discursively achieved agreement that *authorizes* the participants in argumentation, in the role of actors, to accept unreservedly justified assertions as truths. For it is clear from the description from the point of view of action theory that argumentation can fulfill the role of *troubleshooter* with regard to behavioral certainties that have become problematic only if it is guided by truth in a context-independent – that is, unconditional – sense.

Although when we adopt a reflexive attitude we know that all knowledge is fallible, in everyday life we cannot survive with hypotheses alone, that is, in a persistently fallibilist way. The organized fallibilism of scientific inquiry can deal hypothetically with controversial validity claims indefinitely because it serves to bring about agreements that are *uncoupled* from action. This model is not suitable for the lifeworld. Certainly, we have to make decisions in the lifeworld on the basis of incomplete information; moreover, existential risks such as the loss of those closest to us, sickness, old age, and death are the mark of human life. However, notwithstanding these uncertainties, everyday routines rest on an unqualified trust in the *knowledge* of lay people as much as experts. We would step on no bridge, use no car, undergo no operation, not even eat an exquisitely prepared meal if we did not consider the knowledge used to be safeguarded, if we did not hold the assumptions employed in the production and execution of our actions to be true. At any rate, the performative need for behavioral certainty rules out a reservation in principle with regard to truth, even though we know, as soon as the naive performance of actions is interrupted, that truth claims can be vindicated only discursively – that is, only within the relevant context of justification. Truth may be assimilated neither to behavioral certainty nor to justified assertibility. Evidently, only strong conceptions of knowledge and truth – open to the accusation of Platonism – can do justice to the unity of the illocutionary meaning of assertions, which take on different roles in the realms of action and discourse respectively. Whereas in everyday practices 'truths' prop up behavioral certainties, in discourses they provide the reference point for truth claims that are in principle fallible.

The Epistemic Conception of Truth in a Pragmatic Perspective

The stubborn problem of the relation between truth and justification makes understandable the attempt to distinguish 'truth' from 'rational acceptability' through an idealization of the conditions of justification. This attempt proposes that a proposition justified according to "our" standards is distinguished from a true proposition in the same way that a proposition justified in a given context is distinguished from a proposition that could be justified in any context. A proposition is 'true' if it could be justified under ideal epistemic conditions (Putnam)[41] or could win argumentatively reached agreement in an ideal speech situation (Habermas)[42] or in an ideal communication community (Apel).[43] What is true is what may be accepted as rational under ideal conditions. Convincing objections have been raised to this proposal, which dates back to Peirce. The objections are directed in part against conceptual difficulties with the ideal state adopted; in part they show that an idealization of justificatory conditions cannot achieve its goal because it either distances truth too far from justified assertibility or nor far enough.

The first kind of objection draws attention to the paradoxical nature of the notion of "complete" or "conclusive" knowledge fixed as a limit concept – that, when its incompleteness and fallibility is taken away from it, would no longer be (human) knowledge.[44] Paradoxical, too, is the idea of a final consensus or definitive language that would bring to a standstill all further communication or all further interpretation, "with the result that what is *meant* as a situation of ideal mutual understanding stands revealed as a situation beyond the necessity for (and the problems connected with) linguistic processes of reaching understanding."[45] This objection is directed not just against an idealization that hypostatizes final states *as attainable* states in the world. Even if the ideal reference points are understood as aims that are not attainable in principle, or attainable only approximately, it remains "paradoxical that we would be obliged to strive for the realization of an ideal whose realization would be the end of human history."[46] As a regulative idea, the critical point of the orientation toward truth becomes clear only when the formal or processual properties of argumentation, and *not its aims*, are idealized.

The second kind of objection leads to the same conclusion. These objections are directed not against the incoherent results of the idealization of the targeted states but against the operation of idealization itself. No matter how the value of the epistemic conditions is enhanced through idealizations, either they satisfy the unconditional character of truth claims by means of requirements that cut off all connection with the practices of justification familiar to us, or else they retain the connection to practices familiar to us by paying the price that rational acceptability does not exclude the possibility of error even under these ideal conditions, that is, does not simulate a property "that cannot be lost": "It would be apparent either that those conditions allow the possibility of error or that they are so ideal as to make no use of the intended connection with human abilities."[47]

In his debates with Putnam, Apel, and me, Rorty makes use of these objections not in order to discredit the epistemization of truth but in order to radicalize it. With his opponents he shares the view that the standards for the rational acceptability of propositions, although they change historically, do not always do so arbitrarily. At least from the perspective of the participants, rationality standards are open to critique and can be 'reformed,' that is, improved on the basis of good reasons. Unlike Putnam, however, Rorty does not want to take account of the fact of learning processes by conceding that justificatory practices are guided by an idea of truth that transcends the justificatory context in question. He completely rejects idealizing limit concepts and interprets the difference between justification and truth in such a way that a proponent is prepared in principle to defend her views not only here and now but even in front of another audience. Whoever is oriented toward truth in this sense is willing "to justify his convictions in front of a competent audience" or "to increase the size or diversity of the conversational community."[48] On Rorty's view, every idealization that goes beyond this will founder on the problem that in idealizing we must always take something familiar as our point of departure; usually it is 'us,' that is, the communication community as we are familiar with it: "I cannot see what 'idealized rational acceptability' can mean except 'acceptability to an ideal community.' Nor can I see, given that no such community is going to have a God's eye view, that this ideal community can be anything more than us as we should like to be. Nor can I see what 'us' can mean here except: us educated, sophisticated, tolerant, wet liberals, the people who are always willing to hear the other side, to think out all their implications, etc."[49]

Of course, it can be objected to this that an idealization of the justificatory conditions does not in any way have to take the 'thick' characteristics of one's own culture as its point of departure; rather, it can start with the formal and processual characteristics of justificatory practices in general that, after all, are to be found in all cultures – even if not by any means always in institutionalized form. The fact that the practice of argumentation compels the participants themselves to make pragmatic assumptions with a counterfactual content fits in well with this. Whoever enters into discussion with the serious intention of becoming convinced of something through dialogue with others has to presume performatively that the participants allow their "yes" or "no" to be determined solely by the force of the better argument. However, with this they assume – normally in a counterfactual way – a speech situation that satisfies improbable conditions: openness to the public, inclusiveness, equal rights to participation, immunization against external or inherent compulsion, as well as the participants' orientation toward reaching understanding (that is, the sincere expression of utterances).[50] In these unavoidable presuppositions of argumentation, the intuition is expressed that true propositions are resistant to spatially, socially, and temporally unconstrained attempts to refute them. What we hold to be true has to be defendable on the basis of good reasons, not merely in a different context but in all possible contexts, that is, at any time and against anybody. This provides the inspiration for the discourse theory of truth: a proposition is true if it withstands all attempts to refute it under the demanding conditions of rational discourse.[51]

However, this does not mean that it is also true *for this reason*. A truth claim raised for 'p' says that the truth conditions for 'p' are satisfied. We have no other way of ascertaining whether or not this is the case except by way of argumentation, for direct access to uninterpreted truth conditions is denied to us. But the fact that the truth conditions are satisfied does not itself become an epistemic fact just because we can only *establish* whether these conditions are satisfied by way of discursive vindication of truth claim – whereby we have already had to interpret the truth conditions in light of the relevant sorts of reasons for the claim in question.

A consistently epistemic reading of the discourse-theoretical explanation of truth already founders on the problem that not all of the processual properties mentioned retain a "connection with human abilities." Nonetheless, with regard to the argumentative presuppositions of general inclusiveness, equal rights to participation, freedom from repression, and orientation toward reaching understanding, we can imagine in *the present* what an approximately ideal satisfaction would look like. This does not hold for anticipation of the future, of future corroboration (*Bewährung*).[52] To be sure, the orientation toward the future, too, *essentially* has the critical point of reminding us of the ethnocentric limitation and the fallibility of every actually achieved agreement, no matter how rationally motivated; that is, it serves as a reminder to us of the possible further decentering of the perspective of our justification community. Time, however, is a constraint of an ontological kind. Because all real discourses, conducted in actual time, are limited with regard to the future, we cannot know whether propositions that are rationally acceptable today will, even under approximately ideal conditions, assert themselves against attempts to refute them in the future as well. On the other hand, this very limitedness condemns our finite minds to be content with rational acceptability as *sufficient proof* of truth: "Whenever we raise truth claims on the basis of good arguments and convincing evidence we *presume* . . . that no new arguments or evidence will crop up in the future that would call our truth claim into question."[53]

It is not so difficult to understand why participants in argumentation, as subjects capable of speech and action, have to behave in this way if we look at a pragmatic description of their discourses, which are embedded in the lifeworld. In everyday practices, as we have seen, socialized individuals are dependent on behavioral certainties, which remain certainties only so long as they are sustained by a knowledge that is accepted unreservedly. Corresponding to this is the grammatical fact that, when we put forward the assertion 'p' in a performative attitude, we have to believe that 'p' is true unconditionally even though, when we adopt a reflexive attitude, we cannot rule out that tomorrow, or somewhere else, reasons and evidence could emerge that would invalidate 'p.' However, this does not yet explain why we are *permitted* to regard a truth claim explicitly raised for 'p' as vindicated as soon as the proposition is rationally accepted under conditions of rational discourse. What does it mean to say that truth claims can be "vindicated" discursively?

The Pragmatic Conception of Truth

It is still unclear what it is that *authorizes* us to regard as true a proposition that is presumed to be justified ideally – within the limits of finite minds. Wellmer speaks in this regard of a 'surplus' residing in the "anticipation of future corroboration." Perhaps it would be better to say that participants in argumentation who convince themselves of the justification of a controversial validity claim have reached a point where they have been brought by the unconstrained force of the better argument to a certain *shift in perspective*. When, in the course of a process of argumentation, participants attain the conviction that, having taken on board all relevant information and having weighed up all the relevant reasons, they have exhausted the reservoir of potential possible objections to 'p,' then all motives for continuing argumentation have been, as it were, used up. At any rate there is no longer any rational motivation for retaining a hypothetical attitude toward the truth claim raised for 'p' but temporarily left open. From the perspective of actors who have temporarily adopted a reflexive attitude in order to restore a partially disturbed background understanding, the de-problematization of the disputed truth claim means that a license is issued for return to the attitude of actors who are involved in dealing with the world more naively. As soon as the differences in opinion are resolved between 'us' and 'others' with regard to what is the case, 'our' world can merge once more with 'the' world.

When this shift takes place we, who as participants in argumentation accept the truth claim for 'p' as justified, reappoint the state of affairs "that p" – problematized up to now – with its rights as an assertion Mp that can be raised from the perspective of the first person. An assertion that has been *disposed of* argumentatively in this way and returned to the realm of action takes its place in an intersubjectively shared lifeworld from within whose horizon we, the actors, refer to something in a single objective world. It is a matter here of a *formal* supposition, not one that prejudges specific content nor one that suggests the goal of the "correct picture of the nature of things" that Rorty always connects with a realist intuition. Because acting subjects have to cope with "the" world, they cannot avoid being realists in the context of their lifeworld. Moreover, they are allowed to be realists because their language games and practices, so long as they function in a way that is proof against disappointment, "prove their truth" (*sich bewähren*) in being carried on.

This pragmatic authority responsible for certainty – interpreted in a realist way with the help of the supposition of an objective world – is suspended on the reflexive level of discourses, which are relieved of the burdens of action and where only arguments count. Here, our gaze turns away from the objective world, and the disappointments we experience in our direct dealings with it, to focus exclusively on our conflicting interpretations of the world. In this intersubjective dimension of contested interpretations, an assertion "proves its truth" solely on the basis of reasons, that is, with reference to the authority responsible for possible refutation, not for practically experienced disappointment. Here, however, the fallibilist consciousness that we can err even in the case of well-justified beliefs depends on an orientation toward truth whose roots extend into the realism of everyday practices – a realism no longer in force within discourse. The orientation toward unconditional truth, which compels participants in argumentation to presuppose ideal justificatory conditions and requires of them an ever-increasing decentering of the justification community, is a reflex of that other difference – required in the lifeworld – between believing and knowing; this distinction relies on the supposition, anchored in the communicative use of language, of a single objective world.[54] In this way, the lifeworld with its strong, action-related conceptions of truth and knowledge projects into discourse and provides the reference point – transcending justification – that keeps alive among participants in argumentation a consciousness of the fallibility of their interpretations. Conversely, this fallibilist consciousness also reacts back upon everyday practices without thereby destroying the dogmatism of the lifeworld. For actors, who as participants in argumentation have learned that no conviction is proof against criticism, develop in the lifeworld, too, rather less dogmatic attitudes toward their problematized convictions.

This stereoscopic perception of processes of cooperation and communication, layered according to action-contexts and discourses, allows us recognize the *embeddedness* of discourses in the lifeworld. Convictions play a different role in action than in discourse and "prove their truth" in a different way in the former than in the latter. In everyday practices, a prereflexive "coping with the world" decides whether convictions "function" or are drawn into the maelstrom of problematization, whereas in argumentation it depends solely on reasons whether controversial validity claims deserve rationally motivated recognition. It is true that the question of the internal relation between justification and truth poses itself only on the reflexive level; however, only the interaction between actions and discourses permits an answer to this question. The contextualist doubt cannot be dissipated so long as we persist in remaining on the level of argumentation and neglect the transformation – secured by personal union, as it were – of the knowledge of those who act into the knowledge of those who argue, while equally neglecting the transfer of knowledge in the opposite direction. Only the entwining of the two different pragmatic roles played by the Janus-faced concept of truth in action-contexts and in rational discourses respectively can explain why a justification successful in a local context points in favor of the context-independent truth of the justified belief. Just as, on the one hand, the concept of truth allows translation of shaken-up behavioral certainties into problematized propositions, so too, on the other hand, does the firmly retained orientation toward truth permit the *translation back* of discursively justified assertions into reestablished behavioral certainties.

To explain this we have only to bring together in the right way the partial statements assembled here up to now. In the lifeworld actors depend on behavioral certainties. They have to cope with a world presumed to be objective and, for this reason, operate with the distinction between believing and knowing.[55] There is a *practical* necessity to rely intuitively on what is unconditionally held-to-be-true. This mode of unconditionally holding-to-be-true is reflected on the discursive level in the connotations of truth claims that point beyond the given context of justification and require the supposition of ideal justificatory conditions – with a resulting decentering of the justification community. For this reason, the process of justification can be guided by a notion of truth that *transcends justification* although it is *always already operatively effective in the realm of action.* The function of the validity of statements in everyday practices explains why the discursive vindication of validity claims may at the same time be interpreted as the satisfaction of a pragmatic need for justification. This need for justification, which sets in train the transformation of shaken-up behavioral certainties into problematized validity claims, can be satisfied only by a translation of discursively justified beliefs back into behavioral truths.

Because it is, in the end, this interaction that dissipates the contextualist doubt about everyday realist intuitions, an objection seems likely that the whole dispute is prejudiced by my tendentious description of the embedding of discourses in the lifeworld. Rorty would certainly not deny the connection between rational discourse and action. He would also agree with our establishing a connection between the two perspectives: between the perspective of the participants in argumentation who seek to convince each other of the correctness of their interpretations, and the perspective of acting subjects involved in their language games and practices. However, Rorty would not distinguish these perspectives from each other in such a way that the one is relativized against the other. For the purpose of his description, he borrows from the perspective of participants in argumentation the imprisonment in dialogue that prevents us from breaking free from contexts of justification; at the same time, he borrows from the perspective of actors the mode of coping with the world. It is through the *blending into one another* of these opposing perspectives that the ethnocentric certainty is formed – a certainty that prompts Rorty to ask the question of why we should in the first place attempt to bring the contextualist knowledge obtained through reflexive experiences in argumentation into harmony with the everyday realism ascribed to the lifeworld. If the actors in the lifeworld – temporarily – cannot avoid being 'realists,' so much the worse for them. In that case it is up to the philosophers to reform the misleading commonsense conception of truth.

To be sure, deflationism, operating along the lines of Michael Williams with a semantic conception of truth, is still too strong for this purpose. Instead, Rorty rigorously carries through to its conclusion an epistemization of the concept of truth. Because there is nothing apart from justification, and because nothing follows for the truth of a proposition from its justified assertibility, the concept of truth is superfluous. "The difference between justification and truth is one which makes no difference except for the reminder that justification to one audience is not justification to another."[56] Even the only nonredundant use of the truth-predicate – the 'cautionary' one – requires reinterpretation. It is a matter of inventing and implementing a new vocabulary that does without a concept of truth and eliminates realist intuitions (such as the supposition of an objective world, talk of representing facts, and so forth): "We simply refuse to talk in a certain way, the Platonic way . . . Our efforts at persuasion must take the form of gradual inculcation of new ways of speaking, rather than of straightforward argumentation with old ways of speaking."[57]

The Naturalization of Linguistified Reason

Rorty's program of reeducation has provoked questions and objections.[58] In the first instance, Rorty himself must shoulder the burden of proof for his unwillingness to leave the language of common sense as it is. As a rule, pragmatists make substantial allowances for themselves on the basis that their views are at one with common sense. Strangely enough, neopragmatists boast of their role as "atheists in an overwhelmingly religious culture." Their therapy is supposed to reach through the pathological language games of philosophers to the distortions for which Platonism is responsible in daily life itself. In order to make plausible Platonism's idealist violence, Rorty has to let himself in for a diagnosis of the history of Western metaphysics as a history of decline. However, what Heidegger or Derrida, for example, have to say in their own fairly metaphysical ways about the critique of metaphysics is, on Rorty's estimation, more part of the 'edifying' literature that is supposed to be reserved for private perfection of the self and cannot, at any rate, serve the public critique of alienated living conditions.[59]

  Of course, more important than the motivation for this enterprise is the question of its viability. I would like to conclude with just two questions in this regard:

(a) Is the envisaged revision of our self-understanding compatible with the fact of an ability to learn that is not already constricted *a priori*?

(b) What is to happen to the normative character of reason, and how counterintuitive is the proposed neo–Darwinist self-description of rational beings?

(a) The program of a rational revision of deeply rooted Platonic prejudices presumes we are capable of a learning process that not only can take place within a given vocabulary and according to the standards prevailing in a given context but that seizes hold of the vocabulary and standards themselves. This reason alone requires Rorty to provide a suitable equivalent for an orientation toward truth that aims beyond the prevailing context of justification. If, however, the distinction between 'true' and 'justified' shrinks to the fact that the proponent is prepared to defend '*p*' even in front of a *different* audience, the reference point for such an anticipation [of truth] is missing. Rorty counters this objection by conceding a cautious idealization of justificatory conditions. He allows that what traditionally was called the "pursuit of truth" might just as well be described as the "pursuit of intersubjective, unforced agreement among larger and larger groups of interlocutors": "We hope to justify our belief to as many and as large audiences as possible."[60] Rorty, it is true, does not want this to be understood as an orientation toward an "ever-retreating goal," that is, as a regulative idea. Even the larger audience and the overarching context are supposed to be no more than a different audience and a different context. Nonetheless, Rorty adds to this description the qualifications mentioned: ever-expanding size and ever-increasing diversity – that is, conditions that hamper the possible success of argumentation in certain, not completely arbitrary, ways.

Rorty cannot explain this impediment to the success of argumentation that is unnecessary from a functional point of view. With the orientation toward "more and more," "larger and larger," and "increasingly diverse" audiences, Rorty brings a weak idealization into play that, on his premise, is far from self-evident. As soon as the concept of truth is eliminated in favor of a context-dependent epistemic validity-for-us, the normative reference point necessary to explain why a proponent should endeavor to seek agreement for '*p*' *beyond the boundaries of her own group* is missing. The information that the agreement of an increasingly large audience gives us increasingly less reason to fear that we will be refuted presupposes the very interest that has to be explained: the desire for "as much intersubjective agreement as possible." If something is 'true' if and only if it is recognized as justified "by us" because it is good "for us," there is no rational motive for expanding the circle of members. No reason exists for the decentering expansion of the justification community especially since Rorty defines "my own ethnos" as the group in front of which I feel obliged to give an account of myself. There is, however, no normative justification for any further orientation toward the agreement of 'strangers,' merely an explanatory pointer toward the arbitrary features of a "liberal Western culture" in which "we intellectuals" adopt a more or less undogmatic attitude. But even we are assured by Rorty that, "we must, in practice, privilege our own group, even though there can be no noncircular justification for doing so."[61]

(b) In losing the regulative idea of truth, the practice of justification loses that point of orientation by means of which standards of justification are distinguished from 'customary' norms. The sociologizing of the practice of justification means a naturalization of reason. As a rule, social norms can be described not merely from the point of view of a sociological observer but also from the perspective of participants in light of the standards they hold to be true. Without a reference to truth or reason, however, the standards themselves would no longer have any possibility of self-correction and would thus for their part forfeit the status of norms capable of being justified. In this respect, they would no longer even be customary norms. They would be *nothing more than* social facts, although they would continue to claim validity "for us," the relevant justification community. If, despite this, the practice of justification is not to collapse, and if the predicate 'rational' is not to lose its normative character – that is, if both are to continue to be able to function – the rationality standards valid for us have to be, if not justified, then at least explained.

For this Rorty falls back on a naturalist description of human beings as organisms that develop tools in order to adapt themselves optimally to their environment with the aim of satisfying their needs. Language, too, is such a tool – and not, for instance, a medium for representing reality: "No matter whether the tool is a hammer or a gun or a belief or a statement, tool-using is part of the interaction of the organism with its environment."[62] What appears to us as the normative dimension of the linguistically constituted human mind merely gives expression to the fact that intelligent operations are functional for the preservation of a species that, through acting, must 'cope' with reality. This neo-Darwinist self-description demands an ironic price. For Rorty, in replacing the "correct description of facts" with "successful adaptation to the environment," merely exchanges one kind of objectivism for another: the objectivism of 'represented' reality for the objectivism of instrumentally 'mastered' reality. Although admittedly, with this, the direction of fit for interaction between human beings and world is changed, what remains the same is the reference point of an objective world as the totality of everything that we can, in the one case, 'represent,' in the other, 'deal with.'

The pragmatic turn was supposed to replace the representationalist model of knowledge with a communication model that sets successful intersubjective mutual understanding (*Verständigung*) in the place of a chimerical objectivity of experience. It is, however, precisely this intersubjective dimension that is in turn closed off in an objectivating description of processes of cooperation and communication that can be grasped as such only from the perspective of participants. Rorty uses a jargon that no longer permits any differentiation between the perspectives of the participant and the observer. Interpersonal relationships, which are owed to the intersubjective possession of a shared language, are assimilated to the pattern of adaptive behavior (or instrumental action). A corresponding de-differentiation between the strategic and the nonstrategic use of language, between action oriented toward success and action oriented toward reaching understanding, robs Rorty of the conceptual means for doing justice to the intuitive distinctions between convincing and persuading, between motivation through reasons and causal exertion of influence, between learning and indoctrination. The counterintuitive mingling of the one with the other has the unpleasant consequence that we lose the critical standards operating in everyday life. Rorty's naturalist strategy leads to a categorial leveling of distinctions of such a kind that our descriptions lose their sensitivity for differences that do make a difference in everyday practices.[63]

Notes

1   R. Rorty, "Trotsky and the Wild Orchids," *Common Knowledge* 3 (1992): 140–53.
2   R. Rorty, ed., *The Linguistic Turn. Recent Essays in Philosophical Method* (Chicago, 1970), p. 33.
3   T. W. Adorno, *Negative Dialectics*, trans. by E. B. Ashton (London, 1973), p. 408 (amended translation).
4   M. Williams, *Unnatural Doubts* (Princeton, NJ, 1996), p. 365 (n. 51). Cf. also R. Rorty, "Is Derrida a Quasi-Transcendental Philosopher?," *Contemporary Literature* (1995): 173–200.
5   Cf. The exchange between T. McCarthy and R. Rorty in *Critical Inquiry* 16 (1990): 355–70, 633–41.
6   R. Rorty, *Linguistic Turn*, p. 39.
7   R. Rorty, *Philosophy and the Mirror of Nature* (Princeton, NJ, 1979), p. 261.
8   [Editor's note:] Habermas notes that in English the word 'representation' is used to refer to both *Darstellung* and *Vorstellung*.
9   R. Rorty, *Philosophy and the Mirror of Nature*, p. 170.
10 H. Putnam, *Realism with a Human Face* (Cambridge, MA, 1990), p. 28; R. Rorty, "Putnam and the Relativist Menace," *Journal of Philosophy* 90 (1993): 443.
11 R. Rorty, *Philosophy and the Mirror of Nature*, p. 390.
12 Ibid., p. 179: "[The contexualist view] threatens the neo-Kantian image of philosophy's relation to science and to culture. The urge to say that assertions and actions must not only cohere with other assertions and actions but 'correspond' to something apart from what people are saying and doing has some claim to be called the philosophical urge."

13 Ibid., p. 171.

14 Cf. H. Schnädelbach, "Philosophie," in E. Martens and H. Schnädelbach, eds. *Grundkurs Philosophie* (Hamburg, 1985), pp. 37–76.

15 [Editor's note:] Habermas remarks that the subtitle to the German translation of *Philosophy and the Mirror of Nature* is *A Critique of Philosophy* (*Eine Kritik der Philosophie*).

16 R. Rorty, Philosophy and the Mirror of Nature, p. 263.

17 Ibid., p. 339.

18 Ibid., p. 338.

19 R. Rorty, *Philosophical Papers I: Objectivity, Relativism, and Truth* (Cambridge, 1991), p. 23.

20 Only the empiricists were prepared to call 'objective' the experience (*Erfahrung*) that "corresponds to what is there outside" (Rorty). The transcendental idealists, by contrast, reduce even the objectivity of experience to necessary subjective conditions of possible experience.

21 L. Wittgenstein, *On Certainty*, trans. by D. Paul and G. E. M. Anscombe (Oxford, 1969), §115, p. 125.

22 H. Schnädelbach, "Thesen über Geltung und Wahrheit," in *Zur Rehabilitierung des animal rationale* (Frankfurt, 1992), pp. 104–115.

23 With respect to a critique of Rorty's approach, I will confine myself in the following to the problem of truth. However, I would like to indicate, at least, that we would not be able to explain the possibility of learning processes without reference to the capacity for recognizing the same entities under different descriptions.

24 E. Tugendhat, *Traditional and Analytical Philosophy*, trans. P. A. Gorner (Cambridge, 1982), pp. 50ff.

25 R. Rorty, *Philosophy and the Mirror of Nature*, p. 178.

26 Cf. Williams, *Unnatural Doubts*, p. 232: "We need only ask whether or not the 'direct' grasping of facts on which such comparison depends is supposed to be a cognitive state with propositional content. If it isn't, it can have no impact on verification. But if it is, what we have been given is another kind of belief."

27 Ibid., p. 267.

28 R. Rorty, "Pragmatism, Davidson, and Truth," in E. Lepore, ed., *Truth and Interpretation* (Oxford, 1986), p. 343.

29 Williams, *Unnatural Doubts*, p. 266.

30 Ibid., p. 249.

31 F. Kambartel, "Universalität richtig verstanden," *Deutsche Zeitschrift für Philosophie* 44 (1996): 249.

32 It is no accident that I introduced the formal-pragmatic concept of the grammatical supposition of an objective world in the context of the theory of action. Cf. J. Habermas *The Theory of Communicative Action*, trans. T. McCarthy, vol. 1 (Boston, 1984), pp. 75–101; vol. 2 (Boston, 1987), pp. 119ff.

33 Cf. Williams, *Unnatural Doubts*, p. 238: "All that is involved in the idea of an objective world as 'what is there anyway' is that an objective proposition's being true is one thing and our believing it to be true, or being justified in believing it to be true, something else again."

34 R. Rorty, "Is Truth a Goal of Inquiry? Davidson vs. Wright," *Philosophical Quarterly* 45 (1995): 281–300 (here, p. 300).

35 D. Davidson pursues a third strategy that could be called 'theoreticist' or, as he himself proposes, 'methodological'; cf. D. Davidson, "The Folly of Trying to Define Truth," *Journal of Philosophy* 93 (1996): 263–78. Davidson uses the semantic conception of truth, understood in a nondeflationary way, as the undefined basic concept for an empirical theory of language. Both the concept of truth, which is used as a theoretical term in his theory of language, and the theory itself, which is supposed to explain the comprehension of linguistic expressions, can prove their truth (*sich bewähren*) at one and the same time. For this reason, Davidson's implicit "theory of truth" can be discussed only in connection with his theory as a whole. In general, I see the following difficulty: on the one hand, Davidson disputes that

the concept of truth has a content capable of being explicated, to this extent allying himself with the deflationist polemic against attempts to explain the meaning of truth; on the other hand, he has to secure for the truth-predicate, over and above its disquotational function, a certain content as far as the theory of rationality is concerned in order to explain the veridical nature of beliefs. To this extent he joins forces with Putnam and Dummett, who insist that Tarski's Convention T says nothing about the actual meaning of truth. Standing between these two positions, Davidson, instead of merely using the concept, sees himself compelled to write learned treatises on a concept he declares to be 'indefinable' – treatises in which he does, at least, in a metacritical way, isolate the realist intuitions bound up with truth. Cf. D. Davidson, "The Structure and Content of Truth," *Journal of Philosophy* 87 (1990): 279–328. Davidson holds onto the idea that we can know something of an objective world "which is not of our own making." This view separates him from Rorty who attempts in vain to pull Davidson over to his own side of an abolitionist understanding of truth. Cf. D. Davidson, "A Coherence Theory of Truth and Knowledge," in A. Malachowski, ed., *Reading Rorty* (Oxford, 1990), pp. 120–39; cf. also Rorty, "Pragmatism, Davidson, and Truth." For a comparison of Davidson's and my own approaches to the theory of language, see B. Fultner, *Radical Interpretation or Communicative Action* (PhD dissertation, Northwestern University, 1995).

36   K. R. Popper, "Truth, Rationality and the Growth of Scientific Knowledge," in *Conjectures and Refutations* (London, 1963), pp. 215–50.

37   E. Tugendhat, "Tarskis semantische Definition der Wahrheit," *Philosophische Rundschau* 8 (1960): 131–59, reprinted in his *Philosophische Aufsätze* (Frankfurt, 1992), pp. 179–213.

38   I refer here to positions held by P. Horwich and A. Fine; cf. M. Williams, "Do We (Epistemologists) Need a Theory of Truth?," *Philosophical Topics* 14 (1986): 223–242.

39   I introduced this distinction in the Christian Gauss Lectures on founding sociology in the theory of language (1971); cf. J. Habermas, *Vorstudien und Ergänzungen zur Theorie des kommunikativen Handelns* (Frankfurt, 1984), pp. 1–126, especially pp. 104ff.

40   Habermas, *Theory of Communicative Action*, vol. 1, pp. 22–42.

41   H. Putnam, "Introduction," in *Realism and Reason* (Cambridge, 1983).

42   J. Habermas, "Wahrheitstheorie," in Habermas, *Vorstudien und Ergänzungen zur Theorie des kommunikativen Handelns.*

43   K. O. Apel, "Fallibilismus, Konsenstheorie der Wahrheit und Letztbegründung," in Forum für Philosophie, ed., *Philosophie und Begründung* (Frankfurt, 1987), pp. 116–211.

44   C. Lafont, "Spannungen im Wahrheitsbegriff," *Deutsche Zeitschrift für Philosophie* 42 (1994): 1007–23; Williams, *Unnatural Doubts*, pp. 233ff.

45   A. Wellmer, "Ethics and Dialogue," in *The Persistence of Modernity*, trans. D. Midgley (Cambridge, MA, 1991), p. 175 (amended translation).

46   A. Wellmer, "Wahrheit, Kontingenz, Moderne," in *Endspiele* (Frankfurt, 1993), p. 162. English translation as *Endgames: Essays and Lectures on the Irreconcilable, Nature of Modernity* (Cambridge, MA, 1998).

47   Davidson, "The Structure and Content of Truth," p. 307.

48   R. Rorty, "Sind Aussagen universelle Geltungsansprüche?," *Deutsche Zeitschrift für Philosophie* 6 (1994): 982f.

49   R. Rorty, "Putnam and the Relativist Menace," pp. 451f.

50   J. Habermas, "Remarks on Discourse Ethics," in *Justification and Application*, trans. C. Cronin (Cambridge, MA., 1993), pp. 30ff., pp. 58f.

51   L. Wingert, *Gemeinsinn und Moral* (Frankfurt, 1993), p. 277.

52   [Editor's note:] The German term "*sich bewähren*" and its cognates have generally been rendered here as "prove to be true" (in the sense of "turn out to be true"), so as to preserve in translation its connection with "*wahr*," true. *Sich bewähren* is proving to be true in the sense of standing the test, withstanding critical scrutiny. However, because it is the term that Albrecht Wellmer used to render "corroboration" in his influential discussion of Popper, where the reference is clearly to Wellmer's idea of anticipating future "Bewährung,"

"corroboration" is used. See A. Wellmer, *Critical Theory of Society*, trans. J. Cumming (New York, 1974).

53 A. Wellmer, "Wahrheit," p. 163; cf. the corresponding reflections on "superassertibility" in C. Wright, *Truth and Objectivity* (Cambridge, MA, 1992).

54 Cf. Lafont, "Spannungen im Wahrheitsbegriff," p. 1021: "Only the presupposition of a single objective world . . . permits [us] to make the unconditional validity of truth compatible with a fallible understanding of knowledge."

55 I cannot in the present context deal with moral and other normative validity claims that have a built-in orientation toward discursive vindication. They lack the property of "transcending justification" that accrues to truth claims through the supposition of a single objective world built into the communicative use of language. Normative validity claims are raised for interpersonal relationships within a social world that is not independent of "our making" in the same way as is the objective world. The discursive treatment of normative claims is, however, "analogous to truth" insofar as the participants in practical discourse are guided by the goal of a commanded, permitted, or forbidden "single right answer." The social world is intrinsically historical, that is, ontologically constituted in a different way than the objective world. For this reason, in the case of the social world, the idealization of the justificatory conditions cannot include an "anticipation of future corroboration (*Bewäh-rung*)," in the sense of an anticipated refutation of future objections (Wingert), but only in the critical sense of a proviso concerning approximation, that is, a proviso concerning the justification community's actually achieved state of decentering. The discursive indication of a truth claim says that the truth conditions, interpreted as assertibility conditions, are satisfied. In the case of a normative validity claim, the discursively achieved agreement grounds the corresponding norm's worthiness to be recognized; to this extent the agreement itself contributes to the satisfaction of the norm's conditions of validity. Whereas rational acceptability merely indicates the truth of a proposition, it provides a constructive contribution to the validity of norms.

56 R. Rorty, "Is Truth a Goal of Inquiry?," p. 300.

57 R. Rorty, "Relativism: Finding and Making," Ms. (1995), p. 5.

58 T. McCarthy, "Philosophy and Social Practice: Richard Rorty's 'New Pragmatism,'" in *Ideals and Illusions* (Cambridge, MA, 1991), pp. 11–34.

59 R. Rorty, "Habermas, Derrida, and the Functions of Philosophy," *Revue Internationale de Philosophie* 49 (1995), 437–60; cf. my reply in ibid., pp. 553–6.

60 R. Rorty, "Is Truth a Goal of Inquiry?," p. 298.

61 R. Rorty, *Philosophical Papers* I, p. 29.

62 R. Rorty, "Relativism: Finding and Making," pp. 11f.

63 The same objectivism and the same kind of insensitivity could be shown through reference to Rorty's egocentric or ethnocentric description of processes of interpretation, for example, of hard cases of intercultural understanding (*Verständigung*). Unlike Gadamer, Rorty does not have recourse to the symmetrical conditions for an adoption of perspectives learned by speakers and hearers in learning the system of personal pronouns and making possible a reciprocal convergence of interpretive horizons that, initially, are far apart. Instead, he takes as his starting point an asymmetrical relationship between "us" and "them," so that we have to judge their utterances according to our standards and assimilate their standards to ours; cf. J. Habermas, *Postmetaphysical Thinking*, trans. W. M. Hohengarten (Cambridge, MA, 1992), pp. 135ff. This assimilatory model of understanding (*Verstehen*) partially coincides with Davidson's model of interpretation. However, what for Davidson is the result of a methodological decision to view the interpretation of linguistic expressions as the application of the hypotheses of an empirically turned theory of truth, results for Rorty from the decision (of strategic significance for his theory) in favor of a naturalist descriptive vocabulary.

RESPONSE TO JÜRGEN HABERMAS

The initial sections of Jürgen Habermas' paper provide a very sympathetic and perceptive account of the motives which led me to hold my present philosophical views. I understand the course of my own thinking much better after reading this account. Those sections also illustrate the extent to which Habermas and I see the history of philosophy, and the current situation of philosophy, in similar terms.[1] His *The philosophical discourse of modernity* made an enormous impression on me. Ever since I read it I have thought of the "linguistic turn" as subsumable within the larger movement from subject-centered rationality to communicative rationality. But the motives Habermas has for commending this movement are the same as those which lead me to take what he calls "the pragmatist turn" – that is, to exalt solidarity over objectivity, to doubt that there is such a thing as "desire for truth" distinct from desire for justification, and to hold that, in Habermas' words,

> 'being in touch with reality' has to be translated into 'being in touch with a human community' in such a way that the realist intuition, to which mentalism wanted to do justice with its mirror of nature and its correspondence between representation and represented object, disappears completely.

The remaining disagreements between us begin to emerge at the beginning of the section of Habermas' paper called "Truth and Justification." There he says that "the correspondence idea of truth was able to take account of a fundamental aspect of the meaning of the truth predicate" – the notion of unconditional validity. This is a notion for which I can find no use. In an article called "Universality and Truth?"[2] to a version of which Habermas refers, I argued that the switch to "communicative rationality" should lead us to drop the idea that when I make an assertion I am implicitly claiming to be able to justify it to all audiences, actual and possible.

That claim would, I urged, be like the village champion, swollen with victory, predicting that he can defeat any challenger, anytime, anywhere. Maybe he can, but he has no good reason to think so, and it would be pointless for him to make such a claim. Analogously, I argued, when we have finished justifying our belief to the audience we think relevant (perhaps our own intellectual conscience, or our fellow-citizens, or the relevant experts) we need not, and typically do not, make any further claims, much less universal ones. After rehearsing our justification, we may say either "That is why I think my assertion true" or "That is why my assertion is true," or both. Going from the former assertion to the latter is not a philosophically pregnant transition from particularity to universality, or from context-dependence to context-independence. It is merely a stylistic difference.

So when Habermas says that there is an "internal connection between justification and truth," one which "explains why we may, in light of the evidence available to us, raise an unconditional truth claim that aims beyond what is justified," I protest that the explicandum is just not there. We do not aim beyond what is justified. No unconditional claim has been made. It is not the case, as Habermas says, that "What we hold to be true has to be defendable on the basis of good reasons, in all possible contexts." If it were, I would, whenever I acquired a belief, be tacitly making an utterly unjustified empirical prediction about what would happen in a potentially infinite number of justificatory contexts before a potentially infinitely diverse set of audiences.

I find this as implausible as the suggestion notoriously made by the logical positivists: that every empirical assertion is an empirical prediction about a potentially infinite number of future sense-data.

Again, when Habermas makes a distinction between "two pragmatic roles ... played by the Janus-faced concept of truth in action-contexts and in rational discourses respectively," and when he goes on to say that "the concept of truth allows translation of shaken-up behavioral certainties into problematized propositions", I would rejoin that he is ignoring Peirce's point that beliefs are just habits of action. A rational discourse is just one more action-context in which a behavioral certainty evinces itself. There is no Janus-like role to be played, and no translation to be performed.

Rational discourses are the species of action-context in which you are trying to acquire better habits of action by comparing and contrasting your own habits with those of others. In such contexts, your behavioral certainty makes itself evident in your attempt to justify your belief. You may well change your belief as a result of participation in rational discourse, just as you may change it as a result of its lack of success in dealing with the non-human enviroment. But when you turn from encounters with the non-human, non-linguistic part of your environment to encounters with the human, language-using, arguing part, there is no transition that needs explanation or mediation. The passage from the one action-context to the other raises no philosophical problems which could be solved by a better understanding of the concept of truth.

There is nothing to be understood about the concept of X except the various uses of the term 'X.' This goes for the concept of truth as well. 'True' is a term we can, if we like, apply to all the assertions we feel justified in making, or feel others are justified in making. We thereby endorse those assertions. But we can also add, after any assertion we or others make, "But of course somebody someday (maybe we ourselves, today) may come up with something (new evidence, a better explanatory hypothesis, etc.) showing that that assertion was not true." This is an example of 'true's' cautionary use. I do not see why the fact that the term 'true' has both an endorsing and a cautionary use should lead us to think that there is an "internal connection" between justification and truth, or between assertion and unconditionality, or to think that a deflationary account of truth is, as Habermas claims, acceptable only if it "can continue to sustain realist intuitions."

There is, to be sure, something unconditional about of truth. This unconditionality is expressed by the fact that once true, always true: we regard people who use the word in such expressions as "true then, but not now" as using it incorrectly. Since "once justified, always justified" is obviously false, one can indeed express the contrast between truth and justification as a contrast between the unconditional and the conditional. But the unconditionality in question does not provide a *reason* for the fact that the cautionary use of 'true' is always apropos. To say that truth is eternal and unchangeable is just a picturesque way of *restating* this fact about our linguistic practices. The whole pragmatic force of the claim that truth is not conditional is to *express* willingness to change one's mind if circumstances alter, not to explain or justify this willingness. We are not contritely fallible because we are in awe of the unconditionality of truth. Rather, to speak of truth as being unconditional is just one more way of expressing our sense of contrite fallibility (or, more robustly put, our sense of the desirability of comparing one's habits of actions with those of others in order to see whether one might develop some more effective habits). The unconditionality of truth has no positive content over and above the cautionary function of such expressions as "justified, but maybe not true."

As I see it, philosophers who think that we have a duty to truth, or that we should value truth, or that we should have faith in truth, are engaging in needless, and philosophically mischievous, hypostatization.[3] So are philosophers who worry about whether our practices of justification are "truth-indicative" – about whether epistemologists will ever be able to demonstrate that justification will eventually, somehow, God willing, lead to truth. So, it seems to me, is Habermas when he says that it is a "fact" that "a justification is successful in our justificatory context points in favor of the context-independent truth of the justified proposition."

"Our justificatory context." *Whose* justificatory context? Surely not any and every such context has this desirable feature? Have not past justificatory contexts (those of primitive science, racist politics, and the like) pointed us away from truth? In order to deal with such rhetorical questions, Habermas brings in the distinction between rationally convincing people and strategically manipulating them into agreeing with you. He wants to say that only in the former case do we have genuine, and therefore truth-indicative, justification. Some of the so-called "justifications" – the ones which strike us as more like brainwashing than like putting forward arguments – must be ruled out in order to save the claim that "success in our justificatory context points in favor of context-independent truth."

Überzeugen, in short, points in favor of such truth, but *überreden* does not. Thus we find Habermas criticizing me for sweeping this distinction under the rug:

> A . . . refusal to differentiate between the strategic and non-strategic uses of language, between success-oriented and understanding-oriented action deprives Rorty of the conceptual tools to do justice to the intuitive distinctions between rationally convincing and persuading, between motivation through reasons and causal exertion of influence, between learning and indoctrination." (. . . *zwischen Überzeugen und Überreden, zwischen der Motivierung durch Gründe und kausaler Einflussnahme, zwischen Lernen und Indoktrination . . .*)

Habermas and I can agree that certain desirable social practices and institutions could not survive unless the participants could deploy these latter, commonsensical, distinctions. But I see these distinctions as themselves just as context-dependent as the distinction between sufficient and insufficient justification. So I cannot see how they could serve as conceptual instruments for telling us when we are being steered in the direction of context-independent truth. The whole idea of context-independence, in my view, is part of an unfortunate effort to hypostatize the adjective 'true.' Only such hypostatization creates the impression that there is a goal of inquiry other than justification to relevant contemporary audiences.

This hypostatization is exemplified by Habermas' claim that "true propositions are resistant to spatially, socially and temporally unconstrained attempts to refute them."[4] But propositions are just hypostatized assertions. Endowing them with causal powers, such as the ability to resist, is the same move that Plato made when he hypostatized the adjective 'good' and gave causal power to the resulting Idea. Plato thought that only by giving the Good power he explained the appeal of moral virtue. Habermas thinks that only by giving true propositions power can he explain the appeal of such intellectual virtues as eagerness to hear the other side. But "Truth resists attempts to refute it" or "Truth cannot lose in a free and open encounter" is as pragmatically empty as "Healthy people do not get sick." If they get sick, they weren't healthy. What is refuted was never true. An intrinsic property called 'truth' no more explains resistance to refutation than one called "health explains resistance to disease."[5]

Habermas says, correctly, that I am trying to substitute a neo-Darwinian description of human beings for one which distinguishes sharply between what animals do (causal manipulation) and what we do (offering rationally convincing arguments). To effect this substitution, I need to claim, first, that all argumentation is, under one useful description, causal manipulation (*kausaler Einflussnahme*). Second, I need to assert that some sorts of causal manipulation by means of language are highly desirable. The difference between strategic and non-strategic uses of language is the difference between the kind of causal manipulation we are glad to have practiced on us and the kind we resent having practiced on us. In this respect it is like the difference between having our body manipulated by a knowledgeable doctor, one who has our interests at heart, and having it manipulated by a quack chiropracter trying to make a quick buck.

As I see it, the philosophical distinction between non-strategic and strategic uses of language adds nothing to the commonsense distinction between dishonesty and sincerity. You are being what Habermas calls "non-strategic" if the arguments you offer others – mere rhetorical diatribes though they may seem to your critics – are ones you yourself find entirely persuasive. You are being what he calls "strategic" if you say to yourself something like "My interlocutor either would not understand or refuse to accept the arguments that convinced me, so I shall use premises he will grant, and terms he understands, even though I should disdain to use either when talking to myself."[6] In the latter case, your interest in your interlocutor is like the quack chiropractor's interest in her patient. But a sincere, ignorant, chiropractor is no more being "strategic" than is a sincere, ignorant Nazi orator. Both are being honest and non-strategic, though neither is likely to do you any good.

The distinction between honesty and sincerity is not itself context-dependent (or at least no more so than the distinction between the straight and the crooked). The distinction between logic and "mere rhetoric," on the other hand, is just as context-dependent as that between the presence and absence of adequate justification. For a sincere Nazi can successfully use really pitiful arguments to justify infamies – arguments that nobody outside his remarkably provincial, illiterate, and stupid audience would take seriously. They are arguments which *we* rightly describe as 'mere' causal manipulation or 'mere' rhetoric, even though to the Nazi and his stupid audience they seem paradigm cases of rational persuasion, *überzeugende Argumentation*.

From a pragmatist perspective, to describe someone as succumbing to the appeal of "the better argument" is to describe her as being convinced by the sort of reasons that have convinced us, or would convince us, of the same conclusion. Our criteria for betterness of argument are relative to the range of arguments at our disposal, just as our criterion for betterness of tool are relative to the technology at our disposal. To describe someone as having come to a certain conclusion for bad reasons is simply to say that the reasons which convinced her would not convince us.

Habermas, however, says that when we enter into a serious discussion we "presume performatively that the participants allow their 'yes' or 'no' to be determined by the force of the better argument." But this is to hypostatize arguments as he elsewhere hypostatizes true propositions. Arguments no more have a context-independent property of betterness than propositions have a context-independent resistance to refutation. When we enter into a serious discussion we of course hope that our interlocutors will find the same sorts of considerations convincing that we do; indeed, we are not sure whether or not the discussion will count as serious until we have discovered that this hope will be gratified. But that hope is not a presumption about our interlocutors' relation to a natural order of reasons, an order in which the betterness of arguments is apparent without any need to consider the "spatial, temporal, and social restraints" on any actual discussants.

To say that there is no such thing as a proposition being justified *tout court*, or an argument better *tout court*, amounts to saying that all reasons are reasons for particular people, restrained (as people always are) by spatial, temporal, and social conditions. To think otherwise is to presuppose the existence of a natural order of reasons to which our arguments will, with luck, better and better approximate. The idea of such an order is one more relic of the idea that truth consists in correspondence to the intrinsic nature of things, a nature which somehow precedes and underlies all descriptive vocabularies. The natural order of reasons is for arguments what the intrinsic nature of reality is for sentences. But if beliefs are habits of action the one regulative ideal is as unnecessary as the other. Yet Habermas can only go beyond the commonsense distinctions between dishonest and honest use of language on the one hand, and arguments acceptable and not acceptable to us on the other, if he appeals to this implausible idea. For that would be the only way to make plausible the claim that there is a non-context-dependent distinction between real and apparent justification, or that the *überzeugen–überreden* distinction is not just in the ear of the audience.

From my neo-Darwinian perspective, of course, the Cartesian idea of a natural order of reasons is as bad as the suggestion, mentioned by Wittgenstein, that the great advantage of the French language is that words occur in the order in which one naturally thinks them. Familiar French words do indeed occur in the order in which the French typically think them, just as arguments which strike us as *überzeugend* rather than merely *überredend* have premises we accept arranged in the order in which we ourselves would arrange them. But what counts as rational argumentation is as historically determined, and as context-dependent, as what counts as good French.

Habermas gives, in his paper, excellent reasons for abandoning as useless Peirce's notion of "the end of inquiry." But it seems to me that these are also reasons for abandoning all similar idealizations. They all sound inspiring, but they all deflate on closer inspection, in the same way that Peirce's notion deflates. The notions of a natural order of reasons, of the way things really are apart from human needs, of an ideal language, and of universal validity can only be explicated by invoking the notion of the ideal audience – the audience that has witnessed all possible experiments, tested all possible hypotheses, and so on. To explain what any of these idealizations amount to you have to resort to the idea of an audience whose standards of justification cannot be improved on. But such an audience seems to me as hard to envisage as the largest number, the largest set, or the last dialectical synthesis – the one which cannot become the thesis of a new dialectical triad. Our finitude consists in the fact that there can never be an ideal audience, only more spatially, temporally, and socially restrained audiences. So the idea of "universal validity claims" seems to me one more attempt at the sort of evasion of finitude Heidegger rightly criticized.

My conclusion is that what is needed is not an attempt to get closer to an ideal, but rather an attempt to get farther away from the parts of our past that we most regret. We should give up on the Kant-Peirce-Apel strategy of finding regulative ideas to serve as surrogates for the authority of some non-human power, thereby replacing metaphysics with transcendental philosophy. Instead, we should answer the questions "What breaks us out of our parochial contexts and expands the frontiers of inquiry?" "What keeps us critical rather than dogmatic?" with "The memory of how parochial our ancestors have been, and the fear that our descendants will find us equally so." In short, *we should be retrospective rather than prospective: inquiry should be driven by concrete fears of regression rather than by abstract hopes of universality.*

This substitution of fear for hope is my strategy for answering another criticism made by Habermas. He says "As soon as the concept of truth is eliminated in favor of a context-dependent, epistemic validity-for-us, we lack the normative reference-point (*normative Bezugspunkt*) that would explain why a proponent should struggle to secure acceptance for '*p*' beyond the bounds of his own group." (. . . *über die Grenze der eigenen Gruppe hinaus bemühen sollte.*]

Here I need to distinguish between wanting to go beyond those borders and being under an obligation to do so: between *hinaus bemühen will* and *hinaus bemühen soll*. I regard it as a fortunate historical accident that we find ourselves in a culture – the high culture of the West in the twentieth century – which is highly sensitized to the need to go beyond such borders. This sensitization is a result of our awareness of the blind cruelty which has resulted from not doing so in the past, and our fear of falling back into barbarism.

I do not think that we are under an *obligation* to go beyond these borders, but that is simply because I am deeply suspicious of the notion of *obligation*. I tend to agree with Elizabeth Anscombe when she doubts, in her famous essay "Modern Moral Philosophy," that those who do not believe in the existence of God are entitled to use the term "moral obligation."[7] On this point, theists like Anscombe and atheists like myself can make common cause against Kantians who think that you can preserve, and must preserve, a non-prudential "ought." We can line up with Mill and Dewey in being as suspicious of the morality–prudence distinction, when it is given a transcendental twist, as we are of the truth–justification distinction, when it is given the same twist.

However, I would concede, as Anscombe might not, that one can give the notion of "moral obligation" a respectable, secular, non-transcendental sense by relativizing it to a historically contingent sense of moral identity.[8] As someone whose sense of moral identity is tied up with the need to go beyond the boundaries of my own group, I can recuperate the notion of *hinaus bemühen soll*, though perhaps not in a way that Habermas would find adequate. For I can say that I could not live with myself if I did not do my best to go beyond the borders in question. In that sense, I am morally *obliged* to do so, but only in the same sense that a Nazi who could not live with himself if he spared a certain Jew is under a moral obligation to kill that Jew.

But my moral identity is not an expresssion, or an account, of myself as a language-user. So it cannot be incorporated within Habermas' "discourse ethics," or treated as a universal obligations of any language-using being. It is merely a remark about whom I *happen* to be, not about what I must, to avoid performative self-contradiction, conceive myself to be. Perhaps I also could not live with myself if I consumed a rich meal in the presence of a starving child, with whom I refused to share my food. But this too is a fact about the way I happened to be brought up, not a fact about what it is to be a human being.

In short the only *normative Bezugspunkt* that I find myself in need of is something which fits easily into a naturalistic, Darwinian picture of myself: I am an organism whose beliefs and desires are largely a product of a certain acculturation. Specifically, I am the product of a culture which worries about the fact that American black slavery and European pogroms seemed sensible and right to previous generations of white Christians. As such a product, I spend time worrying about whether I may not now be taking similar, current atrocities for granted. I have acquired a moral identity, and a set of obligations, from this culture. I think I am lucky to be have been raised within this culture. But I am well aware that my barbarous ancestors thought themselves lucky to have been raised within their culture, that my cousins in Germany thought themselves lucky to be able to enroll in the Hitler Youth, and that my descendants in a hypothetical fascist culture would have a similarly warm sense of gratitude for their own upbringing.

Philosophers who fear relativism are committed to the idea that we need a criterion for telling real justifications and obligations from apparent ones, and real maturation from apparent maturation. Since the reality–appearance distinction seems to me a relic of our authoritarian past (a secularizing attempt to move the Intrinsic Nature of Reality into the role previously played by the Person Who Must Be Obeyed) I am not worried about relativism. Fear of relativism seems to me fear that there is nothing in the universe to hang on to except each other. As I see it, we do not treat each with respect because we are rational. Rather, 'rationality' is, in our culture, one of our names for our habit of listening to the other side – treating most of our interlocutors with proper respect. There is no faculty called 'reason' which tells us to listen to the other side (tells the slave-owner to listen to the slave, or the Nazi to listen to the Jew). Rather, there are social virtues called 'conversability,' 'decency,' 'respect for others,' 'toleration,' and the like. In our culture, we restrict the term 'rational' to people who exhibit those virtues. That is why Richard Hare's designated monster, the "rational Nazi," is a genuine possibility. It is possible to hear the other side and still do the wrong thing, for it is possible to listen to arguments which *we* know to be *überzeugend*, yet not be *überzeugt*.

Once one accepts the shift Habermas proposes from "subject-centered" to 'communicative' reason, it seems to me, one should be happy with the idea that one's only obligations are to other human beings and to oneself. Habermas, however, believes that Kant was right in thinking that we cannot altogether do without the notion of unconditionality. He sees unconditional, universal validity not only as a useful, but as an indispensable, notion. I not only cannot see why it is indispensable, I cannot even see that it is useful. It seems what Wittgenstein calls "a wheel that turns even though nothing else turns with it, and is therefore no part of the mechanism." The only function it might have is to intimidate us by making us feel that no matter what we do, it is probably not good enough – the function once performed by the doctrine of Original Sin. But once we start thinking of inquiry as a relation between organisms and their environment, rather than as a relation between human beings and something awesome – something like Truth or Reality – we no longer need to be scared.

I see the opposition between Hume and Kant – or, in contemporary moral philosophy, between contemporary Humean moral philosophers like Annette Baier and contemporary Kantians like Christine Korsgaard – as centering around their respective accounts of moral motivation. For writers in the Kantian tradition, the interlocked notions of rationality and universality are indispensable. Baier interprets Hume, "the woman's moral philosopher," as treating the very idea of universal rationality as a relic of patriarchal authoritarianism. That seems to me right, and that is why I see pragmatism, and the neo-Darwinian redescription of inquiry it offers, as part of a more general anti-authoritarian movement – the movement which assumes that if we take care of constitutional democracy, academic and press freedom, universal literacy, careers open to talents, and similar democratic institutions, then truth will take care of itself.

From this Humean point of view, moral progress is what Hume called "a progress of sentiments" – an ability to overlook what one had previously thought to be moral abominations: for example, women speaking in churches, or interracial marriage, or Jews having the same civil status as Christians, or same-sex marriage. From my pragmatist point of view, intellectual progress is a subdivision of moral progress – it is progress in finding beliefs which are better and better tools for accomplishing our communal projects. One of these projects is to replace resentment with good will and authority with democracy.

What Peirce called "blocking the road of inquiry" occurs whenever a given view – Copernicus' theory of planetary motion, or Darwin's theory of the descent of man, or James' pragmatism, or Hitler's racism – is suspected of being a moral abomination. Sometimes, as in the case of Hitler's racism, blocking the road of inquiry is an excellent thing to do. Sometimes, as in the case of Darwin's theory, it is a bad thing to do. Sometimes, as in the case of James' pragmatism, we may be genuinely perplexed about whether we are dealing with a moral abomination, a well-meant but misguided suggestion, or a helpful proposal about how to free ourselves from obsolete ways of thinking.

A lot of powerful philosophical considerations can be brought to bear on such perplexity, and this exchange between Habermas and myself has rehearsed a number of them. But if the pragmatists are right, philosophical reflection will not adjudicate the issue, for such reflections can do little more than rearrange previously existent intuitions, rather than creating new ones or erasing old ones. But erasure is what pragmatists are asking for. Only experiment – trying out intellectual and moral life as it would be lived without the familiar Platonic/Kantian intuitions – will decide the matter.

In a world which had no more urgent tasks than to stage social experiments in order to adjudicate philosophical disagreements, the decision between Habermas' quasi-Kantian way of looking at rationality and morality and my quasi-Humean way would be made after seeing the result of experiments in training a large sample of the rising generation to think in exclusively Humean terms. My prediction is that these experimental subjects would be just as decent people as the control group – the ones who were brought up to understand the term "universal validity."

Notes

1 I entirely agree with Habermas when he says that philosophical "paradigms do not form an arbitrary sequence but a dialectical relationship." I regret having given him the impression that I believe that the Ways of Things, Ideas and Words are incommensurable with one another. I think of them as having succeded one another as a result of the need for a Kuhnian "revolution" in order to overcome piled-up anomalies. Habermas' remark that, just as the scholastic dispute about universals led to the devaluation of objective reason, so "the critique of introspection and psychologism at the end of the nineteenth century contributed to the shaking up of subjective reason" is an admirable account of the relevant anomalies. I agree with Davidson that Kuhn's use of "incommensurable" to describe the difference between pre- and post-revolutionary discourse was unfortunate. Revolutions in science, as elsewhere, are learning experiences, not leaps in the dark.

2 Above, pp. 1–30.

3 The expression "valuing truth" is used by Akeel Bilgrami and the expression "faith in truth" by Daniel Dennett. I criticize their polemical use of these expressions in my "Response to Dennett" below.

4 The original here reads "*wahre Aussagen gegen raümlich, sozial und zeitlich entschränkte Versuche der Widerlegnugn resistent sind*". But Maeve Cook, the translator, is right to render *Aussagen* as "propositions" in this context. For assertions, which are events, are not resistors, though assertors may be. Assertors, however, are always pretty well locked into both spatio-temporal and social situations.

5 See William James, "Pragmatism's Conception of Truth," in his *Pragmatism*, for his use of the analogy between truth, health, and wealth, and for his citation of Lessing's Hanschen Schlau: "Wie kommt es, Vetter Fritzen/dass grad' die Reichsten in der Welt, das Meiste Geld besitzen?"

6 Being strategic in this way is sometimes morally blameable, as when you could easily equip your interlocutor with the ability to understand better arguments. Sometimes it is blameless, as when you are trying to prevent an imminent injustice from being committed, using whatever means will work in the short time available.

7 See G. E. M. Anscombe, *Ethics, Religion and Politics* (Minneapolis: Minnesota University Press, 1981), pp. 29–30.

8 I discuss change of moral identity in my "Justice as a larger loyalty". There I treat it as change in our sense of who counts as "us," of what sort of people need to be consulted in the course of deliberation. The idea is to see moral progress as a result of extending the bounds of our imagination rather than as a result of stricter obedience to a context-independent imperative.

3
Truth Rehabilitated

DONALD DAVIDSON

There is a long tradition according to which the concept of truth is one of the most important subjects for philosophical discussion, but in this century the tradition has come to be seriously questioned by a large number of philosophers, not to mention historians, literary critics, anthropologists, political scientists, sociologists, and others. I think this is because of various tempting errors and confusions. Here I examine a few of the reasons truth has become tarnished, or at least diminished, in the minds of many, and then go on to say why the concept of truth should be restored to its key role in our understanding of the world and of the minds of agents.

Before it could come to seem worthwhile to debunk truth, it was necessary to represent truth as something grander than it is, or to endow it with powers it does not have. When there was no clear line between philosophy and science, it was natural for philosophers to claim to be purveyors of the closest thing to truth on offer. Concentration on epistemology, especially when epistemology seemed called on to provide ultimate grounds of justification for knowledge, encouraged the confused idea that philosophy was the place to look for the final and most basic truths on which all other truths, whether of science, morality, or common sense, must rest. Plato's conflation of abstract universals with entities of supreme value reinforced the confusion of truth with the most eminent truths; the confusion is apparent in the view (which Plato ultimately came to question) that the only perfect exemplar of a universal or form is the form itself. Thus only circularity (the universal or concept) is perfectly circular, only the concept of a hand is a perfect hand, only truth itself is completely true.

Here we have a deep confusion, a category mistake, which was apparently doomed to flourish. Truth isn't an object, and so it can't be true; truth is a concept, and is intelligibly attributed to things like sentences, utterances, beliefs and propositions, entities which have a propositional content. It is an error to think that if someone seeks to understand the *concept of truth*, that person is necessarily trying to discover important general *truths* about justice or the foundations of physics. The mistake percolates down to the idea that a theory of truth must somehow tell us what, in general, is true, or at least how to discover truths.

No wonder there has been a reaction! Philosophy was promising far more than it, or any other discipline, could deliver. Nietzsche famously reacted; so, in a different way, did the American pragmatists. Dewey, for example, quite properly rejected the idea that philosophers were privy to some special or foundational species of truth without which science could not hope to advance. But he coupled this virtuous modesty with an absurd theory about the concept of truth; having derided pretensions to superior access to truths, he felt he must attack the classical concept itself. The attack, in the fashion of the times, took the form of a persuasive redefinition. Since the word "truth" has an aura of being something valuable, the trick of persuasive definitions is to redefine it to be something of which you approve, something "good to steer by" in a phrase Rorty endorses on Dewey's behalf. So Dewey declared that a belief or theory is true if and only if it promotes human affairs.[1]

It would be otiose to review the obvious objections to this view, for both its proponents and critics are familiar with them. Proponents glory in the conflicts with common sense;[2] critics swell with the silly pleasure of having spotted irresponsible rhetoric. It is more interesting to ask why Dewey, and the others Rorty includes in Dewey's camp, James, Nietzsche, Foucault and himself, put forward a thesis so clearly contrary to the ordinary, but philosophically interesting, concept of truth. I think of four related reasons.

According to Rorty, Dewey "agreed with Nietzsche that the traditional notion of Truth, as correspondence to the intrinsic nature of Reality, was a remnant of the idea of submission to the Will of God." Truth as correspondence with reality may be an idea we are better off without, especially when, as in this quotation, 'truth' and 'reality' are capitalized. The formulation is not so much wrong as empty, but it does have the merit of suggesting that something is not true simply because it is believed, even if believed by everyone. The trouble lies in the claim that the formula has explanatory power. The notion of correspondence would be a help if we were able to say, in an *instructive* way, which fact or slice of reality it is that makes a particular sentence true. No-one has succeeded in doing this. If we ask, for example, what makes the sentence "The moon is a quarter of a million miles away" true, the only answer we come up with is that it is the fact that the moon is a quarter of a million miles away. Worse still, if we try to provide a serious semantics for reference to facts, we discover that they melt into one; there is no telling them apart. The proof of this claim is given by Alonzo Church, who credits it to Frege. Church thinks this is the reason Frege held that all true sentences name the same thing, which he called The True. Kurt Gödel quite independently produced essentially the same proof, holding that it was awareness of this line of thinking that led Russell to invent the theory of descriptions (Neale, 1995). Whatever the history of the relevant argument (which is now often called "The Slingshot"), we must, I think, accept the conclusion: there are no interesting and appropriate entities available which, by being somehow related to sentences, can explain why the true ones are true and the others not. There is good reason, then, to be skeptical about the importance of the correspondence theory of truth.

When "truth" is spelled with a capital "T," it is perhaps natural to think there is a unique way of describing things which gets at their essential nature, "an interpretation of the world which gets it right," as Rorty puts it, a description of "Reality As It Is In Itself." Of course there is no such unique "interpretation" or description, not even in the one or more languages each of us commands, not in any possible language. Or perhaps we should just say this is an ideal of which no-one has made good sense. It hardly matters, for no sensible defender of the objectivity of attributions of truth to particular utterances or beliefs is stuck with this idea, and so there is no reason why, if we abstain from the search for the Perfect Description of Reality, we have to buy the thesis that there is no distinction, "even in principle," between beliefs which are true and beliefs which are "merely good to steer by" (Rorty, 1996, p. 7).

We come here to a far more powerful consideration in favor of a somewhat tamer, but clearly recognizable, version of the pragmatic theory of truth. Rorty brings it to the fore when he credits Dewey with the thought that the correspondence theory adds nothing to "ordinary, workaday, fallible ways of telling . . . the true from the false." What is clearly right is a point made long ago by Plato in the *Theaetetus*: truths do not come with a "mark," like the date in the corner of some photographs, which distinguishes them from falsehoods. The best we can do is test, experiment, compare, and keep an open mind. But no matter how long and well we and coming generations keep at it, we and they will be left with fallible beliefs. We know many things, and will learn more; what we will never know for certain is which of the things we believe are true. Since it is neither visible as a target, nor recognizable when achieved, there is no point in calling truth a goal. Truth is not a value, so the "pursuit of truth" is an empty enterprise unless it means only that it is often worthwhile to increase our confidence in our beliefs, by collecting further evidence or checking our calculations.

From the fact that we will never be able to tell which of our beliefs are true, pragmatists conclude that we may as well identify our best researched, most successful, beliefs with the true ones, and give up the idea of objectivity. (Truth is objective if the truth of a belief or sentence is independent of whether it is justified by all our evidence, believed by our neighbors, or is good to steer by.) But here we have a choice. Instead of giving up the traditional view that truth is objective, we can give up the equally traditional view (to which the pragmatists adhere) that truth is a norm, something for which to strive. I agree with the pragmatists that we can't consistently take truth to be both objective and something to be pursued. But I think they would have done better to cleave to a view that counts truth as objective, but pointless as a goal.[3]

Some contemporary pragmatists have moved away from the hopeless idea that a belief is true if it helps us get on with life, or the less foolish, but still wrong, view that truth is no different from what is, perhaps at its practical best, epistemically available. But other philosophers who would not call themselves pragmatists are still rocking in the wake of the legitimate reaction against inflated or misguided theories of truth. The tendency they have joined is a broad one, one which is perhaps now the mainstream of philosophical thought about the concept of truth. The banner under which these debunkers march is *deflationism*. The idea common to the various brands of deflationism is that truth, though a legitimate concept, is essentially trivial, and certainly not worth the grand metaphysical attention it has received. This view receives its strength from two sources. One is wide, and largely justified, dissatisfaction with the standard attempts to define or otherwise explicate, the concept. Probably the most familiar definition, and the most immediately attractive, declares that an utterance or belief is true if and only if it corresponds to the facts, or reality, or the way things are. I have already said why I think correspondence theories are without explanatory content.

Coherence definitions or 'theories' have their attractions, but only as epistemic theories, not as accounting for truth. For while it is clear that only a consistent set of beliefs could contain all true beliefs, there is no reason to suppose every consistent set of beliefs contains only truths. Openly epistemic theories have their powerful support-ers: I think particularly of Michael Dummett and Hilary Putnam, both of whom, with modifications, hold that truth is warranted assertability. I respect this idea for the same reason I respect closely related pragmatic theories, because it relates truth to human attitudes like belief, intention and desire, and I believe any complete account of truth must do this. But theirs cannot be the right way to express the relation. For either the conditions of warranted assertability are made so strong that they include truth itself, in which case the account is circular, or circularity is avoided by making the conditions explicit, and it then becomes clear that a fully warranted assertion may be false.

What, then, is wrong with deflationism? Why shouldn't we accept the view that truth is as shallow as the correspondence theory seems to show it to be? Deflationism has taken a number of forms in recent years. Frank Ramsey, so prescient in many areas, was one of the first to try to make out that, as he says, "[T]here is really no separate problem of truth but merely a linguistic muddle" (Ramsey, 1990, p. 38). His argument begins by noting that "it is true that Caesar was murdered" means no more than "Caesar was murdered": in such contexts, "it is true that" simply operates like double negation, a sentential connective that maps true sentences onto true and false onto false; aside from emphasis and verbosity, the phrase adds nothing to what we can say. Ramsey makes the same point about phrases like "it is a fact that." More perspicuous than others, though, Ramsey notices that we cannot eliminate the truth predicate in this way in sentences like "he is always right," that is, "whatever he says is true." Here the truth predicate seems indispensable.[4] Ramsey makes a confused (and unworkable) proposal for the elimination of the truth predicate in such cases; we have to conclude that he did not prove his case that the problem of truth is merely a linguistic muddle. (Confusions of use and mention make it impossible to be sure what Ramsey had in mind, but one suspects that if he had pursued the subject he would have come out pretty much where Tarski did.)

Ramsey's deflationist attempt, unlike most such attempts, hinged on taking the primary bearers of truth to be propositions. Recently, however, Paul Horwich has revived what we may call propositional deflationism (Horwich, 1990). Horwich's thesis is not that the concept of truth is eliminable, but that it is trivial. He points out that a sentence like "The proposition that Caesar was murdered is true if and only if Caesar was murdered" is surely true, and that such sentences specify precisely the circumstances under which any expressible proposition is true. He then claims that the totality of such sentences provides an infinite axiomatization of the concept of truth (he excludes by fiat sentences that lead to contradiction). Horwich allows that this does not provide an explicit definition of the concept of truth, but it does, he maintains, exhaust the content of that concept. In particular, there is no need to employ the concept in order to explain the concepts of meaning and belief, since these can be explicated in other ways. As will presently be clear, I do not accept these last claims. But it does not matter, since I think we do not understand Horwich's axiom schema or the particular axioms that instance it. The problem concerns the semantic analysis of sentences like "The proposition that Caesar was murdered is true if and only if Caesar was murdered." The predicate "is true" requires a singular term as subject; the subject is therefore "the proposition that Caesar was murdered." Presumably it names or refers to a proposition. But then, what is the role of the sentence "Caesar was murdered" in this singular term or description? The only plausible answer is that the words "the proposition that" are a functional expression that maps whatever the following sentence names onto a proposition. In that case, the sentence itself must be a referring term. If we are Fregeans, we will say it names a truth value. On this hypothesis, the axiom is a straightforward tautology, and explains nothing (since the words "the proposition that" simply map a truth value onto itself).[5] The alternative is that in its first occurrence, the sentence names some more interesting entity. But then we do not understand the axiom, since the sentence "Caesar was murdered" is used once as a name of some interesting entity, and once as an ordinary sentence, and we have no idea how to accommodate this ambiguity in a serious semantics.

Horwich claims both Quine and Tarski as fellow deflationists. But are they? Quine can apparently be quoted in support of the claim. He has repeatedly spoken of what he calls the disquotational aspect of truth, applied, of course, to sentences, not propositions. The truth predicate, applied to sentences, is disquotational in this sense: a sentence like "'Snow is white' is true" is always equivalent to the result of disquoting the contained sentence and removing the truth predicate; equivalent, then, in this case, to "Snow is white." Here we see clearly how we can eliminate the truth predicate under favorable circumstances. Quine knows, of course, that there are contexts in which this maneuver will not remove the truth predicate. Nevertheless, the totality of sentences like "Snow is white' is true if and only if snow is white" exhausts the extension of the truth predicate for a particular language, as Tarski emphasized, and each such sentence does tell us exactly under what conditions the quoted sentence is true.

Disquotation cannot, however, pretend to give a complete account of the concept of truth, since it works only in the special case where the metalanguage contains the object language. But neither object language nor metalanguage can contain its own truth predicate. In other words, the very concept we want to explain is explicitly excluded from expression in any consistent language for which disquotation works. To put this another way: if we want to know under what conditions a sentence containing a truth predicate is true, we cannot use that predicate in the disquotational mode. Disquotation does not give the entire content of the concept of truth.

At best, then, disquotation gives the extension of a truth predicate for a single language; if we ask what all such predicates have in common, disquotation cannot answer. Something analogous must be said about Tarski's truth definitions. Tarski showed how to give explicit definitions of truth for languages satisfying certain conditions, but at the same time he proved (given some natural assumptions) that no general definition was possible; the general concept escaped him. He did go far beyond anything implicit in disquotation, however, for he was able to give proper definitions of truth – relative to specific languages, it goes without saying, which disquotation cannot do. Tarski's truth definitions are not trivial, and they reveal something deep about languages of any serious expressive power. As long as a language has the equivalent of a first order quantificational structure and no decision method, there is no way to define truth for it except by introducing a sophisticated version of reference, what Tarski called satisfaction. Tarski's satisfiers are infinite sequences which pair the variables of a language with the entities in its ontology. The interesting work of the concept of satisfaction comes in characterizing the semantic properties of open sentences, but it turns out in the end that a closed sentence is true if and only if it is satisfied by some sequence. This may suggest that we have here the makings of a correspondence theory, but it would be a Fregean theory, since every sequence satisfies every true sentence. You could say that though this was not his intention, Tarski here indirectly vindicates Frege's slingshot argument.

We must conclude that Tarski's work gives no comfort to those who would like to revive the correspondence theory, nor does it support a deflationary attitude. Given how unsatisfactory the alternatives seem to be, should we nevertheless rest content with the genuine insight Tarski has given us into the nature of truth? I think not, for we have to wonder how we know that it is some single concept which Tarski indicates how to define for each of a number of well-behaved languages. Tarski does not, of course, attempt to define such a concept, though the title of his famous essay is "*The* Concept of Truth in Formalized Languages" ("Der Wahrheitsbegriff . . .") (Tarski

1956a). Various remarks in this work and elsewhere also make clear that Tarski assumes there is one concept, even if it can't be defined. This comes out not only in his stated conviction that his work is directly relevant to the 'classical' concept of truth with which philosophers have always been concerned, but also in his criterion for success in the project of defining truth for particular languages. This (informal) criterion requires that the definition entail as theorems all sentences of the form

$$s \text{ is true-in-}L \text{ iff } p.$$

where s is a description of any sentence of L and p is a translation of that sentence into the language of the defined predicate "true-in-L". Clearly, we cannot recognize that such a predicate is a truth predicate unless we already grasp the (undefined) general concept of truth. It is also significant that Tarski connects the concept of truth with translation: this is essential, since the language for which truth is being defined cannot be the language which contains the defined truth predicate.

This brings me to my positive theme: if all the definitions of the general concept fail, and none of the short paraphrases seem to come close to capturing what is important or interesting about the concept, why do some of us persist in thinking it is interesting and important? One of the reasons is its connection with meaning. This is the connection of which Tarski makes use, for translation succeeds only if it preserves truth, and the traditional aim of translation is to preserve meaning. But to what extent does meaning depend on truth?

Almost everyone agrees that some sentences, at least, have the value true or false, and that for such sentences, we may speak of truth conditions. But deflationists and others tend to doubt whether this fact has much to do with what sentences mean. Meaning, it is frequently said, has to do rather with the conditions under which it is justified or proper to use a sentence to make an assertion; in general, meaning has to do with how sentences are used rather than with their truth conditions. Here I sense two confusions. The first is that truth-conditional and use accounts of meaning are somehow in competition. One can legitimately dispute the claim that a Tarski-type truth definition can serve as a theory of meaning. I think it can, when properly understood, but that is not my thesis here. What is clear is that someone who knows under what conditions a sentence would be true understands that sentence, and if the sentence has a truth value (true, false or perhaps neither) then someone who does not know under what conditions it would be true doesn't understand it. This simple claim doesn't rule out an account of meaning which holds that sentences mean what they do because of how they are used; it may be that they are used as they are because of their truth conditions, and they have the truth conditions they do because of how they are used.

The second confusion is the thought that there is a simple, direct, non-question-begging way to employ 'uses' to provide a theory of meaning. There is not. It is empty to say meaning is use unless we specify what use we have in mind, and when we do specify, in a way that helps with meaning, we find ourselves going in a circle. Nevertheless, it is only by registering how a language is used that we can make it our own. How do we do it? Before we have an idea of truth or error, before the advent of concepts or propositional thought, there is a rudiment of communication in the simple discovery that sounds produce results. Crying is the first step toward language when crying is found to procure one or another form of relief or satisfaction. More specific sounds, imitated or not, are rapidly associated with more specific pleasures. Here use would be meaning, if anything like intention and meaning were in the picture. A large further step has been taken when the child notices that others also make distinctive sounds at the same time the child is having the experiences that provoke its own volunteered sounds. For the adult, these sounds have a meaning, perhaps as one word sentences. The adult sees herself as doing a little ostensive teaching: "Eat," "Red," "Ball," "Mamma," "Milk," "No." There is now room for what the adult views as error: the child says "Block" when it is a slab. This move fails to be rewarded, and the conditioning becomes more complex. This is still pretty simple stuff, for nothing more is necessarily involved than verbal responses increasingly conditioned to what the teacher thinks of as appropriate circumstances, and the child finds satisfying, often enough. There is little point in trying to spot, in this process, the moment at which the child is talking and thinking. The interaction between adult and child in the ostensive learning situation I have described provides the necessary conditions for the emergence of language and propositional thought, by creating a space in which there can be success and failure. What is clear is that we can only say the child *thinks* something is red, or a ball, if it appreciates the distinction for itself: the child thinks something is red or a ball only if it is in some sense aware that a mistake is possible. It is classifying things, and it may have put something in the wrong slot.

It is difficult to exaggerate the magnitude of the step from native or learned disposition to respond to stimuli of a certain sort, to employing a concept with the awareness of the chance of error. It is the step from reacting to proximal stimuli to the thought of distal objects and events, the step from mere conditioned response to what Wittgenstein called "following a rule." This is where the concept of truth enters, for there is no sense in saying a disposition is in error – one cannot fail to 'follow' a disposition, but one can fail to follow a rule.

Here we must ask: how can we reconcile the fact that a general appeal to how language is used cannot be parlayed into a theory of meaning with the present claim that ostensive learning is the entering wedge into language, for surely the ostending teacher is making a use of one-word sentences that the learner picks up? The answer lies in the transition just mentioned. At the start the learner does not register anything more than an association between object or situation and sound or gesture. The value of the association is supplied by the teacher or the environment in the form of reward. In the beginning there is not a word but a sound being given a use. The teacher sees the learner as picking up a bit of language with a meaning already there; the learner has no idea of prior meaning or use: for the learner, what was meaningless before now takes on significance. In the early stage of ostensive learning, error has no point for the learner, for there is nothing for him to be wrong about, and where error has no point, there is not a concept or thought. Once trial and error (from the teacher's point of view) is replaced with thought and belief (from the learner's point of view), the concept of truth has application.

During the learning process, the pragmatist's claim that there is nothing to be gained by distinguishing between success (as measured by the teacher's approval or getting what one wants) and truth is clearly right. This is a distinction that depends on further developments. These are not hard to imagine in rough outline. Ostensive learning works first and best with whole sentences, in practice often represented by what for the experienced speaker are single names, common nouns, verbs, adjectives, and adverbs ("Mama," "Man," "Come," "Good," "Careful"). The child who has no more is still a pragmatist. Once some grammar is in hand, however, separately learned parts can be assembled in new ways, and truth separates from the merely useful or approved.

The references of names, the extensions of predicates, the combinatorial devices themselves, are in the hands of teachers and society; truth is not.

Sentences mean what they do because of the semantic properties of the words and the combinatorial devices they contain. You would not understand a sentence if you did not know to what the names and other singular terms in it purported to refer, or if you were unaware of the extension of its predicates. But to know this is to know that the materials are present which make for truth and falsity. This is so even when we know that a term fails of reference or a predicate has an empty extension. Our understanding of truth conditions is central to our understanding of every sentence. This may escape our notice for many reasons. The first, and most general, reason is that in the normal course of conversation we do not care whether or not a sentence is true; it is a fairly rare occasion when we make an assertion by saying what we literally believe to be true. Our ordinary talk is studded with metaphor, ellipsis, easily recognized irony, and hyperbole, not to mention slips of the tongue, jokes, and malapropisms. But we understand a metaphor only because we know the usual meanings of the words, and know under what conditions the sentence containing the metaphor would be true. There are cases where we may decide a metaphorical sentence is neither true nor false, for example "The sound of the trumpet is scarlet." Our decision that this sentence has no truth value (if that is our decision, for we may choose, with Frege, to count it false) is based on our understanding of the sorts of things of which the predicate 'scarlet' is true or false, and our decision that the sound of a trumpet is not one of them. Interrogatives may not themselves be true or false, but they have answers that are. Indeed, it is clear that one does not understand a yes–no interrogative if one does not know there are two possible answers, one of which is true and one of which is false. Imperatives, if taken to express an order or command, are understood only if one knows what would be true if they were obeyed. Sentences with non-referring names ("Pegasus is a winged horse") may or may not, according to one's semantic theory, have a truth value, but one comprehends such sentences only if one knows what it would be for the name "Pegasus" to name a horse with wings.

Sentences are understood on condition that one has the concept of objective truth. This goes also for the various propositional attitudes sentences are used to express. It is possible to have a belief only if one knows that beliefs may be true or false. I can believe it is now raining, but this is because I know that whether or not it is raining does not depend on whether I believe it, or everyone believes it, or it is useful to believe it; it is up to nature, not to me or my society or the entire history of the human race. What is up to us is what we mean by our words, but that is a different matter. Truth enters into the other attitudes in other ways. We desire that a certain state of affairs be true, we fear, hope or doubt that things are one way or another. We intend by our actions to make it true that we have a good sleep. We are proud or depressed that it is the case that we have won the second prize. Since all these, and many more attitudes have a propositional content – the sort of content that can be expressed by a sentence – to have any of these attitudes is necessarily to know what it would be for the corresponding sentence to be true. Without a grasp of the concept of truth, not only language, but thought itself, is impossible.

Truth is important, then, not because it is especially valuable or useful, though of course it may be on occasion, but because without the idea of truth we would not be thinking creatures, nor would we understand what it is for someone else to be a thinking creature. It is one thing to try to define the concept of truth, or capture its essence in a pithy summary phrase; it is another to trace its connections with other concepts. If we think of the various attempted characterizations as attempting no more than the latter, their merits become evident. Correspondence, while it is empty as a definition, does capture the thought that truth depends on how the world is, and this should be enough to discredit most epistemic and pragmatic theories. Epistemic and pragmatic theories, on the other hand, have the merit of relating the concept of truth to human concerns, like language, belief, thought and intentional action, and it is these connections which make truth the key to how mind apprehends the world.

Rorty doesn't much mind my saying that truth is one concept among a number of other related concepts which we use in describing, explaining, and predicting human behavior. But why, he asks, say truth is any more important than such concepts as intention, belief, desire, and so on? (Rorty 1995, p. 286) Importance is a hard thing to argue about. *All* these concepts (and more) are essential to thought, and cannot be reduced to anything simpler or more fundamental. Why be niggardly in awarding prizes; I'm happy to hand out golden apples all round.

References

Horwich, Paul. 1990. *Truth*. Oxford: Blackwell.

Neale, Stephen. 1995. The Philosophical Significance of Gödel's Slingshot. *Mind* 104:761–825.

Ramsey, Frank Plumpton. 1990. Facts and Propositions. In *Philosophical Papers*. Edited by D. H. Mellor. Cambridge, UK: Cambridge University Press.

Rorty, Richard. 1995. Is Truth a Goal of Inquiry? Davidson *vs.* Wright. *The Philosophical Quarterly* 45 (180):281–300.

Rorty, Richard. 1996. Something to Steer by. *London Review of Books* (June 20):7, 8.

Ryan, Alan. 1996. *John Dewey and the High Tide of American Liberalism*: Norton.

Tarski, Alfred. 1956a. The Concept of Truth in Formalized Languages. In *Logic, Semantics, Metamathematics*, edited by J. H. Woodger. Oxford: Oxford University Press.

Tarski, Alfred. 1956b. On the Concept of Logical Consequence. In *Logic, Semantics, Metamathematics*, edited by J. H. Woodger. Oxford: Oxford University Press.

Notes

1   Most of what I say here about pragmatists early and contemporary is inspired by a review of Alan Ryan (Ryan, 1996) by Richard Rorty [Rorty, 1996 #19]. Rorty writes:

> To take the traditional notion of Truth seriously, you have to do more than agree that some beliefs are true and some false . . . You must agree with Clough that 'It fortifies my soul to know/That, though I perish, Truth is so.' You must feel uneasy at William James's claim that 'ideas . . . become true just in so far as they help us to get into satisfactory relations with other parts of our experience.' You must become indignant when Ryan (accurately paraphrasing Dewey) says that "to call a statement 'true' is no more than to say that it is good to steer our practice by." (Rorty, 1996, p. 7)

> Ryan doesn't buy the idea that what is useful is necessarily true, but this "puts my [Rorty's] pragmatist back up. As I said . . . the whole point of pragmatism is to stop distinguishing between the usefulness of a way of talking and its truth."

2   Thus Rorty, in final praise of the pragmatic attitude to truth, says that "non-competitive, though perhaps irreconcilable, beliefs [may] reasonably [be] called 'true'" (Rorty, 1996, p. 8).

Of course one can imagine circumstances under which it might be reasonable to *say* this (for example to prevent a fist-fight), but could it be reasonable, or even possible, to *think* irreconcilable beliefs are true?

3   Curiously, Rorty sensibly argues that truth is not a norm *and* that there is no difference in principle between what is true and what is justified. "Pragmatists think that if something makes no difference to practice, it should make no difference to philosophy. This conviction makes them suspicious of the philosopher's emphasis on the difference between justification and truth." (Rorty, 1995, p. 281). If there is no difference, truth is identical with what is justified; but Rorty claims there is lots to say about justification, yet little to say about truth. If, as seems right, it *is* a legitimate norm to want to be justified, but not to seek the truth, then there must be a large difference between them.

4   It is also indispensable when we want to explain the validity of logical rules: we need to be able to say why, if *any* sentences of a specified sort are true, others must be (Tarski, 1956b). Rorty wonders why we use the same word, "truth," also to "caution people" that their beliefs may not be justified (Rorty, 1995, p. 286). I doubt we can explain this in a philosophically interesting way; words can be used in many ways without having to change their meaning – that, as I keep saying, is their merit. But it is easy to explain why we use the same word to express validity and to talk about what we have to know to understand a sentence: we prove a rule of inference is valid by appeal to the truth conditions of sentences.

5   I owe this suggestion to Burt Dreben.

RESPONSE TO DONALD DAVIDSON

Davidson says "it may be that they [sentences] are used as they are because of their truth conditions, and they have the truth conditions they do because of how they are used." (p. 70) This sentence troubles people like me – people who think they got the point of Wittgenstein's *Philosophical Investigations* but have never been sure whether they got the point of Tarski's "The Concept of Truth in Formalized Languages." For we are happier with uses than with meanings, and truth conditions make us nervous. Call people who resemble me in this respect "Wittgensteinians."[1]

Wittgensteinians are not sure why, now that Davidson has erased the boundary between knowing a language and knowing our way around the world generally, he still thinks we need a theory of meaning. Why should we suppose that there is a theory which captures this sort of know-how? If we need no theory, maybe we can just set aside Tarski and truth-conditions? Just as Wittgenstein got over his youthful, Tractarian, desire for structure, so maybe we can get over, if not Tarski on formalized languages, at least the desire to carry Tarski over into non-formalized languages.

Wittgensteinians' favorite Davidson essay is "A Nice Derangement of Epitaphs." We like being told that that "there is no learnable common core of consistent behavior, no shared grammar or rules, no portable interpreting machine set to grind out the meaning of an arbitrary utterance." (p. 445). But we are tempted, perhaps foolishly, to better the instruction. We wonder whether there is any point in treating our constant coping with the linguistic behavior of people like Mrs. Malaprop as the constant construction of nonce truth-theories for nonce languages. If there is no such machine, we think, maybe there is no need for a truth-theory. Maybe we can brush Tarski aside.

Davidson reiterates, in "A Nice Derangement," that because "there must be systematic relations between the meanings of sentences," the competent interpreter must be thought of as having

a system for interpeting what he hears or says. You might think of this system as a
machine which, when fed an arbitrary utterance ... produces an interpretation. One
model for such a machine is a theory of truth, more or less along the lines of a Tarski
truth definition ... a recursive characterization of the truth conditions of all possible
utterances of the speaker ... (p. 437)

By the end of the essay, however, the idea of a portable interpreting machine for a
language such as English has been replaced with the suggestion that "a person's ability
to interpret or speak to another person" consists in "the ability that permits him [the
interpreter] to construct a correct, that is, convergent, passing theory for speech
transactions with that person" (p. 445). This replacement epitomizes, Davidson says,
"how far we have drifted from standard ideas of language mastery."

The explicit target of "A Nice Derangement" is the idea of a language as a set of
shared conventions. That essay argues that "what interpreter and speaker share, to the
extent that communication succeeds, is not learned and so is not a langauge governed
by rules or conventions known to speaker and interpreter in advance." What they need
is not such rules or conventions but "the ability to converge on passing theories from
utterance to utterance" (p. 445).

Wittgensteinians, however, wonder if the target should not rather have been the idea
that the ability to act in ways which are capturable in a recursive theory requires one
to describe the agent as applying such a theory. In the case at hand, they wonder
whether the ability to cope with Mrs. Malaprop need be described as the ability to
converge with her on any sort of theory, any more than the ability of two bicyclists to
avoid collision is an ability to agree on a passing theory of passing. Whatever the
competence of these bicyclists consists in, is there any particular reason to think that it
is having a theory?

One can imagine Davidson responding that, although one may learn to cope with
speakers in the same conditioned-reflex way one learns to ride a bicycle, there is
nothing *systematic* about bicycle riding. In "A Nice Derangement" the following is
labeled "Principle (1)":

A competent speaker or interpreter is able to interpret utterances, his own or others, *on
the basis of* the semantic properties of the parts, or words, in the utterance, and the
structure of the utterance. For this to be possible, there must be systematic relations
between the meanings of utterances." (p. 436; emphasis added)

But we Wittgensteinians are dubious. We are tempted to parody "Principle (1)" as
follows:

A competent bicycle-rider is able to cope with a potential infinity of bicycling conditions
(pebbles, sand, other bicyclists, pedestrians, etc.) *on the basis of* the physical characteristics
of the bicycle, his own body, pebbles, sand, etc. For this to be possible, there must be
systematic relations between these properties – the systematic relations which mechanics,
physiology, geology and the rest are devoted to uncovering.

Since nobody suggests that the know-how involved in bicycle-riding is a matter of an
ability to wield a theory of the systematic relations between physical characteristics,
why should we believe that the know-how involved in coping with the potential infinity
of idiolects is a matter of the ability to find a passing recursive theory? Why not treat
the work of grammarians and lexicographers (or their ideal counterparts, the devisers
of Tarskian T-sentences which are adequate to predict the linguistic behavior of

speakers) as bearing the same relation to the speaker on the street as the natural
scientists bear to the bicycle-rider on the road? So why not amend both Principle (1)
and its parody to read "because of" instead of "on the basis of"?

Therapeutic Wittgensteinians who are not sure we need a theory of meaning can
agree with Davidson that there is no "simple, direct, non-question-begging way to
employ 'uses' to provide a theory of meaning" (p. 6). We can also agree that "it is
empty to say meaning is use unless we specify what use we have in mind" (p. 6). But
– being therapeutic rather than constructive Wittgensteinians – we do not say that
meaning *is* use. We would no more say that than we would say that systematic
microstructural relations *are* macrostructural behavior. There is no simple direct way
to employ such behavior to detect microstructure, but there are complicated indirect
ways – those used by natural scientists. There is no way to the meanings save by the
uses, just as there is no way to the micro save by the macro. We emphasize a point
made by Davidson himself; that a Tarskian truth definition is an empirical theory,
designed to find an underlying order behind a lot of confusing uses. Such a theory
bears the same relation to the uses as microstructure to macrostructure.

What, we ask, is a theory of meaning supposed to get us? Why should we not just
do what our guru, Wittgenstein, often did – distinguish between uses of linguistic
expressions as needed? Needed for what? Needed to diagnoses and treat philosophical
complaints. Why view philosophers as having a constructive task, and then be tempted
to view philosophy, of language, Dummett-like, as "first philosophy"? Why not say
that philosophers will have finished with the concept of truth when they have stopped
people from using "truth" in the ways that Davidson thinks they should stop using it
– for instance, as the name of a goal of inquiry (Crispin Wright), or as something
which might prove to be out of reach (Akeel Bilgrami), or something in which to have
faith (Daniel Dennett) or as something great, which will prevail (St. Paul)?

This last rhetorical question brings me, at last, to one of Davidson's main concerns
in "Truth Rehabilitated": how shall we ensure that we have exhausted the concept of
truth?

Wittgensteinians are hesitant to take sides on the question of whether disquotation-
alism does or does not exhaust this concept. For they think it pointless to ask whether
the content of a concept has been exhausted unless we specify which uses of the word
signifying the concept are to be included and which excluded. Davidson excludes quite
a few uses of 'true' and of 'truth' (for instance, "She was a true friend," "Truth is
One," "Fashionable French philosophers do not value truth.")[2] The only two uses he
finds relevant are the cautionary use ("justified, but maybe not true") and the use of
'true' to name the property preserved in valid inference. Davidson doubts that we can
"explain in a philosophically interesting way" (note 4) why the same word has both
uses. But it was the former use which kept truth alive as a stimulating philosophical
topic – for this was the use which was tied up with truth's purported grandeur, power,
value, possible unreachability, and the like (in the way Davidson describes at the
beginning of "Truth Rehabilitated"). Before Wittgensteinians can be confident that
they need think about Tarskian truth-definitions for natural languages, they must be
told why they should now turn their attention to the latter use.

Granted that "words can be used in many ways without having to change their
meaning" (note 4) what is the relation between these manifold uses, the "meaning" of
"true" and the concept of truth? One can imagine people like John Searle protesting
that anybody whose concept of truth has no room for truth as a goal is just plain wrong
about what the concept does and does not include. Such people will see Davidson as

ripping off, and flinging away, great bleeding chunks of this concept, keeping only the few choice bits he likes (while berating those who, like Horwich, are even choosier). We Wittgensteinians, who are dubious about the concept of 'concept', and would be happy to just talk about the utility or disutility of various uses of terms, have some sympathy with this sort of protest.

When Davidson talks about the need to save the concept from those who would give "epistemic or pragmatic" theories of truth, he has in mind the cautionary use of 'true.' When he is saving the concept from disquotationalists like Horwich, however, he talks about the Tarskian what-is-preserved-in-valid-inferences use of 'true'. The only connection between these two uses, apart from the phonetic, seems to be the fact that assertibility is *not* preserved in valid inferences. So both uses of 'true' can usefully be distinguished from assertibility. But then so can the use of 'true' to mean "accurately representing the intrinsic nature of reality." Being different from assertibility is easy.

These various Wittgensteinian doubts boil down to something like this: the question is not whether we have exhausted the concept of truth, or gotten truth right. It is, rather, whether we have sorted out the vairous uses of the word 'true', decided which of them had better be discarded, and specified the functions performed by the remainder. If we look at "Truth Rehabilitated" through those spectacles, it will be read as offering the following advice:

1 Since, as Davidson says, "truth as correspondence with reality may be an idea we are better off without" (p. 66) and since "there is no point in calling truth a goal" (p. 67) and since the pragmatists' "truth is what works" is irresponsible rhetoric (p. 66) we should try to eliminate the relevant uses of 'true' from our idiolects. We should not worry about whether truth-as-correspondence or truth-as-goal or truth-as-what-works is inside or outside the concept of truth. We should drop the inside-outside contrast, and perhaps the 'concept' concept, for the same reason that we have dropped other forms of the scheme–content distinction.

2 We should not let the fact that "truth is objective" in the sense that "the truth of a belief or a sentence is independent of whether it is justified by all our evidence, believed by our neighbors, or is good to steer by" (p. 67) tempt us to retain, in our idiolects, any of the unfortunate uses listed in (1).

3 We should not let the fact that "our understanding of truth conditions is central to the understanding of every sentence" (p. 72) mislead us into thinking that those who understand the sentence have internalized a theory about the relations between a vast number of linguistic expressions, over and above having the know-how necessary to use the sentence in ways that others understand, to justify assertions made with the sentence when required in ways that others accept, and so on. To know under what conditions a sentence is true is not different from knowing what moves to make when justification for such an assertion is demanded. The distinction between truth and justification is not endangered by the fact that the know-how involved in being able to justify a sentence is not a different skill than that involved in knowing when the sentence is true. The systematic relations between linguistic expressions are simply a handy way of getting a grip on the relations of being-frequently-inferred-from-or-to which the radical interpreter, hoping to construct such a definition, must keep track of.[3]

4   "Sentences are understood on condition that one has the concept of objective
    truth". (p. 72, so "without a grasp of the concept of truth, not only language, but
    thought itself, is impossible" (p. 72. But this says no more than that those unable
    to wield expressions like "I believe that *p*, but maybe *p* is not true" should not be
    said to be using language, or thinking. If to wield such expressions as these is all
    there is to having "the concept of objective truth," then indeed such a grasp is
    required for both language and thought.[4] But the question of whether there is more
    or less to the concept than that ability seems idle.

5   Davidson has shown why such deflationary locutions as "truth is trivial" or my
    own "there is nothing much to be said about truth" or "meaning is just use, and
    has nothing to do with truth conditions" are confusing and misleading ways of
    saying that truth is not a value, not a matter of correspondence to reality, and not
    various other things. But one should take care not to create new pseudo–problems
    in the course of dissolving old ones. Davidson runs the risk of doing this, and in
    particular of resuscitating those which cluster around the scheme–content distinc-
    tion, when his anti–pragmatist and anti–deflationist polemic leads him to say things
    like "truth depends on how the world is" (p. 73). For such dicta encourage those
    who still think, as Davidson does not, "that there is something important in the
    realist concept of truth."[5] This risk is increased by such untriangulated remarks as

>   the sort of assertion that is linked to understanding already incorporates the concept
>   of truth: we are *justified* in asserting a sentence in the required sense only if we believe
>   the sentence we use to make the assertion is true; and what ultimately ties language to
>   the world is that the conditions that typically cause us to hold sentences true *constitute*
>   the truth conditions, and hence the meanings, of our sentences." ("The Folly of
>   Trying to Define Truth", p. 275)[6]

6   Davidson's doctrine of triangulation tells us that what ultimately ties language to
    the world is not that various hunks of non–linguistic reality are the conditions of
    the truth of various sentences, but "the triangle that, by relating speaker, interpreter
    and the world, determines the contents of thought and speech."[7]
        The point of this doctrine is that you cannot get along with just holistic
    inferential relations between beliefs and statements (as coherence theorists tried to
    do) nor with atomic relations of being–caused–by (as realists fixated on perception
    still try to do). You have to play back and forth between causation and inference in
    a way which does not permit any of the corners of a triangle to be independent of
    any of the others.

In the bulk of this response, I have left pragmatism pretty much out of the picture. I
have concentrated on the Wittgensteinian, metaphilosophical, question: why need we
go beyond diagnosis to theory? But "Truth Rehabilitated" contains a footnote on a
matter dear to William James' heart: the reconciliation of science and religion: since
the need for such reconciliation was James' principal motive for such "irresponsible
rhetoric" as "truth is what is good for us to believe," I shall conclude by defending my
Jamesian claim that "non–competitive, though perhaps irreconcilable, beliefs [may]
reasonably [be] called 'true'."
    At note 2 in his paper, Davidson cites this claim and incredulously asks "could it be
reasonable, or even possible, to *think* irreconcilable beliefs are true?" Let me try to

explain what James and I have in mind by imagining a very good evolutionary biologist who traces the origins of various species all week long, but takes great comfort from hearing mass on Sundays. She does not see any interesting inferential connections between the beliefs she expresses when reciting the creed and when lecturing on Evolution 101 – though she is vaguely aware that others (for instance, Cardinal Ratzinger) do.

A truth definition for this woman's idiolect would have to take into account the absence of such connections, and the resulting compartmentalization of her beliefs. As an empirical account of her linguistic behavior, such a truth-definition cannot be used to show her that she should be seeing connections she does not see, compartmentalizing when she should not. The radical linguist who produces such a truth-definition must follow the Thomistic maxim: "when you meet an apparent contradiction, make a distinction" (the same maxim that Quine invoked, albeit implicitly, against Lévy-Bruhl).

The effect of compartmentalization is to make beliefs which may prove irreconcilable (once one breaks down walls between the compartments) non-competitive. Such compartmentalization is not uncommon. Most non-philosophers, for example, put their beliefs about the attribution of moral responsibility and their beliefs about the causation of human behavior in separate compartments. When asked to reconcile the two, they are inclined to reply, following Hume's advice, "Why should I?". James recommended that the evolutionary biologist I have described do the same.

James thought that we should treat natural science as performing one function and religion another. They can be made (in Religion 101) to get in each other's way, just as our beliefs about responsibility and about causation can be made (in Philosophy 101) to conflict. In such courses students are told that beliefs they had thought non-competitive should be squared off against each other. Some students make existential acknowledgement of their previous intellectual sloppiness, whereas other students simply continue to compartmentalize when outside of class.

I have argued that one advantage in getting rid of truth-as-accurate-representation, and thereby weakening the attraction of the idea that Truth is One, is that doing so gives us less reason to incite the sort of conflicts traditionally incited in Religion 101 and Philosophy 101. A case can be made that such incitement contributes to clear thinking. But a case can be made that it merely creates pseudo-problems. My phrase "non-competitive, though perhaps irreconcilable" was designed to keep this question open.

If one thinks it desirable to keep this question open, one will have another reason to think of understanding, conversation and inquiry in terms of Davidsonian triangulation. Davidsonians think of "the contents of thought and speech" as determined by whatever it takes to cope simultaneously with non-linguistic causes of belief and with the linguistic behavior of our fellow-humans. Thinking in that way helps one think of inquiry as continual recontextualizaiton, rather than as zeroing in on the way things really are. It thereby makes it easier to see contexts, categories, compartments, and concepts as up for conversational grabs.

Notes

1   It would be more precise, but perhaps needlessly long-winded, to call my own little sect "therapeutic Wittgensteinians." We are not to be confused with the people whom Davidson

describes as "heavy thinkers like Michael Dummett, Putnam and Soames, following various leads suggested by Ludwig Wittgenstein and H. P. Grice." Such thinkers believe that, as Davidson puts it, "an account of meaning can be made to depend on a notion of assertibility or use which does not in turn appeal to the concept of truth ("The Folly of Trying to Define Truth," p. 275). Therapeutic Wittgensteinians do not have an account of meaning to offer, because they agree with Dummett that the moral of *Philosophical Investigations* is that no systematic theory of meaning is possible.

2   Davidson says that "Truth isn't an object . . . truth is a concept" and that to think otherwise is a category mistake. But this begs the question against those who think no analysis of the concept of truth adequate which fails to take account of such hypostatizing uses of 'truth' as those just cited. One philosopher's category-mistake is another's insight. If we could never change categories on our dialectical opponents, intellectual progress would come to a screeching halt. I think of Davidson as making great progress by changing categories, rather than as having accurately described a categoreal fact which others have misdescribed.

3   Through the spectacles I am suggesting we use, Davidson's remark that "we understand a metaphor only because we know the usual meanings of words, and know under what conditions the sentence containing the metaphor would be true" (p. 72) will not be seen to add anything not expressed by "you will not understand uncommon uses of a term unless you understand common uses."

4   Wittgensteinians who are also fans of James and Dewey can agree with Davidson that one who wields these expressions knows that there is a difference between truth and success. But these Wittgensteinians read James and Dewey not so much as people who ignored this difference (although it is true they often did) but as people prescient enough to have said what Davidson was later to say: that since truth swings free of justification, belief, success, and thus of the fortunes of our social practices, truth cannot be a goal or a value. They got a lot of abuse for saying that, for it was widely believed in their day that what Dennett calls "faith in truth" is a prerequisite for moral probity. So the shades of James and Dewey may feel themselves entitled to a bit of credit for softening up Davidson's audience – making it less resistant to his casual iconoclasm than it would otherwise have been.

5   "The Structure and Content of Truth," p. 304. Davidson there explains that that conception is "the idea that truth and therefore reality, are (except in special cases) independent of what anyone believes or can know."

6   Note the word "typically" in this sentence. This word stretches the point which Davidson originally put as follows: "we must, in the plainest and methodologically most basic cases, take the objects of a belief to be the causes of that belief." ("A Coherence Theory of Truth and Knowledge," pp. 317–318). It is a long way from these plainest, perceptual, cases to the typical case. For perceptual reports make up only a tiny fraction of our total linguistic output.

7   "The Structure and Content of Truth," p. 325).

4

Richard Rorty on Reality and Justification

HILARY PUTNAM

In the Introduction to their *Rationality in Question*,[1] Ben-Ami Scharfstein and Shlomo Biderman speak of what they take to be "the increasing sophistication of scientific and philosophical thought, of a kind that allows us to hope – is it against hope? – that in philosophy too there can be a kind of general progress of rationality in the sense of reasonableness." In this essay I shall discuss the thought of a philosopher for whom talk of a "general progress of rationality" is, to put it mildly, problematic.

"Kicking" Discrete Hunks of Reality Versus Referring to Them

Although Richard Rorty is famous for denying that there is any correspondence between our words and elements of reality, virtually all of Rorty's writings contain passages intended to reassure us that he is not denying that there is a world, or even denying that we are in unmediated touch with the world. In *Philosophy and the Mirror of Nature* the idea of language and science as "mirroring" nature is rejected, but they (and we) are nonetheless seen as in contact with nature; science, for example, is to be seen "as a set of working diagrams for coping with nature" (298). In "Pragmatism, Davidson and Truth"[2] the tone of reassurance is strident: "Using those vocables [the words and sentences of 'our language'] is *as direct as contact with reality can get* (as direct as kicking rocks, for instance). The fallacy comes in thinking that the relationship between vocable and reality has to be piecemeal (like the relation between individual kicks and individual rocks), a matter of discrete component capacities to get in touch with discrete hunks of reality." (145–146; emphasis added).

I want to explain why these reassurances seem to me utterly inadequate. My aim will be to show that Rorty's account faces exactly the same problems that were faced earlier in the century by logical positivist accounts, and later by Quinian accounts.[3]

To begin, then, a word about the problems with logical positivist accounts of intentionality. In their phenomenalist period, the positivists were committed to the view that all I am doing when I speak is describing "the" (that is, my own) "*Empfindungen*" or "*Erlebnisse*" – that is, sense data. To the obvious question, "But isn't this solipsism?" the positivists had two famous retorts: (1) "The data have no owner", that is, "the" sense-data have only contingent relations with the person performing the phenomenalist construction of the world,[4] an example of such a contingent relation might be formulated thus: "At times when the eyelids of HP are shut [where this should, of course, be reformulated in phenomenalistic language], there are no visual sense-data." (2) If the construction is successful, such sentences about other people as "I have four children," "My wife is talking to me now," "I am eating with a friend," will all have truth-preserving (or at least verification-by-me preserving) translations into the phenomenalist language, and so I can maintain all of my beliefs about other people, etc.

Suppose, now, that I discover that my spouse is a committed phenomenalist, and really believes that all I am is a logical construction out of *her* sense-data. Should I feel reassured by these responses? My problem isn't that I think that, contrary to the positivists, the entities that she speaks about in her language, the only entities referred to in her primitive notation (namely, her sense data) are "intrinsically" rather than empirically related to her, or that I think they are related to a Kantian transcendental ego; my problem is that those sense data aren't me. If her avowals of love and concern are avowals of an attitude to certain logical constructions out of her sense-data, then, as one says, "we have a problem." And even if all of her sentences about those logical constructions *were* materially equivalent, and equivalent in verification conditions (for her), with the sentences in ordinary language that they replace, sentences about me and our life together, the fact remains that an attitude towards a pattern of regularities in one's own sense-data is not the same thing as an attitude towards another person. Of course (this was another positivist response) she might reply that from her point of view either the difference is merely emotive and not cognitive, or else I am uttering metaphysical nonsense. [In fact, not even the positivists went this far; what a logical positivist spouse who took the line of Carnap's Aufbau would actually have said was, "For you the situation is reversed; it is your data that are 'the' data, and it is I who becomes the logical construction." But that is no better.[5]]

The feature I want to isolate in this dialectic is this: the positivists agreed that there are certain realistic sounding statements in ordinary language that it would be most unreasonable to deny. So they found (or more precisely hoped to find – as we know, their phenomenalist translation project failed) translations of the *sentences* (Rorty calls them the "vocables," or elsewhere "the marks and noises") in question under which they come out true. *But the interpretation they put upon those "vocables" violate our deepest intuitions about what we are doing when we assert them.*[6]

We can see the same pattern reappearing in some of Quine's writing, this time in a materialist rather than a phenomenalist context. On the one hand, Quine is willing to push his own denial that our words stand in a "piecemeal" relation to individual "components of reality" ("like the relation between individual kicks and individual rocks") quite as far as Rorty, though for very different reasons. In one place, for example, Quine has written that there is no fact of the matter as to whether when he speaks of his cat Tabitha he is referring to Tabitha, or the whole cosmos minus Tabitha.[7] Yet Quine also insists that he is a "robust realist." (What this turns out to mean is that Quine is willing to utter the same "vocables" that we all utter, e.g., "Tabitha is a cat," and even to say – with the aid of some Tarskian machinery – "'Tabitha' denotes Tabitha.") Just like the logical positivists,[8] Quine agrees that these realist-sounding statements in ordinary language are ones that it would be most unreasonable to deny. So he finds an account which allows him to utter the "vocables" that we all use to make these statements. But on his own account, all he is doing when he utters those "vocables" is uttering sentences which, when conjoined with other "vocables" he utters and with a certain amount of logical technique, will enable him to derive certain "observation conditionals."[9] Moreover, *a speaker's understanding of those observation conditionals consists simply in the ability to use them as part of a huge linguistic machine which enables the speaker in question to anticipate stimulations of his or her nerve endings* (or so Quine's story runs). Although in a different way the story is as solipsistic as the earlier logical positivist story, and just as unsatisfactory.[10]

Moral: to preserve our commonsense realist convictions it is not enough to preserve some set of "realist" sentences: the interpretation you give those sentences, or, more broadly, your account of what understanding them consists in, is also important. Rorty, however, has never *claimed* to be a realist.[11] So what does all this have to do with him? Well, even if he doesn't like the term "realist" he does insist that his story does give us an account of "the relation between vocables and reality." I repeat my quotation: "The fallacy comes in thinking that the relationship between vocable and reality has to be piecemeal (like the relation between individual kicks and individual rocks), a matter of discrete component capacities to get in touch with discrete hunks of reality." The question is, what – on Rorty's own account of what understanding and using a language amounts to – does even this minimally realistic talk of "the relation between vocables and reality" come to?

On Rorty's view, we have a variety of language games; the use of words in a language game is determined by what Rorty sometimes refers to as "algorithms" or "programs".[12] The inputs to these programs are themselves, Rorty says, always "tailored to the needs of a *particular* input–output function, a *particular* convention of representation,"[13] and the outputs are ways of coping (kicking back), ranging from technological strategies to emotional, aesthetic, even spiritual attitudes. Insofar as I do something that can be called "describing reality" at all, the description is the whole system of vocables I produce. But no word in that system of vocables has a determinate correspondence to a particular set of "discrete hunks of reality," any more than in Quine's story. In particular, even if I speak of my wife or my children or my friend, I am just uttering vocables which help *me* cope. In fact, the *only* difference from Quine's story is that whereas Quine privileges one or two kinds of coping (prediction and the construction of scientific theories which help me predict), Rorty recognizes many desirable forms of coping as more or less on a par.

But, then, how does saying "There is a reality (outside ourselves) which we act on" help Rorty himself to cope? Either this particular "vocable" is merely a trivial consequence of Rorty's currently accepted world picture or else it is merely a futile gesture in the direction of a realism which Rorty has repudiated. If it is the first, then it is too vague; what Rorty should have written is "there are animals, vegetables, minerals, elementary particles, nineteenth-century paintings, etc., that we act on"; and the passage I have quoted twice should have read "the mistake lies in thinking that the relation between vocables and animals, vegetables, minerals, elementary particles, nineteenth-century paintings, etc. [and whatever else his current story posits] has to be piecemeal, etc." – But how would denying that the relation of our "vocables" to these very different sorts of things is "piecemeal" differ from an implausible denial that our ability to get in touch with elementary particles is quite a *different* ability from our ability to get in touch with, say, nineteenth-century paintings? From within our scientific and commonsense descriptions, reality is full of "discrete hunks" (the particles and the paintings). Indeed, Rorty himself uses *kicking a rock* as an example of something that relates a particular kick to a particular rock. Is Rorty claiming that kicking the rock involves a particular rock, but describing the rock does not involve that same particular rock? How can *that* be? How can Rorty so much as use *words* to tell us that kicking a rock involves a particular rock if those very words do not relate particularly to kicks and to rocks?

Rorty's View of Justification

Rorty's view of justification has two aspects, a *contextualist* aspect and a *reformist* aspect.[14] I begin with a brief description of these aspects.

By speaking of Rorty's view as having a *contextualist* aspect, I mean to stress that for Rorty to be a justification is just to be counted as a justification by some bunch of people. What is and what is not a *justification* is, he has claimed, a *sociological* question.

In *Realism with a Human Face*, I asked Rorty[15] whether he does or does not accept five principles[16] concerning justification (warranted assertability), including the following:

(1) In ordinary circumstances, there is usually a fact of the matter as to whether the statements people make are warranted or not.

– and his response was: "I view warrant as a sociological matter, to be ascertained by observing the reception of S's statement by her peers."[17]

Puzzlingly, however, in response to another of my five principles, namely:

(2) Whether a statement is warranted or not is independent of whether the majority of one's cultural peers would say it is warranted or unwarranted.

– he wrote, "Is (2) true? Well maybe a *majority* can be wrong. But suppose everyone in the community, except one or two dubious characters notorious for making assertions even stranger than *p*, thinks S must be a bit crazy . . . Might S still be *warranted* in asserting *p*? Only if there were some way of determining warrant *sub specie aeternitatis*."[18] And he added that he does not see how "one could reconcile the claim that there is this nonsociological sort of justification" with the opposition to metaphysical realism which he and I share.

The reason I speak of this as puzzling is that it is hard to see how the sociologist, qua *sociologist*, could determine that S is warranted in asserting *p when a majority of S's cultural peers disagree*. (How does "'Maybe a majority can be wrong" cohere with the claim that what is and is not a warrant for asserting something is a sociological question? Can a sociologist, qua sociologist, determine that a majority is wrong? How? – by determining that the majority contains some dubious characters? Is "dubious character" a sociological notion?) Perhaps this remark is an expression of what I referred to as the "reformist" aspect of Rorty's view of justification, to which I now turn.

In *Consequences of Pragmatism*, Rorty asserted, ". . . in the process of playing vocabularies and cultures off against one another, we produce new and better ways of talking and acting – not better by reference to a previously known standard, but just better in the sense that they come to *seem* clearly better than their predecessors."[19]

In *Realism with a Human Face*[20] I responded to this by pointing out that it is internal to our concept of reform that whether the outcome of a change is good (a reform) or bad (the opposite) is logically independent of whether most people take it to be a reform. I concluded that Rorty must reject the fifth of my list of five principles,[21] namely:

(5) Our norms and standards of *anything* – including warranted assertability – are capable of reform. There are better and worse norms and standards.

An example I used to try to show that Rorty's criterion cannot distinguish a genuine reform from its opposite was the following: we can imagine that a neo-Nazi tendency wins out, and people cope better in the (Rortian) sense that "it comes to seem to them that they are coping better" by dealing savagely with "those terrible Jews, foreigners and communists," and also imagine that if the forces of good win out it will equally be the case that people cope better in the sense that it comes to seem to them that they are.[22]

In "Putnam and the Relativist Menace," Rorty indicates how he would ward off such counterexamples. "I want to gloss 'come to seem clearly better than their predecessors' as 'come to seem *to us* clearly better than their predecessors'," Rorty writes. He continues, "But 'us' here does not mean 'us humans – Nazis or not,' any more than it means 'whatever otherworlders take over Earth from the humans' or 'whatever nonhuman dominant species evolution next throws up to rule the Earth.' Rather it means 'language users whom we can recognize as better versions of ourselves'."[23]

Now this is extremely strange. It is not the case, after all, that when our children's children or our children's children's children have grown to adulthood and have opted for whatever they will in fact opt for, that any of us will actually be alive to "recognize" them as better versions of "ourselves" or to refuse to so "recognize" them. Does Rorty mean that the criterion for being a reform is that *we would have said they were better versions of ourselves, if, per impossible, we could have known what they were like*? (I once heard Rorty compare appeals to counterfactuals in metaphysics to appeals to "ghost observers.") Perhaps Rorty's criterion is clear enough to uncontroversially exclude some things as possible reforms; for example, if the neo-Nazis win, no-one will suppose – not even the neo-Nazis themselves – that the reasons that have convinced people to support them would have convinced us, or that we would have regarded people convinced by such arguments and appeals as "better versions of ourselves." Perhaps Rorty has dealt with my particular thought experiment of a hypothetical future Nazi take-over. But, to turn to less extreme possibilities, does it make any sense to ask whether our present construals of the American Constitution are the result of arguments that the Founding Fathers would have recognized as appealing to "better versions of themselves"? The counterfactual question is simply too far-fetched. And by the same token, if in a hundred or two hundred years we all become Rortians, or we all become staunch metaphysical realists, the question as to whether the arguments that have been developed over those two centuries and that have won people over are ones that our ghosts can recognize as "better," or whether those people are (in that respect) people that "we can recognize as better versions of ourselves," is simply meaningless as far as I can see. (Certainly it is meaningless as a sociological question.)

In particular, if Rorty's own proposals win out in the future (e.g., the proposal that we give up the idea that there is any such thing as representing individual "hunks of reality," such as Rorty himself, or Quine's cat Tabitha, the proposal that we give up the idea that there is any such thing as "objectivity" and talk about "solidarity" instead, the proposal that we think of "warranted belief" as a purely sociological notion), it does not seem that there is any clear sense in which that victory will represent a *reform* of our standards and ways of thinking *on Rorty's own criterion of reform*. At best, saying that it does will be what Rorty calls a "compliment" that our successors will pay to themselves.

Not only does Rorty (his protests to the contrary) lack any meaningful notion of *reforming* norms and standards; his claim that justification is a "sociological" notion is totally unrelated to Rorty's own practice. When, after all, has Rorty shown the slightest interest in *sociological* description of the *actual* norms and standards current in what he calls "our" societies? But, on reflection, his total disinterest in *empirical* research into norms and standards is not surprising. For if the very idea of *representing* other people (let alone their norms and standards) is a piece of pernicious metaphysics that we have to get out of our system, as Rorty obviously thinks, then any story about what "we" (Western democrats, or "good Europeans," or whatever Rorty wishes to call "us") think is just that: a *story*. And stories, Rorty tells us, cannot represent accurately or fail to represent accurately; they can only enable us (that is, enable Rorty himself, when he is the one telling the story) to "cope" or fail to enable us to "cope" with the flux that bombards our surface neurons (except that, for Rorty, even speaking of "surface neurons" is already telling a story one which Rorty, unlike Quine, does not wish to privilege). If the story about what "we" are like is confirmed by certain characters in the story called "sociologists" (in another mood Rorty calls them "field linguists") that is just a detail in the story. Given *that* view, why *shouldn't* Rorty simply make up his "sociology"?

Notes

1   Published by E. J. Brill (Leiden and New York), 1989. The quote above is from p. xviii.

2   From "Pragmatism, Davidson and Truth," in Ernest Lepore (ed.), *Truth and Interpretation* (Oxford: Blackwell, 1986), p. 351.

3   I compare Rortian and Quinian views of truth and reference in detail in "A Comparison of Something with Something Else," collected in *Realism with a Human Face* (Cambridge, MA: Harvard University Press, 1990).

4   I believe that it was Schlick who used this phrase.

5   Cf. My discussion of this move in "Why Reason Can't Be Naturalized," collected in my *Philosophical Papers*, vol. 3, *Realism and Reason* (Cambridge: Cambridge University Press, 1983), especially pp. 236–7, and also "Logical Positivism Intentionality," in *Words and Life* (Cambridge, MA: Harvard University Press, 1994), especially pp. 89–90.

6   "In Ethics as First Philosophy," collected in Sean Hand (ed.) *The Levinas Reader*, Levinas argues that a profound sense of *responsibility* to the other (the responsibility which is the theme of all of Levinas' philosophy) is precisely what forces us out of such a solipsistic conception of other persons.

7   W. V. Quine, *The Pursuit of Truth* (Cambridge, MA: Harvard University Press, 1990), p. 33.

8   However, the logical positivists did not accept "denotes" and "true" as cognitively meaningful notions until the appearance of Tarski's "The Concept of Truth in Formalized Languages" in 1933. This is collected in A. Tarski, *Logic, Semantics, Metamathematics* (Oxford: Oxford University Press, 1956).

9   The concept of an "observational conditional" is difficult to explain in a brief space. Roughly, such a conditional says that if A (an observable thing or condition) is manifested at any place and time, then B (another observable thing or condition) is manifested at the

same place and time.) (I say "roughly" because strictly speaking it is only the "stimulus meaning" – another of Quine's concepts – of A and B that are determinate.)

10   Quine's response to this criticism is to say that he is not saying the *aim* of science (or of language – for Quine the two are virtually identical) is prediction; the aim is "understanding," or true and comprehensive generalization, or something of that kind. But what does the understanding of that sentence itself consist in? If all there is to understanding is verification, and what is verified is not supposed to have any determinate relation to discrete hunks of reality, then it doesn't matter how "realist" the verified sentences *sound*.

11   In the course of a discussion at Cerisy Lasalle in June 1995, Rorty declared that "commonsense realism is just as bad as metaphysical realism – one leads to the other", and "That's the part of common sense we have to get rid of."

12   "The world does not speak. Only we do. The world can, *once we have programmed ourselves with a language*, cause us to hold beliefs." *Contingency, Irony, and Solidarity*, p. 6 (Cambridge: Cambridge University Press, 1989). Compare also the reference to the standards of a community as "algorithms" in *Philosophy and the Mirror of Nature*, p. 342 (Princeton: Princeton University Press, 1979).

13   "Is Truth a Goal of Enquiry? Davidson vs. Wright," in *The Philosophical Quarterly*, vol. 45, no. 180, 1995, p. 295, emphasis in original.

14   In what follows I shall for the most part confine my attention to two essays by Rorty, namely "Putnam and the Relativist Menace," *The Journal of Philosophy*, vol. 90, no. 9, 1993 and "Is Truth a Goal of Enquiry? Davidson vs. Wright". Jennifer Case's "Rorty and Putnam, Separate and Unequal," *The Southern Journal of Philosophy*, vol. 33, 1995, contains an excellent analysis and criticism of Rorty's arguments in "Putnam and the Relativist Menace."

15   In *Realism with a Human Face*, p. 20.

16   Principle (2) will be quoted immediately, and (5) is quoted in the next section. The remaining principles were: (3) Our norms or standards of warranted assertability are historical products; they evolve in time; and (4) Our norms and standards always reflect our interests and values. Our picture of intellectual flourishing is part of, and only makes sense as part of, our picture of human flourishing in general.

17   "Putnam and the Relativist Menace," p. 450.

18   Ibid.

19   *Consequences of Pragmatism* (Minneapolis: University of Minnesota Press, 1982), p. xxxvii. Emphasis in the original.

20   *Realism with a Human Face*, p. 24.

21   See above for Principles (1) and (2) and note 16.

22   See Realism with a Human Face, pp. 23–24.

23   "Putnam and the Relativist Menace," pp. 453–454.

RESPONSE TO HILARY PUTNAM

I have doubts about Putnam's claim that the phenomenalism of Ayer and Quine is "solipsistic." As I see it, Ayer and Quine simply offered redescriptions of tables and spouses – redescriptions which they regarded as useful for certain epistemological purposes. If you think of your spouse as a logical construction out of sense-data, or of your cat as uttering sentences which will enable you to derive certain observation conditionals, it will be easier, Ayer and Quine thought, to understand how you know as much about your spouse or your cat as you do (despite the veil of ideas which separates you from them). By describing them in such terms, you put yourself in a position to say that talk about what is outside the Cartesian Theatre is just another way of talking about what is inside it.

It would have been inappropriate for Ayer or Quine to have asked themselves, after making one of these anti-skeptical moves "But is my spouse *really* a logical construction out of my sense data?" This question is inappropriate for the same reasons that it would be inappropriate to ask one's surgeon whether one's spouse is *really* just an assemblage of tissues, or a particle physicist whether he or she is *really* just a bunch of quarks.

It may occasionally be useful to describe one's spouse in one or another of these alternative terminologies. But this utility of alternate descriptions does nothing to impugn speaking Ordinary. Noting that the same thing can usefully be described in lots of different ways is the beginning of philosphical sophistication. Insisting that one of these ways has some privilege other than occasional utility is the beginning of metaphysics. Ayer and Quine were, at least part of the time, too canny to insist on anything of the sort.

Consider Putnam's claim that "an attitude toward a pattern of regularities in one's own sense-data is not the same thing as an attitude towards another person." Well, is my attitude toward a collection of elementary particles the same thing as an attitude towards another person? In one obvious sense, yes. I can have an attitude toward an object which is variously described. In another obvious sense, no. The latter sense reflects the fact that I choose my description to suit my attitude, and that I would not use the elementary-particle or sense-data descriptions in most ordinary situations.

What Putnam calls "preserving our commonsense realist convictions" seems to me merely a matter of not letting the fact that non-ordinary descriptions are available prevent us from using ordinary ones for ordinary purposes. Common sense, considered as the beliefs the innocent freshman brings to her first philosophy class, has neither phenomenalist nor realist convictions. Such convictions are opinions on specialized, recondite topics. After she has been asked to take a stand on what is really real, however, the freshman may develop convictions on such topics, just as she may, in her other courses, develop views on the relative merits of Tolstoy and Dostoevsky. But it would be best if her philosophy teachers suggested that she view phenomenalist redescriptions of spouses and cats as as metaphysically innocuous as anti-representationalist redescriptions of true beliefs and sentences. She should view such redescriptions not as claims that ordinary ways of speaking are somehow illegitimate, but as therapeutic devices for dissolving pseudo-problems.

So I disagree with Putnam's "moral." I do *not* think that my account of what understanding ordinary descriptions consists in has any relevance to preserving our realist convictions. Mine is an account given for philosophy-of-language purposes, just as the sense-data account was one given for epistemological purposes. The main purpose of doing this sort of anti-representationalist philosophy of language is the same as the one Quine and Ayer were attempting to serve with their phenomenalistic epistemologies: namely, defeating the skeptic.

Whereas Putnam regards Ayer as wandering pointlessly away from the Ordinary, I think of him as having been fighting the good anti-skeptical fight, but as having used an unnecessarily awkward weapon. I see the progress of analytic philosophy of language from Russellian empiricistic representationalism to Brandom's neo-Hegelian inferentialism as progress from a rather primitive to a fairly sophisticated form of anti-Cartesianism.

By confining my Brandomesque account of what understanding ordinary descriptions consists of to its proper sphere, I am doing something like what Berkeley famously suggested: I am describing with the learned when in their company, and with ordinary people when in theirs. Philosophers have trouble only when this ambidexterity breaks down: only when, succumbing to the metaphysical urge, they start saying that learned purposes have some sort of privilege that ordinary ones do not (because they describe what you "really" see, for example, or because they do not quantify over more things than there are in heaven and earth). Only a metaphysical urge would lead one to say, as Putnam does, that on the view I advocate, "even if I speak of my wife or my children or my friend, I am just uttering vocables which help me cope." It is the "just" which betrays the urge. "Just," like "really," suggests a purpose-transcendent privilege.

Putnam succumbs to this urge again when he says that "any story about what 'we' . . . think is just that: a *story*". I take stories more seriously than Putnam does. One reason is that I think, and he does not, that it makes sense "to ask whether our present construals of the American Constitution are the result of arguments that the Founding Fathers would have recognized as appealing to 'better versions of themselves'." It seems to me that the better sort of judges and politicians ask themselves this sort of question all the time.

So they should, for we often need to imagine ourselves in conversation with those who helped make us what we are in order to help us decide whether we have gone, or are going, in the right direction. I see such conversations, and the stories of progress or regress that result from imagining them, as giving substance and concreteness to the otherwise thin and useless notion of "rationality." This is pretty close to the Hegelian view which Putnam himself once defended. He said, back in 1981, that "Rationality may not be defined by a 'canon' or set of principles, but we do have an evolving conception of the cognitive virtues to guide us." [1] This line of thought meshes with his anti-representationalist claim that ". . . the mind and the world jointly make up the mind and the world. (Or, to make the metaphor even more Hegelian, the Universe makes up the Universe – with minds – collectively – playing a special role in the making up.)" [2]

Once we give up the idea that rationality is a matter of applying ahistorical criteria (as we have to in order to deal with the fact that criteria of choice between theories and policies are as mutable as the theories and practices themselves), we have nowhere to turn except to such stories. Hegel's historicization of philosophy seems to me important precisely because Hegel grasped the emptiness of Kantian attempts to make "Reason" the name of an ahistorical faculty, and to build ahistorical criteria into the structure of the human mind. His solution was to start replacing transcendental arguments with narratives – stories about how we hook up with our past.

My second reason for taking stories more seriously than Putnam does is that Putnam nowadays seems to think it useful to ask, of stories about the historical development of American jurisprudence or about matter as made up of little packets of energy called quarks, whether or not they represent accurately. Although he earlier shared my own doubts about representationalism, in the final paragraph of his contribution to this volume he seems to think that substituting coping for representing is a gesture of despair, a sort of *reductio ad absurdum* of what I am saying.

As I see it, when we want to reassure ourselves of our own rationality – to convince ourselves that we are not being caught up by something merely voguish or merely self-interested – we often hold imaginary conversations with people (our parents, our teachers, our friends) who might be imagined to have doubts about what we are up to. When the novelty in question pertains to US law and politics, such conversations may be with Jefferson or FDR. When it pertains to quarks or superstrings they are, I would imagine, with figures such as Newton and Bohr. These imaginary conversations provide material for the stories we tell ourselves in order to decide whether we are progressing or regressing. (Think of Germans like Heidegger and Tillich holding imaginary conversations in 1933 about Hitler with such figures as Schiller and Fichte. Heidegger convinced himself that Hitler meant progress and thus that he was being rational in turning Nazi. Tillich convinced himself that Hitler meant regress and that he was being rational in preparing for exile.)

Putnam has, in recent years, become convinced that something like direct perceptual realism is the key to avoiding the traps into which he sees me as having fallen. So, as is evident from his Dewey Lectures, he finds McDowell's *Mind and World*, and James' *Radical Empiricism*, much more promising than I do. By contrast, those of us who see Sellars' "Empiricism and the Philosophy of Mind" as pretty much the last word philosophers need utter about perception, and as as devastating a critique of phenomenalism as we shall ever have, see direct perceptual realism as an unfortunate throwback to Cartesianism. We think questions about what we really see as bad as questions about what is really real.

Putnam's recent alliance with Stanley Cavell, Cora Diamond, and James Conant – his emphasis on the Ordinary and on the need to avoid putting forward theses in philosophy – seems to me an unfortunate throwback to pre-Hegelian attempts to find something ahistorical to which philosophers may pledge allegiance. The Ordinary strikes me as just the latest disguise of the *ontos on*. I think Putnam was on the right, historicist, neo-Hegelian track in his *Reason, Truth and History*, and I wish that he had stayed on it. For that book seems to me one of the most heartening and inspiring documents of recent analytic philosophy. When testing myself for rationality, I often find myself conducting imaginary conversations with the Putnam who wrote that book.

I read *Reason, Truth and History* as an (unfortunately unsuccessful) attempt to get analytic philosophers to break away from the scientism of Reichenbach and Carnap – to get them to stop being, in Putnam's words, "too realistic about physics and too subjectivistic about ethics."[3] Almost twenty years after the appearance of that book, alas, we still find philosophers wondering about the objectivity of moral values, the place of value in a world of facts, and so on – the problems that Kant took seriously and Hegel did not. As long as philosophers do so, they will use expressions like "just a story" and 'just conversation," and will exhibit other symptoms of a regression to metaphysics. I regret the reappearance of those symptoms in Putnam's more recent work, but I owe a great debt to his most historicist, least metaphysical, book.

Notes

1   *Reason, Truth and History*, p. 163.
2   *Reason, Truth and History*, p. xi.
3   Ibid., p. 142.

5

The Case for Rorts

DANIEL C. DENNETT

In the late 1960s, I created a joke dictionary of philosophers' names that circulated in samizdat form, picking up new entries as it went. The first few editions were on Ditto masters, in those pre-photocopy days. The 7th edition, entitled *The Philosophical Lexicon*, was the first properly copyrighted version, published for the benefit of the American Philosophical Association in 1978, and the 8th edition (brought out in 1987), is still available from the APA. I continue to receive submissions of further entries, but I doubt that there will ever be a 9th edition. The 8th edition lists two distinct entries for Dick Rorty:

  rort, an incorrigible report, hence rorty, incorrigible.

and

  a rortiori, adj., true for even more fashionable continental reasons.

These were submitted to me years apart, inspired by two distinct epochs of Rorty's work. It may be hard to see the connecting threads between the Princeton professor whose tightly argued "Incorrigibility as the Mark of the Mental" (1970) and "Functionalism, Machines, and Incorrigibility" (1972) were aimed specifically at the smallish clan of analytic philosophers of mind, and the international man of letters described by Harold Bloom as the most interesting philosopher in the world. Can we see the stirrings of Rorty's later ideas in between the lines of his early papers in the philosophy of mind? Perhaps, but that will not be my topic.

  I want to go back to Rorty's papers on incorrigibility,[1] not for historical clues about how to read the later, more widely influential Rorty, but in order to expose an excellent insight lurking in his claim that incorrigibility is the mark of the mental. It went unrecognized at the time, I think, because the reigning methodology in that brand of analytic philosophy ignored the sorts of questions that would have provoked the relevant discussion. While the incorrigibility papers were sufficiently influential – or at least notorious – to anchor an entry in the *Lexicon*, they have never been properly appreciated by philosophers of mind, myself included (of all people). I say "of all people" because Dick Rorty has always drawn explicit links between his ideas and mine, and has played a major role in drawing philosophers' attention to my work. If anybody was in a position to see the virtues of his position, it was I, and while I can now retrospectively see that I did indeed subliminally absorb his message and then re-invent some of it in my own terms (without sufficient acknowledgement), I certainly didn't proclaim my allegiance to, or even deign to rebut, clarify or expand upon, those claims.

If my take on this is right, it means that Dick also didn't quite appreciate the strengths of his own idea, and might even have been misled to some of his more fashionable and famous ideas by a slight misappreciation of the import of his claims about incorrigibility, but I won't pursue that surmise here. If I am right, he will have succeeded in spite of himself in making the sort of contribution to science – to our objective knowledge of the way the world, and the mind, is – that he has abjured as a philosophical aspiration. His own philosophical "conversation" turns out to be more than just conversation. He will perhaps reply that all I have shown is that today his ideas about incorrigibility have more political viability, more charismatic oomph in today's conversations than in those of the early 1970s. But I want to insist that the reason they do is that they show us something interesting about how reality may be represented.

What is the Status of Rorty's Thesis?

His central thesis is as follows:

> What makes an entity mental is not whether or not it is something that explains behavior, and what makes a property mental is not whether or not it is a property of a physical entity. The only thing that can make either an entity or a property mental is that certain reports of its existence or occurrence have the special status that is accorded to, for instance, reports of thoughts and sensations – the status of incorrigibility. (1970, p. 414)

Incorrigibility is to be distinguished from infallibility. It is not that these reports could not possibly be mistaken, but just that "certain knowledge claims about them cannot be overridden" (p. 413). This immediately tilts the playing field, of course, by trading in a host of tempting but indefensible metaphysical claims for an epistemological or even sociological claim. This is just a fact, Rorty suggests, about a "linguistic convention," about the way we treat claims, not a fact about the reality of whatever those claims are about. But at the same time his thesis is not a mere anthropological observation: certain claims cannot be overridden, he suggests, given the role they play in our shared life. (As we shall see, it is this modal claim that never got sufficient attention – from Rorty or his readers – back in the 1970s.)

What goes without saying is that these incorrigible reports are "first person" reports, reports about one's own states and events, to which one is presumed to have one or another sort of "privileged access." This term of art, once so familiar in philosophical writing about the mind, has been eclipsed for some time by other ways of attempting to characterize the crucial asymmetry: Thomas Nagel's (1974) "what it is like" formula or John Searle's (1980, 1983) championing of first person primacy, for instance. It is easy to understand Rorty's lack of sympathy for these later attempts. Far from having overlooked or underestimated the importance of the "first person point of view," he had declared it "the mark of the mental" – but he had also provided a demystifying account of how and why it had emerged, and why it was no bulwark against creeping "third person" materialism. Privileged access is real enough, Rorty was saying, and is indeed the premier feature of mentality, but it is no big deal, metaphysically. It is this deflationary doctrine that I want to re-examine, saving it from some Rortian excesses.

His claim may be expressed with somewhat different emphasis: what makes an entity a "first person," a thing it is like something to be, is that some of its emissions or actions are treated not just as reports, but as incorrigible reports. We vouchsafe an entity a mind by vouchsafing it a certain epistemic privilege with regard to the covert goings-on that control it. A mind is a control system whose self-reports cannot be overridden by third-person evidence.

Could there even be such a control system? One of Rorty's shrewdest observations is that our underlying materialist skepticism about this very possibility is the chief factor that propels us towards dualism and other mysterious doctrines:

> Only after the emergence of the convention, the linguistic practice, which dictates that first-person contemporaneous reports of such states are the last word on their existence and features, do we have a notion of the mental as incompatible with the physical (and thus a way of making sense of such positions as parallelism and epiphenomenalism). For only this practice gives us a rationale for saying that thoughts and sensations must be *sui generis* – the rationale being that any proposed entity with which they could be identified would be such that reports about its features were capable of being overruled by further inquiry. (1970, p. 414)

It does seem at first blush as if the states and events in any material or physical control system would have to be exactly as knowable by "third persons" as by their "owner," and if this is so, then no such states and events could be thoughts and sensations. It seems to follow that in any purely material entity, first-person privilege would evaporate, at which point there would be nothing left to anchor the mental at all. Rorty does not shrink from this implication: in fact, he views his 1970 paper as explicitly arguing for a version of eliminative materialism (p. 401). He has his materialist concede that

> it might turn out that there are no entities about which we are incorrigible, nearly or strictly. This discovery would be made if the use of cerebroscopes (or some similar mechanism) led to a practice of overriding reports about mental entities on the basis of knowledge of brain states. If we should, as a result of correlations between neurological and mental states, begin taking a discovery of a neurological state as better evidence about a subject's mental state than his own report, mental states would lose their incorrigible status and, thus, their status as mental. (p. 421).

He contemplates with equanimity the Churchlandish alternative:

> If it came to pass that people found that they could explain behavior at least as well by reference to brain states as by reference to beliefs, desires, thoughts, and sensations, then reference to the latter might simply disappear from the language. (p. 421).

Here we need to pause and disentangle some issues, for there are apparently more possibilities than Rorty discusses. First, as just noted, there's standard eliminative materialism: the triumph of neuroscience and its "cerebroscopes" would – and should – lead to the demise of mentalistic language, and we would all cease talking *as if* there were minds and mental events, a clear improvement in our conceptual scheme from the perspective of Occam's Razor. But there is another prospect: it could also happen, for all Rorty has said, that people *mistakenly* crown neuroscience the victor, overrating the reliability of third-person theory and abandoning their linguistic practice, coming eventually to treat subjects' self-reports as unprivileged, even though they were in fact reliable enough to sustain (to justify?) the linguistic convention that mentality depends on. This would be the evaporation of the concept of mind from that culture, on Rorty's analysis, but would it also mark the death of the minds themselves? Although people's brains, their hardware, would be up to the task, their attitudes towards their own authority would shift, thereby adjusting the software running on that hardware. Could this diminish their real competence, leading to the loss of the very prowess that is the mark of the mental? As the mind-constituting practice waned, would people lose their minds? What would that be like? Could people come to view all their own first-person reports as unprivileged? What would they say – "We used to have minds, but now we just have brains"?

Would their minds cease to exist once this rush to misjudgment took place? For current Rorty, this is surely a paradigm of a misguided question, assuming, as it does, that there is a neutral standpoint from which the Truth of the ontological claim could be assessed. But many of us unre(de)constructed types may think we can take these questions about the justification and confirmation of our representations more seriously than he now allows. (In fact, he tries to soften this blow by granting scientists and other public and private investigators what he has described to me as a "vegetarian" concept of representation – not the whole ontological hog, but some sort of internal realism in which "facts" may be distinguished from "fictions" – but keep those scare-quotes handy. I think, however, that once this vegetarian concept of representation is exploited to the hilt, we will have enough of a "mirror of nature" in our hands to satisfy all but the most hysterical Realists.)

Back in 1970, the ethos of analytic philosophy let Rorty glide rather swiftly over the question of what the grounds for adopting this linguistic practice might be. In that paper he doesn't emphasize the fact that this innovation might be motivated, or defended against criticism (rightly or wrongly), but he also doesn't treat it as if it would have to be a surd memic mutation, a random happening that had huge consequences for our conceptual scheme but was itself undesigned and beyond defense or criticism. To describe the change in linguistic practices that would amount to the birth of minds, he exploits an elaboration of Wilfrid Sellars' (1963) justly celebrated just-so story about Jones, "the man who invented the concept of mind" (p. 411). Jones, Rorty reminds us, organized his shrewd observations of the comings and goings of people into a theory which postulated covert events and states in people's heads, the history of which would account for all their overt behavior. Jones then trained all the people in the fine art of making non-inferential reports about these states and events he had posited. When the training was complete, he had succeeded in transforming people from relatively inscrutable objects of theoretical analysis into reliable divulgers of their own internal workings.

> According to Rorty, those who went along with Jones found that, when the behavioral evidence for what Smith was thinking about conflicted with Smith's own report of what he was thinking about, a more adequate account of the sum of Smith's behavior could be obtained by relying on Smith's report than by relying on the behavioral evidence. (p. 416).

This passage needs some emendation. Smith's report is part of the behavioral evidence, surely, and a particularly revealing part (when interpreted as a report, not as mere lip-flapping). What Rorty means is that Smith's report, interpreted as a speech act, is recognized as providing a more adequate account than all the other behavioral evidence. He imagines that once this appreciation – it might be misappreciation – of the power of self-reports to trump other evidence was in place,

> it became a regulative principle of behavioral science that first-person contemporaneous reports of these postulated inner states were never to be thrown out on the ground that the behavior or the environment of the person doing the reporting would lead one to suspect that they were having a different thought or sensation from the one reported. (p. 416)

But why should this become a regulative principle? Why turn the recognition of high reliability – what Armstrong had called "empirically privileged access" (Rorty, 1970, p. 417) – into a constitutive declaration of incorrigibility? Is this just an unmotivated overshooting of social practice, a bandwagon effect or other byproduct of enthusiasm for Jones' theory? Or might there be some deeper reason – an actual justification – for thus shifting the very criteria (to speak in 60s-talk) for the occurrence of mental phenomena?

Rorty's linguistic convention is close kin (a heretofore unacknowledged ancestor) to the ploy I attribute to "heterophenomenologists" (1991): deliberately permitting the subject's word to constitute the subject's "heterophenomenological world," creating by fiat a subjective or first-person perspective whose details then become the *explicanda* for a materialist, third-person theory of consciousness. I took the existence of a wide-spread belief in the primacy of the first-person point of view as given, and characterized heterophenomenology as the neutral method science could – and does – use to investigate the relations between the subjective and objective. Rorty's papers suggest that the emergence of a first-person point of view is itself an effect of a similar burden-shifting move.

In his 1972 paper, Rorty hints at the point I now want to examine in more detail:

> if, with respect to a very sophisticated machine, we found that certain states played roles in its behavioral economy very close to those which being frantically hungry, thinking of Vienna, etc., played in ours, then (given that the machine reported on such states and reported making no inferences to such reports) we might decide to extend the same heuristic rule to the machine's reports of those states. But if we then found that the *simplest* and *most fruitful* [emphasis added] explanations of the machine's behavior involved overriding these reports, we should cease to apply this rule. (1972, p. 215)

This suggests that simplicity and fruitfulness were the grounds for "extending the heuristic rule" in the first place, but why? How? Let us expand the account of this intuition pump, guiding and supporting our judgments by some facts that could only have been dimly imagined in 1972. There is today an entity in roughly pre-Jonesian position, a plausible candidate (with some optimistic projections of engineering) for elevation to first-person status: Cog, a "very sophisticated machine" indeed.

The Birth of Cog's Mind: a Just-So Story

At the AI Lab at MIT, Rodney Brooks and Lynn Andrea Stein are leading a team (of which I am a member) that is currently attempting to create a humanoid robot called

Cog. Its name has a double etymology: on the one hand, Cog is intended to instantiate the fruits of cognitive science, and on the other, it is a concrete machine situated in the real, non-virtual world, with motors, bearings, springs, wires, pulleys – and cogs. Cog is just about life-size – that is, about the size of a human adult. Cog has no legs, but lives bolted at the hips, you might say, to its stand. This paraplegia was dictated by intensely practical considerations: if Cog had legs and could walk, it would have to trail a colossally unwieldy umbilical cord, carrying power to the body and input–output to its brain, which is about the size of a telephone booth and stands to the side, along with large banks of oscilloscopes and other monitoring devices. No batteries exist that could power Cog's motors for hours on end, and radioing the wide-bandwidth traffic between body and brain – a task I took for granted in "Where Am I?" (1978) – is still well beyond the technology available.

Cog has no legs, but it has two human-length arms, with hands (three fingers and a thumb, like Mickey Mouse) on the wrists. It can bend at the waist and swing its torso, and its head moves with three degrees of freedom just about the way a human head does. It has two eyes, each equipped with both a foveal high-resolution vision area and a low-resolution wide-angle parafoveal vision area, and these eyes saccade at almost human speed. That is, the two eyes can complete approximately three fixations a second, while you and I can manage four or five. Your foveas are at the center of your retinas, surrounded by the grainier low-resolution parafoveal areas; for reasons of engineering simplicity, Cog's eyes have their foveas mounted above their wide-angle vision areas, so they won't give it visual information exactly like that provided to human vision by human eyes (in fact, of course, it will be vastly degraded), but the wager is that the information provided will be plenty to give Cog the opportunity to perform impressive feats of hand–eye coordination, identification, and search.

Since its eyes are video cameras mounted on delicate, fast-moving gimbals, it might be disastrous if Cog were inadvertently to punch itself in the eye, so part of the hard-wiring that must be provided in advance is an "innate" if rudimentary "pain" system to serve roughly the same protective functions as the reflex eye-blink and pain-avoidance systems hard-wired into human infants. Cog will not be an adult at first, in spite of its adult size. It is being designed to pass through an extended period of artificial infancy, during which it will have to learn from experience, experience it will gain in the rough-and-tumble environment of the real world. Like a human infant, however, it will need a great deal of protection at the outset, in spite of the fact that it will be equipped with many of the most crucial safety-systems of a living being. It has limit switches, heat sensors, current sensors, strain gauges and alarm signals in all the right places to prevent it from destroying its many motors and joints. The surfaces of its hands and other important parts are covered with touch-sensitive piezo–electric membrane "skin," which will trigger signals when they make contact with anything. These can be "alarm" or "pain" signals in the case of such fragile parts as its "funny bones" – electric motors protruding from its elbows – but the same sensitive membranes are used on its fingertips and elsewhere, and, as with human tactile nerves, the "meaning" of the signals sent along their attached wires depends on what the central control system "makes of them" rather than on their "intrinsic" characteristics. A gentle touch, signalling sought-for contact with an object to be grasped, will not differ, as an information packet, from a sharp pain, signalling a need for rapid countermeasures. It all depends on what the central system is designed to do with the packet, and this design is itself indefinitely revisable – something that can be adjusted either by Cog's own experience or by the tinkering of Cog's artificers.

Decisions have not yet been reached about many of the candidates for hard-wiring or innate features. Anything that can learn must be initially equipped with a great deal of unlearned design. That is no longer an issue; no *tabula rasa* could ever be impressed with knowledge from experience. But it is also not much of an issue which features ought to be innately fixed, for there is a convenient trade-off. Any feature that is not innately fixed at the outset, but rather gets itself designed into Cog's control system through learning, can then often be lifted whole (with some revision, perhaps) into Cog-II, as a new bit of innate endowment designed by Cog itself – or rather by Cog's history of interactions with its environment. So even in cases in which we have the best of reasons for thinking that human infants actually come innately equipped with pre-designed gear, we may choose to try to get Cog to learn the design in question, rather than to be born with it. In some instances, this is laziness or opportunism – we don't really know what might work well, but maybe Cog can train itself up. In others, curiosity is the motive: we have already hand-designed an "innate" version, but wonder if a connectionist network could train itself up to do the task as well or better. Sometimes the answer has been yes. This insouciance about the putative nature/ nurture boundary is already a familiar attitude among neural net modelers, of course. Although Cog is not specifically intended to demonstrate any particular neural net thesis, it should come as no surprise that Cog's nervous system is a massively parallel architecture capable of simultaneously training up an indefinite number of special-purpose networks or circuits, under various regimes.

How plausible is the hope that Cog can retrace the steps of millions of years of evolution in a few months or years of laboratory exploration? Notice first that what I have just described is a variety of Lamarckian inheritance that no organic lineage has been able to avail itself of. The acquired design innovations of Cog-I can be immediately transferred to Cog-II, an evolutionary speed-up of tremendous, if incalculable, magnitude. Moreover, if one bears in mind that, unlike the natural case, there will be a team of overseers ready to make patches whenever obvious shortcomings reveal themselves, and to jog the systems out of ruts whenever they enter them, it is not so outrageous a hope, in our opinion. (But then, we are all rather outrageous people.)

One talent that we have hopes of teaching to Cog is at least a rudimentary capacity for human language. And here we run into the fabled innate language organ or Language Acquisition Device (LAD) made famous by Noam Chomsky. Is there going to be an attempt to build an innate LAD for our Cog? No. We are going to try to get Cog to build language the hard way, the way our ancestors must have done, over thousands of generations. Cog has ears (four, because it's easier to get good localization with four microphones than with carefully shaped ears like ours!) and some special-purpose signal-analyzing software is being developed to give Cog a fairly good chance of discriminating human speech sounds, and probably the capacity to distinguish different human voices. Cog will also have to have speech synthesis hardware and software, of course, but decisions have not yet been reached about the details. It is important to have Cog as well-equipped as possible for rich and natural interactions with human beings, for the team intends to take advantage of as much free labor as it can. Untrained people ought to be able to spend time – hours if they like, and we rather hope they do – trying to get Cog to learn this or that. Growing into an adult is a long, time-consuming business, and Cog – and the team that is building Cog – will need all the help it can get.

Obviously this will not work unless the team manages somehow to give Cog a motivational structure that can be at least dimly recognized, responded to, and exploited by naive observers. In short, Cog should be as human as possible in its wants and fears, likes and dislikes. If those anthropomorphic terms strike you as unwarranted, put them in scare-quotes or drop them altogether and replace them with tedious neologisms of your own choosing: Cog, you may prefer to say, must have goal-registrations and preference-functions that map in rough isomorphism to human desires. This is so for many reasons, of course. Cog won't work at all unless it has its act together in a daunting number of different regards. It must somehow delight in learning, abhor error, strive for novelty, recognize progress. It must be vigilant in some regards, curious in others, and deeply unwilling to engage in self-destructive activity. While we are at it, we might as well try to make it crave human praise and company, and even exhibit a sense of humor.

The computer-complex that has been built to serve as the development platform for Cog's artificial nervous system consists of four backplanes, each with 16 nodes; each node is basically a Mac-II computer – a 68332 processor with a megabyte of RAM. In other words, one can think of Cog's brain as roughly equivalent to sixty-four Mac-IIs yoked in a custom parallel architecture. Each node is itself a multiprocessor, and instead of running Mac software, they all run a special version of parallel Lisp developed by Rodney Brooks, and called, simply, L. Each node has an interpreter for L in its ROM, so it can execute L files independently of every other node.[2] The space of possible virtual machines made available and readily explorable by this underlying architecture is huge, of course, and it covers a volume in the space of all computations that has not yet been seriously explored by artificial intelligence researchers. Moreover, the space of possibilities it represents is manifestly much more realistic as a space to build brains in than is the space heretofore explored, either by the largely serial architectures of GOFAI ("Good Old Fashioned AI," Haugeland, 1985), or by parallel architectures simulated by serial machines. Nevertheless, it is arguable that every one of the possible virtual machines executable by Cog is minute in comparison to a real human brain. In short, Cog has a tiny brain. There is a big wager being made: the parallelism made possible by this arrangement will be sufficient to provide real-time control of importantly humanoid activities occurring on a human time scale. If this proves to be too optimistic by as little as an order of magnitude, the whole project will be forlorn, for the motivating insight for the project is that by confronting and solving actual, real-time problems of self-protection, hand–eye coordination, and interaction with other animate beings, Cog's artificers will discover the sufficient conditions for higher cognitive functions in general – and maybe even for a variety of consciousness that would satisfy the skeptics.

Now we are ready to consider Rorty's thesis. At the Royal Society meeting at which I presented the first description of the Cog project, J. R. Lucas embarked on what he took to be the first step of a *reductio ad absurdum*: if a robot were really conscious, we would have to be prepared to believe it about its own internal states. This move delighted me, for not only did Lucas thereby implicitly endorse Rorty's thesis that incorrigibility was the mark of the mental; it also provided an instance in support of his canny observation that it is skepticism about incorrigibility in machines that strikes many observers as grounds for dualism. My response to Lucas was to give the invited implication a warm welcome; we would indeed be prepared to grant this incorrigibility to Cog. How so?

Cog is equipped from the outset with a well-nigh perfect suite of monitoring devices that can reveal all the details of its inner workings to the observing team. In other words, it will be born with chronically implanted "cerebroscopes" that could hardly be improved upon. Add to this the fact that these observers are not just Johnny-come-latelies but Cog's designers and creators. One might well think then that Cog's observers would have an insurmountable lead in the competition for authority about what is going on inside Cog. The prospect of their finding it "simple and fruitful" to cede authority to Cog's own pronouncements may seem dim indeed.

But all the information visible on the banks of monitors, or gathered by the gigabyte on hard disks, will be from the outset almost as hard to interpret, even by Cog's own designers, as the information obtainable by such "third-person" methods as MRI and CT scanning in the neurosciences. As the observers refine their models, and their understanding of their models, their authority as interpreters of the data may grow, but it may also suffer eclipse. Especially since Cog will be designed from the outset to redesign itself as much as possible, there is a high probability that the designers will simply lose the standard hegemony of the artificer ("I made it, so I know what it is supposed to do, and what it is doing now!").

This is a serious epistemological problem even for traditional serial computer programs when they grow large enough. As every programmer learns, it is essential to "comment" your "source code." Comments are lines of ordinary language, not programming language, inserted into the program between special brackets that tell the computer not to attempt to "execute" them as if they were part of the program. By labeling and explaining each subassembly via helpful comments (e.g., "This part searches the lexicon for the nearest fit, and deposits it in the workspace"), programmers can remind themselves and other observers what the point or function of each such part is supposed to be. (There is no guarantee that the assembly in question actually executes its intended function, of course; nothing is more common than false advertising in the comments.) Without the handy hints about how the programmer intended the process or state to function, the very identity of the state entered when a computer executes a line of code is often for all intents and purposes inscrutable. The intrinsic or just local features of the state are almost useless guides, given the global organization on which the proper functioning of the system – whatever it is – depends.

Even in traditional programs, the actual function – and hence actual identity – of a state or event may well evolve away from what is advertised in the accompanying comment, which may remain unchanged in the source code long after it has been rendered obsolete by undocumented debugging efforts. Large programs never work as intended at first – this is a regularity so unexceptioned that one might almost consider it a law of nature, or the epistemological version of Original Sin. By the time they are actually made to work, the adjustments to their original design specifications are so many, and so inscrutable in combination, that nobody can say with confidence and accuracy what the "intended" function of many of the states is. And the only identity that matters in computer programs is functional identity (a point Rorty makes surprisingly well in his 1972 paper, p. 212, in the course of pursuing rather different aims).

In the case of a system like Cog, which is intended from the outset to be self-redesigning on a massive scale, the loss of epistemological hegemony on the part of its "third person" designers is even more assured. Connectionist training regimes, and genetic algorithms, for instance, create competences – and hence states embodying those competences – whose means are only indirectly shaped by human hands. (For that reason, programmers working in these methodologies are more like plant and animal breeders than machine-makers.)

Since, as I noted above, the meaning of signals in Cog's brain is not a function of their intrinsic properties but of their "intended" functions, and since Cog is designed to be indefinitely self-revisable in those functions, Cog's original designers have no secure hold on what the relevant boundaries are between states. What a bit of the system is "supposed to do" is the only anchor for what its meaning is, and when the designers' initial comments about those functions become obsolete, it is open for some new party to become authoritative about those boundaries. Who? Cog itself, the (unwitting) re-designer of its own states. Unlike the genius Jones of Sellars' fable, Cog need have no theory of its own operations (though in due course it might well develop such an auto-psychological interest as a hobby). Cog need only be sensitive to the pressures of training that it encounters "growing up" in a human milieu. In principle it can learn, as a child does, to generate speech acts that do divulge the saliencies of its internal states, but these are saliencies that are created by the very process of learning to talk about them. That, at any rate, is the theory and the hope.

And that is why I gladly defend this conditional prediction: if Cog develops to the point where it can conduct what appear to be robust and well-controlled conversations in something like a natural language, it will certainly be in a position to rival its own monitors (and the theorists who interpret them) as a source of knowledge about what it is doing and feeling, and why. And if and when it reaches this stage of development, outside observers will have the best of reasons for welcoming it into the class of subjects, or first persons, for it will be an emitter of speech acts that can be interpreted as reliable reports on various "external" topics, and constitutively reliable reports on a particular range of topics closer to home: its own internal states. Not all of them, but only the "mental" ones – the ones which, by definition, it is incorrigible about because nobody else could be in a better position than it was to say.

So it is not mere convention that guarantees (while it lasts) that there are minds in this world. There is, as Rorty claims, a convention or something like a convention in the etiology of mind, but it has a natural justification. Ceding authority to a subject-in-the-making is a way of getting it to become a subject, by putting it in a conversational milieu in which its own software, its own virtual Joycean machine (as I called it in 1991), can develop the competence to make self-reports about which it is the best authority because the states and events those self-reports are about get their function, and hence meaning, from the subject's own "take" on them.[3]

"If you called a horse's tail a leg, how many legs would the horse have?" Answer: "Four: calling a tail a leg doesn't make it a leg." True, and calling a machine conscious doesn't make it conscious. Many are deeply skeptical of anti-metaphysical moves such as Rorty's suggestion that a linguistic convention of incorrigibility accounts for the existence of minds, but what they tend to overlook – and what Rorty himself has overlooked, if I am right – is that the existence of such a convention can have effects over time that make it non-trivially self-fulfilling. This is really not such an unfamiliar idea – let's face it: it's Norman Vincent Peale's idea of the power of positive thinking. Or think of Dumbo, the giant-eared little elephant in the Disney cartoon. His friends the crows convince him he can fly by making up a tale about a magic feather that can give him the power of flight just as long as he clutches it in his trunk. By changing Dumbo's attitude, they give Dumbo a power that depends on attitude. Attitudes are real states of people (and elephants – at least in fables – and robots, if all goes well). Changes in conventions can bring about changes in attitudes that bring about changes in competence that are definitive of having a mind.

Could the attitudes lapse? Perhaps they could, but I have shown that Rorty overestimated the power of "cerebroscopes" to trump first-person reports, so there is no good reason to anticipate that the triumph of neuroscience or robotics would bring about the death of the mind.

References

Dennett, Daniel, 1978, "Where Am I?" in *Brainstorms*, Bradford Books/MIT Press.
Dennett, Daniel, 1991, *Consciousness Explained*, New York: Little, Brown.
Haugeland, John, 1985, *Artificial Intelligence: The Very Idea*, Cambridge MA: MIT Press.
McGeer, Victoria, 1996, "Is Self-Knowledge an Empirical Problem? Renegotiating the Space of Philosophical Explanation," *Journal of Philosophy* XCIII, pp. 483–515.
Nagel, T., 1974, "What is it like to be a bat?" *Philosophical Review*, 83, pp. 435–50.
Rorty, Richard, 1965, "Mind-body Identity, Privacy, and Categories," *Review of Metaphysics*, 19, p. 24–54.
Rorty, Richard, 1970, "Incorrigibility as the Mark of the Mental," *Journal of Philosophy*, 67, pp. 399–424.
Rorty, Richard, 1972, "Functionalism, Machines, and Incorrigibility," *Journal of Philosophy*, 69, pp. 203–20.
Searle, J., 1980, "Minds, Brains, and Programs," *Behavioral and Brain Sciences*, 3, pp. 417–58.
Searle, J., 1983, *Intentionality: An Essay in the Philosophy of Mind*, Cambridge Univ. Press.
Sellars, Wilfrid, 1963, "Empiricism and the Philosophy of Mind," in *Science, Perception and Reality*, New York: Humanities Press, pp. 127–96.

Notes

1 See also Rorty, 1965, which I will not discuss, although it is an important paper in the history of the philosophy of mind.
2 For more details on the computational architecture of Cog, see my "The Practical Requirements for Building a Conscious Robot," in the *Philosophical Transactions of the Royal Society*, (1994), 349, pp. 133–46, from which this brief description is excerpted, or for more up-to-date information, consult the World Wide Web site for the Cog Shop at MIT.edu/projects.
3 These points grew out of discussion with Victoria McGeer, of a paper she presented at the Society for Philosophy and Psychology meeting in Vancouver in 1993; the successor to that paper, McGeer, 1996, carries these points further.

RESPONSE TO DANIEL DENNETT

I agree entirely with Daniel Dennett's criticism of my suggestion, in "Incorrigibility as the Mark of the Mental," that the incorrigibility of certain first-person reports should be thought of as the result of adopting a "convention." "Convention" is an unQuinean, unDavidsonian, notion. I should have been more wary of it. It would have been more consistent and more prudent to have spoken of a habit of reliance on such reports – a habit adopted for obvious and good reasons – than of a convention.

When I referred, in a passage Dennett quotes, to a "regulative principle of behavioral science" I should have spoken of a persistent, but revisable, habit of behavioral scientists. Speaking in this way would have made it clear that I wanted to talk about convenience rather than convention, and about the best way to cope with behavior rather than about ontological commitment. On my view, of course, any and every pattern of linguistic practice is an attempt to cope with the behavior (either linguistic or non-linguistic) of things. That is why I have no use for the analytic–synthetic, the fact-vs.-convention, or the "matter of fact-vs.-no matter of fact" distinctions.

Dennett does seem to have a use for such distinctions. For he raises the question "Why turn the recognition of high reliability [of introspective reports] into a constitutive declaration of incorrigibility? Is this just an unmotivated overshooting of social practice . . .? Or might there be some deeper reason – an actual justification – for thus shifting the very criteria (to speak in 60s-talk) for the occurrence of mental phenomena?"

In posing these questions Dennett seems to want to let go of 60s-talk, which was still pervaded by the distinctions I have just deplored, with one hand while holding on to it with the other. He shares this ambivalence with many other contemporary philosophers: they would not be caught dead invoking the analytic–synthetic distinction, but nonetheless want to preserve a distinction between assertions made for the sake of convenience and assertions that have "an actual justification."

As I see it, one can describe any true assertion as a convenient tool for coping with reality, or as a good move in a language-game, or even as a reasonably accurate representation of reality, just so long as one does make invidious distinctions between kinds of assertions (so that true political or literary or moral judgments, for example, are tools and moves but not representations, for example, whereas true physical theories are all three). Describing true assertions as representations of reality, or as corresponding to reality, is harmless if the metaphors of representing and corresponding are not pressed.

Not pressing them is the pragmatic cash-value of using what Dennett calls a "vegetarian" notion of representation. I would prefer, however, to describe this not as a notion of representation – a rather complex and novel one, which may require a theory of "internal realism" to explicate – but simply as a dead metaphor. There is no harm in saying of good tools and good moves that they are also good representations, but nothing interesting is conveyed by this choice of idiom, and its employment should not tempt us to construct theories about how representation works. For it is no more useful to ask "what bits of a physical theory represent what bits of non-linguistic reality?" than to ask "who passed the law of gravity?"[1]

Another way of putting the difference between Dennett's views and mine is that mine allow no room for the notion of "more than just conversation" which he invokes when discussing the "more fashionable and famous ideas" which, in my later years, I have been "misled" into adopting. I see no way to make a principled distinction between conversation about politics and literature, on the one hand, and scientific inquiry on the other except in sociological terms. (The natural scientists, for example, can predict better than the other conversationalists, are more likely to agree among themselves, and so on.) But I take it that Dennett wants to say that there are (what he calls) "deeper reasons – actual justifications" why these sociological facts obtain. That makes him what I call a "scienticist." Scienticists think that they are paying a high compliment when they say of someone, as Dennett says of me, that he "succeeded in spite of himself in making . . . [a] contribution to science – to our objective knowledge of the way the world, and the mind, is." I regard this compliment as like a decoration bestowed by a king who, with any luck, will soon be forced into exile by a citizenry exasperated with monarchic pretensions. The medal is gaudy, and its award was a nice gesture, but it does not mean much.

Part of my ambition, to paraphrase Freud, is to help it come to pass that where epistemology and metaphysics were, sociology and history shall be. So, as Dennett correctly says, I want to "trade in a lot of tempting but indefensible metaphysical claims for an epistemological or even sociological claim." "Sociological" is a much better term than "epistemological" because the fact that, in Dennett's words, "certain claims [for instance, first-person reports of thoughts and sensations] cannot be overriden . . . given the role they play in our shared life" is, given the Myth of Jones, a socio-historical fact. Epistemology has always had pretensions to ahistoricity.

Dennett says that he wants to save my neo-Sellarsian "deflationary doctrine" about first-person reports of the mental from "some Rortian excesses." But I have trouble seeing just what these excesses are supposed to be. This is because I have trouble seeing what it is to "take these questions about the justification and confirmation of our representations more seriously than he [Rorty] now allows." Presumably my lack of seriousness, and at least one of my excesses, consists in not facing up to the question "Would minds cease to exist if the sociological facts changed?"

Dennett correctly says "for current Rorty, this is surely a paradigm of a misguided question." He suggests that I would find it misguided because it assumes "that there is a neutral standpoint from which the Truth of the ontological claim could be assessed." I would prefer to say that it is misguided because it tries to drive a wedge between being an assertion that has an unquestioned and useful role in our language-game and being an assertion which is ontologically correct. It abandons the vegetarian, philosophically banal, ontological attitude which Arthur Fine has called "natural" in favor of invidious comparisons between various sorts of entities. It tries to make the invidious distinction I described above as "scientistic": the distinction between true assertions which are good moves and good tools but not necessarily representations, and assertions which are all three.

I take it that the example of Cog's possible future incorrigibility is supposed to give me reason to take questions like "Would they still have minds? When did they start having minds?" more seriously. But I am not sure exactly how the argument from Cog goes. I am happy to agree that "there is a high probability that the designers [of Cog] will simply lose the standard hegemony of the artificer ('I made it, so I know what it is supposed to do, and what it is doing now!')." As I said at the outset, I quite agree that "it is not mere convention that guarantees that there are minds in the world" but rather success of the sort of training program which Sellars' Jones, and Cog's interlocutors, conduct. But I am not sure about the claim that "the saliencies of its [Cog's] internal states . . . are saliencies that are created by the very process of learning to talk about them."

The question "does talking about X's create the X's, or were they there already?" is one I have discussed elsewhere.[2] The line I take is that although in some cases the question is easily and commonsensically answered (mountains were there already, bank accounts weren't), in many other cases the question is pointless. It is pointless because the choice of answer makes no difference. I cannot see that it matters whether the pre-Jonesians had minds and Jones simply trained them to report on them, or whether the training created the minds. Here, as in the case of Cog, I should have to be told more about why the question is being raised.

So, though I can agree (barring some quibbles with the term "conventions") with Dennett's penultimate claim that "changes in conventions can bring about changes in

attitudes that bring about changes in competence that are definitive of having a mind,"
I would not be perturbed to be told that all that is brought about by the changed
attitudes is a change in competence that is definitive of having knowledge that one has
a mind. When it comes to his final sentence, I am inclined to say that the relevant
triumph of neuroscience might be described either as "the death of the mind" or as
"the obsolescence of mentalistic reports," and that it would not make much difference
which description is chosen. If one does not care about whether or not a good tool or
good move is also a good representation of "the way the world, and the mind, is," then
one will not care about the choice between these alternative descriptions. My attitude
is: give us the tools, make the moves, and then say whatever you please about their
representational abilities. For what you say will be, in the pejorative sense, "merely
philosophical."[3]

****

I want now to turn away from Cog and mentality to some issues about scientism. This
will permit me to take up a line of thought found in the final pages of Akeel Bilgrami's
paper, that I leave undiscussed in my response to him. Bilgrami says that in the
contemporary academy there are some bad people, whom he calls "bullshitters," and
who do not value truth. In a paper called "Faith in Truth," which contains considerable
discussion of my views, Dennett has said much the same. Like Bilgrami, he is appalled
by the "postmodernist" types who seem not to know the difference between seriousness
and frivolity. The fear and loathing of "postmodernism" which is explicit in "Faith in
Truth" can be found between the lines of the paragraph in "The Case for Rorts" in
which Dennett refers to my "more fashionable and famous ideas."

In "Faith in the Truth," Dennett makes clearer what he takes these ideas to be.
There he criticizes what he calls my "attempt to show that philosophers' debates about
Truth and Reality really do erase the gulf [between being serious and being frivolous],
really do license a slide into some form of relativism." In the end, Dennett continues,
the Rortian view is that "it is all just conversations, and [that] there are only political
or historical or aesthetic grounds for taking one role or another in an ongoing
conversation."

In this article, echoed in a later paper called "Postmodernism and Truth," Dennett
joins the chorus of people who see "postmodern relativism" as a subversive and
dangerous movement, and who see me as aiding and abetting this movement. Obviously, I prefer Dennett's avuncular warnings to the scornful ridicule of my more
virulent critics. But, being avuncular in my turn, I would caution both Dennett and
Bilgrami against aiding and abetting the Blimpishness which characterizes many
polemics against "postmodernism" by analytic philosophers. I see both philosophers as
exhibiting the sort of cultural chauvinism which I call "scientism." The sort of
chauvinism I have in mind is illustrated by the many viewings-with-alarm we are
getting nowadays about the insidious influence of "fashionable Continental ideas." ("By
gad, sir! The enemy is at the gate! Time for all decent chaps to rally round! We must
defend Truth and Science against those frivolous, deconstructing, relativists!")

I have no wish to cast doubt on the distinction between the frivolous and the
serious. That is a serious and important distinction. It is well exemplified in the
contrast between the silliest, least literate, members of academic departments of
literature and honest, hard-working, intellectually curious, laboratory scientists – just
as the distinction between self-righteous priggery and tolerant conversability is well
exemplified by the contrast between the sulkiest, least literate, members of analytic

philosophy departments and honest, hard-working, intellectually curious, literary critics.

Neither of these distinctions, however, has any connection with the difference of philosophical opinion between those who do and those who do not believe that truth consists in accurate representation of the intrinsic nature of reality. This latter difference can also be described as that between people who think that justification to all comers is the only goal of inquiry and those who think that there is an additional goal, namely getting things right. People who hold the latter view typically hold the view which I call "scientistic": they believe that this goal is often achieved by natural science but not by those who debate political or literary matters.[4] This difference in philosophical outlook divides people who can see Dennett's point when he contrasts "just conversation" with something better, from people like me, who cannot. So we are the ones who agree with Brandom that "Conversation is the highest good for discursive creatures". So we are puzzled by the term "just."

Akeel Bilgrami sees a connection between philosophical error and bullshit that I cannot spot. He thinks it is "a matter of some importance in our culture, especially our academic culture, that we see the nature and the great importance of truth as a value in a further sense than the moral value of truth-telling." I suspect that Dennett (and probably James Conant as well) would agree with Bilgrami on this point. They might also agree with him when he goes on to say that "the bullshitter" is prepared to speak and write in the requisite jargon, without any goal of getting things right. But Bilgrami, as far as I can see, tells us nothing more about how to tell bullshitters from non-bullshitters. All we can do is watch for indications of whether their actions are directed to this goal.

But what indications are those? What behavioral evidence is relevant? I doubt that there is more hope of accumulating relevant behavioral evidence here than there is when attempting to answer the question "Is he saved?" or "Does he love the Lord his God with all his heart and soul and mind?". The question "Do you value truth?" seems to me as about as pointless as these latter questions.

Nevertheless, I quite agree with Bilgrami that there is a difference between the sort of people he calls "bullshitters" and others. This difference, however, has nothing to do with a person's goals. In particular, it has nothing to do with whether she thinks of herself as trying to make contributions to "our objective knowledge." Rather, the people whom Bilgrami describes as bullshitters are distinguished by being unconversable, incurious, and self-absorbed.

Unconversable people are the ones you cannot talk profitably with on matters of common interest, no matter how hard you try: you finally are forced to conclude that persistent failure to get on the same wavelength is their fault rather than yours. More specifically, you tell the serious inquirers from the frivolous "bullshitters" by finding out who makes a serious effort to hitch his jargon, his interests, and his goals, up with yours – who is willing to go to considerable effort to build conversational bridges. Someone who seems to be making as sincere and determined an effort to do these things as you yourself are will count as "serious." Somebody who doesn't may reasonably be called "frivolous," though perhaps "self-centered" or "intolerant" are more appropriate terms. This test will work on Cog as well as on protoplasmic language-users, and will work no matter what reply either sort of interlocutor makes to catechismic questions like "Do you value truth?" "Do you have faith in truth?" and "Do you aspire to objective knowledge of how the world is?".

Asking such questions of someone one suspects of being frivolous is like a departing representative of the British Colonial Office testing whether a certain native can be trusted to help run his country by inquiring as to whether he is a good Anglican. Such an official (someone like David Low's cartoon figure, Colonel Blimp) sees an obvious connection between reading from the Book of Common Prayer, dressing for dinner, not shooting foxes, abiding by various other British customs, and being a decent, trustworthy chap. Dennett and Bilgrami see an obvious connection between having the right "realist intuitions" and therefore making the right scientistic noises – reading from the analytic philosopher's version of the Book of Common Prayer, so to speak – and being a non-bullshitter. Dennett's conviction that I am aiding and abetting bullshitting can, I think, only be explained by this sort of chauvinism.

Cultural chauvinism consists of the view that one who does not conform to certain traditional practices (sartorial, sexual, gustatory, conversational, or sacramental, for example) is likely to lack such desirable features as seriousness, decency and trustworthiness. I think that Dennett and Bilgrami are guilty of cultural chauvinism when they assume that people who differ from them on philosophical questions, or in the sort of compliments they offer laboratory scientists, lack some sort of moral probity.

The test of the relevant sort of moral probity is whether or not one does one's honest best to break out of one's own parochial little language-game (Foucauldian culture criticism, possible-world semantics, Scientology, superstring theory, British middle-class morality, Anglican worship, Brandomian social-practice semantics, whatever). In testing for such probity, the right question to ask is whether the person in question does his best to find a way to talk about matters of common concern with people who are not accustomed to playing his own preferred game.

These are the sorts of reasons why I think that questions like Bilgrami's "Does she value truth?" and Dennett's "Does she have faith in truth?" are irrelevant to the distinction between seriousness and frivolity. I cordially agree with Bilgrami and Dennett that much current conversation among academics (particularly those accustomed to using the term "postmodern" in full seriousness) is jargon-ridden, profitless, and an unfortunate diversion of libidinal energy from more worthwhile projects. But I do not think that colleagues who go in for these profitless activities are at fault because they fail to grasp the need to get things right. They are trying to get things right too, but the things in question are artifacts which nobody else can see much use for. Their unconversability, and their social uselessness, are results of their failure to see any need to convince a larger circle of the utility of their new toys.

Rather than saying that these people do not value Truth, I would say that they do not have enough intellectual curiosity. They do not try hard enough to find out what is going on elsewhere in the intellectual world. They do not attempt a Gadamerian fusion of horizons. Similar rebukes apply to members of the many little cults (or, if you prefer, "schools") which have grown up within analytic philosophy. Like the worst of the "cultural studies" Foucauldians, lots of analytic philosophers think that if they can make sufficiently clever moves within their own cult's language-game they need not worry about what anybody else in academia, or the larger world, is saying or doing.

To sum up, I see an important sociological distinction between incurious cultists and more conversable sorts of people – a distinction that is important for our practical decisions about whom to talk with about what. But I do not think that this sociological difference reflects the difference between valuing and failing to value something called "Truth" or something else called "Reason." To believe that it does seems to me as chauvinistic as the view that moral probity depends upon belief in the existence of a divinity to whom we owe obedience. One important discovery of recent centuries is that atheists can be just as decent chaps as theists. It is time to follow this up with the realization that literary critics can be just as rational as experimental physicists, even those literary critics who remain in what Dennett calls (in "Faith in Truth") "flatfooted ignorance of the proven methods of scientific truth-seeking and their power."[5]

The religious chauvinism we loathe when it appears in national politics should not be mimicked by a scientistic chauvinism in academic politics. Carnap's and Popper's concern with "the demarcation problem" is, unfortunately, still alive and well within analytic philosophy. But that philosophical tradtion will never become mature enough to make a contribution to the conversation of the intellectuals until it gets over this youthful obsession. Until it does, it is likely to retain its jejune self-image as "more scientific," and therefore more morally virtuous, than non-analytic philosophy. It will continue to combine juvenile arrogance with Blimpish self-satisfaction.

There is, to be sure, a sense in which analytic philosophy is indeed more scientific than other kinds of philosophy. Most analytic philosophers are puzzle-solvers, in the sense in which Kuhn said that natural scientists were puzzle-solvers.[6] They find contradictions between our intuitions, and ways of resolving those contradictions, just as natural scientists find contradictions between theories and observations, and then think up ways of resolving those contradictions. Non-analytic philosophers, on the other hand, typically do not solve puzzles.

They do other things. Some of them try to change our intuitions (by, for example, getting us to think of the idea that true beliefs are accurate representations of reality as an optional metaphor rather than as an important insight). Others tell stories about the history of thought (of the grand, *geistesgeschichtlich*, Hegel–Heidegger, sort). Still others (Derrida, for example) offer remarkable new readings of old philosophical texts. There is plenty of room in the intellectual world for all these activities, and it is hard (unless one thinks that no intuition should ever be erased, nor any text recontextualized) to see why they should be thought of as in competition with analytic philosophy. But as long as analytic philosophers cling to the chauvinist idea that they, together with their colleagues in the natural sciences, have a special relation to "Truth" (valuing it more, for example, or having more faith in it) that their more "literary" colleagues lack, they will be tempted by the unconversability, and the arrogant frivolity, that they decry in others.

Notes

1 Does this mean that there is, as Dennett says, a vegetarian use of "mirror of nature" which could satisfy "all but the most hysterical Realists"? Sure. One can vegetarianize any dead metaphor simply by refusing to press it – refusing to analyze its meaning, determine its transcendental conditions of possibility, or otherwise philosophize about it. But, as I see it, the hysteria is not about realism but about scientism – about the need to make the natural sciences look good by setting them apart from the rest of high culture with the help of heavyweight philosophical, rather than lightweight sociological, distinctions.

Where Dennett sees a scale with hysterical realism at one end and what he thinks of my own hysterical, albeit fashionable, anti-realism at the other, and himself holding to the virtuous non-hysterical mean, I see a fairly sharp break between the people who want to make natural science wonderful and different from the rest of high culture, and those who, like myself, view it as a portion of the conversation which serves certain purposes (e.g., prediction) and does not serve others (e.g., figuring out what to do with our lives). I return to this topic below, in my concluding paragraphs.

2   See "John Searle on Realism and Relativism" in my *Truth and Progress*.

3   I see the question about whether Cog's trainers are "getting it to *become* a subject by putting it in a conversational milieu" as like the question "Do we make our children, or our slaves, subjects by putting them in a conversational milieu?" Maybe we do, or maybe we just gain access to their pre-existing subjectivity. How could it matter? I cannot see how the question would come up unless one thought that the question of whether fetuses, or illiterate slaves, have rights is to be answered by figuring out whether they contain an ineffable whatsis called "subjectivity" or "personhood." Those who do think so hope that metaphysics will guide us when we make moral and political decisions. This hope strikes me as pathetic.

4   This difference is discussed at length in my "Is Truth a Goal of Inquiry: Donald Davidson vs. Crispin Wright," included in my *Truth and Progress*.

5   Dennett says that this ignorance deprives these people of "the leverage provided by scientist's faith in the truth." Lack of this leverage explains the fact that whereas "again and again in science, yesterday's heresies have become today's new orthodoxies," "no religion exhibits that pattern in its history." Historians of religion will have bones to pick here.

6   This is not true, however, of the greatest and most imaginative analytic philosophers – those who, like Sellars, Kripke and Davidson, start by moving the pieces around and wind up knocking over the chessboard.

6

Towards Rehabilitating Objectivity

JOHN McDOWELL

1. Richard Rorty is notorious among philosophers for his campaign against epistemology practiced in the manner of the Cartesian and British-empiricist tradition. But
putting it like that underplays how drastic Rorty's thinking about epistemology is. For
Rorty, an activity in that vein is simply what the label "epistemology" means. He has
no time for a different, and perhaps useful, kind of reflection that might still deserve
to count as epistemological. My main aim in this paper is to urge that what I take to
be Rorty's basic convictions, with which I sympathize, do not require so completely
dismissive a stance towards the very idea of epistemology. Indeed, I want to urge that
Rorty's basic project positively requires a more hospitable attitude to something that
may as well be counted as epistemological reflection.

An illuminating context for Rorty's campaign against epistemology is a Deweyan
narrative of Western culture's coming to maturity.[1] For Dewey's own growing-up, it
was important to disburden himself of the oppressive sense of sin inculcated into him
by his mother, and this feature of his own life shaped his picture of what it would be
for humanity at large to come of age.

In simple outline, the story goes like this. The sense of sin from which Dewey freed
himself was a reflection of a religious outlook according to which human beings were
called on to humble themselves before a non-human authority. Such a posture is
infantile in its submissiveness to something other than ourselves.[2] If human beings are
to achieve maturity, they need to follow Dewey in liberating themselves from this sort
of religion, a religion of abasement before the divine Other.[3] But a humanism that goes
no further than that is still incomplete. We need a counterpart secular emancipation as
well. In the period in the development of Western culture during which the God who
figures in that sort of religion was stricken, so to speak, with his mortal illness, the
illness that was going to lead to the demise famously announced by Nietzsche, some
European intellectuals found themselves conceiving the secular world, the putative
object of everyday and scientific knowledge, in ways that paralleled that humanly
immature conception of the divine. This is a secular analog to a religion of abasement,
and human maturity requires that we liberate ourselves from it as well as from its
religious counterpart.

What Rorty takes to parallel authoritarian religion is the very idea that in everyday
and scientific investigation we submit to standards constituted by the things themselves,
the reality that is supposed to be the topic of the investigation. Accepting that idea,

Rorty suggests, is casting the world in the role of the non-human Other before which we are to humble ourselves. Full human maturity would require us to acknowledge authority only if the acknowledgement does not involve abasing ourselves before something non-human. The only authority that meets this requirement is that of human consensus. If we conceive inquiry and judgment in terms of making ourselves answerable to the world, as opposed to being answerable to our fellows, we are merely postponing the completion of the humanism whose achievement begins with discarding authoritarian religion.

The idea of answerability to the world is central to the discourse of objectivity. So Rorty's call is to abandon the discourse, the vocabulary, of objectivity, and work instead towards expanding human solidarity. Viewed in the context I have just sketched, this invitation has a world-historical character. As Rorty sees things, participating in the discourse of objectivity merely prolongs a cultural and intellectual infantilism, and persuading people to renounce the vocabulary of objectivity should facilitate the achievement of full human maturity. This would be a contribution to world history that is, perhaps surprisingly, within the power of mere intellectuals.

2.   I share Rorty's conviction that we ought to try to get out from under the seeming problems of epistemology in the Cartesian and British-empiricist vein, rather than taking them at face value and attempting to solve them. (It was largely from him that I learned to think like that.) I think, too, that there may be illumination to be had from a parallel between the conception of the world that figures in epistemology in that vein, on the one hand, and a certain conception of the divine, on the other. But it is possible to go that far with Rorty and still dissent from his suggestion that, in order to avoid entanglement in that familiar unprofitable epistemological activity, we need to discard the very idea of being answerable to something other than ourselves.

What gives the seeming problems of mainstream modern epistemology their seeming urgency is not the sheer idea that inquiry is answerable to the world. The culprit, rather, is a frame of mind in which the world to which we want to conceive our thinking as answerable threatens to withdraw out of reach of anything we can think of as our means of access to it. A gap threatens to open between us and what we should like to conceive ourselves as knowing about, and it then seems to be a task for philosophy to show us ways to bridge the gulf. It is this threat of inaccessibility on the part of the world that we need to dislodge, in order to unmask as illusory the seeming compulsoriness of mainstream epistemology. And the threat of inaccessibility is not part of the very idea of the world as something other than ourselves to which our investigative activities are answerable.

This allows us to make the parallel between epistemology and religion more pointed. The world as it figures in mainstream epistemology is a counterpart, not to just any idea of the divine as non-human and authoritative, but to the conception of *deus absconditus*, God as withdrawn into a mysterious inaccessibility. A telling Deweyan protest against epistemology, as practiced in the Cartesian and British-empiricist style, can be cast as a protest against the idea of philosophy as priestcraft, supposedly needed to mediate between this *mundus absconditus* and ordinary human beings who aspire to knowledge of it.

The idea that inquiry is answerable to the world does not by itself commit us to believing that there is a need for philosophy as priestcraft. We can accept that inquiry is answerable to the things themselves and still suppose, correctly, that the resources of ordinary investigative activity can suffice to put us in touch with the subject matter of investigation, without need of special philosophical mediation. That is: we can follow Dewey in rejecting philosophy as priestcraft, without needing to abandon the very vocabulary of objectivity. What we need to dislodge is the idea of the world as withdrawn into inaccessibility, and that is quite another matter.

3. If we separate the idea of objectivity from the threat of withdrawal on the part of the world, we can make better sense of the position of Cartesian and British-empiricist epistemology in the history of philosophy.

For one thing, this makes it easier to ensure that a Deweyan protest against an epistemology with priestly pretensions is aimed in an appropriate historical direction. The idea of being answerable to the subject matter of inquiry is surely not new with modern philosophy. Rorty sometimes cites Plato's manipulation of the contrasts between knowledge and opinion, and between reality and appearance, as a paradigm of what goes wrong in the metaphysics of objectivity.[4] But the familiar supposed problems of modern epistemology are not just more of something that we already find in Plato. That would make it a mystery that two more millennia had to pass before philosophy began to be obsessed with the anxieties of Cartesian epistemology. It took something further and more specific to make what people wanted to think of as the target of their investigations threaten to withdraw out of reach of what they wanted to think of as their means of access to it.

What figures in Plato as a distance between mere appearance and reality is not the distance that generates the characteristic anxiety of modern epistemology. Perhaps both the Platonic and the Cartesian conceptions can be captured in terms of an image of penetrating a veil of appearance and putting ourselves in touch with reality, but the image works differently in the two contexts. In the Platonic context, appearance does not figure as something that after all constitutes access to knowable reality, although it takes philosophy to show us how it can do so. Philosophy in Plato does not show how to bridge a gulf between appearance and an empirically knowable reality; it does not picture appearance as an avenue to knowledge at all. Correspondingly, the acknowledged and embraced remoteness of the knowable in Plato is quite unlike the threatened, but to be overcome, remoteness of the knowable in modern philosophy. Plato is nothing like a Cartesian skeptic or a British empiricist.

Attacking the vocabulary of objectivity as such, as Rorty does, rather than the conception of the world as withdrawn, distracts attention from a necessary task. If we are to achieve a satisfactory exorcism of the problematic of mainstream modern epistemology, we need to uncover and understand the specific historical influences – which, as I have been insisting, are much more recent than the vocabulary of objectivity itself – that led to a seeming withdrawal on the part of what we wanted to see as the empirically knowable world, and thus to philosophy's coming to center on epistemology in the sense of the attempt to bridge the supposed gulf.[5] Freeing the vocabulary of objectivity from contamination by the threat of withdrawal can be the project of epistemology in a different sense. This is an activity whose very point would converge with the point Rorty is making, when he rejects the idea that philosophy holds the secret to the possibility of empirical knowledge.

If we focus on the threat of withdrawal, we not only enable ourselves to raise diagnostic questions at the right point in history, the beginning of modern philosophy; we also make room, perhaps usefully, for a conception of Kant that differs from Rorty's. Rorty finds figures congenial to his world-historical conception of what philosophers ought to be doing only quite recently in the history of philosophy, with the emergence of self-consciously subversive thinkers such as Nietzsche. The only significance Rorty finds in Kant is that Kant's enormous prestige enabled the professionalization of philosophy, in the sense of the activity Rorty deplores as merely prolonging human immaturity.[6] But Kant precisely aims to combat the threat of a withdrawal on the part of the world we aspire to know. Kant undermines the idea that appearance screens us off from knowable reality; he offers instead a way of thinking in which – to put it paradoxically from the point of view of the style of epistemology he aims to supersede – appearance just is the reality we aspire to know (unless things have gone wrong in mundane ways). It is a fundamentally Kantian thought that the truth about the world is within the reach of those who live in the realm of appearance – to use a Platonic turn of phrase that is now rendered safe, deprived of any tendency to encourage the idea that we need philosophical gap-bridging. This is fully in the spirit of a Deweyan protest against the idea that epistemology is needed for a priestly mediation between us and a world that has withdrawn from us.[7] So if we reconceive Rorty's world-historical project, so as to direct it specifically against the epistemological problematic of withdrawal rather than the vocabulary of objectivity, we can see Kant as an ally, not an enemy. For what it is worth, this version of the crusade might do better at engaging professors of philosophy.

4.   One aspect of the immaturity that Rorty finds in putting objectivity rather than solidarity at the focus of philosophical discourse is a wishful denial of a certain sort of argumentative or deliberative predicament. On the face of it, certain substantive questions are such that we can be confident of answers to them, on the basis of thinking the matter through with whatever resources we have for dealing with questions of the relevant kind (for instance, ethical questions); there is no need for a sideways glance at philosophy. But even after we have done our best at marshalling considerations in favor of an answer to such a question, we have no guarantee that just anyone with whom we can communicate will find our answer compelling. That fact – perhaps brought forcibly home by our failing to persuade someone – can then induce the sideways glance, and undermine the initial confidence. Rorty's suggestion is that the vocabulary of objectivity reflects a philosophical attempt to shore up the confidence so threatened, by wishfully denying the predicament. The wishful idea is that in principle reality itself fills this gap in our persuasive resources; any rational subject who does not see things aright must be failing to make proper use of humanly universal capacities to be in tune with the world. If we fall into this way of thinking, we are trying to exploit the image of an ideal position in which we are in touch with something greater than ourselves – a secular counterpart to the idea of being at one with the divine – in order to avoid acknowledging the ineliminable hardness of hard questions, or in order to avoid facing up to the sheer contingency that attaches to our being in a historically evolved cultural position that enables us to find compelling just the considerations we do find compelling.[8]

Here too we can make a separation. This wishful conception of attunement with how things really are, as a means of avoiding an uncomfortable acknowledgement of the limitations of reason and the contingency of our capacities to think as we believe we should, can be detached from the very idea of making ourselves answerable to how things are. We can join Rorty in deploring the former without needing to join him in abandoning the very idea of aspiring to get things right.

I can bring out how these are two different things by looking at a feature of Rorty's reading of Plato.

Rorty follows Nietzsche in suggesting that Platonic conceptions in ethics reflect an inability to face up to the kind of hard choices that are the stuff of an ethically complex life – as if the idea were that getting in touch with the Forms would carry one through life without need for the effort of deliberation.[9] But I think this reading misses the point of Platonic ethics. Being in touch with the Forms is not meant to be a substitute for hard thinking about what to do. On the contrary, the Forms are an image to enable us to sustain the idea that there is such a thing as getting things right, precisely in the absence of ways to make answers to ethical questions universally compelling. It is not a Platonic thought that putting someone in touch with the Forms is in principle a way to compel assent, on disputed questions about how to live, from anybody at all who is rational enough to engage in discussion of the questions.

I think this is brought out by the treatment of Callicles, in the *Gorgias*, and Thrasymachus, in the *Republic*: places where, on Rorty's reading, one would expect to find Plato wheeling in a reality larger than mere human beings, as if it could fill gaps in the arguments that we can come up with apart from resorting to it. That is not what happens in those dialogues. Each of those opponents of ethical orthodoxy is reduced to a sulk, before anything specifically Platonic even appears on the scene, by arguments whose quality is quite uneven, but which are, at the worst, transparently sophistical (so that one can easily sympathize with the sulking). Thrasymachus introduces the question whether one should live in accord with what Socrates would recognize as virtue, but is himself driven into an angry silence in the first book of the *Republic*. Thereafter Plato turns to something that does not look like even a promissory note for a way of rendering an affirmative answer to the question universally compelling, compelling even to people like Thrasymachus. Instead, with Thrasymachus himself conspicuously taking no part in the conversation, Plato has Socrates characterize the knowledge that matters for knowing how to live as what results from a proper education. And education here is not, as Rorty's reading might lead one to expect, a honing of purely intellectual capacities, to put them in tune with a reality one might conceive as accessible independently of contingencies of cultural position. Plato insists that a proper education is an education of the sentiments no less than the intellect (to put it in eighteenth-century terms). There is a similar structure in the *Gorgias*, with Callicles figuring in the conversation as a patently unconvinced "yea"-sayer – remarkably enough, in view of the fuss Plato has Socrates make, earlier in the dialogue, about how important it is to him to secure the sincere assent of his interlocutors (compare 472b with 501c). I think the moral, in both dialogues, must be meant to be something on these lines: people who raise such questions are dangerous, and should be forced into silence, or acquiescence, by whatever means are available; people whose character is in good order will have confidence in right answers to the questions, a confidence that should not be threatened by the fact that questioners such as Callicles or Thrasymachus cannot be won over by persuasive argument.[10]

It is true, of course, that Plato gives a cognitive slant to his picture of what it is to have one's character in good order; he sees it as a capacity to arrive at the truth about a certain subject matter. But there is no implication that this capacity to arrive at the truth somehow insures one against tragic predicaments, or bypasses the need for hard thinking about difficult questions.

One would not expect Plato to have had the sort of concern Rorty has with contingency. But it is one thing to lack that concern, and quite another to have a metaphysical picture that excludes it. Plato's metaphysical picture can perfectly well accommodate the thought that it is a contingency that certain people can get things right; this formulation smoothly combines an acknowledgement of contingency with an employment of the vocabulary of objectivity, in a way that ought to be incoherent if Rorty were right about the vocabulary of objectivity. There is nothing alien to Plato in supplying, say, Glaucon and Adeimantus in the *Republic* with a thought on these lines: "How fortunate we are to have been born Greeks, not barbarians, and thus to have had an upbringing that made us capable of seeing things aright on these matters."

Of course it would be absurd to suggest that one can set aside Rorty's reading of Plato on the strength of a few quick sentences. But I do not need to carry conviction on the alternative I have sketched; it is enough for my purposes here that it should be so much as intelligible. This shows that the very idea of aspiring to get things right, of making ourselves answerable to how things are, has no necessary connection with what Rorty deplores: an inability to face up to contingency, and the fantasy of transferring the burden of hard thinking to the world itself.[11]

5.   So far I have been taking issue, at a general level, with Rorty's suggestion that the very vocabulary of objectivity commits us to a wishful denial of contingency, and that it saddles us with the idea that philosophy is needed, in order to supply a guarantee for the capacity of inquiry to make contact with its subject matter. I agree with Rorty that we should be open-eyed about contingency, and hostile to philosophy's claim to be a necessary underpinning for other sorts of intellectual activity, but I have urged that this does not warrant his dismissive attitude to the very idea of making ourselves answerable to the world.

I want now to point to a flaw in the way Rorty treats the vocabulary of objectivity when he goes into analytical detail about it.

Hilary Putnam has argued, to put it in Rorty's words, that "notions like 'reference' – semantical notions which relate language to nonlanguage – are internal to our overall view of the world."[12] Rorty cites Putnam's argument with approval. He writes, giving more examples of the notions to which the argument applies: "From the standpoint of the representationalist, the fact that notions like representation, reference, and truth are deployed in ways that are internal to a language or a theory is no reason to drop them."[13] The figure here labeled "the representationalist" is someone who refuses to give up the vocabulary of objectivity in favor of the vocabulary of solidarity. Of course Rorty is not suggesting we should drop the uses of these semantical notions to which Putnam's argument applies, uses that are internal to a world view. But he thinks "the representationalist" tries to use the notions in a way that is not internal to a world view. It is this supposed external use, according to Rorty, that is in question in the discourse of objectivity. So his view is that we need to distinguish the discourse of objectivity from the innocent internal use of the semantical notions that Putnam discusses.

One could define the discourse of objectivity as involving a certain supposed external use of the semantical notions, and in that case I would have no problem with Rorty's attitude to it. But Rorty suggests that rejecting these supposed external uses requires rejecting any form of the idea that inquiry is answerable to the world. I think this deprives us of something that is not inextricably implicated with what Putnam unmasks as illusion, and in depriving us of something we can innocently want, the move is damaging to Rorty's own philosophical project.

Rorty's picture is on these lines. If we use an expression like "accurate representation" in the innocent internal way, it can function only as a means of paying "empty compliments" to claims that pass muster within our current practice of claim-making.[14]

Now "the representationalist" finds a restriction to this sort of assessment unacceptably parochial. Recoiling from that, "the representationalist" tries to make expressions like "true" or "accurate representation" signify a mode of normative relatedness – conformity – to something more independent of us than the world as it figures in our world view. This aspiration is well captured by Thomas Nagel's image of "trying to climb outside of our own minds."[15] The image fits a conception, or supposed conception, of reality that threatens to put it outside our reach, since the norms according to which we conduct our investigations cannot of course be anything but our current norms. Recoiling from the idea that we are restricted to paying "empty compliments" to bits of our world view, "the representationalist" tries to conceive the relation between what we want to see as our world view and its subject matter from sideways on, rather than from the vantage point of the world view – now only problematically so called – itself. This way, it comes to seem that referential relations – to focus on the case that originally figured in Putnam's argument – would have to be intelligible in the "Augustinian" way Wittgenstein considers at the beginning of *Philosophical Investigations*; not, that is, from the midst of an understanding of linguistic practice as a going concern, but as if they could be prior building blocks in an explanation, from first principles, of how language enables us to give expression to thought at all.

This conception is naturally reflected in just the sorts of philosophical wonderment at, for instance, the meaningfulness of language, or the fact that we so much as have an "overall view of the world," that Rorty tellingly deplores. In this conception, being genuinely in touch with reality would in a radical way transcend whatever we can do within our practices of arriving at answers to our questions. Thus a familiar gulf seems to open between us and what we should like to be able to think of ourselves as able to get to know about. And the only alternative, as Rorty sees things, is to take our inquiry not to be subject to anything but the norms of current practice. This picture of the options makes it look as if the very idea of inquiry as normatively beholden not just to current practice but to its subject matter is inextricably connected with the "Augustinian" picture and the impulse to climb outside of our own minds. But a piece of mere sanity goes missing here.

6. It will help to focus on just one of the notions that figure in this line of thought, the notion of truth.

Rorty thinks there are three potentially relevant "uses" of "true": a commending or normative use, a "disquotational" use, and a "cautionary" use.[16]

The "cautionary" use is employed when we say, of some claim that we have so far not managed to find anything wrong with, that it may, even so, not be true. Rorty thinks such a remark is a reminder that, even though the claim's credentials have passed muster in the eyes of all qualified audiences to whom we have so far exposed it, we may in the future encounter an audience who finds fault with it, in a way that, as we shall acknowledge, reflects the fact that the future audience is better qualified.

So far, Rorty thinks, so good. The trouble comes if we take this "cautionary" use to be expressive of a norm. That way, we persuade ourselves that we understand compellingness to any audience as a norm for our activities of inquiry, and for the claim-making that gives expression to their results. And now we are liable to picture this universal compellingness in terms of a conformity to reality that would need to be contemplated from outside any local practice of investigation.

No doubt it is a good thing to aspire to overcome parochiality in the persuasiveness of the warrants we can offer for what we believe; that is part of the content of Rorty's own praise of solidarity. But this does not make universal compellingness intelligible as a norm. Rorty writes: "to say something like 'we hope to justify our belief to as many and as large audiences as possible' . . . is to offer only an ever-retreating goal, one which fades for ever and for ever when we move. It is not even what common sense would call a goal. For it is not even something to which we might get closer, much less something we might realize we had finally reached."[17] Trying to identify this "ever-retreating goal," only dubiously conceivable as a goal at all, with truth as a norm for inquiry and judgment is a way into a picture of the obligations of inquirers that has nothing to do with devising arguments in order to convince particular groups of human beings – a picture in which aiming at being genuinely in touch with reality seems appropriately captured by the image of trying to climb outside our own minds. The aspiration to overcome parochiality, then, is all very well; but the only norm, at this level of generality, that intelligibly governs inquiry is that of coming up with claims that our peers, competent in the norms of our current practices of claim-making, will let us get away with.[18] If we try to make sense of a further norm, involving responsibility to the subject matter of inquiry, we land ourselves in the "Augustinian" or sideways-on picture of our relation to that subject matter.

Now, to begin with, there is something unsatisfactory about the way Rorty separates the first two of these three uses of "true," the normative use and the "disquotational" use. Rorty claims that the "disquotational" use of "true" is "descriptive," and as such not merely to be distinguished from, but incapable of being combined in a unified discourse with, any use of "true" that treats truth as a norm for inquiry and claim-making.[19] But this makes no room for such truisms as the following: what makes it correct among speakers of English to make a claim with the words "Snow is white" (to stay with a well-worn example) is that snow is (indeed) white.

The idea of disquotation, literally interpreted, fits the "T-sentences" that are to be provable in a Tarskian theory of truth for a language, formulated in a metalanguage that expands the object language only by adding semantic vocabulary. But we can extend the idea of disquotation to fit the case of a Tarskian theory whose object language is not contained in the metalanguage in which the theory is stated – a theory that might be put to the Davidsonian purpose of capturing an interpretation of one language in another.[20] Here what figures, not quoted, on the right-hand side of a T-sentence is no longer the very same sentence that appears between quotation marks, or otherwise designated, before "is true if and only if" on the left-hand side. But it is a sentence that, if the theory is a good one, has the same effect; its use here cancels the semantic ascent effected by the quotation marks or other method of designation, and so disquotes in an extended sense. A sentence that is true, in the sense of "true" whose conditions of application to the sentences of this or that language Tarski showed how to pin down in a theory (provided that we can find a suitable logical form in, or impose a suitable logical form on, the sentences of the language), is – we can naturally say – disquotable. And this idea of disquotability is not separate, as Rorty suggests, from anything normative. For a given sentence to be true – to be disquotable – is for it to be correctly usable to make a claim just because . . ., where in the gap we insert, not quoted but used, the sentence that figures on the right-hand side of the T-sentence provided for the sentence in question by a good Tarskian theory for its language (the sentence itself, in the case in which we can exploit the unextended idea of disquotation). Truth in the sense of disquotability is unproblematically normative for sentences uttered in order to make claims.[21]

Now let us reconsider Rorty's treatment of the "cautionary" use. In a passage in which he is explicitly wondering whether he suffers from a blind spot, Rorty writes that, apparently unlike Davidson, he sees "no significance in the fact that we use the same word to designate what is preserved by valid inference as we use to caution people that beliefs justified to us may not be justified to other, better, audiences."[22] But what is preserved by valid inference, which is presumably truth as expressed by a commending or normative use of "true," is simply disquotability. That disquotability is normative for conclusions of inference, and hence that disquotability must be preserved by good patterns of inference, is just part of what it means for disquotability to be normative, in the unproblematic way it is, for claim-making. Moreover, disquotability yields a straightforward gloss on the cautionary use of "true" as well. One can express the cautionary point not only with an explicit use of "true," but also with a kind of augmented disquotation: that is, by making a claim in which one modifies a non-quoting use of the words that figure in the original claim, or the words that appear on the right-hand side of a non-homophonic T-sentence for the sentence uttered in making it, by adding a modal operator and a negation sign. Rorty's cautionary use is exemplified in a form of words such as "'All life forms are carbon-based' may not (after all) be true"; but one could achieve exactly the same effect by saying "There may (after all) be life forms that are not carbon-based." What one warns oneself or others that a claim may not have, in spite of its passing muster so far, is just disquotability. I think this shows that the blind spot Rorty wonders about is indeed there. That we use the same word simply reflects the fact that it is the same status, disquotability, that is, on the one hand, preserved by valid inference and, on the other, possibly lacked by beliefs, or claims, on which there is present consensus among qualified judges.

The same blind spot is operative in a thesis Rorty puts by saying "justification is relative to an audience."[23] Taken one way, indeed, the thesis is obviously correct; whenever one carries conviction by giving reasons, it is some particular audience that one persuades. Now Rorty thinks that is the only way to take the thesis; he thinks the only hygienically available conception of what it is for, say, a claim to be justified (or warranted, or rationally acceptable) must be relative to some particular audience, on pain of our purporting to have an idea of justification that is implicated with the sideways-on picture and the aspiration to climb outside our own minds. Failing the sideways-on picture, he suggests, "the terms 'warranted,' 'rationally acceptable,' etc., will always invite the question 'to whom?'."[24] This idea is what underwrites the argument I rehearsed a few paragraphs back, that, although persuasiveness to audiences other than our peers is a worthy aspiration, the only way justification (or warrant, or rational acceptability) can constitute a norm for claim-making is in the guise of ability to pass muster with our peers. But here the norm constituted by disquotability goes missing. An utterance of "Cold fusion has not been achieved, so far, in the laboratory" has (if I am right about the physics) a warrant, a justifiedness, that consists not in one's being able to get away with it among certain conversational partners, but in – now I disquote, and implicitly make a claim – cold fusion's not having been achieved, so far, in the laboratory. Here the terms "warranted," "rationally acceptable," etc., have collected an obvious answer, not to the question "to whom?," but to the question "in the light of what?," and the question "to whom?" need not be in the offing at all.

Notice that in order to insist on these lines that we can make sense of a notion of justification for which the relevant question is "in the light of what?," all I need is my (rather rudimentary) ability to make claims about whether or not cold fusion has occurred. Rorty thinks any purported notion of warrant or justifiedness that is not relative to an audience would have to be implicated with the sort of philosophy that involves trying to climb outside our own minds. But one does not pretend to climb outside one's own mind if one gives expression, as I just did, to the norm constituted by disquotability. One formulates the relevant normative condition on a given assertoric utterance by disquoting (possibly in the extended sense) the words whose assertoric utterance is governed by the norm one is invoking; that is, by using words (for instance, "Cold fusion has not been achieved") that would figure on the right-hand side of the relevant T-sentence, words in whose norm-governed employment one is (more or less) competent.

It is true that we have only whatever lights are at our disposal to go on in bringing such a norm to bear – which involves deciding what to say about, for instance, whether or not cold fusion has occurred. We understand what the norm of disquotability comes to, potential utterance by potential utterance, from the midst of a current practice of claim-making; we understand it by the lights constituted by being a (more or less) competent party to the practice. But it does not follow that nothing can be normative for moves within the practice except ensuring that one's peers will let one get away with them. There is a norm for making claims with the words "Cold fusion has not occurred" that is constituted by whether or not cold fusion has occurred; and whether or not cold fusion has occurred is not the same as whether or not saying it has occurred will pass muster in the current practice. On topics on which there is no dispute, it will always seem from within a practice of investigation that the answers to such pairs of questions coincide, but that should not prevent us from seeing that the questions differ. Moreover, anyone who can be recognized as self-consciously participating in a practice of claim-making must be able to see that the questions differ. Without this difference, there would be no ground for conceiving one's activity as making claims about, say, whether or not cold fusion has occurred, as opposed to achieving unison with one's fellows in some perhaps purely decorative activity on a level with a kind of dancing. The distinguishability of the questions amounts to the availability of the notion of a claim's being justified in the light of how things stand with its subject matter. And the questions are distinguishable from within our practice of claim-making; insisting on the distinction is not an expression of the fantasy that one can conceive the practice's conformity to reality from sideways on.

Seeing how the questions differ, we can see how the thought that some claim is true is not – as in Rorty's "empty compliment" idea – the thought that it would pass muster in the relevant claim-making practice as presently constituted. It is the thought that things really are a certain way: for instance, that cold fusion really has not occurred. To insist on this distinction is not to try to think and speak from outside our practices; it is simply to take it seriously that we can really mean what we think and say from within them. It is not just "the representationalist," someone who thinks we need to climb outside our own minds in order to understand how thought and speech relate to reality, who can be expected to recoil from a denial of this.

There are two different things that might be meant by saying, as Rorty applauds Putnam for saying, that norms expressible with notions like that of truth are internal to our world view. Putnam's insight is that we must not succumb to the illusion that we need to climb outside our own minds, the illusion that though we aim our thought and speech at the world from a standpoint constituted by our present practices and competences, we must be able to conceive the conformity of our thought and speech to the world from outside any such standpoint. But to unmask that as an illusion is not to say, with Rorty, that the norms that govern claim-making can only be norms of consensus, norms that would be fully met by earning the endorsement of our peers for our claims. We must indeed avoid the illusion of transcendence that Putnam's insight rejects, but we do not put our capacity to do so at risk if we insist that in claim-making we make ourselves answerable not just to the verdicts of our fellows but to the facts themselves. That is, if you like, to say that norms of inquiry transcend consensus. But this transcendence is quite distinct from the transcendence Putnam unmasks as an illusory aspiration. These norms are internal to our world view, just as Putnam urged that the relevant norms must be. It is just that the world view to which they are internal has the world in view otherwise than as constituted by what linguistic performances will pass muster in our present practice. But that is merely a requirement for us to have the world in view at all – for moves within the relevant practices to be expressive of a world view, as opposed to merely aspiring to vocalize in step with one another. Taking this transcendence in stride requires no more than confidence in our capacity to direct our meaning at, say, whether or not cold fusion has occurred.[25]

7. What I have been urging is that truth as disquotability is a mode of justifiedness that is not relative to some particular audience; the question that this mode of justifiedness raises is not "to whom?" but "in the light of what?". This mode of justifiedness is, innocuously, normative for inquiry and the judgments and claims it aims at. For all the efforts of philosophers to put it in doubt, something we can conceive in terms of satisfaction of such a norm is unproblematically achievable from the local standpoints that are the only standpoints we can occupy in intellectual activity.

Contrast Rorty's picture, in which there is nothing for truth, as a mode of justifiedness that is not relative to a particular audience, to be except the "ever-retreating goal" of being convincing to ever more and larger audiences. Of course the "ever-retreating goal" cannot be achieved, and Rorty says as much. But his blind spot about disquotability leads him to think this correct point can be put by saying something to this effect: if we conceive truth as a mode of justifiedness that transcends consensus, we are conceiving something that would not be achievable. This rejects the innocuous transcendence along with the illusory one. And the effect is to make urgent just the sorts of question that Rorty wants to discourage.

As I said, taking the innocuous transcendence in stride requires no more than confidence in our capacity to direct our meaning at, say, whether or not cold fusion has occurred. Philosophers have contrived to shake this confidence, to make such a capacity look mysterious, by moves whose effect is to make it seem that comprehension of how inquiry, judgment, and claim-making are related to reality would require the other kind of transcendence, the kind that is an illusory aspiration. Rorty's own refusal to countenance norms for claim-making that go beyond consensus is of course motivated by his well placed hostility to this idea, the idea that we need to climb outside our own minds in order to occupy a point of view from which to conceive the relation of thought to reality. But throwing out the innocuous transcendence along with the illusory aspiration has exactly the effect he deplores; it makes a mystery of how we manage to direct our thought and speech as it were past the endorsement of our fellows and to the facts themselves. Rorty is committed to taking imagery on those lines as irredeemably expressive of the hankering after climbing outside our own minds. But the imagery comes to nothing more than an insistence that we speak and think – of course from the midst of our practices – about, say, whether or not cold fusion has occurred. And Rorty's own move makes a mystery of how we manage to do that, in just the sort of way in which he rightly wants not to let philosophy make a mystery of such things.

If one has a steadfast understanding of truth as disquotability, one can be immune to philosophically induced anxiety about how thought and speech, undertaken from the midst of our local practices, can make contact with reality. But consider someone who has a merely inchoate understanding of truth as disquotability, a norm for inquiry concerning which the relevant question is not "to whom?" but "in the light of what?". Suppose such a person is confronted with Rorty's pronouncement that there is no attaining truth except in the guise of convincingness to one's peers. The pronouncement puts in question the achievability of a kind of conformity of thought and speech to the world that – as such a person realizes, though *ex hypothesi* only inchoately – ought to be unproblematic. It would be only natural to recoil into just the kind of gap-bridging philosophical activity that Rorty deplores.

8. Rorty aims to discourage a certain genre of philosophy, and I have been urging that his treatment of truth is counter-productive by his own lights. It is a connected point that this treatment of truth is, I believe, fundamentally unDeweyan. Philosophers seduce people into the kind of anxiety Rorty follows Dewey in deploring; they induce anxiety by manipulating the thought that we have only our own lights to go on in any inquiry. The thought is actually innocent, but it can be made to seem that having only our own lights to go on is a confinement, something that would threaten to cut us off from reality itself. This makes it seem that we need a special philosophical viewpoint, one that contemplates inquiry's relation to reality from sideways on, so that we can be reassured that ordinary inquiry makes contact with its intended subject matter. On this kind of conception, it is only by the grace of philosophy that truth is attainable in ordinary investigative activity. Rorty follows Dewey in his hostility towards this kind of pretension on the part of philosophy, and as I have indicated, I have no problem with that. But Dewey put the point by saying such things as this: "Truth is a collection of truths; and these constituent truths are in the keeping of the best available methods of inquiry and testing as to matters-of-fact; methods which are, when collected under a single name, science."[26] As Davidson comments: "Dewey's aim was to bring truth, and with it the pretensions of philosophers, down to earth."[27] Dewey insisted that truth is within the reach of ordinary inquiry. Rorty, quite differently, thinks he can achieve the desired effect – cutting down the pretensions of philosophy – by cheerfully affirming that truth in the relevant sense is not within reach at all. That is just the sort of pronouncement that triggers the kind of philosophy Dewey and Rorty deplore, and it is not an effective consolation, or deterrent, to add "not even within the reach of philosophy."[28]

What about the idea that the vocabulary of objectivity reflects an intellectual and cultural immaturity? I have been urging that disquotability is unproblematically normative, and that a proper understanding of the point yields a good gloss on the idea that inquiry is answerable to the world. It seems to me that it would be absurd to equate accepting this simple thought with abasing ourselves before the world, so as to fail to live up to our capacity for human maturity. Indeed, I am inclined to suggest that the boot is on the other foot. If there is a metaphysical counterpart to infantilism anywhere in this vicinity, it is in Rorty's phobia of objectivity, and the suggestion that we should replace talk of our being answerable to the world with talk of ways of thinking and speaking that are conducive to our purposes.[29] This fits a truly infantile attitude, one for which things other than the subject show up only as they impinge on its will. Acknowledging a non-human external authority over our thinking, so far from being a betrayal of our humanity, is merely a condition of growing up.[30]

I applaud Rorty's hostility to the sort of philosophy that sets itself up as providing necessary foundations for intellectual activity in general. But I think he is wrong in supposing that the way to cure people of the impulse towards that sort of philosophy is to proscribe, or at least try to persuade people to drop, the vocabulary of objectivity, and centrally the image of the world as authoritative over our investigations. I think this policy of Rorty's involves a misconception of an innocuous notion of truth. Once we understand that, we can see why Rorty's attempt to dislodge people from the vocabulary tends to have an effect that is exactly opposite to the one he wants. The way to cure ourselves of unwarranted expectations for philosophy is not to drop the vocabulary of objectivity, but to work at understanding the sources of the deformations to which the vocabulary of objectivity has historically been prone. If we could do that, it would enable us to undo the deformations, and see our way clear of the seemingly compulsory philosophical problematic that Rorty wants us to get out from under. This would be an epistemological achievement, in a perfectly intelligible sense of "epistemological" that does not restrict epistemology to accepting the traditional problematic. It is the deformations, to which Rorty's discussions of truth reveal him to be a party, and not the vocabulary itself, that lead to philosophical trouble.

Notes

1   Elaborating this context was a central theme in the stimulating lectures Rorty delivered, under the overall title "Anti-Authoritarianism in Epistemology and Ethics," in Girona, Catalonia, during his 1996 tenure of the Ferrater Mora Chair in Contemporary Thought. My formulation of the Deweyan narrative is a simplified version of the way Rorty presented it in those lectures. See also, e.g., "Solidarity or objectivity?," in Rorty's *Objectivity, Relativism, and Truth* (Cambridge University Press, Cambridge, 1991), pp. 21–34.

2   This phase of the story invites a Freudian formulation, which Rorty gave in his Girona lectures. There are also obvious resonances with Nietzsche.

3   Notice that this is not the same as liberating ourselves from religion *tout court*, as Dewey's own example makes clear.

4   See, e.g., "Solidarity or objectivity?," p. 22.

5   In *Philosophy and the Mirror of Nature* (Princeton University Press, Princeton, 1979) Rorty did concern himself with the historical question I am pointing to here (though I do not think he got the answer right). In respect of responsiveness to this historical question, more recent writings like "Solidarity or objectivity" seem to represent a backward step.

6   See chapter III of *Philosophy and the Mirror of Nature*.

7   See, e.g., *Experience and Nature* (Dover, New York, 1958), p. 410: "the profuseness of attestations to supreme devotion to truth on the part of philosophy is matter to arouse suspicion. For it has usually been a preliminary to the claim of being a peculiar organ of access to highest and ultimate truth. Such it is not." See the opening remarks in the written version of Donald Davidson's Dewey Lectures, "The Structure and Content of Truth," *Journal of Philosophy* 87 (1990), 279–328, from which I have borrowed this quotation.

8   This theme is central in Rorty's *Contingency, Irony, and Solidarity* (Cambridge University Press, Cambridge, 1989).

9   See "Solidarity or objectivity?," p. 32.

10   Rorty says of Orwell's O'Brien: "Orwell did not invent O'Brien to serve as a dialectical foil, as a modern counterpart to Thrasymachus. He invented him to warn us against him, as one might warn against a typhoon or a rogue elephant." (*Contingency, Irony, and Solidarity*, p. 176.) I think that makes O'Brien pretty much exactly a modern counterpart to Thrasymachus as Plato actually uses him.

11 "Fantasy" is not the way Rorty would put this; he thinks such terms of criticism concede too much to the metaphysics of objectivity, and he would simply say that such conceptions have not proved useful. This seems to me to be pragmatism gone over the top, depriving itself of a useful critical notion. But this depends on something I am about to argue, that it is only by way of a conflation that Rorty comes to think resisting the kinds of philosophy he rightly sees as unprofitable requires resistance to the very vocabulary of objectivity.

12 *Objectivity, Relativism, and Truth*, p. 6. See, e.g., Putnam's Meaning and the Moral Sciences (Routledge and Kegan Paul, London, 1978).

13 Ibid.

14 For the phrase "empty compliment," see *Philosophy and the Mirror of Nature*, p. 10.

15 *The View from Nowhere* (Oxford University Press, New York, 1986), p. 9; see *Objectivity, Relativism, and Truth*, p. 7.

16 See "Pragmatism, Davidson and Truth," in *Objectivity, Relativism, and Truth*, pp. 126–50, at p. 128.

17 "Is Truth a Goal of enquiry? Davidson vs. Wright," *Philosophical Quarterly* 45 (1995), 281–300, at p. 298.

18 Rorty writes: "I view warrant as a sociological matter, to be ascertained by observing the reception of S's statement by her peers." ("Putnam and the Relativist Menace," *Journal of Philosophy* 90 (1993), 443–61, at p. 449.) At a different level, we would have to specify the norms of the current practices themselves.

19 See "Pragmatism, Davidson and Truth."

20 See Davidson's writings on interpretation, collected in his *Inquiries into Truth and Interpretation* (Clarendon Press, Oxford, 1984). For the extended notion of disquotation (cancellation of semantic ascent), see W. V. Quine, *Philosophy of Logic* (Prentice-Hall, Englewood Cliffs, N.J., 1970), pp. 10–13.

21 Rorty thinks he is following Davidson in glossing disquotation in terms of a causal relation between bits of language and things that are not bits of language, and concluding from the gloss that "the disquotational use of 'true'," so far from being normative itself, cannot even be coherently combined with normative talk. I think this pretty much misses the point of Davidson's writings about interpretation. I urged this at pp. 152–3 of my *Mind and World* (Harvard University Press, Cambridge, MA, 1994). I think this feature of Rorty's thinking descends directly from the frequent, and never satisfactory, engagements of Wilfrid Sellars with Tarskian semantics; it would be an interesting exercise to trace the line of descent in detail.

22 "Is Truth a Goal of Enquiry?," p. 286. For the belief that the "cautionary" use of "true" "is captured neither by a common-sensical account of its approbative force nor by a disquotational account," see also "Putnam and the Relativist Menace," p. 460.

23 "Is Truth a Goal of Enquiry?," p. 283. See also the passage quoted in n. 18 above.

24 "Putnam and the Relativist Menace," p. 452.

25 Rorty makes a helpful distinction between relativism and ethnocentrism, and disavows relativism. (See "Solidarity or objectivity?") Ethnocentrism is the insistence that we speak from the midst of historically and culturally local practices; it amounts to a rejection of the illusory transcendence involved in the image of trying to climb outside of our own minds. But in refusing to allow the in fact perfectly innocent thought that in speaking from the midst of the practices of our ethnos, we make ourselves answerable to the world itself (for instance, to how things stand with respect to cold fusion), Rorty makes a move whose effect is to collapse his own helpful distinction. The thesis that "justification is relative to an audience" is, as explicitly stated, relativistic, not just ethnocentric. This is at least some excuse for what Rorty complains of (e.g. in "Putnam and the Relativist Menace"), namely Putnam's continuing to count Rorty as a relativist even in the face of Rorty's disclaimer.

26 *Experience and Nature* (Dover, New York, 1958); quoted by Davidson, "The Structure and Content of Truth," p. 279.

27 Ibid.

28 Rorty writes: "To try to make truth approachable and reachable is to do what Davidson deplores, to humanize truth" ("Is Truth a Goal of Enquiry?," p. 298). I think this is a misreading of Davidson's opposition to an "epistemic" conception of truth. Davidson opposes the idea that an account of what it is for a claim to be true needs to incorporate a reference to, for instance, human powers of recognition. That is not at all to say that it is all right to conceive truth as out of reach of human powers of recognition.

29 For a sounding of this note in the context of Rorty's anti-authoritarianism, consider the following passage: "my preferred narrative is a story of human beings as having recently gotten out from under the thought of, and the need for, authority. I see James's suggestion that we carry utilitarianism over from morals into epistemology as crucial to this anti-authoritarianism of the spirit. For James shows us how to see Truth not as something we have to respect, but as a pointless nominalization of the useful adjective we apply to beliefs that are getting us what we want. Ceasing to see Truth as the name of an authority and coming to see the search for stable and useful beliefs as simply one more part of the pursuit of happiness are essential if we are to have the experimental attitude toward social existence that Dewey commended and the experimental attitude toward individual existence that Romanticism commended." ("Response to Bernstein," in Herman J. Saatkamp, Jr., ed., *Rorty and Pragmatism: The Philosopher Responds to His Critics* (Vanderbilt University Press, Nashville and London, 1995), pp. 68–71, at p. 71.)

30 This thought too could be put in Freudian terms.

RESPONSE TO JOHN McDOWELL

Anyone who reads my response to Michael Williams' contribution to this volume will get a good sense of the anti-authoritarianism to which John McDowell refers at the beginning of his contribution. McDowell thinks that this anti-authoritarianism leads me to confuse "the very idea of aspiring to get things right, of making ourselves answerable to how things are" with "an inability to face up to contingency." Whereas I see this inability as beginning with Plato's fear of the plurality and contingency of *nomoi*, McDowell thinks that Plato was OK, and that the rot began to set in only in the seventeenth century. He thinks that Plato's idea of objectivity, of answerability to the non-human, should be preserved, even after we "get out from under the seeming problems of epistemology in the Cartesian and British-empiricist vein" (p. 110).

My culprit is Plato's idea that the varying *nomoi* are, like variation in general, a symptom of separation from the thing with which we ought to be in touch. McDowell's culprit is "a frame of mind in which the world to which we want to conceive our thinking as answerable somehow threatens to withdraw out of reach of anything we can think of as our means of access to it" (p. 110). He thinks that Plato was not troubled by the idea of a *mundus absconditus*, but that post-Cartesians have been.[1]

I think that the way out of both Cartesian and Platonism is to view human *nomoi* – human languages and practices – as as natural as the beaver's teeth, and equally in touch (causal touch, rather than any sort of "answerability" touch) with the world.

He thinks that the way out of Cartesianism is to follow Kant in saying that "the truth about the world is within the reach of those who live in the realm of appearance – to use a Platonic term that is now rendered safe, deprived of any tendency to encourage the idea that we need philosophical gap-bridging" (p. 112).

I think that Kant simply provides sugar coating for the bitter Platonic pill: "Of course," Kant assures us, "you are not in touch with things *as they are in themselves,* but don't worry: you were only *supposed* to be in touch with appearance." I simply cannot read Kant as McDowell does, and I should argue that my way of reading is closer to that of two of Kant's earliest readers. The first part of Fichte's *Vocation of man* is filled with moaning and groaning about a *mundus absconditus*. Hegel (like Dewey later on) saw Kant as opening a whole series of gaps which need to be philosophically bridged.

We shall fear that the world is on the verge of absconding as long as we think that causal connection with the world is not a tight enough way of bonding with it. If one wants to read Kant sympathetically, one should forget about the question of what does or does not constitute what, and also about the distinction between transcendental ideality and empirical reality. One should just cling to the thought that what Kant calls our "empirical" self – the only one we have – is the causal product of the "empirical" world, the only world there is. I think of McDowell as, contrary to his own best intentions, keeping alive the pathos of possible distance from the world. He does this when he insists, in *Mind and World*, that merely causal relations with the world do not suffice. This claim keeps alive the pathetic Kantian question about the "transcendental status" of the world.[2]

McDowell thinks that I would do better to compromise with the Kant-worship endemic among contemporary analytic philosophers. I think the purported Kantian cure is just another form of the Platonic disease. He thinks that the purposes he and I share would be better served by getting over the "phobia of objectivity" and ceasing to insist that "things other than the subject show up only as they impinge on its will" (p. 120). I think that such things show up only as they causally impinge on *us*, and that the volition–cognition distinction (one more unfortunate dualism common to Plato and Kant) should be set aside.

I am less sure of my ground, however, when it comes to Plato than I am when discussing Kant. McDowell's interpretation of the way Socrates handles Thrasymachus and Callicles is very convincing. He is probably right that Plato never believed that "any rational subject who does not see things aright must be failing to make proper use of humanly universal capacities to be in tune with the world" (p. 112). (If so, then Descartes made a fatal egalitarian move in the first sentence of his *Discourse on Method*.) McDowell may also be right that "the acknowledged and embraced remoteness of the knowable in Plato is quite unlike the threatened, but to be overcome, remoteness of the knowable in modern philosophy" (p. 111). But I still think that philosophical attempts, such as Plato's, to generate the pathos of remoteness should be nipped in the bud. We should save sublimity for the arts, and keep philosophy useful.

My way of doing this is to put increasing utility in the place of us for answering better to the world. McDowell thinks that this strategy will just keep the dogmatism–skepticism pendulum swinging. I think the same of his strategy. He thinks that when people hear me "cheerfully affirming that truth in the relevant sense is not within reach at all" they will "flock back to the kind of philosophy Dewey and Rorty deplore" (p. 120). I think that if enough young philosophers are persuaded by *Mind and World* that causal relations are not enough, the epistemology industry may survive for several more generations.

Despite all these disagreements, McDowell and I are united in support of a whole series of Sellarsian and Davidsonian anti-empiricist views. I find about ninety percent of *Mind and World* very appealing indeed. Sometimes McDowell almost persuades me that I should back off from my highly unpopular attempt to replace objectivity with solidarity. I am properly chastened by his reminder that the charge of infantilism is a two-edged sword. Sometimes I think that I really must have the blind spot he diagnoses.

Nevertheless, I would be lying if I said that this blind spot had gone away, and that I now see what McDowell thinks I have so far failed to see. I still have trouble with the central thesis of McDowell's paper: that "in claiming, we make ourselves answerable not just to the verdicts of our fellows but to the facts themselves" (p. 119). I still cannot see the difference between "expressing a world view" and "merely aspiring to vocalize in step with one another." What, I still want to ask, is so "mere" about getting together with your fellow inquirers and agreeing on what to say and believe?

Consider the following passage:

> There is a norm for making claims with the words "Cold fusion has not occurred" that is constituted by whether or not cold fusion has occurred; and whether or not cold fusion has occurred is not the same as whether or not saying it has occurred will pass muster in the current practice. On topics on which there is no dispute, it will always seem from within a practice of investigation that the answers to such pairs of questions coincide, but that should not prevent us from seeing that the questions differ. Moreover, anyone who can be recognized as self-consciously participating in a practice of claim-making must be able to see that the questions differ. Without this difference, there would be no ground for conceiving one's activity as making claims about, say, whether or not cold fusion has occurred, as opposed to achieving unison with one's fellows in some perhaps purely decorative activity on a level with a kind of dancing.

To begin at the end of this passage: why should the relevant example of achieving unison with one's fellows be thought of as a purely *decorative* activity? Why not think of it as serious as warfare, or commerce, or organizing a labor union, or some other workaday activity? Why *dancing*? The cognitive–aesthetic, workaday–weekend, compulsory–optional contrast which McDowell's draws is a misleading context in which to place the issue. It begs the question of whether my view can acknowledge the seriousness of inquiry. It does so by suggesting that to recognize only one norm of inquiry (as I do) rather than two (as McDowell does) will license unseemly frivolity.

Going further back in the passage: I can agree that "Did X happen?" is not the same question as "Can saying X happened pass muster in the current practice?" But of course, as we pragmatists always say on these occasions, the difference is not one that makes a difference. For anything that helps you decide to answer either question in the affirmative will, assuming that you yourself are a participant in the current practice, let you answer the other question the same way. Pointing out that two questions differ in meaning is not, in itself, enough to show a difference between two norms.

McDowell's reference to "topics on which there is no dispute" suggests that the duality of norms becomes clearer when we discuss topics on which there *is* dispute. Such dispute may make us dubious about the current practice, and lead us to murmur things like "*Eppur se muove.*" Presumably his point is that when we say "current practice tells us to affirm that X happened, but the facts may be otherwise" we become more aware of what McDowell calls "the norm constituted by disquotability" (p. 117).

I see no norm relevant to assertibility save those set by one or another social practice – either the current practice or some possible better alternative. So where McDowell sees a distinction between two questions – "to whom?" and "in the light of what?" (p. 117) – I see a distinction between two answers to the question "to whom?". The answer may be "current practitioners" or "some other, better informed or more enlightened practitioners".

As far as I can see, the term "disquotability" adds nothing to the term "truth." Since I want to follow Davidson in treating truth as a primitive term, I see no way to offer an analysis of it which would help us milk some normativity out of it. McDowell says, however, that "what is preserved in valid inference, which is presumably truth as expressed by a commending or normative use of 'true,' is simply disquotability." So presumably the normativity is to be milked out of the *use* of the term rather than of its unanalyzable meaning. But McDowell's phrase "commending or normative use" begs the question in dispute.

I commend 'S' to you as a belief when I say "'S' is true". But do I invoke a norm whenever I commend? Suppose I say that I do. My interlocutor may then ask me to spell out the norm I have just invoked, and tell her how to obey it. If I respond with McDowell's statement that "what makes it correct among speakers of English to make a claim with the words 'S' is that S" (p. 116), my interlocutor may well complain that she asked for a norm, not a platitude. She can reasonably say that the only way to find out whether S is to follow the same old norm she has been following all the time – getting on with current attempts to justify belief that S.

For McDowell, the facts themselves – whether glimpsed by us or not – constitute a norm. "[I]n claim-making we make ourselves answerable not just to the verdict of our fellows but to the facts themselves." (p. 119) What McDowell thinks of as my blind spot prevents me seeing how a "fact" can be anything except a hypostatized true sentence, and how anything can be relevant to deciding whether a sentence *is* true except the outcome of actual or possible practices of justification to our fellows.

To cure my blind spot, I should need to be told more about the analogy between the respect I owe to my fellows and the respect I owe to such hypostatized sentences. But I cannot respect a hypostatized sentence until I think the relevant sentence true, and I cannot figure out whether a given sentence is true without turning away from its hypostatization to the reasons which some practice or other makes relevant to thinking it so.

Nor does it help cure my blind spot to be told that my view denies that "we have the world in view otherwise than as constituted by what linguistic performances will pass muster in our present practice." Like everybody else in the philosophy business, I have (may Dewey forgive me!) tossed around the Kantian metaphor of "constitution" with insouciance. But I have no more idea how to cash out this metaphor than do Kant and McDowell.

How do I tell a world constituted by linguistic practices from a world constituted by facts – facts which somehow (despite the sentence-like appearance) are not themselves "constituted" by any such practices? I have no idea. I get no better idea when McDowell tells me that "to have the world in view otherwise than as constituted by linguistic performances" is a "requirement for us to have the world in view at all – for moves within the relevant practices to be expressive of a world view, as opposed to merely aspiring to vocalize in step with one another."

"Vocalize in unison" carries the same suggestion of frivolity as did "decorative" and "dancing." But suppose I have staked my professional reputation on my claim to have achieved cold fusion, and hope that the Fellows of the Royal Society, after looking into the matter, will not vocalize in unison "Cold fusion has not been achieved." Unfortunately, however, they do. That is no *mere* vocalization: it casts me out from the social practice to which I have committed myself.

Can I console myself with the thought that all those FRSs may not have the world in view otherwise than as constituted by linguistic practices? How do I know whether they do or not? To find out, I should have to find out whether they are, as McDowell puts it, "directing their meaning at ... whether or not cold fusion has occurred" (p. 119). Their vocalizations *sound* as if they were doing that. But who knows? Maybe they have all been reading too much Rorty, and as a result have come to believe that the world *is* "constituted by linguistic practices." Maybe they are somehow managing to direct their meaning elsewhere.

Here again the question is whether we have a difference that could ever make a difference. McDowell's problem is that every time he tells me that I am, or should be, doing something that I do not think I know how to do (regarding something as constituted or not constituted by something else, directing my meaning in the right way) I will ask him, in my tiresome verificationist fashion, for a criterion for having done it. My problem is that practically everybody agrees with McDowell that I have a blind spot, one which makes me insist on criteria where nobody else sees any need for them.

McDowell thinks me both unDeweyan and unDavidsonian in "cheerfully affirming that truth in the relevant sense is not within reach at all," (p. 120) and as pronouncing that "there is no attaining truth except in the guise of convincingness to one's peers" (p. 120).[3] I do not see what "the relevant sense" is. I do not think of myself as encouraging the pathos of distance by saying "settle for convincingness to your peers," but rather as saying, in a bracing and uplifiting tone "Worry about convincing your peers, and truth and the world will take care of themselves." The "guise" of convincing your peers is the very face of truth itself. For there is no way to drive a wedge between convincing your peers and directing your meaning to the world. The moral of Davidson's metaphor of triangulation is that you can never do either without doing both.

I think that if we do our best with our peers, we need not worry about answering to any other norms, nor to the world. For, as Davidson teaches us, you and your peers and the world are always bouncing off each other in causal ways. That causal interaction – that perpetual triangulation – is as intimate as connection with either world or peers can get. Plato and his followers encouraged you to hope for a yet more intimate bonding. But this hankering for sublimity should be confined to weekends spent in art colonies. It is out of place in weekday inquiry.

Notes

1   McDowell says that "the familiar supposed problems of modern epistemology are not just more of something that we already find in Plato. That would make it a mystery that two more millennia had to pass before philosophy began to be obsessed with the anxieties of Cartesian epistemology" (p. 111). My explanation for the Cartesian switch is that Plato and Aristotle yearned for identity with the known, and that after corpuscularianism became entrenched the yearning for *identity* turned into a yearning for accurate *representation*. Identity with a bunch of boring corpuscles is not nearly as attractive as yearning for identity with Platonic Forms or with Aristotelian pure actuality (thought thinking itself). But one can still yearn for the sort of mastery over those corpuscles that comes from knowing their intrinsic nature clearly and distinctly.

2   For more on this point, see "The Very Idea of Human Answerability to the World" in my *Truth and Progress* (Cambridge: Cambridge University Press, 1998). I think that the problematic of nature and freedom which dominates *Mind and World* would only be taken

seriously by someone still worried by the possibility that the world may abscond. I regard Hume's causal compatibilism about free will and determinism as a key pragmatist move: it is a way of saying that we do not have to have what Kant thought morality demanded, a self that swerves free of nature's laws. As long as we yearn to be such a self, we may well suspect that our bond with the world is insufficiently tight.

3   In note 28 to his paper, McDowell quotes me as saying "To try to make truth approachable and reachable is to do what Davidson deplores, to *humanize* truth." Humanization in this sense is to run truth together with justification, and my point was that anybody who says "the better we justify to each other, the closer we are to truth" is running the two together. The metaphor of "closeness" to truth is not one either McDowell or I can use. The difference between us is better stated as the issue of whether there is any use to be made of any spatial metaphor in describing our relation to the world: e.g., "directed to."

7

Reading Rorty:
Pragmatism and its Consequences[1]

JACQUES BOUVERESSE

In *Consequences of Pragmatism* (*CP*), Rorty suggests we give up once and for all trying to answer a question that probably has no meaning, and indeed, may never have had any: namely, the question of what philosophy really is, or of who really ought to be considered a philosopher. He thinks the time has come to end the continuing contestations over the territory of 'philosophy,' a territory defined academically, in any case, and guarded as such against intrusions from the outside. The only thing that liberal institutions should try to guarantee is that, sooner or later, a student be able to hear about all those recent or traditional thinkers who have something original and important to say – regardless of whether these thinkers be deemed philosophers by the usual criteria, or whether they appear within the context of a single, well-defined discipline.

To this effect, Rorty writes:

> I have heard analytic philosophers get furious at comparative literature departments for trespassing on philosophical turf by teaching Nietzsche and Derrida, and doubly furious at the suggestion that they might teach it themselves. Conversely, I have heard fans of Continental philosophy be obnoxious about the 'mere logic-chopping' with which their analytic colleagues waste students' time and dehydrate their minds. Like reciprocal charges of incompetence, this sort of rhetoric is pointless. It is also dangerous, for it can actually result in colleges and universities not having people on the faculty who can explain certain books to interested students. Yet the only way in which institutions of liberal learning can justify their existence is to be places in which students can find practically any book in the library – Gadamer or Kripke, Searle or Derrida – and then find somebody to talk with about it. When all the jockeying to decide which department's budget will bear the freight is over, we have to make sure the result has not been to limit the possibilities open to the students. (*CP*, p. 225)

Rorty not only claims that this is the ideal we ought to pursue, but also that things are heading irresistibly in this direction, at least as far as 'post-phenomenological' Continental philosophy and 'post-analytical' philosophy are concerned. On his view, analytical philosophy proper constitutes the last bastion of resistance to this idea, resistance supported by certainty in the existence of a set of well-defined problems that one can call 'philosophical,' as well as by the conviction that analytical philosophy possesses the one and only method of treating these problems adequately. With the exception of

Husserl, whom, Rorty tells us, we must consider a "brief and futile interruption of the Hegel-Marx-Nietzsche-Heidegger-Foucault sequence," one can say that "what distinguishes Nietzsche, Heidegger, and Foucault from Hegel and Marx is precisely the increasingly wholeheartedness with which they *give up* the notions of 'system,' 'method,' and 'science,' their increasing willingness to blur the lines between disciplines, their refusal to insist that philosophy be an autonomous *Fach*" (*CP*, p. 226).

At first glance, however, it would seem rather that Heidegger, more than anyone, emphasized that which makes philosophy fundamentally different from all else, assigning it an absolutely separate and unique position as a distinct genre among the whole of intellectual activities and cultural productions of an era. It would probably be more correct to say, then, that philosophy has not yet found a middle road between two extreme options, one of which apparently can no longer seriously be defended, and the other of which seems at first glance intrinsically unacceptable to it. The first option involves maintaining the claim over a dominant position in relation to the whole of cultural production; the second option is to consent (whether willingly or in resignation) to a process that entails the complete dissolution of philosophy within this cultural whole, a dissolution which means it would no longer exist except in the guise of 'nowhere and everywhere.' In spite of the fact that some philosophers often present this new situation as a considerable advantage and an opportunity, for the most part they are in no way resigned to seeing their discipline's status within culture become more and more uncertain and unstable. Indeed, most of them have tried not to make it even more indeterminate than it already is, if possible, but rather to delimit it afresh by erasing or more or less ignoring certain previously imposed lines of demarcation. Dividing the philosophers on this question is the fact that, unfortunately, the new boundaries they envisage are not the same for all. According to a common depiction, analytical philosophers are those who would like to make the borders that separate philosophy from science, and philosophical method from that of science, much more fluid and permeable. Heidegger would like to do a similar thing, but he has another type of border in mind: the one separating philosophy from poetry. It seems, however, that philosophy hasn't yet found a way of defending its identity against the threat of absorption coming from the sciences, except by moving closer to literature and art. Nor, for that matter, has it found a way to escape the risk of transforming itself into a simple literary or artistic genre, except by seeking proximity to the sciences.

What makes Rorty unique is that he thinks the time has come to give up the attempt to preserve any boundary at all: the best option would probably be to ignore *all of them*. For Rorty, there is really nothing (not even science) from which we should try to 'keep philosophy pure.' One might say that for Rorty the 'humanities' in general and philosophy in particular continue to belong to a universe which should be fundamentally distinct from that of the sciences. But the difference between the two may be much less important than one generally thinks, if one admits, as he suggests, that what makes the physicists physicists, for example, "is that their writings are commentaries on the writings of earlier interpreters of Nature, not that they all are somehow 'talking about the same thing,' the *invisibilia Dei sive Naturae* toward which their inquiries steadily converge" (*CP*, p. 90). Scientists, philosophers, moralists, and writers, etc., are all somehow engaged in the same enterprise: they all invent new vocabularies and tell new stories about things which, though no doubt different, are not so much so that the conventional distinctions one usually makes about their activities needs to be taken seriously. Certainly, Rorty suggests that at times an important disparity exists between the sciences and humanities, a disparity which might be expressed by saying, "with our colleagues in history and literature, . . . we in the humanities differ from natural scientists precisely in *not* knowing in advance what our problems are, and in not *needing* to provide criteria of identity which will tell us whether our problems are the same as those of our predecessors" (*CP*, p. 218). But it's hard to forget that, in regards to the natural sciences as well as to philosophy, Rorty believes neither in the permanence of problems nor in the convergence of attempts by successive generations to resolve them. Scientists may indeed *need*, as Rorty proposes, the sort of criteria that philosophers can do without. Nothing, however, proves that scientists actually *do* have these criteria.

Rorty's official position is that there is no longer any reason to defend philosophy as an autonomous discipline. Philosophers who find this suggestion unacceptable and scandalous should think about the fact that what for them appears to be the 'hard core,' or even the essence, of what philosophy claims to be today, might be maintained precisely in accordance with such a suggestion. As Rorty says, "Professions can survive the paradigms which gave them birth. In any case, the need for teachers who have read the great dead philosophers is quite enough to insure that there will be philosophy departments as long as there are universities" (*Philosophy and the Mirror of Nature* (*PMN*), p. 393). It's certainly no exaggeration to say that the need to teach the history of the discipline (and to preserve the memory or celebrate the cult of a certain number of great figures who have shaped this history) constitutes about the only thing that still justifies the existence of a good number of philosophy departments in French universities; and the need to teach the history of philosophy, along with the idea that the history of philosophy can only be done by professional philosophers, is what maintains the idea of philosophy as a distinct and autonomous discipline. Of course this doesn't mean that those for whom philosophy only exists today as an obligation to redeem past prestige wouldn't be the first to wax indignant over Rorty's proposals. To perpetuate philosophy as a specific academic speciality probably demands more serious justification than what the philosophers in question would agree to provide. From the institutional point of view, the standing justification is certainly sufficient: it is surely capable, as Rorty remarks, of assuring the survival of philosophy as a '*Fach*' for quite some time – and in the absence of philosophy itself, 'a *Fach*' is precisely what the history of philosophy is.

Be this as it may, I'm far from sharing Rorty's remarkable optimism on this point, as indeed on many others. I don't believe that if philosophy gave up its claim as autonomous '*Fach*,' this would of itself improve the possibility of achieving the conditions of wider practical (rather than of simply theoretical) access to authors and books, access essential to a liberal education and for which the university must constantly strive. From what I understand, these conditions are far from being fulfilled by American philosophy departments. Philosophers like Rorty, however, probably overestimate the degree to which French and other continental European philosophy departments do so, as those who have tried to introduce analytical philosophy there well know. Indeed, on the whole, the position of analytical philosophy in France seems to me clearly less favorable than that of Continental philosophy in the United States. As much as I agree with Rorty on the goal to be pursued, I am equally forced to admit that I have no precise idea about which type of institutional arrangement would best achieve the ideal situation he describes. The only thing that appears clear to me is the absolutely disastrous nature of the solution usually adopted in France. This involves the multiplication of institutions outside the university in which students may supposedly hear about all those new and important things that, it is well understood, cannot be discussed in university departments of philosophy. For as everyone knows, these university departments only tolerate, or teach, the most classical and traditional things, and are condemned by definition to conformity and immobility. From this point of view, the creation of the *Collège International de Philosophie*, above all else, represents to me one more blow to the already foundering University. It would be more consequential to provide the material and intellectual means capable of establishing the 'free space' the University is supposed to be, and that it could be, rather than seeking such a space elsewhere.

Among the many reasons I have always had for deeply admiring Rorty, the first is that he is one of those rare philosophers, and perhaps the only one, to truly practice what he preaches. Harold Bloom described him as 'the most interesting living philosopher in the world today.' I myself wouldn't hesitate to call him one of the most interesting philosophers one can read today – even if not necessarily the most convincing. In any case, I generally find him much more interesting than some of the contemporary French philosophers he most admires. Yet I'm astonished that someone so reasonable and considered in his judgments, so tolerant of colleagues whose conceptions of philosophy differ from his own, and someone for whom the possibilities and reality of dialogue today matter more than anything else, could be so fascinated by all those forms of thought representing exactly the opposite: fascinated, in other words, by those thinkers who (like most major figures in contemporary French philosophy) consider, and sometimes even admit, that they see neither the necessity nor the utility of discussion in philosophy.

One reason for Rorty's superiority seems to me precisely the extraordinary breadth and diversity of his philosophical learning. In this regard, he completely ignores the usual boundaries and divisions, the habitual incompatibilities and antagonisms. I also admire his success in consistently performing philosophical work in a way that agrees perfectly with the liberal, democratic, pluralist ideals to which he adheres politically. Rorty doesn't limit himself, as do many others, to theoretical hopes that students might read and discuss almost any book with someone competent. He himself has read with equal meticulousness and sympathy Heidegger and Dewey, Husserl and Russell, Gadamer and Kripke, Derrida and Searle (among others). That he is, moreover, capable of speaking knowledgeably of them all is perhaps the least one might expect of a philosopher today, but is nonetheless extremely rare. I myself know of no contemporary philosopher whom one can credit with an effort comparable to Rorty's in this respect. Indeed, I sometimes wonder if he realizes to what extent the thinkers he most admires are generally removed from what he advocates and practices, and, furthermore, that they find it absolutely natural to ignore almost everything outside their own philosophical world.

All this must of course come at some cost: the price is accordingly paid by Rorty's tendency to apply systematically the most charitable (one might well say, the most Rortian) reading possible to the authors he critiques, and his tendency to background or present as minor those disagreements which might seem rather to be quite significant. It is astonishing, for example, that certain of Rorty's seemingly devastating critiques against philosophers such as Heidegger and Derrida should nevertheless leave more or less intact both their philosophical reputation and the admiration Rorty holds for them. In regard to Derrida, for example, Rorty writes:

> There is no topic – and in particular not that of the relation between sign and signified, language and the world – on which Derrida holds a different view than that of any of the

philosophers of language I have mentioned. Nor does he have any insights which complement theirs. He is not, to repeat, a philosopher of language. (*CP*, p. 105)

Rorty thinks that we need to give up "the attempt to say, with Gasché and Culler, that Derrida has demonstrated anything or refuted anybody (for instance, Austin)." "It also means," as Rorty goes on to say, "giving up the idea that Derrida has developed a 'deconstructive method' which 'rigorously' shows how the 'higher' of a pair of opposed concepts (e.g. form–matter, presence–absence, one–many, master–slave, French–American, Fido–'Fido') 'deconstructs itself'" (*Contingency, Irony and Solidarity* (*CIS*) p. 134) Rorty takes no more seriously the idea, held by a good number of Derrida's disciples, that Derrida has decisively revolutionized the philosophy of language, than he does deconstructionist claims to political virtue or to the revolutionary socio–cultural effects that it considers itself capable of producing. He simply doesn't believe that the Derridian revolution, any more so than any other philosophical invention or discovery of this genre, can have anything other than indirect political and social implications, implications that are, in any case, much more indecisive and modest than its promoters maintain. "The later Derrida," Rorty writes,

> privatizes his philosophical thinking, and thereby breaks down the tension between ironism and theorizing. He simply drops theory – the attempt to see his predecessors steadily and whole – in favor of fantasizing about those predecessors, playing with them, giving free rein to the trains of associations they produce. There is no moral to these fantasies, nor any public (pedagogic or political) use to be made of them; but, for Derrida's readers, they may nevertheless be exemplary – suggestions of the sort of thing one might do, a sort of thing rarely done before. (*CIS*, p. 125)

I would not of course deny that Derrida's books can be exemplary in many ways or, in any case, unique in their genre. But Rorty by no means helps us understand how they might be *philosophically* exemplary. Once one abandons the idea that Derrida's writings might be exemplary in any one of the first two ways just indicated, ways which (with all due respect to Rorty) have been fundamental to their spectacular success, one must admit that the essential merit of a philosopher like Derrida is to have succeeded in effectively inventing a new genre – in writing books that, as Rorty says of *La Carte Postale*, cannot be classified in any known category: "*All* that connects him with the philosophical tradition is that past philosophers are the topics of his most vivid fantasies" (*CIS*, p. 126). But this is precisely what would be said by those who strongly doubt that simply having philosophers as the main characters of this sort of fantasy suffices to render Derrida's work of real philosophical importance. For reasons that are difficult to discuss, those doubters lack the good fortune of being seduced, as is Rorty, by the new genre that Derrida is supposed to have inaugurated. Generally one might say that Rorty's favorite technique, when reading authors like Derrida or Foucault, is to move into the sphere of private self-expression and self-determination, and, on this level, to redeem and recuperate everything which, when judged from the point of view of philosophical discourse destined for public use (as one is in principle meant to do), risks immediately appearing excessive, unacceptable or absurd. He has indisputably found a possible use for Derrida, one which involves reading him as one reads Proust rather than as one reads any philosopher of the tradition (authors such as Nietzsche, Wittgenstein or Heidegger included): "Derrida is coming to resemble Nietzsche less and less and Proust more and more. He is concerned less and less with the sublime and the ineffable, and more and more with the beautiful, if fantastical, rearrangement of what he remembers" (*CIS*, p. 136). But overall one might do better to ask oneself what those 'abnormal' and unclassifiable authors whose cause he takes up might think of Rorty's treatment of them, and of the way he attempts to save them from the reprobation of the philosophical community. When reading texts like 'Deconstruction and Circumvention,' for example, one can't escape the notion that, after having risked appearing as some sort of analytic philosophy renegade, now Rorty has every chance of being treated by the Continental philosophers that he tries to defend (or, in any case, treated by their disciples), as the sort of friend against whom it is essential and urgent to be protected.

Nominalists like himself, Rorty tells us, "cannot make sense of Hegel's claim that a concept like 'Being' breaks apart, sunders itself, turns into its opposite, etc., nor of Gasché's Derridian claim that 'concepts and discursive totalities are already cracked and fissured by necessary contradictions and heterogeneities'" (*Essays on Heidegger and Others* (*EHO*), p. 126).[2] I myself can only approve of his reaction, one that I find extremely healthy. Similarly laudable is his reminder that concepts of themselves make nothing, but are essentially the instruments we use, and that it is always we who make something of concepts. For as far back as I remember, what always prevented me from being a Derridian was my extreme inability to understand how one could claim to have escaped onto-theological metaphysics (or, in any case, to be trying to do so) and at the same time speak in all innocence of agencies such as '*différance*,' whose differentiating 'movement' is "the common root of all conceptual oppositions that mark our language, such as, to take only a few examples, sensible/intelligible, intuition/signification, nature/culture, etc." Rorty has every reason, it seems to me, to refuse to take Derrida's repeated denials seriously: to refuse, in other words, the exceptional status of a certain number of 'magic words' like '*différance*,' which, Derrida claims (giving the impression that his assertion suffices for truth) is 'neither a word nor a concept.' The difference between my view and Rorty's is that Derrida's protestations here seem to me to have far more radical consequences than those Rorty draws from it, when, for example, one asks if the Derridian project is as revolutionary as it seems and as important as it pretends to be. According to Rorty: "One of the barriers to Derrida's understanding of Austin was that he did not realize how thoroughly this idea had been extirpated from Oxford in the 1950s, thanks to Gilbert Ryle. One of the barriers to Anglo-Saxon understanding of Derrida is the assumption that all he can possibly be doing is to discover belatedly what Austin and Quine already knew" (*EHO*, p. 103, note 19). I must admit to wondering sometimes whether, apart from the more literary, more ambiguous and more extreme formulations which he himself often finds questionable, Rorty really has found in the Continental philosophers who inspire him (Heidegger, Derrida, Foucault, etc.) anything very different from what he might have learned independently from Anglo-Saxon thinkers such as Dewey, Wittgenstein, Austin, Quine, Sellars, Davidson, and so on.

Rorty's charitable readings of authors like Heidegger and Derrida do carry evident drawbacks: such readings run the risk of considerably relativising their philosophical importance, and of confirming the suspicions which might provoke, and indeed often have provoked, much more malevolent readings. Above all, Rorty risks reinforcing the already widespread conviction that, in regards to these matters, everything is a simple question of subjective attraction, indifference or distaste. As he says: "From the later Wittgenstein's naturalistic and pragmatic point of view, we can be grateful to Heidegger for having given us a new language-game. But we should not see that language-game as Heidegger did – as a way of distancing and summing up the West. It was, instead, simply one more in a long series of self-conceptions. Heideggerese is only Heidegger's gift to us, not Being's gift to Heidegger" (*EHO*, p. 65). Supposing that one can indeed speak of a 'new language game' – which seems to me a very un-Wittgensteinien use of the expression 'language game' – about all one can say on the question is that either one finds it interesting or doesn't, that one wants to play it or doesn't. This is certainly the best way one can find to encourage philosophers to tolerate each other. It demands, unfortunately, a price philosophers are probably unwilling to pay, a price that they perhaps are not even able to pay. To say that Heidegger invented a new language game, a better one than the others, can mean only one thing for Rorty: namely, that this game will also probably seem the better one to our successors; and this, in turn, simply means that this is the game they will actually then play. On Rorty's view, however, those others who fail to be seduced by this prospect also need not explain themselves; they are quite justified in using any means at their disposal to keep the Heideggerian game from being played. This said, I must admit that I envy Rorty's goodwill. I am personally incapable of practicing the type of charitable reading at which he excels. Indeed, I generally prefer to believe that philosophers really mean to say what they seem to be saying, even when, as in the standard examples just given, they say things that begin to be acceptable only when one decides they are not serious. If one believes Valéry,

> *Illusion is stimulation.*
> What we *really* think when we say the soul is "immortal" can always be conveyed in less ambitious terms. All metaphysics of this kind may be written off as inaccuracy, linguistic incapacity, a tendency to inflate thought *gratuitously*, and, in short, to get from a phrase one has formulated *more than one has put into it and expended in constructing it*.

What strikes me is the even greater disproportion (if such a thing is possible) between what authors like Heidegger, Foucault and Derrida have got back thanks to ambitious phrasing and what they have actually given. Similarly, such disproportion exists between what they think they are doing and what, if one interprets them in the modest and charitable manner suggested by Rorty, they actually have done. Valéry no doubt would say that, in this respect at least, they are at least as metaphysical as the purest representatives of that tradition they believe themselves to have moved beyond. He might also add that the 'stimulation' which made such a success of their discourse cannot really be separated from its power of illusion.

Some people are astonished by the fact that, when commenting upon certain contemporary French philosophers, I have done so most frequently by offering the sort of 'reasonable' reading Rorty suggests. There are two simple reasons for this. The first is that Rorty generally has the benefit of making otherwise unintelligible things understandable for me: he makes sense of them, even if it is perhaps not the sense intended. The second reason is that discussing our most revolutionary thinkers in light of Rorty's account of their ideas or of their most provocative claims is precisely the most understanding approach I can adopt. My own spontaneous reaction would probably be much less charitable. The principal lesson Rorty draws from the work of these noteworthy authors (logicians, epistemologists, philosophers, writers, etc.) is, however, rather surprising and quite different from the lesson they thought themselves to be proposing. Take Freud, for example, who by most accounts seems the prototype of the scientist, or even of the classic scientist: he is convinced of the discovery of something essential about the 'true nature' of mental life, and believes to have cleared, in territory traditionally claimed by metaphysics and religion, a new space for an authentically scientific psychology. According to Rorty, however,

> The increased ability of the syncretic, ironic, nominalist intellectual to move back and forth between, for example, religious, moral, scientific, literary, philosophical, and psycho-analytical vocabularies without asking the question "And which of these shows us how things *really* are?" – is Freud's major legacy. He broke some of the last chains that bind us to the Greek idea that we, or the world, have a nature that, once discovered, will tell us what we should do with ourselves. He made it far more difficult than it was before to ask the question "Which is my true self?" or "What is human nature?" By letting us see that even in the enclave which philosophy had fenced off, there was nothing to be found save traces of accidental encounters, he left us able to tolerate the ambiguities that the religious and philosophical traditions had hoped to eliminate. (EHO, p. 158)

The authors Rorty most appreciates are invariably those he can retrospectively credit for having contributed to the advent of the sort of intellectual he most favors: syncretic, ironic, distanced, nominalist and instrumentalist. But the question arises of why exactly these authors often seem the most perfect examples of what Musil called, thinking precisely of thinkers like Heidegger and Freud, 'intellectual dictators.' Rorty thinks we are now witnessing the emergence of a generation of scientists who have ceased to believe that they can discover anything like the true nature of reality, of philosophers who no longer believe that philosophy has an historical essence allowing them to distinguish the true philosophers from those who are not, and so on. I take all this to be simply a dream. For reasons that are not merely historical, reasons which Rorty would do well to consider more seriously than he does, this dream has no practical chance of being realized. Indeed nothing, above all the examples Rorty uses to support his diagnosis and prognosis, allows us to believe in its current realization.

It must be said, however, that Rorty does not belong among those philosophers who seek a kind of ecumenical consensus between analytical and Continental philosophy. He thinks that these two traditions simply do not share enough problems to permit an interesting and productive confrontation. He does, furthermore, have the rare advantage of being able to speak knowledgeably about both these traditions. Just as he doesn't believe that philosophy has an essence, a nature or an historical mission, so he doesn't believe, and refrains from suggesting, that either one might be suspected or accused of having somehow betrayed philosophy. There's no doubt that the philosophical community would be singularly more habitable and pleasant to encounter if all philosophers were capable of adopting an attitude similar to Rorty's. But, then again, if such a development doesn't occur, I don't think it's simply because philosophers haven't yet grasped the paradigm shift Rorty describes. In fact, I'm not at all certain such a shift has taken place or indeed can take place. The stories told by Rorty and by all the historians who think like him run as follows: 'once we believed in God, then we renounced our belief in God, but we continued to believe in things like reason, truth, history, etc.; finally today we are abandoning our belief in things of this sort as well.' The problem with such stories is that one doesn't know exactly who 'we' may be understood to be, nor to what extent the changes described have been accomplished. I think even Rorty himself doesn't completely escape the temptation of treating philo-sophical revolutions as supposed scientific revolutions. To put things a little crudely, Rorty doesn't explain why there are still Aristotelian philosophers, but no longer any Aristotelian physicists, or why today there are still so many philosophers who persist in believing in reason and even in God. (One might ask, "Were there really so many more such believers in the past?" Or again: "Is not the unanimity that in ancient times supposedly reigned over such questions completely illusory?"). If one could assume that philosophers like Heidegger and Derrida really did 'prove' certain things, one could equally say that at the same time they rendered other things impossible or ridiculous, things that philosophers before them were able to do with ease. From Rorty's point of view, however, they have done no such thing – nothing, in any case, so clear cut or decisive.

As is probably already quite evident, the reservations and objections I have when reading Rorty are not particularly original. They are by and large very close to those of Bernard Williams and Charles Taylor. Like the former, I don't believe that Rorty has satisfactorily accounted for that which fundamentally distinguishes a scientific program of research from one that should be, on his view, the program of a future philosophy. As Williams writes:

> In a very revealing passage Rorty says that 'pragmatism denies the possibility of getting beyond the . . . notion of 'seeing how things hang together' – which, for the bookish intellectual of recent times, means seeing how all the various epochs and cultures hang together.' That may be a programme for the successor of philosophy, or for the sort of literary criticism from which he does not want that successor to be distinct, but it is certainly no programme for science. The sense that one is not locked in a world of books, that one is confronting 'the world', that the work is made hard or easy by what is actually there – these are part of the driving force, the essential consciousness of science; and even if Rorty's descriptions of what science really is are true, they are not going to be accepted into that consciousness without altering it in important ways – almost certainly for the worse, so far as the progress of science is concerned.

Rorty argues that since the world neither is a language, nor is written in language, and since it can thus offer us no self-descriptions and can tell us nothing about what it really is, we must therefore abandon the idea of science as the search for progressively closer approximations to something like the 'real nature of reality.' Like Goodman, he thinks there is no such thing as "'nature proper,' no one way the world is, nothing already formulated or framed and waiting to be transcribed" (Goodman, p. 132). Rorty maintains that we ought to give up any philosophical attempt to make our criteria appear to be more than simply *our* criteria, but in addition the right criteria, somehow belonging to nature itself, and thus capable of leading us towards truth:

> Nature may, for all we know, necessarily grow knowers which represent her, but we do not know what it would mean for Nature to feel that our conventions of representations are becoming more like her own, and thus that she is nowadays being represented more adequately than in the past. Or, rather, we can make sense of this only if we go all the way with the Absolute Idealists, and grant that epistemological realism must be based on personalistic pantheism. (*PMN*, p. 299)

In other words, nature might be the cause of the appearance or the formation of certain conceptions and beliefs, but it cannot be the cause of the fact that certain conceptions are better than others, or certain beliefs are true. As Rorty says, "The history of science tells us only that one day Newton had a bright idea, namely *gravity*, but stays silent on how gravity caused Newton to acquire the concept of itself – or, more generally, how the world 'guides' us to converge on 'absolute' rather than merely 'perspectival' terms" (*ORT*, p. 57). The reason we must stop thinking that the progress of scientific knowledge allows us to claim that we are closer today to the truth than yesterday,

seems for Rorty essentially to be because the world has no way of 'telling us' whether
we are or not. The world has no way of letting us know that the conventions that allow
us apparently more convenient and increasingly better control over the problems it
presents us, also tend to become more and more like those conventions according to
which the world itself acts. This argument is further proof that truth is a property of
our representations of the world, and not something we can hope to find 'in' the world.
It proves, as Rorty says, that "where there are no sentences there is no truth, that
sentences are elements of human languages, and that human languages are human
creations" (*CIS*, p. 5). In other words, reality can only let us know that our representations need to be improved; it can never tell us they can no longer be replaced by
even better ones because they finally represent the world as it really is. A Popperian
epistemologist could accept all of this perfectly well, yet still claim that in saying that a
better theory may be distinguished from the one it replaces in being closer to (or in
any case, less distant from) objective reality, one says something both sensible, and, at
least in some of the most typical cases, entirely justified. Rorty suspects that realists
(scientific or otherwise) who believe true utterances are true by virtue of something
outside themselves to which they "correspond" (according to the still widespread
'correspondence' theory of truth), must also then be claiming that "the final vocabulary
of future physics will somehow be Nature's Own . . ." (*CP* xxvi). Or, furthermore, that
a vocabulary "is somehow already out there in the world, waiting for us to discover it"
(*CIS*, p. 6). But no form of scientific realism (at least none of those currently being
defended) seems to depend on such an absurd supposition. To hold that the objective
truth of which realism speaks cannot be a property of our representations simply
because these representations will always be by definition our own work and not that
of nature itself, is to hold over realism a victory that is frankly much too easy not to be
held suspect.

For Rorty, the idea that matter, spirit, the self or other such things have an intrinsic
nature that in principle is in no way dependent upon our activities of knowing and that
we attempt to represent in increasingly better ways, represents the secular descendent
of a conception which should not have survived the era of the theological world-view
from which it emerged. Following Blumenberg, one can say that the era of belief in
God as creator of the world has bequeathed to our own questions we feel obligated to
answer, an obligation that holds despite the fact that we no longer have the means our
predecessors had to deal with it. As Wittgenstein says:

> There was an idea that Newtonian mechanics *must* explain everything; and that it must be
> founded on principles that, so to say, would be sensible laws for a Creator to make (Laws
> of Minimum This, of Conservation of That). Why this idea? 'Because everything pointed
> to it.' Everything? No, only everything that they concentrated on.

There was indeed a time when the task of science could be understood as the attempt
to discover the principles and laws according to which the world before us was
conceived, to discover how, in other words, an all-knowing, all-powerful author must
have created it. In principle, today's scientists have had to renounce such claims. But
this doesn't mean they should abandon as a simple theological relic the fundamental
conviction motivating the majority of them: that there are laws of nature we must try
to discover rather than simply inventing them. Einstein explained his famous declaration, "*Raffiniert ist der Herrgott, aber boshaft ist er nicht*," as meaning the following:
"Nature hides its mystery by the sublimity of its being, not by trickery." One might

take Einstein's adoption of such formulas, or even his stating in less anthropomorphic language that the universe is a realization of the most simple mathematical ideas, to indicate the thoughts and words of a theologian rather than a scientist. But indeed, Einstein always recognized that the certainty inhering in such claims actually did have the nature of religious belief, of a conviction with no rational foundation. There are doubtless few scientists who are realists in the Einsteinian sense. I don't think, however, that the scientific community would long carry out its activities, or that they wouldn't undergo a significant change, if these activities no longer found their ultimate support in some form or other of realism. Neither the modifications Rorty describes, nor the philosophical critique that supports them, have any effect upon realism in this sense.

In the end, the type of realism that for a pragmatist like Rorty "does not make any difference" and can be considered superfluous (without consequence or justification), might be more like a myth than a philosophically founded conviction. This myth of realism, if it is one, is in some way constitutive of the scientific project itself. Here of course I'm thinking about the philosophical reasons we might have for abandoning realism, and not about the problem Arthur Fine presents when he writes: "One can hardly doubt the importance of a non-realist attitude for the development and practically infinite success of the quantum theory. Historical counterfactuals are always tricky, but the sterility of actual realist programs in this area at least suggests that Bohr and company were right in believing that the road to scientific progress here would have been blocked by realism." It may be that even Einstein's famous realism was in the end essentially of the sort Fine calls "motivational realism," rather than a realism constituted by a group of specific beliefs about reality. But it seems to me that even if we accepted "motivational realism" as the only serious successor of its older, long dead counterpart, we would be very far from the attitude Rorty proposes. In other words, Rorty advocates something quite different from the minimal realism implied by what Fine calls the "natural ontological attitude" ("Try to take science on its own terms, and try not to read things into science"). There is one thing we might possibly say about moral, social and cultural reality: it does not pre-exist our own creative acts and as such, it is in some way entirely made by us. I don't think, however, that scientists one day will be able to say the same thing of natural reality or will treat their own creations in the same way as philosophers, writers or moralists. In other words, I'm not convinced by the efforts Rorty, following many others, makes to rise above, or to deny, the division between scientific and literary culture.

As I've indicated above, I'm generally far from sharing Rorty's optimism about the benefits of post-philosophical culture. In this regard, my position is similar to that of Bernard Williams, who writes: "I doubt, in fact, whether Rorty has extracted from the ruins, as he sees it, of Philosophy any activity that will sustain a post-philosophical culture of the kind he sketches. It is not very realistic to suppose that we could for long sustain much of a culture, or indeed keep away boredom, by playfully abusing the texts of writers who believed in an activity which we now know to be hopeless." I willingly admit that my position here is largely determined by the particularities of the French situation and by my own past, one which follows an almost exactly opposite philosophical trajectory to that of Rorty. It's easy to understand how philosophers like Rorty became so tired and frustrated by the constraints analytic philosophy imposes upon philosophical writing and research, that they decided to attempt something radically different. But I belong to a generation of philosophers who, given the socio-cultural context wherein philosophical problems arise for them, have every reason for, in Rorty's words, "casting longing glances toward analytical philosophy – and particularly toward the 'realist' analytic philosophers who take Philosophical problems seriously" (*CP*, p. xxii). For those like myself, who found the politico-philosophical terrorism beginning its reign at the beginning of the 1960s intolerable, analytic philosophy in contrast could not but offer the comforting image of what a democratic philosophical community should be: civilized and tolerant, where all citizens equally must offer arguments and be willing to listen to and discuss possible objections. This sort of community was the last thing we could hope to ask for in the philosophical milieu of that time. It goes without saying that our conception of analytic philosophy then owed much to idealization and naivety. But I'm still convinced today that for someone like Rorty (and myself) who holds democracy to be of the highest importance (even more important than philosophy itself), the scientific community and its methods should continue to offer an example from which philosophy might draw inspiration. It is an example, in any case, that philosophy should not allow itself to ignore, as happens most of the time in France. As Bernard Williams has it:

> it is certainly true that the discourse of analytic philosophy, its argumentative procedures, are more continuous with those of scientists. It seems to its practitioners more responsible, more consequential, less open to arbitrariness, whimsicality and rhetoric than other styles of philosophy, and I suspect that it seems so to scientists as well, in so far as it does not seem to them, along with most other philosophy, merely pointless. [. . .] But analytic philosophy does hold that it offers a very abstract example of certain virtues of civilized thought: because it gives reasons and sets out arguments in a way that can be explicitly followed and considered; and because it makes questions clearer and sorts out what is muddled. [. . .] Both in this philosophy and in the sciences, the ideal is the old Socratic ideal that mere rhetoric and the power of words will not prevail.

As everyone knows, Rorty has radically contested this image of analytical philosophy and its virtues. At the same time, he has tried to make the differences upon which analytical philosophy attempts to base its superiority and its specificity seem illusory or unimportant. As a number of critics have suggested, the weakness of Rorty's conception lies in his failure to indicate how things should work in a post-philosophical world where one will no longer refer to such things as reason, truth, and objectivity. Open to equal criticism is the fundamental optimism with which Rorty envisions the 'progress' that should result from such a liberation. I'm tempted to say that in recent decades in France we've already had a hint of what the discourse, method and behavior of philosophers would be like in the universe Rorty wishes for. We have some experience of what happens when rhetoric, the power of words, and the cult of personality prevails over reason, logic, and the rules of argumentation. Rorty is content to find ideas like truth and objectivity useless. But it was not long ago when these ideas were considered, among other things, oppressive and dangerous and when it was deemed necessary for progress to abandon all the rules which allowed the intellectual world to resemble a democratic community. The image I have of this period is indeed rather more like one of a religious confession unified by obligatory belief in a certain number of heroes, saints and revolutionary philosophical discoveries of the day. Mach's response to Planck, who had called him a 'false prophet', was that if the scientific community was becoming a church in which one had to believe in the existence of atoms, he preferred to no longer consider himself a scientist. He was wrong about the point in contention, but right in principle. For philosophy, I don't think that things can be thought of any other way. This is the reason that at the time I chose to become part of the 'secular,' republican community of analytic philosophers, at the risk of no longer being considered a philosopher at all. The serious reservations I have about the ability of principles and maxims like those offered by Rorty to sustain a community of "post-Philosophical" intellectuals are not deductions *a priori*. They are based on concrete experience of the type of result such principles and maxims would be likely to produce if they really were applied. Given the situation in France over these last years, the success of a "post-philosophical community" would seem, indeed, extremely unlikely: all those 'humanist' notions that were once the target of philosophical criticism are returning in full force, and the idea is dawning even on French philosophers that we may have something to learn from the example and methods of analytic philosophy.

Rorty, who also unquestionably speaks from experience, believes the supporters of the analytic tradition have considerably overestimated the importance of argumentation to philosophy. He thinks that the philosophers he calls "poetic world-disclosers" like Hegel, Heidegger and Derrida, "have to pay a price, and part of that price is the inappropriateness to their work of notions like 'argumentation' and 'rigor' (*EHO*, p. 124). Philosophers who propose new ways of talking are precisely those against which it becomes impossible to argue from within the framework of our accepted ways of speaking. This goes hand in hand with the idea that, for such authors, philosophy operates on an essentially sub-propositional level, one given by the creation of a new vocabulary. On this level, questions of truth and justification cannot really be asked. Rorty declares his "sympathy with Ernst Tugendhat's nominalist, Wittgensteinian rejection of the idea that one can be non-propositional and still be argumentative" (*EHO*, p. 124). I wonder to what extent Rorty thinks that if one wants to be propositional, one still needs to be argumentative. In any case, Rorty has no objection to the existence of a category of professionals who, as is the case with analytic philosophers, distinguish themselves above all by having at their disposal particularly refined argumentative skills which can be applied to just about any subject. Indeed, he even explicitly emphasizes that such skills are a precious advantage, a resource that democratic societies like ours should take more advantage of. This point deserves to be highlighted, as I don't know whether Rorty realizes how much his position on this question differs from that of his favorite Continental philosophers: the latter would be more likely to see such professionals, and the real or imagined prestige which they enjoy, as simply another example of technocratic imperialism, rather than as an eventual trump for democracy.

If one takes the task of philosophy to be principally that of innovation in the realm of language (or, in Deleuze's less nominalist terms, of the 'creation of concepts'), it follows that argumentation is not of primary importance. I'm not as certain as Rorty seems to be, however, that efforts to argue for or against the introduction of a new vocabulary are incongruous or impossible, and that we must simply content ourselves just to wait and see if such a new vocabulary sticks or not. I readily admit that arguing against a new vocabulary is quite different from trying to argue about propositions made in the terms normally used. The difficulty seems to me to lie in the fact that the failure of philosophers to keep discourse at a sub-propositional level is not due simply to lack of care or thought, as the authors cited by Rorty well show. Indeed, that it is at all possible to accomplish such an endeavor in a consistent and convincing fashion is by no means certain. Derrida himself, for example, and not only his disciples and sycophants, as Rorty likes to say, offers a good number of perfectly contestable and extreme theses, and even affirms that he has "proved" them (the quotations, of course, do nothing to rectify such assertions). Certainly, a moment could occur in philosophy, as it might in any other intellectual endeavor, when it is unreasonable and absurd to want to continue discussion. At this point, demanding that discussion happen at any price only results in making impossible the type of creativity that has always distinguished great philosophers from simple commentators or epigones. But the difficulty here, as always, is in recognizing the point when one should stop. Just as it is possible to go beyond what one might reasonably demand, it's also possible to settle for much less than what could be, or indeed, should be, asked. Personally, I think this last option holds the more likely danger, as demonstrated now by the eagerness with which one exempts certain philosophers from providing any reasonable justification at all.

My disagreement with Rorty then comes from the fact that, with some of the most typical continental philosophers, he is convinced that what needs to be encouraged in philosophy is not the tendency to offer and ask for reasons and arguments. Rather, it is the opposite tendency whose development is encouraged as having only positive and "liberating" consequences. On the basis of what we have known in France over the last years, however, in some and perhaps even most cases, philosophers seem so little inclined towards discussion and even find it so abnormal that inciting them to go further in that direction would be quite useless. I don't know what Rorty might think of an opinion like the one Deleuze offers here concerning the fundamental uselessness of discussion in philosophy:

> It's already hard to understand what someone is saying. Discussion is a narcissistic exercise, where each person takes turns showing off: quite soon, no one knows what they are talking about. The real difficulty is determining a problem to which one or another proposition responds. But if one understands the problem someone poses, one has no desire to discuss it with him. Either one presents the same problem, or else one presents another and would rather move forward in this direction. How does discussion take place if there is no common set of problems and why should discussion occur if there is one? One always gets the solutions one deserves for the problems one presents. Discussions represent a great deal of time lost over indeterminate problems. Conversations are another matter. We must have conversations. But the littlest conversation is a highly schizophrenic exercise that takes place between individuals possessed of a common heritage and a great taste for ellipsis and short cuts. Conversation is rest cut by long silences. Conversation can produce ideas. But discussion is in no way part of philosophical work.

It seems to me that while philosophers had a common set of problems (as was the case a certain number of times in the history of philosophy), they could at least, and indeed did, effectively discuss the merits of their respective solutions. But I offer this citation of Deleuze here above all because it is quite representative of the methods used by many of the great thinkers of contemporary philosophy: they make their refusal to discuss appear in the guise of a theory implying that discussion in philosophy is futile. The secondary benefit (or perhaps the primary one?), is the possibility of finding oneself once and for all immune to the objections other philosophers might be inclined to make. What I find remarkable about Deleuze is his at least apparent conviction that every time a philosopher claims to be inventing a new concept, he really is inventing one. Whether a new concept actually has been created or whether it has simply been proposed that one adopt a new word which no-one can do anything useful with, or a deviant use of an old one, seems the crucial question here. It is also of course the question which must not be asked.

What the exact place of discussion in philosophy should be is most likely a problem that philosophical discussion won't bring much closer to resolution. But there is nonetheless an important and serious side to this problem, one having to do with the fundamental disagreement between analytical and Continental philosophers about how to approach the history of philosophy. Unlike analytical philosophers, Continental philosophers generally don't believe that such a thing as an error (or *a fortiori*, non-sense) can exist in philosophy. This is indeed what one would be forced to admit, if things were to happen entirely at a sub-propositional level, at a level, in other words, where there is no question of being cognitive or argumentative. In order for there to be refutations, there must be possible errors; and for there to be errors, there must be propositions. There is no real place for refutation if interesting philosophy is essentially "a contest between an entrenched vocabulary which has become a nuisance and a half-formed new vocabulary which vaguely promises great things" (*CIS*, p. 9). Like the majority of Continental philosophers, Rorty considers the will to refute to be at best a lack of originality, and at worst a simple waste of time. As Deleuze would say, the only correct way to react to what great philosophers tell us is to try to do the same thing as them, namely, to take our turn at inventing concepts. And as Rorty says, "I take refutation to be a mark of unoriginality, and I value Derrida's originality too much to praise him in those terms. So I find little use, in reading or discussing him, for the notion of 'rigorous argumentation'" (*EHO*, p. 121). Rorty doesn't go as far as to say, as Heidegger does, that in the realm of essentialist thought, refutation is nonsensical. This is because Rorty doesn't in fact believe in the existence of a mode of knowledge, opposed and superior to that of science, that one could call 'essentialist.' In *Philosophy and The Mirror of Nature*, Rorty emphasizes that,

> the positivists were absolutely right in thinking it imperative to extirpate metaphysics, when 'metaphysics' means the attempt to give knowledge of what science cannot know. For this is the attempt to find a discourse which combines the advantages of normality with those of abnormality – the intersubjective security of objective truth combined with the edifying character of an unjustifiable but unconditional moral claim. (*PMN*, p. 384)

Consequently even Heidegger can't pretend to have received from Being the sort of special knowledge that is reserved to a few great thinkers. For Rorty, Heidegger really did nothing more than propose a new way of describing what we had done until then and what we could now envision doing afterwards. My own impression is that in saying this sort of thing, Rorty asks philosophers to give up something perhaps as indispensable to their activities as motivational realism is for scientists, without for all that increasing in any way our possibilities of discussing what they propose. Indeed, the possibility for discussion might even seem more reduced than before, since the only thing that could eventually lend itself to discussion (and that Rorty effectively discusses), is the way in which philosophers perceive and present what they do. I myself don't believe that originality is the only thing that really counts in philosophy: we have seen some good examples of the excess and aberration this type of idea leads to. Nor do I believe that refutation is as useless as Rorty thinks: if there are errors, it is important to refute them, even if those who refute them are generally less original than those who produce them. But this is obviously a point which demands a more lengthy discussion than I can offer here.

My perplexity, I should hasten to add, doesn't extend to knowing whether authors like Foucault, Derrida, Deleuze, etc. should be counted among the most creative and original minds of our time. No-one, I should think, can have serious doubts about this point. For me, the question is only whether such great originality can justify the pure and simple refusal of philosophical dialogue with which they regularly oppose potential contentions. In any case, I don't think the example of the great philosophers of the past generally proves them right in this regard. At a time when such prophesy was almost a habit, Foucault announced that perhaps one day the era would be Deleuzian. It is indeed possible. As Rorty would say, what today is considered 'abnormal,' can very well become normal and perfectly conventional tomorrow. But in the meantime, to ask contemporaries to silence their reservations and objections and to simply wait for the future to confirm the prediction, is not only disagreeable and humiliating. To my mind, it also asks for the pure and simple sacrifice of the philosophical intellect. For me, it is problematic to wish to enjoy all the privileges of an inspired and charismatic thinker addressing a community of believers, while at the same time claiming that what is being done, precisely because it is 'philosophy,' is fundamentally different from religious or political rhetoric. Newton Garver, who is certainly no enemy of Derrida, remarks that, "Derrida's style is inimical to philosophy, because it is inimical to dialogue" [Garver, p. 194]. Indeed I also think that even if Derrida himself is not entirely an enemy of philosophy, as some would have him be, his style certainly is.

The last point I'd like briefly to make is the following. Rorty has in theory no sympathy for the Heideggerian notion that philosophy determines the course of an era, and that the worth of an era is in some way given by the worth of its philosophy: "For Heidegger, other human beings exist for the sake of the Thinker and the Poet. Where there is a Thinker or a Poet, there human life is justified, for there something Wholly Other touches and is touched. Where there is not, the wasteland spreads" (*EHO*, p. 76).

But Rorty also believes that the heroes of liberal society are not scientists or philosophers in the traditional sense, but those figures he calls, "the strong poet and the utopian revolutionary" (*CIS*, p. 60). As many of his commentators have remarked, Rorty's evident predilection for 'abnormal' thinkers causes quite noticeable tension between his elitist 'romantic impulse,' and his pragmatic, democratic and egalitarian tendencies.[3] The first leads him to consider the goal of liberal society to be to "make life easier for poets and revolutionaries" (*CC*, p. 13); the second prevents him from believing that what is good for poets and revolutionaries should at the same time necessarily be good for all ordinary people. To use a language now no longer current, one might say that Rorty sometimes hesitates between the theory of "influential minorities (or singularities)," and that of democratic reform, which privileges free debate and consensus. French disciples of Nietzsche and Heidegger have been severely criticized by Habermas (and in some fashion by Rorty himself) because of their tendency to think that open solidarity with the principles and institutions of the liberal democratic society to which they belonged would be a betrayal of the cause of philosophy. Rorty also has a similar problem. He claims that for him, democracy has priority over philosophy, a point on which I agree entirely. Yet at the same time he holds as the most important thinkers of our era those authors whose principles would more likely have them declare (even if some would not willingly admit it): "Let democracy perish, as long as philosophy still lives!" Rorty of course is not so naive as to overlook the problem posed by his use of thinkers like Foucault: "Foucault would not appreciate my suggestion that his books can be assimilated into a liberal, reformist political culture" (*CIS*, p. 64). But the same thing ('*mutatis mutandis*') might be said of Derrida. As Descombes remarks, there are two Foucaults: the French, or Nietzschean, Foucault, and the American Foucault, one who resembles overall a kind of modernized

Dewey. For the two Foucaults, as Rorty notes, the problem is that of the "romantic intellectual who is also a citizen of a democratic society" (*EHO*, p. 193). It seems to me that there are also two Derridas who differ in much the same way. (I am, of course, overlooking the fact that there are also at least two very different American Derridas.) I don't think that Rorty has for the moment found a truly satisfying solution to a problem that evidently is also his own: namely, the problem of the place of the romantic intellectual in democratic society, and that of the place of the democratic intellectual in a philosophical community whose inspiration remains fundamentally romantic, the paradigm being that of the extraordinary individual capable of imagining and causing radical ruptures and transformations. In a certain sense, philosophy has never mixed well with democracy. Democracy, in turn, has often been considered incapable of producing a truly great philosophy. As Musil says:

> Philosophers are violent and aggressive persons who, having no army at their disposal, bring the world into subjection to themselves by means of locking it up in a system. Probably that is also the reason why there have been great philosophic minds in times of tyranny, whereas times of advanced civilization and democracy do not succeed in producing a convincing philosophy, at least so far as one can judge from the lamentations one commonly hears on the subject.

Perhaps this also explains the contempt the French philosophers most favored by Rorty generally seem to think it necessary to show for 'American-style' theorists of liberal democracy. These latter theorists are perhaps in the last instance Rorty's true heroes, and are those to whom he is trying to bring the French philosophers closer. It would seem, however, that Rorty's friends are, in general, far from being the friends of his friends.

By proposing to philosophers that remaining, or once again becoming, heroes of liberal society, requires them to be more like the 'strong poet,' or like the 'utopian revolutionary,' Rorty seems at first glance to make an offer rather more typically Continental than Anglo-Saxon. Liberal societies in general no longer tend to think they have real revolutions to wage or that the solution to their most urgent problems depends directly or indirectly upon the contribution of poets (in the strict or in the larger Rortian sense of the term). One might well then suggest that if Rorty in some way needs pragmatist reformers like Dewey for public use, he needs revolutionary thinkers like Heidegger, Foucault and Derrida essentially for the private sphere. So long as one remains within the private sphere, one can be as irrationalist, poetic, prophetic, individualist, anarchist, anti-democratic and anti-humanist as one wants.

Rorty's romantic optimism is something I've always admired, even if I personally am quite unable to share it. When discussing the recent problem in America of the obligatory political correctness being imposed upon philosophers and writers, such optimism allows him to conclude: "There are already indications that leftist political correctness is becoming a criterion for faculty hiring. But, with luck, these injustices will be no worse than those which contemporary academic leftists endured from exponents of 'traditional humanistic values' in the course of their own rise to power" (*EHO*, p. 139). I'm tempted to point out that we too have had a taste of such things. During the time when it was understood that 'everything is political,' philosophers were judged essentially according to the real or estimated political impact they might have had, an impact estimated, furthermore, by the professional revolutionaries who thought themselves experts in this area. Overall this type of behavior seems to me to have caused more injustices than it corrected. It led above all to a significant, and sometimes quite disastrous, drop in the standards of philosophical excellence. Within a few years, these very same revolutionary theorists and their supporters returned with unsettling candor to celebrate things like competence, hard and fast knowledge, and the authority of the recognized masters. Today one still hardly dares to remind people that a philosophical problem might have political significance, or that the motives of philosophers might have a political aspect. Not only political Marxism but the concepts and philosophical culture of Marxism as a whole seem to have disappeared without a trace from the mental universe of our intellectuals. To the American universities now apparently undertaking a form of the experiment already familiar to us, I can only say I wish them well. To me, what has occurred over these last decades unfortunately cannot be seen as the development of the sort of post-philosophical culture Rorty tells us about: namely, a post-philosophical culture that is skeptical, sage, moderate and reasonable while at the same time less inhibited, more imaginative, creative and revolutionary than its predecessors. Rather, what we have now seems more the expression of a fairly banal and primitive dialectic, or, to put things more bluntly, what Bergson calls the "law of double frenzy."

Notes

1 This paper appeared in *Lire Rorty*, ed. Jean-Pierre Cometti (Paris: Editions de l'Eclat, 1992), together with a French translation of the appended response by Richard Rorty. This translation of Jacques Bouveresse's text was prepared by Adrienne Janos. (A response which has not previously appeared in English.)
2 Gasché, Rodolphe. *The Tain of the Mirror*. Cambridge: Harvard University Press, 1986, p. 136.
3 See for example Nancy Fraser's, "Singularity or Solidarity? Richard Rorty between Romanticism and Technocracy" in *Reading Rorty*, 303–321.

RESPONSE TO JACQUES BOUVERESSE

At present, as Jacques Bouveresse says, we have two sorts of philosophy professors: those who would like to nudge philosophy over to the side of poetry and those who would like to nudge it over to the side of science. Bouveresse and I disagree about the extent to which it is necessary or desirable to choose between these two alternatives. Bouveresse agrees with my analytic colleagues that the science side has obvious advantages, and the poetry side obvious dangers. I think that both sides have advantages and dangers in approximately equal measure, and that it would be a bad idea for philosophers ever to come down firmly on either side.

The poetry–science opposition has often been explicated in terms of the distinction between beauty and truth, or between fantasy and reality, or between taste and method. I have urged that we explicate it instead in terms of the distinction between private and public needs: needs that cannot easily be made evident to our fellow humans and needs that can. This latter distinction is obviously one of degree rather than kind, and that seems to me one of its advantages for the purpose to which I wish to put it. The private–public distinction separates the sort of thing we do in order to expand ourselves by expanding our imaginations from the sort of thing we do in order to achieve common-sensical, familiar purposes. It separates what Habermas calls "world-disclo-sure" from what he calls "action-coordination." These two activities obviously blur together in all sorts of ways; but the opposite ends of the spectrum are clearly distinct.

These two sorts of needs call forth two different sorts of moral virtues. The moral virtues of the typical scientific community are those which Bouveresse says prevail among the analytic philosophers. They are the virtues of a "democratic philosophical community, civilized and tolerant, where the citizens are obliged to furnish arguments and to understand and discuss whatever objections to those arguments are put forward." Bouveresse admits that his conception of analytic philosophy may be a little idealistic and naive, and that his preference for this sort of philosophy is influenced by his own unfortunate experiences with the other sort.

I, in turn, must admit that if I had been exposed to what Bouveresse calls "the politico-philosophical terrorism" to which French philosophers were subjected in the 1960s, I should probably be less prone than I am to make heroes of Derrida and Foucault, and more enthusiastic about analytic philosophy than I am. Bouveresse and I both know horror stories about what philosophy professors in our respective countries have done to each other, stories of which the other is blissfully ignorant.[1] But despite the stories I could tell, I can agree that my own English-speaking philosophical community has many social virtues that seem to be lacking in France. By and large, I agree with Bouveresse that the effect of taking science as the model which philosophy should imitate has produced, among the analytic philosophers, a civilized and tolerant community.

Still, such communities have the vices of their virtues. Occasionally a revolutionary comes along and says to such a community, "You think you are civilized and tolerant, but actually you are time-serving bores, congratulating each other on skill in the performance of complicated rituals which have no relevance to anything outside your own tiny, useless, circle." Communities attacked in this way will typically exhibit incredulity, defensiveness, disdain, and contempt. Nine times out of ten, these reactions are entirely appropriate. The tenth time – as when this sort of thing was said by Galileo and Hobbes to the universities of their time, or by Hegel or James or Wittgenstein to the philosophy professoriates of their times – future generations may wind up agreeing with the revolutionary outsider. Those generations will tend to see, in hindsight, the social virtues of the civilized and tolerant community in question as unimportant, in comparison with the beneficial effects produced by the revolution which undermined that community. They will see the moral virtues of the revolution-ary – self-confidence, the courage to go it alone by speaking in an idiom that nobody else is (as yet) using, a willingness to risk everything on the chance one might be right – as at least as essential to the progress of civilization as the social virtues of the *ancien régime*.

The principal vice of the community of analytic philosophers is that its members do not read much outside of analytic philosophy. Graduate study in philosophy in most American philosophy departments is largely a matter of going over the publications of the last ten or twenty years in order to get the background necessary for throwing oneself into the "hot topics" of the last one or two years – the topics currently being discussed on the preprint circuit. Since some first-rate people still go into analytic philosophy, the best philosophy PhDs of a given year form a cohort of sharp, lively minds, united by a sense of being the vanguard of an ancient discipline and buoyed by high morale. Yet they have very little sense of what that ancient discipline was. They will typically have read either Plato's *Republic* or Aristotle's *Metaphysics*, but probably not both. They will almost certainly have read parts of *The Critique of Pure Reason*, but they are unlikely to have a coherent story to tell about how philosophy got from the Greeks to the German idealists, nor about what happened between Kant and Frege. Nor do they have much sense of what is going on in the history, political science, literature, or sociology departments of the universities in which they teach. This is why they are baffled and annoyed when they find that contemporary French and German philosophers are being admired, discussed, and taught in those departments. When they try to read somebody like Gadamer or Heidegger or Derrida they just do not have enough background to get the point. Typically, they react to their confusion by saying "Well, as a trained philosopher, I can tell good from bad philosophy, and this stuff is *bad*."

What they should say – what would improve and expand their community if they did say – is, "There is a lot about philosophy that I don't know." This is also what should be said by Continental philosophers who are repelled by the technicality – the lack of romance, drama, and verve – when they pick up a book by Searle, Rawls, Davidson, Dennett, or Putnam. But neither sort of philosopher is willing to say this, because both insist that they *know what philosophy is*. They are both wrong. Nobody knows what philosophy is, any more than anybody knows what poetry is or what science is. All three of these are cultural traditions with many contemporary growing points – so many that no single person can keep track of them all. Nobody is in any position to generalize about "all possible" philosophy or poetry or science, because brilliant innovators will always think up new things for any of these three to be.

The biggest difference between Bouveresse and myself is that he uses terms like "philosophical content" and "philosophical importance" in a way that I would not. Thus, when Bouveresse says that "Rorty certainly gives us no help in understanding in what respect that [Derrida's books] are *philosophically* exemplary," I should reply that there is, indeed, a great deal of philosophy to which these books are irrelevant. On the other hand, they *are* relevant to what one thinks about Heidegger, Nietzsche, Hegel, and Plato; nothing more than that relevance, it seems to me, is required to make them useful contributions to philosophy.

Bouveresse seems to share with my analytic colleagues the idea that a contribution to philosophy should come in the form of an argument for the truth of a proposition. I think that that is just one of the many forms in which such contributions are made. Contributions are also made by, for example, Kierkegaardian and Derridean jokes, Aristotelian and Heideggerian neologisms, and Hegelian and Habermasian *Geistesgeschicten*. As I see it, there is just no point in trying to decide whether a given article or book about some figure or topic traditionally labeled "philosophical" is itself a piece of philosophy. It may or may not be, depending upon whether people pick it up and run with it, and whether the people who do run with it are called "philosophers" by future generations. (For example: Galileo's attack on Aristotle is not called "philosophy" but "physics." Heine's spoof of Hegel is not called "philosophy" but "cultural criticism." In contrast, however, Wittgenstein's renunciation of the *Tractatus is* called "philosophy" rather than "a renunciation of philosophy." But this is simply because a lot of people in philosophy departments have [contrary to Bertrand Russell's hopes and expectations] found it useful to gloss, and enlarge upon, the *Philosophical Investigations*).

Perhaps I can clarify my way of looking at the matter by taking up Bouveresse's question about whether "once one puts aside more literary, ambiguous and extreme formulations" I have really found in people like Heidegger, Derrida, and Foucault "anything very different from what I might have learned from various figures within Anglo-Saxon philosophy (Dewey, Wittgenstein, Austin, Quine, Sellars, Davidson, etc.)." I see what he means, and he has a point. As far as doctrines within what we Anglo-Saxons call "the philosophy of mind" or "the philosophy of language" go, the views I attribute to these "Continental" figures are, indeed, best expressed in "Anglo-Saxon" terms. But such doctrines – such arguable-for propositions – are not all you get out of these writers. From Heidegger and Derrida you get a brilliantly original idiom (Heideggerese, Derridean) of which it is useful to have a command.[2] From Foucault you get a kind of know-how, a way of looking askance and obliquely at contemporary institutions and practices, analogous to the kind of know-how you pick up from Marx and Weber. Had these three thinkers had to write in the idiom of analytic philosophy, we would have lost a lot. They would have found the idiom imprisoning, just as Peirce and Frege would have chafed at having to write in the idiom of the philosophy professors who made up their proximate intellectual environments.

So I want to resist Bouveresse's suggestion that we divide up the work of people like Heidegger, Derrida, and Foucault into the good, philosophical, arguable-for stuff, and the bad, poetic, unarguable-for, literary, ambiguous, extreme stuff. We have to take enlightenment where and as we find it. We shall not get it if we worry too much about whether what is offered is poetry rather than philosophy, or pedantic, ritual, hair-splitting rather than philosophy. We should suspend judgment on the "philosophy or something else" question until we have done our best to try to put the new, strange, hard-to-place, material to use. We should not try to settle this question either (like many analytic philosophers) on the basis of the presence of argument nor (like some Continental philosophers) on the basis of the presence of romance.

Bouveresse puts a fair question when he asks whether I can say anything more about whether or not to bother with people like Derrida and Foucault than "I find this interesting" or "I don't want to play this game." No, I cannot. But then one cannot do much more than this for many other things. Consider our attitude toward a field of learning that we have the option of studying, or a whole culture (the Chinese, say) which we have the option of learning something about, or a foreign language (reputed to contain magnificent poetry) that we could master if we took the time and energy to do so. I would suggest that the post-Frege tradition in philosophy and the post-Nietzsche tradition in philosophy both invite this sort of attitude from those who were raised in the alternative tradition. It is quite reasonable to say, "No, life is too short." But it is also reasonable to say, "Well, there might be something over there in the alternative field/tradition/culture/language that would change my life; it's worth the effort; I'll give it a try."

There is no obvious reason why someone inflamed by Heidegger should master the Frege-Russell-Carnap-Quine-Davidson sequence, nor any obvious reason why someone inflamed by Davidson should master the Hegel-Nietzsche-Heidegger-Gadamer-Derrida sequence. Nor will someone who tries to get a feel for both traditions (as Bouveresse and I have) necessarily benefit by doing so. I am, of course, delighted and encouraged by Bouveresse's saying that I handle texts from both traditions "*en connaissance de cause*," but I recognize that by trying to do so I may have merely fallen between two stools. One can write as pointlessly in a melange of two distinct idioms as one can when confined to a single idiom. There is no guaranteed benefit to be had from extending one's philosophical range of acquaintance. But there is also no harm in trying to do what both Bouveresse and I have tried to do. Ecumenicism can be a futile exercise and a bore, but it can also, occasionally, produce something exciting.[3]

Let me conclude this section of my response by saying something more about the particular case of Derrida. As Bouveresse notes, Derrida has not said what he thinks of my attempt to read him as one reads Proust. It is quite possible, even likely, that he hates it. However this may be, I entirely agree with Bouveresse that Freud *would* hate to be read as I read him – with no attention to his pretensions to "science," and thus little interest in, for example, Grunbaum's criticisms of him. But even if Derrida's attitude is "God save me from 'friends' like Rorty," my admiration and respect for him would probably not deter me from continuing to read him, and to write about him in much the same vein. I find much (though not everything) that Derrida writes engrossing and exciting, as I do much (though not everything) that Freud wrote. As with Freud, I use Derrida's writings as grist for my own mill – taking what I want and setting aside what I find pointless.

Reading authors against their own expectations, against the grain of their intentions, is often a profitable exercise, no matter how annoyed the authors get at finding themselves so read. Certainly authors are not the best authorities on how to use their own books. More generally, philosophy professors may not be the best authorities on which philosophy books can do most for the progress of human civilization. Once we write our books, we should, I think, sit back and say, "*Habent sua fata libelli*; anybody who cares enough to read them can do what they want to with my books, and good luck to them." I admit that it is often exasperating to read other people's summaries of what one has said; I have frequently experienced this exasperation myself. But I do not think there is much point in insisting that the only legitimate *Rezeptionsgeschichte* is one in which authorial intention is respected.

The best service we authors can do one another is to treat each other's books not as monoliths but rather as (to use Wittgenstein's image) ropes made up of overlapping strands, any assortment of which can be picked out and woven together with strands picked out from other ropes. Bouveresse says that such an attitude may be "the best way to encourage philosophers to tolerance" but that "unhappily it is at a price which they are not disposed to pay, and which perhaps they *cannot* really pay." I think they *can*, and that their dispositions do not matter. If an interesting philosopher chooses to behave like an "intellectual dictator," so much the worse for him or her. That bad behavior should not deter us from doing what we like with his or her writings.

I turn now to the question of scientific realism, which is at the center of the second section of Bouveresse's paper. Bouveresse thinks that the notion of "objective truth" can be given a clear and interesting sense (one which is not simply "beliefs acceptable to a civilized and tolerant community of inquirers"), and I do not. He thinks that there is a point in saying that the laws of nature are discovered rather than invented, and I do not. He thinks that the scientific community would falter if it no longer had a sense of being "*soutenue en dernier ressort par une forme quelconque de realisme,*" whereas I think that this community would probably continue its work unperturbed. I think, and Bouveresse does not, that there is a possible world in which natural scientists treat "their own creations exactly as they do those of philosophers, creative writers and moralists," and that the culture of this possible world has various advantages over that of the actual world.

How are Bouveresse and I to resolve these issues? By applying the powerful methods of analytic philosophy? What methods? Our disagreements about these matters can as easily be phrased in the jargon of analytic philosophy of science and philosophy of language as in any other. Restatement in a given jargon does not insure the availability of a method for resolving disagreement. (One of the few things Thomas Nagel and I agree about, for example, is that argument is over-rated in philosophy and, in particular, that the central issues on which he and I disagree – whether experience goes beyond language, and whether reality may not extend beyond the reach of any possible human language – are pretty well unarguable.)

I would suggest that these issues can only be resolved, as Dewey would say, *experimentally*. That is, we can only resolve them by trying to *create* a culture in which the science–poetry distinction is not explicated in terms of the distinction between reality and fantasy, between "the world" and "us," but rather – as I suggested above – in terms of the distinction between different sorts of human needs. This would be a great big cultural change – as big as the one that was brought about by the secularization of morality and of social institutions – but is worth a try. Perhaps my conviction that this experiment would succeed is due to being an American who has read too much Emerson, Whitman, James, and Dewey – just as Bouveresse admits that his conviction that such an experiment is bound to fail may be the result of certain particular aspects of the French situation and of his personal history. But, however this may be, there is no substitute for trying the experiment and observing the result.

I can, however, say something to defend myself against Bouveresse's suggestion that I want to try giving up on "reason, truth, and objectivity." I do not want to give up on these, any more than secularists like Hume wanted to give up on charity, benevolence, and fellow-feeling. Hume just wanted to reinterpret these notions naturalistically. I want to give terms like 'reason,' 'truth,' and 'objectivity' senses that are compatible with Nietzsche's Darwinian claim that we are just "clever animals." I do not think that this can be done without giving up on the notion of scientific truth as accurate representation of (in Bernard Williams' phrase) "what is there anyway," nor without giving up on the idea that the world (or humanity, or philosophy, or anything else) has an intrinsic nature (an idea that Bouveresse emphatically endorses).[4]

I think that Nietzsche and Foucault were right in saying that truth is always an effect of power, and that it is a waste of time to try to replace power with truth, or "mere" intersubjectivity with "real" objectivity. Rather, we should try to keep power (and, thus, the decision about which intersubjective decisions count) in the hands of us good guys (the people with the social virtues characteristic of most natural scientists and of many analytic philosophers). We should not aim at replacing "social constructs" with something better, but just aim at social constructs that will facilitate the practices of a better (fairer, more just, more open) society than we have now. So I recommend getting rid of correspondence theories of truth and representationalist theories of knowledge. Getting rid of these means rejecting Bouveresse's thesis that "things like matter, mind, the self and whatever have an intrinsic nature that in principle owes nothing to our cognitive activities."

Having said this, however, I still would not want to claim that, as Bouveresse puts it, "the task of philosophy consists principally of linguistic innovation." Linguistic innovation is the task of anyone who happens to have a gift for it, and one of the many advantages of a democratic society is that it gives more people more opportunities for employing that particular gift. Nor do I think that (quoting Bouveresse again) "what ought to be encouraged in philosophy is not the tendency to give and ask for reasons and arguments, but rather an inverse tendency."

Some people – those drawn to analytic philosophy and constitutional law, for example – are good at giving and getting reasons and arguments. Other people – those drawn to literary criticism and "Continental" philosophy, for example – may not be. These two sorts of people are of equal utility to culture in general and to philosophy in particular, at least if philosophy is defined as I would define it, as a continuation of a conversation that began in the Platonic dialogues. Given that definition, one will reject any claim that begins "the task of philosophy is . . ." or "what ought to be encouraged in philosophy is . . ." Free and open conversations take unpredictable directions, swerve in unforeseeable ways for unforeseeable reasons. There is no way to rise above the conversational moment in which one finds oneself, survey the conversation as a whole, and make principled recommendations. The most one can do is say something like: "This segment of the conversation (for example, the French segment or the American segment) is getting a bit boring; it might profit from a little attention to what is going on in another segment."

There is no more reason for pitting the world-disclosing "poetic" philosophers against action-coordinating "scientific" philosophers than there is for pitting construction workers against ballet dancers, or accountants against comedians. The two may not be able to work together, but culture and society will always need to have both on hand. I quite agree with Bouveresse about the silliness of Deleuze's characterization of discussion as a "narcissistic exercise," but I do not think that one need try to delimit what will count as "philosophy" in order to counteract this silliness. Deleuze's attempt to make a theoretical virtue out of a personal preference is just as bad as claims that, for example, nobody can do philosophy who does not know Greek, or who cannot follow Goedel's incompleteness proofs.[5] It is almost as foolish as my own remark (quoted by Bouveresse) about refutation being a mark of lack of originality.[6] To stop ourselves from saying such silly things, we philosophy professors have to keep reminding ourselves that we should not encode a commendation of our own particular skills or habits or preferences (or those of our heroes) in the form of a persuasive redefinition of our discipline.

I turn now to the end of Bouveresse's paper, where he discusses the turn toward Continental ways of thinking in American universities. Here, I think he has a good point; we in the United States should indeed learn from the French experience what can happen when an academic discipline goes sour as a result of attempts to make it relevant to political struggle.

Fifteen years ago, when I found that almost the only other American academics who were reading the Hegel-Nietzsche-Heidegger-Derrida sequence were people who taught literature rather than philosophy, I optimistically assumed that this European cultural tradition would now, at last, be represented in American universities, to everyone's benefit. I foresaw a happy and harmonious division of labor between philosophy departments (which would stay analytic, and continue to neglect both the history of philosophy and Continental philosophy) and other departments (which would take up the resulting curricular slack). That was one of the reasons I switched jobs, moving from the Princeton philosophy department to a nondepartmental job at the University of Virginia (a university that has distinguished departments of literature, and that I thought might be filled with students who would want to learn about the Hegel-Derrida sequence).

I did not foresee what has actually happened: that the popularity of philosophy (under the sobriquet "theory") in our literature departments was merely a transitional stage on the way to the development of what we in America are coming to call "the Academic Left."[7] This new sort of "left" has been called, by Harold Bloom, "the School of Resentment," and the name fits. Its members are typically no more interested in the romance of the Nietzsche-to-Derrida tradition than in that of the Shakespeare-Milton-Wordsworth tradition or the Jefferson-Jackson-Teddy Roosevelt-John F. Kennedy tradition. They prefer resentment to romance. They view themselves as "subverting" such things as "the humanist subject" or "Western technocentrism" or "masculist binary oppositions." They have convinced themselves that by chanting various Derridean or Foucauldian slogans they are fighting for human freedom. They see the study of literature and philosophy *simply* as a means to political ends.

The political uselessness, relative illiteracy, and tiresomely self-congratulatory enthusiasm of this new Academic Left, together with its continual invocation of the names of Derrida and Foucault, have conspired to give these latter thinkers a bad name in the United States. This complicates my own situation, since I have to keep insisting that my admiration for these two men does not extend to an admiration for their disciples, the resentful specialists in subversion. Nevertheless, philosophical colleagues who have remained resolutely analytic often say to me: "See what you've done! You helped smooth the way for these creeps! Aren't you ashamed of yourself?"

I am, I must admit, chastened. But I am not ashamed. I can only repeat once again: *Habent sua fata libelli.* One cannot judge an author or a book by what a particular set of readers do with it. That would be like judging Pasteur by the development of germ warfare, or Aristotle by the Inquisition. There are other things to do with Foucault and Derrida than are currently being done with them by the School of Resentment, just as there are other things to be done with Nietzsche than to use him as the Nazis used him. There is no need to solemnly expel Derrida and Foucault from a temple labeled "philosophy" in order to show one's dislike for the uses to which their work has been put by others. The question of whether they are "really" philosophers is, for all the reasons I have offered above, without interest. The question of whether they provide a "model" for philosophy should be answered by saying: of course they do, and so do Plato, Hobbes, Kierkegaard, Nietzsche, Wittgenstein, and Davidson. There are as many models for participation in the conversation that Plato began as there are past participants. But there is no way to simplify one's life and one's philosophical activity by ascertaining, in *advance* of such participation, who the best models are.

I would not wish to end without thanking Jacques Bouveresse for his very sympathetic, patient, and helpful paper. I am not only flattered by the attention he has paid to my books, but delighted to find someone with whom, despite all our disagreements, I can share so many attitudes, concerns, and experiences. I have rarely read a discussion of one philosopher's work by another that is so clearly aimed at facilitating mutual understanding, as opposed to achieving a dialectical victory. Whatever the vices of the community of analytic philosophers, Bouveresse splendidly exemplifies the virtues of that community.[8]

Notes

1 Bouveresse seems to think that we Anglo-Saxon philosophers are blessedly free from cults of personality. He could not be more wrong. An adequate history of the American philosophical profession in this century would have to take account of many such cults, and of lots of nasty little quarrels about individual and institutional pecking-orders. It is perfectly true that we contemporary Anglo-Saxon philosophers discuss each other's work charitably, sympatheti-

cally, and in detail. But this does not restrain us from spiteful academic politicking, or from spirited attempts to marginalize one another. We're only human, after all.

2 Bouveresse is right that "form of life" is not the right term for a jargon like Heideggerese. 'Idiom' is perhaps better – it means much the same thing as 'jargon,' but without the pejorative implications.

3 See Pascal Engel, "Interpretation with Hermeneutics: A Plea against Ecumenicism,"*Topoi* 10 (1991) 137–46. Engel here criticizes Bjorn Ramberg's attempt (in his excellent book *Davidson's Philosophy of Language*) to bring Davidson and Gadamer together. I agree with some of Engel's points about the dissimilarities between the two thinkers, and disagree with others. But it seems to me that hammering out the similarities and dissimilarities in detail, in the way that Ramberg and Engel do, is very enlightening. Further, I think that Engel is quite wrong in saying that "if the ecumenical enterprise is not backed by a proper willingness to promote, within continental philosophy, the standards and style of analytic philosophy – which are the standards of good professional and serious philosophy – it is of no use trying to create a 'dialogue' between the two traditions, because the very conditions of such a 'dialogue' would simply not exist." I see no reason why Gadamer should have to learn to write like Davidson, rather than Davidson learning to write like Gadamer. Why shouldn't there be give and take – a bit of stylistic loosening-up – on both sides? Surely notions like "the standards of good professional and serious philosophy," by begging all questions, estrange the parties from the outset?

   In his "French and American Philosophical Dispositions" (*Stanford French Review* 15.2 [1991] 177), Engel objects to my description of philosophy as an "ongoing conversation" by saying that this conversation is "bound to be abstract and unrealistic if it is not put into practice within philosophical institutions and if there is no real agreement on the standards of rationality in philosophy." I do not think that there are any such standards except mutual good will – good will that extends to a willingness to master unfamiliar idioms, rather than waiting to have what is said in those idioms translated into one's own.

4 For an account of what I think is wrong with the idea of intrinsicality see my "Holism, Intrinsicality, and the Ambition of Transcendence," edited by Bo Dahlbom in *Dennett and his critics* (Blackwell, 1995).

5 At certain times and places in the history of modern philosophy, the skills valued in graduate students of philosophy were those of the classical philologist. At others, they were those of the mathematical logician. At still others, they were those of the intoxicated revolutionary. At still others, those of the prosecuting attorney. None of these skills seem to me more or less appropriate than any other. "Philosophy" is something so big and diffuse that it can use *all* these skills.

6 My enthusiasm for Derrida carried me away, on this occasion, into fatuity. There have been, of course, plenty of highly original philosophers (Kant, for example) who were terrific at refutation. There have even been highly original philosophers (J. L. Austin, for example) who were not good at much else.

7 For a description of the contemporary American Academic Left, see the final chapters of John Patrick Diggins, *The Rise and Fall of the American Left* (New York: Simon and Schuster, 1992) as well as chapters 1, 3, and 5 of David Bromwich, *Politics by Other Means* (New Haven: Yale University Press, 1992). See also my article "Intellectuals and Politics," *Dissent* (Autumn 1991) and Andrew Ross's reply to my criticisms of him (with my rejoinder) in *Dissent* (Spring 1992).

8 Footnote added in 2000: Since this response to Jacques Bouveresse was written (in 1991) things have changed a bit – both within analytic philosophy and in my understanding of non-analytic philosophy. I offered a slightly different view of the contrast between the two sorts of philosophy in a paper called "Analytic Philosophy and Transformative Philosophy" written in 1998. That paper is forthcoming in *Stanford Humanities Review*. Jacques Bouveresse offered further reflections on this contrast in his inaugural lecture at the College de France, an enlarged version of which appeared as *Le Demande philosophique*; *Que veut la philosophie et*

que peut-on vouloir d'elle? (Paris: Editions l'Eclat, 1996). A view similar to Bouveresse's is offered in Pascal Engel's very intriguing book *La Dispute; introduction à la philosphie analytique* (Paris: Editions de Minuit, 1997) – a book written in the form of a dialogue between representatives of the two philosophical traditions.

8

Vocabularies of Pragmatism: Synthesizing Naturalism and Historicism

ROBERT B. BRANDOM

I

The concept of a *vocabulary* plays a pivotal role in the philosophical world-view – and the vocabulary articulating it – that Rorty has been developing over the past three decades.

His use of this trope has its roots in Quine's critique of attempts by Carnap and other logical positivists to divide the explanatory labor addressed to linguistic practice between *meanings* and *beliefs*. At issue was the Kantian strategy of sharply distinguishing between the activity of *instituting* conceptual norms (fixing meanings) and the activity of *applying* those norms (forming and expressing beliefs). The idea was, first, that it is entirely up to us what we could and would mean by our words – here no 'should' gets a grip, beyond the subjective 'should' that reflects our convenience or arbitrary preference. But, second, once we have committed ourselves in this regard by free stipulation of meanings, the world imposes itself on us, constraining what we should believe, what meaningful sentences we should endorse. For in the context of a settled association of meanings with linguistic expressions, how it is with the things the meanings fix it that we are talking about determines which sentences are objectively *correct*, in the sense of *true*. Our talk is to be explained by factoring it as the product of our free meaning-creating activity and the world's brute, stubborn actuality – again following Kant, what we can know *a priori* because we have *made* it, and what we can know only *a posteriori*, because it can only be *found*.

Quine pointed out that this model overdescribes actual linguistic practice. For we simply do not see sharp differences between changes of meaning and changes of belief of the sort that model predicts. Both on the side of what motivates such changes, and on the side of what follows from them, changes in linguistic practice seem rather to be arrayed along a continuous dimension accordingly as we are more or less sure how to go on, as the norms already in play seem to have a firmer or a looser grip on the case at hand, as we are more or less inclined to say that we are going on in the same way or changing how we do things. We can present this dimension, if we like, at most as having a change-of-belief pole at the less radical end and a change-of-meaning pole at the more radical end. (In much the same way, I want to say, Hegel responded to the Kantian precursor of this positivist explanatory structure by insisting that all our discursive activity can be construed *both* as the application of previously constituted conceptual norms – phenomenal activity – *and* as the institution of new ones – transcendental activity. There is no such thing either as the mere application of a previously determinate conceptual content nor as the institution of a wholly novel conceptual content. Every application of a concept develops its content. More on the significance of this thought later.)

If Quine is right, then we should not commit ourselves to a way of talking about our linguistic practices that distinguishes between languages, as structures of meanings, and theories, as structures of beliefs. 'Vocabulary' is Rorty's suggestion for a successor notion to do the work for which the positivists appealed to those concepts. Thus where before taking Quine's point on board we would have had to distinguish change of language or meaning from change of theory or belief, in Rorty's recommended idiom we can just talk about change of vocabulary. Of course, to say this much is not yet to outline a view, it is only to point to a task: the task of articulating and teaching us how to use the idiom of vocabularies, of exploring its utility for organizing our thinking about our cognitive and practical activity as knowers and agents. A great deal of Rorty's philosophical work can usefully be seen as responding to this challenge. Indeed, I think that one of the major reasons underlying the deep affinity Rorty feels with Davidson's thought is that Davidson is the other major philosopher whose work is oriented in large part by this particular Quinean legacy.

II

Rorty originally came to public prominence as a philosopher (and not coincidentally, to Princeton as it was becoming the premiere department of its time) in the late 1960s, as the author of the first genuinely new response to the traditional mind–body problem that anyone had seen in a long time: eliminative materialism.[1] Just as Nietzsche had o'erleaped the classical alternatives of theism and atheism by suggesting that at one time God did exist, but that he had died – indeed that we had killed him by coming to talk and think differently, without thereby ceasing to be us – Rorty transcended the classical alternatives of materialism and dualism by suggesting that although at one time we did (and still now do) genuinely have minds, we can make sense of changes in our vocabulary that would have the effect of destroying them, so that afterwards we would no longer count as having minds, also without thereby ceasing to be us. The argument, characteristically, grew out of a reading of the history of philosophy informed by a reading of contemporary work. Puzzling over the question of why the mind–body problem becomes urgent for modern philosophy in a way that it was not for ancient philosophy, Rorty came to a new way of thinking about one of Descartes' central innovations: his definition of the mind in *epistemic* terms. Descartes defined the mind in terms of its relation to our knowledge of it; it is what is best known to itself. Indeed, the mental is defined by its *perfect* epistemic accessibility; it is the realm where error and ignorance are impossible – what is happening in one's own mind is exactly whatever one *thinks* is going on. Rorty called this defining epistemic feature 'incorrigibility.'

Adapting some of Sellars' ideas, Rorty construed incorrigibility in *normative* terms as a structure of *authority*, as according some representations a distinctive sort of epistemic *privilege*. And he went on to understand this special sort of normative status in *social* terms: we treat sincere first-person claims about the contemporaneous contents of consciousness as incorrigible by agreeing to count nothing as overriding them, that is, as providing decisive evidence against them. So long as we deploy a vocabulary that accords some reports the status of having the right sort of incorrigibility, we *are* incorrigible and *do* have minds. If, as Rorty further argued, it is coherent to conceive of circumstances in which we alter our vocabulary to allow sincere first-person reports of mental happenings to be overruled, say by the deliverances of cerebroscopes, then by doing so we are conceiving of circumstances in which we would have come not to have minds in the specifically Cartesian sense. Since this process need not affect our capacity to deploy the vocabulary of psychological states about which no-one these days takes us to be incorrigible – beliefs, desires, intentions, and so on – to envisage the loss of mind in this sense need have no impact on our sense of ourselves as intelligent or rational, that is as sapient. Nor need it affect our capacity to understand ourselves as sentient: as sharing that characteristic sort of responsiveness to environing stimuli that we evidently share at least with other mammals – as even the Cartesians admitted, while they still withheld the attribution of genuine mentality to such nondiscursive creatures, on the grounds that they were incapable of knowledge, indeed, of the sort of conceptually articulated judgments of which incorrigible ones form an epistemically limiting case.

This rich and original line of thought is developed in the form of a single sustained argument, each of whose steps involves conceptual moves that are potentially controversial. It has set off significant reverberations in many different quarters, but I do not think we are yet in a position to see to the bottom and assess its significance and success once and for all. One aspect of the argument, which has not been much remarked upon, is, I think, particularly important for understanding the subsequent course of Rorty's intellectual development. For that argument purports to portray a particular case in which a change of vocabulary – from one that accords incorrigibility to some reports to one that does not – brings with it a change in the objects talked about. And the point of the eliminativist alternative is that this change should *not* be assimilated to more familiar cases in which what there is to talk about remains the same, but with a change in vocabulary we stop talking about some bits of it, and start talking about some other bits. The claim is not just that we could stop talking about our minds. The claim is that our having minds in the first place is a function of speaking a vocabulary that incorporates a certain sort of epistemic authority structure. That structure is optional, and speakers of a different sort of idiom simply would not have minds to talk about. If the idea of eliminative materialism is coherent, then we must reconceive the possible relations that vocabularies can stand in to what they enable us to talk about. That is just what Rorty sets out to do.

III

The way of thinking about the relations between vocabularies and the world in which they are deployed that has been standard since Descartes takes *representation* as its master-concept. Beginning with *Philosophy and the Mirror of Nature* (*PMN*) Rorty embarks on an extended investigation of the possibility and advisability of moving beyond that model. The point is not to surrender the idea that vocabularies answer to things that are not vocabularies, but to reconstrue that idea in terms other than the representational. Rorty's development of this line of thought has both a critical and a constructive phase. I think it is useful to see the critique of representational models of vocabularies as centering on a particularly pregnant idea that is implicit already in the work on eliminative materialism: his pragmatism about norms, paradigmatically epistemic ones. By this I mean the thought that any normative matter of epistemic authority or privilege – even the sort of authority exercised on what we say by what we talk about – is ultimately intelligible only in terms of social practices that involve implicitly recognizing or acknowledging such authority. On the constructive side, Rorty began to explore the consequences of replacing the representational model by modeling the use of vocabularies on the use of *tools*. This idea, common to the classical American pragmatists and Wittgenstein, might be called 'instrumental pragmatism.'

The first move in the critique of representationalism about the semantic and epistemic functioning of vocabularies concerns the notion of epistemically *privileged* representations. This takes the form of a brilliant rational reconstruction of what was progressive in American philosophy in the late 1950s and early 1960s, epitomized by the work of Sellars and Quine. Rorty sees those thinkers as spearheading a pragmatist dissolution of neoKantian positivism. For he reads them as undermining the foundationalist picture of justificatory regresses as halted on the side of premises by the pure contribution of the constraining *world* in the form of what is *given* in perception, and as halted on the side of inferences by the pure contribution of the unconstrained *mind* in the form of its chosen *meanings*. The point of attributing special sorts of epistemic authority to the perceptual given and to inferences underwritten by meaning-analytic connections among concepts must, on the pragmatist line, be to explain features of the use of linguistic expressions – the deploying of a vocabulary – in which such authority is acknowledged in practice. But our linguistic practices turn out not to exhibit the sorts of features that would express such implicit acknowledgment: the perceptually given cannot coherently be understood as cognitively significant apart from its role in an inferentially articulated practice of applying empirical concepts, and inferences supposedly underwritten by connections among meanings alone are no more immune to revision in the face of recalcitrant experience than are those evidently underwritten by general matters of fact.

Although Rorty did not put the point just this way, I take it that it is specifically pragmatism about epistemic norms that structures this diagnosis of the conceptual bankruptcy of epistemological foundationalism. The target is philosophical invocations of representations supposed to be epistemically privileged solely by their relations to certain kinds of *things* – perceptible facts and meanings – apart from the role those things play in practices of acknowledging them as authoritative. So regarded, the Sellarsian and Quinean critiques belong in a box with the later Wittgenstein's investigations of the kind of social practical background against which alone items such as sentences, mental images, and consciously framed intentions can be understood as normatively binding on our activity, in the sense of determining what according to them it would be *correct* to go on to do. The real issue concerns what sort of larger practical context we are presupposing when we think of something as (functioning as) a representation. For to treat something as a representation is to treat it as subject to a distinctive sort of normative evaluation as correct or incorrect. One lesson of the rational reconstruction of Sellarsian and Quinean critiques of the notion of intrinsic epistemic authority uncritically relied upon by foundationalist epistemologists is that the idea that the world *by itself*, or a mental act *by itself*, engendering norms determining the correct use of vocabulary is a radical mistake. This lesson is the opening salvo in an assault on the usefulness of the Kantian project of factoring the norms governing our deployments of our vocabularies into those due to the way the world is and those due to the activity of the mind.

The role of this discussion in the larger project of reconceptualizing the constellation of freedom and constraint characteristic of vocabularies was obscured, I think, by its occasioning a series of casually incendiary metaphilosophical speculations about its significance for the shape and future of the discipline of philosophy: that without that Kantian project, philosophy would find itself with nothing to do. This line of thought was always at best tangential to the central philosophical thrust of the argument of *PMN* – a dispensable peripheral frill one could take or leave according to taste without prejudice to the main point. Distracted by all the metaphilosophical dust and dazzle in the air, however, it was all too easy to dismiss the discussion of privileged representations with the observation that semantic representationalism does not, after all, entail epistemological foundationalism, and to console oneself accordingly with the thought that a critique of the latter falls far short of a critique of the former. Indeed it does, but this is the move that opens the argument, not the one with which it closes.

IV

Rorty's master-strategy in the book is to use a Kantian conceptual tool to undermine a (broadly) Kantian representationalist picture. That tool is the distinction between *causal* considerations and *justificatory* considerations. Kant accused his predecessors of running together causal and conceptual issues, largely through insufficient appreciation of the normative character of the 'order and connection of ideas.' It is one thing, he says to Locke, to exhibit the grounds for our ideas or beliefs by saying where they come from, that is, what matter-of-factual processes in fact give rise to them. It is quite another to exhibit grounds for those beliefs by saying what reasons justify them. Rorty appeals to this Kantian distinction to enforce a strict separation between the foreign and domestic affairs of vocabularies. Under the banner "Only a belief can justify another belief" – epitomizing a view he shares with Sellars and Davidson – Rorty insists that inferential or justificatory relations obtain only between items *within* a vocabulary (that is, between different applications of a vocabulary). The relations between applications of a vocabulary and the environing world of things that are not applications of a vocabulary must be understood exclusively in nonnormative causal terms. The application of any empirical vocabulary is indeed constrained by the world in which it occurs, but that constraint should be understood as a kind of causal constraint, not a kind of normative constraint. In a nutshell, this is how I think Rorty's critique of semantic representationalism goes: Normative relations are exclusively intravocabulary. Extravocabulary relations are exclusively causal. Representation purports to be *both* a normative relation, supporting assessments of correctness and incorrectness, *and* a relation between representings within a vocabulary and representeds outside of that vocabulary. Therefore, the representational model of the relation of vocabularies to their environment should be rejected.

For those – evidently not readers of such canonical texts as "Nineteenth Century Idealism and Twentieth Century Textualism" – who are pleased to think of Rorty as a kind of linguistic idealist, burdening him with the worst excesses of some of the literary theorists he has the audacity to write about, it may come as a surprise that his critique of representationalism is founded not on denying or ignoring the causal context in which our talk takes place and to which it ultimately answers, but precisely on a hard-headed insistence and focus upon the significance of that context. What distinguishes his view is rather his claim that the sense in which the talk answers to its environment must be understood *solely* in causal terms, and his determination to follow out the consequences of that claim wherever they lead. Why should one think that? Rorty reads Sellars in "Empiricism and the Philosophy of Mind"[2] as enforcing this point. Failure to observe the sharp distinction between epistemic, inferential, normative relations, on the one hand, and causal ones, on the other, leads to the myth of the given: the idea, most broadly, that some *thing*, a mere occurrence, or process, could by itself have normative (specifically, epistemic) significance, bind us, oblige us, or entitle us to do something. This is the idea I have called pragmatism about norms: only in the context of a set of social practices – within a vocabulary – can anything have authority, induce responsibility, or in general have a normative significance for us. More specifically, the key idea is that justification is an *inferential* affair. What justifies a claim or a belief must be another claim or belief, for only those have the right conceptual shape to serve as premises from which it could be inferred. The world consists of things and their causal relations, and they can only cause and not justify a claim or a belief – cannot make it correct or incorrect.

It might seem that a crucial distinction is being ignored here. It might be acknowledged that a worldly fact could not, by itself anyway, *justify* a claim or belief, and so make it correct in the sense of justificatory entitlement. But it need not follow that the fact could not make a claim or belief correct in the sense of *true*. The representational model, after all, does not purport to tell us about justification (at least, not directly); its claim is that the use of our empirical vocabularies stands in normative semantic relations to the world, in that how things are determines the correctness of our claims in the sense of their truth. This is indeed a point at which some misgivings are warranted, but the distinction in question is not simply being overlooked. Rorty strenuously resists the possibility of the radical decoupling of the concept of truth from practices of justification that is implicitly being put in play at this point.[3] His pragmatism about epistemic norms is not restricted to norms of justification, but extends to the norms invoked in appeals to truth and correctness of representation.

The question is why we shouldn't think of our claims as standing in normative relations to facts, which make them correct or incorrect in the sense of true or false. Rorty rejects the idea of facts as worldly items that make our claims true or false. Once again, this is not because he ignores or denies the existence of everything other than vocabularies. Precisely not. It is rather a consequence of his anti-idealist commitments to the world of causally interacting things that causally constrains our applications of vocabulary not having a conceptual structure. It is because to talk of facts is to talk of something that is conceptually structured, propositionally contentful, something, that is, with the right shape to stand in inferential and hence justificatory relations. And that is a shape something can only be given by a vocabulary. Conceptual norms are creatures of vocabularies: no vocabularies, no conceptual norms. Rorty can explain our talk of facts: to treat a sentence as expressing a fact is just to treat it as true, and to treat a sentence as true is just to endorse it, to make the claim one would make by asserting the sentence. But he rejects the idea of facts as a kind of thing that *makes* claims true. This is why he endorses the argument he sums up as "Since truth is a property of sentences, since sentences are dependent for their existence upon vocabularies, and since vocabularies are made by human beings, so are truths."[4] Before there were humans, there were no truths, so no true claims, so no facts.

Now I think that at this point something has gone wrong with the argument But before saying what, I want to stress that Rorty ends up saying these odd things just because they seem to him to be required in order to secure his prosaic, never-questioned commitment to the existence of a world of causally interacting things that existed before there were vocabularies, that was not in any sense constituted by our vocabulary-mongering, and that goes its way in large part independently of our discursive activity (sometimes regrettably so). I think one can understand facts as true claims, acknowledge that claiming is not intelligible apart from vocabularies, and still insist that there were true claims, and hence facts, before there were vocabularies. For we should distinguish between two senses of 'claim': on the one hand there is the act of claim*ing*, and on the other there is what is claim*ed*. I want to say that facts are true claims in the sense of what is claimed (indeed, of what is claimable), rather than in the sense of true claimings. With this distinction on board, there is nothing wrong with saying that facts *make* claims true – for they make claimings true. This sense of 'makes' should not be puzzling: it is inferential. "John's remark that [*p*] is true because it is a fact that *p*," just tells us that the first clause follows from the second (assuming that the singular term in the first has a referent).

There were no true claimings before there were vocabularies, because there were no claimings at all. But it does not follow that there were no true claimables. In fact, we can show that we ought not to say that. Here is an argument that turns on the grammatical transformations that "It is true that . . ." takes.

Physics tells us that there were photons before there were humans (I read a lot about them in Stephen Weinberg's account of the early history of the universe, *The First Three Minutes*, for instance). So if before time V there were no humans, so no vocabularies, we do not want to deny that

1   There were (at time pre-V) photons.

We can move the tense operator out front, and paraphrase this as:

2   It was the case (at time pre-V) that [there are photons].

By the basic redundancy property of 'true', we can preface this with "It is true that . . .":

3   It is true that [It was the case (at time pre-V) that [there are photons]].

Now we can move the tense operator out to modify the verb in "It is true that . . .":

4   Was [It is true (at time pre-V) that [there are photons]].

This is the key move. It is justified by the observation that *all* sentential operators can be treated this way, as a result of deep features of the redundancy of 'true.' Thus one can transform "It is true that Not [*p*]," into "Not [It is true that *p*]," "It is true that Possibly [*p*]," into "Possibly [It is true that *p*]," and "It is true that Will-be [*p*]," into "Will-be [It is true that *p*]." But now, given how the tense operators work, it is straightforward to derive:

5   It was true (at time pre-V) that [there are photons].

And again invoking the features that make 'true' redundant, we get:

6   It was the case (at time pre-V) that [It is true that [there are photons]].

These uniformities involving the interaction of 'true' with other sentential operators tell us we are committed by our use of those expressions to either deny that there were photons before there were people – which is to deny well-entrenched deliverances of physics – or to admit that there were truths about photons before there were people to formulate them. Taking the latter course is entirely compatible with acknowledging that the notion of a fact (true claimable) is only intelligible relative to that of a vocabulary.[5]

  That old semanticist and modal logician Abraham Lincoln asked "If we agreed to call the tail a 'leg', how many legs would horses have?" His answer was: "Four, because you can't change how many legs horses have by changing the way we use words." This is surely the right response. One cannot change the nonlinguistic facts, in the unloaded sense, by changing linguistic ones. In the counterfactual situation envisaged, the words "Horses have five legs," would be true, but only because it would not say that horses have five legs, and so would not conflict with the fact that horses would still have four legs. When we specify a counterfactual situation and go on to reason about it, our suppositions should not be thought of as altering the meaning of the words we use now to talk about it. The right thing to say using our concept of *photon* is that these things would have been there even if no language users had ever existed to undertake commitments regarding them. For facts are true claims in the sense of what is claim*ed*, not in the sense of claim*ings*. If we had never existed, there would not have been any true claimings, but there would have been facts (truths) going unexpressed, and in *our* situation, in which there *are* claimings, we can say a fair bit about what they would have been.

V

If this is right, then we are not, as Rorty claims, precluded from talking about facts making our claimings true. We can only understand the notion of a fact by telling a story that makes reference to vocabularies – though notice, it is a consequence of the Quinean point with which we began that we can also only understand the notion of a vocabulary as part of a story that includes facts. But this does not entail that there were no facts before there were vocabularies. We can understand those true claimables as (when things go right) making our claimings true. But what about the original point that only beliefs can justify beliefs, and its generalization to the claim that we should only see causal, and not normative relations between the causal order and our applications of vocabularies? This is a complex issue. Here I can only outline some of the considerations that bear on it. The crux of the matter, I think, is to enforce what Sellars calls the 'ing'/'ed' distinction that was invoked in the previous section, now as applied to 'belief.' Subjective idealism of the Berkeleyan sort resulted from failure to observe this distinction with the term 'experience,' thereby underwriting a slide from the true, or at least not obviously false, "All we know is what is experienced ('experience')," to the false "All we know is experiencings ('experience')." Believings can justify other believings, and believables can justify other believables. These two senses of 'justify' are different, but intimately related. (Just *how* they should be understood to be related, and which is more usefully regarded as prior in the order of explanation, are deep and interesting questions.) But can believables (which, if true, are facts) justify believings? To ask that question is to ask whether something that is not the application of a vocabulary can justify (and not merely cause) the application of a vocabulary. This Rorty and Davidson deny.

I want to suggest one way in which one might take issue with the claim that only causal relations, and not also normative relations of justification, ought to be admitted to obtain between items that are not applications of vocabularies and items that are:[6]

(a)   There are facts, that is, conceptually structured truth-makers,

(b)   Applications of vocabulary must answer to those facts in a not strictly causal but also in an inferential-justificatory sense, and

(c)   In a central range of favored cases of perceptual experience, the facts *are* the reasons that entitle perceivers to their empirical beliefs.

I indicated in the previous section how someone who shared Rorty's basic commitments might come to be committed and entitled to (a); (b) is just the denial of the general thesis in question, which distinguishes vocabularies' extramural and intramural relations as causal and normative respectively; (c) then specifies the sense in which justificatory relations are to be discerned in addition to causal ones. I claim that one can maintain all of these consistently with pragmatism about norms (and hence without falling into the myth of the given).

Consider what I am doing when I attribute knowledge to someone. I am first of all attributing a propositionally contentful *commitment* – a taking-true – to the candidate knower. One cannot be taken to know what one does not take to be true. This corresponds to the belief condition on the classical conception of knowledge as justified true belief (the JTB conception). Second, I am attributing some sort of epistemic *entitlement* to that commitment. Unwarranted or merely accidentally correct takings-true do not count as knowledge. This corresponds to the justification condition on the classical conception, though I am purposely using the somewhat broader notion of epistemic entitlement so as not to prejudge the issue (contentious between epistemological internalists and externalists) of whether one can *be* justified in holding a belief without being able to justify the belief). What about the truth condition on knowledge, the demand that the belief correspond to or express a *fact*? In taking the candidate knower's belief to amount to knowledge, I am taking it to be true. That is, I take it to be an expression of a fact: a true claim (in the sense of what is claimed or claimable). Doing that is not *attributing* anything to the knower above and beyond the proposition-ally contentful commitment and epistemic entitlement to it already mentioned. It is doing something else. It is *endorsing* the claim, *undertaking* the commitment myself. The standard of correctness I apply is just correspondence to (in the sense of expression of) the facts as I take them to be. Of course, I may be wrong, as the putative knower may. But the meaning of the truth condition on knowledge, the sense of 'correct' in which the correctness of a belief is being assessed (by contrast to the sense of correctness assessed by attributions of epistemic entitlement), derives ultimately from this comparison between commitments *attributed* to another, and those *undertaken* oneself.[7]

Such a story underwrites assessments of normative relations obtaining between applications of vocabulary – claims that are candidate expressions of knowledge – and facts with respect to which they are true or false. But it does not violate the claims of pragmatism about norms. For the how things are is allowed to have normative significance for the correctness of someone's sayings and believings only in the context of someone else's *attitudes* toward how things are, that is, only as filtered through the takings-true of the one assessing the knowledge-claim. The facts are caught up in social practices by being endorsed by the one attributing knowledge. So there is in this picture no contact between naked, unconceptualized reality and someone's application of concepts. The sort of semantic correctness involved in truth assessments can be made intelligible as comparisons of one application of vocabulary (by the candidate knower) with another (by the one assessing the candidacy). Surely such an account satisfies the scruples that motivate Rorty's rejection of normative word–world relations, in spite of its invocation of facts and its underwriting of talk of 'making-true' and 'correspondence.'

VI

But it is one thing to produce a sanitized notion of the correctness of claims being settled by the facts where 'correct' is understood in the sense of *true*. It is a taller order to produce a corresponding notion of correctness of claims as being settled by the facts, where 'correct' is understood in the sense of *justified*. This is what is at issue in claims (b) and (c) above; it is what Sellars' arguments against the myth of the given in terms of the confusion of non-normative causal with normative inferential–justificatory relations apparently militate against; and it is what the principle that only a belief can justify a belief directly rules out. In fact, the same strategy applied above to domesticate epistemic correctness as truth can be extended to domesticate epistemic correctness as justification or warrant. We can see the facts as standing in normative relations of justification to our claimings as well as in causal relations of triggering them. Indeed, we can see them as standing in the normative relations precisely *because* and insofar as they stand in the causal relations.

Epistemological externalists claim that it can be appropriate to attribute the sort of epistemic entitlement required to distinguish mere true beliefs from true beliefs that amount to knowledge even in cases where the candidate knower cannot offer reasons justifying her belief. A paradigm case is where the belief is in fact, whether the believer knows it or not, the output of a reliable belief-forming mechanism. Thus someone who is being trained to distinguish Toltec from Mayan potsherds by eye may in fact acquire the reliable differential responsive dispositions required for her noninferential reports of Toltec fragments to count as perceptual knowledge before she realizes that she is reliable. She may at that point be inclined to call something Toltec, without being able to give any reason for that inclination. If she is in fact sufficiently reliable in distinguishing Toltec from Mayan bits, reliabilist epistemologists argue that when she is right, she genuinely knows she is looking at a Toltec bit, even though she cannot justify that claim, even by an appeal to her own reliability as a noninferential reporter. After all, beliefs acquired in this way are not merely accidentally true.

This sort of epistemological reliabilism, it seems, is a paradigm case of what Rorty is committed to treat as the mistaking of a causal relation for a justificatory one. For what counts as justifying the reporter's belief (and so qualifying it as knowledge, if it is true) is the merely causal relation of reliable noninferential triggering of response (classification as Toltec) by stimulus (Toltec potsherds). But if we look at things from the point of view of the one *attributing* knowledge (as we did before), this appearance vanishes.

For what I am doing in *taking* the reporter to be reliable, *attributing* reliable differential responsive dispositions to produce noninferential reports, is precisely *endorsing an inference* myself. I am taking it that the inference from 'She is disposed noninferentially to report that the pottery is Toltec' to 'The pottery is (probably) Toltec' is a good one. This is an inference *from* a commitment *attributed* to the reporter *to* a commitment *undertaken* by the attributor. I can treat the report as expressing knowledge even though the reporter cannot offer reasons for it because *I* can offer reasons for it. Although she cannot invoke her reliability, I can – and if I could not, I could not, even by the reliabilist externalists' lights, attribute knowledge. The causal relation can underwrite a justification just because and insofar as those assessing knowledge claims *take* it as making good a kind of *inference*. Non-normative causal relations between worldly facts and someone's claims do not exclude normative epistemic justificatory relations between them, since others can *take* the causal relations *as* reasons for belief, by endorsing reliability inferences. This story about assessments of epistemic entitlement, like the one about truth assessments, is couched entirely in terms of discursive commitments and entitlements. It shows how the difference in social perspective between assessor and assessed can bring relations between the vocabulary and the causal environment in which it is applied within the scope of the vocabulary itself.

I said above that basing the sharp separation of the foreign and domestic relations of vocabularies by distinguishing exclusively causal external relations normative justificatory internal relations, on the principle that only a belief could justify a belief, runs the risk of seeming to ignore the distinction between two sorts of correctness-assessments of beliefs for which the facts might be invoked. To say that a worldly fact could not *justify* a claim or belief, and so make it correct in the sense of justificatory entitlement is not to say that the fact could not make a claim or belief correct in the sense of *true*. I pointed out that Rorty would not accept a radical decoupling of justification and truth – to justify a claim is, after all, to give reasons to think it is *true*. I have now sketched a story about assessments of truth and assessments of reliability (and hence epistemic entitlement) that respects the pragmatism about norms that I see as underlying Rorty's scruples, that does not decouple truth radically from giving and asking for reasons, and that shows how causal relations between applications of vocabulary and the facts to which those applications answer (in both the sense of 'answer' given by assessments of truth and that given by assessments of entitlement or justification) can support conceptually structured inferential relations between facts and claims. This story denies that we must understand the relations between vocabularies and the world they address in exclusively causal terms, restricting normative talk of semantic and epistemic assessment to relations within the vocabulary. At the same time, it accepts a version of the principle that only beliefs can justify (or make true, in the sense of giving inferential grounds for) beliefs. It does so by distinguishing what is believ*ed* (or believ*able*) from believ*ings*, and appealing to the distinction of social perspective between *attributing* commitments and inferences, on the one hand, and *endorsing* commitments and inferences, on the other. Together, these moves let us talk about facts, as true believables, in favored cases both justifying believings and making them true.

I have been urging, in the spirit of friendly amendment, that the scruples that lead Rorty properly to insist that semantic and epistemic, as opposed to causal, relations are intelligible only when thought of as obtaining between relata that all have conceptual shape can be satisfied without our having to deny that our claims answer normatively to the facts – both for their truth and for their justification – as well as being causally conditioned by them. The key is to look more closely at the *social* articulation of our linguistic practices of making and assessing claims, of giving and asking for reasons. However, even if this reconstruction is successful, Rorty may well still think that attempting to tame such dangerous idioms as "truth as correspondence to the facts" and "reliable causal connections providing reasons" is a foolish task to take on: no matter how docile training may seem to have made them, they are always liable to reassert their wild nature and turn on their supposed master. At any rate, the remainder of this discussion will not presuppose the acceptability of these suggestions.

VII

A dualism is a distinction drawn in such a way as to make unintelligible the relation between the two sorts of thing one has distinguished. Rorty distinguishes vocabularies, within which various distinctive sorts of normative assessment are in order, from things like photons and butterflies, which interact with each other only causally. Things of this kind do not *normatively* constrain each others' activities; they are not in the business of obliging and entitling themselves or each other to do things one way rather than another. A distinction of this sort is recognizably central in the thought of figures otherwise as diverse as Kant, Frege, Wittgenstein, and Sellars. Does Rorty's use of 'vocabulary' commit that great foe of dualisms to a dualism of norm and cause? I don't think so. But pursuing the issue opens up some interesting avenues through his thought.

If we take a step back, we can say that there is the *vocabulary* of causes, and there is the *vocabulary* of vocabularies (that is, of implicitly normative discursive practices). What can we say about the relations between them? First of all, they are *different* vocabularies. It may be that all Rorty needs of the Kantian distinction between the order of causation and the order of justification is this fact: these 'orders' are specified in different vocabularies.[8] It would be a mistake to confuse, conflate, or run them together. But they are not just different. For one thing, the vocabulary of causes is a vocabulary. It is something we can discuss in the metavocabulary of vocabularies. We can ask such questions as how the vocabulary of Newtonian causes arose, and how it differs from the vocabulary of Aristotelian causes in the questions it prompts us to ask about ourselves and our activities. Rorty himself often pursues such questions, and thereby affirms his practical commitment to historicism. But developing and applying vocabularies is something that we, natural creatures, do. Our doing of it consists in the production of causally conditioned, causally efficacious performances. That is to say that using vocabularies is one among many other things that is describable in the vocabulary of causes. Rorty never loses sight of this fact. In his insistence on reminding us of the causal relations between our applications of vocabulary and the world in which we apply it, he affirms his practical commitment to naturalism.[9]

The fact that we can use the vocabulary metavocabulary to discuss the causal vocabulary (its emergence, peculiarities, practical virtues and vices, and so on), and the causal metavocabulary to discuss vocabularies (the role of reliable differential responsive dispositions in empirical vocabularies, the practical capacities they enable, and so on) shows that the distinction between the vocabulary of causes and the vocabulary of vocabularies is not drawn in terms that make relations between them unintelligible. So it is not playing the functional expressive role of a dualism. From the point of view of this question, when we have remarked on the complementary perspectives these metavocabularies provide on each other, we have said everything there is to say – at any rate, everything we need to say – about the relations between the two.

Rorty's positive suggestion is that we can make sense of normative evaluations of vocabularies on the model of assessing tools as more or less useful in pursuit of certain *goals* or *purposes*. One of the cardinal benefits he sees stemming from the adoption of the vocabulary of instrumental pragmatism is the *discursive pluralism* that idiom encourages. It makes sense to make normative comparisons of tools once a task is specified. Hammers are better than wrenches for driving nails. But it makes no sense to ask whether hammers or wrenches are better, simply *as tools*. Assessment of tools is always relative to a purpose; to describe something as a tool is only to say that it has a purpose, not to specify some particular purpose. Similarly, Rorty wants to teach us not to ask whether one vocabulary is better than another simply *as a vocabulary*. We can say that the causal vocabulary is the better one to apply if one's purpose is to predict which way one billiard ball will move when struck by another, or to get someone to say "Ouch." And we can say that the vocabulary vocabulary is probably better if we want instead to discuss the relations between Blake's poetry and Wordsworth's.[10]

One of the main indictments of the metavocabulary of representation is that it tempts us to think that we can make sense of the question "Which vocabulary is better as a *representation*?," without having to specify a further purpose.[11] "Mirroring the world" is intelligible as such a purpose only as an element of some larger practical context. The root commitment of the representational metavocabulary as a metavocabulary is the idea that 'representing the world' specifies a purpose that all vocabularies share – or at least a purpose to which they could all be turned, a dimension along which they could all be compared. But insofar as this is true, the purpose in question is devoid of any content common to the motley of vocabularies with which we are familiar. It is an empty formal compliment that can be paid to any set of practices that deserve to be called 'linguistic,' in virtue simply of some performances counting within them as having the significance of assertions. The compliment is empty because promiscuous. It affords no grounds for comparison, for assessments of better and worse.[12] For assertions just are claims about how things are. That is, we derive our practical grip on the notion of 'representing how things are' from our practical mastery of assertion: representing how things are is what we are doing when we make claims.

So Rorty's purpose in introducing the vocabulary vocabulary is not to recommend it as a replacement for or competitor of the causal vocabulary. It is introduced as useful for some purposes, and not for others. It *is* intended to replace the metavocabulary of representations. For that one turns out, Rorty argues, to have outlived its usefulness for the purposes for which philosophers introduced it: understanding how vocabularies work in general (and in particular the relationship between the causal vocabulary of modern physics and the intentional vocabulary of everyday life). My purpose in the remainder of the essay is not further to examine that critical argument, but rather further to explore the instrumental pragmatism Rorty recommends to replace the representationalism of our philosophical fathers.

VIII

If we should think of vocabularies instrumentally, as tools, what should we think of them as tools for doing? The purposes with respect to which we assess vocabularies as better and worse, more and less successful, come in two flavors. For we can think of purposes either as they come into view from the perspective of the *naturalist*, or as they come into view from the perspective of the *historicist*. Vocabularies can be viewed as evolutionary coping strategies. As determinately embodied organisms, we come with interests in survival, adaptation, and reproduction. Vocabularies can be useful tools for pursuing those inbuilt ends – particularly the causal vocabularies that enable prediction and secure control over the natural environment. Broadening the focus somewhat, *whatever* it is that we find ourselves wanting or pursuing – whether rooted in our biology, in the determinate historical circumstances under which we reproduce our social life, or in idiosyncrasies of our individual trajectories through the world – deploying vocabularies can be a useful means for getting what we want. This thought is the lever with which classical American pragmatism sought to move the conceptual world. To think of vocabularies this way is really to think of them in the terms of the metavocabulary of causes (of already describable effects).

But vocabularies can do more than just help us get what we already want. They also make it possible to frame and formulate new ends.[13] Rorty says:

> The Wittgensteinian analogy between vocabularies and tools has one obvious drawback. The craftsman typically knows what job he needs to do before picking or inventing tools with which to do it. By contrast, someone like Galileo, Yeats, or Hegel (a 'poet' in my wide sense of the term – the sense of "one who makes things new") is typically unable to make clear exactly what he wants to do before developing the language in which he succeeds in doing it. His new vocabulary makes possible, for the first time, a formulation of its own purpose.[14]

No nineteenth-century physicist could have the goal of determining whether neutrinos have mass. No ancient Roman governor, however well-intentioned, could resolve to respect the human rights of the individuals over whom he held sway. No medieval poet could set out to show the damage wrought on an individual life by the rigidity of gender roles inscribed by an archetypal family romance. In fact, pragmatism itself is a prime example: Raymond Williams points out that the words 'problem' and 'solution' had only such rare and specialized uses (in mathematics) at the time that they do not even occur in the King James version of the Bible. (Nor, indeed, does 'happiness.') Can we post-Deweyans so much as understand the way of being in the world natural to ones whose personal, professional, and political activities are not structured by the seeing of problems and the seeking of solutions to them?

And as purposes wax, so they wane. No physician can any longer so much as try to isolate the choleric humour in a feverish patient. No statesman can aim, like Metternich, to re-establish recognition of the divine right of kings. And it would be a rare contemporary poet who could adopt Milton's goal and write so as "to justifye the wayes of God to man." A distinctive feature of Rorty's discursive pragmatism is how seriously he takes this historicist point about the role of alterations of vocabulary in altering the purposes accessible to us – both by engendering novel ones and by rendering familiar ones obsolete or irrelevant. To think of vocabularies this way is to think of them in terms of the metavocabulary of vocabularies, rather than the metavocabulary of causes. For to do so is to focus on bringing about new descriptions, rather than new effects.

This insight provides another reason to reject the monolithic representationalist answer to the question: What are vocabularies *for* – that is, what purpose do they serve *as* vocabularies? For the representationalist response is that vocabularies are tools for representing how things always already in any case are. It entails that vocabularies can be partially ordered depending upon whether they do that job better or worse. Such a response is at least intelligible so long as we restrict our attention to the role of vocabularies in pursuing the sort of goals that come into view from the broadly naturalistic perspective. Insofar as the point of vocabularies is conceived as helping us to survive, adapt, reproduce, and secure antecedently specifiable wants and needs, limning the true vocabulary-independent structure of the environment in which we pursue those ends would evidently be helpful. It is much less clear what the representationalist picture has to offer if we broaden our attention to include the role of vocabularies in *changing* what we want, and even what we need. From the historicist perspective, insofar as it makes sense to talk about what all vocabularies are for, simply as such, the answer must give prominent place to the observation that they are for engendering new purposes. This function of vocabularies is simply not addressed by representationalist totalitarianism.[15]

These two sorts of purposes – those that loom largest from the perspective provided by the commitments implicit in the naturalist's preferred vocabulary, and those that loom largest from the perspective provided by the commitments implicit in the historicist's preferred vocabulary – fund structurally different sorts of assessments of more and less successful vocabularies, and consequently structurally different notions of conceptual or discursive *progress*. Assessments of the relative success of various vocabularies at achieving purposes of the first kind are at least in principle available *prospectively*. Assessments of the relative success of vocabularies at achieving purposes of the second kind are in principle only available *retrospectively*.

Interests rooted in fundamental features of our embodiment and activities as social creatures transcend more parochial features of our vocabularies. They put even practitioners of discarded vocabularies in a position to assess with some authority the relative success of different attempts at pursuing them. Thus Aristotle would not, without complete re-education, be able to appreciate much of the conceptual progress we have made in physics since his time. But he would immediately be able to appreciate our greater facility at making large explosions, constructing tall buildings, traveling and transporting cargo by air, and so on. For our techniques are simply and evidently better at doing things he could already perfectly well understand wanting to do – in a way that more accurately measuring the charge on an electron is not something he could already understand wanting to do. We owe the preservation of the bulk of classical Greek philosophy and literature – the repository of their vocabularies – to the admiration of the early Arabs for the practical achievements of Greek medicine. Greek doctors could save warriors from the effects of battlefield wounds and diseases the Arabs knew would otherwise be fatal. That gave them a reason to treasure and translate works of Greek theory that would otherwise have left them unmoved. For the medical practice answered to interests the Arabs shared, while the theory – which the Greeks insisted was inseparable from the practice – answered to interests formulable only in an alien vocabulary. In cases like these, progress in achieving ends can be visible even from the point of view of those speaking a *less* successful vocabulary.

By contrast, the sophisticated interests that are intelligible only as products of particular vocabularies give rise to assessments of success and progress that are essentially available only retrospectively. From the privileged vantage point of (what we take to be) a mature atomic theory of the nature of matter, we can retrospectively discern (indeed, in an important sense, constitute) a progressive path trodden by Democritus, Lucretius, Dalton, and Rutherford, and contrast it with the mistakes of the fans of infinitely divisible cosmic goo. Nineteenth-century realist painters, having won their way clear to the purpose of conveying in a picture exactly the visual information available to an observer from a point of view fixed in space and time could then rewrite the history of art Whiggishly, seeing it as structured by such epoch-making events as the discovery of the laws of perspective; medieval painters would not and could not have seen the later productions as doing better what they were trying to do. Assessments of progress in realism of portrayal are essentially retrospective.[16]

Assessments of technological and theoretical progress are evaluations of the relative success of different vocabularies at achieving a fixed constellation of goals. Such evaluation requires that the goals be specified in some vocabulary. The structural difference I am pointing to reflects the difference between goals that are specifiable in all the vocabularies being evaluated, and those that are specifiable only in a privileged subset – in the limit, in one of them. Naturalistic pragmatism allows vocabularies to be evaluated only with respect to their utility for accomplishing the first sort of end. Historicist pragmatism allows vocabularies to be evaluated also with respect to their utility for accomplishing the second sort of end. Naturalistic pragmatism courts the dangers of reductionism and philistinism – as though we could safely dismiss Romantic poetry by asking what contribution it has made to the adaptability and long term survivability of human beings. Historicist pragmatism courts the dangers of smugness and empty self-satisfaction. For it is far too easy to tell Whiggish retrospective stories, rationally reconstructing one's tradition as a monotonic approach to the pinnacle of one's current vocabulary. We can all too easily imagine our scientific institutions falling into the hands of theological fanatics who can describe in excruciating detail just how the revolutionary change from present day science to their loopy theories represent decisive progress along the essential dimension of pleasingness to God – a purpose unfortunately and pitiably no more available from within the impoverished vocabulary of TwenCen natural science than that of measuring the charge of electrons was from within Aristotle's vocabulary.

Once these two sorts of purposes have been distinguished, it is obviously important to try to say something about how they ought to be understood to be related. It is a central and essential feature of Rorty's developing philosophical vocabulary that it strives to keep both the perspective of the naturalist and the perspective of the historicist fully in view at all times. The reductive naturalist must be reminded that she is leaving out of her story an absolutely crucial *practical* capacity that vocabularies give us: the capacity to frame genuinely novel purposes, and so in a real sense to remake ourselves. The uncritical historicist must be sprung from the dilemma of flabby relativism, on the one hand, and self-satisfied parochialism, on the other, by the reminder that there *are* purposes that transcend vocabularies and permit us to make comparative assessments. The theological fanatics should not be permitted to claim theoretical progress over traditional natural science until and unless that progress can be certified technologically as well. The question is: can they on the basis of their theories both keep the machines running and continue to make the sort of progress at securing common practical ends that would have convinced Aristotle of our greater prowess, and ought to convince contemporary scientists that their successors had indeed made corresponding progress? Pragmatism ought to be seen as comprising complementary vocabularies generated by the perspectives of naturalism and historicism, of common purposes and novel purposes, rather than as restricting itself to one or the other.

IX

One arena in which Rorty explicitly confronts this challenge may seem initially surprising: political theory. A distinctive feature of Rorty's thought is his conviction that adopting a philosophical vocabulary that treats people as incarnated vocabularies[17] has specifically political implications. This shared conviction is one of the deep underpinnings of his identification with Dewey, and a warrant for the assertion of kinship implicit in adopting-and-transforming the tag 'pragmatism,' even in the face of the many important differences between the two thinkers' use of it. Again, this commitment marks a significant point of contact with Habermas. Though both philosophers are quick to insist on the magnitude and import of the issues that divide them, they are each concerned to extract substantive political conclusions from a philosophical investigation of language. It is easy to see how an intellectual whose research as a philosopher has led him to view philosophy as one form of writing among others – distinguished by the vocabularies it has inherited and the texts to which it owes allegiance rather than by a distinctive task or timeless essence – should address himself to its relations to other sorts of literature and criticism. Seeking to situate one's research area in, and develop its significance for the culture more generally is, after all, the distinctive calling of the intellectual as such. It is perhaps more difficult to see how the vocabulary vocabulary could be thought to teach us lessons concerning our relations to institutions that articulate *power*, traditionally distinguished from mere talk. But for Rorty, it is vocabularies all the way down.

Many of the lessons he extracts are critical, by way of ground-clearing: for instance, don't think that the propriety and the utility of the vocabulary of rights, or of obligations, must be grounded in the existence of a distinctive kind of *thing* (rights, obligations), which another vocabulary must be getting wrong, or at least ignoring, insofar as it leads us to speak otherwise. After all, for Rorty mindedness turned out to consist in an authority structure instituted by an optional vocabulary, rather than in an antecedent structure of facts specifiable in a causal vocabulary. But the most basic positive suggestion that Rorty makes in this area is that political wisdom begins with a sharp distinction between the *public* and *private* use of vocabularies.[18] The vocabularies in which we conduct our public business with each other must be shared. They answer to the goals of minimizing cruelty, humiliation, and injustice, and of creating a space in which individuals can pursue their private ends with as little interference from others as is compatible with minimizing cruelty, humiliation, and injustice. Our private vocabularies need not be shared. They answer to the goals of re-creating ourselves individually by redescribing ourselves – transforming our inherited vocabularies in novel and unpredictable ways and pursuing idiosyncratic personal goals that come into view through the medium of those new vocabularies. Aristotle, Locke, Marx, Mill, Dewey, Rawls, and Habermas are theorists, practitioners, and admirers of the kinds of public vocabularies whose job it is to sustain and perfect communities, making possible the formulation and pursuit of shared goals and projects. Thoreau, Kierkegaard, Nietzsche, Baudelaire, Heidegger, Proust, and Nabokov are theorists, practitioners, and admirers of the kinds of private vocabularies whose job it is to transform and perfect individual selves, making possible the formulation and pursuit of novel personal goals and projects. Public vocabularies articulate the norms that govern our answering to each other; private vocabularies articulate the norms that govern our each answering to ourselves.

Rorty sees the distinction between public and private discourse as a special case of the distinction between thought and talk that takes place *within* a stable, shared vocabulary, on the one hand, and thought and talk that transcends such a vocabulary by creating a new, individualized vocabulary, on the other. Community-constitutive acts of forming 'we' intentions, and the giving and asking for reasons that such acts are embedded in, are made possible by the shared norms and commitments implicit in our use of a public vocabulary. Poets and revolutionary scientists break out of their inherited vocabularies to create new ones, as yet undreamed of by their fellows. The creation of novel vocabularies is an activity we can all partake in to one degree or another, but we should recognize the incommensurability of the vocabulary in which we publicly enact our concern for the development of the 'we' and that in which we privately enact our concern for the 'I.' Rorty says:

> There is no way to bring self-creation together with justice at the level of theory. The vocabulary of self-creation is necessarily private, unshared, unsuited to argument. The vocabulary of justice is necessarily public and shared, a medium for argumentative exchange . . .

He recommends that we

> begin to think of the relation between writers on autonomy and writers on justice as being like the relation between two kinds of tools – as little in need of synthesis as are paintbrushes and crowbars. One sort of writer lets us realize that the social virtues are not the only virtues, that some people have actually succeeded in re-creating themselves. We thereby become aware of our own half-articulate need to become a new person, one whom we as yet lack words to describe. The other sort reminds us of the failure of our institutions and practices to live up to the convictions to which we are already committed by the public, shared vocabulary we use in daily life. The one tells us that we need not speak only the language of the tribe, that we may find our own words, that we may have a responsibility to ourselves to find them. The other tells us that that responsibility is not the only one we have. Both are right, but there is no way to make both speak a single language . . .
>   The demands of self-creation and human solidarity [are] equally valid, yet forever incommensurable.[19]

Here the tool metaphor is brought in to make intelligible the practical compatibility of both undertaking the shared commitments implicit in deploying the vocabulary of liberal community and adopting the attitudes of ironic detachment and playful creativity expressed in deploying idiosyncratic vocabularies that bring novel possibilities and purposes into view. These two forms of life are equally near and dear to Rorty's heart, and central to his wider vision of our situation as incarnated vocabularies. We can lead these two lives if we keep a strict separation between the vocabularies of public and private life. The vocabulary that construes vocabularies as tools is Rorty's primary tool for construing that split coherently and nondualistically. For if there is no one thing that vocabularies as vocabularies are *for* – for instance, mirroring nature, representing how the *things*, from which we should read off our responsibilities, really are – then we can simply see tradition-sustaining and tradition-transforming vocabularies as serving different purposes, and hence as not competing.

What more can we say about the relationship between these two discursive aspects of our lives, beyond the observation that they are distinct and do not compete with one another? I think they can be understood as expressions of the two dimensions of pragmatism noted in the previous section: public discourse corresponding to common purposes, and private discourse to novel purposes. The novel vocabularies forged by artists for private consumption make it possible to frame new purposes and plans that can be appreciated only by those initiated into those vocabularies. The re-creation of the individual they enable makes possible a distinctive sort of assessment of success that is essentially retrospective – since prospectively, in the terms of the vocabulary that has been transformed and transcended, one cannot in general so much as understand the ends toward which one's efforts are now bent. By contrast, the overarching goals that structure and orient the public vocabulary Rorty envisages are common to, or at least intelligible in the terms of, a wide variety of vocabularies. Minimizing cruelty is an aim rooted ultimately in our biological encoding of pain as the mark of harm for creatures like us. A baseline or default abhorrence of the infliction of pain on one of *us* (though possibly not on one of those *others*) is accordingly one of the most basic attitudes instituting and sustaining an *us*. And just as pain is the paradigm of felt harm to an essentially biological creature, so is humiliation the paradigm of felt harm to an essentially social one. These are just the sort of vocabulary-transcendent common purpose highlighted by the pragmatist-as-naturalist.

Can the same be said of the other common civic aims that Rorty, as liberal theorist, insists should be basic to our public discourse? On the face of it, the aspiration to *justice*, in the sense that those affected by plans for communal action should have a voice in the deliberation that leads to the adoption of those plans, and the aspiration to *freedom*, in the sense of ensuring to each individual appropriate behavioral and discursive space in which to pursue purely private ends (where that pursuit does not infringe on the corresponding space of others) have a different status. These aims evidently are not shared by inhabitants of all political vocabularies – either historically, or on the contemporary scene. And Rorty is constitutionally suspicious of the heroic efforts of thinkers like Rawls and Habermas (following such models as Locke, Kant, and Hegel) to exhibit commitments to goals like these as always already implicit in giving and asking for reasons in a vocabulary at all. For him, the practical efficacy of appeals to this sort of concern is always relative, not only to our embodiment and social nature, but also to our historical circumstance. That we cannot and need not insist that these considerations can be shown to be pressing from the vantage point provided by *every possible vocabulary* whatsoever is the upshot of the realization of the contingency of the conditions that make even a liberal polity possible. Nonetheless, though the goals of justice and freedom in these minimal senses may not *move* all those to whom we would in our actual circumstances, and with our actual traditions, like to address political claims in a public vocabulary, those goals are evidently *intelligible* to them. The problems posed by the collision of the aims of justice and freedom with the ruthless public pursuit of private interest by an arbitrarily privileged few, whether in Athens or in Washington, is not that the parties to the dispute cannot *understand* one another's goals. They understand each other all too well. The problems are rather practical: the wrong side too often wins. Disagreements of this sort do not belie a shared public vocabulary. (Indeed, a striking feature of contemporary political discourse – and not only in the developed, prosperous part of the world – is the extent to which debates are framed in terms of the opposition between justice and freedom in these minimal senses, on the one hand, and the ruthless public pursuit of private interest by an arbitrarily privileged few, on the other. The disputants just disagree about who is who.)

X

Lining up the public/private split in this way with the two sorts of purposes pragmatists can appeal to – those that are most salient from the perspective of the naturalist, who starts out employing the metavocabulary of causes, and those that are most salient from the perspective of the historicist, who starts out employing the metavocabulary of vocabularies – suggests a way of using the vocabulary vocabulary to conceptualize the complementary relation between these perspectives. For this way of thinking about them emphasizes the divide between routine purposes and novel ones, and hence between shared, tradition-sustaining norms and idiosyncratic, tradition-transforming performances. And the way in which these two presuppose and involve one another is of the essence of specifically *linguistic* practices.

For the characteristic feature distinguishing vocabularies from nondiscursive tools is their function in generating novel claims, and hence novel purposes. Forty years ago Chomsky made the epochal observation that novelty is the rule, rather than the exception, in human languages. In fact, almost every sentence uttered by an adult native speaker is new – not only in the sense that that speaker has never uttered it before, but more surprisingly, also in the sense that *no-one* has ever uttered it before. A relatively few hackneyed sentences may get a lot of play: "Have a nice day," "I'm hungry," "You'll be sorry," and so on. But it is exceptionally unlikely that an unquoted sentence chosen at random from an essay such as this one will ever have been uttered before. Nor is this preponderance of novelty a feature special to the special vocabularies and complex sentences of professor-speak. Even the chit-chat we use to organize routine enterprises in our everyday lives consists largely of strings of words that have never before appeared together in just that order. Almost surely, no-one has ever before said exactly "If it rains, we'll have to take both the baseball equipment and the picnic stuff out of the trunk of the car, because it leaks." That is, even where the sentiment is routine, the expression of it seldom is. (How much more unlikely is it that anyone before Sam Johnson had ever described an acquaintance as "obscurely wise and coarsely kind"!) This phenomenon has been repeatedly confirmed empirically, by searches of large corpora of spoken and written sentences. And it is easily deduced almost from first principles by a comparison of the number of sentences of, say, 20 words or fewer, generated by simple grammatical constructions from the very limited 5,000-word vocabulary of Basic English (readers of this essay probably not only passively understand, but actively use an order of magnitude more English words than that), with the number of sentences there has been time for all human beings to utter in the history of the world, even if they all always spoke nothing but English, and did nothing but utter sentences.

Now some of this novelty is conceptually trivial – a matter of there being many ways to convey (what we want to call) essentially the same thought. But a great deal of it is not. As one moves away from the careless imprecision that can be perfectly in order in casual conversation, either in the direction of literature (with poems as the textual pole defining the dimension I mean to be pointing at) or in the direction of a technical discipline such as metallurgy (with equations couched in the mathematical language of fundamental physics as the textual pole defining that dimension), one finds more and more that to use a different string of words is to say something importantly different. The more specialized the vocabulary, the more likely it is that lexical or syntactic differences carry with them substantial differences in *inferential* behavior, and hence conceptual significance. Far more often than not, the uttering of novel sentences is the making of novel claims. The difference between ordinary and specialized idioms in this regard is only one of degree: intensified, the phenomenon that is already evident in everyday life becomes more striking still in more specialized disciplinary idioms.

Novel claims have novel inferential consequences, are subject to novel challenges, require novel justifications. The game of giving and asking for reasons largely consists in the entertainment of the possibilities for such novel commitments, and the exploration both of their consequences and of what would be required in order to become entitled to them. We spend most of our time on untrodden inferential ground. Although what else a novel claim would commit one to, what it would be incompatible with, and what would entitle one to it must in some sense be *controlled* by shared norms that antecedently govern the concepts one deploys in making such a claim, in the sense that the inferential moves are answerable for their correctness to those norms, it is simply a mistake to think of the antecedent norms as *determining* the process. In exploring the inferential significance of novel claims, we are not simply tracing out paths already determined in advance. For the inferential norms that govern the use of concepts are not handed down to us on tablets from above; they are not guaranteed in advance to be complete or coherent with each other. They are at best constraints that aim us in a direction when assessing novel claims. They neither determine the resultant vector of their interaction, nor are they themselves immune from alteration as a result of the collision of competing claims or inferential commitments that have never before been confronted with one another.

Philosophy proper was born when Plato took as an explicit topic of understanding and explanation the Socratic procedure of exploring, querying, and grooming our concepts by eliciting novel claims and producing novel juxtapositions of commitments his interlocutors were already inclined to undertake so as to expose their potentially incompatible consequences. Socrates showed how it was possible for us to investigate the cotenability, by our *own* lights, of our various commitments, and indeed, of the coherence of concepts we deploy. Engaging in these characteristic exercises in Socratic rationality typically changes our dispositions to endorse claims and make inferences. Where these changes are substantial, the result is a change in the conceptual norms to which one acknowledges allegiance: a change in vocabulary. Such changes can be partially ordered along a dimension that has something that looks like change of meaning at one end, and something that looks like change of belief at the other.

Dummett points to the (now happily archaic) expression 'Boche' as a useful paradigm of inappropriate pejoratives: its circumstances of appropriate application are that someone is of German nationality, and its consequences of application include being barbarous or more prone to cruelty than other Europeans.[20] Using the word, applying the concept, commits one to accepting the propriety of the inference from the circumstances to the consequences of application. If, once Socratic exploration of the inferential and doxastic potential of this concept has made this implicit inferential commitment explicit, one does not endorse that inference, then one must relinquish the concept and refuse to apply the term at all. This is most like a change of meaning – but notice that it is occasioned by confronting that meaning with substantive beliefs, perhaps about the Germany of Bach, Goethe, and Kant. Again, I may be committed to the inference from something's tasting sour to its being an acid, and also to the inference from something's being acid to its turning litmus paper red. If I then run across something that tastes sour and turns litmus paper blue, I have a problem. Whether what I do should count as a change of belief about acids or a change in what

I mean by acid is just not clear. My discovery that not *all* green tractors are made by John Deere, and not *all* red ones by International Harvester presumably belongs pretty close to the change-of-belief end of the spectrum. But as we saw in Section I, the vocabulary vocabulary was originally introduced precisely to express our acknowledgment of the practical inadequacy of the theoretical vocabulary of meaning and belief that committed us to answering one way or the other to the question: change of meaning or change of belief?

So Quine's original point should be developed further. Every claim and inference we make at once sustains and transforms the tradition in which the conceptual norms that govern that process are implicit. The vocabulary vocabulary that replaces meaning-belief talk must incorporate and express our realization that *applying* conceptual norms and *transforming* them are two sides of one coin. (This is the point of Hegel's talk about the "restless negativity of the Concept.") The only practical significance of conceptual norms lies in the role they play in governing the use and application of those concepts, in concert with their fellows. That use consists largely in making novel claims and novel inferences. And doing that leads inexorably to changes, not just in the claims we are disposed to make, but thereby in the concepts themselves. To use a vocabulary is to change it. This is what distinguishes vocabularies from other tools.

I mentioned in the previous section that in employing the vocabulary vocabulary as he does to distinguish the public from the private dimension of our discourse, Rorty is placing himself in a tradition whose most influential contemporary practitioner is Habermas. It is a tradition that pursues a Kantian project with more contemporary tools – a tradition that seeks at least to explicate (and in its stronger versions, which Rorty does not endorse, even to justify) the fundamental commitments of its *political* theory in terms of an account of the specifically *linguistic* practices that structure our discursive activity. The considerations advanced above provide the raw materials for a pragmatist in Rorty's sense to develop this project along lines he has not pursued.

For perhaps the fundamental challenge of traditional (Enlightenment) political philosophy is to explain exactly why it is rational (if it is rational) for an individual to surrender any freedom of action by constraining herself by communal norms.[21] What, it is asked, is in it for her? The most natural answers all seem to justify only the conclusion that it would be in her interest for most or all *others* to do so. But our discussion of what is distinctive of vocabularies as tools – their essential self-transcendence as systems of norms that maintain themselves only by the generation of novelty that transforms them, their status, in short as engines that generate and serve the novel, idiosyncratic purposes highlighted by the historicist, as well as the familiar, common ones highlighted by the naturalist – suggests that things will look different if the communal norms in terms of which we address the challenge are modeled on *linguistic* norms. For when the question "What purpose of the individual would be served by trading away some freedom for constraint by communal norms?" is asked, it has usually been assumed that the purpose in question must be one that is *antecedently* envisageable by the individual: security, access to collective means, the sentimental rewards of engagement in a common enterprise, and so on. This is to view community, with its normative demands on the behavior of individuals, as a tool subserving purposes that come into view from the standpoint of the naturalist.

Linguistic norms are special, in that being *constrained* by them gives us a distinctive sort of *freedom*. Subjecting oneself to linguistic norms by embracing a vocabulary is undeniably a form of constraint. It involves the surrender of what Isaiah Berlin calls negative freedom – that is, freedom *from* constraint. Not just anything one does counts as making a move in the language game. But since it also enables one to make and understand an indefinite number of novel claims, formulate an indefinite number of novel concepts, frame an indefinite number of novel purposes, and so on, subjecting oneself to constraint by the norms implicit in a vocabulary at the same time confers unparaleled positive freedom – that is, freedom *to* do things one could not only not do before, but could not even *want* to do. As Sellars says: "Clearly human beings could dispense with all discourse, though only at the expense of having nothing to say."[22] The point of speaking the common language of the tribe, binding oneself by the shared norms of a public vocabulary, is not limited to the capacity to pursue shared public goals. It consists largely in the private (in the sense of novel and idiosyncratic) uses to which the vocabulary can be put. Not the least of these is the capacity to generate new specialized vocabularies, the way in which private sprouts branch off of the public stem. Likening the point of constraining oneself by political norms to the point of constraining oneself by linguistic norms[23] opens up new theoretical possibilities for a response to the traditional challenge of political philosophy – possibilities that come into view only from the perspective of the historicist pragmatist. This model promises a different way of pursuing what I called in Section III above "the larger project of reconceptualizing the constellation of freedom and constraint characteristic of vocabularies."

I am inclined to extract more specific political claims from this observation by following the model of Kant and Habermas. Doing that is thinking of our moral value – in terms of which the purpose and limitations of political institutions and activities are to be understood – as deriving from our nature as essentially discursive creatures: vocabulary-mongers. What matters about us *morally*, and so ultimately, *politically* is not ultimately to be understood in terms of goals available from the inevitably reductive perspective of the naturalist: paradigmatically the avoidance of mammalian pain. It is the capacity each of us discursive creatures has to say things that no-one else has ever said, things furthermore that would never have been said if we did not say them. It is our capacity to transform the vocabularies in which we live and move and have our being, and so to create new ways of being (for creatures like us). Our moral worth is our dignity as potential contributors to the Conversation. This is what our political institutions have a duty to recognize, secure, and promote. Seen from this point of view, it is a contingent fact about us that physiological agony is such a distraction from sprightly repartee and the production of fruitful novel utterances. But it is a fact, nonetheless. And for that reason pain, and like it various sorts of social and economic deprivation, have a second-hand, but nonetheless genuine, moral significance. And from that moral significance these phenomena inherit political significance. Pragmatist political theory has a place for the concerns of the naturalist, which appear as minimal necessary conditions of access to the Conversation. Intrinsically they have no more moral significance than does the oxygen in the atmosphere, without which, as a similar matter of contingent fact, we also cannot carry on a discussion. What is distinctive of the contemporary phase of pragmatism that Rorty has ushered in, however, is its historicist appreciation of the significance of the special social practices whose purpose it is to create new purposes: *linguistic* practices, what Rorty calls 'vocabularies.' There is no reason that the vocabulary in which we conduct our public political debates and determine the purposes toward which our public political institutions are turned should not incorporate the aspiration to nurture and promote its citizens' vocabulary-transforming private exercises of their vocabularies. The vocabulary vocabulary brings into view the possibility that our overarching *public* purpose should be to ensure that a hundred private flowers blossom, and a hundred novel schools of thought contend.

XI

I have been urging that the public, tradition-sustaining, and the private, tradition-transforming sorts of practices that Rorty discusses are two aspects of all discursive activity, neither intelligible apart from the other. This is to say that we should not think of the distinction between routine speaking of the language of the tribe and creative discursive recreation of the individual – pursuit of old purposes and invention of new purposes – in terms of the distinction between discourse that takes place *within* the boundaries of a vocabulary and discourse that *crosses* those boundaries and enters a new vocabulary. For that way of putting things owes its force to nostalgia for the distinction between deliberating about what we ought to believe, within a set of rules fixed by what we mean, on the one hand, and creating a new set of meanings, on the other. And that is the very picture the vocabulary vocabulary was introduced to overcome. *Every* use of a vocabulary, every application of a concept in making a claim, *both* is answerable to norms implicit in communal practice – its public dimension, apart from which it cannot mean anything (though it can cause something) – *and* transforms those norms by its novelty – its private dimension, apart from which it does not formulate a belief, plan, or purpose worth expressing.

To propose this sort of friendly amendment to Rorty's use of the vocabulary vocabulary is not to deny that it makes sense to talk about different vocabularies: that there is no difference between two conversations being conducted in (and so liable to assessment according to the norms implicit in) some *one* vocabulary, and their being conducted in *different* vocabularies. Although to treat something as a vocabulary is to treat it as a fit object to be *translated* (as to adopt the causal vocabulary is to treat it as fit to be in a distinctive way *explained*), this claim does not entail that any two vocabularies must be intertranslatable. Rorty argues forcefully and to my mind convincingly that any two, as we might call them, *fundamental* vocabularies – autonomous language games that one could play though one played no other, vocabularies in which one pursues the common interests that come into view from the perspective of the naturalist – must be at least largely intertranslatable.[24] But *parasitic* vocabularies need not: the vocabulary of quantum mechanics and the vocabulary Eliot puts in play in "The Wasteland" are not in any recognizable sense intertranslatable. Remarks made or conversations conducted in these idioms simply come from different discourses. The purposes they subserve, the norms they answer to, are internal to those vocabularies; they are of the sort that come into view only from the perspective of the historicist. It makes perfect sense to call such vocabularies 'incommensurable,' if by that we mean just this: they are not intertranslatable, and not evaluable as alternative means to a common end, tools adapted to some one purpose specifiable from outside them both.

It does *not* follow, however, that they are incommensurable in the sense that "there is no way to bring them together at the level of theory," as Rorty claims in one of the passages quoted above in Section IX. That is, it does not follow that they cannot be articulated in some one metavocabulary. I have been arguing that public and private vocabularies are not incommensurable in this sense. To pick two examples not entirely at random: either the causal vocabulary or the vocabulary vocabulary can be used to encompass both sorts of vocabulary. Though one surely does not learn *everything* about them by doing so, one can sensibly discuss the social and economic conditions that causally occasioned and conditioned, say, Wordsworth's poetry or Dalton's atomic theory, and the effects those new vocabularies then had on other things. And we need not see two vocabularies as serving the *same* purposes in order to see them as serving some purposes in the way distinctive of vocabularies. Indeed, one of the cardinal virtues of Rorty's vocabulary vocabulary is precisely that it lets us talk about vocabularies – including both the differences and the intimate relations between their public and their private aspects – in just such a general way.

This claim raises the issue of just what status what I have called the 'vocabulary vocabulary' has for Rorty. The characterization I have offered of the role it is intended to play – as an overarching metavocabulary – may well be one he is inclined to resist. For that way of putting things seems to place this idiom in the context of a sort of metaphysical project that Rorty explicitly and strenuously rejects as a matter of deep methodological and metaphilosophical principle. I would like to close by attempting to resolve this contradiction by the traditional irenic Scholastic method of making a distinction.

Systematic metaphysics is a peculiar literary genre, to be sure. It may be thought of as distinguished by its imperialistic, even totalitarian, discursive ambition. For the task it sets itself is to craft by artifice a vocabulary in which everything can be said. This enterprise can be interpreted in two ways: modestly, or maniacally. On the maniacal reading, the project is to limn the boundaries of the sayable. What cannot be formulated in its preferred vocabulary is to be rejected as nonsensical. Thought of this way, metaphysics has two characteristics that are seen as objectionable from the point of view of the more modest reading. First, it aims at sculpting a vocabulary adequate to what can be said in every possible vocabulary. Second, it arrogates to itself a distinctive sort of privilege: the authority to determine (on the basis of translatability into its favored terms) what is genuinely sayable, and hence thinkable, and what would be sham saying and the mere appearance of thought.

Now it is the first lesson of historicist pragmatism that the notion of "all possible vocabularies" is one to which we can attach no definite meaning. Every new vocabulary brings with it new purposes for vocabularies to serve. These purposes are not in general so much as formulable in the antecedently available vocabularies. They are the paradigm of something that Rorty claims (I suggested at the outset, as a lesson drawn from his eliminative materialism) we should not think of as part of the furniture of the world patiently awaiting our discovery of them, but as genuinely *created* by our new ways of speaking. As such, there is no way to throw our semantic net over them *in advance* of developing the languages in which they can be expressed. Further, to be a pragmatist about norms is to insist that every claim to authority or privilege be grounded in concrete practices of articulating and acknowledging that authority or privilege – that no normative status at all is conferred simply by *things*, not even by the whole universe, apart from their uptake into and role in some determinate vocabulary. That principle, rooted in Sellars' critique of the ideology of givenness, expands for Rorty into a view of metaphysics (in the maniacal sense) as the pursuit of theology by other means. He has relentlessly pointed out how pervasive are metaphysical claims that some vocabulary possesses a special sort of cognitive authority stemming from ontology alone.

On the modest reading of metaphysics, by contrast, the task of this genre of creative nonfiction writing is still understood as the engineering of a vocabulary in which everything can be said. But, first of all, the quantifier is understood differently. The modest metaphysician aims only to codify the admittedly contingent constellation of vocabularies with which her time (and those that led up to it) happens to present her – to capture her time in thought. She sees her task as that of constructing a vocabulary that will be useful for the purposes of the contemporary intellectual: the one who by definition is concerned with seeing the culture whole, trying to make the vocabularies it now seems useful to employ to get various sorts of practical grips on things hang together. As Rorty has pointed out in another connection, one should distinguish the enterprise of such intellectuals from the enterprise of various sorts of researchers, who work within definite disciplinary matrices, pushing back the frontiers of their particular portion of the culture, without in general needing to be concerned with how their area relates to the rest. The special research interest of the metaphysician, I am suggesting, is to build vocabularies useful for the purposes of intellectuals. The only authority such vocabularies can claim is derived from the success of the various vocabularies they address, and the illumination it can provide concerning them. Insofar as there are vocabularies that are practically successful but not codifiable in a particular metaphysical vocabulary, it has failed. And here the measure of success is not only achievement of the sort of goals to which the naturalist draws our attention, but also of those to which the historicist does. But the sortings of vocabularies into those that fit smoothly into the regimented form and those that fit less well can still be valuable. In the past such reorganizations have taught us a lot, even in cases where the metaphysical vocabulary generating those sortings patently fails to fulfill its imperialist ambitions. Once the metaphysician renounces the adoption of an exclusionary or dismissive attitude toward non-conforming vocabularies, the project of metaphysics modestly understood represents one potentially useful discursive tool among others for getting a grip on our multifarious culture. This is not an enterprise that the enlightened pragmatist ought to resist. Indeed, I have been claiming that that is precisely the enterprise on which the most prominent and accomplished such pragmatist has in fact been successfully embarked for the past three decades.

Notes

1 This terminology has since been kidnapped (shades of Peirce's complaints about James) and pressed into service as the label for a distinct position it inspired – one that addresses propositional attitudes such as beliefs and desires, rather than the occurrent mental events that were Rorty's target. Although the later pretender to the title is also an interesting philosophical position, and although both trace their ancestries in significant ways to Sellars, the confusion that inevitably results from the adoption of this terminology is a shame. One of its effects, I think, has been to distract attention from the most interesting issues about the relations between vocabularies and what they are about that Rorty's version raises. For those issues are raised precisely by the radical suggestion that materialism could *become* true upon our changing our vocabulary in determinate ways. Those issues do not arise for the successor notion of eliminative materialism about beliefs and desires. For if that view is correct, materialism was *always* true – what a change in vocabulary gets us is *only* a change from a worse to a better vocabulary, given how things always already were.

2 Reprinted in *Science, Perception, and Reality* (Routledge, Kegan, Paul, 1963).

3 This is a theme that Putnam has been much concerned to develop, and a deep point of affinity between these two thinkers – though it would take us too far afield to pursue the point here.

4 *Contingency, Irony, and Solidarity* (Cambridge University Press, 1989 – hereafter *CIS*),

p. 21. See also "Pragmatism, Davidson, and Truth," reprinted in *Objectivity, Relativism, and Truth* (Cambridge University Press, 1991), pp. 126–150. Davidson (I think injudiciously) also says things like this in his Dewey lectures on truth.

5   I explain in detail how I think this story goes in *Making It Explicit* (Harvard University Press, 1994), hereafter *MIE*.

6   One of the central tasks McDowell sets himself in the opening chapters of his pathbreaking book, *Mind and World*, is to take issue with this claim in a far more radical way than I sketch here. McDowell, like Sellars, is an *internalist* about justification: to *be* justified one must be *able* to justify, to offer reasons oneself for one's beliefs. The view I am sketching attempts to split the difference between this sort of internalism and the sort of justificatory externalism of which epistemological reliabilism is a paradigm. He and I explore some of these issues (as well as what is involved in not decoupling truth and justification) in his "Knowledge and the Internal" and my "Knowledge and the Social Articulation of the Space of Reasons," both in *Philosophy and Phenomenological Research* (December, 1995). McDowell and I are both concerned, as Rorty is, to avoid the myth of the given, and to abide by the larger lessons Sellars' discussion of it teaches.

7   It does *not* follow from this claim that 'true' just means 'whatever I believe.' It evidently does not mean that, or I couldn't wonder about whether all my beliefs are true. It takes a bit of work to develop the view forwarded in the text so as to avoid commitment to such an unwelcome consequence. I show how this can be done in *MIE*, especially chapters 5 and 8. These discussions culminate in the *objectivity proofs* (pp. 601–607) which show that the view does not identify the facts with anyone's commitments or dispositions to apply vocabulary – not with mine, not with all of ours, not with those of any ideal community.

8   If we were to try to be even a little more careful about pinning this general distinction on Kant, we would have to acknowledge that causation is itself a thoroughly normative (rule-governed) affair for Kant – indeed, explaining the significance of this fact is an absolutely central task of the first *Critique*. But the distinction between things that act only according to rules and things that act according to conceptions or representations of laws, the realm of nature and the realm of freedom, will do pretty well. Rorty sometimes (e.g., in "The World Well Lost") distinguishes these two by saying that what it is for us in practice to *treat* something as belonging to the first realm, is to see its antics as fit to be *explained* (which is the cash-value of adopting the causal vocabulary), while to treat something as belonging to the second realm is to see its antics as fit to be *translated* (which is the cash-value of adopting the vocabulary vocabulary).

9   Recall Rorty's observation in *Philosophy and the Mirror of Nature* (Princeton University Press, 1979, pp. 166–7) that near the end of the nineteenth century philosophy was left with two approaches, historicism and naturalism, neither of which gave philosophical understanding any special dispensation. Russell and Husserl, each in his own way, responded to this situation by coming up with something for philosophy to be apodeictic about in the Kantian manner. It has taken us the better part of a century to see through their fascinating fantasies, and work our way back to historicism and naturalism.

10   Though that is not to say that causal vocabularies are useless in this case, since we can learn a lot about the vocabularies of these poets by studying the social and political influences to which they were subject, the effects of their early familial experiences, and so on.

11   See for instance, the discussion that culminates at *CIS*, p. 21.

12   Of course, to say this is not to say that there is no point in coming up with some more limited theoretical notion of representation of things that applies to some vocabularies and not others, specifying a more specific purpose to which some but not all can be turned. But such a notion is not Rorty's target, for it does not aspire to being a metavocabulary – a vocabulary for talking about all vocabularies, the essence of what being a vocabulary is.

13   Of course, the development of nonlinguistic tools can also make new purposes possible, though it is seldom possible to separate this phenomenon firmly from the discursive context in which it takes place.

14 *CIS*, pp. 12–13.

15 Notice that this point is independent of, and less radical than, the lesson I suggested at the outset Rorty learned from his treatment of the mind in terms of incorrigibility. That case is different from the engendering of new (and obsolescing of old) *purposes*, since it purports to show how *representeds* can be brought into and out of existence by changes in vocabulary. It would accordingly be an even more extreme variety of alteration that could be wrought by changes in vocabulary. In Rorty's view, for us to have minds just is for us to use vocabulary that incorporates a certain structure of authority.

16 I'm waving my hands here at the story Gombrich tells in his magisterial *Art and Illusion: a study in the psychology of pictorial presentation* (E.H. Gombrich: Phaidon, London, 1968).

17 "Private Irony and Liberal Hope", in *CIS*.

18 It should be clear throughout the discussion that Rorty's talk of 'private' uses of vocabulary does not fall foul of the considerations advanced in Wittgenstein's arguments against the intelligibility of private languages. Rorty's private vocabularies are private only relatively and *de facto*, not absolutely, or *de jure*.

19 *CIS*, pp. xiv–xv.

20 Michael Dummett, *Frege's Philosophy of Language* (Harper & Row, 1973) p. 454. See also the related discussion in Chapter Two of *MIE*.

21 Of course the terms of this question are infinitely contentious. They remain so even when it is not taken to presuppose that this is an issue anyone ever actually faces, but merely a hypothetical whose answer can illuminate the normative status of political institutions. It is not obvious that the validity of political claims depends on their being an answer to any question analogous to this one. It is not clear why it should be norms of *rationality* that are taken to undergird political norms (though that is the thought of those who adopt the strong version of the Kantian tradition I am discussing). Nor, even supposing that, does it go without saying that the rational norms in question should be assimilated to the model of *instrumental* or means-end reasoning (though that is an orienting commitment of the pragmatist tradition that Rorty shares with Dewey). Again, the idea that the default position is one in which individuals possess maximal freedom of action, their surrendering, relinquishing, or renouncing of which deserves to be classified either as recompensed or unrecompensed presupposes a very specific Enlightenment picture of the human situation – one that we ought to be chary of root and branch. All these challenges I think are well taken. Nonetheless, it is instructive to see how the considerations assembled above permit a novel response to the question of the nature of the authority of political norms even in the broad classical form in which not only Hobbes but Kant can be seen to be addressing it.

22 In "A Semantical Solution to the Mind–Body Problem," reprinted in *Pure Pragmatism and Possible Worlds*, ed. Jeffrey F. Sicha (Ridgeview, 1980).

23 As before (see note 21) we need not think it is so much as coherent to conceive of this as a choice anyone ever actually confronts – no nonlinguistic creature would be in a position to weigh the various considerations. But – as was pointed out above in discussing the perspective of the historicist – that does not mean that the costs and benefits of such a 'decision' cannot sensibly be assessed *retrospectively*, from the point of view of someone who can frame the purposes that only become available along one path.

24 In "The World Well Lost", reprinted in *Consequences of Pragmatism* (University of Minnesota Press, 1982).

RESPONSE TO ROBERT BRANDOM

I shall first respond to what Brandom says in the sections of his paper about which I have doubts – sections IV–VI, in which he tries to rehabilitate the notion of "fact" by treating facts as true claimables. Then I shall try to enlarge and develop what he says in various other sections, sections with which I am in enthusiastic agreement.

Brandom says that I "strenuously resist the possibility of radical decoupling of truth from practices of justification" (p. 161). I used to resist this, until Davidson showed me how to render the decoupling harmless by making "true" unanalyzable. But Davidson's strategy depends on getting rid of facts. Since "truths" and "facts" are pretty nearly equivalent notions, I think it important to get rid of both. So I still want to defend the claim that there were no truths before human beings began using language: for all true sentences S, it was true back then that S, but there were no "wordly items" – no facts, no truths – of the sort Brandom believes in.

I think that the claim that "If we had never existed . . . there would have been facts (truths) going unexpressed" (p. 163) is at odds with the another claim Brandom makes: that "the notion of a fact (true claimable) is only intelligible relative to that of a vocabulary" (p. 163). Brandom denies that the second claim makes trouble for the first. He thinks I have no good reason to "reject the idea of facts as worldly items that make our claims true or false" (p. 163).

Brandom's strategy of treating truths, and facts, as true claimables, seems to me like saying that the rules of baseball were there, but unexpressed, before baseball was played. To be sure, it is true now, and was always true, that a regulation baseball is covered in horsehide. So if, during the first three seconds of the universe's existence, there had been a regulation baseball around, it would indeed have been covered in horsehide. In that sense, there were true claim*ables* way back then, just as there were possible regulation baseballs. In the sense in which there were baseball games going unplayed at the dawn of creation, I would agree that there were, as Brandom says, "facts (truths) going unexpressed" (p. 163). Possibilities, dispositions, and potentialities are cheap.

But worldly items are more expensive. A possible true claiming is not the same thing as, in Brandom's words, a "worldly item" which can make claims true – a *true claimable*. Possibilities are not worldly enough to *do* anything. At pp. 162ff., Brandom offers an demonstration that we "we ought not to say" that "there were no true claimables before there were vocabularies." But we would not need to have this demonstrated to us if "S was an unexpressed true claimable at pre-V" were equivalent to "'S' was true at pre-V." For anybody who believes that all true standing sentences (sentences containing no indexicals) have always been true and always will be is going to admit cheerfully that, if *that's* all it takes there to have been those true claimables, then indeed there have always been plenty of them around. But we shall still dig in our heels when told that those unexpressed true claimables (those facts, those truths) *do* anything – for instance, that they make claims true.

Since he believes that he has a controversial thesis to demonstrate, Brandom must believe that "S was an unexpressed true claimable at pre-V" *adds* something to "'S' was true at pre-V." The only way I can think of to explicate the purported extra is to attribute to Brandom the view that

(P)   The unexpressed true claimable S cannot exist at t unless the entities referred to in "S" exist at t.

But (P) seems to entail a view Russell once held: that Xs are ingredients of facts about Xs. I doubt that Brandom agrees with Russell on this point.

Notice that we cannot take advantage of the fact that Brandom's example is an existence-proposition to substitute the following for (P)

(P′)   The unexpressed true claimable *Xs exist at t* cannot exist at *t* unless Xs exist at *t*.

P′ is obviously true, but it can play no role in Brandom's demonstration of the existence of a debatable set of worldy items. Unlike (P) it does not even look like a claim about worldly items. It is obviously just a fancy way of saying, pointlessly, that it would not have been the case at *t* that Xs existed if Xs had not existed at *t*.

Prima facie, it would seem difficult to milk a demonstration of the existence of controversial worldly items out of what Brandom calls "deep features of the redundancy of 'true'" – the features illustrated by his six-step argument about protons. Even after going over it many times, I still do not see that that argument gives him what he needs. The argument seems to me leave the debate about whether (*pace* Davidson and I) to talk about "facts making our claimings true" pretty much where it was.

Heidegger, appreciating the point on which Brandom and I agree – that "the notion of a fact (true claimable) is only intelligible relative to that of a vocabulary" – inferred that before Newton formulated them, Newton's laws were neither true nor false. I once tried to defend Heidegger's audacity, but my defense went over like a lead balloon.[1] So I have resigned myself to intuiting, like everybody else, that a true sentence was true before anybody thought it up. But I cannot resign myself to intuiting that "facts *make* claims true – for they make claimings true" (p. 162).

Brandom says soothingly that "This sense of 'makes' should not be puzzling. It is inferential. 'John's remark that [p] is true because it is a fact that *p*' just tells us that the first clause follows from the second." Well, it is no more or less puzzling that the sense of 'makes' in "Its dormitive power makes opium put people to sleep." A true claimable makes a claim true, in the specified inferential sense. A dormitive power makes a substance put people to sleep, in the inferential sense that "Taking it tends to put people to sleep" follows from "It has a dormitive power."

Why am I so intent on resisting Brandom's attempt to reconcile the fact that facts are intelligible only relative to vocabularies with un-Davidsonian notions like "making-true" and "correspondence"? Because I think that nobody would have had a use for this cluster of notions unless they had a conception of beliefs cutting reality at joints which are not relative to vocabularies – which are Nature's Own, owing nothing to the human needs and interests which led us to dream up photon-talk and baseball-talk. Without this cutting-at-the-joints imagery, nobody would ever have suggested that true beliefs were accurate representations of reality.

I have offered three arguments against this last suggestion.[2] The first argument is that there is no test for whether a belief accurately represents reality except justification of the belief in the terms provided by the relevant community. So Occam's Razor suggests that we skip the representing and just stick to the justifying. The second argument is that the story of biological evolution is helpless to explicate the coping–representing distinction, helpless to say when organisms stopped coping and began copying. In the light of these arguments, we should give up thinking of beliefs as representations. We should think of vocabularies as tools for coping rather than media for copying.

But without representations, the notion of "fact" becomes useless, and misleading. It is misleading because it suggests that our better vocabularies cut at the joints, and our less good vocabularies gerrymander. This suggestion provokes attempts to divide culture into the good fact-finding parts and the less good non-fact-finding parts, the "objective knowledge" part and the other part. The evil consequences of such attempts provide a third argument for following Davidson rather than Brandom: for rejecting the ideas of "representation," "correspondence," and "making true."

Brandom might reply to my third argument, however, by saying that facts as truth-makers, and joints in nature, are harmless if there are enough of them to, so to speak, factualize *every* area of culture. He could argue that the unfortunate consequences of the invidious scientism which I decry (for instance, in my "Response to Dennett," above) can be avoided if one stipulates that *all* true claimables – those about comparative aesthetic worth and about investment opportunities as well as those about baseball and photons – are made true by facts, represent reality accurately, cut nature at the joints, etc.

Brandom might then go on to deal with my first argument by saying that although there is indeed no test for accuracy of representation of reality other than justifiability to a community of inquirers, Ockham's Razor is not a good enough reason to give up a perfectly respectable idiom. Who's afraid of Molière? Why *not* say, that opium's dormitive power makes it put people to sleep, and that the fact that *p* makes 'p' true, without having to give independent tests for the maker and the made?

He could deal with my second argument by saying that the sought-for divide between coping and copying, in the process of biological evolution, is simply the emergence of languages. We can give a good naturalistic account of how languages came into existence as coping devices. If we want to say that linguistic tools cope by copying, no harm is done, and common sense is assuaged.

If Brandom takes the line I have just suggested, most of the differences between us are resolved. The two of us can join forces against those who say that physics represents facts and literary criticism doesn't. We can agree that the only difference between the two fields is sociological – a matter of, for example, the amount of controversy concerning various purported facts. We can say that every area of culture is doing its best to represent reality accurately, cut nature at the joints, and so on. We can say that the interesting question is not "Knowledge or opinion? Objective or subjective?" but rather "Useful vocabulary or relatively useless vocabulary?" We could agree to differ about the extent to which it is prudent to assuage common sense.

But a new disagreement would break out between us if Brandom continued to say that "in a central range of perceptual experience, the facts *are* the reasons that entitle perceivers to their empirical beliefs" (p. 164). I find this shocking, especially when put forward by a fellow Sellars-fan. I had assumed that we Sellarsians all agreed with Armstrong, Pitcher, Dennett, et al., that perceptual experience was simply a matter of physiological events triggering a disposition to utter various non-inferential reports. We all agreed, I thought, that Wittgenstein was right to reply to the question "How do you know that that is red?" with "I know English." To answer "My reason is that fact that it *is* red" would be ludicrous.

I agree with Brandom that, in the case of the reliable Toltec-potsherd-discriminator, there would be nothing wrong with saying that she knows a Toltec potsherd when she sees one, whether she knows that this is the case or not (pp. 165–6). I also agree that what I am doing when I take her to be reliable is endorsing the inference from "She is disposed noninferentially to report that the pottery is Toltec" to "The pottery is (probably) Toltec." I can even agree that "the causal relation can *underwrite* [my emphasis] a justification because and insofar as those assessing knowledge claims *take* it as making good a kind of inference" (p. 166). But that still seems a long way from saying that "the facts are the reasons."

Brandom thinks that this gap can be spanned even if we continue to believe "that only beliefs can justify (or make true, in the sense of giving inferential grounds for) beliefs". For we can

> distinguish between what is believed (or believ*able*) from believ*ings*) and appeal to the distinction of social perspective between *attributing* commitments and inferences, on the one hand, and *endorsing* commimtments and inferences, on the other. Together, these moves let us talk about facts, as true believables, in favored cases both justifying believings and making them true. (p. 166)

I cannot see, however, why one would want to go from

(A)   I use my knowledge of S's reliability to infer from her report to the truth of her claim.

to

(B)   The fact (the truth of her claim) of her claim justifies her in making the claim.

I should have thought that, until she learns that others take her to be reliable, she is no more *justified* in making the claim than the Geiger counter is *justified* in buzzing.

Brandom presciently says that

> Rorty may well still think that attempting to tame such dangerous idioms as "truth as correspondence to the facts" and "reliable causal connections providing reasons" is a foolish task to take on: no matter how docile training may seem to have made them, they are always liable to reassert their wild nature and turn on their supposed master. (p. 167)

Something like that is, indeed, my reaction to sections IV–VI of Brandom's paper. My fear is that countenancing these dangerous idioms will be taken as a concession by the bad guys: the people who still use perceptual experience as a model for "hard facts," and who think that photon-talk is somehow harder than talk about comparative aesthetic worth.

These bad guys are the people I think of as "authoritarians." These guys do not agree with Brandom and myself that increased freedom and richness of the Conversation is the aim of inquiry, but instead think that there is the further aim of getting Reality right (as opposed to getting, for instance, snow, photons, baseball, Cezanne and the best use of the term "fact" right).[3]

****

So much for my reservations about sections IV–VI of Brandom's paper. I have no reservations about his "friendly amendment to Rorty's use of the vocabulary vocabulary" – his claim that

> *Every* use of a vocabulary, every application of a concept in making a claim, *both* is answerable to norms implicit in communal practice – its public dimension, apart from which it cannot mean anything (though it can cause something) – *and* transforms these

norms by its novelty – its private dimension, apart from which it does not formulate a belief, plan, or purpose worth expressing. (p. 179)

Brandom encapsulates this claim in the remark "To use a vocabulary is to change it. This is what distinguishes vocabularies from other tools" (p. 177).

That way of putting it is a neat way of restating part of what Dewey had in mind when he talked about "the means–end continuum." Dewey's point was that it is no easier to draw a neat line between what you want and how you will go about getting it than between the meaning of a word and the beliefs you express with its aid. The more you learn about what it takes to get what you want, the more you may want something slightly different; the more we use a word, the more the dictionary is likely to define that word slightly differently in the next edition.

Examples of both sorts of plasticity lie near at hand. I did not quite realize, until I read Brandom's paper, either that I had adopted a vocabulary vocabulary, or that I was putting it forward as a replacement for the metavocabulary of representations (p. 168). But now that I have learned this I mean something slightly different by "vocabulary" than I did before. My philosophical aims have been slightly altered by having been given a better grip on the tool I have been using to achieve them.[4]

As a result of this alteration, I now think Brandom is right that

we should not think of the distinction between routine speaking of the language of the tribe and creative discursive recreation of the individual . . . in terms of the distinction between discourse that takes place *within* the boundaries of a vocabulary and discourse that crosses those boundaries and enters a new vocabulary. (p. 179)

He is also right that I have been in danger of over-romanticizing novelty by suggesting that great geniuses can just create a new vocabulary *ex nihilo*. I should be content to admit that geniuses can never do more than invent some variations on old themes, give the language of the tribe a few new twists. This admission is compatible with saying we should be profoundly grateful to, for example, Galileo, Yeats and Hegel.

As a further result, I can now boast, with the aid of hindsight, that I have tried to discourage people from asking "whether one vocabulary is better than another simply *as a vocabulary*" (p. 168). I can tie this in, as Brandom does, with my campaign against authoritarianism (one version of which is what Brandom calls "representationalist totalitarianism" (p. 170)). As he says, representationalism leads us to neglect "the role of vocabularies in *changing* what we want and even what we need" (p. 170). Brandom sums up the point of this campaign when he says that "assessments of progress in realism of portrayal are essentially retrospective" (p. 171). (This point ties in with my claim, in "Response to Habermas," that inquiry should be motivated by fear of regression rather than by the hope of reaching the ideal.)

I have sometimes tried to sum up my views on these matters by saying that Freedom is more important than Truth: that it is better to regard inquiry as enlarging our imagination, and thus our alternatives, than to think of it as getting more and more things right. It does, as I admit below in "Response to Ramberg", get things like snow and photons and baseball right. But getting things right is to the point of human life what shooting straight is to the pursuit of happiness. Both are very useful, but they are only means to an ever-changing end. Plato's nerdy conviction that the point of our existence is getting things right *more geometrico* was as blinkered as Achilles' conviction that the point is victory in battle.

Talk of the point of human existence will always be an expression of admiration for the talker's own gifts, or for his own heroes. My own talk on this topic is an expression of admiration for Romanticism, and in particular for the form this movement takes in the best book written by one of my earliest heroes – Hegel's *Phenomenology of Spirit*. Brandom is equally in awe of that book, and so the two of us agree that the point of human life is

> to make and understand an indefinite number of novel claims, frame an indefinite number of novel purposes, and so on, subjecting oneself to constraint by the norms implicit in a vocabulary [which] at the same time confers unparaleled positive freedom – that is, freedom *to* do things one could not only not do before, but could not even *want* to do" (p. 178).

Brandom is a fellow-historicist and fellow-Romantic as well as a fellow-naturalist. I agree with him that

> what matters about us *morally* and so ultimately, *politically*, is not ultimately to be understood in terms of goals available from the inevitably reductive perspective of the naturalist: paradigmatically the avoidance of mammalian pain. It is the capacity each of us discursive creatures has to say things that no one else has ever said, things furthermore that would never have been said if we did not say them . . . Our moral worth is our dignity as potential contributors to the Conversation (p. 178).

In such passages as this, Brandom leaves himself open to the same accusations of pseudo-aristocratic condescension and ivory-tower aestheticism as are frequently leveled at me. He courts them when he sympathizes with my suggestion that "our overarching public purpose should be to ensure that a hundred private flowers blossom" (pp. 178–9). He courts them again when he goes on to say that "pain, and like it various sorts of social and economic deprivation, have a second-hand, but nonetheless genuine, moral significance" (p. 178).

I think that it is worth subjecting oneself to such accusations to insist on this point. "Representationalist totalitarianism," and attempts to claim "that some vocabularies possess a special sort of cognitive authority stemming from ontology alone" (p. 180), are bolstered by the idea that pain is our best example of contact with reality. This idea, in turn, is supported by saying, correctly, that our most pressing moral duty is to relieve the social and economic deprivation which fills so many human lives with unnecessary pain. But if asked why that is our duty, I think the best answer is that we want everybody to be able to lead a specifically human life: a life in which there is a chance to compose one's own variations on old themes, to put one's own twist on old words, to change a vocabulary by using it. *Brave New World* – still the best introduction to political philosophy – shows us what sort of human future would be produced by a naturalism untempered by historicist Romance, and by a politics aimed *merely* at alleviating mammalian pain.

Notes

1   I published this defense in German, and showed it to Brandom. He counseled me to leave it in the decent obscurity of a learned language.
2   None of these arguments is at all original. They can all be found in James or in Dewey.

3   For this opposition, see page 375, in my response to Ramberg.

4   I also have a more flattering view of the course of my work than before. Brandom has suggested a coherence between my earlier and my later writings that had not occurred to me. I had not seen that there was a connection between the eliminative materialism I was urging in the 1960s and the private–public distinction I have been urging since *Contingency, Irony and Solidarity*. My unconscious has been more cunning than I had realized. On the other hand, as I say in my "Response to Dennett," I now think that in the 1960s I was over-ontological, and too inclined to talk about what "really" exists. It now seems to me that we should not worry about whether Jones created or discovered minds in the persons whom he trained to speak about inner episodes. We should be more *jemenfoutiste* about the making–finding distinction than I was back then.

9
Epistemology and the Mirror of Nature

MICHAEL WILLIAMS

1. The Emergence of Epistemology

In *Philosophy and the Mirror of Nature*,[1] Richard Rorty makes the startling claim that epistemology is a *modern* subject. Of course, it is a commonplace that, in the seventeenth century and thanks largely to Descartes, philosophy takes a pronouncedly epistemological turn. But this is not what Rorty is saying. His view is not that epistemology acquires a new level of importance in the period from Descartes to Kant. Rather, that period is when the subject is *invented*. Before Descartes, perhaps even before Kant, there is *no such subject*. Call this the *Emergence Thesis*.

The Emergence Thesis underwrites Rorty's willingness to contemplate the death of epistemology: for Rorty, tantamount to the death of philosophy itself. To appreciate the connection, we must recognize that the death of epistemology is not just the *end* of epistemology. One way to end epistemology would be to solve its problems in some permanently satisfactory way; another would be to convince everyone that its problems, while genuine, are not susceptible of solution.[2] Neither of these ways of ending epistemology answers to what Rorty has in mind. Rorty's project is an exercise in what I call "theoretical diagnosis." He wants to bring to light the unacknowledged presuppositions that he believes generate a whole form of inquiry: the problems to which it is addressed and the theories and methods available for their solution. This is different from the kind of "therapeutic diagnosis" that treats philosophical problems – epistemological problems included – as *pseudo-problems* generated by misuses or misunderstandings of language. Theoretical diagnosis treats the problems as genuine, but only given a definite background of (possibly dispensable) theoretical presuppositions.[3] If those presuppositions can be successfully challenged, then the problems to which they give rise can reasonably be set aside and attempts to solve them on a theoretical level will become otiose. This has happened to other disciplines in the past: demonology and judicial astrology for example. For Rorty, epistemology deserves a similar fate.[4]

The distinction between rejecting and accepting a problem's claim to naturalness is not coextensive with that between approaching it diagnostically rather than constructively. This is because, from the standpoint of therapeutic diagnosis, a problem might be rooted in *a natural illusion*, a perennial temptation to misunderstanding. By contrast, a theoretical diagnostician will suspect the problems that command his attention of having a traceable history, perhaps even a definite point of origin. The availability of an explanatory account of their origin and development will thus confirm the appropriateness of the theoretical diagnostician's approach while serving as the vehicle of his diagnosis. This is what we find in Rorty, who defends the claim *that* epistemology is a modern construction by offering an account of *how* the construction takes place.

Its importance notwithstanding, it is tempting to dismiss the Emergence Thesis out of hand. Isn't it obvious that sophisticated discussions of epistemological issues can be found at least as far back as Plato? And doesn't this make the claim that there is no epistemology before the seventeenth century, let alone the eighteenth, patently absurd? Certainly, there is something right about this reaction. Even so, I shall argue, the Emergence Thesis is by no means as obviously wrong-headed as this quick dismissal imagines. While there may be some things we might want to call "ancient epistemology," they are more distant from their modern counterpart than is generally supposed, though some are more distant than others. Rorty, I shall argue, is right to claim that something new emerged in the seventeenth century. The interesting question is "What?". What exactly emerged when epistemology was constructed and where would we be if it fell apart?

2.   Projection and Reversal

Rorty's account of the nature and origins of epistemology turns on the following sequence of claims, which I present in his own words.

1   [T]o think of knowledge which presents a "problem," and about which we ought to have a "theory," is a product of viewing knowledge as an assemblage of representations – a view of knowledge which . . . was a product of the seventeenth century . . .

2   Descartes's invention of the mind – his coalescence of beliefs and sensations into Lockean ideas – gave philosophy new ground to stand on. It provided a field of inquiry which seemed 'prior' to the subjects on which the ancient philosophers had opinions. Further, it provided a field within which *certainty*, as opposed to mere *opinion*, was possible.

3   Locke made Descartes's newly contrived 'mind' into the subject matter of a 'science of man' – moral philosophy as opposed to natural philosophy . . .

4   This project of learning more about what we could know by studying how our mind worked was eventually to be christened 'epistemology.' But before the project could come to full self-consciousness, a way had to be found of making it a *nonempirical* project . . .

5   Kant put philosophy 'on the secure path of a science' by putting outer space inside inner space (the space of the constituting transcendental ego) and then claiming Cartesian certainty about the laws of the inner for what had previously been thought to be outer . . . The Copernican revolution was based on the notion that we can only know objects *a priori* if we 'constitute' them . . . Once Kant replaced the 'physiology of the human understanding of the celebrated Mr. Locke' with . . .

'the mythical subject of transcendental psychology,' 'epistemology' as a discipline came of age . . .

6   [B]y taking everything we say to be about something we have 'constituted,' [Kant] made it possible for epistemology to be thought of as a foundational science . . . capable of discovering the 'fonnal' . . . characteristics of any area of human life. He thus enabled philosophy professors to see themselves as presiding over a tribunal of pure reason, able to determine whether other disciplines were staying within the legal limits set by the 'structure' of their subject matters. (*PALN*, pp. 136–9)

7   Once Kant had written, historians of philosophy were able to make the thinkers of the seventeenth and eighteenth centuries fall into place as attempting to answer the question "How is our knowledge possible?" and even to project this question back upon the ancients. (*PMN*, p. 132.)

8   [The] picture of "epistemology and metaphysics" as the "center of philosophy" (and of "metaphysics" as something that emerges out of epistemology rather than vice versa) . . . is the one built into philosophy curricula today. (*PAIN*, p. 134). Clearly, Rorty's fundamental diagnostic hypothesis is concerned with the picture of mind as the mirror of Nature: as he puts it here, with knowledge as an assemblage of representations. Without this image, and the theoretical ideas that cluster around it, we would never think of "knowledge" as a suitable object for systematic theory.

This is an intriguing idea. We should not take it as obvious that there can be a systematic theory of "what we can know." Aren't the limits of our knowledge (or ignorance) constantly shifting because subject to innumerable contingencies? Rorty would say "Yes." But he would add that thinking of knowledge as an assemblage of representations opens the way for a systematic theory of "what we can know" based on a general account of our representational capacities. Furthermore, postulating privileged access to our own minds, our knowledge of our representational capacities will be prior to and independent of the natural sciences, hence able to explain the "foundations" of such knowledge. Granted, to become property "philosophical," this theory must be non-empirical. To show how this might be was the contribution of Kant who, by also insisting on a clear distinction between the formal or structural component in our representations and the material or empirical component, finally establishes "knowledge" as an object of distinctively philosophical concern.

Even so, it is hard to resist thinking that the Emergence Thesis must be wrong. Granted that the conception of knowledge as an assemblage of representations offers one way of constituting knowledge as an object of theory, we have no reason to suppose that it is the only way. To return to the objection raised at the outset, what were the ancients doing when they discussed knowledge, if not epistemology?

Rorty is aware of this objection and offers two responses, both of which figure in the narrative sketched above. One is the *Projection Thesis*: that although, with our understanding of "epistemology" in place, we can examine ancient texts for anticipations of the subject we know and love, in so doing we will be "projecting" our concerns back upon our ancestors. The other is the *Reversal Thesis*: that the reconception of mind as the mirror of Nature leads to a reversal in the order of dependence between metaphysics and epistemology. For the ancients, epistemology emerges out of metaphysics whereas, for the moderns, the opposite is true: metaphysics emerges out of epistemology. It is not easy to see how Rorty's three theses can all be true. Most obviously, the Emergence Thesis and the Reversal Thesis seem to be in tension. How can the ancients have made epistemology subordinate to metaphysics if they had no epistemology in the first place? To resolve the tension, we need to distinguish between discussions of *epistemological questions and epistemology*, understood as an autonomous subject distinct from and largely independent of metaphysics. With this distinction in place, we can read Rorty as claiming that, while the ancients occasionally discuss epistemological questions, as an afterthought to metaphysics, these discussions do not amount to anything like what we think of as epistemology. So, we could restate the Emergence Thesis as the claim that, while there may be pre-modern epistemological discussion, there is no pre-modern *subject* of epistemology.

Rorty suggests that the subordinate status of epistemological inquiry is indicated by the fact that the ancients did not recognize any division of philosophy corresponding to what we mark out by the terms "epistemology" or "theory of knowledge," both of which terms are post-Kantian neologisms (*PMN*, p. 135). Possibly, this terminological point will strike some philosophers as irrelevant: if the ancients went in for epistemo-logical discussion, what difference does it make whether or not they felt the need to give what they were doing a name? Maybe none, but the question cannot be settled with a wave of the hand. Rorty is inviting us to take seriously the fact that our current way of dividing up the philosophical terrain – however natural it seems to us – is of fairly recent origin; and he wants to explore the thought that different division-schemes correspond to deeply divergent understandings of philosophical inquiry. To be sure, we may sometimes be able to excise pre-modern epistemological discussions from their original problem-contexts and align them with interests of our own. But to take this to show that the ancients and ourselves are in the same line of business would be just what Rorty thinks of as projection.

True, putting things this way, we shall have to allow that the question "is epistemology of modern origin?" cannot be answered with a simple "Yes" or "No," for our answer will depend on how demanding a conception of epistemology we have in mind. If we are looking for theoretically motivated discussions of questions about human knowledge, the answer will certainly be "No." But if we are looking for "epistemology" as a distinct philosophical sub-discipline, the answer might turn out to be "Yes." And more than a verbal point will be at issue. Either way, however, the Reversal Thesis will have to be qualified. If the Emergence Thesis is correct, the "epistemology" that emerges from metaphysics can't be exactly epistemology. But the Reversal Thesis may still point to an important idea: that reversing the priority of metaphysical and epistemological questions is inseparable from the emergence of epistemology itself.

This idea deserves a closer look. But before getting to this, we must attend to a problem with the Projection Thesis, which now seems to be under threat. If we distinguish between epistemological questions and epistemology – allowing that the ancients discuss epistemological questions even if they do not go in for epistemology – how can we say that we are merely projecting when we attribute to them epistemolog-ical concerns? Rorty will have to argue that they are not concerned with exactly the same questions; or even if the questions are the same, at some suitably abstract level, that they are approached in an importantly different way and accorded a different significance. Such differences, if they went unrecognized, would offer plenty of scope for projection.

The distinction between epistemological questions and epistemology is not something I am imposing on Rorty: something like it is implicit in his own story. The object of his diagnostic attention is not any discussion that is "epistemological" in the generic sense of "about knowledge" but something more narrowly focused. Thus, he tells us

> The . . . demarcation of philosophy from science was made possible by the notion that philosophy's core was "theory of knowledge," a theory distinct from the sciences because it was *their foundation* . . . Without this idea . . ., it is hard to imagine what "philosophy" could have been in the age of modern science . . . Kant, however, managed to transform the old notion of philosophy – metaphysics as "queen of the sciences" because of its concern with what was most universal and least material – into the notion of a "most basic" discipline – a *foundational* discipline. (*PMN*, p. 132)

Modern philosophy's epistemological turn is a new and surprising development since, according to Rorty,

> [t]he dream of a first philosophy firmer than science is as old as the *Republic*, and we may agree with Dewey and Freud that the same primordial urges lie behind both religion and Platonism. But that does not tell us why anyone should think that first philosophy consists in, of all things, epistemology. (*PMN*, p. 223)

This, then, is Rorty's real target: *epistemology as first philosophy*. Still, the question remains that, if Rorty is concerned with the emergence of a certain conception of epistemology, isn't it egregiously misleading of him to suggest that he is accounting for the invention of epistemology *tout court*? In fact, isn't he just offering, in an overly dramatic guise, the familiar story about modern philosophy's epistemological emphasis? Not necessarily. If Rorty can argue that casting epistemology for the role of first philosophy is inseparable from its emergence as a distinct discipline, he will forge an explanatory link between a certain conception of the status of epistemological discussion and the emergence of epistemology as a distinct (and distinctively philosophical) form of inquiry. This thesis is sharper than the familiar idea that modern philosophy is distinguished by its epistemological turn. The standard way of thinking about the epistemological turn does not doubt that the ancients and moderns were concerned with the same issues and in much the same way: modern philosophy's epistemological turn is merely a re-ordering of pre-existing philosophical genres. Though the Reversal Thesis might mislead us into thinking otherwise, this is just what Rorty denies. His thought is that moving questions about knowledge to center stage transforms our understanding of the questions themselves in such a way that, where previously it had been at most an appendix to metaphysics (or physics or psychology), the "theory of knowledge" becomes a subject in its own right. Such a claim is not improperly explored under the heading of "the emergence of epistemology."

I conclude that the Emergence Thesis should not be dismissed out of hand. Still, what does it really mean? In particular, what is involved in thinking of epistemology as "first philosophy"?

3 Problems and Methods

I have allowed that, if we are undemanding in our understanding of epistemology, we can say that Rorty's real target is a certain conception of epistemology rather than epistemology as such. This way of putting things also has its attractions, not the least of which is the hint that other conceptions are possible. Is there some way of understanding what the range of theoretical options might be? Can we construct a broader diagnostic framework that explains how different approaches to epistemological theorizing arise?

I want to distinguish four problems concerning knowledge (really, problem-areas). I do not need to claim that these problems are wholly intuitive, only that they are relatively generic. Anyway, as we shall see, the different ways of giving them more definite content provide plenty of scope for theoretical diagnosis. Nor do I claim that they are the only problems about knowledge that philosophers have taken an interest in. But they will do for now. They are:

1   *The analytic problem.* What is knowledge? (Or if we prefer, what do we, or should we, *mean* by "knowledge"?) For example, how is (or should) knowledge be distinguished from mere belief or opinion? What we want here, ideally, is a precise explication or *analysis* of the *concept* of knowledge.

2   *The problem of demarcation.* There are two sub-problems here. The first concerns whether we can determine, in some principled way, what sorts of things we might reasonably expect to know about? Or, as is sometimes said, what are the scope and limits of human knowledge? Do some subjects lie within the province of knowledge while others are fated to remain in the province of opinion, or even faith? Since the aim here is to draw a boundary separating the province of knowledge from other cognitive domains, we can call this the "external" boundary (or demarcation) problem. But there is also an internal boundary problem. We may wonder whether we should think of knowledge as all of a piece. Or are there importantly different kinds of knowledge: for example, *a priori* and *a posteriori* knowledge?

3   *The problem of method.* How is knowledge to be obtained or sought? Is there just one way, or are there several, depending on the sort of knowledge in question? (Here the problem of method interacts with the internal demarcation problem.) Furthermore, can we improve our ways of seeking knowledge?

4   *The problem of skepticism.* Given the existence of seemingly intuitive skeptical arguments, why suppose that knowledge is even possible?[5]

This list of problems offers the diagnostic framework we need. Let me explain.

There are three things to notice about the list. The first is that the order in which the problems are listed is entirely arbitrary and implies nothing about their relative importance. This is because there is no fixed order of relative importance. We might suppose that the analytic problem must come first, on the grounds that our views about all the other problems will depend on what we take knowledge to be. But this would be wrong for two reasons. For one, it might be that other problems can be raised and discussed taking for granted only "lowest common denominator" ideas about the nature of knowledge and can thus be approached independently of any fine-grained solution to the analytic problem. This is exactly how many philosophers see the problem of skepticism; and this is part of the reason why they see that problem as natural or intuitive. For another, we may want to use ideas about demarcation – about the sorts of claims with respect to which knowledge – talk is most appropriate – to refine (or even reform) our understanding of the concept of knowledge, in which case the analytic problem has no built-in methodological primacy. But more importantly still, neither does skepticism.

The second point is that, not only do my questions stand in no fixed order of importance or priority, there is no requirement that a philosopher interested in one or another of them take an interest in the rest. No question on the list is of mandatory concern. For example, a philosopher interested in demarcation or method may or may not take skepticism seriously, and vice versa. However – and this is the third point – which questions a philosopher takes seriously, together with the order of importance or priority he assigns to them, will shape decisively his approach to epistemological theorizing. So while not all the problems on the list are distinctively modern – indeed, it is arguable that none is – a certain way of bringing them into alignment may be.

This suggestion reinforces a point made earlier, that the Projection Thesis should not be taken to mean that seeing any epistemological concerns whatsoever in the ancient philosophers is always a matter of anachronistically projecting our interests on to our forebears. If we distinguish epistemological questions from "epistemology" (as an autonomous philosophical discipline), and if we find reason to associate epistemology (so conceived) with a certain alignment or prioritization of such questions, we can and should detach the thought that epistemology is a relatively recent arrival on the philosophical scene from what would in any case be an implausibly over-generalized claim about projection. Rorty can concede that the ancients addressed recognizably epistemological questions, including some or all of those addressed by the moderns. All he needs to claim is that they handled them in a fundamentally different way: so fundamentally different that they were not engaged in what we think of as epistemology.

Though this is the line Rorty should take, it is not always the one he actually follows. He qualifies the Projection Thesis, albeit implicitly, in a different way. When he speaks of projecting our concerns on to the ancient philosophers, he has in mind a specific concern and specific ancient philosophers: not my list and not just any philosophers. The question is "How is knowledge possible?" and the philosophers are Plato and Aristotle. This is the wrong way to go. For one thing, Plato provides as good an example as we could wish for of why we should distinguish epistemological questions from "epistemology," in the more demanding sense that Rorty wants us to attach to that term. According to Rorty himself, Plato's *Republic* provides an example of non-epistemological first philosophy. But it is surely evident that the metaphysics of the *Republic* are closely interwoven with undeniably epistemological concerns. Moreover, this defense of the Projection Thesis has nothing to say about the point that skepticism is only one epistemological problem area that philosophers concerned with knowledge have tried to address. Indeed, as we shall see, Rorty's own views about what is involved in the emergence of epistemology themselves depend on embedding the skeptical question in a wider range of epistemological interests.

At this point, we can return to the Reversal Thesis. Read in the light of Rorty's concern with epistemology as first philosophy, it amounts to the claim that when epistemology gets cast for that role, metaphysics arises out of epistemology rather than vice versa. This reversal is also supposed to distinguish ancient philosophy from modern. But none of this is quite right, as we can see from a brief glance at some of the epistemological ideas of Plato and Locke.

Both Plato and Locke put forward views that embody responses to all four problems on my list. Thus:

The analytic problem

According to Plato, knowledge is distinguished from opinion, even true opinion, by being infallible. Locke, too, with some qualifications, accepts a demonstrative conception of knowledge.

The problem of demarcation

Partly because of his acceptance of the Heraclitean doctrine of flux, Plato restricts knowledge to Forms: "knowledge" of the material world is really opinion. Though his metaphysical starting point – the corpuscular–mechanical view of nature – is quite different, Locke too is pessimistic about our attaining genuinely scientific knowledge of material things. For one thing, such knowledge would require knowledge of "real essences" – the distinctive corpuscular microstructures of various natural kinds of stuff. Locke's views about the nature of our "ideas" make him dubious about our prospects in such matters.

The problem of method

For Plato, the proper method for seeking knowledge is not observation but demonstrative proof, or perhaps some other form of *a priori* reasoning. (As is well known, Plato thinks that even mathematical "knowledge" is not the real thing.) Ideally, Locke agrees. But he thinks that, in scientific matters, we will have to content ourselves with an experimental approach. This will acquaint us with what properties in fact go together in various natural kinds ("substances"), though it will not yield understanding of why, say, gold is both yellow and soluble in *aqua regia*. Only knowledge of real essence, which we don't have and are unlikely to get, would provide that. We must be empiricists *faute de mieux*.

The problem of skepticism

For Plato, knowledge is possible but, since there is no knowledge of the material world, it will be is less extensive than we like to think. Locke has similar doubts. There is some demonstrative knowledge: of the existence of God, for example. For the rest, experience will yield as much certainty as our condition needs, though not knowledge in the full sense. What we can neither demonstrate nor experience, we must leave to faith.

Note that for both Plato and Locke, metaphysical views play an essential role in generating epistemological conclusions. Accordingly, the idea of a metaphysically conditioned approach to epistemological questions does not trace a bright line between ancient philosophy and modern. A more interesting question, however, concerns the relation between these philosophers' metaphysical and epistemological positions. In either case, do we see epistemology simply "emerge" out of metaphysics?

In Plato's case, the answer is plainly "No." What we find in Plato is a complex interaction of metaphysical and epistemological considerations, not a clear one-way relation of dependence. In the *Republic*, Plato argues that the material world is not to be identified with ultimate reality because it is, in an important sense, less than fully real: only the Forms, idealized abstract objects existing outside space and time, are fully real. This metaphysical picture arises out of reflection on a certain paradigm of knowledge – the geometrical theorem – without which it would scarcely be intelligible. But although, given the state of Greek science, this choice of paradigm is not surprising, it leads easily to a very demanding conception of knowledge. Geometrical theorems are established, not by casual observation but by logical proof from self-evident premises or axioms. Accordingly, the argument goes, they are certain and infallible. Taking the theorem, so conceived, as the paradigm of knowledge, it is natural to identify infallibility – taken as implying *necessary* truth – as that which distinguishes knowledge from opinion. It seems clear, however, that our "knowledge" of the material world, encountered through our senses, does not live up to this standard. To Plato, anyway, it is evident that it does not. Accepting, as he does, Heraclitus's idea that the material world is in constant flux, it is clear to him that no natural object corresponds perfectly to a mathematically tractable shape. Identifying definiteness with mathematical intelligibility, he concludes that natural objects have no definite character and so are not even potential objects of knowledge. Knowledge demands a world of changeless objects, located in a dense network of necessary inter-relationships: the world of the Forms. In Plato, metaphysics and epistemology are reciprocally influential.

Locke – the modern – comes closer to the idea of epistemology's emerging out of metaphysics. To the extent that Locke argues at all for the corpuscular-mechanical conception of nature, he does so by way of pouring scorn on its Aristotelian rival. But for the most part, it functions as the essential, largely unquestioned background to his epistemological inquiries. His main interest is in tracing its epistemological consequences. This is why, though his concerns are far more purely epistemological than Plato's, he disclaims all pretensions to be pursuing first philosophy. The philosopher of human understanding is an "under-laborer," not a master builder. Nevertheless, not even Locke's epistemological conclusions simply "emerge" from his metaphysics. How could they? Epistemologically speaking, Locke is something of a pessimist, but why should his corpuscular-mechanical picture of the world suggest *anything* about the limits of human knowledge? Two further elements are needed: some views about human cognitive capacities and some solution, however schematic, to the analytic problem. These are provided, respectively, by his account of the experiential origin of ideas and his conception of knowledge as deriving from our perception of "agreement" and "disagreement" between the ideas experience furnishes us with.

So much for epistemology's emerging out of metaphysics. How about the claim that, for the moderns, the direction of dependence is reversed? We have already seen that not all the moderns fit this pattern. But do any? If Rorty is right in his account of the origins of modern epistemology, none should, not even Descartes. After all, Rorty's central diagnostic claim is that a new metaphysical picture – mind as the mirror of Nature – creates the very possibility of thinking of knowledge as an object of systematic theory. He further thinks that the conception of knowledge that this image of mind sponsors – knowledge as an assemblage of representations – makes knowledge seem in urgent need of theorization. This is because thinking of knowledge in terms of accuracy of representation causes the threat of skepticism to arise in a newly dramatic form. However, he does not think that any metaphysical picture is, by itself, capable of turning knowledge into a problem. As he says, "The seventeenth century gave skepticism a new lease on life because of its epistemology, not its philosophy of mind" (*PMN*, p. 113). What he must mean here, I think, is that the fatal step is taken when the idea of knowledge as an assemblage of representations is combined with the idea

that what we immediately and certainly know is only the contents of our representational states. But if this is right, we do not find a simple case of metaphysics emerging
out of epistemology any more than, in the case of Plato, we find a simple case of
epistemology emerging out of metaphysics.

Rorty would reply, I think, that the reason he thinks that, in modern philosophy,
metaphysics emerges out of epistemology is that the new line between the mental and
the physical, the "inner" and the "outer," is itself drawn epistemologically: incorrigibility is "the mark of the mental." But this, too, is an oversimplification. As Rorty
himself recognizes, the thought that the "inner" is the arena of certainty is largely
sustained by the counterpart thought that knowledge of the "outer" is especially
vulnerable to skeptical doubt. But, as he also recognizes, the problem of the external
world – where the knowledge in question is concerned not merely with the real nature
of things but extends to the very existence of a world "without the mind" – is a
distinctively modern invention.[6] The skepticism that arises from the idea of the inner
as the locus of epistemological privilege also sustains that very metaphysical boundary.
In other words, post-Cartesian discussions of knowledge are also shaped by a complex
pattern of interaction between metaphysical and epistemological ideas. As stated, the
Reversal Thesis trails to capture the distinction Rorty needs.

The important point about Plato and Locke is not that they put metaphysics first
but that, in their approach to epistemological questions, skepticism comes last. While
the views of both philosophers display a notably skeptical strain, the skepticism is
entirely consequential, growing out of independently established results regarding
demarcation. We could even say that these philosophers, well aware that their
demarcational ideas collide with pre-theoretical inclinations, do not treat skepticism as
a *problem* at all. Certainly Locke, like Hobbes before him, finds Descartes's interest in
extravagant forms of skepticism risible.[7] Whether or not we want to describe demarcational ideas as "skeptical," for philosophers who approach demarcation in the spirit of
Plato and Locke, skepticism comes last, if it comes in at all.

Of course, it is entirely possible to reverse the Plato–Locke order of priority: to map
the scope and limits of human knowledge by exploring, independently of metaphysical
or scientific preconceptions, the limits of skeptical argumentation. Indeed, some will
argue, our explorations had better be independent of such preconceptions, if (contrary
to what a theoretical diagnostician will claim) skeptical arguments are genuinely
intuitive: such arguments will throw all our views about the world into suspense. This
is, of course, the procedure advocated by Descartes though, admittedly, if his skeptical
investigations are surreptitiously shaped by metaphysical ideas, his procedure will not
be quite what it appears to be. But, however that may be, what makes Plato's and
Locke's approach to epistemological questions "metaphysical" is not that they unqual-
ifiedly put metaphysics first but that neither even pretends to be a *methodological*
skeptic.

That the key element in the emergence of epistemology, as Rorty conceives it,
concerns the methodological role of skepticism could have been inferred from his
insistence that epistemology is an essentially nonempirical discipline. The Emergence
Thesis, we may recall, has to do with epistemology's emergence as a distinct,
independent form of philosophical inquiry, separate from both metaphysics and
empirical science. This independence is of a piece with the requirement that epistemology be a nonempirical subject: a discipline devoted to explaining the possibility of
knowledge of the world cannot take any such knowledge for granted. It is, therefore,
no surprise to find that, according to Rorty, epistemology begins to take shape when

the most important question for philosophy to answer becomes "How is our knowledge possible?" Indeed, Rorty's tendency is to use "epistemologically centered" and "skeptically centered" more or less interchangeably. But in light of this, his claim that epistemology is a modern phenomenon comes into question all over again; for although modern philosophy sees a massive resurgence of interest in skepticism, neither skepticism nor philosophical opposition to it is a modern invention. Rorty is of course well aware of this. Nevertheless, he continues to insist that epistemology is a modern subject. It follows that taking skepticism seriously will not, by itself, turn epistemology into first philosophy, hence epistemology as Rorty believes we should understand it. The question is: why not?

4. Skepticism Ancient and Modern

When Rorty was writing *Philosophy and the Mirror of Nature*, no one took much interest in Hellenistic philosophy. This is unfortunate since a case can be made that, in the later Hellenistic period when skepticism had developed into a sophisticated school of thought, those who accepted the skeptical challenge felt obliged to put epistemology first. As Sextus Empiricus tells us,

> The Epicureans start off with Logic, for they expound "Canonies" first, treating of things evident and non-evident and allied matters. The Stoics themselves, too, say that Logic comes first . . .

Skeptics agree with this, at least conditionally. This is because

> if truth is to be sought in every division of Philosophy, we must, before else possess trustworthy principles and methods for the discernment of truth.[8]

The background to this talk of beginning with "logic" is the standard Hellenistic division of philosophy into logic, ethics and physics. However, "logic" is understood in a wider-than-contemporary sense. Logic "includes the theory of criteria and proofs" and so covers issues that we would assign to epistemology. So Sextus is rather naturally read as testifying to wide agreement that, within the accepted divisions of philosophy, epistemology comes first.

It is hard to see what would account for this Stoic-Epicurean acceptance of the priority of epistemology if not the confrontation of those schools with a sophisticated skeptical opposition. The pressure to begin with a systematic account of "things evident and non-evident" is created by the existence of systematic arguments for the claim that nothing is "evident," the overcoming of such arguments being the standard that such an account must meet. Descartes could not have put it better. But if this is right, Rorty's attempt to line up the distinction between ignoring/rejecting and endorsing methodological skepticism with that between ancient and modern approaches to questions about knowledge fails in both directions. Not only does the supposedly ancient, Platonic approach to epistemological questions persist into modern times – as we see in Locke and, for that matter, contemporary epistemological naturalists – its supposedly modern alternative, epistemology-as-first philosophy, is anticipated in later antiquity.

A reply to this might be that, while these points show that Rorty needs to adjust his chronology, neither is fatal to the theoretical–diagnostic argument that his narrative is intended to sustain. What matters is whether Rorty is right to connect the emergence of epistemology with certain definite – possibly dispensable – theoretical preconceptions, not whether those preconceptions are wholly modern. Abstractly viewed, this is fair enough. But it ignores the fact that Rorty's central diagnostic hypothesis traces "epistemology" to an idea of unquestioned modernity: knowledge as an assemblage of representations, mind as the mirror of nature. This is not an idea that can plausibly be attributed to either the ancient skeptics or their chief opponents. Certainly, Rorty would not wish to defend any such attribution. But if, nevertheless, they anticipated the idea of epistemology as first philosophy, the objection to Rorty's narrative has much more than chronological significance.

Or so it would seem. In fact, however, the situation is not so straightforward. We need to look again at the fact that the Hellenistic philosophers assign the investigation of "things evident and non-evident" to "logic." It is easy to say that they are operating with a more encompassing sense of "logic" that covers topics we would think of as belonging to epistemology. But perhaps there is more to it than that. Perhaps epistemology, as part of logic, adds up to something less than epistemology as the moderns understand it. Clearly, that this is what Rorty needs to argue.

The claim that epistemology-as-first-philosophy is anticipated in later antiquity ties this conception of epistemology to an acceptance of "refuting the skeptic" as philosophy's first order of business. Rorty's emphasis of "showing how knowledge is possible" suggests that this is his view too. But closer examination of his position reveals a more complicated and more interesting view. Rorty does not of course deny that epistemology has been much concerned with skepticism. Nor is he unaware that there were ancient skeptics or that the sixteenth-century recovery of the writings of Sextus Empiricus had an important impact on the subsequent development of philosophical thought. However, like Locke (or Hobbes), he does not think that skeptical arguments are self-evidently interesting or important. Accordingly, he does not see the seventeenth century's sudden interest in skepticism as explaining how philosophy-as-epistemology came to dominate the modern philosophical imagination. Rather he sees it as in itself an extraordinary fact, crying out for explanation. "Why," he asks, "did the theory of knowledge become more than the languid academic exercise of composing a reply to Sextus Empiricus" (*PMN*, p. 223)?

This is a good question. Part of Rorty's answer is that the seventeenth-century idea of knowledge as an assemblage of representations "gave skepticism a new lease on life." It did so because

> [a]ny theory which views knowledge as accuracy of representation, and which holds that certainty can only be rationally had about representations, will make scepticism inevitable."
> (*PMN*, p. 113)

Here Rorty is thinking of skepticism in the generic sense of a philosophical challenge to the possibility of knowledge; and his thought seems to be that the image of the mirror of Nature strengthens immeasurably the skeptic's case. In fact, as I have already mentioned in passing, Rorty argues for a much greater divergence between post-Cartesian skepticism and its ancient forebear. Modern philosophy does not see a only revival of interest in old skeptical problems: it sees the invention of a range of problems unknown to the ancient skeptics. As Rorty puts the point:

> [W]e should distinguish traditional Pyrrhonian skepticism about our ability to attain certainty from the new veil-of-ideas skepticism which Descartes made possible by carving

out inner space. Traditional skepticism had been principally troubled by the "problem of the criterion" – the problem of validating procedures of inquiry while avoiding either circularity or dogmatism. This problem, which Descartes thought he had solved by "the method of clear and distinct ideas," had little to do with the problem of getting from inner space to outer space – the "problem of the external world" which became paradigmatic for modern philosophy. The idea of a "theory of knowledge" grew up around this latter problem . . . (*PMN*, p. 139–40)

Or again:

[t]he veil-of-ideas epistemology which took over philosophy in the seventeenth century transformed skepticism from an academic curiosity (Pyrrhonian skepticism) . . . It did so by giving rise to a new philosophical genre – the system which brings subject and object together again. (*PMN*, p. 113.)

The image of mind as the mirror of Nature does not simply revive skepticism by breathing new life into old problems. Rather, it creates new problems, thereby giving rise to a new theoretical discipline devoted to their solution.

In one way, Rorty is on strong ground: the problem of our knowledge of the external world is unknown to the ancient skeptics. But in another way, he seems to have presented an argument that subjects the Emergence Thesis to severe qualification. To be sure, the claim that the problem of the external world is of modern origin is interesting and significant. Moreover, it certainly implies that a good deal of epistemological theorizing – all the theorizing devoted to solving that problem – must be modern as well. Nevertheless, there seems to be no reason to claim that epistemology *as such* is a distinctively modern subject: not even when epistemology is taken as first philosophy. In fact, on Rorty's own showing, there seems to be reason not to. Rorty argues that Descartes creates the problem of the external world by treating his newly reconceived mind as the arena of certainty. But, also according to Rorty, the question of how we can attain certainty is the central problem presented by Pyrrhonian skepticism. It appears to follow that Cartesian skepticism arises out of a particular response to Pyrrhonian skepticism. This points to an important continuity in the skeptical tradition. And once this continuity is admitted, it seems far more accurate to say that Descartes sends skeptically centered epistemology off in new directions than that he invents the subject.

To see what we can salvage from Rorty's claim that epistemology as first philosophy is a modern creation, we need to delve a bit more deeply into the differences between skepticism ancient and modern. In particular, we need to look again at the fact that the ancient skeptics and their opponents assign epistemological questions to "Logic." The possibility I want to explore is that, while for the Hellenistic philosophers Logic is the division of philosophy that *comes first*, it falls far short of what Rorty thinks of as "first philosophy." As a result, "logic" does not amount to what, according to Rorty's story, the moderns come to call "epistemology." I want further to suggest that this shortfall reflects the character of the skepticism that the ancient theorists felt they needed to overcome. Pyrrhonian skepticism, I claim, is *essentially dialectical*. Because of this, the problem it presents remains *theoretically isolated*.

The problem of the external world is not the only problem that the ancient skeptics appear to have missed. The problem of induction, too, is either missed or anticipated in an uncertain and fragmentary form. Either way, it is accorded little significance.[9] In general, the ancient skeptics are not concerned with problems that depend on assigning knowledge-claims to discrete epistemic domains. As Rorty says, the object of their attention is the "problem of the criterion": the question of whether it is possible to state, in general terms, how the "evident" (or sometimes the true) is to be distinguished from the "non-evident." This problem is the fundamental concern of logic: "the study of things evident and non-evident." And their most powerful weapon against the solutions to the problem offered by their dogmatic opponents is a series of variations on the theme that no criterion can be defended without a self-defeating lapse into circular reasoning or the opening up of a vicious infinite regress.

This is a significant difference and Rorty is right to emphasize it. But it does not, by itself, indicate a radically divergent understanding of skepticism. The emergence of domain-specific skeptical problems, we might say, added to the skeptical problematic: it did not lead to a permanent loss of interest in the regress problems that dominated ancient discussions. However, the divergence between ancient skepticism and modern goes much deeper than this talk of adding problems suggests. It is important to understand not only what skeptical arguments the ancients skeptics used, but how they used them; and this means attending to what was subtracted from the skeptical tradition, as well as what was added.

When we think of epistemology as "refuting the skeptic" we have in mind the need to come to terms with certain canonical epistemological arguments: skeptical arguments. But such arguments, though they have an important place in Pyrrhonian skepticism, are not in any straightforward sense its basis. Rather, the basis of Pyrrhonian skepticism is a highly developed dialectical practice: the method of opposition. The Pyrrhonian skeptic is one who has perfected the art of meeting any given opinion, theory or observation with a countervailing opinion, theory or observation of roughly equal persuasiveness. These "oppositions" can be constructed in any way at all: observation against observation, observation against theory, theory against theory, and so on. All that matters is that the opposed views, because of their comparable appeal, neutralize each other, leaving the skeptic unable to assent to either. Naturally, these suspense-inducing oppositions are subject-matter specific: an ethical opinion will be met by an alternative ethical opinion, a physical theory by an alternative physical theory, and so on. Moreover, since "persuasiveness" is not objective credibility, no "theory of evidence" is presupposed. Finally, there is no recipe for constructing effective oppositions. This is an ability to be acquired: it neither has nor needs a theoretical rationale. Putting these points together, we see that the Pyrrhonian skeptic's dialectical practice is not based on epistemological theory at all. Indeed, it has no immediate connection with what we think of as skeptical argumentation. It presupposes not so much theoretical views about human knowledge as a certain intellectual environment one characterized by competing schools of thought, none enjoying a decisive persuasive edge over its rivals.

What, then, is the place of skeptical argumentation in Pyrrhonian dialectical practice? Does its development mark a departure from – or perhaps a theoretical rationalization of – the oppositional skepticism just described? I do not think so. For the Pyrrhonian skeptic the function of skeptical arguments is not to *defend* the method of opposition but to *extend* it to Logic. The need for this extension is Pyrrhonian practice is readily understood in the context of the Stoic-Epicurean proposal that philosophy should begin with the investigation of things evident and non-evident: that Logic should come first. This proposal is a reasonable response to the intellectual environment that sustains oppositional skepticism and it puts the skeptic on the defensive. The Pyrrhonian countermove, however, is ingenious. The skeptic admits that it is plausible to suppose that there is some criterion of evidence or truth. However, he notes that there are certain problems – and here he trots out his general skeptical arguments – that need to be overcome by an acceptable account of the criterion. Since no account currently on the market seems able to overcome them, the skeptic finds himself unable to say whether there is really such a criterion or not. As Sextus tells us towards the end of his discussion of the problem of the criterion, the skeptics

> do not propose to assert that the criterion of truth is unreal (for that would be dogmatism); but since the Dogmatists appear to have established plausibly that there really is a criterion of truth, we have set up counter-arguments which appear to be plausible . . .[10]

To sum up, for the Pyrrhonian, skeptical arguments do not rationalize the method of opposition: they extend from Ethics and Physics into Logic, thereby neutralizing attempts to escape its effect by moving the debate to the level of epistemological theory. The introduction of explicitly epistemological arguments does not change the essentially dialectical character of Pyrrhonian skepticism.[11]

Modern skepticism, as Rorty understands it, is not in this way dialectical. His theoretical diagnosis ties it to a specific theoretical perspective – "veil of ideas epistemology" – which is taken to be the last word on "our epistemic situation." With this conception in place, the skeptic is transformed from a tiresome interlocutor, bent on arguing interminably about any claim anyone puts forward, into someone who has exposed what threatens to be an irremediable defect in our epistemic position: a threat built into the relation between "mind" and "world."

Doubtless, one factor in the transformation of skepticism is the rise of modern science, which changed the intellectual environment in ways that made the Pyrrhonian method of opposition seem, for large areas of inquiry, no longer a live option. Freed from subordination to Pyrrhonian dialectical practice, skeptical arguments come to represent freestanding theoretical problems. To the extent that they threaten to afflict areas of inquiry that embody consensus-commanding claims to knowledge, there *must* be something wrong with them: in these areas, the interest of skepticism can only be methodological. Physics itself – now in the form of definitely established views – is always to be saved, even at the cost of metaphysical re-interpretation: for example, in idealist or instrumentalist terms. But it is important that not all subject-matters provoke this reaction. Perhaps there are types of would-be knowledge for which the traditional approach to skepticism, rooted in unresolvable conflicts of opinion, remains very much in play. Perhaps this differential vulnerability to dialectical forms of skepticism is an index of an important difference in epistemic status. Perhaps, too, in such cases, general skeptical arguments do not need to be so decisively refuted. Indeed, it may turn out that the accounts of knowledge we are led to in our attempts to insulate our paradigm knowledge claims from skeptical undermining do not apply to all subject matters. They may even reveal some subject-matters are not genuinely "cognitive." Such possibilities also do their part in investing skepticism with new significance.

Now, in Rorty's story, it is Kant who works epistemology-as-first-philosophy into its definitive shape. Kant's achievement is to put philosophy in the positions of "judging other areas of culture on the basis of its special knowledge of the 'foundations' of these areas" (*PMN*, p. 8). In my terms, Kant links the project of "refuting the skeptic" with the problem of demarcation: for instance, tracing the boundaries between reason and faith. In effect, we trace such boundaries by exploring the limits of skepticism. As we can see, this approach to demarcation is quite different from the "metaphysical" strategy of Plato or Locke. For these philosophers, as we have seen, the skeptical element in their thought is consequential on certain demarcational ideas. Moreover, so far as I can see, neither the ancient skeptics nor their opponents envisaged a *discriminating* use of skeptical problems. Again, this is not surprising. The intellectual world of late antiquity was, as we have said, one of competing philosophical schools, each with its distinctive views in physics *and* ethics. Adherents of such schools needed to dispose of the Pyrrhonian's blanket threat to claims to knowledge. But neither they nor the skeptics had a motive to put the skeptic's explicitly epistemological arguments – which in any case covered a narrower range than skeptical arguments of the modern period – to demarcational use: say, to make an invidious distinction between their physical and ethical views. As Rorty remarks, "the ancient schools had each a view of human virtue designed to match their view of what the world was like" (*PMN*, p. 138). Such an approach to philosophy does not encourage an interest in demarcation, at least along anything like modern lines.[12]

The ancient approach to positive philosophy reflects an intellectual environment in which physics and ethics are equally up for grabs: the very environment that sustains the Pyrrhonian approach to skepticism. We can find a similar environment in the sixteenth century, which is why Montaigne can revive skepticism in its authentically Pyrrhonian form. For Montaigne, Copernicus is not so much the herald of a new dawn as someone with the ingenuity to have plausibly controverted one of the most deeply entrenched views imaginable: Copernicus simply adds to the welter of conflicting opinions. However, once Newton put physics *hors de combat*, the situation was changed in ways that suggested a more discriminating use for skeptical argumentation. But the possibility of putting skeptical arguments to such use has the consequence that "refuting the skeptic" is no longer a self-contained academic exercise: it makes philosophy-as-epistemology an undertaking of profound cultural importance.

The connection with the problem of demarcation is important but does not exhaust modern skepticism's philosophical significance. For Rorty, as we just saw, linking skepticism with demarcational concerns – in effect reversing the previous order of dependence – depends on the use of methodological skepticism to identify the foundations of knowledge. However, there are three aspects to this talk of "foundations," which Rorty would have done well to distinguish more sharply:

1 *Epistemic Foundations.* Methodological skepticism is a device for identifying the "foundations" of *knowledge in general*, including (or perhaps especially) scientific knowledge. The idea is to determine what sorts of claims are "epistemologically basic," hence capable of standing to "inferential" claims as evidence to conclusion.

2 *Metaphysical Foundations.* In exploring the limits of skepticism, we are led to certain general and fundamental principles which provide the framework within which all detailed empirical inquiry is to be conducted. The quest for epistemic foundations aims to identify the *types* of claims or beliefs that are intrinsically credible. By contrast, the quest for metaphysical foundations aims at uncovering *specific propositions* which function as the "presuppositions" of whatever else we might come to know. For example, Descartes presents his confrontation with skepticism as leading him to the discovery that the essence of matter is extension. In a similar vein, Kant argues that causal determinism is presupposed by any claim to knowledge of an objective world. Closer to our own time, philosophers have taken the position that

we can defend the possibility of knowledge of the world only by recognizing that physical objects are logical constructions out of sense-data.

3 *Epistemology as the Foundation of Philosophy.* As the subject that determines the "foundations of knowledge" in both an epistemological and a metaphysical sense, epistemology becomes the foundation or centre of philosophy. Epistemology is not just the first but the most basic division of philosophy in that the other divisions are dependent on its results.

This multiple-aspect concern with "foundations" is crucial to the emergence of epistemology as first philosophy.

Once more, the Hellenistic philosophers provide the contrasting background against which the distinctive contours of modern philosophy become visible. For both the Pyrrhonian skeptics and their dogmatic opponents, logic is "first philosophy" only in the sense that skepticism constitutes a dialectical challenge that must be dealt with *before* particular views in ethics and physics can be advanced. Logic is thus *a propaedeutic* to the other divisions of philosophy, not their foundation. If we are to defend metaphysical (or physical or ethical) views, we will need to be able to refute the skeptic. But refuting the skeptic is not the key to determining what our metaphysical (or physical or ethical) views should be in the first place. Ancient "logic," as the study of things evident and non-evident, is concerned with epistemic foundations only. It is, in this way, more purely epistemological than modern "epistemology." The way in which the ancients "put epistemology first" does not have the effect of making metaphysics something that emerges out of epistemology. Accordingly, it does not make "logic" into first "philosophy," in the rich sense Rorty attaches to that term. By Rorty's standards, Hellenistic logic is not modern epistemology.

5. Epistemology in Transition

Where does this rather involved discussion leave us? I shall begin by summarizing its results. Then I shall say something about their implications for Rorty's claim that epistemology is (or deserves to be) on the brink of death.

Beginning with the Emergence Thesis, I think that Rorty is right to suggest that the subject which, after Kant, we came to know as "epistemology" represents a new theoretical configuration, without any exact counterpart in antiquity. Admittedly, if we take "epistemology" in a liberal sense, using it to cover any theoretically motivated discussion of questions about knowledge, we shall have to say that what began to emerge in the seventeenth century was a new approach to epistemology, rather than epistemology as such. But Rorty's more dramatic way of putting things has a point, for it calls attention to epistemology's emergence as a distinct subject, no longer an addendum to metaphysics, physics or psychology but, at least in aspiration, prior to them. Rorty's view is that epistemology only really comes into its own when promoted to the rank of first philosophy. This promotion, he thinks, not only ends it subordination to metaphysics but separates it from what might otherwise seem to be relevant scientific disciplines, such as empirical psychology. The Emergence Thesis is therefore not just an exercise in hyperbole.

There is something to the Projection Thesis too. Of course, if I am right to distinguish my relatively generic epistemological questions from the particular theoretical configurations that result from different ways of weighting and prioritizing them, seeing ourselves as sharing epistemological interests with the ancients need not be a matter of projection. But we would be equally mistaken to suppose that they went in for what, in Rorty's story, is the modern form of epistemology-as-first-philosophy. So the projection Thesis can be taken as a salutary, if somewhat overstated, warning not to take for granted a greater continuity of interests than is really there.

I have been rather hard on the Reversal Thesis. I have argued that the key reversal has to do with the place of skepticism in philosophical theorizing, not with subordinating epistemology to metaphysics or vice versa. The Platonic approach to epistemological questions cannot properly be described as putting metaphysics first since it involves complex interactions among metaphysical and epistemological ideas. But neither can "modern" philosophy be straightforwardly understood as the genre that puts epistemology first. Locke thinks of himself as an under-laborer and, in any case, operates more in the metaphysical than in the skeptical tradition. And as for the Cartesian tradition, Rorty is committed to the view – which I do not dispute – that the methodological skepticism that lies at its heart is heavily freighted with metaphysical commitments. To be sure, there is, in the modern period – or more precisely in the Cartesian tradition that eventually comes to dominate it – a dramatic re-weighting of epistemological considerations. Nevertheless, if Rorty is right to connect skepticism in its modern form with the image of mind as the mirror of Nature, then even in the Cartesian tradition, there is no simple way in which epistemology is wholly prior to metaphysics.[13]

This latter claim appears to be in tension with my reading of the Emergence Thesis, which ties the emergence of epistemology to a demanding conception of first philosophy. It looks as if, according to me, Rorty is committed to arguing that skeptically centered epistemology is both metaphysically loaded (*via* the image of mind as the mirror of Nature) and the metaphysically neutral key to all further philosophizing. Quite so, but this does not mean either that I am wrong about Rorty or that Rorty is wrong about modern philosophy. Rorty holds that the form of skeptical questioning we inherit from Descartes is heavily indebted to metaphysical preconceptions. He does not hold that this is how it is presented by Descartes or understood by most philosophers today. On the contrary, it is because problems like that concerning our knowledge of the external world are generally taken to be natural or intuitive that there is work for the theoretical diagnostician to do. If anything like Rorty's story is true, the problem is with philosophy in the Cartesian vein, not with Rorty's reading of modern philosophy or my reading of Rorty.

In the light of these amendments and qualifications, what should we make of Rorty's speculations about the death of epistemology? This question deserves much more careful consideration than I can give it here. But I should like to offer a few suggestions.

If my reading of the Emergence Thesis is correct, we must recognize that Rorty's conception of epistemology-as-first-philosophy is very demanding. Rorty tends to downplay just how demanding by talking of epistemology as "foundational," without calling attention to the multiple senses attaching to that term. However, as we have seen, he puts three conditions on epistemology's functioning as first philosophy. The first is that epistemological inquiry be guided by methodological skepticism. The second and third are that methodological skepticism be the key to answering both further epistemological questions (in particular questions about demarcation, though questions about method may also be on the agenda) and further metaphysical questions. These conditions are not essentially interconnected. This means that epistemology, in its Cartesian configuration, is subject to fragmentation. Indeed, I think that it has already fragmented. However, recognizing this gives no insight into the likely fate of the fragments.

Few philosophers today think of epistemology as first philosophy, in Rorty's demanding sense. But there are two main ways of denying it this status. One is to retain an interest in skepticism, as the theory of knowledge's central problem, while ceasing to think that answering the skeptic is the key to answering every other problem currently thought of as "philosophical." In effect, this returns epistemology to the status of what the ancient opponents of skepticism thought of as "Logic." The other is to downgrade the importance of answering the skeptic, possibly abandoning methodological skepticism as a device for exploring epistemological questions. This is typical of contemporary "naturalized" epistemology. Since this approach blurs the distinction between philosophical and scientific questions, Rorty can argue that it amounts to a roundabout way of conceding that epistemology, as a distinctively philosophical enterprise, is dead. Perhaps. But given my list of epistemological questions, a naturalistic epistemologist can argue for more continuity of interest with our philosophical tradition of reflection on questions about knowledge than Rorty's talk about the death of epistemology is naturally understood to imply. Indeed, whatever its merits, contemporary naturalism falls squarely within the Plato–Locke approach to epistemological questions, which has a longer history than the Cartesian problematic that Rorty has made it his business to dismantle.

It is possible, of course, that both of these options represent blind alleys. But an argument for this would have to go beyond the diagnostic story of *Philosophy and the Mirror of Nature*. Take the problem of skepticism: Rorty may want to argue that detaching this problem from demarcational and metaphysical questions reduces "refuting the skeptic" to the "languid academic exercise" it once was. However, this is more an expression of taste than an argument. It is not clear that skepticism depends for its theoretical interest on being seen as the key to lots of other, *prima facie* independent problems. This is not how it was regarded in late antiquity and it is not clear that this is how it should be regarded today. Nor can Rorty claim to have undermined this problem's urgency by tracing it to questionable metaphysical preconceptions: as we have seen, Rorty's theoretical diagnosis, which traces skepticism to the image of mind as the mirror of Nature, applies at best to skepticism about our knowledge of the external world. The central Pyrrhonian problem of the regress of justification is independent of that image and is thus left untouched.[14]

In this connection, it is worth noting that Rorty has difficult relations with Pyrrhonism. The regress problem is often thought to force a choice between a broadly foundational and a broadly coherentist conception of knowledge. *Philosophy and the Mirror of Nature* contains much to suggest that, at the time of writing, Rorty took himself to have chosen the coherentist option. This looks less like arguing for the death of skeptically centered epistemology than the adoption of a standard anti-skeptical strategy, though whether it is a workable strategy is another question. But, at best, this is ending epistemology by solving its fundamental problem, not killing it off by way of theoretical diagnosis.

Rorty would resist this description of his position. In his eyes, coherentist epistemology is not really epistemology. This is evident from his willingness to equate "the demise of foundational epistemology" with the demise of epistemology *tout court* (*PMN*, p. 315). Because holistic constraints on belief-revision are only loosely constraining, they do not offer "a set of rules which will tell us how rational agreement can be reached on what would settle the issue on every point where statements seem to conflict" (*PMN*, p. 316). *A fortiori*, they do not divide culture into areas where such algorithmically enforced agreement can be expected and where it cannot, which makes a holistic approach to justification apparently inhospitable to demarcational ambitions: there is no saying, in general terms, what can and cannot be coherently woven into someone's web of belief. All we see here, however, is how closely Rorty's sense that coherentist epistemology is not really epistemology is tied to his demanding conception of epistemology as first philosophy. We are given no reason to suppose that the problem of skepticism – detached from overweening ambitions – has been decisively undermined. Rorty himself appears to be continuing anti-skeptical theorizing, hence epistemology of a more modest kind.

Rorty might claim that the demise of foundational epistemology signals the end of Pyrrhonian as much as Cartesian concerns. Pyrrhonian skepticism, he might say, will appear as a threat only to those who feel the need for rules guaranteeing in advance that any dispute can be rationally resolved. But this distorts our contemporary understanding of skepticism. The quest for certainty having been largely abandoned, skepticism today is radical skepticism: not the claim that nothing is certain but that nothing is ever so much as justified. Accordingly, the problem facing constructive epistemologies is not to guarantee decisive resolutions to any conceivable dispute but to say something about the factors relevant to justifying taking one position rather than another, the working assumption being that not all positions are always equally justifiable.

At the very outset, I mentioned two ways of ending epistemology that would not amount to its death. One was to claim to have solved its problems and we have just seen that, in spite of himself, Rorty shows some affinities with philosophers who make such a claim. The other was to admit that the "problems" are really insoluble, thus not so much problems as facts of life. Perhaps surprisingly, Rorty has tendencies in this direction too. Thus, in a later work, he adopts the position of the "ironist," defined as one who entertains "radical and continuing doubts" about his "final vocabulary." The mark of a "final" vocabulary item is the impossibility of defending its use in a "noncircular way"; and the source of the ironist's doubts is acquaintance with other, competing final vocabularies. The affinity with Pyrrhonian skepticism in both its dialectical and theoretical-epistemological dimensions hardly needs spelling out: irony is skepticism by another name. This is not to deny that the Pyrrhonian problematic, as much as the Cartesian, is better approached diagnostically than theoretically, only that the diagnosis must be sought outside the image of mind as the mirror of Nature. Accordingly, even for the diagnostically inclined, there is theoretical work that remains to be done.[15]

So much for the option of continuing to take skepticism seriously, while detaching the problem from the multiply foundational ambitions that Rorty assigns to first philosophy. What about the option of downgrading its importance even within the arena of epistemological inquiry? Here I shall be brief. Let me just say that in arguing for the death of epistemology, Rorty ties all epistemological questions – including the problems of method and demarcation and method – to methodological skepticism. I have argued that this is misleading: theoretically and historically. As our brief glance at Plato and Locke revealed, there are other ways of articulating demarcational and methodological ideas. So we cannot assume that all epistemological concerns stand or fall with the problem of skepticism. Not even a fully convincing diagnosis of skepticism in all its forms would rule the pursuit of other traditional epistemological questions permanently out of court.[16] Perhaps these interests, too, are concerns we would be better off without. But Rorty's account of the emergence of epistemology does not tell us why. This account – I hope I have shown – is immensely subtle and important. Much remains to be learned from it. But it is not the last word. There are other stories that remain to be told.

Notes

1 Richard Rorty, *Philosophy and the Mirror of Nature* (Princeton University Press: Princeton, NJ 1979). Subsequent references given in the text by *PMN* and page number.

2 This is Thomas Nagel's attitude to skepticism. See *The View from Nowhere* (Oxford: Oxford University Press 1986), ch. V. For some remarks on Nagel's position, see my *Unnatural Doubts*, (p/b edition, Princeton: Princeton University Press 1996), p. 247f.

3 For more on the distinction between therapeutic and theoretical diagnosis, see *Unnatural Doubts*, p. 3 If. My terminology departs from Rorty here. Rorty expresses the hope for his project's being "'therapeutic' in the way that Carnap's original dissolution of standard textbook problems was 'therapeutic' . . ." (*PMN*, p. xiii–xiv). The Principle of Verifiability brands as meaningless all statements that are neither analytically true (or false) nor empirically confirmable (or disconfirmable). Its demarcational bite is thus wholly derivative from its adherents' views about confirmation: that is to say, from their epistemological theories. Since Rorty wants a way out of epistemological problems that leaves no residue of epistemological theorizing, the comparison with Carnap is unfortunate. On the other hand, the comparison should not be taken too seriously. Rorty thinks of his project as therapeutic because "pictures rather than proposition, metaphors rather than statements . . . determine most of our philosophical convictions" (*PMN*, p. 12) and exposing the influence of pictures is not like refuting theories. This form of therapy is more reminiscent of Wittgenstein than of Carnap. Nevertheless, I still want to say that he is engaged in what I think of as theoretical diagnosis. Not only are the pictures Rorty has in mind closely allied with theses that can be fairly precisely articulated, his preference for talking about pictures is a way of drawing attention to an important feature of what I think of as theoretical diagnosis: that it differs from straightforward refutation by aiming to bring to light preconceptions that generate the entire space of accepted theoretical alternatives. The point is not that such preconceptions do not embody theoretical ideas but that those ideas function differently from the explicit claims, the development or denial of which leads to one or another theory within that space.

4 Problems that seem to arise independently of contentious, theoretical ideas will have an air of being wholly "natural" or "intuitive." This aura of naturalness will make them seem compelling, even if seemingly insoluble. Theoretical diagnosis aims to dispel this aura. This sheds light on one of Rorty's favourite eye-brow raising claims: that concern with this or that problem is "optional." To a philosopher under the spell of the apparent intuitiveness of a particular problem, Rorty's *insouciance* can only look like intellectual irresponsibility. But if the problem can be revealed as an artifact of theoretical ideas that, once made explicit, are anything but compelling, it is the diagnostician's "irresponsibility" that turns out to be the illusion.

5 There is a fifth problem that a more satisfactory account of the emergence (or transformation) of epistemology would have to take into account: the question of the value of knowledge. None of the other problems would be interesting unless knowledge were in some way valuable (though not all philosophers have valued it in the same way). Preserving the value of knowledge is an underappreciated constraint on answers to the other questions. Changing conceptions of the value of knowledge may have more to do with the contrast

between ancient philosophy and modern than the epistemology-centeredness that is the main topic of Rorty's investigation. See n. 12 below.

6 See Myles Burnyeat, "Idealism and Greek Philosophy: What Descartes Saw and Berkeley Missed," *Philosophical Review* (1982).

7 Locke: "[I]f . . . any one will be so sceptical, as to distrust his Senses, and to affirm that all we see and hear, feel and taste, think and do, during our whole Being, is but the series and deluding appearances of a long Dream, whereof there is no reality; and therefore will question the Existence of all Things, or our Knowledge of any thing: I must desire him to consider, that if all be a Dream, then he doth but Dream, that we makes the Question; and so it is not much matter, that a waking man should answer him." *Essay Concerning Human Understanding*, ed. P. Nidditch (Oxford: Oxford University Press 1975), p. 634 (IV.XI.8).

8 Sextus Empiricus, *Against the Logicians*, 1.22, 24; in R. G. Bury trans., *Sextus Empiricus*, vol. 2 (London/Cambridge MA: Heinemann/Harvard University Press 1967).

9 See Ian Hacking, *The Emergence of Probability* (Cambridge: Cambridge University Press 1975).

10 Sextus Empiricus, *Outlines of Pyrrhonism* 2, 79; in R. G. Bury, trans., *Sextus Empiricus* vol. 1 (London/Cambridge MA: Heinemann/Harvard University Press 1967).

11 This reading of Pyrrhonian skepticism is controversial. For a detailed defense, see my "Scepticism without Theory," *Review of Metaphysics* (1988).

12 A stronger claim could be made for why the ancient philosophers would not have been interested in the sorts of demarcational issues that are so central to modern discussions. This is that, for the ancients, it is not just that physics and ethics are tailored to fit together in sustaining a certain picture of the good life but rather that, strange as it sounds, all three divisions of philosophy are of fundamentally ethical significance. The function of logic is to discipline the intellect and of ethics to discipline the will. And physics? To discipline desire: reflection on the physical nature of nature of things peels away adventitious human valuations, helping us to become indifferent to things that are in fact indifferent. See Pierre Hadot, *Philosophy as a Way of Life* (English edition, Oxford: Blackwell 1995), ch. 3. Also Hadot, *Qu'est-ce que la philosophie antique?* (Gallimard: Paris 1995), ch. IX.

13 Though I do not dispute the claim that Cartesian skepticism is metaphysically loaded, my own theoretical diagnosis differs markedly from Rorty's. For me, the essential element in the Cartesian problematic is a certain metaphysics of knowledge which I call "epistemological realism." This is the idea of an objective "order of reasons," existing independently of our contingent situations, interests, background beliefs, and so on. This idea – the central theoretical commitment of foundationalist theories of justification – is the driving force behind the modern list of canonical skeptical problems. From my standpoint, the epistemo-logical significance of the Cartesian view of mind is to rationalize this metaphysical-epistemological doctrine. However, epistemological realism is detachable from the Cartesian view and so able to survive assaults on it. I therefore find it significant that Rorty himself recognizes that the Cartesian metaphysics of mind, taken alone, is of limited diagnostic importance. Thus he writes that "The seventeenth century gave skepticism a new lease on life because of its epistemology, not its philosophy of mind" (*PMN*, p. 113). As he goes on to explain, the Cartesian tradition both identifies knowledge with accuracy of representation and holds that certainty is restricted to the contents of representations. From my point of view, it is the second proviso that really does the work. Remove it and the idea of knowledge as accuracy of representation is harmless. Indeed, it can be re-interpreted along impeccably pragmatists lines. I defend this account of Cartesian skepticism in *Unnatural Doubts*. A richly detailed account of how a pragmatist might think about representation, without falling into skeptical traps, is given by Robert Brandom in *Making it Explicit* (Cambridge MA: Harvard University Press 1994).

For another view entirely of the metaphysical background to the problems of modern philosophy – one that emphasizes the rise of philosophical naturalism, the disenchantment of Nature resulting from the Scientific Revolution – see John McDowell, *Mind and World* (Cambridge MA: Harvard University Press 1994). For some critical comments on McDowell, see my "Critical Notice," *Philosophical Quarterly* (1995). But my reservations notwithstanding, McDowell's emphasis on the importance of modern naturalism brings out an element in the formation of modern philosophy which, though understressed in both Rorty's diagnosis and my own, unquestionably needs to be taken into account.

14 In Ayer's *The Problem of Knowledge* (London: Pelican 1956), the problem of skepticism is identified with an array of foundational problems: the external world, induction, etc. Contrast this with a recent work like Bonjour's *The Structure of Empirical Knowledge* (Cambridge MA: Harvard University Press 1985), where the ancient problem of the regress is firmly back in first place. As Cartesian skepticism has come under a cloud, owing to the work of critics like Rorty, the Pyrrhonian problem has grown in importance. For a brilliant demonstration of how inadequate recent attempts to solve it have been, see Robert Fogelin, *Pyrrhonian Reflections on Knowledge and Justification* (Oxford/New York: Oxford University Press 1995), Part II.

15 McDowell's diagnosis of the ills of modern philosophy is notable for taking seriously the problems of falling in with radically holistic forms of coherentism. See, for instance, his criticisms of Rorty in *Mind and World*, Afterword Part 1.

16 For an example of how demarcational questions might be pursued independently of standard skeptical problems, see Crispin Wright's recent discussion of how to distinguish between areas of discourse for which a "realist" conception of truth is appropriate and those for which it is not: Wright, *Truth and Objectivity* (Cambridge MA: Harvard University Press 1994). Unsurprisingly, Rorty has no sympathy with this sort of thing, holding that a pragmatist or deflationary approach to truth takes the steam out of the issues that concern Wright. My point here is only that, whatever the merits of Wright's arguments, he is not doing the sort of epistemology that is the focus of attention in *PMN*. Rorty would probably deny this, on the grounds that anyone who takes questions about realism seriously must be trying to breathe life into the idea of truth as correspondence. Accordingly, there is a definite continuity between "epistemology" and project's like Wright's *via* the notion of truth as accurate representation, a direct descendant of the image of the mirror of Nature. However, I doubt that this is fair to Wright's views about truth, which are minimalist. But more than that, the real center of attention in *PMN* is, as we have seen, often less the idea of knowledge as an assemblage of representations than various epistemological theses grafted on to it. (If I am right about the real source of Cartesian skepticism, this is no accident: see n. 13 above.) If it turns out that criticisms of these additional epistemological theses, none of which Wright is committed to, carry the burden of Rorty's attack on "epistemology," the argument of *PMN* can be largely successful while leaving Wright's approach to demarcational questions untouched.

RESPONSE TO MICHAEL WILLIAMS

Williams is putting it mildly when he says that there is a tension between my Emergence Thesis (epistemology was invented in the seventeenth century) and my Reversal Thesis (the moderns reversed the ancient order in which metaphysics was prior to epistemology) (p. 194). The latter thesis is hopeless, and I wish I had never advanced it. To have made it plausible I should have had to give suitable definitions of "metaphysics" and "epistemology." I had, and have, no such definitions.

It is not clear that either word is worth defining. Both words have come to be little more than the names of pigeon-holes into which curricular odds and ends can be stuffed. We philosophy professors, who are nothing if not creatures of habit, still set examinations titled "Metaphysics and Epistemology." But when sitting on committees to write these examinations we ask each other dumb questions like "Isn't a question about rigid designation philosophy of language rather than metaphysics?". We give silly answers like "Well, it could count as metaphysics if we threw in something about real essences." We find ourselves saying things like "That question about Kuhn and Popper is really philosophy of science rather than epistemology, but it could count as an epistemology question if we rephrase it using the term 'scientific knowledge'."

If I were writing *Philosophy and the Mirror of Nature* (*PMN*) now, I would do my best to avoid the words "metaphysics" and "epistemology." I would try to tell the story entirely by reference to dominant metaphors and images and not by reference to distinctions between disciplines. For using the names of purported disciplines buys in on exactly the understanding of the history of philosophy that I was trying to reject: the history of philosophy as a series of attempts to deal with familiar sets of problems – some ethical, some epistemological, some metaphysical.

I am suspicious whenever somebody lists, as Williams does, "four problems concerning knowledge." (I shall say more about that list later.) My reaction to the items on such lists is typically "But how did anybody come to see *that* as a problem?" and then to try for what Williams calls a "theoretical diagnosis" of the willingness to take the problem seriously.[1]

I hoped, when writing *PMN*, to treat the history of philosophy in the way Dewey treated it, as a series of reactions to events taking place outside of philosophy. I had hoped to write about the genesis of philosophical problems in a Deweyan way – to show such problems as epiphenomena of attempts to reconcile old metaphors and old ways of thinking with new and startling cultural developments (the Athenian Empire, the Christian religion, the New Science, the French Revolution, Darwin, Freud, and the like).[2] But I got distracted, and the book fell between two stools. In the event my book was partly amateurish cultural history and partly an attempt to dissolve certain very particular problems which were being discussed by analytic philosophers in the 1970s.

One of the big questions I was trying to answer for myself when I wrote *PMN* was: how did philosophy survive the New Science? Why didn't the success of corpuscularian physics make philosophy obsolete? How did philosophy extricate itself from what the eighteenth century called "natural philosophy," and set up in business on its own? My answer ("because they invented the veil of ideas, and thereby produced a new field of inquiry to replace the one that physics had taken over") had some merit, but it dodged around an important topic.

That was the topic of how philosophy managed, among the educated classes, to take over some of the functions of religion. Religion was barely mentioned in *PMN*. Like too many other contemporary writers on the history of philosophy, I thought that it was enough to grasp the interaction of scientific and philosophical change. I did not see the need to bring in the changes in moral and political thought which resulted from the interaction of scientific and religious changes with one another.[3] It now seems to me that to think properly about the kinds of questions I was trying to answer in *PMN* one needs to keep three balls in the air at once – science, philosophy, and religion. My current way of thinking about these three areas of culture was suggested to me by Heidegger's account of the history of philosophy from Plato to Nietzsche as "humanism" – as a series of attempts to put more and more power in the hands of human beings. Heidegger thought this attempt was bound to come to a bad end, whereas I agree with Dewey that it is a good project, worth pressing ahead with.[4] But whether good or bad, it provides a useful thread with which to connect episodes in the history of culture.

Thinking of the various peripities of Western thought in Heidggerian terms has led me to think of these areas of culture in the following way. The scientific question is "how do things work?". The religious question is "what should we be afraid of?"[5] and the philosophical question "Is there something non-human out there with which we need to get in touch?"

All three are questions about the whereabouts of power, and they obviously interlock. If it turns out that things (for instance, diseases, volcanoes, the wind and the rain) work without the intervention of invisible persons, we may eventually have less to be afraid of than we had once thought. If it turns out that the only reason for getting in touch with something non-human is to adapt it to our needs (the Deweyan view, which Heidegger despised), then our sense of the human situation will change. We shall become secularists, who let art and politics fill the gap left by God. We may also become pragmatists, who deny that truth is a matter of accurate representation of the intrinsic nature of reality. The idea of such an intrinsic nature may come to seem a shibboleth.

Of all the cultural changes that the West has experienced, the New Science was by far the most important. It gave us moderns what the ancients never had – a universally accepted, confidence-inspiring, account of how things worked. Corpuscularianism went from being one more philosophical guess at the riddle to being everybody's platitude. Williams takes note of this shift when he says that as a result of the rise of modern science

> To the extent that they [skeptical arguments] threaten to afflict areas of inquiry that embody consensus-commanding claims to knowledge, there *must* be something wrong with them. Physics is always to be saved, even at the cost of metaphysical re-interpretation: for example, in idealist or instrumentalist terms" (p. 205).

I agree with what Williams says here except for the term "metaphysical." The idealist and instrumentalist treatments of physics were not, it seems to me, *metaphysical* reinterpretations. Kant would have resisted being described with the help of that adjective. He thought he was doing something very different from Leibniz. For Leibniz contrasts a physical description of how things work with a metaphysical description of what they really are. Kant and Fichte contrast physical knowledge with something that is not knowledge: namely, morality. James and Dewey would not have liked that adjective either: when they say physical science is a tool for fulfilling certain human needs, they are not contrasting it with something that is not a tool, but only with other tools.

Because he is commenting on a book which saddled itself with the terms "metaphysics" and "epistemology," Williams too saddles himself with them. I think both of us would do better to forget these terms and just talk about the Appearance–Reality distinction on the one hand and the Veil of Ideas idea on the other. Both of these ideas have a traceable history, both are dispensable, and both are part of the history of affirmative answers to questions like: Is there something non-human out there with which we need to get in touch? Are we ever going to get in touch with it? Are we so constituted as to be unable to get in touch with it?

I now think that the emergence of epistemology as first philosophy should be seen as an answer to the question: how can we keep the pathos of distance, our sense of something non-human toward which we reach but which we may never grasp, even after we have gotten a pretty good idea of how things work? The idea of mental representations, and of the veil of ideas, helped fill the need for an abyss to be crossed – a need which the pagans filled by the sense of helplessness before elemental powers, and the Christians by the sense of Sin. This is my answer to Williams when he asks: granted that something new emerged in philosophy in the seventeenth century, what was it?

Williams then goes on to ask "What exactly emerged when epistemology was constructed, and where would we be if it fell apart?" Williams gives a very judicious account of the continuities and discontinuities between Plato and Locke, and between Pyrrhonian and Cartesian skepticism, but he leaves untouched *PMN*'s claim that *representationalism* – the doctrine that our knowledge of the world passes through a representing medium which may or may not distort what the world is really like – comes to center stage only after the New Science begins to get a grip on the minds of educated Europeans. The story Williams tells is a more balanced story than the one I told, and is a useful corrective to mine. But it is compatible with my claim that this new way of maintaining the pathos of distance between the human and the non-human shoved aside the older problematic of Appearance and Reality.

This Greek problematic re-emerged briefly in Kant and his German Idealist successors. Hegel, in particular, tried to brush representationalism aside, and to go back to Greek (and, more specifically, Aristotelian) forms of pathos. But his attempt had, even among the Germans, only a short-lived success. When people started crying "Back to Kant!," and when Frege and Peirce updated representationalism by suggesting that we concentrate on linguistic rather than mental representations, Hegel (and the Aristotle of *Metaphysics* XII) began to sink beneath philosophers' horizon of consciousness.[6]

Because I think "representationalism" is a good answer to Williams' question "What exactly emerged when epistemology was constructed?," I think that the answer to his question "Where would we be if it fell apart?" goes like this: we would be left with less encouragement to cling to the pathos of distance. We should be more Nietzschean in our willingness to say "Thus I will it" rather than "Thus the Intrinsic Nature of Reality obliges me." We should be more "humanist" in the sense of that term which Heidegger endeavored to make pejorative – more willing to take power into our own hands.

What would happen to philosophy as an academic discipline if epistemology fell apart? I think it has already fallen apart, and that this devolution is illustrated by Williams' comments on his own list of "four problems about knowledge." Williams says that "there is no fixed order of relative importance" among these problems and that "there is no requirement that a philosopher interested in one or another of them take an interest in the rest" (pp. 196–7). I quite agree, but I would use both points to argue that "epistemology" is now the name of a pigeon-hole rather than of an area of inquiry. One can tuck anything said about knowledge by anybody who has ever been called "a philosopher" into one of the four smaller pigeonholes into which Williams has subdivided the larger one: Carneades and Gettier, Locke and Plato, Lehrer and St. Augustine, Quine and Cavell. As sets of pigeonholes go, Williams' is fine. But no such unordered set is of much use when one is trying to construct a dramatic narrative of cultural change.

Once upon a time, I should argue, it would have been much easier to see a fixed order of priority among Williams' four problem. The demarcation problem came first. If we had not felt the need to say such things as "this part of our culture [theology, physical science, morality, art, whatever] is closer to the non-human power that we need to get in touch with" we should never have started in on demarcation. Had we not, I doubt that we should ever have found ourselves talking about the other three problems on Williams' list, except perhaps for skepticism in its specifically Pyrrhonian form.

We should certainly have talked about the difference between knowledge and opinion, but this would have been a practical, rather than a theoretical matter: a discussion of the amount of confidence you can place in various people's views. This discussion would not have linked up with the question of our relation to Reality. Without the pathos of distance, the same pathos as is invoked in the Appearance–Reality distinction, I doubt that we should have had many books about the nature of knowledge, or the right method of seeking knowledge. We should have been in the position of readers of Williams' *Unnatural Doubts*, who lay that book down wondering why anyone would ever think that "knowledge" was the name of a natural kind, the name of something whose nature we have not yet adequately grasped.

I shall conclude by using another handle to pick up the question "Where would we be if epistemology fell apart?" – if all the epistemology professors read *Unnatural Doubts* and then went into other lines of work. This handle is the realism-vs.-antirealism debate. That debate is a downmarket version of the nineteenth-century debate between those who did not want to let go of religion and those who thought that, now that we knew how things work, we could forget God.

Nowadays the role once played by defenders of religious belief is played by defenders of realism. These people are the defenders of what they call "sound common sense" against radical innovation. They think they know the answer to the demarcation problem: the natural sciences are in touch with the Intrinsic Nature of Reality, and perhaps no other portion of culture is. In their view, people who do not accept this answer are undermining civilization as we know it (the same view that Wilberforce took of T.H. Huxley). Such people lack humility; they lack respect for non-human Reality. To have this humility is to grant the knowledge-claims of the natural scientist a special character – "objectivity," or "objective truth." (As I say in my "Response to Daniel Dennett," many contemporary calls to resist the subversive power of "post-modernism" are expressions of scientistic cultural chauvinism.)

People who, like me, see only a sociological sort of demarcation between the knowledge-claims of physicsts and those of moralists do not usually call themselves "antirealists." They try to dismiss the realist–antirealist debate as pointless. Philosophers like Arthur Fine, Donald Davidson, and me see no point in drawing philosophical demarcation-lines through culture. They treat all knowledge-claims as on a par, and none of them as standing in a special relation to Reality. They are all causally related to reality, but none of them are representationally related to Reality.

In this respect, the current realist–antirealist debate differs from the religion–science debate of the previous century. It is not a debate about which area of culture gets in touch with the non-human entity most relevant to human flourishing, but rather about whether we need to think in terms of a non-human reality at all – whether we can now do without the pathos of distance. If we ever did lose this sense of pathos, then the question I suggested was definatory of philosophy would be answered. The answer would be "No, there is nothing non-human out there with which we need to get in touch, because human beings have always been in causal touch with the rest of the universe, and that it is the only kind of touch there is."

Would that be the end of philosophy? Certainly not. There would still be the need to reconcile the old and the new – to reshape old metaphors and vocabularies so as to accommodate them to new insights. That is why philosophy will last as long cultural change does. But philosophy may eventually cease to be thought of as a super-science, or as supplying a foundation for science, or as a substitute for religion, or as supplying weapons to be used to defend either religion or science against their cultured despisers. Philosophy would be a matter of conciliating the human present with the human past. If this comes to pass, the science–religion debate and the realism–antirealism debate will seem equally quaint.

Notes

1   Williams contrasts therapeutic with theoretical diagnosis: diagnoses of a "natural illusion, a perennial temptation to misunderstanding", "perennial illusions" with diagnoses of illusions which have "a traceable history." He says, correctly, that in *PMN* I was trying to trace the history of the beliefs which made it possible to treat epistemology as first philosophy. I was attempting the sort of theoretical diagnosis of skepticism which Williams later offered, with considerably greater precision and success, in his *Unnatural Doubts*.

I am, however, dubious about Williams' therapeutic–theoretical distinction. I doubt that there are any natural illusions, and am suspicious of the idea (championed by Stanley Cavell) of perennial, inevitable, temptations. The notion that philosophy should be therapy is plausible if "therapy" means something like "freeing up the imagination to contemplate alternatives not previously envisaged." It is not plausible if it means something like "restoring health" or "clearing away illusion." There is no philosophical analog of the "inevitable" Mueller-Lyon illusion, because there is no analog of the ruler which tells us that the two lines are, visual appearances to the contrary, of equal length.

2   For a quick sketch of this Deweyan approach see my "The Future of Philosophy" in *Rorty and the Pragmatists*, ed. Herman Saatkamp (Nashville, TN: Vanderbilt University Press, 1995).

3   I have been helped to see this by J.B. Schneewind's insistence that treating the history of philosophy as the history of metaphysics and epistemology is dumb, and that treating the history of ethics apart from the history of religion is impossible. Schneewind's *The Invention of Autonomy* is the history of that part of what we now call "seventeenth and eighteenth century philosophy" which really made a difference to the way the self-image of European humanity changed. But the traditional insistence that "metaphysics and epistemology" make up the "core" of philosophy has given us histories of philosophy which marginalize the history of ethics.

4   For a quick sketch of Heidegger's reading of the history of philosophy as the history of power-plays, see "Heidegger, Contingency and Pragmatism" in my *Essays on Heidegger and Others* (Cambridge: Cambridge University Press, 1991), pp. 27–49.

5   I know that there are religions of love as well as religions of fear. But, for reasons set out in "Pragmatism as Romantic Polytheism" (in my *Philosophy and Social Hope*) and in my discussion of Dewey in Lecture I of *Achieving Our Country*, I think that the religion of love has gradually moved out of the churches and into the political arena. That religion is in the process of being transfigured into democratic politics. What is left behind in the churches is the fear that human beings may not be able to save themselves without help – that social cooperation is not enough.

6 Their influence survived, however, in writers who tried to recapture Aristotle's notion of
   knowledge as identity of subject and object rather than representation of object by subject –
   notably idealists such as Royce and process philosophers such as Whitehead. G.R.G. Mure's
   writings on Aristotle and Hegel are particularly helpful in tracing the connections between
   these two knowledge-as-identity theorists.

10

What was Epistemology?

BARRY ALLEN

Epistemology is not something which results from a natural desire to answer a natural question. (Richard Rorty)

The concern of epistemology, or the theory of knowledge, is to draw normative lines around its subject, to deduce the formal conditions of knowledge, and define the terms of justification. The result may be Hume's natural history of knowledge or Kant's transcendental project, Fichte's *Wissenschaftslehre* or the reconstruction of science by the logical positivists. The questions these different projects pursue may not be natural ones. Rorty thinks they are questions we do not need to take up anymore, if we ever did. They involve optional assumptions which we can and should drop. These assumptions include the idea of mind as the mirror of nature, of knowledge as "privileged representations," and philosophy as knowledge about knowledge, its "transcendental conditions of possibility" or its "scope and limits."

Not to credit these ideas is no doubt to bid adieu to epistemology. But the significance of this gesture depends on the implicit philosophy of knowledge which evaluates and dismisses the assumptions of epistemology: Rorty's positive, pragmatic, "holistic approach to knowledge" (*PMN*, p. 181). He says he does not want "to substitute one sort of account of human knowledge for another, but . . . to get away from the notion of 'an account of human knowledge'" (*PMN*, p. 180). Yet his writings articulate a number of claims which obviously add up to a substantial (if controversial) account of knowledge. The following passages sound the main themes:

> Knowledge . . . [is] what we are justified in believing . . . [and] "justification" [is] a social phenomenon rather than a transaction between "the knowing subject" and "reality". (*PMN*, p. 9)

> Justification is not a matter of a special relation between ideas (or words) and objects, but of conversation, of social practice (*PMN*, p. 170). Conversation [is] the ultimate context within which knowledge is to be understood (*PMN*, p. 389). The community [is the] source of epistemic authority (*PMN*, p. 188). Everything which is not a matter of social practice is no help in understanding the *justification* of human knowledge. (*PMN*, p. 186)

> Pragmatism views knowledge not as a relation between mind and object, but, roughly, as the ability to get agreement by using persuasion rather than force (*ORT*, p. 88). Insofar as

pragmatists make a distinction between knowledge and *opinion*, it is simply the distinction between topics on which such agreement is relatively easy to get and topics on which agreement is relatively hard to get. (*ORT*, p. 23)

Rorty likes Wittgenstein's point that any knowledge philosophy may have cannot be more than a platitude, a reminder about how we use words, and *knowledge* is first of all a word, not a thing-in-itself about which we should expect an interesting theory. In particular, there is nothing behind the word which, if only we knew it better, could spell it out in a formula, would make us better knowers. From this perspective, the problem with epistemology is that its subject-matter – knowledge "itself" – is illusory and does not exist. Yet in the remarks I cited, Rorty goes beyond the platitudes of ordinary language, and it is this implicit philosophy of knowledge which concerns me. I shall steer around Rorty's critique of traditional epistemology (briefly discussed in the next section), and concern myself mostly with the substantial conception of knowledge which it presupposes.

Pragmatism and Epistemology

In *Philosophy and the Mirror of Nature* Rorty criticizes a number of ideas that have found a home in philosophy's "epistemological project":

"Knowledge as accurate representation, made possible by special mental processes, and intelligible through a general theory of representation". (*PMN*, p. 6)

Epistemological skepticism, and the project of refuting the skeptic. (*PMN*, p. 114)

Locke's idea of "learning more about what we could know and how we might know it better by studying how our mind worked." (*PMN*, p. 137)

The idea that armed with a theory of knowledge, philosophy can define a "permanent neutral matrix" for the adjudication of any claim to know. (*PMN*, p. 211)

A common thread among these is the idea of knowledge as "cognition," by which I mean a mental state that qualifies as knowledge by having been caused "in the right way." Whatever is defined as the right way becomes our source of "privileged representations," which are the best knowledge, uniquely deserving the name of science (*epistem*). Rorty seems to assume that epistemology in any usual form presupposes this "cognitive" concept of knowledge, presupposing that knowledge is distinguished from non-knowledge by its being caused in an appropriate way. That is why "the notion of a 'theory of knowledge' will not make sense unless we have confused causation and justification" (*PMN*, p. 152). If epistemic quality depends on causal provenance, then we are dealing with the epistemology of "privileged representations," that is, mental states "which are certain because of their causes rather than because of the arguments given for them" (*PMN*, p. 157).

The idea of knowledge as "cognition" animates philosophy's oldest analogy for knowing – seeing something clearly and distinctly, more so than you could with the eye of the body. This is Plato's purely intellectual gaze, directed upon immaterial forms, whose abstract changelessness lets us see them steady and whole. Aristotle's hylomorphism was an effort to replace the optical analogy with something technical and precise. Later philosophers rang changes on Plato and Aristotle. Medieval thinkers worked Aristotle's notion of *phantasia* (without which there is no thought) into a theory of mental representations, or what they called objective (that is, subjective) ideas functioning in cognition as rational signs of extra-mental reality. Descartes and Locke popularized this scholasticism. Their "idea idea" combined the Platonic assumption that knowledge is a kind of vision with Aristotle's idea that knowing requires some sameness, an isomorphism or formal correspondence between a psychical item (Cartesian idea) and the external *presence* (Platonic idea) it re-presents. Hume exposed the unfortunate implications of this view of knowledge. If an idea is the first or immediate object of understanding, then obviously there is nothing with which we may compare an idea except another idea. So we have no right to call ideas "representations." *We* are presented with them, but *they* do not "present" anything other than themselves. True and false, therefore, like good and evil, must consist entirely of relations *among* ideas, including the sentiments and passions they provoke. Perception, understanding, knowledge, meaning, and value are all limited to ideas, to subjective patterns, feelings, and habits.

Kant absorbed and transformed Hume's subjective internalism. He agrees that it makes no sense to think of ideas or *Vorstellungen* as quasi-pictures whose truth depends on their resemblance to the things they are about. Unlike Hume, however, who (like Rorty) abandons the whole idea of representation, Kant comes up with a new theory about how ideas are amenable to epistemic evaluation as objective, veridical, true, and so on, without anybody having to lift a veil and compare an idea with a thing-in-itself. Ideas, perceptions, experiences are not pictures of independently present things. They are logical judgments, propositional components of the theory through which we understand and become conscious of what we know. These components (the content of empirical knowledge) acquire significance from their place in the theory, and are justified as knowledge by their logical coherence. The idea of *resemblance* plays no role in Kant's theory of empirical knowledge. Concepts are rules for connecting sensations rather than abstractions from sense, and representations are rational constructions driven by human need, not a disinterested imitation of being.

Rorty praises "Kant's advance in the direction of taking knowledge to be of propositions rather than of objects – his step away from the attempts of Aristotle and Locke to model knowing on perceiving" (*PMN*, p. 154). Kant is the first philosopher "to think of the foundations of knowledge as propositions rather than objects" (*PMN*, p. 160). Yet Kant only "advanced half of the way toward a conception of knowledge as fundamentally 'knowing that' rather than 'knowing of' – half way toward a conception of knowledge which was *not* modeled on perception" (*PMN*, p. 147). Kant still wanted to deduce the "scope and limits" of knowledge, and to do so in terms of a "framework of causal metaphors – 'constitution,' 'making,' 'shaping,' 'synthesizing,' and the like" (*PMN*, p. 161). Kant thus remains caught in the assumptions of the epistemological or "cognitive" conception of knowledge, defining a mental state as knowledge because of its cause (transcendental conditions) rather than because of the arguments that can be given for it.

What would a full-blown conception of knowledge as fundamentally "knowing that" look like? Sentences replace experiences and justification is carefully distinguished from causation. Conversation, the exchange of statements, replaces the contemplative monologue of mimesis and the mentalism of transcendental synthesis. This is Rorty's anti-epistemological argument: Hume without the subjectivism, Kant without the monologism or the pseudo-problem of transcendence, the objectivity of knowledge being achieved dialogically, through the publicity of language. Knowledge has to be true, of course, but there is no significant practical difference between a true belief and one which passes for true because it is so well justified.[1] "True" does not have the same logical meaning as "justified," but the logical distinction between them makes no difference in practice and can be dropped. Knowledge is "what we are justified in believing" (*PMN*, p. 9). The justification of belief is the dialectical defensibility of statements of belief. Knowledge chases agreement up the tree of conversation.

Rorty "goes all the way" from presence and representation to an entirely linguistic and anti-representational view of knowledge. Knowledge does not require that a Real Something transcend belief and measure the cognitive quality of our conversations. Knowledge revolves entirely within discourse. It is entirely a matter of sentences people believe true, the statements they make, the interlocutors who receive and criticize such statements, and the standards they go by. In the eighteenth century it was said that nothing but an idea can be like an idea. Rorty transcribes this insight in the register of language: Nothing but a sentence can justify a sentence. Showing that a sentence is warranted (or true) means showing its connection with other sentences assumed to be warranted (or true). Furthermore, since a perception is evidence for a sentence only when it is described or interpreted with a sentence, verification revolves entirely within language.

Knowledge and Conversation

Rorty identifies as his "crucial premise" in *Philosophy and the Mirror of Nature* the assumption that "we understand knowledge when we understand the social justification of belief, and thus have no need to view it as accuracy of representations." The social justification of belief, he says, is "not a matter of a special relation between ideas (or words) and objects, but of conversation, of social practice" (*PMN*, p. 170). This premise entails a number of consequences. Some are negative; for instance that "there is no such thing as a justified belief which is nonpropositional," nor "justification which is not a relation between propositions" (*PMN*, p. 183). Also that "everything which is not a matter of social practice is no help in understanding the *justification* of human knowledge" (*PMN*, p. 186). More positively, conversation is said to be "the ultimate context within which knowledge is to be understood" (*PMN*, p. 389). Justification is relative to the different conversations we can have. "Alternative standards of justification" (*PMN*, p. 380) make knowledge depend on what "a given society, or profession, or other group, takes to be good ground for assertions of a certain sort" (*PMN*, p. 385).

Hasty critics assume Rorty has reduced justification to *de facto* agreement, anybody's agreement reached any way. Bernard Williams rhetorically asks why, if all you need to establish something as knowledge is agreement, Crick and Watson might not "have economised on all that trouble with the x-ray photographs . . . and just spread some gossip about the helix?"[2] The answer is because it wouldn't have worked, would not have persuaded those who mattered. The agreement that defines knowledge cannot have been produced in any old way. Knowledge is (only) what *we* agree is justified by *our* standards, *our* methods, concepts, evidence, and styles of reasoning. The difference between "relativism" and Rorty's *ethnocentric* pragmatism has misled more than one critic. Putnam thinks he is taking a stand against Rorty and relativism when he defines knowledge as belief which has attained ideal rational acceptability. But take the idea one step further. How do we assess rational acceptability? As Putnam says, it is by referring to traditions, to historical styles and paradigms of rationality, or in other words, ethnocentrically. There is no misunderstanding when Rorty says to Putnam that he "cannot see what 'idealized rational acceptability' can mean except rational acceptability to an ideal community . . . [or] how, given that no such community is going to have a God's eye view, this ideal community can be anything more than *us* as we should like to be." Or when he adds that "identifying 'idealized rational acceptability' with 'acceptability to *us* at our best' is just what I had in mind when I said that pragmatists should be ethnocentrists rather than relativists."[3]

The source of Rorty's ethnocentric view of knowledge runs deep in pragmatism, linking Dewey and Peirce to Hegel. Dewey believed that "inherent in all social life [is] an intimation of what it would be at its best."[4] Rorty makes explicit the implication that "our only useful notions of 'true' and 'real' and 'good' are extrapolations from practices and beliefs" (*PMN*, p. 377). To extrapolate our use of the word "true," say, would require that we use it in new cases with the same normative meaning as in the past. Such "extrapolation" is not going to be predictable from information about a past pattern of agreement – unless, of course, the predictor is one of us, a member of our community, following our rules, attuned to our way of going on. As far as knowledge, truth, and rationality are concerned, there is as Hegel said no "out and out Other" by which they are measured. They are *ours* or *for-us*. In the words of another Hegelian-cum-pragmatist, "the theoretical attempt to track down the 'source' of the normative dimension in discourse leads us right back to our own implicitly normative practices. The structure of those practices can be elucidated, but always from within normative space, from within *our* normative practices of giving and asking for reasons."[5]

Ethnocentrism is supposed to be bad. No one ever calls himself "ethnocentric." We reserve this term for our opponents; it is always someone else, with whom you disagree, who is ethnocentric. But Rorty is not advocating the fallacy that anthropologists (and others) love to denounce – the colonialist assumption that unlike the savage our way of doing things is especially favored by reason, nature, or God. It is, however, especially favored by *us*, and Rorty thinks the difference is important. This point has often been missed. His endorsement of ethnocentrism does not make sense without liberalism; without liberalism, ethnocentrism would be awful. But Rorty sees nothing objectionable about ethnocentrism when the ethnos at the center is a liberal democratic society that makes openness to others central to its own self-image (*ORT*, p. 204). *Our* ethnocentrism is different from everybody else's. When *we* are ethnocentric, we are not ethnocentric. When we are true to our traditions, we are open to other traditions, when we are interested in ourselves, we are interested in what is new and different, happy (at our best) to accommodate and learn from it.

Let me return to the "crucial premise" of Rorty's argument in *Philosophy and the Mirror of Nature*. It is that there is nothing more to knowledge than "the social justification of belief," and the corollary, that conversation is "the ultimate context within which knowledge is to be understood." Why buy this premise? Reading *Philosophy and the Mirror of Nature* with this question in mind drew my attention to four lines of argument.

1   How Else? Assuming it is not "by virtue of relations of 'acquaintance' between persons and, for example, thoughts, impressions, universals, and propositions" (*PMN*, p. 177), *how else* would a claim acquire the authority of knowledge? Knowledge is not an impossible transaction between the mental mirror and things-in-themselves. So *what else* could it be if not just what you can (appropriately) get

interlocutors to agree with? "We can only come under epistemic rules when we have entered the community where the game governed by those rules is played" (*PMN*, p. 187). "All matters concerning epistemic status . . . [are] a sociological rather than metaphysical concern" (*PMN*, p. 219).

But isn't that really the question – whether ruling out the epistemology of mirrors as good as proves the pragmatism of conversation? Have we an exclusive choice to make between metaphysics and sociology, mimesis and conversation, Platonism and Pragmatism? Isn't the real question whether Rorty makes a good case for knowledge as ethnocentric consensus? Why is rejecting "the pseudo-explanation of epistemic authority through the notion of 'direct acquaintance' by the 'Eye of the Mind' with mental entities such as sense-data and meanings" (*PMN*, p. 209) supposed to favor the claim that "the community [is the] source of epistemic authority" (*PMN*, p. 188)? Rorty's discussion of knowledge is laced with dichotomous reasoning which avoids outright fallacy only on the unargued assumption that we face an exclusive choice between two well-defined alternatives:

> We can think of knowledge as a relation to propositions, and thus of justification as a relation between the propositions in question and other propositions from which the former may be inferred. Or we may think of both knowledge and justification as privileged relations to the objects those propositions are about. (*PMN*, p. 159)

> Can we treat the study of "the nature of human knowledge" just as the study of certain ways in which human beings interact, or does it require an ontological foundation . . .? Shall we take "S knows that p" . . . as a remark about the status of S's reports among his peers, or shall we take it as a remark about the relation between subject and object, between nature and its mirror? . . . To choose between these two approaches is to choose between truth as "what it is good for us to believe" and truth as "contact with reality." (*PMN*, pp. 175–176)

The "how else?" argument is not as strong as it needs to be. The oppositions Rorty presents are not logically exclusive, so no objection against one side favors the other, and *no* argument can prove the negative proposition that there is no understanding of knowledge apart from the antithetical ones Rorty considers. It is not for a critic to defend a third option (though I will do so later); the arbitrariness of the dichotomies argues against shifting the burden of proof. The question is not "how else?" It is why saying *no* to the epistemology of privileged representations is supposed to be as good as saying *yes* to Rorty's pragmatism?

2   Ockham's Razor. "Once we understand (as historians of knowledge do) when and why various beliefs have been adopted or discarded, there is [not] something called 'the relation of knowledge to reality' left over to be understood" (*PMN*, p. 178). To posit an unverifiable difference between "true knowledge" and what seems well justified and thus passes for known would be superfluous, redundant, a source of pseudo-problems. Yet only someone already convinced of Rorty's dichotomies will think it is simpler to explain knowledge in terms of conversation.

3   "Justification is public" (*PMN*, p. 254). Frege taught analytic philosophers to make a sharp distinction between norm and causation. Attend to the sentences of public language, not subjective ideas or private mental representations. Since the concern to hold justified beliefs or to justify statements is a concern with how one stands in

another's eyes, the difference between knowledge and error is to be sought not in a solitary transaction with mute reality but in a normative difference between sentences realized in actual or possible conversations. Again, though, I am unhappy with the implicit dichotomy. Do we really have to choose between private mental events and public discourse? What about public things, like artifacts, whose use is as social as a conversation though there need be nothing linguistic or conversational about it. Later I shall argue that knowledge figures in any and all our transactions with artifacts. The artifacts of language and what we do with them are not unique in the expression of knowledge. That is why I am unsatisfied with Rorty's idea that *conversation* is where the difference between knowledge and non-knowledge is ultimately decided.

4   Meaning Holism. Rorty agrees with "the holistic point that words take their meaning from other words rather than by virtue of their representative character, and the corollary that vocabularies acquire their privileges from the men who use them rather than from their transparency to the real" (*PMN*, p. 368). Why do vocabularies acquire epistemic privilege from the men who use them? Apparently it is because once we "drop the notion of correspondence for sentences as well as for thoughts," we see that sentences are "connected with other sentences rather than the world" (*PMN*, pp. 371–372). The argument seems to be that since words acquire meaning by relations to other words rather than to things, things cannot enter into the rationale for anything that we say or mean. Perhaps meaning-holism implies that words are not representations, which may further imply that justification has nothing to do with a representation's adequacy to the thing it represents. But from these (again) entirely negative inferences nothing follows about what justification *is*. The holistic criticism of knowledge or truth as "a special relation between ideas (or words) and objects" does not prove Rorty's crucial premise that justification *is nothing but* "a matter . . . of conversations, of social practice."

The Biases of Epistemology

I think Rorty needs a better reason than he has explained for choosing to see knowledge as he does, and not only because of the inconclusiveness of the arguments I have discussed. His pragmatism shares a number of biases with the epistemology it seeks to overcome, and consequently retains some of epistemology's presuppositions and deficiencies.

(a)   Propositional bias. The most important knowledge, or the knowledge that most repays philosophical consideration, is propositional knowing-that, knowledge of truth, of a proposition that is true, or is suitable for evaluation in terms of true and false.

(b)   Belief-*plus*. The presumption that knowledge begins with belief, which rises to knowledge through the addition of extra factors. Most epistemologies add justification, many add truth. For Rorty, knowledge is ethnocentrically justified belief, which pragmatically entails its passing-for-true among the interlocutors who matter. The shared assumption concerns the continuity of knowledge and belief, the idea that knowledge is some form of belief-*plus* (whatever).

(c)   Discursive bias. Knowledge as *claims*, as linguistic, discursive, dialogical expressions of belief; as statements, appropriate objects for dialectical challenge and defense. The best knowledge is consequently logical, rational, discursively articulated, its value realized in rational discourse. There may be no privileged representations, but Rorty blatantly privileges discourse in the wide sense that includes discussion, demonstration, dialectic, and dialogue or conversation.

(d)   The misplaced good of knowledge, and a posture of indifference toward Nietzsche's question concerning this good. Why care for knowledge? Why prefer it over ignorance, error, or fantasy? Rorty's pragmatism is no more help in understanding this preference than any of the traditional theories of knowledge, while the suggestion that we merely drop the preference is empty.

Propositional bias

The principal reason for the propositional bias in epistemology is the assumption that the unit of knowledge must admit of evaluation in terms of true and false, which is a functional definition of a proposition. Even if Rorty does not distinguish between a proposition's "really being true" and its merely passing or being well justified, he does assume that the unit of knowledge is something believed-true, which ensures that his pragmatism shares epistemology's propositional bias.

Why must knowledge be true (or even believed-true)? "Well, (it may be said), if we discover that something we thought we knew is wrong, that it is an error and is false, we revoke our belief and speak no more of it as knowledge." That is right as far as it goes. What it shows is not that knowledge must be true, but that something we consider an error is not, of course, something we are going to count as knowledge. Certainly knowledge cannot be false. But "true" and "false" are contrary, not contradictory, terms. Knowledge does not have to be one or the other. From the mere fact that no knowledge *is false* nothing follows about truth as a logical ingredient of knowledge.

Consider this inference: (1) *Socrates knows that p*; so, (2) *p*. Many find the inference valid, and it might occur to a philosopher to adduce it as proof that knowledge has to be true.[6] On the face of it though, the inference is contrived. Who would reason this way and to what purpose, especially since it is no easier to determine when somebody (really) knows that *p* than it is to determine whether *p* is true? Perhaps the intuitive validity of the inference reveals what Wittgenstein called logical grammar. Attributing knowledge to another usually carries an implicit claim to know the same yourself. But that does not show that a logical property of *being true* partly constitutes knowledge, or that knowledge could not be what it is were it not *knowledge of the truth*.[7]

If knowledge must be true, then a claim to know must be a claim to know that something is true. Not that it is warranted, reasonable, or justified – those would be different claims – but that it is *knowledge* and as such is the very truth. But knowledge that has to be true cannot be fallible. The only claim you could reasonably assert as knowledge would be one that (you suppose) could not possibly be incorrect. So the more implausible it is to believe in infallible truth, the more doubtful it should be that truth is a condition on knowledge. But why fallibility? What recommends this attitude toward knowledge? As Hume and Kant argued, knowing is not to enjoy a specular representation of a thing-in-itself apart from its relation to anything else. Instead, as Nietzsche and Dewey say, it is to know the relations, to know some cross-section of relations among an entire ensemble of things (including sentences). Since such relations are constantly changing, so must knowledge change to confront novelty without loss of reliability. The structure and content of knowledge can be no more immutable than the environment in which it makes sense. This vital flexibility distinguishes knowledge from belief, doctrine, or genetic hard-wiring. But it also means that merely to retain empirical reliability the practice of knowledge requires what Peirce called the attitude of contrite fallibilism.

The assumption that knowledge has to be true, or that the most important instances of knowledge are propositional, makes the distinction between knowing-that and knowing-how seem greater than it is. Of course propositions, sentences, statements are all artifacts, things we must know how to make before we can know that they are true. Also the knowledge it takes to know that a proposition is true is not itself propositional knowledge. To know, say, *that Australia lies in the Southern Hemisphere* is true, you have to know how to discover and assess evidence, weigh plausibility, consult authorities, refute objections, and so on, including perhaps knowing how to get there from here.[8] All knowledge is like that, building on operational, effective know-how, and the artifacts (including but not limited to those of conception and communication) that we know how to use.

Belief-plus

The propositional bias in epistemology stands on two legs. One is the conviction that knowledge has to be true. The other is that belief (conceived as a kind of propositional registration) is a necessary ingredient of knowledge, that knowledge is some form of belief-*plus*. Most disputes in epistemology concern the further factors that raise belief up to knowledge. No-one (Rorty included) questions the assumption that knowledge not only begins in belief but never leaves it behind.

How could it? "Surely if I know that *p*, I must believe that *p*!" Or at least not disbelieve it. But what continuity between knowledge and belief does that prove? Not that knowledge is a logical complex of which belief is a logical element. Belief is what we have to fall back on where we want knowledge. Only those who *want* knowledge believe in God. A denizen of the equatorial zone may believe snow is white, but those for whom winter is a fact of life do not believe snow is white. They know it. Anybody who *believes* snow is white does not know much about snow, and those who know it at all know it is white (as they know it can be other than white). Such knowledge is not an impeccably justified belief. It is not a belief at all. It is non-propositional, perceptual, kinesthetic knowledge.

The difference between belief and knowledge is a difference between the sources and limits of competence. If your belief arises not from your own experience, but from reading something in a book, and if all that your belief allows you to do is speak plausibly, then it is just a belief, not knowledge. If with experience, you are reliably able to do something well, you do not have a terrifically well-justified belief – you have knowledge. As for talking plausibly, the communicative skills by which someone makes a case and persuades others are certainly knowledge, however sophistical or erroneous the claim defended may be.

Rorty sounds one of pragmatism's founding ideas when he says that beliefs are not mental representations but rules for action.[9] Does this idea diminish the argument against belief-*plus* conceptions of knowledge? I don't think so. Peirce says that "the whole function of thought is to produce habits of action," which is his definition of belief. But since a belief is also something that can be true or evaluated for truth (as Peirce insists, calling it a tautology), the upshot of this pragmatism is a logocentric propositionalizing of action and habit rather than a de-propositionalizing or anti-representational account of belief.[10]

Can the belief queried and attributed in what Quine and Davidson call radical translation or interpretation be a "rule of action"? It has to be a disposition to assent to a sentence, which makes it a rule of speech-action, a habitual response to linguistic prompting. If *that* is what belief is, then belief shrinks to what you can have a conversation about, and if knowledge is belief-*plus* (whatever), then knowledge is an even smaller part of what you can have a conversation about. At this point knowledge has become confused with prestigious talk.[11]

Combining the pragmatic conception of belief as a rule or habit of action with a belief-*plus* conception of knowledge assumes that knowledge is rule-like or habitual, when it is precisely the distinction of knowledge that it can deal with cases at the limit of rules, where habitual responses break down. The difference between knowledge and belief shows up clearly when success in an endeavor calls for action that is *not* rule-governed or habitual, not following mechanically from anything we have already seen. The most important knowledge is always knowledge of (and at) the limits of rules. If belief is a rule of action, knowledge (or at least the best knowledge) cannot be a belief at all. It is not the same sort of thing as belief only better, improved by the addition of a further factor. Belief is *faute de mieux*, something we may have a right to (as James argued) when we badly *want* knowledge we do not have. When we have it, however, knowledge has lost this and every other characteristic of belief.

The bias of discourse

The epistemology of propositional belief-*plus* offers an entirely discursive conception of knowledge. Knowledge is limited to propositions that stand up to methodological, logical, or conversational tests. Such propositions withstand objections and triumph in debate by the unforced force of the better argument. But like the concepts of truth, proposition, and belief, those of argument, logic, proof, discursive articulation, and verbal justification are less central to knowledge than logocentric philosophers from Parmenides to Rorty assume.[12]

The reduction of knowledge to a discursive value may only be a scholar's implicit assumption that words are the most important things in the world. Yet there is more to *sapiens* than *logos*. Lots of knowledge is never discursively articulated, not translated into sentences, or defended with reasons, and it is usually doubtful that it could be. No amount of true sentential knowledge enables one to use a tool well, and trying to translate such know-how into sentences is largely pointless. The knowledge itself is the capacity to perform well with some range of (mostly non-linguistic) artifacts. Sentences with which somebody might describe the action or its upshot do not take us closer to the essence of the knowledge.

The privilege of discourse is no more defensible in the form of Rorty's pragmatic conversations. He claims to extend "wholehearted acceptance to the brute, inhuman, causal stubbornness" of things (*ORT*, p. 83). But he also wants to say that "there are no constraints on inquiry save conversational ones – no wholesale constraints derived from the nature of the objects, or of the mind, or of language, but only those retail constraints provided by the remarks of our fellow inquirers" (*CP*, p. 165). How stubborn can inhuman causality be if it can't even constrain an inquiry or what inquiry proves? The "hardness of facts" is supposed to be "an artifact produced by our choice of language game ... simply the hardness of the previous agreements within a community about the consequences of a certain event" (*ORT*, p. 80). Yet brute causality limits what we can make and do in ways which unfortunately can have surprisingly little to do with "agreements within a community about the consequences of a certain event" (*ORT*, p. 80). The statement and justification of beliefs is no doubt a social practice but causation is not, and neither is knowledge.

Misplaced good of knowledge

Why prefer knowledge? Rorty has nothing to say to this question except perhaps that we *do* prefer it. We prefer knowledge because of who we are – children of Platonism and the Enlightenment, of Socrates and Locke, Mill and Freud. Solidarity with this heritage counts for more than the (platitudinous) reasons we could give for preferring knowledge.

Is that really the best we can do? We are those children, but our forebears thought there was an excellent reason for preferring knowledge: knowledge is truth and, if not divine, truth is at least "the most valuable, [and] pleasantest thing in the world" (Locke).[13] Take away this reason and you threaten the coherence of the preference for knowledge. For it is hardly true that we esteem knowledge unconditionally. We are also the inventors and lusty practitioners of advertising and propaganda.[14] We have more secrets, more strategic non-knowledge, more floridly rhetorical communication than ever before. Merely because in some of our moods we have honored knowledge does not provide us with a coherent understanding of this preference today, not if we *think* about our commitment, and do not merely cling to it without reasons.

What is lacking from Rorty's pragmatism is some idea of why, if all there is to knowledge is belief-plus-(ethnic)consensus, we should prefer it. Why should one *want* to believe what others readily accept? Why not shed the bad taste of wanting to agree with the many, as Nietzsche recommended? To come at the same point from another direction, were knowledge as Rorty describes it, it would be difficult to understand our preference for it. As difficult, ironically, as it was for William James to understand the good it would do knowledge to copy a transcendent reality. Rorty reduces the value of knowledge to no more than what the Irishman got from being carried to the banquet in a sedan chair with no bottom. "Faith! If it wasn't for the honor of the thing, I might as well have come on foot!" So with knowledge after Rorty. But for the honor of being agreed with, we might as well remain ignorant.[15]

Why prefer knowledge? An obvious answer is, prudence, of course. Rorty might like this answer. He seems to have adopted what Charles Taylor calls "the prudent strategy." This is "a stripped-down secular outlook, without any religious dimension or radical hope in history ... advis[ing] us to scale down our hopes and circumscribe our vision ... [and] remove the burden of impossible aspirations."[16] The question is whether thinking about knowledge in terms of ethnocentric consensus is wise or even prudent.

Of course prudence has something to do with the value of knowledge. When we do not act with knowledge success is no more likely than chance. Yet this much prudence cannot entirely motivate our doing what has to be done to make new knowledge or keep knowledge we have. To be reproduced without loss and survive another generation knowledge must not only be in constant use, but used *well*. Such use requires action that goes beyond the utilitarian preoccupation with prudence, requiring the peculiar indifference to prudence or utilitarian rationality that Nietzsche called the daring of the lover of knowledge.[17] The result is work whose aesthetic quality has left the calculations of prudence and utility far behind. The continuing existence of knowledge requires both the capacity and the desire to attain such finesse, and that is why prudence is not wise or even ultimately prudent. It is a terminally short-term strategy, whose long-term effect is not to preserve knowledge but to lose it, waste it, forget it.

Rorty banalizes technical or artifactual practice by redescribing it in his relentlessly linguistifying terms. Superiority becomes essentially rhetorical, innovation reduces to the appearance of a new vocabulary. Yet the knowledge mostly responsible for present-day technological civilization does not have this rhetorical, linguistic, verbal character. Our best examples of structural art, such as Hagia Sophia or the Brooklyn Bridge, do not have that character, nor do inventions as far-reaching as the wheel or as singular as the clothesbutton. Nothing is clarified, and a lot is made obscure, by the suggestion that innovations in reinforced concrete were really just a new way of talking. We learned a new way of talking as a result of living with Maillart's concrete bridges, but to confuse a new language-game with the artifactual innovation that gives it a point and material reference is to confuse a parasite with its host and make a mystery of both language and technics. We do not get a *truer* account of what is *really going on* by redescribing the reliability or effectiveness of artifacts or the knowledge that they express and presuppose in terms of beliefs, sentences, or linguistic dispositions. Of course a vocabulary is an artifact and description can be a tool. I do not want to forget about language, only to question Rorty's assumption that there is practically no difference between words and things, a thing is as good as a description, as well as the assumption that sentences are the units of knowledge, descriptions the artifacts that matter most. As if the more material artifacts and techniques upon which we daily depend were byproducts of language and not, as is likely, the other way around.[18]

Knowledge and Human Existence

Were knowledge as Rorty supposes – ethnocentric, conversational, agreeable belief – its superior value (in contrast to opinion, doctrine, conviction, error, myth, and the like) would be a mystery if not a mistake. Is the appropriate attitude toward knowledge one of "less is more" – ask less from knowledge, cultivate lower expectations, then we cannot be let down? What if the only way to ensure that knowledge does not disappoint us is by expecting a lot from it? That is our plight – let me explain why.

Homo sapiens is one of several overlapping hominid mutations of *Homo erectus*, and the only one to survive. Knowledge, embodied in superior artifacts, seems to have figured in our success at the expense of competing hominids.[19] Passing for true does not make a statement true, but then for Rorty (as for Davidson) *nothing* "makes" a statement true. See Donald Davidson, *Inquiries Concerning Truth and Interpretation* (Oxford: Oxford University Press, 1984), p. 194. Rorty thus departs from the pragmatic tradition of a "theory of truth." I discuss this tradition in *Truth in Philosophy* (Cambridge, MA: Harvard University Press, 1993). One thing paleoanthropology has shown is the superiority of the artifacts associated with the first *sapiens* over other contemporary hominid species. Since artifacts are worthless without the knowledge that attends their use, superior artifacts and superior knowledge are two aspects and descriptions of the same existential reality for evolving hominids, and may have made the competitive difference between us and unsuccessful species in other ways very like us. This would mean that a rich artifactual environment has been among the ecological conditions of human adaptation. It was from within this already significantly artifactual environment that spoken language would have arisen. Superior artifacts and the knowledge they presuppose and generate have made us the adaptable animals that we are. The only way we survive as much change as we do is by constantly changing our environment, remaking it (with artifacts) as it remakes us, in a relationship that is probably symbiotic. What continues to make us adaptable is our capacity to change, and what guides that change so far as it *is* guided and not left up to chance is knowledge.

Perhaps the connection between these reflections on artifacts and the question of the value of knowledge is obvious. Knowledge belongs to the human ecology, as do the artifacts our very existence co-evolutionarily entails. Human beings need superior artifacts no less than a suitable atmosphere. Hence the value of knowledge. What makes knowledge good, what makes it desirable and worth cultivating, is that it enhances the reliability with which we operate in an artifactual environment. When we do not act from knowledge success is no likelier than chance. The value of knowledge is the value of any capacity to perform reliably with artifacts. If you want an obvious example of knowledge, don't think of an obviously true sentence. Think of an obviously sophisticated artifact, or any artifact used in a sophisticated, artful, excellent manner. It is this performative quality that makes the difference between knowledge and belief, and proves that it is the artifact, not the sentence or belief, which is the unit of knowledge, the foci around which all our practice of knowledge and all its results gravitate.

Despite our deep dependence on them, there is nothing instinctual about knowledge or the superior artifacts which sustain it. No gene ensures that despite the negligence of previous generations the next will have knowledge without which it cannot survive. Nothing mechanically guarantees that human beings will cultivate an ethos of knowledge appropriate to survival. Neither is it enough that people are constantly using knowledge for it to be reproduced without loss of competence. As I have suggested, knowledge has the peculiarity that it has to be used well merely to be reproduced without degrading loss. That is why we cannot ensure that knowledge does not let us down except by expecting a lot from it and from those who claim it, and by caring about the difference between knowledge and opinion or belief.

Some definite cultural (one might better say ethical) presuppositions are probably required to sustain any powerful, flexible, adaptation-enhancing, artifactual ecology. Just having the knowledge around and using it is not enough to ensure continuing empirical reliability. The use of knowledge can become self-parasitical, worming away at reliability and competence by over-reliance on extrapolation or pointless formality. The only way to reproduce knowledge and keep it superior is through a culture or ethos of superior technical practice. Epistemic or artifactual stasis, routine without change, is ultimately not viable. We cannot stay where we are in knowledge without trying to know more and better than we have. We cannot preserve knowledge to be used without doing more than merely using what is already known.

When we remember what impressed our forebears and had better still impress us about knowledge, we do not find what Rorty describes. We do not find agreeable conversation. The important thing is the quality of the performance that puts knowledge into practice. Such performances are at most occasionally dialogical, and are usually evaluated not by conversational consensus but artifactual reliability – not by anybody's *agreeing* that a work is reliable or well done, but by its *being* so.

Let me give an example to help suggest that there is a significant difference between being reliable and what even well-informed or qualified opinion agrees is so. When first built, practically all American structural engineers would have agreed that the Tacoma Narrows Bridge was twentieth-century engineering at its best, the work of a master designer. Some continue to believe this, despite the fact that the 1500-meter bridge collapsed in 1940, four months after it was opened. It collapsed for a reason that the designer could and obviously should have taken into account. But the entire profession of structural engineering in America had adopted a simplistic aesthetic of slimness in bridges, rationalized by a faulty doctrine and specious mathematical analysis, which obfuscated known lessons concerning the effect of wind on the suspended deck.

Although it was precisely this aerodynamic effect that was responsible for the Tacoma Narrows failure, one observer suggests that if the relevance of aerodynamics to the design "had been suggested by a person outside the network of 'leading structural engineers,' the advice would have been considered an attack on the profession of civil engineering." Which is exactly what happened. Shortly after the collapse, an article in *Engineering News-Record* argued that had the designer (Leon Moisseiff) taken appropriate notice of a whole documented series of wind failures in similar bridges both in America and Europe he might have changed the design and prevented the failure. Two weeks later the profession extracted this retraction: "The casual reader [of the critical article] may infer . . . that the modern bridge engineer, in view of the earlier failures of bridges, was remiss . . . The author . . . did not suggest or intend the reader to imply that the modern engineer should have known the details of the earlier disasters."[20]

Reflection on such examples should disabuse philosophers of the notion that knowledge is nothing but the consensus of disciplinary or professional peers. There is a palpable difference between the collapse of a bridge and the collapse of engineering belief in the principles of its design. What experts agree is well done need not be so, nor need what they call knowledge be the real thing. Conversation is not the context in which it is ultimately decided what is knowledge. That is decided where the reliability of knowledge is decided, which is ultimately nothing short of the entire environment where knowledge makes us effective.

✳✳✳✳✳✳✳✳✳✳✳✳✳✳✳✳✳✳

What was epistemology? An exaggeration. An exaggerated importance for "science," for the value of deduction, proof, truth, and for the importance of dialectics and theory to intelligence and knowledge. Pragmatists decry the craving for certainty, finding in it the otherworldly indifference to practical life which is anathema to them.[21] Rorty suggests that apart from the metaphor of mind as mirror of nature there would be no topic for a "theory of knowledge." Only if knowledge is taken for a quasi-visual reflection of things-in-themselves would the idea arise of a project to enhance knowledge by learning more about how our cognition-causing mechanism works. Of course the mind is not really a mirror. That's just a metaphor. If it creates more trouble than it is worth, which is how Rorty judges the metaphors that sustain the impression that epistemology is possible or desirable, then drop it. You need not worry about dropping some portion of The truth, for truth is no more than what passes for true, and that changes with our historical conversations. As Dewey suggested, and Rorty concurs, intellectual progress "usually occurs through sheer abandonment of questions . . . We do not solve them; we get over them."[22] That is how Rorty must view the questions of epistemology. He sees a bad answer and infers that the question must be bad too. But however objectionable the metaphors that have solidified into epistemology may be, the importance of the questions to which they were addressed remains.

What was epistemology? A bad answer to a good question. The bad answer, or at least Plato's, was to misunderstand artisanship as copying forms that already exist in an immaterial realm which can be explored more directly by philosophical dialectic. But the question is not a misunderstanding too. It concerns the value of knowledge, its ecological singularity, the inextricability of its and our flourishing. We do not understand that much better than the Greeks did, and in the mean time knowledge has become more complicated. Plato was not wrong to let his attention be drawn to artisanship when he thought about knowledge, nor was he wrong to let the question of *what knowledge is* be directed by the question why it is *good*. The force of either question comes from the insight, which Rorty has said nothing to discredit, that the knowledge of superior artifacts plays an incomparable role in adapting us to our environment and maintaining that adaptation in the face of ceaseless change.

To remain adaptable in the way knowledge makes us requires an appropriate ethos or ethic of knowledge, and that is where Rorty's pragmatism is deficient. It obscures and mystifies the value of knowledge, the valuable difference between it and its pretenders, and is no help in understanding what it requires of us against the entropic tendency of time toward the loss of knowledge. My argument with Rorty's pragmatism is an argument for the primacy of artifacts over language-games or discourse, for performative reliability over conversational consensus, for knowledge over belief-plus-whatever, and for the superior good of knowledge over hope and solidarity.

Notes

References to the following works by Rorty are parenthetically embedded:

CIS   *Contingency, Irony, and Solidarity* (Cambridge: Cambridge University Press, 1989).

CP   *Consequences of Pragmatism* (Minneapolis: University of Minnesota Press, 1982).

ORT   *Objectivity, Relativism, and Truth*, *Philosophical Papers*, vol. 1 (Cambridge: Cambridge University Press, 1991).

PMN   *Philosophy and the Mirror of Nature* (Princeton: Princeton University Press, 1979).

1   Passing for true does not make a statement true, but then for Rorty (as for Davidson) *nothing* "makes" a statement true. See Donald Davidson, *Inquiries Concerning Truth and Interpretation* (Oxford: Oxford University Press, 1984), p. 194. Rorty thus departs from the pragmatic tradition of a "theory of truth." I discuss this tradition in *Truth in Philosophy* (Cambridge, MA: Harvard University Press, 1993).

2   Bernard Williams, "Getting It Right," review of *Contingency, Irony, and Solidarity*, *London Review of Books* 11, no. 22 (23 Nov. 1989), p. 3.

3   Hilary Putnam, *Realism and Reason* (Cambridge: Cambridge University Press, 1983), p. 299; and *Realism with a Human Face* (Cambridge, MA: Harvard University Press, 1990), pp. 157, 159. Rorty, "Putnam and the Relativist Menace," *Journal of Philosophy* 90 (1993), 451–452. Kai Nielsen also overlooks the difference between ethnocentrism and relativism in his critique of Rorty; see *After the Demise of the Tradition: Rorty, Critical Theory, and the Fate of Philosophy* (Boulder: Westview, 1991), pp. 154–155. I discuss Putnam and Rorty in "Putnam und Rorty über Objektivität und Wahrheit," *Deutsche Zeitschrift für Philosophie* 42

(1994):989–1005, and "Critical Notice of Putnam," *Canadian Journal of Philosophy* 24 (1994):665–688.

4   Robert B. Westbrook, *John Dewey and American Philosophy* (Ithaca: Cornell, University Press, 1991), p. 171. On Dewey and Rorty, see Carroll Guen Hart, *Grounding Without Foundations: A Conversation Between Richard Rorty and John Dewey to Ascertain their Kinship* (Toronto: Patmos Press, 1993).

5   G. W. F. Hegel, *Encyclopedia* §377 (*Zusatz*). Robert Brandom, *Making It Explicit: Reasoning, Representation, and Discursive Commitment* (Cambridge, MA: Harvard University Press, 1994), p. 649 (my emphasis).

6   For instance, Gilbert Harman, *Thought* (Princeton: Princeton University Press, 1973), pp. 114–115.

7   Brandom observes that "attributions of knowledge . . . are hybrid deontic attitudes in the sense that they involve both attributing and acknowledging commitments." "In taking someone to be a knower, one *attributes a commitment*, *attributes entitlement* to that commitment, and acknowledges commitment to the same content oneself." *Making It Explicit*, p. 202; see also p. 515.

8   See Gilbert Ryle, "Knowing How and Knowing That," *Collected Papers*, vol. 2 (London: Hutchinson, 1971), esp. pp. 224–225. Compare Michael Oakeshott's distinction between "technical" and "practical" knowledge; *Rationalism in Politics and Other Essays* (London: Methuen, 1962), p. 9. By contrast, Wilfrid Sellars writes: "anything which can properly be called 'knowing how to do something' presupposes a body of knowledge *that*; or, to put it differently, knowledge of truth or fact." *Science, Perception, and Reality* (London: Routledge & Kegan Paul, 1963), p. 1.

9   On beliefs as rules of action, see *CIS*.65; *ORT*.65, 118. Alexander Bain defined belief as "that upon which a man is prepared to act." Peirce, who first put the point in terms of rules/habits of action, said that "from this definition pragmatism is scarce more than a corollary." *The Collected Papers of Charles Sanders Peirce*, ed. Hartshorne and Weiss (Cambridge, MA: Harvard University Press, 1935), vol. 5, p. 7.

10 Peirce, "How to Make our Ideas Clear," *Collected Papers*, vol. 5, p. 256; and "The Fixation of Belief," ibid., p. 232.

11 The concept of belief, on which so much recent philosophy of mind and action uncritically depends, is treated with refreshing skepticism by anthropologist Rodney Needham. Flying in the face of everything philosophers say about radical interpretation, he observes that since "statements of belief are the only evidence for the phenomenon" and "the phenomenon itself appears to be no more than the custom of making such statements," belief "has no logical claim to inclusion in a universal psychological vocabulary." It "does not constitute a natural resemblance among men," nor does the practice of making statements of belief belong "to the common behavior of mankind." The very *having* of beliefs "is not in fact a conceptual capacity common to all men," and in ethnographical reports the word (and concept) "should be quite abandoned." *Belief, Language, and Experience* (Oxford: Blackwell, 1972), pp. 108, 151, 188, 200, 193.

12 On the Greek origins of the discursive bias see David Furley, "Truth as What Survives the *Elenchus*: An Idea in Parmenides," *The Criterion of Truth*, ed. P. Huby and G. Neal (Liverpool: Liverpool University Press, 1989).

13 Locke, Letter to Molyneux, January 1689. The good of truth is a theme of Locke's *Essay Concerning Human Understanding*; see for instance the Epistle to the Reader, and I.iv.23

14 James Rorty attributes an "axiom" to a former advertising colleague: "Always tell the truth. Tell a lot of the truth. Tell a lot more of the truth than anybody expects you to tell. Never tell the whole truth." *Our Master's Voice: Advertising* (New York: John Day, 1934), p. 176.

15 William James, *Pragmatism* (Cambridge, MA: Harvard University Press, 1978), p. 112.

16 Charles Taylor, *Sources of the Self* (Cambridge, MA: Harvard University Press, 1989), pp. 519–520.

17 Nietzsche, *The Gay Science*, §343.

18 On the relationship between tools and language in human evolution, see Merlin Donald, *Origins of the Modern Mind* (Cambridge, MA: Harvard University Press, 1991), pp. 113–115. For a survey of recent research, see K.R. Gibson and T. Ingold, ed., *Tools, Language, and Cognition in Human Evolution* (Cambridge: Cambridge University Press, 1993).

19 In part, this is the argument of Clifford Geertz, "The Impact of the Concept of Culture on the Concept of Man," *The Interpretation of Cultures* (New York: Basic Books, 1973). It is also, though only in part, the argument of Henry Plotkin, *Darwin Machines and the Nature of Knowledge* (Harmondsworth: Penguin, 1994). Plotkin finds knowledge *wherever* there is adaptation (so plants "know" how to photosynthesize nutrients), while I suggest that knowledge is as uniquely human as our neurology. And while Geertz speaks not of knowledge or superior artifacts but simply of culture, another anthropologist finds it convenient to *define* culture as "whatever it is one has to know or believe in order to operate in a manner acceptable to [a] society's members" (W. Goodenough, in Plotkin, p. 214). See my "Forbidding Knowledge," *The Monist* 79 (1996), and "Knowledge and Adaptation," *Biology and Philosophy*, 12 1997.

20 E. S. Ferguson, *Engineering and the Mind's Eye* (Cambridge, MA: MIT Press, 1992), pp. 190–192, 227. For an account of the Tacoma Narrows failure, see Henry Petroski, *Engineers of Dreams: Great Bridge Builders and the Spanning of America* (New York: Knopf, 1995), pp. 294–308. Professional insiders *still* maintain Moisseiff's blamelessness for Tacoma Narrows; see M. Levy and M. Salvadori, *Why Buildings Fall Down* (New York: Norton, 1992), chap. 7. The authors also refuse to fault Helmuth Jahn's "superb" and "brilliantly conceived structure" for a Kansas City arena (1973), despite the fact that days after the American Institute of Architects held their 1979 convention there the roof collapsed (pp. 57–59).

21 James, *Pragmatism*, pp. 111–112, 115, 123–125; and John Dewey, *Reconstruction in Philosophy* (New York: Henry Holt, 1920), chap. 5.

22 John Dewey, "The Influence of Darwin on Philosophy," cited in Rorty, *ORT*.96n. The significance of Dewey's remark for the traditional problems of epistemology is complicated by a remark elsewhere to the effect that "modern philosophic thought has been so preoccupied with these puzzles of epistemology . . . that many students are at a loss to know what would be left of philosophy if there were removed both the metaphysical task of distinguishing between the noumenal and phenomenal worlds and the epistemological task of telling how a separate subject can know an independent object. But would not the elimination of these traditional problems permit philosophy to devote itself to a more fruitful and more needed task?" (*Reconstruction in Philosophy*, pp. 123–124).

RESPONSE TO BARRY ALLEN

Barry Allen's *Truth in Philosophy* builds on Wittgenstein's insight into the nature of identity. Wittgenstein's point was that, although every question of the form "Is X the same as Y?" (e.g., "Is it the same time on the sun as it is here?") has a sense if we give it one, it has no sense until then. Allen combines this point that identity and difference come and go with redescription with Quine's insistence on "no entity without identity." The result is his claim that the self-identity, and thus the entitative status, of anything you can mention is up for conversational grabs. In that sense, everything – including clouds and rocks – is an artifact. To deny this, as philosophers usually have, is to be committed to what Allen calls "onto-logic" – the idea that being, *to on*, imposes criteria of sameness and difference all by itself, and that *logos* (human thought and talk) simply plays catch-up.

In his second book, *Knowledge and Civilization*, Allen proposes that we capitalize on the realization that clouds and concepts are as artifactual as beaver dams and quarks by attempting a general theory of "superb artifactual achievement" – Allen's surprising definition of the term "knowledge." His contribution to this volume echoes his criticisms of me in that book.

I agree with pretty much everything Allen says in *Truth in Philosophy*. I learned a lot from reading his very imaginative and acute summary of the assumptions about the relation between reality and language which we inherited from the Greeks. These assumptions were the target of both *Sein und Zeit* and *The Quest for Certainty*. Reading Allen's first book is perhaps the best way of grasping what Heidegger and Dewey had in common, and thus of understanding the leitmotif of twentieth-century philosophy – the motif that links Hegel with Brandom and Nietzsche with Davidson.

I have trouble, however, with *Knowledge and Civilization* – perhaps more trouble than Dewey would have had. Dewey would have liked the idea of replacing epistemology with a general theory of artifacts. He might have shared Allen's doubts about the "conversationalism" Brandom and I share, and, more generally, of what Allen calls our "discursive bias." He might have agreed with Allen that this bias continues the Platonic/Aristotelian preference for the mathematician over the artisan. But even the fear of being unDeweyan cannot persuade me that Allen's redefinition of "knowledge" is a useful way to continue his criticism of the philosophical tradition. My hunch is that it will work better just to drop knowledge as a topic rather than to say that I, and other critics of the Cartesian/Kantian epistemological problematic, have gotten knowledge wrong.

One way of expressing my doubts is to urge that Allen runs together two senses of the term "belief" – the one we employ when we ascribe beliefs to organisms in order to explain behavior and the one we use when we are distinguished "mere" belief from genuine knowledge. When we try to cope with an organism or other entity whose behavior is quite complex, we often attribute beliefs and desires to it. This lets us explain portions of its behavior as actions – as the outcomes of practical syllogisms. For this explanatory purpose, we do not need the term "knowledge" at all.

But when we are making comparative evaluations of success, as opposed to explaining behavior, we need to distinguish those who know from those who do not: the beavers that build tight dams from those that build leaky dams, the people who know that a certain mushroom is non-poisonous from those who merely believe that it is. The invidious sense of "believe," in which it is opposed to "know", does not have much in common with the purely descriptive sense, the one we use when we construct practical syllogisms. Belief-as-opposed-to-knowledge is not what is being attributed in the major premise of the practical syllogism. There seems no particular reason why the same term – "belief" – is used in these two different ways, any more than why we anglophones make do with a word which is ambiguous between *connaitre* and *savoir*.

I suspect that trying to bring both uses of "belief" under the same philosophical tent may be fruitless – as fruitless as trying to bring together "true statement," "true friend" and "true gold" (*wahr*, *treu*, and *echt*, roughly speaking). I cannot see why Allen would want to mingle the sense of "believe" in which (as he puts it) "anybody who *believes* that snow is white does not know much about snow" with the sense in which anybody who knows anything much about snow believes that it is white. Once we distinguish these two senses, I doubt that we need to say anything synoptic which applies both. Nor should we favor the former as ordinary and dismiss the latter as contrived.

I also doubt that we have, or need, a "philosophy of knowledge" hovering in the background of epistemology, and perhaps capable of surviving epistemology's demise.

Allen says that I have such a philosophy, because my dismissive treatment of epistemology "presupposes" a "substantial conception of knowledge" (p. 221). He also says that my "pragmatism shares a number of biases with the epistemology it seeks to overcome" (p. 226). My suggestion that "the most important instances of knowledge are propositional," Allen says, makes "the distinction between knowing-how and knowing-that seem greater than it is" (p. 228).

As I see it, however, that distinction remains both great and useful even after we grant to Allen that most of "the knowledge it takes to know that a proposition is true is not itself propositional knowledge" (p. 228). My pragmatism, like Dewey's, treats the historian's justified belief that a certain event took place as continuous with the architect's skill, the caveman's spear and the beaver's dam. A skilled architect and a disciplined historian are as reliable instruments for certain purposes as a sharp spear or a sturdy dam are for others.

Dewey, like Heidegger, spent a lot of time saying that it pays, for certain purposes (for instance, getting rid of epistemology) to view the *Vorhanden* as a species of the *Zuhanden*. Perhaps I should have spent more time doing the same. If I had, I would have said that sentences, skills, and disciplines (such as historiography) can all be treated as artifacts. All three can, like the spear and the dam, be evaluated in terms of reliability. But I would also have said that, so treated, artifacts are continuous with organs: the beaver's teeth and its dam, the human hand and the tools it grasps, can all be so evaluated.

This means that when we forget about practical syllogisms, and just talk about know-how, the distinction between the human and the non-human fades out. For know-how goes a long way down the great chain of being. (Think, for example, of all those insidiously clever viruses.) When we want to zero in on the human, however, we have to go propositional and start talking about knowing-that. This is because only language-users have that sort of knowledge.[1] The linguistic turn helped us preserve a Deweyan continuity between biology and culture by letting us see mind as a matter of behaving so complexly as to demand what Dennett calls the adoption of the intentional stance, rather than as the eruption of something new and strange in the midst of the protoplasm. But it also helped us emphasize the discontinuity between ourselves and the brutes by directing attention to the irreducibility of intentional to non-intentional discourse.

When one does take the intentional stance, it is natural to zero in on knowing-that, and to neglect know-how. For the advantage of that stance is that it enables us to bring in the vocabulary of inference – to talk about practical and other syllogisms. Allen sees focusing on knowing-that at the expense of knowing-how as the consequence of a bad philosophy of knowledge. I see it as just a way of highlighting the problems which are important to epistemologists, preparatory to explaining how (by getting rid of the notion of representation) these problems can be dissolved.

But Allen is quite right that a lot of things I have said sound as if they were generalizations intended to cover both knowing-how and knowing-that. When so read, they are indeed biased, and seriously misleading. If I had written "knowledge-that" instead of "knowledge," these passages might have seemed unobjectionable. They might not have led Allen to ascribe to me "the assumption that there is practically no difference between words and things that . . . descriptions [are] the artifacts that matter most. As if the more material artifacts and techniques upon which we daily depend were byproducts of language and not, as is likely, the other way around" (p. 231).

But not all the differences between Allen and myself can be ironed out by such a rewriting. For Allen thinks that we need a radically new "philosophy of knowledge," one which takes account of the probability that "the more material" artifacts gave rise to language rather than vice versa. But I think it fruitless to ask whether non-linguistic artifacts gave rise to linguistic ones, or vice versa. That seems like asking which of two symbiotes is more truly host and which more truly parasite. On the one hand, it is hard to improve your non-linguistic artifacts unless your peers can deploy critical remarks about their design; for lack of linguistic artifacts to use in making such remarks, the beaver dams of our own day are no better than those of old. On the other hand, it is hard to have the leisure for language-building if you lack non-linguistic artifacts with which to defend yourself against the climate and the predators. One can see why the two kinds of artifacts are likely to have been produced around the same time, and to have developed in tandem.

If I understand Allen's project, he thinks that we shall only understand "the value of knowledge, its ecological singularity, the inextricability of its and our flourishing" better than the Greeks did (p. 234) if we set conversation in the context of the production of artifacts and skills. Such understanding will, Allen believes, be blocked as long as we say, as I did, that "conversation is the ultimate context in which knowledge should be understood." I should be happy to change "knowledge" to "knowledge-that" in that over-ambitious remark, but this would not eliminate my differences with Allen. For I do not see that there is anything about the value of knowledge and its ecological singularity that we do not already sufficiently understand.

In particular, I do not see why we need to draw any line between the knowing animals and the non-knowing animals other than the line between the sentence-wielding knowers-that and the non-sentence-wielders who only know how.

Allen seems to want the former sort of line, for he says that plants, *pace* Plotkin, do not know how to photosynthesize. Presumably he would also deny that beavers know how to build dams, for he suggests that "knowledge is as uniquely human as our neurology" (n. 19). Admiring the beavers as I do, I cannot see anything especially human about knowing how to get things done. Attributing knowledge-that, on the other hand, seems useful only when explaining ourselves, and perhaps our computers. We attribute knowledge-how wherever telic description seems appropriate, but knowledge-that only when intentional description does.

Allen takes seriously Nietzsche's question "Why prefer knowledge to ignorance?" Unlike me, he thinks the obvious answers – "utility" and "prudence" – insufficient. This is because he thinks that

> To be reproduced without loss and survive another generation knowledge must not only be in constant use, but used *well*. Such use requires action that goes beyond the utilitarian preoccupation with prudence, requiring the peculiar indifference to prudence or utilitarian rationality that Nietzsche called the daring of the lover of knowledge. The result is work whose aesthetic quality has left the calculations of prudence and utility far behind. (pp. 230–1)

Many of Allen's sentences would be more plausible if "knowledge" were replaced by "know-how" just as many of mine would be more plausible if it were replaced by "knowing-that." In particular, Allen's claim about reproduction without loss and inter-generational survival works only for know-how, and not for knowledge that. (We may not make use of our knowledge that a nasty event happened in the woodshed in early

March of 1497 for a long time. That knowledge may repose in a dusty muniment room for generations before it becomes relevant to some historian's researches.)

As for the motives and attitudes of lovers of knowledge, it is certainly true that many craftspersons, like many historians, never think twice about the utility of their productions. They regard attention to that question as a boorish distraction. Allen's invocation of aesthetic quality pumps up the same intuitions as those which make scientists resent being viewed as mere predictors, mere handmaidens of technological progress. Getting control of the environment and improving man's estate, these scientists say, is not their motive. They are after *knowledge* and *truth*. In the same spirit, Allen says that indifference to utilitarian rationality is required to produce work "whose aesthetic quality has left the calculations of prudence and utility far behind."

My reaction to the resentful scientists goes like this: reference to utility will not adequately describe your motives, but it will be a sufficient explanation of why we call you "scientists." For if your work doesn't, sooner or later, help us improve our estate we shall find something else to call you ("dreamer," "pure mathematician," "crank," or "mere philosopher," for example). My reaction to Allen's parallel claim is that what Veblen called "the instinct of workmanship" does indeed produce work with an aesthetic quality that goes beyond fulfillment of easily describable needs. Still, we should not call it craftsmanship (but rather, perhaps, "fine art") if that work does not help us improve our estate. Any human activity – the production of TV commercials, pimping, mathematical physics – can be given an aesthetic quality. But we can understand all there is to understand about both knowing-how and knowing-that without attention to this possibility.

****

What was epistemology? A bad answer to a bad question – a question as bad as "What is the good?" Knowledge, like goodness, is a good thing. So it was thought, in both cases, that by having a theory of this good thing we might be able to acquire more of it. Neither project panned out. Allen thinks that Plato was right "to let the question of *what knowledge is* be directed by the question why it is *good*" (p. 234). But neither question seems to me likely to have an interesting answer. I quite agree with Allen that "the knowledge of superior artifacts [including, presumably, superior sentences] plays an incomparable role in adapting us to our environment and maintaining that adaptation in the face of ceaseless change." (p. 234) But I cannot see why that fact should lead us to ask the sort of question which Plato became famous for asking.

However, I am not sure that I have adequately grasped the scope and motive for Allen's project – a new philosophy of knowledge, distinct both from epistemology and from the pragmatists' dismissal of epistemology. It may be that the foregoing responses to his paper largely miss his point. But I hope that they may encourage him to explain more clearly what is likely to be gained from commingling the two senses of "belief" which I distinguished at the outset.

Notes

1   Those who hunt for inferences lurking behind behavior acquire what Allen calls a "discursive bias." For they specialize in breaking know-how down into knowing-that. Interest in such breakdown begins at the border between zoology and anthropology. Ornithologists are

content to say that bower-birds know how to build bowers, but anthropologists are not content to report that a certain wise woman knows how to cure diseases. They want to say more: that she believes this disease is caused by a certain demon, believes that this demon is repelled by a specific herb, and so on.

11

Is Truth a Goal of Inquiry?:
Rorty and Davidson on Truth[1]

AKEEL BILGRAMI

I

For some time now, Rorty's philosophical relation to Davidson has been one of an admiring but nagging disciple. The general message of some recent papers on Davidson has tended to be: if only this man who has got so much right would not stubbornly continue to say some of the things he says. Many of the complaints come from a perspective that Rorty announces as being pragmatism. This paper takes up Rorty's relations with Davidson on one very central theme, that of truth. It is not a defense of either. It takes the study of these relations as an occasion to explore some very large and vexed questions in the philosophy of recent times about realism and objectivity, but it does so keeping firmly in mind the perspective that Rorty favors, and takes these questions up with a view only to exploring what sort of thing a pragmatist position on these themes might shape up to be.

Though there will be some points of fundamental disagreement with Rorty's thinking on this subject, this paper is intended as a tribute to the vigilant critical guidance that Rorty has given us against a certain historically and presently pervasive picture of truth and knowledge and reality. Rorty's great importance for these subjects within analytic philosophy (by contrast with his widely acknowledged influence in other disciplines and among philosophers hostile to analytic philosophy) has tended to get a little lost. This is partly because of the distracting irritation caused in many by the flamboyant and exaggerated way he sometimes describes his conclusions, by his (often quite justified) dismissiveness of the professional cliquishness among analytic philosophers, by the compensating cozy and excluding idiom he adopts ("We pragmatists." "We liberals." "We quietists" . . .), and perhaps most of all by the fact that his influence in other disciplines, while often salutary and interesting, has also been on those who sometimes do bad and sloppy philosophy under the claim of doing those other disciplines in non-traditional "post-modern" modes. Although I do remorselessly consider myself to be a run-of-the mill analytic philosopher, I will not be distracted by these irritations since I simply do not feel them. Why should a philosopher (Rorty) have to trim his manners to win the applause of analytic philosophers? And why should he ungenerously disown those whom he might have influenced in unfortunate ways? (As Hume once said to Rousseau, "Honest men don't give alibis.") The present volume is a conspicuous and fitting reflection of the fact that philosophers will refuse to be distracted in these ways because such distractions are superficial and anxiously defensive, even as they are smug.

The chief and most explicit source of disappointment on the matter of truth for Rorty is Davidson's failure to have come around to what he sees as a more fully pragmatist position on it.

As Rorty says "Pragmatists think that if something makes no difference to practice, it should make no difference to philosophy."[2] He then applies this principle to the concept of truth and finds that various treatments of the concept are guilty of neglecting this principle. And though there is a source here of disagreement between him and Davidson, it is also clear that they agree on a lot of assumptions despite their disagreement. It is worth making some of this clear.

Even at first sight it would seem as if his complaint against Davidson is relatively minor. It is not so much that Davidson violates the principle, but that his own self-description is one that misdescribes what he himself believes. Rorty thinks that nothing important in Davidson's detailed views amounts to a neglect of this principle, but when he represents his own position Davidson falls into such misrepresentations as: "Since the concept of truth is central to the theory [that is, to an empirical theory of an agent's overall behavior], we are justified in saying that truth is a crucially important explanatory concept."[3] The reference here is to Davidson's long-standing claim that a theory of truth along modified Tarskian lines is one of the components in an overall theory of a subject's behavior (including linguistic behavior) along with other components such as those which attribute beliefs and desires to the subject. Rorty asks: "Certainly the sort of empirical theory to which Davidson thinks 'the concept of truth' central, serves explanatory purposes, but why should one pick out one of the many concepts explicated by reference to such theories and say that it has a crucial explanatory role?" To this complaint Davidson replies: "Rorty doesn't much mind my saying that truth is one among a number of other related concepts which we use in describing, explaining, and predicting human behavior. But why, he asks, say truth is any more important than such concepts as intention, belief, desire, and so on? Importance is a hard thing to argue about. All these concepts (and more) are essential to thought, and cannot be reduced to something simpler or more fundamental. Why be niggardly in awarding prizes; I'm happy to hand out golden apples all around."[4]

So far the disagreement does not seem to be about anything very significant. It seems as if this concept of truth *does* meet the pragmatist demand of making a difference to practice since a theory of truth (of course among other things) is what explains an agent's behavior. Once the demand is met, the dispute about whether you think it central (among those other things), or whether you think them all central, is not a dispute that goes all that deep.

The source of the general agreement here perhaps flows from a prior agreement on one of the properties of truth which is sometimes described (and by Rorty himself) as "disquotation."[5] In disquotation, we specify a sentence's truth-condition as follows: we first put the sentence in quotation marks (this being a standard way of talking about the sentence) and then we append the words "is true" followed by the bi-conditional logical connective, and then the very same sentence whose truth-condition we are thus specifying, but without the quotes. Thus the familiar bi-conditional: "'Snow is white' is true if and only if snow is white." Sentences such as this are the provable sentences of a Tarski style theory of truth for a natural language. Tarski took it for granted that in the bi-conditional the right hand sentence was a translation of the quoted sentence on the left, and so Tarski's idea can be expressed by saying that disquotation of this sort is a special case (if you like, a degenerate and limiting case) of translation. That is to say, the right hand side of the T-sentence which specifies the truth-condition of the quoted sentence on the left is a special case of translation of that quoted sentence. When, unlike the example above, the object language is not contained in the meta-language, what is on the right hand side of the bi-conditional, what specifies the truth-conditions of the quoted sentence, will be in a different language from the quoted sentence. And then the fact of its being a translation will be worn on the sleeve, as it were, in a way that it is not in the example above. As, for instance, in: "La neige est blanche," is true if and only if snow is white. I have said that disquotation is a limiting case of translation. But we can put the point conversely: the latter sort of sentence in which the right hand side is more manifestly a translation of what is quoted on the left, exemplifies, as McDowell points out in his paper in this volume, an *extended sense of disquotation.*[6] It has been Davidson's novel and important contribution to further point out that, when the object language is not contained in the meta-language, then were one to give empirical support to these bi-conditionals in the behavior of speakers functioning as intentional agents in their environment, one would thereby be giving empirical support to a theory of truth which could serve in successful interpretation of those speakers. It is for this reason, as I quoted him saying earlier, that Davidson insisted that truth is an essential component in any account that makes sense of agents' behavior, and, as I also said, Rorty was happy to grant this so long as it was clear that it was one among various other components in the account. Rorty is happy for the pragmatist to embrace this disquotational property of "is true" because it brings with it no large claims about the "representational" nature of thought and language, and therefore no claims to how truth is a form of "correspondence" to the world. The role of truth is justified only as feeding into our grasp of a subject's behavior, and so it meets the pragmatist demand that it make a difference to practice. It is not surprising then that Rorty thinks that disquotation is an acceptable characterization of "is true" for the pragmatists. It yields, after all, a special case of translation, and therefore with the right empirical support it has a practical significance which emerges in successful interpretation. I will return to this point some pages later.

In addition to disquotation, Rorty and Davidson agree that truth has another property. Rorty describes this as the "cautionary" aspect of "true." This is the claim that truth cannot be *strictly reduced* to any other concepts (such as justification). This is for reasons that echo G.E. Moore's argument regarding the indefinability of 'good.' To those who thought 'good' was reducible or definable (say in terms of social aggregate utility), Moore retorted that one could show the distance between good and such a purported defining property by pointing out that one could always ask *non*-trivially: "But is *x* (say, an action or the adoption of a rule) which does have high social aggregate utility, good?" Similarly, following Putnam, Rorty admits that one may non-trivially ask "is a sentence (or belief) that is justified, true?," thereby mimicking Moore to show the distance between truth and justification. He says this constitutes the "cautionary" aspect or use of the predicate "is true" since it tells inquirers that they must step with caution in case things they consider quite justified may not be true.

On the basis of their agreement on this property, Davidson and Rorty draw one identical conclusion: Truth cannot be a goal of inquiry. (In concluding this with Davidson, Rorty seems to have departed from some positions which might properly be described as pragmatist.[7] And Davidson who is happy not to be described as a pragmatist, explicitly says that he is opposing precisely pragmatism when he concludes that truth cannot be a goal of inquiry.)

Why do Rorty and Davidson conclude that truth cannot be a goal of inquiry on the basis of what Rorty calls the "cautionary" aspect of truth? Each of them presents their arguments in slightly different terms for this identical conclusion.

It is worth quoting Davidson at length here from the same paper I cited earlier:

> We know many things, and will learn more; what we will never know for certain is which of the things we believe is true. Since it is neither a visible target, nor recognizable when achieved, there is no point in calling truth a goal. Truth is not a value, so the "pursuit of truth" is an empty enterprise unless it means only that it is often worthwhile to increase our confidence in our beliefs, by collecting further evidence or checking our calculations.
>
> From the fact that we will never be able to tell which of our beliefs are true, pragmatists conclude that we may as well identify our best researched, most successful beliefs with the true ones, and give up the idea of objectivity. (Truth is objective if the truth of a belief or sentence is independent of whether it is justified by all our evidence . . .) But here we have a choice. Instead of giving up the traditional view that truth is objective, we can give up the equally traditional view (to which the pragmatists adhere) that truth is a norm, something for which to strive. I agree with the pragmatists that we can't consistently take truth to be both objective and something to be pursued. But I think that they would have done better to cleave to a view that counts truth as objective, but pointless as a goal.

The so-called cautionary aspect of truth yields a crucial and remarkable premise for both Davidson and Rorty and that is the claim that we *cannot ever tell which of our beliefs are true*. This, says Davidson, is what makes truth *objective*, and truth, Davidson says, is indeed objective. And the conclusion drawn from this premise is that if truth is objective in this sense, then it cannot possibly be a goal to pursue. If we cannot possibly know when we have achieved a goal, it cannot with any point remain a goal of ours. So we have a choice, according to Davidson. Either we embrace the objectivity of truth and give up the idea of many pragmatists that truth is a goal, or we give up the idea that truth is objective and retain truth as a goal. Davidson opts for the former.

Rorty articulates his agreement with the premise as follows. The cautionary aspect of truth shows that truth is beyond all justification and that is why we cannot ever know when any of our beliefs is true, as opposed to justified. For Rorty justification is always to an audience (something that does not surface particularly in anything Davidson has ever said). And so Rorty says that the gap between justification and truth emerges when we find that even when we have satisfactorily justified a certain belief or sentence to the currently available audience, there can always be newer and more imaginative audiences to whom we have still to justify it. The idea of truth will then have to be the impossible ideal of a justification after which no further justification is needed. Truth is not a reachable goal, so no goal at all. The premise is couched in terms of justification to audiences but in effect it says the same thing as Davidson: we can never know when one of our beliefs (however justified we take it to be) is true. Rorty, like Davidson, is happy therefore to jettison truth as a goal, and he says that the only goal can be justification. They both go from the so-called cautionary aspect of truth to the conclusion that truth cannot be a goal of inquiry, on the ground that the cautionary aspect of truth forces the idea that we can never tell which of our beliefs is true (or, in Rorty's rhetoric, on the ground that there are inexhaustible audiences to whom we might have to justify a belief of ours).

Rorty draws a *further* conclusion that Davidson does not (and this I suppose is his complaint against Davidson after so much agreement on so much else so far), which is that if truth is not a goal of inquiry, there is much less interest in the notion of truth than philosophers have taken it to have. This is Rorty's version of pragmatism. Pragmatism lays it down that any bit of philosophy which is not relevant to practice is not of genuine interest. A specific gloss on being "relevant to practice" when applied to truth is that truth should be a goal of inquiry, if it is to be relevant to practice. It is not such a goal, so it's of no particular interest. Davidson makes no commitment to Rorty's specific gloss on the idea of "relevant to practice" which requires that truth be a goal of inquiry to be so relevant. Thus Davidson does not draw anything like Rorty's further conclusion.

So far as I can tell that fairly summarizes the agreements and disagreement between Rorty and Davidson on this subject.

Lots of questions remain.

It immediately occurs to ask what interest and relevance does Davidson think that truth has for philosophers, if it is objective in the sense that he defines it to be and which leads him to say that it is not a goal of inquiry. We have seen that Davidson has claimed that even if it is not a goal of inquiry, it is of interest and relevance to the explanation of agents' behavior. It is the central concept (*truth*-conditions) in the stating of meanings of their sentences (and therefore, as a corollary, central to specifying the contents of their beliefs). But is it so obvious that conditions of truth (where truth is understood in the sense that Davidson has defined in the way he has, as objective) can specify an agent's meanings and intentional contents in a way which explains his behavior? I think that this is highly doubtful. For one thing such a notion of truth-conditions could not possibly solve the Frege and Kripke puzzles about identity and belief. And I think that it is quite clear that any notion of truth-conditions that cannot cope with these puzzles cannot possibly play a central role in explaining agents' behavior. I have argued this at length elsewhere and I will not do so again here. I will only say that if my argument, which I am not giving here, is right, then anyone who embraces Davidson's version of the objective notion of truth would have to be quite skeptical of any relevance that such a notion of truth could have to explaining behavior. So when Rorty conceded to Davidson that truth is one among several other concepts that went into explaining behavior, he was either being too concessive or he was looking just at disquotation and not the further feature that defines truth as being objective for Davidson.

Another question might arise out of a surprise that many readers may feel on finding that someone like Davidson should define the objectivity of truth in this way. Does this picture of truth not look very much like the kind of realism that Davidson has often disavowed? Doesn't it look a lot like what Putnam and others have called 'metaphysical' realism? What did Davidson have in mind when he denied these things? He often mentions two sorts of doctrines when he characterizes the kind of realism he shuns. One is the idea of a traditional correspondence notion of truth. The other is the idea of a "full and complete description of reality." Davidson dismisses both these ideas on grounds that he has himself now made familiar. I won't rehearse them here. What he is clear about is that his rejection of these ideas is intended as a rejection of what Putnam calls 'metaphysical' realism, or, as McDowell following Kant calls it, 'transcendental' realism.

Nevertheless it does seem as if the claim that we could never know when and which of our beliefs are true, is one that, though different from these ideas that Davidson has dismissed, all the same conveys a conception of truth whereby it is out of our reach, in just the way that a realism of the sort that is called 'metaphysical' or 'transcendental' would have it. McDowell describes this position well in the essay I have cited earlier, as a picture of representation which relates our thought and language "to something more independent of us than the world as it figures in our world view." That, it would seem, is a very accurate description of what we must think of representation as being if we thought, with Davidson, that "we could never tell which of our beliefs are true." As McDowell says (in sympathy with Rorty and Davidson) expressions like 'true,' *on this picture*, could not possibly signify a "mode of normative relatedness" that our language or thought could have to the world. But, and here he is totally out of sympathy with both Davidson and Rorty, he quite rightly thinks that there is no need to give truth over to such a picture. And so he says there is no reason to deny that expressions such as 'true' do signify a "mode of normative relatedness" to the world, nor any reason to deny that truth could be a goal of inquiry.

What is it to be out of sympathy with a picture in which truth (and therefore the world which true statements and beliefs describe and capture) is out of reach in the way Davidson does? That is of course the deep and hard question of how to demarcate a ground that is properly described as "transcendental idealism." (The reader should not be put off by this bit of Kantian terminology, which I follow McDowell in using. She could use her own term to describe the intended ground.) McDowell has demarcated this ground at length and in depth in several papers, and others too have done so in somewhat different versions, disagreeing with McDowell perhaps on some details.[8] What I am interested in doing in the rest of this paper on Rorty, who has so valiantly and interestingly tried to revive the interest and importance of pragmatism, *is to see what version of transcendental idealism makes possible a position that is plausibly described as pragmatism.* Central to that position is the idea that both Rorty and Davidson deny – that truth is a goal of inquiry.

II

Let me start with a demarcated ground that may be described as "transcendental idealism" of a sort that is distinctly not hospitable to the pragmatism I have in mind. In fact it is a ground that even Davidson, despite his remarks about not being able to tell which of our beliefs are true (remarks that suggest that truth and the world are out of reach in a way that at first sight seems to imply transcendental *realism*) could plausibly occupy. This is a position which says roughly this. Yes, it is the case that we can never tell which of our beliefs are true, but that does not mean that Descartes is right in thinking that all our beliefs could be false. There may be a reason or an argument to show that all our beliefs cannot be false, and so the world (and truth) are in a sense not out of reach, since on the basis of this argument we know that many of our beliefs and statements will capture and describe it correctly.[9] On the assumption that such an argument exists, we would have defined an anti-Cartesian position, which many may wish to say recovers the world from the loss it suffered from being placed out of reach in the First Meditation. This recovery may with some right be described as constituting a version of transcendental idealism. And it is a recovery of the world, which is compatible with Davidson's claim that we could never tell which of our beliefs is true. It is *only a global* recovery, and is, as it were, *an epistemologically blind* recovery, since *no particular* truth about the world is known to be a truth by inquirers. But recovery it is. Truth cannot any longer be described as being out of reach in the way that a strict transcendental realism would have it.

That such a position is possible, of course, turns on there being an argument for, over and above assertion of, the following conclusion: that the idea that we can never know which of our beliefs about the world are true does not inevitably force the Cartesian idea that perhaps all of our beliefs about the world may be false. But if such an argument existed, then we would have to relax our own claim made above that Davidson's conception of the objectivity of truth is what transcendental idealism is defined against. For such an argument would show transcendental idealism in at least this version to be compatible with the idea that we could never tell which of our beliefs is true. The fact is, however, that it is very hard to give a non-question begging argument for this conclusion. It is not obvious that anyone has done so, thus far, or at any rate done so in a way that would satisfy most philosophers.[10] For this reason, I think it is worth exploring the possibility of a version of transcendental idealism which does not grant to Davidson the claim that "we can never tell which of our beliefs is true." Such a transcendental idealism would not merely recover the world in the weak and global sense mentioned above. It would not be an epistemologically blind recovery of the world, in the very sense I also mentioned above. This would surely be a distinctly superior version of transcendental idealism.

Not only would it be superior in this way, the task of seeking such a version of transcendental idealism would also have the distinct advantage of not having to find a non-question begging argument against the Cartesian possibility that all our beliefs about the world may be false. That possibility only arises because of the sort of picture of objective truth that Davidson's claim defines. It is only his claim that we could never tell which of our beliefs about the world are true that threatens the Cartesian possibility that perhaps none are. (This is just the familiar transition from: if no particular belief about the world could be established to be true, then it is possible that all are false.) But if we never granted him that initial claim, if we resisted his picture of what makes truth objective, then we would not be landed in the seemingly impossible position of having to come up with a non-question begging argument against that possibility. We could instead attempt the task of demarcating a ground properly described as transcendental idealism, which did not have to face the Cartesian threat in the first place. (It simply won't do to say here that the resistance to this picture of what makes truth objective itself amounts to begging the question against the Cartesian skeptic. The skeptic's position lies in its conclusion that all of our beliefs about the world could fail to be true. To point out that his understanding of 'true' is going to be resisted, does not amount to begging the question against him, it is rather to try and show that the question only arises under conditions which one is resisting. This is not to be in a position of someone – like Davidson – who buys into rather than resists this picture of objective truth, and in doing so has allowed the question to have arisen. Once arisen, it has to be answered. And I am doubting that it can be non-question-beggingly answered. But if there is no question in the first place, no question can be begged.)

It is worth pointing out that were we to succeed in this resistance, we would have lived up to an instruction of Rorty's which he has long given to Davidson. For some years now Rorty has been saying to Davidson that we should tell the Cartesian skeptic to get lost, and not try and give a philosophical answer to him or her. This instruction now has a clear and good interpretation, which does have a point as an instruction *to Davidson*. If we accept Davidson's claim that "we can never tell which of our beliefs is true" we are threatened with a Cartesian skeptical possibility, to which we must find a philosophical answer. But if we rejected that claim, if we rejected the objectivity of truth in the sense defined by that claim, then we would not be threatened by the skeptical possibility in the first place. Such a distinction between preempting a possibility and answering it gives a clear interpretation to Rorty's instruction as being applicable to Davidson.

I have been careful to say repeatedly above that we are exploring a transcendental idealism that rejects *Davidson's version* of what makes truth objective as defined by his claim that we can't tell which of our beliefs is true. This suggests that there is another way of thinking of the objectivity of truth. Rorty himself nowhere sees things this way. For him, there is no other version, and since *this* version is of no particular substantial interest our focus should rather simply turn to justification. Truth in this sense provides no norm nor is it a goal of inquiry. Thus for him, all that remains once we see that the only notion of objective truth there is lacks any interest for the pragmatist, is to give up any philosophical interest in truth. What philosophers should understand is that in inquiry we only justify our beliefs to the best of our ability against audiences which may find them unjustified.

In his most interesting paper in the present volume, McDowell makes an eloquent effort to convince Rorty that truth does not lose its objectivity nor its interest as providing a norm simply because we might reject various versions of its objectivity that put it out of reach. Though Rorty is the stated target, it is clear that the Davidson who articulates his version of the objectivity of truth only to say it cannot be a goal of inquiry, would equally be a target of McDowell's efforts. McDowell clearly wants to retain the objectivity of truth, and do so in a form that allows us to see it as a goal of inquiry.

McDowell first describes the following train of thought in Rorty: Putnam must be applauded for showing that notions like truth, reference and representation, are "internal to our overall view of the world." But even philosophers who agree with this refuse to give up the vocabulary of objectivity. Rorty himself is not suggesting that we do not use these semantical notions. But we must be watchful and use these notions in a way that is not external to a world view as many philosophers end up doing. Thus we must be watchful that we don't slip into the vocabulary of objectivity, we must use terms like truth and reference only in Putnam's innocent internal sense. McDowell adds: "One could *define* the discourse of objectivity as involving a certain supposed external use of the semantical notions, and in that case I would have no problem with Rorty's attitude to it. But Rorty suggests that rejecting these supposed external uses requires rejecting any form of the idea that inquiry is answerable to the world. I think that this deprives us of something that is not inextricably implicated with what Putnam unmasks as illusion . . ."

What is it that McDowell does not want us to be deprived of? He says that it is quite wrong to think that just because words like "true" do not signify a mode of "conformity" that our beliefs or sentences have to "something more independent of us than the world as it figures in our world view," they also fail to signify a mode of conformity to the world as it *does* figure in our world view. It is this idea of objective truth of which McDowell does not want us to be deprived that underlies the prospect of a plausible transcendental idealism. Whereas, conformity to something *more* independent of us than the world as it figures in our world view would lead to a transcendental realism, conformity to something *no more* independent of us than the world as it figures in our world view would give us just the notion of truth that underlies transcendental idealism.

The key idea then is that of (the) truth (of our beliefs and sentences) as *conformity to the world as it figures in our world view*. Though McDowell does not mention Davidson we can point out that it is this key idea, this notion of truth, which finds no place for the Davidsonian claim that we could never tell which of our beliefs is true. For conformity (of our beliefs) to things as they figure in our world view, is surely a conformity that we do not have to be in the dark about. This allows for not just the global idea that somewhere among all our beliefs there are some (or other) beliefs which must be true, but we are in the dark as to which.[11] Rather, cases of conformity are capable of being in full view, something which I described as a conception of truth and of the world that does not put us in a position in which we are "epistemologically blind." Thus what McDowell wants to allow for is a transcendental idealism quite different from the one that is compatible with Davidson's position, and one which does not fall in with Rorty's despair with the notion of truth in the face of Davidson's claim that we can never tell which of our beliefs are true.

A good place to situate this quite other version of objective truth than Davidson's is in a famous and familiar statement of Quine's which, though it is very underdescribed, has many of the elements that McDowell aspires to. I will quote it at length. In the closing pages of Chapter I of *Word and Object*, Quine says:

> It is rather when we turn back into the midst of actually present theory . . . that we can and do speak of this or that sentence as true. To say that the statement 'Brutus killed Caesar' is true or 'The atomic weight of sodium is 23' is true, is in effect simply to say that Brutus killed Caesar, or that the atomic weight of sodium is 23. [Here Quine in a footnote cites Tarski for a way of developing the last point.] . . . the truth attributions are made from the point of view of the same surrounding body of theory . . .
>
> . . . Have we now so lowered our sights as to settle for a relativistic doctrine of truth, rating the statements of each theory as true for that theory and brooking no higher criticism? Not so. The saving consideration is that we continue to take seriously our own particular aggregate science, our own particular world-theory, or loose total fabric of quasi-theories, whatever it may be. Unlike Descartes, we own and use our beliefs of the moment, even in the midst of philosophizing, until by what is vaguely called scientific method we change them here and there for the better. Within our own totally evolving doctrine, we can judge truth . . . subject to correction, but that goes without saying. (pp. 24–5)

Quine says here that we judge truth from within our current ongoing theory of the world. This may not sound very interesting since it is merely a point about *judging* truth, not about the sort of conformity that truth itself amounts to. But he does also say something which suggests a way of resisting the notion of objective truth that we want to resist. He says that, "unlike Descartes, we own and use our beliefs of the moment, even in the midst of philosophizing . . ." One way to be guided by this thought is to lay claim to the idea that from the point of the view of those who judge truth, that is to say from the point of view of the inquirer, her current theory of the world is put to "use" in inquiry in the following way: it sets the standard for what is and is not to be counted as true. That standard comes from nowhere else, and no other standard is necessary. The reference to Descartes can be used to support this reading.[12] Descartes, because he was "cautioned" (Rorty's word) by the fact that any one of our beliefs could be false, was not in a position to use any of our beliefs as setting this standard of what is to count as true and what not. To lay claim to this idea is to say with McDowell that the expression 'true' signifies a kind of conformity our beliefs or sentences have "to things as they figure in our world view," and to "nothing more independent of our world view."

This way of opposing Descartes is quite distinctive. Here is a way of seeing what is distinctive about it. Take again the idea Davidson insists on, which is that we can never tell which of our beliefs are true. This, as we saw a while back, is an idea that for him grew out of what Rorty called the cautionary aspect of truth. As we also saw, this idea, though it is quite different from those ways of invoking metaphysical realism such as "correspondence" notions of truth or visions of a complete description of reality, nevertheless approximates something of the "out of reach" conception of reality that metaphysical realists embrace. It is this conception that Bernard Williams described as "the objective conception of reality" which he attributed to Descartes, and then made the point that it is this conception that gives rise to Descartes' own threat to our knowledge of the external world. So the search for arguments against Descartes' skeptical threat is one way of being an anti-Cartesian. What is distinctive and different about the anti-Cartesianism we are reading into Quine's negative reference to Descartes is brought out well by comparing it with this. If my reading of Quine is correct, then Quine far from responding to a threat of skepticism prompted by the objective conception of reality, is instead saying something like this. Since we (inquirers) use our own theory of the world (McDowell's "world view") as the standard for what is true (McDowell's "normative relatedness of our beliefs to things as they figure in our world view"), there is *nothing* from the point of view of the inquirer that can be *cautionary* about our conception of truth. And since it is the allegedly cautionary aspect of truth that gave rise to Descartes' (and Davidson's) objective conception of the world in the first place, this way of opposing Descartes repudiates him at a prior place and stage.

The picture is this. The inquirer has various states of mind, some of which are cognitive. Among these latter are some which are the beliefs that count as her current theory of the world, as Quine puts it. These set the standard by which truth is judged. There may be various other cognitive propositional attitudes which the inquirer entertains, which are not beliefs in this sense, and about which inquiry is undertaken by her as to whether they should become part of her theory of the world. In this inquiry about these states which are not (or in some cases not yet) beliefs in the sense of constituting one's world view, all sorts of caution may be advisable. But about beliefs in the sense that do constitute one's world view, there is nothing that counts as cautionary from the inquirer's point of view. The inquirer could not use these in the sense Quine suggests on this reading, that is, as the standard or norm inherent in the concept of truth, if he was so cautioned. Even from an inquirer's point of view, of course, it is *logically* possible that beliefs in this sense be false, but the point is that the acknowledgment that there is that logically possibility, does not lead to the kind of epistemological blindness that Rorty's and Davidson's cautionary idea suggests, that is, it does not lead to the concession that we can never tell which of our beliefs are true, and it does not lead us to doubt these beliefs. The acknowledgment therefore does not have any epistemological implications for inquiry. We still continue to use them confidently as the standard or norm just mentioned. To put it ironically in Rorty's own pragmatist terms, if the so-called cautionary aspect of truth does not caution us in the practice of inquiry, if it does not caution us into refraining from confidently using the beliefs which constitute our world-view in our inquiry, then it is merely 'cautionary' *so-called*.

(It might be thought that though any particular belief that constitutes our world-view may not be something that we may doubt or be cautioned about, it is surely the case that inquirers know that some of these beliefs are bound to be false. But even if that lottery-paradoxical kind of effect is so, it is not clear how this cautions the *inquirer*. An inquirer is only cautioned by doubt about any particular proposition. It is not clear how it could affect inquiry if one acknowledged some of our doubt-free beliefs might be false, without knowing which. What serious and specific cautionary instruction might this give an inquirer?)

So far I have given Quine a certain reading to support McDowell's idea that there is an alternative picture to Davidson's idea of objective truth, and on this reading the idea of truth gets to be something no more independent of us than the world as it figures in our world-view. This notion of truth I have said does not have the cautionary aspect claimed by Rorty and Davidson. It is a different way of rejecting Descartes, one inconsistent with his (and Davidson's) objective conception of truth and reality, not one consistent with it and merely answering the skeptical threat it raises. I recognize that there will be a tendency to reject the claim that any of this gets us to something that has the full prestige of "truth." A Davidsonian might display this tendency by saying something like this: all that has been shown is that our judgments of truth are made in the light of our best evolving doctrine. But that is not much more than trivial. By what other light could they be made? The point would only be non-trivial if this taught us something about the role and nature of truth, as opposed to judgments of truth. An account of the latter is an account merely of beliefs, not of truth. What was promised is something about truth that is an alternative to Davidson's objective conception of it. What has been delivered are just some truisms about the nature of beliefs or judgments of truth.

To say this would be to miss the point that Quine, over and above saying that we judge truth by the light of our evolving current doctrine, also says that unlike Descartes we are not cautioned by any logical possibility of error, and in fact we "use" the beliefs that constitute our world-view in a certain way, as the standard for truth. This is just the idea that not judgments of truth, but truth is being a given certain characterization, one in which it amounts to a conformity of our beliefs with something no more independent than things which figure in our world-view. Something which is "used" in this way is not, *qua being so used*, anything that we *could* possibly be cautious about in the way required by Rorty and Davidson. Being cautious would be precisely to be halted or paused in such a use of it.

Another way of putting the point is this. What this response on Davidson's behalf fails to see is that once Rorty has brought in the inquirer and raised the question of the nature and role of truth in the context of inquiry, then what comes onto centre-stage is *the point of view of the inquirer*. From this point of view, which *in inquiry* will be the *first*-person point of view, to believe without doubt (that is, not in the sense say of an hypothesis, but in the sense that constitutes one's world view) is to believe *true*. So if Davidson challenges us to say which of our beliefs are true (something he thinks we can never say), the answer is quite unproblematically that (from the first-person point of view) these are true. It's only from the third-person point of view that someone may wonder whether some of a person's beliefs are true. But for a third person to wonder this cannot, even if communicated to the inquirer concerned, amount to cautioning the inquirer in anything but an illocutionary sense. It would not have cautioned the inquirer in the sense that the inquirer was now (just by the fact of having been communicated to in this way) going to be cautious and refrain from using his beliefs (that amounted to a world view) in the way being suggested by Quine and McDowell. That is, the cautioning communication by itself would not have succeeded in making the inquirer cautious in what might (bending the original idea a bit) be described as a "perlocutionary" case of cautioning. (Cautioning communication here would not be like persuading). For it to be successful, the cautioning third person would have had to have the effect of sowing doubt in the inquirer about some belief that he held without doubt prior to the cautioning. But for this to have happened would mean that the inquirer was in some way made by the third person to give up one of his beliefs on the basis of some *particular* reason presented to him that opened up his mind and got him to deliberate and change his beliefs. But this is not the sowing of doubt that issues from any cautionary aspect of 'truth' of which Rorty and Davidson speak. Their idea of a cautionary aspect of truth is just the idea that any of our beliefs could be false, so we better be cautious about the beliefs we take to be justified. Such a *general* form of caution cannot have any place in inquiry because once we introduce the idea of inquiry, we introduce the crucial distinction between an inquirer's or first-person point of view and a third-person point of view. From a first-person point of view, there is no scope at all for caution about the beliefs we use in the way Quine and McDowell require. And from the third person point of view successful cautioning of an inquirer may of course take place but it cannot by the nature of things be caution in the sense Rorty and Davidson think is built in a *general way* into the nature of truth, seen as objective in their sense. It can only be caution prompted by the injection of serious and specific doubt by the citing of particular reasons to the inquirer by the third person. It is simply impossible therefore for there to be any clear and intelligible place for their cautionary aspect of truth once inquiry is the subject. It is Rorty's innovation in recent times to once again subject the concept of truth to the pragmatist's context of inquiry. But once this is done, his own agreement with Davidson on the consequences of the cautionary aspect of truth is made questionable and unnecessary.

Again the Davidsonian will respond: But all you have done is characterized truth from a first-person point of view. And truth from a first-person point of view is not truth, it is judgment of truth or belief. And again we must respond: once you have accepted Rorty's innovation that truth be discussed within the pragmatist's context of its place and role in inquiry, then to insist on the first-person point of view is just to insist on what you have accepted, viz, what role it has in the point of view of inquiry. And so again we must repeat what McDowell says: truth here is conformity to something no more independent of us (inquirers) than the world as it figures in our world view.

In a related point, it would now seem that having introduced the context of inquiry, and therefore the point of view (first-person) of the inquirer, Rorty's own view that the only goal that inquirers can have is justification is made unnecessary. From her point of view what the inquirer seeks is truth, she seeks to know which among the propositional states of mind which are not truths, but merely hypotheses, supposals, etc., should be counted as truths. As Peirce would say she wants to relieve doubt, she wants to know which one of these various propositions she entertains as hypotheses she can be certain about and put into "use" as part of the standard by which we judge truth. The standard contrast between truth and justification is no longer possible in this context and framework. The standard contrast has it that truth and justification apply to the same things, states like beliefs. And those who wish to reduce truth to justification argue that the concept of truth that transcends all justification is incoherent, while those who want to say that truth cannot be so reduced, stress what underlies the cautionary point that Rorty has conceded to Davidson, viz, that our best justified beliefs can fail to be true, and so we cannot ever know which of our beliefs is true. But this standard contrast has no comfortable place in the pragmatist framework of asking questions about truth in the context of inquiry. The pragmatist is of course keen to deny that truth is not "out of reach" in the sense that the inquirer cannot tell which of our beliefs are true. But this, in this changed context of inquiry, is not to be understood at all as the pragmatist saying that truth is reducible to justification; in denying that truth is out of reach, the pragmatist is not saying that the inquirer has to now settle for justification of her beliefs as a goal. *From the inquirer's point of view* (first-person), her beliefs (those cognitive states of mind which are doubt-free and which constitute her world view, unlike those propositions that are merely hypotheses) *are* true. They are not "merely" justified. In fact since we are certain of these beliefs, since they constitute our 'world-view' (as McDowell calls it), since we don't grant anything but an epistemologically irrelevant logically possibility of their being false, we are not cautious regarding them, we "use" them (in Quine's sense), and don't justify them at all. The Rortian retreat to their being "merely" justified as opposed to being true thus throws up the wrong contrast. The right contrast is that they are not something that the inquirer thinks of as the sort of thing that gets justified because she believes them *true*. If the inquirer justifies anything it's not these things, not beliefs.

Rorty has not embraced this much more Peircean version of pragmatism, since he continues to stress the standard contrast between truth and justification. In a sense I think that is to have failed to fully exploit his own framework which stresses inquiry and the inquirer. His version of pragmatism also stresses inquiry, but holds on to the standard contrast because it argues that if truth is not a goal of inquiry, being out of reach, then justification alone is that goal. In this other version of pragmatism, from the first person point of view, beliefs of which an inquirer is doubt-free are true. And it is not as if this other version is a position owing only to Peirce and others in the pragmatist tradition. It is a position that echoes epistemological attitudes and remarks that are to be found in both Austin and Wittgenstein. Austin often puts the point in terms of knowledge rather than our subject, truth, but the point carries over to our subject without much strain. He says: "The expression, 'When you know, you can't be wrong' is perfectly good sense. You are prohibited from saying 'I know it is so, but I may be wrong' . . ." He also makes the distinction a little later: "Being aware that you may be mistaken doesn't mean merely being aware that you are a fallible human being; it means that you may be mistaken in this case."[13] Both these points were made in our repudiation above of the cautionary aspect of truth, and in our stressing the distinction between beliefs and other states of mind such as hypotheses, for being aware that one is mistaken in a particular case is not to believe in the sense of belief that goes into our world view, but in the sense of hypothesis. And being aware that one is fallible but not in any particular case, brings no particular caution to inquiry in which particular cases of belief in our world-view are "used" as a standard. In general, the pragmatist point that no kind of caution turns "true" to "justified," echoes an Austinian insight that "I know" does not mean something like "I claim to know but possibly do not know since I could be wrong."

It should be made clear that this refusal to see the impact of Rorty's cautionary point about truth as being relevant to the inquirer (and therefore refusing to see it as relevant to truth once its role in inquiry has become the framework for discussing truth) does not amount to denying that the inquirer's doubt-free beliefs are not revisable. But revisability of what we believe *true* does not amount to saying that we are at most justified in our beliefs. Both Quine and Austin are explicit about this. In the quoted passage, Quine says, "Unlike Descartes, we own and use our beliefs of the moment, even in the midst of philosophizing, until by what is vaguely called scientific method we change them here and there for the better. Within our own totally evolving doctrine, we can judge *truth* . . . subject to *correction*, but that goes without saying" (my emphases). And Austin says: "It seems a serious mistake to suppose that language (or most language, language about real things) is 'predictive' in such a way that the future can always prove it wrong. What the future can always do, is to make us revise our ideas about goldfinches . . . or anything else." So the point is: from the point of view of our *current* but *evolving* doctrine, our doubt-free beliefs have the full prestige of truth, not the mere justification of the cautionary idea.

I have been arguing that a standard distinction in standard debates between realism and anti-realism, the distinction between truth and justification, does not carry over to questions about truth once we ask them in the framework of a fully pragmatist setting of the context of inquiry. In the standard form of those debates, where the issue is "Is truth a coherent and intelligible notion even if it is supposed to transcend all justification?", perhaps the standard distinction is unavoidable. But that is because in that standard format, there is no first-/third-person point of view distinction. That distinction only enters if the issue is something like the pragmatist's issue that Rorty raises: "what place does truth have in inquiry?" Once inquiry has been introduced as the context in which the issue of truth is to be raised, then we have to take seriously the point of view (first-person) of the inquirer. It is true of course that philosophers like Dummett who wanted to address the standard format issue by saying that truth, if it transcends all justification, violates Wittgenstein's demand that meaning *is use*, were close to saying something like what the pragmatist says. Close, but no cigar. For it is not yet to have introduced the inquirer's point of view In any explicit way as the pragmatist has done, and so philosophers like Dummett continue to discuss the issue in terms of the standard distinction between truth and justification. Thus when I say that Rorty fails to fully exploit the framework he has himself introduced, the diagnosis may be that he is still half seeing the debate in the standard format where there is no first- and third-person point of view distinction, even as he has changed its context to a pragmatist one where there is such a distinction to be exploited.

Now, a perfectly good question remains, as to what, in this revised pragmatist framework, *is* the distinction between truth and justification. Just because we have been saying that an inquirer does not justify her doubt-free beliefs and the question of justification for them does not even arise, surely we are not saying that there is no place for justification in inquiry. Surely the distinction between truth and justification does not disappear. No it does not. It is just that it does not take the form of saying what Davidson and Rorty say, which is that we can only know whether our beliefs are justified not that they are true, so we only can seek their justification not their truth. What form, then, does the distinction take, if not this one? Remember, the claim of this kind of pragmatist is to say that (from the point of view, inquiry) our doubt-free beliefs are true. For her, like for Quine and Austin and Wittgenstein and McDowell, we do not need to justify these beliefs, they constitute our world view, and we simply 'use' them as the standard, by which we judge truth, by which we inquire and try and relieve the doubt that we have in the hypotheses we entertain, and so on. I do not justify my belief that the earth is round or that I have a hand or . . . anything else that is part of my current best doctrine. I believe them true. There is no question of justification. Of course if somebody were to ask me to justify these beliefs, if she asked me for reasons or evidence, I might give them to her, but that is a bit of politesse, of good social relations, and of no epistemological interest. The point of epistemological interest is that we neither need nor do anything by way of deliberation to justify these beliefs because we hold them without doubt. Audiences are not to the point here. It is because Rorty has stressed audiences so much that he does not exploit the real epistemological arena, the point of view of the inquirer, a (first-person) point of view within which nothing needs justification once it is held without doubt. But in epistemology audiences are not to the point. They do not play any constitutive role for any element of inquiry. If we deal with them it is not for the sake of inquiry, it is for the sake of advancing our careers, getting research funds, fulfilling public responsibilities, or generally spreading the word which we cherish. If justification to audiences has no epistemological relevance, justifying doubt-free beliefs within inquiry (not to audiences, but from the point of view of the inquirer and her inquiry) makes no epistemological sense. Why justify any thing that is not being doubted? The only thing to say about these beliefs as inquirers is that they are true, To say that any one of them is true is to say, as McDowell does, that they conform, they have a particular form of normative relatedness, to the world as it figures *in our own world view*. So, to repeat, the question is: what does justification apply to, if it does not apply to these beliefs? For surely there must be some distinction between truth and justification.

It may be thought that "justified" applies to those cognitive states that are not beliefs in this sense, but things that we entertain and which are not doubt-free. But that cannot be exactly right either, since if they are not doubt-free they are not 'justified.' Are they the sorts of things that we *try* and justify? Well, if trying to "relieve our doubt" about them is to try and justify them, the answer might be yes. But the fully right thing to say is this. Suppose we were to remove doubt about some state of mind that we do not believe but entertain only as an hypothesis, and as a result come to believe it without doubt, we would have then made a change in our "evolving" (as Quine calls it) world-view, however slight and fragmentary the change might be. From the point of view of the state of the evolving doctrine before that change was made, that change, that bit of evolution, would need a justification. At any given, current state of the evolving doctrine, and from the point of view of that current state of the doctrine, no justification is required for the beliefs that are not in doubt and which constitute that current state of the doctrine. But equally, therefore, from that same point of view, from the point of view of that current state, any decision to change the current doctrine by adding or subtracting from it would need justification. That is why Isaac Levi, who has studied the revision of belief with more rigor and intellectual detail than any one I know, has claimed that justification applies to *changes* in our doubt-free beliefs.[14] What we need to deliberate about and justify as inquirers (and not to audiences but in the practice and pursuit of inquiry about the world) is not our doubt-free beliefs, rather we need to deliberate about and justify whether we should in any way make any changes in such beliefs, add to them or subtract from them in the light of new incoming states of information, etc. Some changes in beliefs are justified, others may be irrational and unjustified and unwarranted. We can add to Levi's point that justification applies to change of belief the following point which is of interest to the debates about truth and justification. In the standard distinction, both truth and justification apply to the same animal, beliefs. For this reason, it is possible to even raise the question whether truth is reducible to justification or not. It is possible to ask whether all there is to truth, in any intelligible sense, is justification, even if we say no by way of an answer. But in the revised distinction as it shows up in this other version of pragmatism, it is not even possible to ask that question since truth and justification apply to two altogether different kinds of things that are relevant to inquiry. The former apply to beliefs, the latter apply to changes in beliefs. The idea that they are (or are not) reducible is not an idea that can even be formulated in this framework.

While we look at the question of whether truth is a goal of inquiry from still half within the standard form of the debate about truth and justification, as Rorty does, it is hard to deny his conclusion that truth and justification are not different goals of inquiry. And if we also accept the so-called cautionary aspect of truth and say that we can never know which of our beliefs are true, as Rorty also does, then it is hard not to be sympathetic with his conclusion that the goal of inquiry is justification not truth. But if McDowell and Quine (on my reading) are right, we do not have to accept that idea of truth according to which we cannot know which of our beliefs are true. And it is McDowell's point against Rorty that if we give up these assumptions, then there *is* a perfectly good sense that truth is a norm and a goal of inquiry. But here I think we have to tread carefully. In the rest of the paper, I will try and get clear about the exact sense or senses in which truth is a value and a goal of inquiry.

III

What McDowell says is that even if we give up the idea that truth is out of reach in this way, we still have something that Rorty himself endorses wholeheartedly, which is the property of truth we call "disquotation." And McDowell thinks that Rorty does not fully exploit the normative and goal-directing element that is inherent in the very idea of disquotation. Rorty's mistake is apparently to see it as purely descriptive and without this normative element. He says: "Rorty claims that the 'disquotational' use of 'true' is 'descriptive' and as such not merely to be distinguished from, but incapable of being combined in a unified discourse with, any use of 'true' that treats truth as a norm of inquiry and claim-making." And McDowell protests this by saying immediately after: "But this makes no room for such truisms as the following: what makes it correct among speakers of English to make a claim with the words 'Snow is white' (to stay with a well-worn example) is that snow is (indeed) white." He adds a little later something which again stresses the element of norm: "For a given sentence to be true – to be disquotable – is for it to be *correctly* usable to make a claim just because . . ., where in the gap we insert, not quoted but used, the sentence that figures on the right hand side of the T-sentence provided for the sentence in question by a good Tarskian theory of language. Truth in the sense of disquotability is unproblematically normative for sentences uttered in order to make claims."[15]

This is a very interesting point, but it is not clear that it will satisfy Rorty. For it is not clear whether the sense of norm or goal that Rorty is denying to truth in inquiry is what McDowell has here established as "truth as a norm of inquiry and claim-making." The sense of norm that McDowell has established comes in the use of 'correctly' in the following thought: "for a given sentence to be disquotable (that is true) is for it to be correctly usable to make a claim just because . . .". But this does not by itself establish a norm in the sense of goal of inquiry in the further sense that we *actually seek to be* correct in this way in our inquiry. The sense of norm that he has established is just the sense of norm that comes with the true/false distinction, and it becomes clear then that disquotation (if it helps characterize truth) should carry that sense of norm. But the idea that we should seek truth and avoid falsehood (or error) is the sense of norm that the pragmatist in Rorty wants to bring onto the center stage of discussions of truth. It is not enough for Rorty that truth carries with it a norm in the sense that it divides all our beliefs into those which have the property of correctness, and those which lack it. But that is all that 'correct' gets one in the thought above from McDowell that I cited. The pragmatist wants to know whether we should be seeking to acquire beliefs in one of those divisions and shun those in the other. And some pragmatists (Peirce for instance) say yes to this question, and others (Rorty) say no, truth is not such a goal.

One way of bringing out this point about why what McDowell says about the normativity of truth in inquiry does not come up to the concern that the pragmatist has about the norms of inquiry can be brought out as follows. Burnyeat[16] has shown that Cartesian skepticism was different and more radical from Ancient skepticism in claiming that if we put into question that we have *knowledge* of the external world, then the existence of the external world can be put into doubt. To put it in terms of truth and inquiry which is our present subject, if it is the case that all the beliefs in our inquiry about the external world could be false, then we put into doubt the existence of the external world. For the ancient skeptic there was no such radical loss of the world as a result of loss of knowledge of the world, since for him, knowledge-seeking inquiry was not the only way of relating to the world, one also related to it by living in it. Heidegger,[17] as is well-known, made much of this distinction, describing it in terms of the world being "ready-to-hand" (lived in) rather than "present-at-hand" (known), and one of the things that may be made of it is precisely the idea that the norm that truth provides for our beliefs as they occur in our ready-to-hand relations is quite different from the norm that truth provides when it directs our inquiry. It is not as if beliefs about the world are not in play in the former kind of relations, and it is not as if truth therefore is not in play. It is rather that any notion of normativity that applies to truth here is no more than what McDowell claims for it, but that is not yet the norm or goal that pragmatists discuss and that Peirce and others take to be a goal of inquiry, but which Rorty does not because he thinks that justification is a good enough goal. The disagreement between Rorty and Peirce here is over a matter that is over and above the idea of correctness that applies even to beliefs in our *ready-to-hand* level relations with the world. Our beliefs at this latter level are susceptible to normative assessment of correctness and incorrectness, truth and falsity. But seeking the correct ones and avoiding the incorrect are not goals in *themselves*. The only real goals are the goals that we have in living in the world, the practical ends that such living involves. But these are not *cognitive* goals. What I am stressing when I talk of the goals of inquiry are the latter. It is perfectly possible that claim-making in our inquiry cannot be kept apart too much from the claim-making in our non-knowledge-seeking but lived relations with the world. That is, if we make claims at all in the ready-to-hand level dealings with the world, (as surely we must), then it may be that *we are already* incipiently embarked in the sort of truth-seeking goals that are involved more fully in the present-to-hand level relations with the world, such as seeking scientific knowledge of it, and so on. But there is still a gap between what McDowell establishes as a norm, that is, the idea of "correctness" inherent in truth and disquotability, and the further sense of norm, that is, the value of gaining such correctness and therefore the goal of seeking it. That we must seek to be correct in the sense that McDowell has established is not an idea that is simply built-in to the idea of the disquotation.[18] But disquotation is the only site and source of correctness and normativity that McDowell cites. So, that we might seek to be correct (in the sense of 'correct' that McDowell has established) is a further cognitive goal, and that was what the pragmatist was interested in when she asked whether truth was a goal of inquiry.

In any case, whether McDowell has built it in or not in his remarks on disquotation and norms, what is clear is that both he and I and many pragmatists want to say that we can (and do) have goals of inquiry which are fully cognitive, and that do not just make inquiry subservient to the practical ends of living in the world. And if I am right over the last many pages, it is a transcendental idealism of the sort that we have been sketching that allows us to have these goals, for it puts truth within our reach, so as to be able to make it a goal of this kind. I will close this paper by clarifying in what sense truth is a goal and a value, over and above the sense that McDowell has firmly established.

That pragmatists have cognitive goals is sometimes obscured by talk of truth being valuable, and it will be a minor service to remove these obscurities. The popular caricature (no doubt often fed by careless remarks in James and Dewey, though not Peirce) is that a belief is true if it is useful, or some slightly (though not much) more refined version of that. Here, for instance, is Davidson on the pragmatist in his paper in this volume. "Since the word 'Truth' has an aura of something valuable, the trick of persuasive definitions is to redefine it to be something of which you approve, something "good to steer by" in a phrase Rorty endorses on Dewey's behalf. So Dewey declared that a belief or theory is true if and only if it promotes human affairs." The last statement is the caricatured view. But it does not even follow from the idea that truth is good to steer by. For what we could be steering is our inquiry, not our practical goals. What we take to be true (our doubt-free beliefs), our world-view, is, if Quine is right, exactly what we steer our inquiry by. So it by no means reduces truth to what promotes human affairs. It provides the background standard by which we steer and seek to relieve doubt on matters about which there still is doubt, that is, hypothesis, conjecture, etc. It steers such cognitive activity undertaken for such cognitive ends. It is a failure to appreciate that the pragmatist can be interested in *cognitive* goals of this kind that leads one to attribute to them this caricatured idea of the value of truth.[19]

Even if we do not, as in the caricatured view, *reduce* true belief to beliefs that turn out to be useful, we may still be blind to the pragmatist interest in cognitive values. If we think that the only values there are values that are utilitarian or more generally values that promote well-being and "human affairs," then we are bound to think that if truth is a value, a goal of inquiry, it must just be another way of saying that we seek truth because the deliverances of inquiry (say, scientific inquiry), that is, truths (which are not in themselves an end), help us eventually to travel faster, combat ill-health, etc., all of which are ends and values of ours. This does not reduce the concept of truth to usefulness (it does not say "a belief is true if and only if it is useful"), but it subserves truth as a value to other sorts of values. We do not need to deny that the true deliverances of inquiry may have these instrumental effects to insist that truth is a value in its own right and not instrumental and subservient.

The sense in which truth is such a non-instrumental value surfaces differently when we talk of our beliefs and when we talk of linguistic things such as utterances, written or verbal. It is the former that we have been mostly discussing when we discussed inquiry. And in my discussion, I have tried to defend the idea that truth is a norm or goal of inquiry in a sense over and above what is established by McDowell's remarks about the norm inherent in the idea of disquotation and claim-making. I have tried to defend the idea that apart from the norm in the idea of *correctly* believing or claiming something, truth is a norm in that we seek to arrive at correct beliefs. It is the latter idea that Rorty was denying when he said that truth is not a norm or goal of inquiry. But the idea does not carry over so neatly to our utterances.

To say exactly why not and to say exactly what sort of value truth has in the matter of utterances rather than beliefs, reveals a fascinating and, I believe, very important feature of the sense in which truth is a value in our culture. Actually what I just said is misleading. It is not as if there is a different sense in which truth has a value when it comes to belief from when it comes to utterances. It is rather that the value of truth, in the one philosophically important sense of value there is to truth, surfaces very differently in utterances than it does in inquiry and belief. In the matter of beliefs, we can capture the idea that truth is a value by saying that we seek true beliefs in inquiry. But this does not carry over into anything like: we utter or seek to utter only true sentences when we communicate. It is not a goal of communication to say true things, in a way that seeking true beliefs and avoiding false ones is a goal of inquiry. There is no such parity of goal in communication and inquiry. This is because it is very often a goal of speakers to say things which conceal the truth rather than to convey it. But, on the other hand, just because there are frequent intended lies and misleading statements among our utterances does not show that truth is not a value. The value of truth (the very same value that is found in belief and inquiry) surfaces in utterance and communication, not in the pat form of making us seek to utter true things in the way we seek true beliefs. The reason for this is that the value of truth (as regards belief in inquiry) does surface in the utterances and communications of *liars as well*. What does not surface in the utterances of liars is the value of truth-*telling*. Now, Rorty has often denied that there is any value to truth, and said that there is only value in truth-telling and said that the value of truth-telling is not different in kind from the value, say, of being kind or generous. It is of moral interest but has no other interest. For Rorty, truth itself if it was a value would have an interest over and above a moral interest – but truth is not a value.

I will conclude with a plea for not following Rorty on this since I believe that it is a matter of some importance in our culture, especially our academic culture, that we see the nature and the great importance of truth as a value in a further sense than the moral sense of value in truth-telling. Indeed if it was not for having read a great deal of Rorty over the years, I would not have been instructed into the importance and concern of this point, which he explicitly denies, but which his work nevertheless deeply exemplifies. The sense in which truth is a value which stands apart is that it is a much more abstract sense of value than is possessed by truth-telling or considerate-ness or generosity. And its abstractness lies in the fact that I have already hinted at, the fact that the liar who violates the moral norm of truth-telling *nevertheless values* truth. In fact it is partly because he values it (in this abstract sense) that he tries to conceal it or invent it. What is this more abstract value which even the liar has? Rorty might understandably protest and ask: if there is this abstract value to truth, and if even the liar values it, someone must surely in principle be able to *fail* to value it, else how can it be a value?

This is a good question. And the answer is yes, someone does indeed fail to value truth in this more abstract sense, but it is not the liar. It is the equally common sort of person in our midst, it is the bullshitter. This is the person who merely sounds off at parties or, alas, gets published in some academic journals just because he is prepared to speak or write in the requisite jargon, without any goal of getting things right nor even (like the liar) concealing the right things which he thinks he has got. The so-called Sokal hoax on which so much has been written I suspect leaves precisely this lesson to be drawn. I don't want to get into a long discussion about this incident since I think that it has become a mildly distasteful site for people making careers out of its propaganda and polemical potential. But I will say this briefly. Everything that I have read on the subject of this hoax, including by Sokal himself, takes up the issue of how Sokal exposed the rampant and uncritical relativism of post-modern literary disciplines.

Though I don't doubt that literary people in the academy have recently shown a relativist tendency, I wonder if that is really what is at stake. The point is analogous to the one I just made about the liar. The relativist also does value truth, in the abstract sense that I have in mind, even if he has a somewhat different gloss on it from his opponents. In fact he too, precisely because he does value truth in this abstract sense, wishes to urgently put this different gloss on it. I believe it quite likely that the journal in which Sokal propagated his hoax would have been happy (at least before the controversy began) to publish a similarly dissimulating hoax reply to his paper in which all kinds of utterly ridiculous arguments were given, this time for an anti-relativist and objective notion of truth, so long as they were presented in the glamorous jargon and with the familiar dialectical moves that command currency in the discipline. If so, the lesson to be learnt from the hoax is not that relativism is rampant in those disciplines (which it may be), but that very often bullshit is quite acceptable, if it is presented in the requisite way. To set oneself against that is to endorse the value of truth in our culture in a way that amounts to valuing *truth* over and above truth-telling, for a bullshitter is not a liar. I don't think Rorty should deny this. It defines the possibility of philosophy as he practices it, and as it is done in this volume of papers about him, but also (despite the propaganda generated by the Sokal hoax) as it is done in Continental Europe, where it *is* for the most part done quite interestingly and profoundly.

Notes

1 I am grateful to Donald Davidson, Ihsan Dogramaci, Isaac Levi, David Maier, John McDowell, Gurpreet Rattan, Richard Rorty, Carol Rovane, Stephen White, and Lee Whitfield for critical and instructive discussions on the subject of this paper.

2 See the opening sentence of his "'Is Truth a Goal of Enquiry'? Davidson vs. Wright," *Philosophical Quarterly*, vol. 45, no. 180, July 1955. All other quoted references to Rorty will be from this paper.

3 Quoted in Rorty *ibid.*, from p. 313 of Davidson's Dewey Lectures "The Structure and Content of Truth" given at Columbia University and published in the *Journal of Philosophy*, 87 (1990).

4 See the closing sentence of "Truth Rehabilitated" in this volume. All other quoted references to Davidson will be from this paper.

5 I should make clear that though Davidson accepts that disquotation is a property of truth, he does not think that it exhausts our notion of truth, as the doctrine of 'deflationism' claims.

6 See McDowell "Toward Rehabilitating Objectivity". All quoted references to McDowell will be to this paper.

7 Most of the approving references to pragmatism in this paper are to Peirce. The paper of Peirce that I have in mind in my passing references to him is "The Fixation of Belief" in his *Collected Papers*, (Harvard University Press, 1978). Vol. V, Bk.2, ch.iv.

8 I have tried to do this over the various chapters of my book *Belief and Meaning* (Blackwell, 1992).

9 The claims of charity in one of its two versions is supposed to yield this outcome in Davidson. I think it is not so obvious that one of the versions does so, nor that the other does so without begging the question. But I will not elaborate these doubts here.

10 In Chapter 5 of *Belief and Meaning*, I give an argument which I frankly grant as not being a knock-down argument of the sort philosophers call "transcendental."

11   I repeat that even this global idea is one that we have a right to only if we have an argument that establishes it without begging the question against the skeptic.

12   This reading of Quine is something I could not have made if I had not read Isaac Levi's very attractive pragmatist reconstructive analysis of Peirce's belief-doubt model of inquiry. See among other things of Levi, *The Enterprise of Knowledge* (MIT Press, 1983).

13   Austin "Other Minds," *Philosophical Papers*, (OUP, 1960) p. 98. I have not cited Wittgenstein for reasons of space, but similar attitudes may be found in *On Certainty* (Blackwell, 1969).

14   See Levi, ibid.

15   Quine too stresses in the passage I quoted that this idea of judging truth by the light of our own current doctrine gives us a perfectly objective notion of truth (not parochial or relativistic, as he explicitly says) and spelt out in terms of disquotation, as he also explicitly says.

16   "Idealism and Greek Philosophy" in Godfrey Vesey, *Idealism: Past and Present* (CUP, 1982).

17   *Being and Time* (Harper and Row, 1962).

18   When I put my point to McDowell, in conversation, he himself expressed the opinion to me that it is built-in, and said that he did not in his paper make explicit that it is nor how exactly it does. It is not very clear to me how it is built-in, but it will not be possible for me to pursue this interesting issue any further in this paper. I will leave it as a challenge for him (and me, and anyone else who is interested).

19   I don't mean to suggest that Davidson has been unfair to pragmatists in these remarks. He in fact is quite fair and goes on as Rorty does to take up the question of whether truth can be a goal of inquiry and a value in the cognitive sense of value, and like Rorty denies that it can.

RESPONSE TO AKEEL BILGRAMI

As Bilgrami says, Davidson and I agree in asserting two counter-intuitive propositions:

1   we can never tell which of our beliefs are true;
2   truth is not a goal of inquiry.

These sound counter-intuitive as soon as one takes what Bilgrami calls "the inquirer's or first-person point of view" (p. 253). " For taking this stance means using "true" to characterize beliefs I currently have no reason to doubt: those which make up what Bilgrami calls my "world-view." "*From the inquirer's point of view* (first-person)," Bilgrami writes, "her beliefs (those cognitive states of mind which are doubt-free and which constitute her world view, unlike those propositions that are merely hypotheses) are true. They are not 'merely' justified" (p. 254).

From this point of view, these beliefs "are not something that the inquirer thinks of as the sort of thing that gets justified because she believes them *true*, If the inquirer justifies anything it's not these things, not beliefs" (p. 254). Bilgrami thinks it appropriate for pragmatists to assume this point of view, and to abandon the conventional philosophical view that "truth and justification apply to the same things, states like beliefs" (p. 253). For "this standard contrast has no comfortable place in the pragmatist framework of asking questions about truth in the context of inquiry."

Bilgrami seems to think that pragmatists should do this because they believe that what doesn't make a difference to practice should make no difference. But pragmatists like Dewey were interested in making very long-term differences to very large practices, not just in the sort of inquiry which can be traced back to a particular occasion of doubting. When Bilgrami evokes "the context of inquiry" he does it in such a way as to shove aside specifically philosophical contexts. But in books like *The Quest for Certainty* and *Reconstruction in Philosophy* Dewey spent a lot of time talking about the long-term need to create a culture in which the question of whether "truth" is "within our reach" would not arise. It would not arise because nobody would attempt to define "truth" either as Bilgrami does (as the property had by beliefs which "have a particular form of normative relatedness to the world as it figures in our own world view" (p. 256) or in any other way. The image of thoughts or words answering to the world would go by the board, and be replaced by images of organisms coping with their environment by using language to develop projects of social cooperation.

I read Davidson as contributing to this Deweyan enterprise and I do not find Peirce's "The Fixation of Belief" particularly relevant to it. So I do not think it reasonable to fasten on that paper of Peirce's as a way of showing that purported pragmatists like Davidson and myself should stop saying counter-intuitive things. About all "The Fixation of Belief" does is to point out that we think for the sake of removing the irritation of doubt. Dewey felt that his culture was irritated by Cartesian and Kantian doubts about the relation of its beliefs to reality, irritations which could be removed by getting rid of questions about mind–world, word–world, and scheme–content relationships.

Dewey would, I think, be distressed by Bilgrami's attempt to revive the scheme–content distinction in the form of a divide between doubt-free items (the ones to which Bilgrami wants to restrict the application of the term "belief") and dubitable ones, with the former serving as a "standard" for the latter. The distinction between items presently being doubted and those not being doubted is unproblematic, but for Dewey as for Davidson, this is not a distinction between the field of application of a standard and a standard, nor between something that is not a "theory of the world" and something that is. By bringing in notions like "standard" and "theory," and by restricting "belief" to doubt-free items, Bilgrami makes needlessly heavy weather out of the shifting boundary between the items inquiry is presently moving about and those it is presently leaving alone.

Further, I fail to see what is especially first-person or agent-like about the point of view Bilgrami describes. For purposes of his argument, it would be enough to say, correctly, that there is an unphilosophical use of the term "true" in which "is true" is used interchangeably with "is certain," and both are used interchangeably with "is among my beliefs." The laity do indeed speak this way. But why should the mind of this stolid layperson, the person who has what Bilgrami calls "a (first-person) point of view within which nothing needs justification once it is held without doubt," be described as "the real epistemological arena" (p. 256)? Would it not be better described as a mind undisturbed by epistemological reflection? It only takes an hour with Socrates, or the first two weeks of philosophy 101, to change this mind into one eager to distinguish between truth and certainty, quite willing to grant that its doubt-free beliefs may not be true, and capable of seeing the point of Davidson's counter-intuitive claims. Dewey was speaking to such a student. He did not use the Narodnik tactics preferred by Austin and Bilgrami, and I think he was wise to eschew them.

Consider Bilgrami's claim that "in epistemology audiences are not to the point . . . If we deal with them it is not for the sake of inquiry, it is for the sake of advancing our careers, getting research funds, fulfilling public responsibilities or generally spreading the word that we cherish" (p. 256). I am tempted to call this separation of inquiry from audiences a flamboyant exaggeration. But it might better be treated as a result of Bilgrami's surprising, undefended, redefinition of the term "epistemology." Much of what usually counts as "epistemological" discussion is about the relationship between truth and justification. It revolves around the fact that both justification and certainty may be transitory, whereas truth is eternal. Bilgrami simply rules out this discussion as non-epistemological, and invites pragmatists to join him in doing so. But most of the philosophers who have called themselves "pragmatists" have prided themselves on leaving behind both Cartesian methodological solipsism and Descartes' confusion of knowledge with certainty. They have viewed inquiry as a thoroughly social phenomenon, one in which audiences clamoring for justification fill every epistemological arena.

Viewing inquiry that way can reasonably be called a "third-person" view – looking down from above on something that can be described as a person trying to get a world right, or an organism trying to cope with its environment, or in various other ways. Bilgrami is right to say that we must take such a view before we can swallow such counter-intuitive claims as "we can never tell which of our beliefs are true" and "truth is not a goal of inquiry." But it is not clear why the view of the unreflective agent, who brushes these claims aside, is to be preferred to the view of the reflective Davidsonian, who makes them. Pragmatists can happily agree that these claims will always sound absurd to people who use "true" interchangeably with "undoubted by me." But why are such people relevant? Why should a pragmatist view with suspicion someone who speculates that a lot of presently doubt-free beliefs will turn out to be false?

When conducted by philosophers, to be sure, most such speculation is what Peirce called "make-believe doubt." But his criticism of such doubt was aimed at its use by the skeptic, not at people like Dewey and Davidson who are trying to get rid of skepticism. Bilgrami, however, takes Davidson and me to hold that "truth is out of our reach" (p. 246), thereby making us sound like skeptics. His argument for doing so is that we are attempting, over ambitiously, to view our thought and our language as attempting to represent what McDowell calls "something more independent of us than the world as it figures in our world view."

Bilgrami says that he finds this phrase of McDowell's "a very accurate description of what we must think of representation as being if we thought, with Davidson, that 'we could never tell which of our beliefs are true'" (p. 247). But in the first place, neither Davidson nor I think that thought or language *represents* a world. We are trying to get rid of the very idea of representation. In the second place, it is hard to figure out what McDowell could mean by "more independent of us than the world that figures in our world view." All sides to all these disputes agree that the world that so figures is mostly causally independent of us: that is, most of it would be as it is had we never existed.

To get an interesting further degree of causal independence we should have to imagine a situation in which it was no longer the case that our beliefs changed as our causal relations with the world changed, or perhaps a world where we had no causal relations at all to anything we have beliefs about. But has not Davidson shown that the latter situation cannot obtain? Is either suggestion coherent? Or is some sort of non-causal independence in question? What sort?

I am not sure how Bilgrami would answer these rhetorical questions, but I am also not sure that further exegesis of McDowell would pay off. For I cannot see the connection between the Sellarsian–Davidsonian claim that inquiry "can put *any* claim in jeopardy, but not *all* at once" and the idea of something being out of reach. It is even more obscure how Davidson, the philosopher who has insisted, notoriously, that most of our beliefs must be true, can be said to think truth out of reach. There is no mention of this latter Davidsonian doctrine in Bilgrami's paper, except in the severly etiolated form "not all of our beliefs can be false." Mention of the full-strength doctrine (to which I too adhere, faithfully following in Davidson's tracks) would, I think, have made it very difficult to portray Davidson or myself as people worried about something being out of our reach.

Having once introduced the idea that Davidson and I portray truth as out of reach, Bilgrami goes on to suggest that the only way to get it back within reach is to solve "the deep and hard question of how to demarcate a ground that is properly described as 'transcendental idealism'" (p. 247). He proceeds to formulate the project of his paper as "seeing what version of transcendental idealism makes possible a position that is plausibly described as pragmatism" (p. 247). Maybe some version of Peirce, a devout Kant-worshipper, could be so described, but I doubt that any version of Dewey could. For transcendental idealism makes essential use of the reality–appearance distinction, whereas Deweyan pragmatism eschews that distinction in favor of the distinction between more and less useful descriptions.

Bilgrami says that "it is not obvious" that anyone has given a "non-question-begging argument" for the claim that "all of our beliefs about the world may be false" does not follow from "we can never know which of our beliefs about the world are true" (p. 248). I think there is such an argument. The first step in this argument goes from the claim that coherence among propositional attitudes is our only test of truth to Sellars' conclusion that "empirical knowledge . . . is a self-correcting enterprise which can put *any* claim in jeopardy, but not *all* at once." ("Empiricism and the Philosophy of Mind", sec. 38). The second step is provided by Davidson's argument against the scheme–content distinction: viz, that if you abandon all or most of your previous beliefs about Xs (cows, electrons, or epistemology, for example) then you are no longer talking about Xs, and *a fortiori* do not have false beliefs about them. You have changed the subject.

Bilgrami presumably finds this two-step argument question-begging because he would not accept the claim that there is nothing to say about the connection between our justifying activities and truth – no way to cross the gap between the contingent and temporal and the eternal. His motive for not accepting it is that, like McDowell, he does not wish to be deprived of the claim that the word "true" signifies "a mode of conformity to the world as it *does* figure in our world-view" (p. 249). Anyone who cannot put up with this deprivation – that is to say, anyone who thinks that conformity to, or answerability to, this world is insufficiently insured by our constant causal interaction with the world will, like McDowell, have go in quest of something like transcendental idealism.

Bilgrami's reason, as opposed to his motive, for being suspicious of coherence as the sole test of truth is that "our current theory of the world . . . sets the standard for what is and is not to be counted as true" (p. 250). Here the difference between his view and the one I share with Davidson is that we see no point in dividing up our propositional attitudes into the standard-setting ones that form part of a "theory of the world" and the non-standard-setting ones that do not. We see this as just the sort of scheme–content distinction which leads to skepticism, relativism, representationalism, and a lot of other terrible things. Following Quine's lead, we insist that there are no pure white doubt-free beliefs to form the scheme or set the standard, but only shades of grey – only degrees of actual and potential doubtfulness, of centrality to our belief-systems.

Bilgrami's only concession to this sort of anti-dualistic holism is to grant that "it is *logically* possible that beliefs in this sense [the standard-setting ones] be false." But, he goes on to say, that possibility will not "caution us into refraining from confidently using the beliefs which constitute our world-view in our inquiry" (p. 251). He is certainly right on this point: as he says, the Davidsonian claim that any of our beliefs can be false provides no "serious and specific cautionary instruction" to an inquirer (p. 252). But it was not supposed to. It was supposed rather to remind us of the puzzle that called epistemology (and much of the rest of philosophy) into existence in the first place: the puzzle created by the fact that there will always be a gap between temporary coherence, temporary justification, and its (purported) goal of eternal truth.

This merely philosophical point that "any of our beliefs could be false" was not, *pace* Bilgrami (p. 253), intended to carry the corollary that "we better be cautious about the beliefs we take to be justified." Pointing to that gap provides no specific help to any specific inquirer. Does that mean that pragmatists, who prize concreteness and specificity, should stop calling attention to it? Bilgrami thinks so: he says that "once Rorty has brought in the inquirer and raised the question of the nature and role of truth in the context of inquiry, then what comes onto center-stage is the *point of view of the inquirer*" (p. 252).

As I said earlier, I think Bilgrami's "crucial distinction between an inquirer's or first person point of view and a third-person point of view" comes down to no more than the distinction between the lay and the philosophical uses of the word "true." So when Bilgrami says that "it is Rorty's innovation in recent times to once again subject the concept of truth to the pragmatist's context of inquiry," I cannot accept this well-meant compliment. The pragmatist *philosopher*'s context of inquiry is the one shared by Kant, McDowell and everybody else who is attracted by transcendental idealism: it is the context in which one wonders whether and why justification should be thought to lead to truth. If, as Bilgrami says, "the distinction in standard debates about realism and anti-realism, the distinction between truth and justification, does not carry over to questions about truth once one asks them in the framework of a fully pragmatist setting of the context of inquiry" (p. 255), then so much the worse for that "fully pragmatist setting." That is not the setting in which to discuss the issues that divide Davidson and Brandom from McDowell and Wright.

Bilgrami sees more in Peirce's "Fixation of Belief" essay than I do. All I get out of it is the thought that the point of inquiry is problem-solving, that we only have doubts about our propositional attitudes when we have a problem to solve, and that inquiry ceases when doubts and problems vanish. If that were all there were to pragmatism – or if Austin's Narodnik endorsement of the lay idiom were sufficient to give philosophy peace – then we should long ago have heard the last of "the standard debates about realism and anti-realism." On my view of pragmatism, however, it is not an attempt to get back in touch with the attitude of "the inquirer" or "the first person" but something much more ambitious – an attempt to get us not to hypostatize the adjective 'true," and thereby avoid having to ask whether "truth" is or is not "in reach." Dewey did not just say that once you stop speaking Philosophical instead of Lay your problems will dissolve. Rather, he gave an account of how the fixation of belief by language-using organisms can be treated without reference to the accuracy of representations, and thus without raising the question of how we can guarantee such accuracy. Following up on Dewey in Davidson's way, rather than on Peirce in Isaac Levi's way, seems to me a more effective way to ensure that both transcendental idealism and epistemology will eventually be seen as quaint antiques.[1]

Notes

1 For the sake of convenient packaging, I have relocated the discussion of the last few pages of Bilgrami's paper. I take up his claim that the people he describes as "bullshitters" fail to value truth in the second part of "Response to Daniel Dennett." Dennett and Bilgrami hold similar views on these matters.

12

Freedom, Cruelty, and Truth:
Rorty versus Orwell

JAMES CONANT

Liberal . . . [F]rom the Latin *liberalis*, pertaining to a free man.

Oxford English Dictionary

[L]iberals are people who think that cruelty is the worst thing we do . . . Somewhere we all know that philosophically sophisticated debate about . . . objective truth . . . is pretty harmless stuff.

Richard Rorty[1]

There is some hope that the liberal habit of mind, which thinks of truth as something outside yourself, something to be discovered, and not as something you can make up as you go along, will survive . . .

[T]he feeling that the very concept of objective truth is fading out of the world . . . frightens me much more than bombs.

George Orwell[2]

This paper compares and contrasts Richard Rorty's and George Orwell's respective conceptions of what it means to be a liberal – their respective views of the relation between preservation of freedom, prevention of cruelty, and regard for truth. In his book, *Contingency, Irony and Solidarity*, Rorty reads Orwell as espousing the variety of liberalism that Rorty himself seeks to champion. The aim of this paper is to suggest, not only that what is offered there is a misreading of Orwell, but that it is a singularly instructive misreading – one which illuminates the shortcomings of Rorty's preferred method of dissolving philosophical problems.

I.   The Aims and Method of this Paper

There are few contemporary philosophers who have been criticized from as many different quarters as Richard Rorty has. There are also few contemporary philosophers who have been as generous and patient in replying to their critics as he has. In preparation for writing this paper, I read through some of Rorty's many replies to his critics. I was struck by how completely unfazed Rorty remains in the face of most criticisms of his work. (This failure on his part to be impressed by a criticism of his work naturally impresses me most when I am impressed by the criticism.) His reply to every critic is thoughtful and gracious, sometimes repeating things he says elsewhere, but never with any trace of a suggestion that he secretly thinks the critic a moron. Still, many of the replies are pervaded by a common mood and tone. The mood is one of weariness (of having heard it all before) and the tone is one of forbearance (of wishing the topic under discussion were more interesting). And, to some extent, even the content of many of the replies is similar: it is a content which could be most economically expressed simply through a shrug of the shoulders.

The common subtext of these extended verbal shrugs of the shoulders might be put as follows:

> Yes, yes, you want to accuse me of having made a *philosophical* mistake, or of slighting the importance of a *metaphysical* insight, or of violating *common sense*, or of being out of touch with *reality*, or . . .; but don't you see that criticism of this sort is only effective against someone who *cares* about philosophical correctness, metaphysical insight, common sense, being in touch with reality, or . . .; and don't you see that my whole goal is to try to get you to stop caring about the problems to which these ways of talking give rise and to start caring about problems that are worth caring about. My whole point is that we don't *need* to care about the sorts of problems that philosophers say we have to care about – we only think we have to; and my aim is to demonstrate the utter dispensability of caring about such problems by offering a practical demonstration of how well one can get on without caring about them.

Though I sympathize with many of Rorty's specific criticisms of the post-Cartesian metaphysical tradition, I also sympathize with many of the critics who find his own putatively non-metaphysical views as philosophically unsound as those he opposes. But the fact remains that criticisms to the effect that his views are philosophically unsound are bound to strike Rorty as point-missing. So what sort of criticism might strike home? What sort of criticism has a hope of eliciting from him something other than a verbal equivalent of a shrug of the shoulders? Rorty himself likes to recommend his epistemological doctrines on *therapeutic* and on *political* grounds – that is, on the ground that their adoption will liberate us from disabling metaphysical obsessions, and on the ground that they cohere more comfortably with the sort of politics that we (that is, citizens of our sort of liberal democracy) cannot help wanting. This suggests two possible avenues of criticism which might provoke a more searching response from Rorty: (i) a criticism which could succeed in demonstrating to him that his way of leaving philosophy behind fails to accomplish its purpose, and (ii) a criticism which could succeed in demonstrating to him that his way of rejecting philosophical problems does not enable us to care about the very sorts of goods that he thinks we should care about instead. The most effective way of making out the former criticism would be to show that, his sincere belief to the contrary notwithstanding, his thought remains controlled by the philosophical controversies he wishes to put behind him. The most effective way of making out the latter criticism would be to show that the consequences of his views for the things he thinks we should care about are not only not what he believes and wants them to be, but are in fact roughly the opposite of what he believes and wants them to be.[3]

The aim of this paper is to mount a version of each of these criticisms in tandem with the other. The strategy for doing this will be to juxtapose Rorty's reading of Orwell with the texts of Orwell's he purports to read and with passages from Orwell which comment or otherwise bear on those texts. I hope to show that there is a fairly literal sense in which Rorty is *unable to read* Orwell and that this inability is tied to an inability to free himself from certain philosophical preoccupations. It will also emerge that many of the things that Orwell himself is most concerned to be able to say – and to preserve as sayable for future generations – turn out to be things that Rorty's strategy for dissolving philosophical problems (namely, one of "vocabulary replacement"), if successful, would deprive us of the resources for saying.

Rorty tends to see philosophers as *obsessed* with unprofitable controversies, and prides himself on having liberated himself from those obsessions. But there remains something obsessive about Rorty's own relation to these unprofitable controversies.[4] Consider the following syndrome: someone does not believe certain doctrines, thinks that much time has been wasted trying to refute them, and that we should no longer occupy ourselves with them; yet this person's thought remains controlled by the worry that he might be falling back into the very doctrines he wishes no longer to occupy himself with. I will refer to a syndrome of this sort when it is directed towards doctrines of an epistemological nature as *epistemologism*.[5] Epistemologism is a species of *fixation* – an inability to detach one's mind from certain ideas (however much one may claim to be no longer interested in attending to them). The strategy of this paper will be to treat Rorty's writing on Orwell as a field within which the symptoms of his epistemologism manifest themselves.

The attempt to mount a criticism of Rorty which Rorty himself might find compelling encounters an additional obstacle in Rorty's views on philosophical *method*. Rorty frankly admits to no longer being much interested in either offering or responding to philosophical arguments *per se*. He sometimes seems to claim to find the arguments of a philosopher persuasive only to the extent that they can be shown to be *parasitic upon* or *abbreviations for* a claim to the effect that a certain old way of talking leads to intellectual dead-ends, whereas a proposed new way of talking assists in the avoidance of those dead-ends.[6] The method of philosophical persuasion that Rorty himself officially favors in his recent work is that of *redescription*:

> On the view of philosophy which I am offering, philosophers should not be asked for arguments against, for example, the correspondence theory of truth or the idea of the "intrinsic nature of reality" . . . Interesting philosophy is rarely an examination of the pros and cons of a thesis. Usually it is, implicitly or explicitly, a contest between an entrenched vocabulary which has become a nuisance and a half-formed vocabulary which vaguely promises great things . . . Conforming to my own precepts, I am not going to offer arguments against the vocabulary I want to replace. Instead, I am going to try to make the vocabulary I favor look attractive by showing how it may be used to describe a variety of topics.[7]

The method of this paper, accordingly, will be to offer a redescription of Rorty's doctrines. In particular, starting in the section on Rontian Totalitarianism of the paper, the goal is to furnish a description of how Rorty's doctrines appear when viewed from the perspective of Orwell – an author Rorty professes to admire and whose work he views as innocent of the sort of philosophy he deplores. My aim, in offering such a redescription, will be roughly the opposite of Rorty's own: to try to make "the vocabulary" he favors look unattractive by showing how poorly it describes a variety of topics he himself uses it to describe.[8] The point of the exercise is to suggest that Rorty's own attempt to junk an "entrenched vocabulary" (which has allegedly become a nuisance) in favor of a "half-formed vocabulary" (which vaguely promises great things) deprives us of the very resources we require to address some of "the great things" the pared-down replacement "vocabulary" was supposed to help us address.

II.   The Genre of Realism

Rorty's favorite label for the view which he is most concerned to oppose is *Realism*. It is not at all easy to say what Rorty thinks Realism is. There are two aspects of his employment of the term that are responsible for this: (i) sometimes the term seems to denote a fairly *narrow* epistemological or metaphysical thesis, while, at other times, it seems to denote an extraordinarily *broad* doctrine encompassing a variety of theses in ethics, aesthetics and political philosophy,[9] (ii) in both its narrow and its broad employment, the term appears alternately to denote quite different doctrines – doctrines which are not only distinct but mutually *inconsistent*. One might be led to conclude on these grounds that the term 'Realism' as it figures in Rorty's writings simply has no clear meaning.

I do not think this is true. Although it is by no means readily apparent to me how to define the term as it figures in Rorty's writings, I can readily perceive affinities between the various doctrines that Rorty groups together under this heading. More-over, I take myself to be able to tell which doctrines Rorty himself would and which ones he would not count as examples of Realism; that is, I take myself to have acquired a practical mastery of Rorty's use of the term, as I imagine many of Rorty's other readers also have (though without necessarily being able to formulate a definition which is sufficiently inclusive to cover all of his uses of the term.) For the purposes of this paper, I propose to offer a partial reconstruction of Rorty's employment of the term by construing the set of doctrines which it comprehends as collectively comprising a philosophical *genre*.

Membership in a genre is not achieved by satisfying certain necessary or sufficient conditions for membership. A genre is defined by *features*. But each feature is in principle optional. (There is no *one* thing, for instance, that makes a film a *western* – for any feature you name, I can name a film that is recognizably a western but lacks the feature in question.) And no feature suffices for membership. (A film can have, for instance, cowboys in it and yet not be a western.) Certain features are, admittedly, more basic than others – more central to the structure of the genre than others. But even in the absence of an apparently fundamental feature, membership in the genre can still be achieved through the presence of a compensating feature. Such pairs of compensating features can be mutually incompatible with one another. Most impor-tantly, membership in a genre is not an all or nothing affair: it is a matter of *degree* – the greater the number of generic features an object exhibits, the more fully it exemplifies the genre in question.[10]

I propose, for the purposes of this paper, to define Realism as a genre of philosophical doctrine.[11] All subsequent references to Realism in this paper are to this genre of doctrine.[12] I have specified eight characteristically Realist theses below. No one of them is a necessary feature of the genre.[13] Some of them are mutually incompatible; some are limiting cases of others. My aim in distinguishing these eight theses has not been to capture the full extent of Rorty's use of the term,[14] but to isolate those features of (what Rorty calls) Realism which play – either directly or indirectly – an important role in his discussion of Orwell.

1   *The thesis that the Thing-in-Itself is a condition of the possibility of knowledge.* All our experiences of the world are of appearances, views of it from some particular point of view. The only sorts of truths we are able to formulate are truths about the

world under some description. But we should not mistake the limitations of our knowledge, imposed on us by our finite cognitive capacities, for limitations that are inherent in the nature of reality as such. The idea that our experience is *of* the world (that the appearances are *appearances* and not mere illusions) – that is that there is something which our descriptions are *about* – presupposes the further idea that there is a way which is *the way the world is in itself.* For the world to be a possible object of knowledge there must be such a way that it is, apart from any description of it – a way the world is when "viewed from nowhere", that is from no particular point of view (or, alternatively, from a God's-eye point of view). Moreover, though such knowledge of the world (as it is in itself) is in principle unattainable for us, we are able to *think* what we cannot know: we are able to grasp in thought that there is such a way the world is, apart from the conditions under which we know it. It is only by postulating the existence of such a noumenal reality that we render coherent the supposition that all our apparent knowledge of reality is indeed *knowledge* of a genuinely mind-independent external reality.[15]

2   *The thesis that objectivity is non-perspectival.* Some descriptions of the world are to be preferred to others. Descriptions can be more or less accurate. Descriptions of the world are more accurate – that is, better *mirror* the actual structure of reality – to the extent that they are *purified* of everything in them that is an artifact of our partial parochial perspectives on reality. Though it is not possible for us to describe reality without using concepts which human beings can understand, it is possible for us to use concepts which are *not peculiarly ours* – concepts which every properly conducted inquiry into the ultimate nature of reality, be it conducted by humans or non-humans, is eventually fated to converge upon. In so far as our aim is to achieve a knowledge of things as they really are, a description of reality formulated solely in terms of concepts of this latter sort represents a *metaphysically privileged mode of description.* Such concepts furnish us with the means to achieve a non-perspectival, transparent mode of access to how things really are in themselves. The resulting descriptions are descriptions of objective reality.[16]

3   *The thesis that the fabric of reality is value-neutral.* A description of objective reality must be purged of all concepts that involve a reference to subjective properties. Subjective properties are those which are extrinsic to reality and only intelligible with reference to the effects of reality on sentient beings. The *objective properties* of reality are those which are not subjective but inherent in reality itself. Evaluative concepts – since they are only intelligible with reference to human needs, interests and desires – do not describe objective features of reality. A description of the objective features of reality must confine itself to employing purely descriptive, *value-neutral concepts.*

4   *The thesis that there exists an independent moral order.* True moral statements correspond to an independent moral reality or moral order. The aim of moral enquiry is (a) to arrive at a set of *metaphysically privileged moral concepts* for describing or characterizing this reality or order,[17] and (b) to answer all genuine moral questions, that is, all genuine questions which can be formulated employing such concepts. The existence of an independent moral order guarantees that every such question, no matter how seemingly difficult, has a right answer. For every genuine moral statement, there is a self-subsistent moral fact or truth corresponding

either to it or to its negation. There are *no hard moral cases* – that is, cases which do not admit of unequivocal resolution. There are only apparently hard cases. The apparent hardness of a genuine moral case is due (never to the nature of the case itself, but rather) always to our clouded or otherwise distorted view of moral reality.[18]

5   *The thesis of anti-historicism.* There is such a thing as *the* actual course of history; but it can only come into view in a narrative which furnishes an *objective description* of the unfolding of historical processes. Such a description of historical processes is "objective" in the sense defined in the section above on the thesis that the fabric of reality is value-neutral. The processes which figure in such a description are fully intelligible without the mediation of our own (present) needs, values and interests or of the (past) needs, values and interests of the communities caught up in the processes which are the target of description. The aim of historical understanding, in so far as it aims at objective truth, is to achieve such an unmediated understanding of past events.

6   *The thesis of the commensurability of goods.* All fundamental goods are commensurable. There are, in reality, *no tragic conflicts* – situations in which we can only pursue one fundamental good by compromising our allegiance to another. If the demands of happiness, truth, and justice appear to pull in opposite directions, this can only be because we have failed properly to understand the nature of the Good, the True, or the Just. The central task of philosophy is to formulate a *single unifying vision* which, while fully respecting each distinct kind of good, harmoniously synthesizes the (only apparently incompatible) sorts of demands imposed by each.

7   *The thesis of the criterial nature of moral status.* We form a moral community with all other beings who share *morally relevant properties* with us. (Favorite candidates for morally relevant properties include: an essential humanity, a rational nature, a capacity for self-consciousness, personhood, membership in a biological species, sentience.) Possession of the relevant property or properties is *the criterion* for being an appropriate subject of moral concern. A morally relevant property is an *objective property* (in the sense defined in the paragraph on the thesis that the fabric of reality is value-neutral) and thus *ahistorical* and *transcultural* in nature. The existence of such properties is the source of all moral obligation and entitlement. We owe moral obligations to all and only those beings who possess the relevant properties. Every being who possesses the relevant properties possesses thereby certain *rights*, and each of us has an obligation to see that those rights are upheld to the best of her ability.

8   *The thesis of the possible transparency of language to fact and the relative non-transparency of literature.* *Transparent prose* is the linguistic medium which permits the formulation of undistorted descriptions of objective reality of the sort specified in the section above on the thesis that objectivity is non-perspectival. Literary works – since they deal with actions, persons and events that are fictional and employ imprecise or innovative uses of language – do not offer transparent representations of objective reality. The legitimate aims of literary works are threefold: (i) *decorative* – to entertain, divert, or prettify, (ii) *emotive* – to address

our non-cognitive faculties (iii) *illustrative* – to exemplify an antecedently understood principle, for instance by telling a story that has a moral.[19]

Any doctrine which embraces a version of one or more of the above eight theses
qualifies for the purposes of this paper as a species of Realism. The greater the number
of the above theses a doctrine embraces, the more central a member of the genre – the
more Realist – it is.

Any of the above eight theses could be formulated in a more sympathetic and
nuanced manner. I have intentionally formulated each so as to render it maximally
vulnerable to Rorty's arguments against Realism. I will make no attempt in this paper
to rehearse the arguments that Rorty employs against these theses or to justify the
claim that these theses are indeed vulnerable to his arguments. I shall simply express
my sympathy with Rorty's work in so far as that work is animated by a desire to help
us see that we can reject all eight of the above theses without thereby giving up
anything we should want. I shall therefore not be concerned in this paper to criticize
Rorty on the grounds on which his Realist critics do. The preliminary point of
identifying the eight theses listed above as instances of philosophy gone wrong is to
define a *space of agreement* between Rorty and myself.[20] The eventual point of the
exercise will be to demonstrate how much room that still leaves for disagreement. I
turn now to the more delicate task of indicating our space of disagreement.

III.   Rorty's Metaphysics

The title of this section of the paper is intentionally provocative. Rorty would bristle at
the suggestion that he has a metaphysics. Rorty counts philosophers such as Wittgenstein and Heidegger among his heroes and says that he shares their avowedly anti-
metaphysical aims – aims such as that of "showing the philosopher the way out of the
philosophical fly-bottle" and of "deconstructing the Western metaphysical tradition."
But whenever Rorty enters into a detailed engagement with Realist theses, such as the
eight listed above, he does not tend to do what these two of his heroes represent
themselves as attempting to do. He does not show us why apparently compulsory
philosophical problems (for which the Realist purports to offer solutions) are not
compulsory[21] or how we can get out from under the questions (which the Realist
purports to answer) by coming to see what is wrong with the questions.[22] When Rorty
stands back from his arguments with Realism and pronounces on the nature of his
objectives, he tends to characterize his aims in terms which echo those of philosophers
such as Wittgenstein and Heidegger. He describes himself as wanting to dissolve
philosophical problems and unmask philosophical questions. But such pronouncements
are generally at odds with the actual character of Rorty's detailed engagements with
Realism. In his criticisms of Realism, Rorty invariably formulates his rejection of a
thesis of Realism in terms of a counterposed thesis. He thus invariably ends up
affirming a thesis that has the same logical form as a thesis which the Realist affirms,
but with one difference: a negation operator has been introduced into the content-
clause of the thesis. Rorty does not merely refuse to affirm what the Realist says, but
ends up affirming an alternative answer to the Realist's question. He ends up claiming
that there is something we cannot do or have which the Realist claimed we can do or
have. More significantly, where the Realist purports to offer an explication of some
notion – such as objectivity, knowledge, or representation – Rorty invariably ends up

rejecting not merely the explication of the notion but the notion itself. Despite his protestations that he has no interest in the activity of constructive philosophizing, Rorty often goes on to elaborate the outlines of an alternative theory showing how we can make sense of our existing practices (of assertion, description, justification, criticism, etc.) in the absence of the seemingly indispensable notion. This inevitably involves him in the elaboration of further theses, as metaphysically contentious as any of those he sought to reject. Rorty thus ends up enunciating what certainly appear to be (at least partially) worked-out metaphysical doctrines of his own – doctrines which he opposes to those of the Realists and which (at least appear to) offer alternative answers to the Realist's questions.

There follow eight examples of such theses. I will refer to the conjunction of these eight theses as *Rortianism*. I do not thereby mean to suggest that these eight theses encompass either everything that Rorty himself takes to be central in his work or everything that I myself take to be centrally contentious in Rorty's work. Rortianism, as defined here, is simply the complement of Realism, as defined above. The aim, in thus defining 'Rortianism', is to isolate those of Rorty's own substantial metaphysical commitments which play – either directly or indirectly – an important role in his discussion of Orwell. In characterizing the eight theses listed below, I have tried to remain close to Rorty's own presentation of his views and to furnish some hint at the motivation for each thesis by indicating the sorts of views each is concerned to repudiate.

1'   *The thesis that solidarity should replace objectivity.* To aspire to *objectivity* is to aspire in making claims to make oneself answerable to the world itself.[23] To aspire to *solidarity* is to aspire in making claims to make oneself answerable to nothing further than the verdicts of the members of one's community.[24] The idea that a claim can stand in a normative relation to the world – a relation which would make the claim correct or incorrect (true or false) *in light of how things are with the world* – is to be rejected.[25] Since claims cannot be justified in the light of how things are, the only way for a claim to be justified is by its being justified *to some other person(s)*.[26] Justification is a sociological matter, a matter of seeing whether something is acceptable to my peers.[27] Solidarity (agreement with one's community) should therefore replace objectivity (agreement with how things are) as the end of inquiry. Inquiry should aim not at Truth, but at ever-widening circles of consensus.[28] The traditional distinction between knowledge and opinion should be re-interpreted as the distinction between topics on which it is comparatively easy to achieve agreement and those on which it is comparatively difficult to achieve agreement.[29]

2'   *The thesis of linguistic idealism.* Only descriptions of the world can be true or false, and descriptions must be formulated in sentences. Thus where there are no sentences there is no truth. Sentences, however, are elements of human languages, and human languages are human creations. Truth cannot exist independently of the human activity of employing language to make claims because sentences cannot so exist. Apart from the activity of human beings there is no language, hence no true claims, hence no truths.[30]

3'   *The thesis of instrumentalism concerning linguistic norms.* The aim of employing a vocabulary is to achieve not the accurate representation of how things are but rather the satisfaction of our needs, interests and purposes. Vocabularies should be thought of not as mirrors but as *tools*. The assessment of the adequacy of a vocabulary – like that of a tool – is always relative to a purpose.[31] Not only is there no such thing as a value-neutral description of the world that can be understood without reference to human interests, but the adequacy of any description – however apparently value-free – can only be assessed with reference to such interests. Alternative descriptions should be compared not with reality, but with each other, and evaluated not according to how well they enable us to represent the world, but according to how well they help us *cope*.[32]

4'   *The thesis of the conversational basis of moral belief.* The only sense in which a moral belief can "get things right" is for it to be a belief which those of my peers who are competent in the norms of my community's current practices of claim-making will let me get away with.[33] These communal norms furnish a limited pool of persuasive resources: certain disputes may remain inadjudicable. In the absence of agreement, all we can do is to continue to participate in an ongoing *conversation* – a conversation in which we try to bring our conversational partners over to our point of view. To think that a moral belief can be "right" or "true" in some further sense – to think that it can be answerable to how things are – is to think that there is some non-human authority to which we should appeal in order to resolve moral disputes. To think this is to fail to acknowledge the *contingency* of our historically evolved practices of moral claim-making and the ineliminable *hardness* of the "hard" moral questions we confront when working within such practices. It is to fail fully to *de-divinize the world*: to continue to yearn for a secular surrogate for the concept of the Divine – a non-human entity onto which we can transfer the burdens of hard moral thinking and ongoing moral conversation.

5'   *The thesis of historicism.*[34] Historical processes are not governed by laws. They are fundamentally *contingent*, influenced by human agency and unforeseeable chance events. Historical understanding is always *situated* and necessarily colored by our present values and interests. Historical accounts are stories we tell to provide a coherent narrative about who we are and how, through interacting with each other and the world, we got here. Such stories are inherently *retrospective* – each community in each age will tell the story differently – and they are *constructed*.[35] The only sense in which a historical narrative can "get things right" is by telling a story which proves to be both acceptable and enabling to the members of a community; and the only sense in which one such narrative can be "better" than another is – not by offering a more faithful description of the objective sequence of events, but rather – by *redescribing* the events in a novel and helpful way.[36]

6'   *The thesis that public and private goods are incommensurable.* The relation between the significant products of human reflection concerning *autonomy* and those concerning *justice* is like the relation between two kinds of tools. They are no more in need of synthesis than are paintbrushes and crowbars. Autonomy has to do with our interest in self-creation; justice with our interest in fostering human solidarity. These interests are equally valid, but forever *incommensurable*. There is no useful way to bring them together at the level of theory. They point in opposite directions: the one away from others to private pursuits and the cultivation of individuality; the other outwards to the community at large and the amelioration of its public institutions and shared practices. The vocabulary of self-creation is necessarily *esoteric*: difficult to share and unsuited to argument. The vocabulary of justice is necessarily *exoteric*: susceptible of being widely shared and able to serve as a medium for argumentative exchange. The latter furnishes us with the means to join in a common purpose and thus to *preserve our community*, the former with the means to discover novel purposes and thus to *transform ourselves*.[37]

7' *The thesis of Rortian liberalism.* A moral status is not something one possesses simply in virtue of possessing certain "objective" properties. A moral community is something that is *forged* rather than found, something which is *produced within historically evolved practices*, not something which exists simply as a function of brute ahistorical fact. Moral status is thus conferred and moral concern acquired *through a cultural process* – through participation in certain kinds of communities: communities which have evolved vocabularies which enable one (a) to engage in the activity of moral reflection and deliberation, (b) to express one's solidarity with fellow members of one's community (for instance, by using expressions such as 'we' and 'us' for insiders and 'them' for outsiders), and (c) to view those with whom one expresses solidarity as appropriate subjects of moral concern. One such vocabulary our community has evolved is *the vocabulary of liberalism*. A liberal is someone who thinks *cruelty is the worst thing we can do* and that 'morality' should not be taken to denote anything other than our abilities to notice, identify with, and alleviate pain and humiliation.[38] Someone who is committed to the vocabulary of liberalism thinks that there is *no noncircular theoretical justification* for his belief that cruelty is a horrible thing. He thinks and talks from within the midst of certain historically and culturally local practices. He does not take the validity of those practices to rest on an ahistorical or transcultural foundation. He takes his commitment to liberalism to be nothing more than a function of his commitment to his community.[39]

8' *The thesis of ironism.* Ironism is *opposed to common sense*. To be commonsensical is to take for granted that statements formulated in one's current vocabulary – the vocabulary to one which one has become habituated – suffice to describe and judge the beliefs, actions and lives of those who employ alternative vocabularies. An ironist is someone who thinks there is no single preferred vocabulary. No vocabulary is closer or more transparent to reality than any other. An ironist realizes that anything can be made to look good or bad by being redescribed in an alternative vocabulary. She renounces the attempt to formulate neutral criteria of choice between vocabularies. While provisionally continuing to employ her present vocabulary, she nourishes radical and abiding doubts concerning it, and has no truck with arguments phrased in it which seek either to underwrite or to dissolve these doubts. She cherishes works of literature as precious cognitive resources because they initiate her into *new vocabularies*, furnishing her with novel means – not for seeing reality as it is, but rather – for *playing off descriptions against redescriptions*.[40]

Two comments are in order on the numerically correlated pairs of Realist and Rortian theses – that is (1) and (1'), (2) and (2'), etc. First, none of these pairs stand to one another in a straightforward relation of thesis to antithesis. On the contrary, the pairs have been constructed in such a way that a modicum of reflection should suffice to establish that there is plenty of room to maneuver between the Realist and Rortian members of each pair. (The point of constructing these pairs is to show that Rorty's thought is pervasively controlled by them, with the result that the intervening space of intellectual options remains invisible to him.)[41] Second, the Rortian member of each pair is motivated in part by an implicit proposal for how to go on talking without having to employ vocabulary which plays a crucial role in the formulation of the Realist member of each pair – vocabulary such as "objective truth," "the way the world is," "transparency to fact," etc.[42]

The Rortian theses all participate in a single underlying strategy for bringing fruitless forms of philosophical controversy to an end. The strategy is to adopt a mode of discourse from within which one no longer has any occasion to call upon the vocabulary requisite for the formulation of Realist theses.[43] The underlying injunction concerning how to dissolve philosophical problems might be summed up as follows: "Free yourself from the problems by *jettisoning the vocabulary* in which the problems are couched!" Rorty's confidence in the wisdom of this strategy encourages a blindness to intellectual options that occupy the intervening space between the rejection of Realist theses and the affirmation of their Rortian counterparts. When Rorty encounters occurrences of vocabulary which he would, on philosophically prophylactic grounds, prefer to jettison, he tends to become immediately suspicious. He tends to assume that the motivation behind calling upon the vocabulary must be an attachment to some Realist thesis in the neighborhood; and he tends to proceed to argue as if the only way to steer clear of the Realist thesis in question were to adopt its Rortian counterpart. But Rorty's preferred strategy for dissolving philosophical problems is a wise one only if the sole function within our linguistic community of the vocabulary in which Realist theses are formulated is to enable such theses to be formulated. If there are other discursive possibilities – apart from the formulation of Realist theses – whose availability depends upon the availability of that vocabulary,[44] then a pragmatist has no business enjoining us to jettison that vocabulary unless he can first demonstrate that the loss of those other discursive possibilities is vastly outweighed by the gain of rendering ourselves immune to the temptations of Realism.[45]

IV.   Enter Orwell

Orwell's biographer Bernard Crick claims that Orwell "would have been incapable of writing a contemporary philosophical monograph" and that he was "scarcely capable of understanding one."[46] Crick documents this claim with examples, anecdotes and testimony.[47] In a footnote, Rorty refers to Crick's evidence for this claim.[48] The claim, as we shall see, is important to Rorty. He adduces Orwell's lack of taste for or skill at constructing philosophical arguments[49] as a ground for thinking that standard readings of Orwell must be wrong. I think that Rorty is right that Orwell's writings are innocent of the philosophical obsessions which Rorty deplores. This renders Orwell's writings potentially useful in two ways. They can furnish: (i) a measure of Rorty's epistemologism, and (ii) a ground for questioning the wisdom of Rorty's strategy of dissolving philosophical problems. They can furnish (i) if it can be shown that Rorty's reading of Orwell remains controlled by the very obsessions which he takes to be irrelevant to an understanding of Orwell. It is the task of the sections on Rorty on Orwell's Admirers and An Outline of Rorty's reading of *Nineteen Eighty-Four* of this paper to show this. They can furnish (ii) if it can be shown that they make generous use of the vocabulary in which Realist theses are formulated, but exclusively in the service of discursive ends which have nothing to do with the formulation of such theses. It is the task of the sections on Orwell on Totalarianism, Rortian Totalitarianism, and Politics and Literature (VII, VIII, and IX) of this paper to show this.

Below is a list of eight examples of the sorts of things which we will encounter Orwell saying in the sections VII, VIII, and IX of this paper. Versions of all eight of these remarks recur throughout Orwell's corpus.[50] They are examples of (what I take to be) *ordinary* uses of language[51] – but each of them contains occurrences of the sort of vocabulary which Rorty views with great suspicion (vocabulary such as "truth," "facts," "independent," "wrongness," "objectivity," "human") and which he urges us to learn to dispense with.[52]

1″ The feeling that the very concept of objective truth is fading out of the world is – and should be – frightening.

2″ Facts exist independently of us and are more or less discoverable.

3″ One should constantly struggle to efface the distortions in one's view of the facts that are due to one's personality and to the varieties of bias and self-deception from which every observer necessarily suffers.

4″ Some moral cases are not hard cases. It is possible to see the unspeakable wrongness of an act.

5″ There are objective historical truths. Historical facts are independent of what we say or believe happened in the past.

6″ There is an important connection between politics and literature. Literature provides a means for fighting a kind of corruption of language which facilitates the task of those who seek to hide the truth. The enemies of intellectual liberty thus seek to keep the issue of truth-versus-untruth as far in the background as possible in their discussions of both politics and literature.

7″ The protagonist of *Nineteen Eighty-Four* is the last human being in Europe – the sole remaining guardian of the human spirit. A liberal is someone who thinks that the human spirit will only survive as long as we think of truth as something to be discovered, and not as something we make up as we go along. The worst thing we can do is – not cruelty, but – to undermine someone's capacity to think of truth in these terms.

8″ Good prose is like a window pane. It places the truth in plain and open view.

Since I agree with Rorty that Orwell's work is innocent of any militantly metaphysical preoccupations, I think (1″)–(8″), as they occur in Orwell's writing, are *not* happily characterized as *metaphysical theses*.[53] But, regardless of how one chooses to characterize (1″)–(8″), the fact remains that they are examples of things that Orwell has it at heart to say.

One aim of this paper is to show – by looking first (in the sections on Rorty and Orwell's Admirers and An Outline of Rorty's Reading of *Nineteen Eighty-Four* in this paper) at what Rorty says about Orwell and then (in sections VII–IX of this paper) at what Orwell himself says – that (1″)–(8″) are *inaudible* to Rorty. They are literally inaudible to him in the sense that he simply never hears Orwell saying most of these things. With respect to most of these remarks, as far as I can ascertain, Rorty manages to read Orwell without ever realizing that such remarks recur throughout his corpus. With respect to the two remarks that Rorty does realize are in Orwell – namely (3″) and (8″) – he views them as unfortunate and dangerously misleading rhetorical flourishes. But (1″)–(8″) are also inaudible to Rorty in a more irremediable sense. Even if Rorty were brought to see that Orwell really does want to say these things, I think it would be difficult for Rorty to see how these remarks could be innocent of Realist metaphysics: (1″) would appear to him to presuppose a commitment to (1), (2″) a commitment to (2), etc. Moreover, (1″) certainly appears to be something that a proponent of (1′) should not want to say, and similarly for (2″) and (2′), etc. Sections VII and IX of this paper will seek to show that when our intellectual options are confined to a forced choice between Realist and Rortian theses – between members of the pairs (1) and (1′), (2) and (2′), etc. – we are unable to recover the thoughts Orwell sought to express in (1″)–(8″).

We are now in a position to offer the following more precise characterization of Rorty's epistemologism: when Rorty comes across remarks such as (1″)–(8″), he assumes that they must either be attempts to assert (1)–(8) or bits of mere rhetoric; he is thus unable to read an author, such as Orwell, who is concerned neither to attack nor to defend (1)–(8), but whose writings abound with remarks such as (1″)–(8″) and who attaches great importance to the thoughts which such remarks express.

V.   Rorty on Orwell's Admirers

The aim of this section of the paper is twofold: first, to furnish some examples of Rorty's concluding that a commentator on Orwell must be concerned to recommend some form of Realism on the ground that the commentator employs certain vocabulary; second, to provide an overview of the reading of Orwell which Rorty assumes such commentators must endorse and which serves as the foil for his own reading of Orwell.

Indeed, it would be difficult to outline Rorty's own reading of *Nineteen Eighty-Four* without first discussing the reading of the novel he opposes. Rorty's discussion of Orwell is structured around the assumption that there are two natural ways to read Orwell: either as a Realist or as a Rortian. Though Rorty himself never explicitly represents the issue of how to read Orwell in such bald terms, such a view of the issue implicitly structures his entire discussion. Thus Rorty's procedure for justifying his own reading turns in no small part on entering objections to a Realist construal of Orwell's texts. But this is a reasonable procedure only if these two readings exhaust the field of promising possible readings of Orwell. That Rorty should think that they do is itself a striking symptom of his epistemologism.

Rorty takes the following claim to be an uncontroversial point of common ground between himself and those readers of Orwell with whom he disagrees: the major aim – or at least one of the major aims – of *Nineteen Eighty-Four* is to offer an imaginative redescription of Soviet Russia.[54] The disagreement, as Rorty represents it, turns on how to answer the following two questions: (i) how is such a redescription accomplished and (ii) what is the point of furnishing such a redescription? As regards (i), this is how Rorty describes what the readers of Orwell with whom he disagrees think:

[Orwell] accomplished the redescription by reminding us of some plain truths – moral truths whose obviousness is on a par with "two plus two is four."[55]

As an example of a reader of Orwell who says things like this, Rorty quotes the following extract from an essay by Lionel Trilling:

Orwell's native gifts are perhaps not of the transcendent kind; they have their roots in a quality of mind that is as frequent as it is modest. This quality may be described as a sort of moral centrality, a directness of relation to moral – and political fact.[56]

This suggests that Orwell is especially good at doing something which, for the moment, we may provisionally gloss as "getting at the truth." This, in turn, suggests the following answer to (i): it is Orwell's "gift" for "getting at the truth" which allows him to furnish a compelling redescription. Rorty takes this to be the answer to (i) that readers such as Trilling endorse.[57] Rorty, moreover, thinks it a terrible answer because he takes it to rest on a *Realist conception* of what it is that makes descriptions (or redescriptions) compelling.[58] How is Rorty able to tell that readers of Orwell such as Trilling are captivated by Realism? By the vocabulary they employ. The two passages above contain words like "plain truths," "moral truths" (worse still: "moral truths" which are *obvious*), "a directness of relation to fact" (and worst of all: "a directness of relation to *moral* fact") – words which trigger Rorty's philosophical alarms.

As regards (ii), here is how Rorty summarizes what he thinks Trilling et al take the point of Orwell's novel to be:

Orwell teaches us to set our faces against all those sneaky intellectuals who try to tell us that truth is not "out there," that what counts as a possible truth is a function of the vocabulary you use, and what counts as a truth is a function of the rest of your beliefs. Orwell has, in short, been read as a realist philosopher, a defender of common sense against its cultured, ironist despisers.[59]

Rorty concedes that there are some passages which, when taken out of context, appear to support this reading. He mentions two examples of such passages. The first is a set of remarks from Orwell's essay "Why I Write." Rorty concedes that in this particular set of remarks "Trilling's way of speaking is echoed by Orwell himself."[60] The remarks that Rorty particularly has in mind in this connection are Orwell's remark that "good prose is like a window pane" and the remark that the effort to write prose of this sort requires that one "strive constantly to efface one's own personality."[61] These remarks, according to Rorty, are "often read together" by Orwell's Realist admirers with the following passage from *Nineteen Eighty-Four*:

The Party told you to reject the evidence of your eyes and ears. It was their final, most essential, command. [Winston's] heart sank as he thought of the enormous power arrayed against him, the ease with which any Party intellectual would overthrow him in debate . . . And yet he was in the right! . . . The obvious, the silly, and the true has got to be defended. Truisms are true, hold on to that! The solid world exists, its laws do not change. Stones are hard, water is wet, objects unsupported fall towards the earth's centre. With the feeling that he was speaking to O'Brien, and also that he was setting forth an important axiom, [Winston] wrote: "Freedom is the freedom to say that two plus two make four. If that is granted, all else follows."[62]

Rorty takes this passage to be the main support of the Realist reading of *Nineteen Eighty-Four*. Thus, when giving his own reading of the novel, Rorty takes some trouble to sketch his own (purportedly) non-metaphysical alternative interpretation of the passage. Rorty concurs that this is a pivotal passage,[63] but he takes its concern to be with *freedom* rather than *truth*. Since this passage occupies a central place in the quarrel Rorty takes himself to have with other readers of Orwell, and since we will often have occasion to recur to it, I will henceforth refer to it as "the focal passage."

Rorty takes the focal passage to supply admirers of Orwell with a pretext for attributing certain Realist theses to Orwell.[64] But he also thinks that these admirers attribute Realist theses to Orwell of a sort which the focal passage taken by itself would hardly seem to invite. Rorty adduces the following passage from Samuel Hynes as evidence of the popularity of a broader Realist construal of *Nineteen Eighty-Four*:

> Winston Smith's beliefs are as simple as two plus two equals four: the past is fixed, love is private, and the truth is beyond change. All have this in common: they set limits to men's power; they testify to the fact that some things cannot be changed. The point is beyond politics – it is a point of essential humanity.[65]

When Rorty hears someone talking about "a point of essential humanity," he assumes that what must be at issue is a Realist thesis to the effect that what confers moral worth upon each of us is our partaking of an indestructible human essence.[66] Central to the reading of the novel that Rorty wishes to ward off is the claim that there is something deep down within each of us – our essential humanity – which we all share and the presence of which guarantees that the actual future of humanity cannot ever resemble the future depicted in *Nineteen Eighty-Four*. On Rorty's reading of the novel, one of its central concerns is to urge that whether our future rulers turn out to be like O'Brien does not depend – "as metaphysicians generally suggest" – on "deep facts about human nature."[67] In taking Orwell to be urging such an anti-metaphysical view, Rorty takes himself to be at odds with the proponents of accepted interpretations of the novel. For the proponents of accepted interpretations all declare Orwell to be concerned with something they are happy to call the "preservation of humanity." Rorty takes such talk to be of a piece with the following sort of reading of the novel:

> On this reading, the crucial opposition in Orwell's thought is the standard metaphysical one between contrived appearance and naked reality. The latter is obscured by bad, untransparent prose and by bad, unnecessarily sophisticated theory. Once the dirt is rubbed off the windowpane, the truth about any moral or political situation will be clear. Only those who have allowed their own personality . . . to cloud their vision will fail to grasp the plain moral facts . . . Only such people will try to evade plain epistemological and metaphysical facts through sneaky philosophical maneuvers . . . Among such facts are that truth is "independent" of human minds and languages, and that gravitation is not "relative" to any human mode of thought.[68]

Some of what Rorty says here leaves no doubt that a proponent of this reading would be committed to Realist theses.[69] It is also true that much of what Rorty says here echoes remarks that commentators such as Trilling and Hynes actually make.[70] Rorty takes the presence of such remarks in their writings to be evidence of their desire to offer a Realist reading of Orwell;[71] and, as a matter of charity to Orwell, he thinks one ought to consider whether a "non-metaphysical" reading of *Nineteen Eighty-Four* might not be available instead.[72]

I don't think Rorty is right about Trilling and Hynes.[73] But this is not to deny that someone could advance a Realist reading of *Nineteen Eighty-Four*. The prose of such a reader of Orwell would not sound like prose which is animated by the concerns of a Trilling or a Hynes. It would sound like prose which is animated by the concerns of someone who shares Rorty's obsessions. Peter Van Inwagen is such a reader of Orwell. His reading of the focal passage is the mirror-image of the one Rorty advances:

> One important component of the Common Western Metaphysic is the thesis that there is such a thing as objective truth . . . Philosophers who deny the existence of objective truth are today usually called "anti-realists" – in opposition, of course, to "realists," who affirm the existence of objective truth . . . [T]he greatest of all attacks on anti-realism [is] George Orwell's novel *1984*. Anyone who is interested in Realism and anti-Realism should be steeped in the message of this book. The reader is particularly directed to the debate between the Realist Winston Smith and the anti-Realist O'Brien that is the climax of the novel. In the end, there is only one question that can be addressed to the anti-Realist: How does your position differ from O'Brien's?[74]

Rorty and Van Inwagen both assume that an affirmation of the sentiments which Winston expresses in the focal passage reflects his commitment to Realism and that the author of the novel's stance towards Realism can be gauged by determining whether he wishes to distance himself or whether he wishes to identify himself with the sentiments of his protagonist.[75] Neither Van Inwagen nor Rorty is able to envision the possibility that what is at stake in Winston's remarks – remarks such as "The obvious, the silly, and the true have got to be defended" or "The solid world exists, its laws do not change" – is not the truth or falsity of a metaphysical thesis.[76] Both Van Inwagen and Rorty seek to enlist Orwell on their side of a metaphysical dispute between a Realist and an anti-Realist.[77] Due to their shared obsession with Realism, neither allows for a reading of the novel which takes the author to identify with the sentiments of his protagonist but doesn't take such an identification to commit the author to Realism.

VI.   An Outline of Rorty's Reading of *Nineteen Eighty-Four*

The aim of this section of the paper is threefold: first, to sketch an overview of Rorty's own reading of *Nineteen Eighty-Four*, second, to provide some indication of the manner in which Rorty motivates that reading, and third, to lay some groundwork for the charge that Rorty's epistemologism renders him unable to read Orwell's novel.

As soon as we cease to read Orwell's texts through Realist spectacles, Rorty suggests, we will see that Orwell's concern lies with cruelty rather than truth. The underlying charge is that only someone committed to Realism could possibly be led to think that it was Orwell's view that the possibility of sustaining the ideals of liberalism depends on preserving a respect for "truth" or "humanity"; only someone who approached Orwell's texts with Realist spectacles would be led to read the texts as Trilling and Hynes do. One reason Rorty adduces for preferring his own "non-metaphysical" reading of Orwell has already been touched on in section IV: Orwell doesn't seem to be a writer who has much taste for philosophical argument. This allows Rorty to challenge Realist readers of Orwell with the question: is it not perverse to read this author as centrally concerned with mounting a defense of a metaphysical doctrine? Given the reading of Orwell that Rorty himself offers, however, this challenge to Realist readers of Orwell threatens to boomerang back on him: is it not equally perverse to read this author as centrally concerned with defending theses whose motivation depends on the desire to distance oneself as far as possible from Realism? We shall see that it is Rorty who reads every line of Orwell (and every line of Orwell commentary) through philosophical spectacles, and that it is Rorty – not Trilling or Hynes – who attempts to enlist Orwell on one side of an argument between a Realist and an opponent of Realism.

Rorty offers a very particular gloss on where Orwell's concerns as an author do lie: Orwell's main concern is to "sensitize an audience to cases of cruelty and humiliation which they had not noticed." Orwell is to be read, above all, as a good "liberal ironist": someone whose aim is to "give us an alternative context, an alternative perspective, from which we liberals . . . could describe the political history of our century."[78] Rorty's subsequent characterization of what is involved in "sensitizing an audience" to cases of cruelty and humiliation clearly bears the marks of a Rortian recoil from Realism. Rorty explains:

> [T]he kind of thing Orwell . . . did – sensitizing an audience to cases of cruelty and humiliation which they had not noticed – is not usefully thought of as a matter of stripping away appearance and revealing reality. It is better thought of as a redescription of what may happen or has been happening – to be compared, not with reality, but with alternative descriptions of the same events.[79]

We are offered here a *contrast* between two ways of understanding what is involved in evaluating a description of an event: the description is to be compared with reality or the description is to be compared with alternative descriptions. Throughout his essay on Orwell, Rorty writes as if these constituted mutually opposed ways of understanding what it is to evaluate the adequacy of a description of an event,[80] and as if we must take Orwell to be always doing only the one and never the other:

> Deciding between the descriptions [which Orwell and others offer of Communism] . . . is not a matter of confronting or refusing to confront hard, unpleasant facts. Nor is it a matter of being blinded, or not being blinded, by ideology. It is a matter of playing off scenarios against contrasting scenarios, projects against alternative projects, descriptions against redescriptions.[81]

Enabling his readers "to confront hard, unpleasant facts," enabling them to recognize their own individual strategies for "refusing to confront the facts," depicting what it is to be "blinded by an ideology" and what it is not to be so blinded – all such characterizations of Orwell's activity as an author, Rorty claims, are misplaced since they involve the attribution to Orwell of a commitment to Realism. Orwell, according to Rorty, has no use for the idea of truth – for the idea that some descriptions are superior to others in virtue of the relation in which they stand to the subject matter which they describe. According to Rorty's Orwell, some descriptions just happen to be more *useful* than others. This leaves Rorty in the somewhat awkward position of having to conclude that Orwell's own characterizations of the sort of prose he aspires to write (prose that has the transparency of a window pane) must be mischaracterizations of his own writing:

> Redescriptions which change our minds on political situations are not much like window-panes. On the contrary, they are the sort of thing which only writers with very special talents, writing at just the right moment in just the right way, are able to bring off.[82]

As candidate explanations for Orwell's success as an author, we are asked to choose between (i) Orwell's having succeeded in revealing "certain facts" or "moral truths" and (ii) Orwell's "special talents" as a writer. As Rorty sees the matter, in order to save Orwell from Realism we must opt for (ii) as opposed to (i).[83] This, of course, leaves Rorty with the problem of why Orwell says things that sound like (i). Rorty suggests that whenever Orwell says such things he is best read as not really meaning them:

> In his better moments, Orwell himself dropped the rhetoric of transparency to plain fact, and recognized that he was doing the same *kind* of thing as his opponents, the apologists for Stalin, were doing.[84]

This is, it seems to me, an extraordinary sentence. There are three claims here about Orwell which, for the moment, I will simply note in ascending order of extraordinariness. First, talk of "transparency to plain fact" figures in Orwell's writing as mere *rhetoric*. Second, in his better moments, Orwell is happy to *drop* this rhetoric. Third, Orwell understood himself to be doing the same *kind* of thing as his opponents, the apologists for Stalin, were doing – offering persuasive redescriptions of recent events. (We will return to these claims in section VII.)

Over and above offering a persuasive redescription of Soviet Russia, according to Rorty, Orwell also had a second aim in *Nineteen Eighty-Four*: to invent O'Brien.[85] This latter aim occupies the last third of the novel:

> Orwell did not invent O'Brien to serve as a dialectical foil, as a modern counterpart to Thrasymachus . . . Orwell is not setting up a philosophical position but trying to make a concrete political possibility plausible . . . He does not view O'Brien as crazy, misguided, seduced by a mistaken theory, or blind to the moral facts. He simply views him as *dangerous* and as *possible*.[86]

Rorty identifies a potentially metaphysically innocuous characterization of O'Brien "as misguided, seduced by a mistaken theory, and blind to the moral facts" with a tendentious characterization of O'Brien as "a modern counterpart to Thrasymachus," a dialectical foil for Orwell's quasi-Platonic philosophical agenda.[87] Having made this identification, Rorty opposes to this his own claim that Orwell simply views O'Brien as *dangerous* and as *possible*. But in the absence of an identification of the innocuous and tendentious characterizations, why should one think that these two views of O'Brien cannot easily be made to harmonize? Why can't Orwell view O'Brien as misguided, seduced by a mistaken theory, blind to the moral facts *and* dangerous and possible?

Rorty insists that what is supposed to be really *scary* about the prospect with which the novel presents us is that it forces on us the thought that "as a matter of sheer contingent fact" the future could, at least in principle, resemble the future depicted in the novel.[88] The thought is, no doubt, scary. In insisting upon this, what Rorty is most concerned to deny is an alternative view of what might be scary about the possible future that the novel depicts: that what is scary is the demise of "the possibility of truth." Rorty knows that Orwell's admirers somehow manage to be frightened by the idea of living in a society in which our leaders have the power to deprive us of our hold on the concept of objective truth. But only a Realist, Rorty thinks, could find *that* prospect frightening. What such readers of Orwell fear losing Rorty regards as well lost. Whenever he hears someone using words such as "objective truth" or "the world" or "reality" as terms for something with which we might lose touch and which we should respect, Rorty hears truth or the world or reality being anthropomorphized – being turned into something personlike. Rorty is aware that people tend to find his own deflationary accounts of truth and empirical knowledge unsatisfying; and he senses, quite correctly, that there is something about his attitude to truth and reality which strikes some of these people as insufficiently respectful. But he can only see one reason why someone should think this: because she still yearns for a privileged mediator (the scientist, or the philosopher, or the poet, or *somebody*) who can discharge the priestly function of putting us in touch with a realm which transcends the human. Loss of contact with truth or the world or reality could only be frightening to such a person – someone who has failed to realize that the idea of answerability to the world is a secular surrogate for the idea of answerability to an infallible Deity. The only way Rorty can see of ever giving content to such talk of "answerability to something non-human" is through an appeal to Realist theses (such as the thesis that the world has a preferred description of itself). Hence he concludes: once we abandon such theses, there is no longer any reason to think it would be *hubris* on our part to abandon the traditional language of "respect for fact" and "objectivity."[89] He identifies a continued attachment to such ways of speaking as a sure sign that the speaker has failed to take the final and crucial step in the post-Enlightenment project of attaining to full intellectual maturity. The speaker still longs for something outside our contingent historically situated practices. He longs for something transhuman which would underwrite practices of which he approves and would condemn practices – such as the practices of the community depicted in Orwell's novel – of which he disapproves. Rorty cannot see how such a person could, in speaking this way, possibly be speaking for Orwell. Rorty, rightly, takes Orwell to be of the view that the practices of our community are utterly contingent: there is a small but not insignificant possibility that they might be replaced by practices utterly reprehensible to us in the near future. Rorty sees a connection between the repudiation of the (Realist) longing for something transhuman which would underwrite our practices and Orwell's particular way of illustrating the contingency of those practices. By illustrating the radical contingency (that is the extreme fragility and plasticity) of our present practices of claim-making in the particular way that he does – namely, by making palpable how genuine the possibility is that our society might develop into a future society which rejects so many of our present claims concerning "the obvious, the silly, and the true" – Orwell's novel reveals that there is nothing outside our current practices of claim-making to which those practices are answerable and which could constrain the direction of their future evolution.[90] Rorty is thus able to conclude that there is a natural fit between the manner in which Orwell himself illustrates the contingency of our practices and Rorty's own interpretative claim that Orwell's admirers distort the concerns of Orwell's novel when, in characterizing its concerns, they deploy the traditional language of "respect for fact," "objectivity," "being in touch with reality," etc.

Orwell's view of history, as presented by Rorty, sometimes seems to involve not only a thesis about the contingency of our practices but an additional thesis about the dependence of large-scale historical outcomes on small-scale events not subject to the influence of human agency. It sometimes sounds as if Orwell's point, according to Rorty, is that only an attachment to a bad metaphysical view would lead us to think that we, readers of the novel, bear a *responsibility* for whether our future will turn out to resemble the one depicted in the novel. Gripped by the worry that someone infatuated with Realism might overlook Orwell's emphasis on the contingency of our practices, Rorty overlooks the possibility of a reading of Orwell that turns on the (not necessarily Realist) claim that it is only by cherishing and nurturing certain of our present values and ideals that we can forestall the triumph of totalitarianism. Rorty's reading invites a gratuitously quietest construal of Orwell's view of the possible influence of human agency on the course of history:

> History may create and empower people like O'Brien as a result of the same kind of accidents that have prevented those people from existing until recently . . . What Orwell helps us see is that it may have *just happened* that Europe began to prize benevolent sentiments and the idea of a common humanity, and it may *just happen* that the world will wind up being ruled by people who lack any such sentiments and any such moralities. On my reading, Orwell's denial that there is such a thing as the autonomous individual is part of a larger denial that there is something outside of time or more basic than chance which can be counted on to block, or eventually reverse, such accidental sequences.[91]

This makes it sound as if the *overriding* determinants of history are mere matters of chance – outcomes that depend upon *accidents* beyond human control. In his eagerness to oppose a very dubious thesis ("the continuation of civilization as we know it is metaphysically guaranteed") with an alternative thesis ("nothing is guaranteed: accidents just happen"), Rorty tends to slide from an unobjectionable construal of the exegetical claim that Orwell believes in the contingency of history to what appears to be a far less plausible construal of that claim. He slides – or at least seems to slide – from the claim that Orwell believes that nothing guarantees that things will develop one way rather than another to the claim that Orwell believes that the future outcome of history is essentially *out of our hands*. Rorty never explicitly endorses this fatalistic construal of Orwell's view of history; but, as we shall see, Rorty's slanting of the rhetoric of contingency in the direction of such a construal leaves him with a reading of Orwell's novel which manages completely to overlook Orwell's own ethical and political motivations in writing the novel.[92]

Rorty cites the following remarks from a 1944 newspaper article by Orwell as further evidence of the soundness of his reading of the novel:

> The fallacy is to believe that under a dictatorial government you can be free *inside* . . . The greatest mistake is to imagine that the human being is an autonomous individual. The secret freedom which you can supposedly enjoy under a despotic government is nonsense, because your thoughts are never entirely your own. Philosophers, writers, artists, even scientists, not only need encouragement and an audience, they need constant stimulation from other people . . . Take away freedom of speech, and the creative faculties dry up.[93]

Rorty seizes on this remark because of its emphasis on the importance of *conversation*.[94] He takes the passage to express a repudiation of the notions of inner freedom and the autonomous individual,[95] with the aim of making the same sort of point against the Realist that a Rortian critic seeks to make: truths are not discovered, they are forged; and they are forged in communities through a process of conversation. Apart from joint participation in such an ongoing conversation, nothing binds us together: the mere fact of being human does not assure us of a common bond with others.[96] Rorty goes on to suggest that the 1944 passage should be read in conjunction with the focal passage, and that these two passages taken together can be seen as pointing the way to the reading of Orwell which Rorty himself favors. On the basis of these two passages, Rorty concludes that Orwell's views swing free of the suspect ideas which Orwell's admirers, such as Trilling and Hynes, try to foist on him – such as the idea that truth is independent of what we say and think, the idea that the possibility of freedom and morality are tied to such an understanding of truth, and the idea that simply by being human we have some common bond.[97] The real point of the novel, according to Rorty, lies not in a preoccupation with such ideas but rather in a defense of Rortian liberalism – specifically, in a defense of the ideas that cruelty is the worst thing we do and that what matters is freedom rather than truth.

Cruelty certainly does figure prominently in one of the climactic scenes of *Nineteen Eighty-Four*. Through the infliction of much pain and humiliation, O'Brien eventually succeeds in getting Winston Smith to believe that he is speaking the truth when he says "2+2=5". Rorty's discussion of the pivotal scene is structured around an opposition of two ways of understanding what is horrifying about this scene: either the horror derives from O'Brien's success in destroying Winston's hold on the concept of objective truth or the horror derives from the spectacle of O'Brien's practicing his talent for "tearing human minds to pieces and putting them together again in new shapes of [his] own choosing."[98] In the absence of further elaboration, this opposition is bound to seem forced and to beg the question against the proponent of a Realist reading of Orwell[99]: what if (something which can be described as) "undermining someone's hold on the concept of objective truth" is the best way there is of tearing a human mind to pieces? Rorty does elaborate further. But, in developing his reading of the scene, Rorty introduces a new wrinkle into his conception of liberalism which might at first seem only to exacerbate this problem:

> [T]he worst thing you can do to somebody is not to make her scream in agony but to use that agony in such a way that even when the agony is over, she cannot reconstitute herself. The idea is to get her to do or say things – and, if possible, believe and desire things, think thoughts – which later she will be unable to cope with having done or thought.[100]

The worst thing you can do to somebody is to make her scream in agony in such a way that it has the effect of leaving her unable to reconstitute herself. Beneath the surface one glimpses – both here and throughout Rorty's subsequent discussion – the thought that what is really the worst thing you can do to somebody is (not cruelty *per se*, but rather) to bring it about (by whatever means) that someone is unable to reconstitute herself (cruelty simply being one extremely effective *means* of achieving this end). This thought is unquestionably central to Orwell's novel; but taken by itself it hardly speaks in favor of a Rortian reading of the novel. The question remains: what is the most effective means of rendering someone unable to reconstitute herself? The first sentence of the focal passage appears to suggest a direction in which to look for an answer: "The Party told you to reject the evidence of your eyes and ears. It was their final, most essential, command." Winston's subsequent thought appears to offer a suggestion about how to defend oneself against the Party's strategy for leaving one unable to reconstitute oneself: "Truisms are true, hold on to that!"

Rorty himself sees the possibility of such a construal of the focal passage. But he can't see a way to separate such a construal from a Realist reading of the novel. This places Rorty in the position of having to argue that the falsity of the propositions of whose truth O'Brien seeks to convince Winston is irrelevant to an understanding of O'Brien's project (of seeking to tear Winston's mind apart and put it together again in a new shape). Rorty insists that on a proper understanding of the pivotal torture scene, it does not matter to the scene that "two plus two is four" happens to be true. All that matters for the scene, according to Rorty, is that Winston believes what he says (when he says "two plus two is four"). The horror of the scene lies entirely in the fact that he is not permitted to say what he believes without getting hurt. What Orwell cares about is your ability to talk to other people about what seems to you to be true; it doesn't matter in the least for Orwell's purposes whether what is believed is in fact true:

> [I]t does not matter whether "two plus two is four" is true, much less whether this is "subjective" or "corresponds to external reality." All that matters is that if you do believe it, you can say it without getting hurt. In other words, what matters is your ability to talk to other people about what seems to you to be true, not what is in fact true. If we take care of freedom, truth can take care of itself. If we are ironic enough about our final vocabularies, and curious enough about everyone else's, we do not have to worry about whether we are in direct contact with moral reality or whether we are blinded by ideology, or whether we are being weakly "relativistic."[101]

Rorty here confronts "Orwell's admirers" with two options for how to think about what matters in this scene: either (i) what matters is that "2+2=4" is *true* (that is, that what we say is answerable to something beyond what our community holds to be true), or (ii) what matters is *freedom* (that is, the freedom to say 2+2=4 if that is what you believe, or to say 2+2=5, if that is what you believe). Rorty represents the options for reading Orwell as requiring a choice between (i) and (ii) and concludes that Orwell's view is that what matters is freedom and not the answerability of what we say to something outside of what we say. What, Rorty in effect asks, do we lose if we conclude that what destroys Winston is not loss of the concept of objective truth, but rather the loss of his freedom? We lose nothing, Rorty suggests, and we save Orwell from the charge of being needlessly preoccupied with metaphysical issues such as "truth." Winston's real loss – his loss of freedom – is to be traced not to his "losing touch with external reality" but to his loss of overall coherence. I lose my freedom to say and think what I believe, according to Rorty's Orwell, not when I fail to be answerable to something outside of a human community, but when the failure of my beliefs to cohere with each other results in the loss of my ability to justify myself to myself:

> The *only* point in making Winston believe that two and two equals five is to break him. Getting somebody to deny a belief for no reason is a first step toward making her incapable of having a self because she becomes incapable of weaving a coherent web of belief and desire. It makes her irrational, in a quite precise sense: She is unable to give a reason for her belief that fits together with her other beliefs. She becomes irrational not in the sense that she has lost contact with reality but in the sense that she can no longer rationalize – no longer justify herself to herself.[102]

Rorty is undoubtedly right that it is Orwell's view that a person becomes incapable of sustaining a self if she becomes systematically unable to give reasons for her beliefs that fit together with her other beliefs. Rorty, however, identifies "constituting oneself as a coherent self" with success in "rationalizing" one's beliefs. Now what does it mean to "rationalize" one's beliefs? Is the criterion of my having successfully rationalized my beliefs the attainment of a web of belief in which all my beliefs in fact stand in rational relations to one another or is it merely that I and my peers take my beliefs to stand in such relations to one another? Much that Rorty says elsewhere suggests that he would reject this as a spurious question. His rejection of such a distinction (between my beliefs' universally seeming and actually being justified) plays a crucial role in his reading of the novel. According to Rorty, at the beginning of their conversation, O'Brien and Winston have equally coherent but distinct sets of beliefs; and, by the end of their conversation, only one of them – namely, O'Brien – continues to have a coherent set of beliefs. Now it is certainly right that O'Brien does not *experience* any lack of coherence in his web of beliefs. He is in this sense able to justify himself to himself. Does that mean his beliefs are justified? Since Rorty assumes that only someone mired in Realism could be of the view that O'Brien's beliefs remain open to some further criticism, he concludes that Orwell neither wants nor should want to be able to rebut O'Brien's claim to be able to justify himself to himself.

Rorty's argument that the *truth* of "2+2=4" drops out as irrelevant turns on a point that is sound in itself but hardly sufficient to establish his reading of the pivotal scene: namely, that O'Brien could have succeeded in "breaking" Winston without getting him to believe something false. If it were true that O'Brien's only purpose in his treatment of Winston was to achieve a certain "effect," and if it were further true that the desired effect was simply to "break" Winston (by any means possible), then Rorty would be right to conclude:

> If there were a *truth*, belief in which would break Winston, making him believe that *truth* would be just as good for O'Brien's purposes . . . The effect would be the same, and the effect is all that matters to O'Brien. Truth and falsity drop out.[103]

The question is whether O'Brien's concern is merely with "breaking" people (in which case truth and falsity can drop out as irrelevant), or whether it is with breaking them in a very particular way, namely in such a way that their minds can subsequently be enslaved. If the aim is to break Winston in such a way that he is able to believe only what the Party wants him to believe, then breaking his hold on the distinction between truth and falsity might not be irrelevant. What does it take to enslave a mind? (One might have thought that the novel as a whole was concerned to explore this question.) It is at this point that Rorty's reading takes a quite surprising turn – one which renders this question utterly otiose. According to Rorty, the ultimate end O'Brien seeks to effect through his torture of Winston is merely to break him: he has no interest in bringing Winston's own ideas into line with those of the Party. This interpretative claim has (what Rorty might regard as) the virtue of making it the case that truth and falsity can drop out as utterly irrelevant to an understanding of the pivotal scene, but only at the apparent cost of rendering much of the action of the latter third of the novel utterly mysterious. If the point is just to "break" Winston, then why does O'Brien spend so much of the final portion of the novel doing things like arguing with Winston whether various historical events happened in the manner in which Winston remembers them to have happened or in the manner in which the Party (currently) decrees that they happened? Why does he spend so much time trying to deprive Winston of his conviction that he once saw a photograph of Rutherford which falsified the Party's official account of Rutherford's demise? Why does O'Brien invest so much energy trying to destroy Winston's ability to arrive at a view of the truth which is independent of the Party's version of the truth? O'Brien seems to take an extraordinarily circuitous route towards his end, if his end is merely to "break" Winston. Rorty's reading threatens to leave O'Brien appearing peculiarly obsessed with getting Winston to assent to falsehoods for no particular reason. Rorty sees the problem this poses for his reading and draws the only conclusion he consistently can in light of his interpretative claim: the obsession with getting Winston to assent to falsehoods is simply O'Brien's obsession and has nothing to do with O'Brien's own attachment to the beliefs of whose truth he tries to convince Winston (let alone, with the novel as a whole seeking to make some point about the importance of "the possibility of truth"). According to Rorty's reading, O'Brien just enjoys torturing people in this particular way. He has very perverse tastes with regard to the kinds of suffering he most enjoys causing and he likes to find ways to draw the process out . His aim is to afford himself the pleasure of contemplating the spectacle of the particular sort of mental pain which, through his interrogation, he induces in Winston:

> The point of breaking Winston is not to bring Winston into line with the Party's ideas. The Inner Party is not torturing Winston because it is afraid of a revolution . . . It is torturing Winston for the sake of causing Winston pain, and thereby increasing the pleasure of its members, particularly O'Brien. The only object of O'Brien's intensive seven-year-long study of Winston was to make possible the rich, complicated, delicate, absorbing spectacle of mental pain which Winston would eventually provide . . . [T]he last third of *1984* is about O'Brien, not about Winston – about torturing, not about being tortured.[104]

This passage is a breathtaking example of how far Rorty is prepared to go in his reading of the novel to minimize the significance of the constant occurrence throughout the novel of vocabulary such as "truth," "reality," and "objectivity." The only way Rorty sees to accord such vocabulary pride of place in a reading of the novel is to opt for a Realist reading. To steer as clear of such a reading as possible, Rorty goes to the length of construing this vocabulary instead as belonging to O'Brien's arsenal of instruments of torture. This leads Rorty to embrace the following exegetically stunning conclusion: the concern of the last third of *Nineteen Eighty-Four*, in which this vocabulary figures so prominently, has nothing to do with the concepts denoted by this vocabulary.[105] The last third of *Nineteen Eighty-Four* is concerned solely with O'Brien and his pleasure in torturing. Thus Rorty sums up his view of the novel as follows: "I think that the fantasy of endless torture . . . is essential to *1984*, and that the question about 'the possibility of truth' is a red herring."[106]

VII.   Orwell on Totalitarianism

Orwell summed up what he "really meant to do" in *Nineteen Eighty-Four* by saying that his aim was to display "the *intellectual* implications of *totalitarianism*."[107] Properly understood, this remark expresses the aim of the novel quite precisely. The two words I have italicized in the quotation, however, are liable to misinterpretation when viewed through Rortian spectacles. A comment on each is in order.

"Intellectual" for Orwell does not mean what "philosophical" does for Rorty. Its reference is not restricted to "fruitless philosophical controversies" of the sort which Rorty identifies, above all, with metaphysical debates concerning Realism. The intellectual implications of X, for Orwell, have to do with X's implications for the possibility of carrying on an intellectual life.[108] No commitment to highflown metaphysical doctrines is presupposed by such an employment of the locution 'intellectual implications.' Something which renders the pursuit of poetry, chemistry or archaeology impossible is something which has negative intellectual implications. Conversely, something has positive intellectual implications if it enables such pursuits to flourish. One can in this sense speak of the intellectual implications of allocating national resources, of passing a law, or of starting a war. What interests Orwell, in much of his work, is the most fundamental way in which something can have negative intellectual implications: namely by undermining the conditions of the possibility of having an intellectual life altogether. It is "intellectual implications" of this latter sort with which Orwell is, above all, concerned in *Nineteen Eighty-Four*. What is harder for a reader of Orwell (such a Rorty or Van Inwagen) who is obsessed with Realism to see is that no highflown metaphysics is required to understand the sorts of things which Orwell counts, in this latter sense, as conditions of the possibility of having an intellectual life.[109]

The central topic of Orwell's novel – the abolition of the conditions of the possibility of having an intellectual life – fails to come into view on Rorty's reading. This happens for two reasons. First, the vocabulary Orwell employs to characterize many of these conditions is vocabulary which Rorty supposes only someone with Realist motivations would want to put to (any but a merely rhetorical) use. (Rorty therefore, as we saw in section VI, tries to minimize the significance of the numerous passages in the novel in which such vocabulary occurs.) Second, the sorts of tactics which Orwell sees as directed towards undermining these conditions are not ones which Rorty is apt to associate with what goes on in "philosophically sophisticated debate" precisely because such tactics are, as they figure in Orwell's descriptions of them, highly effective. Rorty tends to picture such debate as an intrinsically barren and ineffectual activity. Orwell, however, is evidently concerned with tactics which can wreak profound and very concrete transformations in our social, cultural and political lives. This encourages Rorty to conclude that Orwell's concern in the novel must lie not with sophisticated philosophy, but rather with something entirely unrelated: matters of politics and history – matters such as redescribing Soviet Russia and illustrating the contingency of our practices. But, without additional assumptions, one cannot move – as Rorty tends to – from the observation that certain tactics are able to effect concrete changes in our lives to the conclusion that these tactics must therefore not employ the resources of philosophically sophisticated theory. Orwell thinks that some of the most far-reaching transformations of human social, cultural and political life can be brought about only with the aid of a totalitarian tactical employment of sophisticated forms of philosophical pseudotheorizing.[110]

The following remark structures Rorty's entire view of the options for how to read Orwell: "Somewhere we all know that philosophically sophisticated debate . . . is pretty harmless stuff."[111] The argumentative relevance of this observation to Rorty's discussion of Orwell lies in the implicit assumption that only a Realist would think that such debates are not "pretty harmless stuff" (and Orwell is no Realist). But what Orwell's work brings out so powerfully is that a stretch of theorizing which, in one context, has a "merely philosophical" import can, in another context, be tied to modes of thought and action which can have substantial and harmful effects on human lives. One therefore cannot tell whether some stretch of philosophically sophisticated theorizing is pretty harmless stuff without looking (a) to the *uses* to which that theorizing is put, (b) to the institutional and political contexts within which those uses proceed, and (c) to the practical consequences that those uses prove to have in those contexts.[112] (If that isn't a pragmatist point, I don't know what pragmatism is.) When Rorty comes across the sort of vocabulary that Realists are fond of employing, he assumes that nothing of genuine consequence could possibly be at issue. Rorty's obsession with Realism thus leaves him unable to identify the concerns which Orwell calls upon such vocabulary to express, even though Orwell himself takes those concerns to be internally related to the very matters which Rorty urges we all should be concerned with (for instance, the prevention of cruelty, the preservation of freedom, and the promotion of conditions under which a liberal polity can flourish).

Even if it were generally true – as Rorty's contends – that "philosophically sophisticated debate . . . is pretty harmless stuff", the question which Orwell's novel forces upon its reader is whether philosophical theory remains harmless when it is exercised in certain institutional settings, backed up by state power and ruthlessly directed towards ideological ends. Consider the following five claims: (i) our social practices do not require metaphysical justification, (ii) we would be better off if we weaned ourselves of the belief that our practices do require such justification, (iii) most contemporary professional philosophical debate about the sort of justification our practices putatively require is pretty harmless stuff, (iv) in certain institutional and political contexts, the belief that our practices do and should rest upon a philosophical foundation is anything but harmless in its effects, (v) the politically responsible intellectual should attend to the negative intellectual implications that this latter sort of recourse to philosophical theorizing can have. Rorty's discussion of Orwell proceeds as if these five claims were incompatible. Rorty argues as if an acknowledgment of the truth of (iv) or (v) would somehow undercut the truth of (i)–(iii). This blind spot leaves him utterly unable to locate one of the central preoccupations of Orwell's work: the totalitarian ends to which the labor of intellectuals can be put. Rorty's work is, of course, animated by a concern to urge (i)–(iii). Rorty insists that Orwell is not much interested in philosophy, yet his reading of *Nineteen Eighty-Four* leaves one with the impression that its author must share Rorty's concerns. But it is hard to imagine that Orwell would have much interest in a project describable in the terms which Rorty often uses to describe his own project: one of urging people (who mostly work in the literature and philosophy departments of universities) to cease engaging in forms of theorizing which are inherently ineffectual and harmless.[113] The kind of critique of the theorizing of intellectuals that Orwell is concerned to mount only has application to forms of theorizing which have potentially harmful practical effects.[114] This raises the question whether the theorizing of a Rorty – however harmless it may be in *his* hands – might be viewed by Orwell as a kind of theorizing which, once it leaves Rorty's hands (and falls into the hands of, say, an O'Brien), can have harmful practical effects.

We come now to the second of the words I italicized in the quotation from Orwell with which this section of the paper began. Rorty is not alone among readers of Orwell in assuming that the term "totalitarian" as it figures in his writing should be understood to denote a certain form of government. This exegetical assumption encourages the following gloss of that quotation (in which Orwell sums what he "really meant to do" in *Nineteen Eighty-Four*): the primary aim of the novel is to say something about the form of government found in Soviet Russia.[115] As we have seen, this assumption structures Rorty's reading of the first two-thirds of the novel. But the assumption is mistaken. It vastly underestimates the scope of the concept *totalitarian* as it figures in Orwell's writing.[116] The term 'totalitarianism', as Orwell uses it, refers to (both practical and intellectual) tactics for "abolishing freedom of thought to an extent unheard of in any previous age"[117] – tactics which are so called because they aim to achieve *total* control of human thought, feeling and action. Orwell's use of the term covers forms of government, but it also covers more pervasive and local sorts of practices and institutions (various journalistic practices are among his favorite examples[118]). Above all, however, Orwell applies the term to *the ideas of intellectuals* – and not just to ideas in currency in (what American journalists are apt to call) "totalitarian countries," but to ideas found throughout the modern industrial world.[119]

Orwell's novel is as much concerned with describing Capitalist Britain as it is with "redescribing" Soviet Russia.[120] The point of the redescription is lost on anyone who fails to grasp that *the triumph of certain ideas* represents a prospect that the author of this novel believes to be possible anywhere, thinks is avoidable, and finds really scary:

> I do not believe that the kind of society that I describe [in *Nineteen Eighty-Four*] necessarily *will* arrive, but I believe . . . that something resembling it *could* arrive. I believe . . . that totalitarian ideas have taken root in the minds of intellectuals everywhere, and I have tried to draw these ideas out to their logical consequences. The scene of the book is laid in Britain in order to emphasize that the English-speaking races are not innately better than anyone else and that totalitarianism, *if not fought against*, could triumph anywhere.[121]

Reading this passage together with the one quoted at the beginning of this section, Orwell can be heard making four observations about the novel here: (i) the aim of the novel is to display the intellectual implications of certain ideas, (ii) these ideas have taken root in the minds of intellectuals everywhere, (iii) the novel displays their implications drawing them out to their logical consequences, (iv) the point of doing this is (not to encourage a fatalistic view of history,[122] but rather) to show that these ideas could triumph anywhere, *if not fought against*.[123]

As Orwell defines the term, "totalitarianism" refers to the abolition of the freedom of thought in a positive as well as a negative respect: the aim of totalitarian intellectual tactics is not only negatively to constrain but also positively to shape the possibilities of thought available to those to whom they are directed.[124] It is in his discussions of the positive control that totalitarianism exerts on thought that one particularly encounters Orwell saying things of a sort that Rorty's Orwell would never want to say:

> [Totalitarianism's] control of thought is not only negative, but positive. It not only forbids you to express – even to think – certain thoughts, but it dictates what you *shall* think, it creates an ideology for you, it tries to govern your emotional life as well as setting up a code of conduct. And as far as possible it isolates you from the outside world, it shuts you up in an artificial universe in which you have no standards of comparison.[125]

Totalitarianism seeks to isolate you from the outside world. This does not mean that the standards of comparison which totalitarianism isolates you from are those of your community of preferred conversation-partners. On the contrary, the problem with totalitarian ideas, according to Orwell, is that they aim to bring it about that the sole available standards of comparison are precisely those which Rorty's Orwell urges are the only ones you should ever want: the standards supplied by the community of "comrades" with whom you express your solidarity. The standards of comparison of which you are deprived by totalitarian ideas, according to Orwell, are the sorts of standards which are only available to someone whose thought is answerable to the facts themselves. Orwell, when he says things like "the facts exist and are more or less discoverable,"[126] is not expressing a commitment to Realism. What other sort of reason could there be for saying things like this?

Orwell's most proximate aims are to warn of the dangers of totalitarianism and to illuminate the cultural, social and political conditions under which freedom and justice can flourish. But why does the prosecution of such aims lead him to employ vocabulary which triggers Rorty's philosophical alarms? Why doesn't he just talk in a sober and sensible fashion about the sorts of freedoms which concentration camps and secret police forces deprive us of? Because he thinks that would be to concentrate only on the most advanced and flagrant symptoms of a malady that is most effectively treated in its less advanced stages. Much of his work is concerned with identifying the early symptoms of the malady. He identifies these with those practices and institutions in our society which cultivate a hostility to "truthfulness."[127] Concentration camps and secret police forces are peripheral to the set of cultural, social, and political phenomena which he wants to identify as totalitarian. What is integral is a kind of "organized lying" which, if the logical consequences of its inherent tendencies were fully drawn out, could be seen to "demand a disbelief in the very existence of objective truth."[128] *This* is what Orwell finds really inimical to the ideals of liberalism in totalitarianism. Totalitarian modes of thought do, in Orwell's view, inevitably lead to the proliferation of atrocities. And still more frightening to Orwell than the forms of cruelty to which they give rise is a further (what Orwell calls) "*intellectual* implication" of totalitarian modes of thought: namely, the undermining of the possibility of your leading a life in which you are free to think your own thoughts – to have your own take on whether, for instance, something is an atrocity or not.[129] But neither cruelty nor loss of freedom is what Orwell considers to be "the really frightening thing about totalitarianism" – they are, in his view, merely inevitable consequences of it.[130] "The really frightening thing about totalitarianism is not that it commits 'atrocities' but that it attacks the concept of objective truth."[131]

In order to see what Orwell takes "the really frightening thing about totalitarianism" to be, it helps to notice how the central themes of his novel emerge directly from his writings about his experiences as a soldier in the Spanish Civil War:

> I have little direct evidence about the atrocities in the Spanish civil war, I know that some were committed by the Republicans, and far more . . . by the Fascists. But what impressed me then, and has impressed me ever since, is that atrocities are believed in or disbelieved in solely on grounds of political predilection. Everyone believes in the atrocities of the enemy and disbelieves in those of his own side, without ever bothering to examine the evidence.[132]

"The really frightening thing about totalitarianism" is not just that it encourages someone self-consciously to misdescribe an event as, say, an atrocity. (There is nothing remarkable or unprecedented about the phenomenon of willful misdescription. The use of language to tell lies has been with us as long as language itself has.) Nor is it just that it encourages someone unwittingly to misdescribe the facts. (Inaccurate reports of events can be found in any newspaper.) Someone who self-consciously lies about whether something is an X or who inadvertently misdescribes something as an X does not thereby damage or eviscerate his capacity to go on in other contexts and correctly apply the concept on his own. Orwell, however, is precisely concerned to draw attention here to a process of belief-formation which does loosen our hold on certain concepts. The above passage is concerned with a state of affairs in which atrocities are believed in or disbelieved in solely on grounds of political predilection, without ever bothering to examine the evidence.[133] But exactly wherein lies the frightening aspect of this? Is it that, if our beliefs about whether an atrocity has been committed are not sensitive to evidence, then the norms for the application of the concept *atrocity* cease to guide the application of the concept? But not all cases of this sort are frightening. There are cases, for example, in which we more or less self-consciously desist in our use of a piece of vocabulary because we realize that our use of it is no longer guided by any clear criteria.[134] In such cases, we realize we are no longer able to express determinately meaningful thoughts employing the vocabulary in question. There are other sorts of cases, in which we continue to employ a piece of vocabulary but fail to realize that we no longer determinately mean anything by it.[135] This latter sort of case is admittedly quite unsettling, but it is not of the sort which Orwell finds really frightening.

The really frightening case is one in which you do retain your original grasp of the concepts in question and continue to use them to form perfectly determinate beliefs about happenings in the world, yet the mechanisms by means of which those beliefs are formed are no longer guided by the happenings which form the subjects of those beliefs. Orwell writes:

> Early in life I had noticed that no event is ever correctly reported in a newspaper, but in Spain, for the first time, I saw newspaper reports which did not bear any relation to the facts, not even the relationship which is implied in an ordinary lie.[136] I saw great battles reported where there had been no fighting, and complete silence where hundreds of men had been killed. I saw troops who had fought bravely denounced as cowards and traitors, and others who had never seen a shot fired hailed as the heroes of imaginary victories; and I saw newspapers in London retailing these lies and eager intellectuals building emotional superstructures over events that had never happened . . . This kind of thing is frightening to me, because it gives me the feeling that the very concept of objective truth is fading out of the world.[137]

During the Spanish Civil War, intellectuals in Britain held certain beliefs about what was happening in Spain and attached great importance to the happenings which formed the subjects of those beliefs. Many acted on those beliefs; some died acting on them. The totalitarian dimension of the situation was a function, on the one hand, of the loyal determination of these intellectuals to believe only accounts accredited by their respective political parties and, on the other hand, of the unwavering determination of their parties to admit only politically expedient accounts of what was happening in Spain. The following situation was therefore in place: the beliefs of these intellectuals were answerable solely to the standards by means of which a prevailing consensus was reached within their party, but the means by which that consensus was reached was not answerable to *what was happening in Spain*. So the beliefs of British intellectuals concerning what was happening in Spain bore no relation to what was happening in Spain, not even the relationship which is implied in an ordinary lie. What's more, by the time the war came to an end, the means by which anyone might be able to discover what had happened in Spain were, in all likelihood, forever lost.[138]

The situation of those intellectuals is the sort of thing Orwell has in mind when he says "the concept of objective truth begins to fade out of the world" – that is, a situation in which belief-formation is subject to the following three conditions: (a) the resulting beliefs are answerable solely to the mechanisms through which consensus is achieved within a certain community, (b) those mechanisms yield beliefs about the facts that do not bear any relation to the facts, not even the relationship implied in an ordinary lie, (c) systematic means are employed by the community to render access to any other standard unavailable. I will henceforth refer to such a state of affairs – in which the formation of someone's beliefs with respect to some subject matter is subject to these three conditions – as "a totalitarian scenario"; and I will henceforth refer to a state of affairs in which the formation of someone's beliefs about a subject matter is not (systematically insensitive to the subject matter of those beliefs because) subject to these three conditions as a non–totalitarian scenario.[139] *Nineteen Eighty-Four* is an attempt to depict a scenario which is totalitarian with respect to an extraordinarily wide class of beliefs – a world in which the formation of as many of a person's beliefs are subject to the above three conditions as can possibly be the case.[140] It is about the possibility of a state of affairs in which the concept of objective truth has faded as far out of someone's world as it conceivably can.[141] The attempt to depict such a state of affairs is one of the central ways in which Orwell's novel seeks "to draw out the logical consequences" inherent in certain modes of thought – modes of thought which Orwell found to be prevalent among British intellectuals during the 1930s.

The exploration of the existential consequences of trying to embrace the Party's doctrine of the mutability of the past represents *Nineteen Eighty-Four*'s most resolute effort to draw out these logical consequences. The Party aims to ensure that the concept of objective truth completely ceases to apply to the way history is recorded or remembered:

> The Party said that Oceania had never been in alliance with Eurasia. He, Winston Smith, knew that Oceania had been in alliance with Eurasia as short a time as four years ago. But where did that knowledge exist? Only in his own consciousness, which in any case must soon be annihilated. And if all others accepted the lie which the Party imposed – if all records told the same tale – then the lie passed into history and became truth. "Who controls the past," ran the Party slogan, "controls the future: who controls the present controls the past." And yet the past, though of its nature alterable, never had been altered. Whatever was true now was true from everlasting to everlasting. It was quite simple. All that was needed was an unending series of victories of your own memory. "Reality control," they called it.[142]

Numerous passages in the novel characterize the purpose of "reality control" as "the denial of objective reality"; and some equate such a denial with the denial of "objective truth."[143] Rorty asks us to view all such talk in the novel as pertinent only to an understanding of the methods of torture which allow O'Brien to get his kicks: "[T]he fantasy of endless torture . . . is essential to *1984*, . . . the question about 'the possibility of truth' is a red herring."[144] But Winston speaks for Orwell when he reflects: "If the Party could thrust its hand into the past and say of this or that event, *it never happened* – that, surely, was more terrifying than mere torture and death."[145] Glimpses into the possibility of such a nightmare scenario figure prominently in Orwell's writings about the Spanish Civil War:

> I am willing to believe that history is for the most part inaccurate and biased, but what is peculiar to our own age is the abandonment of the idea that history *could* be truthfully written. In the past people deliberately lied, or they unconsciously coloured what they wrote, or they struggled after the truth, well knowing that they must make many mistakes; but in each case they believed that "the facts" existed and were more or less discoverable. And in practice there was always a considerable body of fact which would have been agreed to by almost everyone. If you look up the history of the last war [that is, World War I] in, for instance, the *Encyclopedia Britannica*, you will find that a respectable amount of the material is drawn from German sources. A British and a German historian would disagree deeply on many things, even on fundamentals, but there would still be that body of, as it were, neutral fact on which neither would seriously challenge the other. It is just this common basis of agreement . . . that totalitarianism destroys . . . The implied objective of this line of thought is a nightmare world in which the Leader, or some ruling clique, controls not only the future but *the past*. If the Leader says of such and such an event, "It never happened" – well, it never happened. If he says that two and two are five – well, two and two are five. This prospect frightens me much more than bombs – and after our experiences of the last few years that is not a frivolous statement.[146]

When Orwell says here that "in practice there was always a considerable body of fact which would have been agreed to by almost everyone," his point is not that there was some preferred vocabulary upon which all historical investigators are fated to converge. He attributes to the investigators in question nothing more than a shared interest in establishing what actually happened during World War I, a shared set of norms for the employment of concepts for describing what happened, and the shared belief that there was a considerable body of *mundane* facts concerning which near-universal agreement could be attained (even between investigators of radically different political predilections). Yet his point here is not the mere Rortian point that a consensus was attainable; it is the Orwellian point that that consensus was not answerable solely to the demand to achieve consensus within a certain community. The historical research of these investigators did not proceed within the confines of a totalitarian scenario (that is the formation of their beliefs was not subject to the three conditions mentioned above as constitutive of a totalitarian scenario). The formation of their beliefs was sensitive to the demand to achieve consensus with their comrades in arms, but was not so beholden to that demand as to be rendered insensitive to any other. Their beliefs were answerable to a body of fact (records, memories, the existence of graveyards, etc.) which placed constraints on what one could claim: constraints which were equally acknowledged and respected by German and English historians alike. The numerous references in *Nineteen Eighty-Four* to the Party's "denial of objective truth," its "denial of the validity of experience," and its "denial of the very existence of external reality" are connected by Orwell in this passage with the loss of "a considerable body of fact which would have been agreed to by almost everyone." In the world of the novel this loss is reflected not in the absence of a prevailing consensus (about something which even in that world gets called "the facts") but in the loss of the "considerable body of [actual] fact" to which Orwell here refers and to which that consensus should be answerable. When Orwell says the prospect of this loss frightens him much more than bombs, this is not a testament to his insensitivity to cruelty. This passage was written in London in 1942 after the author had witnessed the cruelty inflicted through the bombing of a defenseless urban civilian population. It was the most devastating example of cruelty which Orwell, in his not uneventful life, had witnessed first-hand. The example is chosen in order to anticipate the charge that the author's conclusion is a "frivolous statement" – to make it clear that the author means to be taking the full measure of the horror of cruelty in concluding that cruelty is not the worst thing we do.

The above passage concludes with the claim that "the implied objective" of a totalitarian line of thought is "a nightmare world": a world in which if the Leader says of such and such an event, "It never happened" – well, it never happened; and if he says that two and two is five – well, two and two is five. This passage clearly anticipates the topic (and, to some extent, the exact wording) of the focal passage. The author of the above passage does not intend the truth of "2+2=4" to drop out as irrelevant to an understanding of the point of the passage. *Nineteen Eighty-Four* is an attempt to depict a world which comes as close as any can to being one in which the prospect described in this passage obtains. Two paragraphs before the focal passage in the novel we find this:

> It was as though some huge force were pressing down upon you – something that penetrated into your skull, battering against your brain, frightening you out of your beliefs, persuading you almost, to deny the evidence of your senses. In the end the Party would announce that two and two made five, and you would have to believe it. It was inevitable

that they should make that claim sooner or later: the logic of their position demanded it. Not merely the validity of experience, but the very existence of external reality was tacitly denied by their philosophy . . . And what was terrifying was not that they would kill you for thinking otherwise, but that they might be right. For, after all, how do we know that two and two make four? Or that the force of gravity works? Or that the past is unchangeable? If both the past and the external world exist only in the mind, and if the mind itself is controllable – what then?[147]

What does it mean to say "not merely the validity of experience, but the very existence of external reality was tacitly denied by [the Party's] philosophy"? It means that one is asked to form one's beliefs about how things are in a manner that is no longer beholden to how things are. There are two sorts of examples of truth-claims which figure centrally in this passage (and in the focal passage and, indeed, throughout the novel): perceptual judgments (claims based on "the evidence of your senses") and elementary arithmetical judgments (two and two make four). Why do these two sorts of examples recur throughout the novel? Once a member of our linguistic community has become competent in the application of the relevant (perceptual or arithmetic) concepts, these are the sorts of judgments the truth or falsity of which can easily be assessed by the individual *on her own*. Once having acquired the relevant concepts and having fully mastered them, her ability to arrive at a verdict on such questions does not wait upon the development of a consensus within her community on such questions. (It is this ability on the part of the individual – to arrive at a view of the facts which does not depend on a knowledge of the Party's preferred version of the facts – that the focal passage announces must be undone: "The Party told you to reject the evidence of your eyes and ears. It was their final, most essential, command.") Indeed, when the verdict concerns, say, something you saw and no one else saw, you have excellent *prima facie* reasons to trust your own view of what happened over, say, a conflicting version which appears in the newspaper.[148] It is this capacity of individuals to assess the truth of claims on their own that threatens the absolute hegemony of the Party over their minds. (If the freedom to exercise this capacity is granted, then – as the focal passage says – all else follows.) The "mind itself" is fully "controllable" only when the Party's version of the facts (for instance, that such-and-such never happened) is taken as true even in the face of contradictory testimony from one's own senses (for instance, one's vivid memory that one saw such-and-such happen) and against the grain of the norms built into the concepts employed in the formulation of the Party's version of the facts (for instance, norms that prescribe such things as that this is the sort of case we call a case of "such-and-such," that this is the sort of thing we call "adding" one number to another number, etc.).

Recall now Rorty's reading of the focal passage: O'Brien's object is merely to deprive Winston of the freedom to believe what he wants to believe – the truth of what Winston happens to believe drops out as irrelevant; O'Brien forces Winston to believe "two and two make five" because Winston *happens* to believe that "two and two make four" and Winston *happens* to have attached great importance to this belief. But what the novel says (just prior to the focal passage) is: "in the end" the moment would come when "the Party would announce that two and two made five" because "the logic of their position demanded it." "Two and two make four" figures as a central example of something the truth of which must be denied by the Party because of the kind of claim that it is: one that is true and moreover easily seen to be true by anyone competent in our practices of claim-making.[149] The novel is here working out one of the "intellectual implications of totalitarianism." The Party's practice of wholesale "organized lying" is only sustainable if, in the end, it deprives its members of their ability to autonomously assess the credentials of a claim – any claim: even a straightforward perceptual or arithmetic claim. The reason claims such as "two and two make four" and "I see a photograph before me" figure prominently as examples is (not just because Winston happens to believe them to be true and happens to attach importance to them, but rather) because they are the sorts of claims that can be known to be true by a Winston and, once known to be true, will sometimes inevitably fail to cohere with the rest of the Party's version of the facts.[150] The criteria for determining the truth-value of such claims do not require that prior to arriving at a judgment on such matters one consult the latest bulletin from the Party – unless, that is, the ground-rules for attaining competence in the community's practices of claim-making are radically altered from any practices for making such claims with which we are familiar. This raises the question: does the community described in Orwell's novel have a coherent alternative set of ground-rules for making such claims?

A central point of the novel is to suggest that the ultimate "logic of the Party's position" demands that the ground-rules for the application of concepts and the formation of beliefs have at least apparently been altered from those with which we are familiar. But it would be a tremendous misunderstanding of Orwell's novel to think that, in suggesting this, his aim is merely to describe a set of practices of claim-making which happen to differ radically from our own, and that his point in doing so is to urge that, apart from our culturally and historically provincial predilections, there is nothing that entitles us to prefer our practices to these possible future practices – that there is nothing outside these possible future practices that condemns them. Orwell's point is that "the denial of external reality" demanded by the logic of the Party's position can only be approximated to the extent that members of a community learn to cultivate a tremendously thorough-going form of self-deception – so thorough-going that they succeed in hiding from themselves that "the truth goes on existing, as it were, behind [their] back[s]."[151] If one were to try to formulate the sort of ground-rules which the logic of the Party's position implicitly demands, one might, on a hasty first try, arrive at something like the following three-part recipe for assessing the truth-values of claims:

(a) "Such-and-such" is true if and only if such-and-such.

(b) Whatever the Party says is true is true, and anything the Party has a reason to want to be true is true.

(c) In all cases in which (a) and (b) yield conflicting judgments, (b) takes priority over (a).

This says that we should only judge a claim to be true in accordance with (a) in those cases in which (a) and (b) do not conflict; in those cases in which they do conflict, we should not judge in accordance with (a). But now how are we to understand this recipe? Does it articulate (i) a conception of (what Orwell calls) truth or (ii) merely a revision in the rules for the employment of a piece of vocabulary (that is, 'true'),[152] so that it no longer univocally means what Orwell means by the word when, for instance, he says that "however much you deny the truth, the truth goes on existing, as it were, behind your back"?[153] Understood either way, the recipe hardly succeeds in capturing what the Party wants of its members. Let's consider (ii) first. When O'Brien asks Winston how many fingers he is holding up, he would hardly be satisfied with the reply "You are holding up four fingers, but it is not *true* that you are holding up four fingers." He doesn't merely want Winston to *utter the words* "It is true that you are presently holding up five fingers" and (to desist in uttering the words "It is true that you are presently holding up four fingers"), while continuing, all along to believe that O'Brien is holding up four fingers (as could be easily arranged, if, for instance, it was stipulated that the usual meaning of 'true' was to be suspended and that 'true' should here be taken to mean "it is not the case"). O'Brien doesn't just want Winston to acquiesce in the utterance of certain sequences of words; he wants to alter Winston's *beliefs*. This brings us to (i). Rorty might want to object that (i) involves a red herring: namely, the whole idea of what Orwell calls "truth" (when he says things like "however much you deny the truth, the truth goes on existing, as it were, behind your back").[154] In the service of avoiding this philosophically suspicious bit of a vocabulary, one might attempt to reformulate the above three-part recipe as a series of imperatives (about what one should believe when) which dispenses with any explicit mention of the offending vocabulary:

(a)   Believe "such-and-such" when the pre-Ingsoc criteria for believing that such-and-such are satisfied (if, for instance, relying upon the testimony of your senses, you can plainly see that such-and-such, etc.).

(b)   If the Party says or has reason to want you to believe "such-and-such", then believe such-and-such.

(c)   In all cases in which (a) and (b) conflict, (b) takes priority over (a).

But this still fails fully to capture what the Party wants of its members. For the Party is not prepared to acknowledge that there are cases in which (a) and (b) conflict. When O'Brien asks Winston how many fingers he is holding up, he does not want Winston merely to believe that there are five fingers in front of him because the Party happens to want him to believe that there are five fingers in front of him. He doesn't want Winston simply to overrule the testimony of his senses in favor of what the Party tells him. Nor does O'Brien want Winston, in concluding that there are five fingers in front of him, to be adopting a (post-Ingsoc) wholesale revision in our concepts (of "see," "five," "fingers," etc). In his conversations with Winston, O'Brien does not mean to be engaged in a process of teaching him new concepts and hence, in effect, a whole new language. He doesn't merely want Winston to believe something which can be expressed in Newspeak by saying "I see five fingers," but which has a completely different meaning from its homophonic English counterpart; he wants Winston to believe *that there are five fingers* in front of him. O'Brien wants Winston to look at him holding up four fingers and, if the Party wants him to believe that there are five fingers, to *see* five fingers in front of him, and to have the ground of his belief that there are five fingers in front of him be (not that the Party wants him to believe that, but) that he *sees* five fingers. The Party's ambition is therefore neither so modest as merely to want to change the ground-rules for how to use certain philosophically freighted portions of our vocabulary (for instance, "truth," "reality," etc.) nor so ambitious as to want to effect a wholesale revision of the ground-rules which constitute our entire battery of concepts, completely jettisoning our familiar norms for making claims. The

Party wants us to believe that we are retaining our present ground-rules for employing concepts while also always believing that the Party's version of the facts is true. The ways in which the Party wants its members to think and judge cannot be captured in terms of a coherent set of ground-rules for the application of concepts: Party members are supposed simultaneously to abide by our ordinary norms for making claims and not to abide by those norms.

The Party wants its members to be able to think and judge – which requires that they retain their mastery of our familiar norms for the application of concepts – but never to think or judge in a manner which conflicts with what the Party wants them to think or judge; yet, all along, while thinking and judging in accordance with the Party's decrees, to believe that they are never arriving at a judgment about how things are which conflicts with a judgment at which someone who had no knowledge of the Party's decrees, but who simply abided by the norms built into our concepts, might have occasion to arrive. The Party therefore places an incoherent set of demands upon its members, the incoherence of which must be rendered *invisible* if those demands are to serve the Party's purposes.[155] How is this invisibility to be achieved? The rules for the formation of beliefs that Party members are in fact required to follow and the rules that they are asked to *believe* that they are following cannot be the same.[156] How is it possible for Party members successfully to follow a set of rules that they never believe they are following? By practicing "reality control" and "doublethink." Party members are expected to "adjust" their beliefs about reality in accordance with the Party's decrees but then are asked to believe that the justification for their beliefs lies (not merely in their accord with the Party's decrees, but) in their accord with the facts. Party members are asked, for example, not only to believe that such-and-such happened in the past (if the Party presently decrees that this is what happened), but to adjust their memories of the past so that they now remember such-and-such as having happened in the past and believe that the ground of their present belief that such-and-such happened in the past is (not the Party's present decree to that effect, but rather) their present memory of its having happened in the past.[157] This is why the novel insists that reality control can be successfully practiced only by someone who has become adept in the practice of doublethink. In order to be a Party member, one therefore needs "to deny the existence of objective reality and all the while to take account of the reality which one denies . . . [O]ne must be able to dislocate the sense of reality."[158] One must not only adjust one's beliefs about reality, but one must also be proficient in the art of forgetting that one continuously so adjusts them.[159] Rorty occasionally talks as if our practices and the "practices" of the future totalitarian society depicted in Orwell's novel represented a pair of equally viable alternatives (with the interesting difference that, as it happens, talk of "objective reality" is frowned upon in the future "practices" and all that is thereby lost is a proclivity to engage in fruitless metaphysical controversies). But this is not right. There are overwhelming grounds – as Winston's reflections all too clearly illustrate – from *within* their "practices" for preferring our practices to theirs.[160] What Orwell calls "the denial of objective reality" is a denial which can be at most partially sustained and then only within a set of "practices" regulated by what Orwell calls a "schizophrenic system of thought"[161] – a system that simultaneously respects and disregards our present norms for making claims: claims which are answerable (not only to our peers, but also) to how things are.[162]

When Rorty says that (for the purposes of understanding Orwell's novel) "the question about 'the possibility of truth' is a red herring,"[163] there are two things to which one might take "the possibility of truth" to refer: (a) the possibility of the beliefs of the members of a community concerning how things are being answerable to how things are, (b) the possibility of the members of a community being honest and forthright when they communicate their beliefs to one another. Neither is a red herring. The first possibility is the one that reality control aims to subvert; the second is the one that doublethink aims to subvert.[164] What the novel shows is that the two possibilities are interrelated – that (a) and (b) mutually depend upon one another – and thus that the practices of reality control and doublethink presuppose and mutually reinforce each other. If the Party knowingly falsifies every form of evidence and if every Party member with first-hand knowledge of such acts of falsification withholds his knowledge of such acts, then the beliefs of members of the Party will no longer bear any relation to the facts, not even the relationship implied in an ordinary lie. But it is impossible completely to insulate a Party member from reality. As the novel illustrates over and over again, reality rears its ideologically uncooperative head (for instance, Big Brother's predictions turn out to be false, etc.). Hence "reality control" must be practiced: one's beliefs about reality must be "adjusted." One can continuously adjust one's beliefs to reality in the manner the Party requires of its members only if one cultivates the vice of dishonesty to such a degree that dishonesty and self-deception become second nature. We are now in a position to see the extraordinary perversity of Rorty's claim that Orwell understood himself to be doing the same *kind* of thing as his "opponents" – for instance, the apologists for Stalin – were doing. One of Orwell's aims is to bring out how the practice of his "opponents" (that is, the producers of what Orwell calls "propaganda," or, as Rorty prefers to say, "persuasive redescriptions of events") presupposes the systematic cultivation of reality control and doublethink – arts of deception, conscious and unconscious, practiced on oneself and others. It is a condition of being able to practice the unconscious forms of such arts that one lack the ability to characterize accurately what one is doing while one is doing it. It is therefore a condition of Orwell's achieving the sort of description of the vices of his "opponents" to which he aspires that he himself, in offering such a description, not exemplify those vices – that he not be doing the same kind of thing as his "opponents."

Rorty regards the topic of "the individual's control over her own mind" both as important to Orwell's novel and as important, and he regards the topic of "the concept of objective truth" both as irrelevant to an understanding of the novel and as irrelevant to anything we should care about. He thinks that only a Realist could imagine that the former topic could somehow depend on (something describable employing the vocabulary of) the latter. But Orwell's interests are not those of the Realist; he employs the expression "the concept of objective truth" in the context of seeking to distinguish between totalitarian and non-totalitarian scenarios. When Orwell seeks to explore this distinction he draws on forms of words (such as "a neutral body of fact providing a common basis of agreement") of a sort which Rorty tends either to pounce upon as evidence of a commitment to Realism or (in a misguided attempt at charity to Orwell) to overlook as mere rhetoric. This leaves Rorty unable to read Orwell.[165]

VIII. Rortian Totalitarianism

The aim of this section of the paper is to offer a redescription of Rortianism, as it might appear to someone with Orwell's preoccupations. For Orwell, the distinction

between totalitarian and non-totalitarian scenarios is an important distinction to be able
to draw. It is by no means an idle or merely metaphysical distinction. To inhabit one
of these scenarios rather than the other is to inhabit one of two very different worlds.
The distinction does not trade on a tacit reliance on Realist metaphysics. Yet Rorty's
way of rejecting Realism would, I think, strike Orwell as depriving him of his preferred
resources for drawing this distinction.

Passages such as the following recur throughout *Nineteen Eighty-Four*:

> Being in a minority, even a minority of one, did not make you mad. There was truth and
> untruth, and if you clung to the truth even against the whole world, you were not mad
> . . . [Winston] fell asleep murmuring "Sanity is not statistical," with the feeling that this
> remark contained in it a profound wisdom.[166]

A number of Rortian theses – most notably (1′) – do seem to take sanity to be a
statistical matter: a matter of the congruence of one's beliefs with those of one's peers.
Admittedly, in a non-totalitarian scenario, such congruence is generally a reliable
measure of sanity. But Orwell is concerned to depict a world in which it is not a
reliable measure:

> [Winston] was a lonely ghost uttering a truth that nobody would ever hear. But so long as
> he uttered it, in some obscure way the continuity was not broken. It was not by making
> yourself heard but by staying sane that you carried on the human heritage.[167]

What Orwell's depiction of a totalitarian scenario brings out is that a statistical gloss on
sanity cannot serve as a definition of sanity. Hilary Putnam once asked Rorty – as I
imagine Orwell would have wanted to ask Rorty – if he accepted the following two
principles:

(a)   In ordinary circumstances, there is usually a fact of the matter as to whether the
      statements people make are warranted or not.

(b)   Whether a statement is warranted or not is independent of whether the majority
      of one's cultural peers would *say* it is warranted or unwarranted.[168]

Nineteen Eighty-Four offers numerous illustrations of these principles. In the world of
the novel, there is a fact of the matter as to whether Winston's statement that he saw a
photograph of Rutherford is warranted. (It is warranted, and remains so even after all
the corroborating evidence has been destroyed by the Party.) Moreover, it is important
to the narrative of the novel that whether Winston's statement is warranted or not is
independent of whether the majority of his cultural peers in the Party would *say* it is
warranted or unwarranted. Even though, at the end of the novel, Winston clearly
constitutes a minority of one, his statement remains warranted. Rorty not only fails to
see that such a state of affairs is envisioned in the novel, he fails to see that it can so
much as represent a perfectly coherent possibility. This is how Rorty replies to
Putnam's question:

> There being a fact of the matter about warranted assertibility must, for Putnam, be
> something *more* than our ability to figure out whether S is in a good position, given the
> interests and values of herself and her peers, to assert *p*. But what more . . . can it be?
> Presumably it is whatever makes it possible for a statement not to be warranted even

though a majority of one's peers say it is. *Is* that possible? Is (b) true? Well, maybe a *majority* can be wrong. But suppose everybody in the community, except for one or two dubious characters notorious for making assertions even stranger than *p*, thinks S must be a bit crazy. They think this even after patiently sitting through S's defense of *p*, and after sustained attempts to talk her out of it. Might S still be *warranted* in asserting *p*? Only if there is some way of determining warrant *sub specie aeternitatis*, some natural order of reasons which determines, quite apart from S's ability to justify *p* to those around her, whether she is *really* justified in holding *p*. I do not see how one could reconcile the claim that there is this nonsociological justification with [the rejection of Realism].[169]

Rorty here suggests that a process in which S's peers "patiently sit through S's defense of *p* and [engage in] sustained attempts to talk her out of it" constitutes the sole possible means of establishing whether *p* is warranted. But warrant is not simply a function of the capacity of a speaker to convince his conversation-partners of the truth of his claim. The conversation that takes place between O'Brien and Winston at the end of the novel can be described using the terms that Rorty employs in the above passage: "O'Brien patiently sits through Winston's defense of his claims and engages in sustained attempts to talk him out of them." But the outcome of their conversation – in which Winston recants his claims – is hardly a test of whether Winston's claims are warranted or not. O'Brien demands that Winston's beliefs conform to what the Party would have him believe (and O'Brien has the persuasive resources at his disposal to bring it about that Winston accedes to this demand). Such a demand, however, as we saw in section VII, cannot be cashed out in terms of a coherent set of norms for making claims.

Rorty does not see how to allow for a scenario in which both of the following are true: (i) S's willingness to assert *p* furnishes practically everybody in S's community (except perhaps for one or two dubious characters) with a ground for thinking that S is crazy, and (ii) S is fully warranted in asserting *p*. *But Winston finds himself in just such a situation.* Orwell, in depicting the conversation between Winston and O'Brien, aims to furnish an example of just the sort of case which Rorty (in the passage quoted above) does not allow for: it is Winston – who is in a minority of one – who adheres to the only coherent norms for making claims that he and O'Brien (and other members of their community) share. Winston's claims are warranted because they are in accord – not with what his peers, in fact say, but – with what his peers should say. Winston's statement that he saw a photograph of Rutherford is warranted (not because he possesses some way of determining warrant *sub specie aeternitatis*, but rather) because he faithfully adheres to the only coherent norms members of his community have for applying concepts (such as the concept *photograph*) and for making claims (such as the claim "I saw such-and-such").[170] A state of rationally warranted intellectual isolation – such as Winston finds himself in – can come about whenever what one's peers *ought* to believe (given the norms inherent in the community's practices for making claims) fails to coincide with what they, as a matter of brute sociological fact, happen to believe. If one inhabits a non-totalitarian scenario, then one is not likely to find oneself in such a situation – a situation in which one's community as a whole goes wrong, leaving one in a minority of one. What *Nineteen Eighty-Four* makes vivid, however, is that, if one has the misfortune to be an inhabitant of a totalitarian scenario, then, unless one is adept in practicing the arts of reality control and doublethink, it is not only possible but *probable* that one will find oneself in such a situation a great deal of the time and with respect to a great many of one's beliefs.[171] (The more totalitarian the scenario one inhabits, the greater the number of beliefs one will have which will be both warranted and unacceptable to one's peers.)

In the above passage, Rorty equates the following two things: (i) there is some way of determining warrant *sub specie aeternitatis*, (ii) there is a way of determining the warrant of *p* quite apart from S's ability to justify *p* to those around her. (i) and (ii) are not equivalent. (ii) does not presuppose any Realist metaphysics. It merely presupposes that there is a distinction between justifying a claim to the satisfaction of other people and a claim's being justified in the light of the facts. (1′) precludes the possibility of drawing such a distinction. The distinction is one that it is easier for inhabitants of non-totalitarian scenarios (such as Rorty) to overlook than for inhabitants of totalitarian scenarios (such as Winston). Rorty writes:

> [T]he terms 'warranted,' 'rational acceptability,' etc., will always invite the question 'to whom'? This question will always lead us back, it seems to me, to the answer '*Us*, at our best'. So all 'a fact of the matter about whether *p* is a warranted assertion' can mean is "a fact of the matter about our ability to feel solidarity with a community that views *p* as warranted."[172]

The only sense Rorty can make of notions such as warrant or rational acceptability is in terms of the idea of passing muster with our peers. In the world of the novel, Winston knows that the Party did not invent the airplane.[173] He has clear and vivid memories of airplanes from his childhood, way back before the days of the Party. But his belief will never pass muster with any of his peers. All of the history books and all other forms of documentary evidence have been altered to reflect the Party's version of the facts. Every member of the Party now dutifully believes the official version of the facts (putatively) documented in the history books. Winston's belief to the contrary is an act of thoughtcrime punishable by death.[174] His peers have no interest in entertaining beliefs that might lead to their being vaporized, so they have all internalized the mental habit of crimestop.[175] Under these circumstances, is Winston's belief (that the Party did not invent the airplane) warranted? If the question "Is Winston's belief warranted?" is simply equated with the question "Is it acceptable to his peers?" then the answer clearly is: "No, his belief is not warranted." For Winston, under the totalitarian conditions in which he finds himself, is in no position to bring anyone round to his belief. The only existing "community that views *p* as warranted" in this case is a community of one. There is no larger community with whom Winston can seek solidarity, if to seek solidarity means to seek *de facto* agreement with a present community of peers.[176] What this shows is that there is something missing in Rorty's theory of justification. Implicit in the practices of Winston's community are norms which, if properly abided by, underwrite Winston's belief. Assuming (as the author of the novel clearly intends us to) that Winston's memory does not deceive him (that is, that there were airplanes when he was a child) and given the norms that govern the application of the concept of *invention* (for instance, that it is impossible for X to invent Y if there were Ys before X existed), then Winston's belief is warranted; and it remains warranted even if it also remains the case that none of his peers are willing to (engage in an act of thoughtcrime in which they) credit the possibility that his belief is warranted.

In non-totalitarian scenarios, the following two tasks generally coincide: the task of seeking to justify a claim to the satisfaction of other people and the task of seeking to establish that a claim is justified in the light of the facts. In totalitarian scenarios, these two tasks diverge radically. It is manifest to Winston that the question whether it is true that the Party did not invent the airplane and the question whether or not someone will be allowed to get away with saying "The Party did not invent the airplane" are different questions. In our world, as long as the question "Who invented the airplane?" does not become too ideologically fraught, the tasks of seeking an answer to that question and of seeking an answer to the question "What will my peers let me get away with saying about who invented the airplane?" ought to coincide. In Winston's world they do not coincide. If our world were like Winston's world in the respect in which Rorty suggests that it already is – if our only aim in inquiry were to remain in step with our peers – then there would be no reason to suppose that our claims had any more bearing on the world than the claims which appear in the newspapers in *Nineteen Eighty-Four* have on the "events" which those newspapers report. Yet even the inhabitants of Winston's world are (at least in principle) able to distinguish the questions "Who invented the airplane?" and "Who does practically everyone *say* invented the airplane?". Not even the Party goes quite as far as Rorty! It does not aim to deprive its members of the capacity to distinguish between these questions. What members of the Party believe is that the answers to these two clearly distinct questions happily coincide. As we saw in section VII, the Party does not want its members to believe what the Party says on the ground that the Party says it. The Party, of course, does want them to believe that what the Party says is true; but the Party wants them to believe that their ground for believing what the Party says is that it accords with the facts. Not even the Party aims to do away in theory with (what Orwell calls) "the very concept of objective truth" – that is the very idea of the answerability of claims concerning how things are to how things are. Nevertheless, Orwell's depiction of the world in which Winston lives – a world in which, as Orwell puts it, this concept is on the verge of "fading out" – is perhaps as close as we can come to contemplating in imagination the implications of the adoption of a resolutely Rortian conception of objectivity (that is, a conception in which the concept of objectivity is exhausted by that of solidarity).[177]

Rorty often describes the very prospect that Orwell finds so frightening as if it were a prospect only someone with Realist scruples should have any reason to shrink from. Thus, for example, Rorty suggests that only a Realist would want to hold that the claim "There are rocks" is implied by the claim "At the ideal end of inquiry, we shall be justified in asserting there are rocks." Rorty concludes:

[T]here seems to be no obvious reason why the progress of the language-game we are playing should have anything in particular to do with the way the rest of the world is.[178]

It is precisely in scenarios which approximate the conditions of a totalitarian scenario that the progress of our language-games for making claims is sure to have nothing to do "with the way the rest of the world is" – as, for example, the progress of the highly ideological language-game for making claims about what was happening in Spain played by British intellectuals during the Spanish Civil War failed to have anything in particular to do with what was happening in Spain. In the scenario depicted in *Nineteen Eighty-Four*, abiding by (some of what pass in that world for) norms of inquiry – such as taking newspaper accounts of events as true – does not improve a person's chances of having beliefs about the world which are right about the world. Following those "norms" leaves a person with a set of beliefs about the world that (can, indeed, quite properly be said to) have nothing "in particular to do with the way the rest of the world is." That is the problem with those (putative) norms of inquiry. In a non-totalitarian scenario – that is, the sort of scenario we generally take ourselves to inhabit – the whole point of abiding by (what Rorty calls) "the rules of language-games" for making claims is that, in abiding by them, we strengthen the probability that the claims we come out with will have something to do with the way the world is. If abiding by those rules did not have this consequence, this would reveal that there was something wrong with those rules. We do occasionally discover that our rules for conducting inquiry do not improve our chances of being right about the world; and when we discover this we modify our rules. In the world of *Nineteen Eighty-Four*, the emergence of a felt need for some modification of the prevailing norms of inquiry is forestalled only through a tremendous expenditure of effort – through systematically falsifying the evidence which constantly threatens to accumulate showing that (what pass in that world for) norms of inquiry do not improve one's chances of being right about the world.

Perhaps the single most perverse feature of Rorty's reading of *Nineteen Eighty-Four* is that, in attributing Rortian doctrines to Orwell, it comes extraordinarily close to attributing to Orwell the very views that Orwell chose to put into O'Brien's mouth.[179] O'Brien, in the following portion of his dialogue with Winston, opens with an argumentative gambit strikingly reminiscent of some of Rorty's own tactics:

> O'Brien smiled faintly. "You are no metaphysician, Winston," he said. "Until this moment you had never considered what is meant by existence. I will put it more precisely. Does the past exist concretely, in space? Is there somewhere or other a place, a world of solid objects, where the past is still happening?"
> "No."
> "Then where does the past exist, if at all?"
> "In records. It is written down."
> "In records. And . . .?"
> "In the mind. In human memories."
> "In memory. Very well, then. We, the Party, control all records, and we control all memories. Then we control the past, do we not?"[180]

O'Brien moves here from an affirmation of the hopelessness of a hyper-Realist, hyper-metaphysical construal of the reality of the past (as "a place, a world of solid objects, where the past is still happening") to an unqualified denial of the idea that (what Orwell calls) "the concept of objective truth" has application to the past. According to O'Brien, the Party controls the past because it controls all mechanisms for achieving an informed consensus about the past. It does not take much of a stretch to formulate O'Brien's view in Rortian vocabulary. O'Brien would, I think, find the following reformulation of his view perfectly congenial:

> There is no past, as it were, "out there" against which to assess the veridicality of memories and records. There is nothing independent of the community's present practices of making claims about the past against which to assess the truth-values of such claims. The "truth" about the past is simply a matter of how the community's memories and records as a whole *cohere* and has nothing to do with how well those memories and records "represent the facts." To seek an answer to the question "What happened at such-and-such a point in the past?" is to seek a *consensus* with one's peers. If a Winston Smith comes along and challenges the coherence or integrity of the community's beliefs, the truth is to be arrived at through a process of *conversation* between Winston and his peers. The "true" story will be the one that *prevails* as the outcome of that conversation.

The convergence between O'Brien's and Rorty's views is striking.[181] Hence the perversity of Rorty's reading of Orwell. For O'Brien's answers to his own questions (for instance, "Where does the past exist, if at all?") in his dialogue with Winston represent Orwell's most resolute attempt "to draw out the logical consequences of totalitarianism" to their ultimate conclusion.

The reason that the Party's version of the story will prevail, in the world of *Nineteen Eighty-Four*, is because the Party has the power to make its story prevail. O'Brien is quite blunt about this. Faced with Winston's recalcitrance, his aim – the aim, indeed, of all conversations conducted in the Ministry of Love – is simply to persuade. O'Brien's interest in pursuing his conversation with Winston is not to uphold certain norms of inquiry and see where they might lead. He is not interested in discriminating between the relative epistemic merits of different kinds of persuasion – in discriminating, for example, between brute persuasion (causing someone to change her beliefs through the application of various kinds of force) and rational persuasion (achieved through an appeal to a shared set of norms of inquiry). Rorty equates O'Brien's impatience (with those who might wish to discriminate too finely between kinds of persuasion) with an impatience he attributes to Orwell with readers who demand that he have an answer to O'Brien:

> On the view of *1984* I am offering, Orwell has no *answer* to O'Brien, and is not interested in giving one ... O'Brien regards the whole idea of being "answered," of exchanging ideas, of reasoning together, as a symptom of weakness.[182]

Rorty is certainly right here about O'Brien. But is he right that Orwell has no *answer* to O'Brien and is not interested in giving one? The position O'Brien defends in his dialogue with Winston is very close to the one that Rorty finds in the following passage from Sartre:

> Tomorrow, after my death, certain people may decide to establish fascism, and the others may be cowardly or miserable enough to let them get away with it. At that moment, fascism will be the truth of man, and so much the worse for us. In reality, things will be as much as man has decided they are.[183]

Rorty glosses the point of this passage as follows:

> This means that when the secret police come, when the torturers violate the innocent, there is nothing to be said to them of the form "There is something within you which you are betraying. Though you embody the practices of a totalitarian society which will endure forever, there is something beyond those practices which condemns you."[184]

Orwell's answer to O'Brien could be put using the very form of words that Rorty here claims is of no use.[185] Orwell would be quite happy to say to O'Brien: "Though you embody the practices of a totalitarian society which will endure forever, there *is* something beyond those practices which condemns you." Indeed, the whole point of the novel is that a resolutely totalitarian society has to expend an enormous amount of energy to hide from itself the fact that there is a world going on behind its back – beyond its practices – which condemns those practices. As we saw in section VII, Orwell characterizes what it is that lies beyond those practices which condemns those practices – and hence must be "tacitly denied" – as "the very existence of external reality."[186] As we have now seen in this section, this characterization does not presuppose any commitment to Realist theses. All it presupposes is an appeal to norms internal to our practices of making claims – norms which, as we have seen, the totalitarian society depicted in Orwell's novel can afford neither completely to disregard nor simply to respect.

IX.   Politics and Literature

Liberalism and totalitarianism are antonyms in Orwell's vocabulary. What Orwell calls the "liberal habit of mind" is the habit of mind that seeks to make one's beliefs beholden to something outside one's ideological preferences. As the epigraphs to this paper aim to display, Orwell's definition of a liberal comes close to being the opposite of Rorty's definition of a liberal ironist. A liberal, for Orwell, is someone who thinks of truth as something outside himself – as something to be discovered – and not as something he can make up as he goes along.[187] One merit of Orwell's definition of a liberal compared to Rorty's (that is, someone who thinks cruelty is the worst thing we do) is that it builds on the original meaning of the term.[188] and its cognates.[189] For Orwell, a liberal is someone who is free to arrive at his own verdict concerning the facts, someone who possesses "a free intelligence" – "a type hated with equal hatred by all the smelly little orthodoxies which are now contending for our souls."[190] The assumption underlying Orwell's conception of what it is to be a liberal (as expressed, for instance, in the epigraph to this paper from Orwell) is one which Rorty denies both on his own and on Orwell's behalf: namely, that there is an intimate connection between freedom and truth. According to Rorty's reading of *Nineteen Eighty-Four*, as we saw in section VI, the only thing which matters to Orwell is that, if you believe something, you can say it without getting hurt: what matters is not what is in fact true, but that you retain the freedom to be able to talk to other people about what seems to you to be true. According to Rorty's Orwell, if we take care of freedom, truth can take care of itself. As we shall see in a moment, this is roughly the opposite of Orwell's view. When "the very concept of objective truth begins to fade out of the world," the conditions not only for truth, but also for freedom, are undermined. The capacity to make true claims and the capacity to exercise freedom of thought and action are, for Orwell, two sides of a single coin. What his novel aims to make manifest is that if reality control and doublethink were ever to be practiced on a systematic scale, the possibility of an individual speaking the truth and the possibility of an individual controlling her own mind would begin simultaneously to fade out of the world. The preservation of freedom and the preservation of truth represent a single indivisible task for Orwell – a task common to literature and politics.

A task common to literature and politics? To Rorty, such a statement is bound to seem to involve a crossing of different kinds of discourse, suited to different purposes, and best able to serve those purposes when kept distinct. He identifies politics with the tasks of responding to the demands of justice and seeking to forge solidarity, thereby preserving and strengthening our traditions and practices. He identifies literature with the tasks of creating new vocabularies and responding to the demands of self-creation, thereby transforming our traditions and practices. In thus understanding each, Rorty understands politics and literature to be responding to incommensurable demands:

> [We should] think of the relation between writers on autonomy and writers on justice as
> being like the relation between two kinds of tools – as little in need of synthesis as are

paintbrushes and crowbars ... The demands of self-creation and human solidarity [are] equally valid, yet forever incommensurable.[191]

Rorty takes any claim to the effect that the tasks of literature and politics might in some way not be incommensurable to involve a tacit commitment to Realism.[192] Rorty approaches Orwell's writings with the assumption that Orwell, too, sees the concerns of literature as incommensurable with those of politics. He assumes that for Orwell, as for himself, each of the following pairs is as little in need of synthesis as are paintbrushes and crowbars: autonomy and justice, the creation of new vocabularies and the maintenance of solidarity, the private activity of saying what you like and the public activity of discovering what others will let you get away with saying.

At the beginning of his diary, Winston inscribes the following greetings to his (presently non-existent) potential readers:

> To the future or to the past, to a time when thought is free, when men are different from one another and do not live alone – to a time when truth exists and what is done cannot be undone:
> From the age of uniformity, from the age of solitude, from the age of Big Brother, from the age of doublethink – greetings![193]

Three central concepts of the novel are linked here: freedom, community, and truth. You have freedom of thought only when you are free to arrive at your own verdict concerning the facts (that is, when you are not held captive by an overriding demand to achieve consensus). Such freedom can be exercised only where there is genuine community (that is, a shared set of coherent norms regulating the practices of most members of the community most of the time).[194] As we saw in the last section, such community can be sustained only where the norms that regulate inquiry are guided not only by a demand to remain in step with one's peers but by a demand to make one's claims concerning how things are answerable to how things are. The point of Winston's complex description of his potential readership is that the possibility of freedom, the possibility of community and the possibility of truth are seen by him to stand or fall together. This contrasts starkly with how Rorty sees the relationship between these three concepts. Rorty takes freedom to be the central theme of Orwell's novel; he takes community to be something anyone can get for free (as long as one lives with other people and does things a sociologist might want to study); and, at least as far as the novel is concerned, Rorty declares truth to be a red herring. This misses not only the point of the above passage, but the point of much of Orwell's writing: you have freedom only if you have genuine community, and you have such community only where disagreements concerning how things are can be resolved in a fashion that takes account of how things are. Rorty is certainly right that the novel seeks to "sensitize" its readers to some of the ways in which "cruelty is a bad thing"; but most of the point of the novel is missed if one misses the internal relation between its concern with cruelty and with the possibilities of freedom, genuine community and truth. The novel seeks to exhibit to how cruelty becomes commonplace in a world in which these three concepts no longer have a secure foothold.[195]

In failing to grasp the connection between these three concepts, Rorty misunderstands what freedom, community, and truth are for Orwell. In the latter half of the above passage, Winston employs three other concepts, equally central to the novel, to specify what prevails in the absence of freedom, community, and truth: uniformity, solitude, and doublethink. Freedom of thought is not – as Rorty suggests – merely the freedom to say or think whatever you happen to feel like saying or thinking at a given moment; it is the freedom fully to exercise one's intellectual resources, to make the most of one's capacity for thought. The fundamental deprivation of freedom suffered by a Party member lies not in the prohibitions on what he is allowed to say, but in the undermining of the conditions which would enable him to develop his capacity to arrive at something worth saying. Once such conditions are undermined, you can say whatever you like, but it will hardly differ from what anyone else says. What Orwell dreads most is not just the abolition of our negative liberty to say and think what we like without fear of interference or harm, but the systematic erosion of our positive liberty – our capacity to do or think or want anything other than what those in control want us to do or think or want.[196] The aim of the Party is to bring about a state of affairs in which everyone is free to do and say what they like and yet perfect harmony and consensus reigns.[197] Hence uniformity. A community of genuinely free people is not simply one in which a high level of *de facto* consensus has been achieved and will be sustained, but one in which vigorous disagreement is welcomed as a spur to refining a shared set of norms for adjudicating and resolving present and future disagreements. In the absence of such practices for resolving disagreement, regardless of how much one talks to others, one will always find oneself sealed off by one's heterodox convictions. Hence solitude. Truth is not simply a compliment we pay to those of our assertions which, as it happens, our peers will let us get away with. Regardless of what our peers say, "The Party invented the airplane" is true if and only if the Party invented the airplane. If you know that the Party did not invent the airplane, but in order to survive (in a world controlled by the Party) you have to believe otherwise, then you must believe to be true what you know to be false.[198] Hence doublethink.

One can be of the view that these three inextricably linked capacities – the capacity to exercise one's freedom, the capacity to participate in a community, and the capacity to distinguish between truth and falsity – are characteristically (perhaps even uniquely) *human* capacities, without thereby subscribing to any Realist theses. In Orwell's vocabulary – and not only Orwell's – fully to possess such capacities is to be fully "human," to exercise them is to express one's "humanity," and to engage in acts that aim to undermine their exercise is to engage in acts of "inhumanity." Rorty does not see how there could be anything worth caring about which is at issue in such talk. But, in failing to see this, he fails to see a central topic of Orwell's novel. One can slant the point in a Rortian direction: one of the things that "our capacity for freedom is essential to our humanity" or "our capacity to distinguish truth from falsity is essential to our humanity" means is that we can form a community with other members of the species *Homo sapiens* only to the extent that those members of our biological species can and do exercise these capacities. (This does not involve any denial of contingency: it is not to say either that there always will or that there must be members of the species which are, in this sense of the term, "human.") The normative notion of humanity implicit in such ways of talking is neither a merely biological nor a mysteriously metaphysical one.[199] Yet it is a notion for which Rorty's reading of Orwell leaves no room. Such a notion is in play in Hynes's and Trilling's talk of Orwell's concern with the preservation of humanity. It is in play in the passage from *Nineteen Eighty-Four* (quoted earlier) in which Winston reflects that, in his world, it is simply by staying sane that one carries on the human heritage.[200] Orwell's original title for *Nineteen Eighty-Four* was *The Last Man in Europe*, meaning the last man capable of free thought, conscious of the absence of community, and able to feel horror at the disregard for truth – that is *the last human being*. O'Brien says to Winston:

If you are a man, Winston, you are the last man. Your kind is extinct: we are the inheritors. Do you understand that you are *alone*? . . . You are the last man. You are the guardian of the human spirit.[201]

If Winston is the last guardian of the human spirit, then that means the human spirit is something that can die out. Orwell is afraid, and writes his novel to awaken us to the fear, that (something he is willing to call) our "humanity" can be allowed to wither away. Such an employment of the vocabulary of "humanity" does not trade – as Rorty fears – on a tacit appeal to the idea that there is something deep inside each of us, some indestructible common human nature, some built-in guarantee of human solidarity that will be with us forever.[202] On the contrary, there is nothing built-in or guaranteed about it. That is precisely what worries Orwell. Precisely because it is fragile, he wants us to appreciate that it is also precious.

Rorty is certainly right that Orwell is not interested in constructing some sort of grand philosophical synthesis of literature and politics. But one can reject the possibility of such a synthesis without drawing the Rortian conclusion that all demands pertinent to the one must be incommensurable with those pertinent to the other. In Orwell's vocabulary, the term "totalitarianism" refers to a set of cultural and intellectual tendencies that render genuine literary and genuine political discourse equally impossible. Orwell sees the possibility of either kind of discourse as tied to the very thing Rorty claims Orwell doesn't care about: "the possibility of truth."[203] Almost as if in reply to Rorty, Orwell writes:

The enemies of intellectual liberty always try to present their case as a plea for discipline versus individualism. The issue truth-versus-untruth is as far as possible kept in the background . . . [T]he controversy over freedom of speech . . . is at the bottom a controversy over the desirability of telling lies. What is really at issue is the right to . . . [speak] as truthfully as is consistent with the ignorance, bias and self-deception from which every observer necessarily suffers . . . [A]ny writer who finds excuses for the persecution [of others] or the falsification of reality, thereby destroys himself as a writer.[204]

Orwell does not understand literature to be concerned, in the first instance, with the task of creating new vocabularies, but rather with the task of *reclaiming our present vocabulary*; and he understands that task to be simultaneously a literary and a political one.[205] Rorty, as we saw in section VI, has difficulty seeing how Orwell's own characterizations of the sort of prose he seeks to write could be anything but mischaracterizations, because Rorty associates the vocabulary Orwell thus employs with a Realist conception of "transparency." Rorty concludes that Orwell's characterizations are mere rhetoric which Orwell himself would be happy to drop. Such characterizations, in fact, are tied to a central concern running throughout the whole of Orwell's work: to articulate a (metaphysically innocuous) conception of the moral and political obligations of the writer – the essayist, the poet and the novelist. The task of literature is to undo the corruption of language. The corruption of language corrupts thought.[206] Combating ugliness, inaccuracy and slovenliness in the use of language constitutes, for Orwell, the "first step towards political regeneration."[207] A speaker or writer who does not inhabit his language thoughtfully – who fails to explore and rejuvenate its potential for the vivid yet precise expression of thought – ends up being carried along by forms of expression that mask the unclarity and untruthfulness of his thought both from himself and from others. To the extent that a speaker or writer only parrots hackneyed phraseology, he fails to be in full control of his own mind. "[H]e has gone some distance towards turning himself into a machine."[208] To the extent that his relation to language is one in which pre-existing phrases remain master of his thought, his mind is one that is easily enslaved and, to some extent, one that already is enslaved:

> A scrupulous writer, in every sentence that he writes, will ask himself at least four questions, thus: What am I trying to say? What words will express it? What image or idiom will make it clearer? Is this image fresh enough to have an effect? . . . But you are not obliged to go to all this trouble. You can shirk it by simply throwing your mind open and letting the ready-made phrases come crowding in. They will construct your sentences for you, to a certain extent – and at need they will perform the important service of partially concealing your meaning even from yourself. It is at this point that the special connection between politics and the debasement of language becomes clear.[209]

In *Nineteen Eighty-Four*, the Party has not failed to grasp the special connection between politics and the debasement of language. Hence all novels are written by novel-writing machines, the ultimate crime against the state is to keep a private diary, and the most pressing item on the Party's political agenda is the perfection and implementation of Newspeak.

Among the ironies in Rorty's attempt to find an apologia for his own doctrines in *Nineteen Eighty-Four*, the most wonderful lies in the fact that the novel – under the topic of Newspeak – contains perhaps the most searching meditation ever written on the potential intellectual implications of replacing one vocabulary with another. (Remarkably, Rorty never comments on this topic in the novel.) One purpose of Newspeak is, of course, the production of vocabulary for new concepts – concepts such as *doublethink*, *thoughtcrime*, and *crimestop* – whose daily employment, as we have seen, is essential to maintaining the practices and beliefs of members of the Party. But the most important purpose of Newspeak is the destruction of concepts. It is, above all, this destructive and purportedly liberating potential of Newspeak that is most emphasized in *The Principles of Newspeak*[210] (the appendix to the novel) and which should most interest Rorty. For what appeals to Rorty about vocabulary replacement as a method of dissolving philosophical problems is that it holds open the promise of making it impossible to formulate old useless problems. The underlying premise is that a problem which can no longer be formulated is a problem that no longer exists.[211] Now such a method, no doubt, can sometimes be liberating. A change of vocabulary usually entails a change in the sorts of things we can talk about. If there are no such things as phlogiston or witches, and if the only purpose formerly served by the vocabulary of "phlogiston" and "witches" was to make talk about such things possible, then nothing would be lost and something gained by junking the vocabulary. Moreover, in changing vocabularies, we can also sometimes effect a change in the sorts of things we want. We may discover more interesting things to care about and divert our attention away from less rewarding inquiries. All of these features of vocabulary replacement appeal to Rorty. But the point of the discussion of Newspeak in *Nineteen Eighty-Four* is that all of these features of vocabulary replacement cut both ways. A change in vocabulary can also deprive us of the ability to talk about some things we might still want to talk about, if only we still could. A sufficiently radical change in the discursive resources available to us might also change *us* so radically that we become no longer able even to want to talk about those things which formerly most occupied our thoughts; and it can deprive us of the discursive resources necessary to explore – and thus reopen – the question whether we are now better off in our present condition, in which we are unable to imagine our previous wants and ineluctably stuck wanting what we now want. The feature of vocabulary replacement that most appeals to Rorty is just the one that most appeals to the Party: it renders certain "modes of thought impossible."[212] Winston's colleague in the Ministry of Truth, who is busy at work on the eleventh and definitive edition of *The Newspeak Dictionary*, explains the chief objective of Newspeak to Winston:

> [O]ur chief job is . . . destroying words . . . It's a beautiful thing, the destruction of words . . . [T]he whole aim of Newspeak is to narrow the range of thought. In the end we shall make thoughtcrime literally impossible, because there will be no words in which to express it . . . The Revolution will be complete when the language is perfect . . . Even the literature of the Party will change. Even the slogans will change . . . The whole climate of thought will be different. In fact there will *be* no thought, as we understand it now. Orthodoxy means not thinking – not needing to think.[213]

Some of the concepts which Newspeak aims to abolish – such as the concept of freedom – are ones for which Rorty himself expresses considerable fondness. But, as we have seen, a good many of the forms of words that Newspeak aims to "destroy" are ones that Rorty's own proposals for vocabulary replacement earmark for destruction, like "objective truth," "objective reality," "essential to humanity," etc. One of the intended consequences of the implementation of Newspeak is to render most of the literature of the past utterly incomprehensible. An unintended consequence of Rorty's proposals, were they to be embraced, would be to render some of the literature of the past – notably Orwell's *Nineteen Eighty-Four* – equally incomprehensible.[214]

Notes

1 *Contingency, Irony and Solidarity* (Cambridge: Cambridge University Press, 1989) [henceforth *CIS*], pp. xv, 183.

2 *The Collected Essays, Journalism and Letters of George Orwell*, edited by Sonia Orwell and Ian Angus (New York: Harcourt Brace Jovanovich, 1968) [henceforth *CEJL*], II, pp. 258–9; III, pp. 88–89.

3 In speaking here of "the *consequences* of [Rorty's] views for the things he thinks we should care about," I am permitting myself to pass quickly over the tricky matter of Rorty's own understanding of the relationship between philosophy and politics. The matter is tricky because, on the one hand, given some of what he himself says, one could be forgiven for thinking that Rorty is committed to the view that his own epistemological doctrines are without political import; on the other hand, it often seems to be crucial to Rorty's manner of advertising the merits of his "liberal ironism" that it not merely involve a conjunction of a politics (liberalism) with a philosophical standpoint (ironism) but that there is some sort of internal relation between the former and the latter – that if you are concerned, above all, with promoting the ends of liberalism, then you have good reason to embrace Rorty's ironism. One could therefore be forgiven for concluding that there is a tension in Rorty's understanding of the relation between philosophy and politics: a tension between his willingness to recommend his own philosophical views on political grounds and his willingness to insist that philosophical controversy about the nature of truth and knowledge is a fruitless activity which can have no significant political consequences. Rorty can often be found saying the following sort of thing:

> I do not think that any large view of the form . . . "truth is really . . ." – any large philosophical claim – *could* discredit political beliefs and aspirations . . . I do not think it

is psychologically possible to give up on political liberalism on the basis of a philosophical view about the nature of man or truth or history . . . One would have to be very odd to change one's politics because one had become convinced, for example, that a coherence theory of truth was preferable to a correspondence theory. (*CIS*, pp. 182–3)

How can this be squared with Rorty's equally frequent urging that his own brand of anti-representationalist ironism best suits the needs and aims of the friends of liberal democracy? Rorty's most careful answer to this question runs as follows:

Although I do not think that there is an inferential path that leads from . . . antirepresen-tationalist views of truth and knowledge . . . [such as those common to Nietzsche, James and Dewey] either to democracy or antidemocracy, I do think there is a plausible inference from democratic convictions to such a view. [If] your devotion to democracy is . . . wholehearted, then you will welcome the utilitarian and pragmatist claim that we have no will to truth distinct from the will to happiness. ("Pragmatism as Romantic Polytheism", in *The Revival of Pragmatism*, edited by Morris Dickstein (Durham, *NC*: Duke University Press, 1998); p. 27)

Rorty's understanding of the relation between philosophy and politics allows that – even though no sensible person would change his politics because of the outcome of a metaphysical discussion, and even though there are no strict entailment relations between this or that particular metaphysical doctrine about the nature of truth and knowledge and this or that particular brand of politics – there are particular philosophical views that make for a more *congenial fit* with this brand of politics over that one. Thus, for example, if you believe that "we can have a knowledge of an 'objective' ranking of human needs" then you are at risk of believing that you might be justified in overruling the result of democratic consensus (see ibid., p. 27); and, conversely, if you believe that there is no way things are independently of what your peers will let you get away with saying about how things are, then you are less likely to be led politically astray by your metaphysical convictions. Rorty is thus able to hold without contradiction that, although his own philosophical views do not entail a justification of liberal democracy, they do make the world marginally safer for liberal democracy.

(This way of reconciling the apparent tension in Rorty's writings with regard to the relation between politics and philosophy is tendentious in that it assumes that Rorty's own "views" amount to substantial philosophical views – something that Rorty himself is sometimes at pains to deny. It is the burden of section III of this paper to justify this assumption.) Do Rorty's views make the world safer for democracy? Three central aims of this paper are (1) to challenge Rorty's claim that "antirepresentationalist views of truth and knowledge" make for a congenial fit with a liberal democratic politics, (2) to show that (contrary to Rorty's reading of Orwell) Orwell thought that views such as Rorty's made for a *very* congenial fit with a totalitarian politics, and (3) to argue that seeing why Orwell thought this helps one to see what is misguided in Rorty's own views of truth and knowledge.

4   Dr. Freud tells us that one of the most characteristic features of obsessives is that they passionately and repeatedly insist that they are free of the particular form of obsession from which they suffer. Thus, for a given subject S and subject matter X, the psychoana-lytic measure of S's obsession with X lies not in the extent to which S is prepared to disavow an interest in X, but in the extent to which S is actually capable of ceasing to think about X and capable of getting on with thinking about other things. The classical obsessive is someone who, despite his protestations to the contrary, is unable to cease viewing everything in terms of certain ideas which he insists are of no interest to him. Hence Freud remarks: "Obsessional neurosis is shown in the patient's being occupied with thoughts in which he is in fact not interested . . . The thoughts may be senseless in themselves, or merely a matter of indifference to the subject [yet] . . . he is obliged to

brood and speculate as though it were a question of his most important and vital problems" (*Introductory Lectures on Psychoanalysis*, New York: Norton, 1966; p. 258).

5   To claim that someone suffers from epistemologism, so defined, is not yet to attribute a commitment to any particular doctrine(s) to him. Individuals with very different first-order philosophical commitments may equally suffer from epistemologism.

6   See, e.g., *CIS*, p. 9.

7   *CIS*, p. 9.

8   I find the term 'vocabulary' to be one of the slipperier terms in Rorty's vocabulary. Sometimes it seems to mean (nothing more than) *vocabulary* – i.e. words or sequences of words. Sometimes it seems to mean (something more like) *language* or *linguistic framework* – a terminology plus a set of constraints on its employment which involve doxastic and inferential commitments. Sometimes it seems to mean (something more like) *theory* or *doctrine* – so that more than one of them can be formulated within a single vocabulary in either the first or second sense of 'vocabulary.' And sometimes its seems to mean (something much more comprehensive like) *world view* or *form of life* – a closed system of thought or practice for which no non-circular form of justification is available. Henceforth, when the term occurs in scarequotes it is meant to echo Rorty's own equivocal usage; and when it occurs without scarequotes it should be understood in the first, least committal sense. Thus in some contexts in which Rorty speaks of vocabularies, I will prefer to speak of *doctrines*, partly to avoid equivocation between the first and third senses of the term 'vocabulary' and partly to facilitate the isolation of cases in which two individuals (e.g. Orwell and the Realist) might share a vocabulary without having any metaphysical commitments in common.

9   See "Solidarity or Objectivity" (in *Objectivity, Relativism and Truth*; Cambridge: Cambridge University Press, 1991 [henceforth *ORT*]), *passim*, but especially p. 31, for a good example of a very broad construal of Realism.

10 I am indebted here to the account of genre elaborated by Stanley Cavell in *Pursuits of Happiness* (Cambridge, MA: Harvard University Press, 1981); see especially pp. 27–30.

11 I will place 'Realism' in capital letters throughout to indicate that, as employed here, it signifies a genre of *metaphysical doctrine*. It is thus not to be equated with the use of the term 'realism' by philosophers (such as Cora Diamond, John McDowell, Hilary Putnam, Ludwig Wittgenstein) who wish to refer to the possibility of a perspective on our practices that is neither Realist nor anti-Realist. For further discussion of these two contrasting uses of the term, see my "On Wittgenstein's Philosophy of Mathematics", *The Proceedings of the Aristotelian Society* (Fall, 1996).

12 A "doctrine," as I shall use the term in this paper, consists of a combination of philosophical theses.

13 A much trickier question is whether any of (1)–(8), each taken simply as a paragraph-long series of statements, is by itself *sufficient* to constitute an expression of Realism. Rorty, I think, would view a willingness to come out with anything that sounded at all like any of these eight sequences of words as a sufficient basis on which not only to charge but to convict someone of Realism. I would certainly agree that a speaker who is inclined to call on any one of these eight paragraph-long sequences of words is *very likely* to be guilty as charged. But, on my view, the assessment of such a charge must await an examination of the wider context in which the sentences occur. As I do not agree with Rorty that Realism is helpfully thought of as a matter of employing certain vocabulary, I do not take the occurrence of certain forms of words in a statement ever to constitute a sufficient condition for categorizing a statement as an expression of Realism. What makes someone a Realist, on my view, is not merely a proclivity to call upon certain words or phrases or sentences but rather what he wants to (be able to) mean by the words or phrases or sentences which he calls upon.

14 For that purpose, many more than eight theses would be required (and several of the ones distinguished here would, in principle, be dispensable since they are limiting cases of more

general theses). But my partial reconstruction of Rorty's employment of the term 'Realism' fails, by design, to capture a further aspect of Rorty's employment of the term. Rorty, as indicated in the previous note, sometimes talks as if 'Realism' denoted a category of doctrines which could be individuated by the vocabulary used to formulate them. This way of construing Realism encourages Rorty to view most everyday talk about "truth," "objectivity," or "reality" as itself caught up in Realist metaphysics. Since such a construal begs most of the questions with which this paper will be concerned, I shall construe 'Realism', for the purposes of this paper, as a label for a genre of metaphysical *theses*.

15   In formulating (1), I have tried to stay as close as possible to locutions that Rorty himself employs when characterizing the thesis in question. Hence the (putatively) Kantian terminology. Rorty is, no doubt, right in thinking that a great many philosophers who discuss (1), whether they applaud or deplore it, assume that (1) is a Kantian thesis. Rorty himself shares this view. I do not. Kant himself rarely speaks of "things *as* they are in themselves" (though Kemp Smith's translation regrettably sometimes does where Kant does not), but rather usually only of things-in-themselves *simpliciter*. The most generic distinction which this terminology marks in Kant is between the "thing-in-itself" and the "thing-in-its-relation-to-other-things." The distinction between appearance and reality is a special case of this more general distinction. In each case, the "thing-in-itself" is *one and the same thing* as the "thing-in-its-relation-to-other-things," only considered under an abstraction. The nature and severity of the abstraction varies depending upon the issue under discussion. Even when the terminology marks a distinction between the "thing-in-itself" and the thing *as it appears to a knower*, Kant will, depending upon the issue at hand, abstract more or less severely from the conditions under which the thing is known. In some contexts in *The Critique of Pure Reason* the contrast is one that is drawn within our present experience (e.g., the contrast between the rain and the rainbow in A45–6), in other contexts the contrast is between our present and our possible future knowledge of objects (e.g., between the objects of scientific investigation as they are presently known to us and as they might someday, in principle, be knowable to us), and in yet other contexts, notoriously, the abstraction is yet more severe. But when the abstraction is of the severest possible sort – i.e., when the thing-in-itself is identified with the object of knowledge considered utterly apart from any possible conditions of knowledge – then Kant's point is precisely that the thing, so considered, "is nothing to us," that such a notion of a "thing" is (as he puts it) "without *Sinn* or *Bedeutung*." Kant thus, in effect, rejects (1). He denies that we can assign sense or reference to the notion of a reality which is utterly screened off from us by the conditions of knowledge. Kant was admittedly not always resolutely clear about this issue in the A edition of *The Critique of Pure Reason*; but his B edition revisions of the chapter on "The Ground of the Distinction of All Objects in General into Phenomena and Noumena" are directed precisely at resolutely redressing this unclarity. He there refers to the notion of the thing-in-itself considered utterly apart from our faculty of knowledge as "the negative concept of the noumenon" in order to distinguish it from "the positive concept of the noumenon." And he insists that the former of these notions is the only notion of a noumenon which has any role to play within his theoretical philosophy. (It is only in the context of characterizing the content of the positive concept of the noumenon – whose content derives entirely from the doctrines of Kant's *practical* philosophy B that it remains permissible, in the light of the B edition revisions, to employ the locution "things *as* they are in themselves.") Within the theoretical philosophy, the only role that the notion of a noumenon has to play is to signal the emptiness of such a notion and to warn against the philosophical confusion of thinking that such a notion can be put to work in theoretical philosophy. It is, as Kant puts it, an "entirely *indeterminate* concept," and the confusion results when one "is misled into treating this entirely *indeterminate* concept . . . as if it were a *determinate* concept of an entity that allows of being known in a certain [purely intelligible – i.e., humanly impossible] manner" (B307).

   All subsequent employments of (apparently) Kantian terminology in this paper are consequently to be understood as echoing Rortian terminology for referring to (1), and should not be taken to represent an endorsement of Rorty's reading of Kant.

16 (1) and (2) represent two different ways of attempting to satisfy the philosophical desire to give content to an idea of *the way the world is from no particular point of view*. (1) and (2) are, however, mutually inconsistent. (1) affirms that the ultimate nature of reality is inherently unknowable; (2) that it is, at least in principle, knowable. (2) proceeds from the assumption that the idea – which is central to (1) – of *the way the world is apart from any description* makes no sense. (2) identifies the overcoming of the subjectivity of human knowledge with the attainment of the minimally perspectival point of view afforded by a metaphysically preferred description of the way the world is. Rorty often weaves back and forth between (1) and (2) as if they were equivalent. This is forgivable, in as much as the writings of Realists often hover indeterminately between these two theses. I take the trouble to distinguish (1) from (2) here because I think Rorty recoils from each in an apparently distinct direction – see (1') and (2') below – directions which can be usefully thought of as movements away from (1) and (2) respectively.

17 Thus far, what we have is a version of (2) formulated as a thesis about *moral* reality. I have formulated (4) in this way because it figures in Rorty's writing largely as an application of (2) – an application made available by the assumption that there is such a thing as an "independent moral reality." The remainder of (4) – the claim that there are no hard cases – could, in principle, be treated as an independent thesis (and motivated on other sorts of grounds). I have treated it here as part of a single complex thesis concerning the objects of moral knowledge because this complex thesis figures prominently as a unitary target in Rorty's writing.

18 (3) and (4) are both versions of (2). They are mutually inconsistent. (3) affirms that a metaphysically privileged description of reality will not require moral concepts; (4) affirms that it will.

19 Unlike the preceding seven, thesis (8) figures in Rorty's thought largely as an implicit target. My reconstruction here of what Rorty takes a Realist theory of literature to be is somewhat speculative. Nevertheless, it is clear from Rorty's writings that he takes Realists to be committed to a theory of literature which vastly underrates the potential contribution of poets and novelists to furthering the ends of inquiry, and that he takes his own ironist theory of literature to be a consequence of its rejection.

20 The phrase "philosophy gone wrong" fudges over a disagreement, in so far as it is Rorty's view that these theses should be rejected on the ground that they have failed to prove *useful*, whereas it is my view that a proper ground for a rejection of these "theses" involves coming to recognize each of them as only an *apparent* thesis. (For a brief overview of my differences with Rorty on this point, see my introduction to Hilary Putnam's *Words and Life*, Cambridge, MA: Harvard University Press, 1994; pp. xxiv–xxxii.) But this dimension of my differences with Rorty will not play a weight-bearing role in the argument of this paper.

21 I am assuming here that there is a distinction worth drawing between *showing why* certain apparently compulsory philosophical problems are not compulsory and merely *declaring that* they are not compulsory.

22 I am assuming here that there is a distinction worth drawing between helping someone come to see what is wrong with a question that he thinks both perfectly intelligible and intellectually compulsory and merely encouraging him to stop thinking about the question and advertising the relative advantages of changing the subject of conversation. (I explore this distinction, in the context of contrasting Rorty's and Putnam's respective readings of later Wittgenstein, in my introduction to Hilary Putnam's *Realism With a Human Face*, Cambridge, MA: Harvard University Press, 1990; pp. xxxiv–lvii.)

23 Rorty defines the "the desire for objectivity" as the desire to describe oneself "as standing in immediate relation to a nonhuman reality" (*ORT*, p. 21).

24 "Insofar as a person is seeking solidarity, she does not ask about the relation between

the practices of the chosen community and something outside that community" (*ORT*, p. 21).

25   On the grounds that the only alternative is to opt for some version of (1) or (2). See "Pragmatism, Davidson and Truth", *ORT*, pp. 126–150, for Rorty's most developed version of this argument.

26   "[T]he terms 'warranted', 'rational acceptability', etc., will always invite the question 'to whom'? This question will always lead us back, it seems to me, to the answer '*Us*, at our best'" ("Putnam and the Relativist Menace", *Journal of Philosophy*, Vol. XC, No. 9, September 1993 [henceforth *PRM*], p. 453). I will return to this passage in section VIII of this paper.

27   See, e.g., *PRM*, p. 449.

28   Here are some samples of how Rorty puts this point:

> For pragmatists, the desire for objectivity is . . . simply the desire for as much intersubjective agreement as possible, the desire to extend the reference of "us" as far as we can. (*ORT*, p. 23)

> [We pragmatists] deny that the search for objective truth is a search for correspondence to reality, and urge that it be seen instead as a search for the widest possible intersubjective agreement. ("Does Academic Freedom have Philosophical Presuppositions?", *Academe*, November–December 1994 [henceforth *DAFHPP*], p. 52)

> "Truth" only sounds like the name of a goal if . . . progress towards truth is explicated by reference to a metaphysical picture . . . Without that picture, to say that truth is our goal is merely to say something like "we hope to justify our belief to as many and as large audiences as possible". ("Is Truth a Goal of Inquiry?: Davidson vs. Wright", *Philosophical Quarterly*, Vol. 45, No. 180 [henceforth *ITGE*], p. 298)

29   See, e.g., *ORT*, p. 23. I am attempting, under the heading of (1'), both to parrot various things Rorty himself says (about why we should substitute solidarity for objectivity) and to formulate something that has the appearance of being a single thesis. But, it should be noted, the following are distinct theses:

(a)   There are only causal – and no normative – word–world relations.

(b)   Justification is a matter of acceptability to my peers.

(c)   Justification is a sociological matter.

Rorty sometimes moves between these theses as if (a) entailed (b) and (b) entailed (c). But one can affirm (a) and deny (b) (as do, e.g., certain reliabilists); and one can affirm (b) and deny (c) (by insisting that justification is a matter of what my peers *ought* to accept rather than what they, as a matter of sociological fact, do accept). The latter of these two slides will be taken up in section VIII of this paper.

30   The preceding sentences are largely a paraphrase of *CIS*, pp. 4–5. The gist of (2') is succinctly summarized by Rorty somewhat later on in *CIS* as follows: "[S]ince truth is a property of sentences, since sentences are dependent for their existence upon vocabularies, and since vocabularies are made by human beings, so are truths" (*CIS*, p. 21). I have presented (1') and (2') as if they were distinct theses. I do not believe this is the case – they are, as section VIII aims to show, different expressions of a single confusion.

31   This last way of formulating Rorty's view I owe to Robert Brandom's contribution to this volume. It should be noted, in this connection, that it is crucial to (3'), as formulated here, that it deny that the success of a vocabulary is ever due to its *representational adequacy*. Brandom, in his contribution, suggests that Rorty's attack on representationalism is much

more limited in scope. In a footnote, Brandom says that it is *not* to Rorty's purpose to claim . . .

> that there is no point in coming up with some more limited theoretical notion of representation of things that applies to some vocabularies but not others, specifying a more specific purpose to which some but not all can be turned . . . [S]uch a notion is not Rorty's target, for it does not aspire to being a metavocabulary – a vocabulary for talking about all vocabularies, the essence of what being a vocabulary is. (p. 29n)

Rorty's target, Brandom suggests, is not the very notion of representation – as my formulation of (3′) would have it – but rather the more ambitious philosophical idea that the representational idiom constitutes an appropriate *metavocabulary* – a vocabulary which enables us to assess the adequacy of all other vocabularies (apart from any consideration of the purposes those vocabularies are intended to serve). Thus, according to Brandom, Rorty objects to representation serving as a philosophical master-concept, but not to its serving, if rendered appropriately hygienic, as a means of articulating *one dimension* along which the adequacy of a vocabulary, relative to certain purposes, might be assessed.

Brandom, it seems to me, underestimates Rorty's hostility to the very idea of representation. (See, e.g., all of Part II of *Philosophy and the Mirror of Nature*, and, in particular, Rorty's prospective and retrospective summaries on p. 11 and pp. 371–2 of the moral of Part II.) But even if one dismisses his numerous hostile remarks about the very idea of representation as an overstatement of his position, Rorty, as far as I can see, is in no position to make room for a "more limited notion of representation," along the lines that Brandom proposes, as long as he remains committed to theses such as (1′) and (2′).

Brandom is certainly right that a representationalist metavocabulary is one of Rorty's targets. Indeed, Rorty, in *CIS*, occasionally seems to suggest that *the very idea of a metavocabulary* – a vocabulary which furnishes criteria for assessing the adequacy of all other vocabularies – is something which every good ironist, if she is to remain faithful to her credo, must oppose. It seems to me, though, that one might be forgiven if Rorty's frequent hyper-pragmatist invocations of concepts such as *coping* or *satisfaction* led one to conclude that Rorty's aim, contrary to his own ironist strictures, was precisely to substitute one metavocabulary for another – an instrumentalist for a representationalist one.

32   If Rorty were allowed to speak for himself, in formulating this thesis, he would, no doubt, along the way, work in remarks such as the following:

> Different vocabularies allow us to formulate different truths. Our needs and interests are extremely diverse in nature and vary over time and with circumstances. Which vocabulary we should adopt depends upon which needs and interests we seek to address. Since some vocabularies are better adapted to one purpose than another, we should be linguistic pluralists, alternating back and forth, inventing and discarding vocabularies as best suits our purposes.

I have omitted such remarks from my summary of (3′) because (under a suitable interpretation) I have no quarrel with them. Indeed, I think they are largely truisms which can easily be separated from the features (of this region) of Rorty's thought that I take to be a philosophical overreaction to the failure of Realism.

33   This claim figures in Rorty's writings, for the most part, simply as an application of (1′). It will prove useful in what follows, however, to isolate it as an independent thesis.

34   I note in passing – to avoid unnecessary confusion – that someone like Karl Popper meant something close to the opposite (of what Rorty does) by the term 'historicism': i.e. the thesis that historical processes are governed by laws and cannot be influenced by human agency. I will henceforth only employ the term in Rorty's sense.

35   I take what I have said so far (under a suitable interpretation) to be virtually platitudinous. It is the subsequent glosses on what it means to say such stories are "situated" and "constructed" that render (5′) metaphysically contentious.

36   This final sentence is simply an application of the doctrines of (1') and (4') to the case of history. I have attempted here to characterize what I understand Rorty to mean by the expression "historicism." There is a less committal use of the term, in which people (e.g., Quentin Skinner or Charles Taylor) seek to employ the term, as Rorty does, to signify a thesis opposed to (5), but without intending thereby to commit themselves to theses such as (1') or (4').

37   This paragraph is largely a paraphrase of *CIS*, pp. xiv–xv.

38   The two components of this definition of a liberal are quite independent: (i) a liberal is someone who thinks that cruelty is the worst thing we can do and (ii) a liberal is someone who thinks that 'morality' should not be taken to denote anything other than our abilities to notice, identify with, and alleviate pain and humiliation. I use the complex term 'Rortian liberalism' to refer to the conjunction of (i) and (ii). But one can affirm (i) and deny (ii). Indeed, as far as I can see, (i) is in principle compatible with militantly Realist versions of theses such as (4) and (6). Moreover, Rorty himself often suggests that it suffices for someone to hold (i) to count as a liberal by his lights. Thus, whenever I speak in the paper of "Rorty's definition of a liberal" I mean only to refer to (i).

39   This paragraph is, in large part, a paraphrase of remarks from *CIS*, pp. xv, 189, 193, 195.

40   This paragraph has been constructed by paraphrasing remarks from *CIS*, pp. xv, 73–4, 174.

41   I do not mean hereby to suggest that Rorty himself anywhere explicitly claims that the rejection of the Realist member of any such pair entails the affirmation of its Rortian counterpart, but only that his arguments often implicitly presuppose such an entailment.

42   (1') is implicitly motivated by a proposal for jettisoning talk of "objective truth," "objective reality," etc.; (2') by a proposal for jettisoning talk of "the way the world is," "independent facts," etc.; (3') by a proposal for jettisoning talk of "value neutrality," "freedom from bias," etc.; (4') by a proposal for jettisoning talk of "moral facts," "moral reality," etc.; (5') by a proposal for jettisoning talk of "the immutability of history"; (6') by a proposal for jettisoning talk of a "unifying vision," "grand philosophical synthesis," etc.; (7') by a proposal for jettisoning talk of what is "essential to humanity," talk of "rights," and other sorts of talk indulged in by proponents of (7); (8') by a proposal for jettisoning talk of "transparency to fact," "representational verisimilitude," etc.

43   Though he no longer *requires* such vocabulary, a Rortian may continue to employ it in either of two ways: (i) he may continue to employ it as a means of warding off the enemy (e.g., by saying things like "We should replace objectivity with solidarity"), (ii) he may interpolate a revisionist account of its meaning which enables him to continue to speak with the vulgar (by declaring things like "For the pragmatist, 'knowledge' and 'truth' are simply compliments paid to beliefs we think well justified.").

44   Or more precisely: whose availability depends upon the availability of concepts traditionally expressed by means of that vocabulary.

45   Of course, if there are less drastic and yet equally effective ways of disarming Realism, then there are *no* good reasons to jettison the vocabulary. This is in fact my view. But since my aim in this paper is not to disarm Realism, I shall not argue the point here.

46   Bernard Crick, *George Orwell* (Boston: Little, Brown, 1980), p. xx.

47   Such as the encounter between A. J. Ayer and Orwell which led Ayer to conclude that Orwell "had no interest whatsoever in philosophy" and Orwell to conclude that Ayer ought to "interest himself a bit more in the future of humanity" (Ibid, p. 325).

48   *CIS*, p. 173n.

49   "[Orwell] had no more taste for [philosophical] arguments, or skill at constructing them, than did Nabokov" (*CIS*, p. 173).

50   Orwell kept himself alive for most of his life by furiously writing weekly newspaper columns, editorials, and book reviews, often lifting prose from one piece into another. This led to an extraordinary amount of (often *verbatim*) repetition in his corpus of those thoughts he cared most about. Versions of (1″)–(8″) occur repeatedly in his journalism and – since

he rewrote the journalism into polished meditative essays and transposed whole passages from the essays into the novels – they all recur in his essays and novels.

51 In Wittgenstein's sense of "ordinary" – where *ordinary* contrasts (not with *literary* or *metaphorical* or *scientific* or *technical*, but) with *metaphysical*. In this sense of "ordinary," the uses to which poetry and science put language are as much part of ordinary language as calling your cat or asking someone to pass the butter.

52 One way of putting the topic of this paper would be to say that it is about Rorty's inability – his professed allegiance to the thought of later Wittgenstein notwithstanding – to exercise the sort of discernment that Wittgenstein's later work is centrally concerned to impart: an ability to discern between ordinary and metaphysical *uses* of language, between uses of language in which words are at work in their context of use (expressing a thought) and ones in which language is on holiday (only apparently expressing a thought). Oblivious to the discriminations of use which such discernment discloses – oblivious to how one possibly could do what Wittgenstein says he seeks to do ("bring words back from their metaphysical to their everyday use") for *these* words – Rorty's anti-metaphysical response bears the characteristic earmark of an *anti-metaphysical metaphysics* (be it Berkeley's, Hume's, Carnap's, or Derrida's): a recoil from the ordinary. In attacking (not the *use* that a philosopher makes of his words, but) *the words*, urging us to throw the words themselves away, Rorty would have us destroy (not only metaphysical houses of cards, but) precious everyday discursive resources and along with them the concepts (and hence the availability of the thoughts) which they enable us to express.

53 I would be happy to characterize some of these remarks – e.g. (2″) – as *grammatical remarks*. But that is a story that must await another occasion.

54 Rorty contrasts Orwell's two major novels, *Animal Farm* and *Nineteen Eighty-Four*, with Vladimir Nabokov's *Lolita* and *Pale Fire*. He claims that Nabokov's – unlike Orwell's – novels "will survive as long as there are gifted, obsessive readers who identify themselves with" the respective protagonists of each of the novels. Rorty, in this connection, also quotes with approval Irving Howe's remark that Orwell is one of those writers "who live most significantly for their own age" (*CIS*, p. 169). Rorty's point in contrasting Orwell with Nabokov is that as certain historical events recede into the past, readers of Orwell's novels will be comparatively less able to identify themselves with Winston Smith et al. Similarly, Rorty's point in adducing Howe's remark is that Orwell's work is not primarily concerned with "enduring problems." Both of these points are tied to Rorty's assumption that the major aim – or at least one of the major aims – of *Nineteen Eighty-Four* is to redescribe Soviet Russia. This assumption will be taken up in the later section on Orwell on Totalitarianism.

55 *CIS*, p. 171.

56 Quoted by Rorty in *CIS*, p. 172. Trilling's passage in context runs as follows:

> George Orwell's . . . *Nineteen Eighty-Four* confirms its author in the special, honorable place he holds in our intellectual life. Orwell's native gifts are perhaps not of the transcendent kind; they have their roots in a quality of mind that is as frequent as it is modest. This quality may be described as a sort of moral centrality, a directness of relation to moral – and political – fact, and it is so far from being frequent in our time that Orwell's possession of it seems nearly unique. Orwell is an intellectual to his fingertips, but he is far removed from both the Continental and the American type of intellectual . . . He is indifferent to the allurements of elaborate theory . . . The medium of his thought is common sense, and his commitment to intellect is fortified by an old-fashioned faith that the truth can be got at, that we can, if we actually want to, see the object as it really is. ("Orwell on the Future", in *Speaking of Literature and Society*; New York: Harcourt Brace Jovanovich [henceforth *SLS*]; p. 249)

Trilling says two things here which hardly cohere with Rorty's Realist construal of this passage. Notice, first, that Rorty has cut the passage off in mid-sentence. What Trilling goes on to say in that sentence about the quality of "directness of relation to moral – and political – fact" which Orwell's writing possesses is that "in our time . . . Orwell's possession of it seems nearly unique." This hardly accords with Rorty's hypothesis that the phrase "directness of relation to moral – and political – fact" denotes the kind of relation to fact that, on a Realist account, all veridical instances of moral and political thought possess. Notice, second, that Trilling goes on to make the very point which Rorty himself adduces as a ground for thinking that Orwell is not a Realist: "[H]e is far removed from both the Continental and the American type of intellectual . . . He is indifferent to the allurements of elaborate theory." The feature of Orwell's sensibility that Trilling is struggling to characterize in the above passage is beautifully captured in the following remark by Timothy Garton Ash:

> The unmistakable Orwell voice is one of defiant unvarnished honesty, of the plain man bluntly telling things as they are . . . Orwell was an inveterate diarist, note-taker and list-maker . . . He loved what the English poet Craig Raine memorably calls "the beauty of facts." If Orwell had a God, it was Kipling's "the God of Things as They are". (*New York Review of Books*, October 22, 1998)

Notice: Garton Ash, in seeking to characterize "this quality Orwell's writing possesses" is led (as was Trilling) to call upon forms of words, in this case borrowed from the poetry of Raine and Kipling, that Rorty surely would be unable to hear as anything other than frothing endorsements of a Realist metaphysics.

57 Rorty passes over in silence Trilling's remarks later in the same essay (e.g., "to read *Nineteen Eighty-Four* as an attack on Soviet communism . . . and as nothing else would be to misunderstand the book's aim"; *SLS*, p. 253) which clearly indicate that he does not share Rorty's assumptions concerning what the novel aims to "redescribe." For some indication of what might be moving Trilling in these remarks, see notes 116, 120 and 133.

58 Specifically, a conception which involves a commitment to some version of (4).

59 *CIS*, p. 172.

60 Ibid.

61 The occurrences of these remarks which Rorty cites are from *CEJL*, I, p. 7. These themes are sounded repeatedly throughout Orwell's corpus.

62 Quoted on *CIS*, p. 172.

63 Though, as we shall see, Rorty does not take the passage to be as pivotal as he imagines someone who favors the "realist" reading of *Nineteen Eighty-Four* must.

64 In particular, (2) and (4).

65 Quoted by Rorty, *CIS*, p. 173n. The passage is from Hynes's "Introduction" to *Twentieth Century Interpretations of 1984*, edited by Samuel Hynes (Englewood Cliffs, NJ: Prentice-Hall, 1971), p. 19. Rorty, I surmise, takes the final two sentences of the passage to rest on theses (5) and (7).

66 Such vocabulary also occurs in the article by Trilling that Rorty cites. Trilling says that the citizens of Orwell's dystopia "might actually gain a life of security, adjustment, and fun, but only at the cost of their spiritual freedom, which is to say, of their humanity" (*SLS*, p. 251).

67 *CIS*, p. 187.

68 *CIS*, p. 173.

69 Such as (2), (4) and (8).

70 Rorty embellishes, however, on what these commentators actually say. Thus, for example, in the above passage, Rorty speaks of "plain epistemological and metaphysical facts," assuming that commentators on Orwell, such as Trilling, when speaking of "plain facts" must have *epistemological* or *metaphysical* facts in mind. This seems to me an extraordinary assumption. (Indeed, the notion of a "plain metaphysical fact" strikes me as an oxymoron.)

71 Consider the following six examples drawn from the above passage: (a) that one can distinguish between transparent and untransparent prose, (b) that a fondness for the latter

sort of prose can be a function of clouded vision, (c) that such clouding can be caused by one's personality, (d) that people try to evade the plain facts, (e) that truth is independent of human minds and languages, (f) that gravitation is not relative to any human mode of thought. Rorty is certainly right that most admirers of Orwell – including Trilling and Hynes – say things, on Orwell's behalf, which sound very much like (a)–(f). Must the motivation to (a)–(f) be understood in terms of a commitment to some subset of (1)–(8)? From the rest of Rorty's discussion, it is plain that he takes the motivation on the part of commentators such as Trilling and Hynes to (a) and (b) to be a commitment to some version of (8), the motivation to (c) to be a commitment to some version of (3), and the motivation to (d), (e) and (f) to be a commitment to some version of (1) or (2).

72 "I do not think there are any plain moral facts out there in the world, nor any truths independent of language ... So I want to offer a different reading of Orwell" (*CIS*, p. 173).

73 I take it that, in advancing their readings of Orwell, Trilling and Hynes are not concerned with philosophical controversies such as the one (in which Rorty himself is embroiled) between Realism and Rortianism, and are hence untroubled by the worry that their formulations of Orwellian thoughts could be construed (by someone with epistemologistic obsessions) as enunciations of Realist theses. But this presupposes the claim argued for in sections VII–IX: that the vocabulary which the Realist likes to employ is put by Orwell (and, following him, by his admirers) to other discursive ends.

74 Peter Van Inwagen, *Metaphysics* (Boulder, CO: Westview, 1993), pp. 56, 59, 69.

75 Rorty never claims in so many words that, in the focal passage, Winston's thoughts reflect his commitment to Realist theses. But what Rorty does say about the focal passage would appear to commit him to such a view. Rorty says that if one identifies the sentiments expressed in the focal passage with those of the author one will inevitably be led to conclude, mistakenly, that Orwell is a Realist. It is very hard to see how to reconcile this commitment with Rorty's assertion that he believes Orwell's work to be free of metaphysical concerns. The only apparent route open to Rorty to effect such a reconciliation would be for him to claim that the focal passage appears to support a Realist construal *only when considered apart from the context of the novel as a whole*. But this route is blocked: Rorty cannot afford to make room for an innocent construal of Winston's remarks. Rorty's entire discussion of "Orwell's admirers" turns on the premise that one can identify Realist commitments by attending to the vocabulary a speaker employs. If one affirms that Winston is not here giving voice to Realist theses, then this leaves the door wide open to a reading of Trilling and Hynes according to which, in echoing Winston, they are not either. Indeed, the argument of sections VII and IX of this paper could easily be adapted to mount an argument to the effect that the remarks of Trilling and Hynes about Orwell's novel appear to support a Realist construal only when considered apart from the context of the reading of the novel that each of them seeks to offer.

76 In this respect, as readers of Orwell, Van Inwagen and Rorty are much closer to each other than either is to Trilling or Hynes. My own (Wittgensteinian) view of the structure of this controversy – for which I will not argue in this paper – is nicely summed up by *Philosophical Investigations*, 402:

> [W]e are tempted to say that our way of speaking does not describe the facts as they really are ... As if the form of expression were saying something false even when the proposition *faute de mieux* asserted something true.
>
> For *this* is what disputes between Idealists, Solipsists and Realists look like. The one party attack the normal form of expression as if they were attacking a statement; the others defend, as if they were stating facts recognized by every reasonable human being. (Oxford: Blackwell, 1953)

Rorty fully yields to the temptation "to say that our way of speaking does not describe the facts as they really are." For he, like Van Inwagen, thinks that in order for our ordinary ways of speaking to be on to "the facts as they really are" they would require a metaphysical underpinning. Rorty, in seeking to deny the need for such an underpinning, feels obliged to *attack* our normal modes of expression as if they themselves embodied metaphysical claims; he "attacks the normal form of expression as if he were attacking a statement"; and Van Inwagen, while retaining Rorty's picture of the sort of (super-)facts which would be required to vindicate the normal mode of expression, defends what Rorty attacks, as if he "were stating facts recognized by every reasonable human being." Trilling, Hynes and Orwell simply call upon our normal modes of expression without the least intention of taking sides in such a debate between the Realist and the anti-Realist; Rorty and Van Inwagen are unable to view such a willingness to acquiesce in the normal mode of expression as anything other than an implicit endorsement of a Realist metaphysics.

77   Rorty denies that he wants so to enlist Orwell: "I want to offer a different reading of Orwell. This is not a matter of wanting to have him on my side of a philosophical argument. He had no . . . taste for such arguments" (*CIS*, p. 173). But, given the reading that Rorty goes on to offer, I cannot see how to take this disclaimer seriously.

78   *CIS*, p. 173.

79   Ibid.

80   Rorty, in short, represents the issue here as if our options were exhausted by (5) and (5′).

81   *CIS*, pp. 173–4.

82   *CIS*, p. 174.

83   We are not allowed the option of concluding that Orwell's success is a function of both. The argument here depends on the assumption that the theories of literature implicit in (8) and (8′) represent exhaustive alternatives for understanding Orwell's accomplishment as an author. Rorty identifies (i) with (4) and (ii) with (8′) and sees (4) as belonging with the anti-ironist conception of literature of (8). This allows him to see (i) and (ii) as incompatible and to move swiftly from a rejection of (i) to an endorsement of (ii).

84   *CIS*, pp. 173–4.

85   *CIS*, p. 171.

86   *CIS*, p. 176. It is the burden of the section on Rortian Totalitarianism of this paper to argue not only that Orwell does view O'Brien as "seduced by mistaken theory" but also that the theory by which he is seduced is in important respects indistinguishable from the central tenets of Rortianism.

87   From what one gathers elsewhere about how Rorty reads Plato, it seems safe to conclude that for Rorty what it means to view O'Brien "as a modern counterpart to Thrasymachus" is to view him as "a dialectical foil" for the elaboration of Realist theses – in particular, (4) and (6). In skirting past this issue, I should not be understood to be endorsing Rorty's reading of Plato.

88   See *CIS*, p. 183.

89   The last six sentences are largely a paraphrase of *CIS*, p. 21.

90   This leaves it open that the connection here (between the repudiation of the Realist longing for something transhuman which would underwrite our practices and Orwell's particular way of illustrating the contingency of those practices) is not one that Orwell sees, but one that only Rorty sees. It is, however, difficult to avoid the impression that, according to Rorty, Orwell's whole point in illustrating the possibility of practices that differ from ours in just these respects is to oppose Realist theses such as (1) and (2). But, given Rorty's claim that Orwell's work is free of metaphysical concerns, Rorty is perhaps most charitably read here as maintaining only that Orwell's particular way of illustrating the contingency of our practices can serve as a useful instrument in the arsenal of someone – like Rorty – who (unlike Orwell) is concerned to disenchant us with Realism.

91   *CIS*, p. 185.

92   This elision on Rorty's part of Orwell's political motivations – and, with them, the novel's implicit call for political vigilance – is rather puzzling, given the distance of Rorty's usual views about politics from any form of fatalism.

93   *CEJL*, III, p. 133.

94   Orwell agrees with Rorty that in order to continue to think, you need to be able to share your thoughts with others; and in order to do that you need to possess the freedom to be able to *say* to others what you think. But this by itself hardly amounts to an endorsement of either (4') or (7'), as Rorty goes on to suggest.

95   "I take Orwell's claim that there is no such thing as *inner* freedom, no such thing as an 'autonomous individual', to be the one made by historicist . . . critics of 'liberal individualism'" (*CIS*, p. 177). Orwell's view, however, as we shall see, is not that there is no such thing as inner freedom or an autonomous individual. His point in the sorts of passages in his work to which Rorty (through his use of demonizing scarequotes) here alludes (see, e.g. *CEJL*, II, p. 135) is simply that *under certain political conditions* the sort of freedom or autonomy in question – which Orwell identifies with freedom of thought – ceases to be possible.

96   The slide in Rorty's way of rejecting (7) – so that such a rejection leads immediately into an affirmation of (7') – comes out nicely in the following remark:

> I take Orwell's claim . . . to be the one made by historicist . . . critics of 'liberal individualism'. This is that there is nothing deep inside each of us, no common human nature, no built-in human solidarity, to use as a moral reference point. There is nothing to people except what has been socialized into them . . . Simply by being human we do not have a common bond. (*CIS*, p. 177).

Orwell, as we shall see, agrees with Rorty that there is "nothing deep inside each of us" which guarantees that the political future will resemble the present. Nevertheless, as we shall also see, Orwell's worst fear could aptly be expressed by saying that in the future – unlike the present – there will be nothing to people except what has been socialized into them. We shall also see that Orwell would be quite happy to say that simply by being human we do have a common bond; but what he would mean in saying this does not rest on a metaphysical notion of "our essential humanity" of the sort which figures in (7).

97   The only way Rorty is able to hear any of these three ideas is as a version of a Realist thesis – specifically as versions of (2), (4) and (7) respectively.

98   The quotation is from *Nineteen Eighty-Four* (New York: Harcourt, Brace and Company, 1949 [henceforth *N*]), p. 270; it is cited by Rorty on *CIS*, p. 177.

99   More importantly, for my purposes, it begs the question against any non-Realist reader of Orwell who thinks that a project (which can be described as one) of "undermining Winston's hold on the concept of objective truth" is integral to O'Brien's purpose in seeking to tear Winston's mind apart.

100 *CIS*, pp. 177–8.

101 *CIS*, pp. 176–7. Rorty manages, on the strength of these two passages from Orwell, to attribute to Orwell (1'), (2'), (3') and (8') – and by implication (4'). As noted above, Rorty construes Orwell's views about the contingency of history in terms of (5'); and he takes the 1944 passage by itself to support the attribution of (7') to Orwell.

102 *CIS*, pp. 178.

103 *CIS*, pp. 178–9.

104 *CIS*, pp. 179–180.

105 Equally peculiarly, on Rorty's reading, the last third of novel seems to have almost nothing to do with the narrative of the first two-thirds of the novel (in which Winston repeatedly frames his indictments of the society in which he lives by employing this vocabulary).

106 *CIS*, p. 182. Rorty credits Judith Shklar with formulating the conception of what it is to be a liberal that he himself favors. ("I borrow my definition of 'liberal' from Judith Shklar, who says that liberals are the people who think that cruelty is the worst thing we do;" *CIS*, p. xv). Rorty takes his own reading of Orwell's novel – which foregrounds the theme of cruelty and disparages the theme of "the possibility of truth" (as an interpretative red herring) – to be a reading which makes Orwell out to be "a good liberal." It is thus worth

noting that when Shklar herself writes an essay on *Nineteen Eighty-Four*, she feels no compulsion to choose between a reading of the novel which places the theme of the horror of cruelty at the center of the novel and one which places that of the denial of reality at its center. She sums up her own reading of the novel as follows: "Cruelty *and* especially the denial of reality ... were what made up the political order of *1984*" [my emphasis] ("*Nineteen Eighty-Four*: Should Political Theory Care?" in *Political Thought and Political Thinkers* (edited by Stanley Hoffmann, University of Chicago Press: Chicago, IL, 1998)); p. 344.

107   *CEJL*, IV, p. 460 [my emphases]. This, again, is something that Judith Shklar appreciates: "[W]hat sort of book is it? It is not a prophecy at all, in fact. Orwell meant to draw out the logical implications of the thinking of his fellow intellectuals ... What would a world in which all thinking was really ruling-class ideology involve? After all many theorists claim that this is so always. What would writing about the past and present really amount to if that were indeed the case? It takes real imagination to cope with such propositions and *1984* in fact does that" (*op. cit.*, pp. 341–3).

108   *Nineteen Eighty-Four* is about a community in which that possibility has become so vanishingly small that its absence can not even be experienced (by most people) as a loss: "A person growing up with Newspeak as his sole language would no more know that ... *free* had once meant "intellectually free," than, for instance, a person who had never heard of chess would be aware of the secondary meanings attaching to *queen* and *rook*" (*N*, pp. 312–3).

109   Rorty sees Realists as concerned to argue that our social practices have philosophical, as well as empirical, presuppositions. This leads Rorty to claim that the only sorts of presuppositions our practices have are *empirical* ones. Rorty often argues as if the Realist is shown to be wrong if it can be shown that the alleged presuppositions are contingent. The putative presuppositions are shown not to be *philosophical* presuppositions, if they can be shown to be merely "optional" – i.e. dispensable. (See, e.g., *DAFHPP*, pp. 52–3.) On this conception of what makes something a philosophical presupposition of a practice, the sorts of "presuppositions" (on, e.g., the possibility of free thought and free speech) with which Orwell is concerned evidently do not count as "philosophical": for Orwell's whole point is that they are "optional" – they can be wiped out (though only at the cost of wiping out many of our current practices along with them). But does this mean (as Rorty seems to suppose) that they are therefore "merely empirical" presuppositions of our practices?

110   Thus institutions such as the mandatory telescreen, the thought police, and the two minutes hate would not be able to wreak anything like the harm they do in the world of *Nineteen Eighty-Four*, if they did not afford an effective means of monitoring, enforcing, and reinforcing allegiance to certain ideas – in particular, the three "sacred principles of Ingsoc": the principles underlying Newspeak, doublethink, and the doctrine of the mutability of the past (*N*, p. 27).

111   *CIS*, p. 183.

112   Lest I be misunderstood, let me be clear that I agree with Rorty that our social practices do not rest on metaphysical presuppositions. I also agree with Rorty that within professional academic circles most of the debates concerning some version of a thesis such as (7) tend to be pretty sterile and fruitless. But it does not follow that such debate is necessarily harmless. It depends, as said, upon the cultural, institutional and political context within which such debate proceeds: within the American political context, debate about a version of (7) currently underway between activists on both sides of the abortion controversy is not always harmless in its effects. In the hands of the Nazis, a fanatical commitment to a version of (7) was anything but harmless in its effects.

113   This is not to say that Orwell would disagree with Rorty about (i) and (ii). Nor is it to say – presuming one could hold Orwell's interest long enough to get him to understand what the parties to the debates about Realism now taking place in philosophy departments take

themselves to be debating – that Orwell would disagree with Rorty about (iii). It is only to say that Orwell has other fish to fry.

114   The point (in the last note but one) about (7) might seem to turn on a peculiarity of (7); namely, that any version of (7) is an explicitly moral thesis, and therefore, at least in principle, the sort of doctrine which has potential practical implications. This might appear to suggest that the target of Orwell's critique is restricted to certain forms of moral or political theorizing. But what *Nineteen Eighty-Four* is concerned to bring out is that philosophical doctrines of a sort which appear, on the surface, to involve "purely theoretical" questions – such as doctrines regarding the mutability of the past – can, when put to certain uses in certain political contexts, have practical effects which are at least as far-reaching and devastating as those of any explicitly moral doctrine.

115   On an alternative broader construal of 'totalitarian' common among many American commentators on Orwell, the assumption yields the following (only slightly less confining) gloss: the aim of the novel is to say something about the form of government common to, say, Franco's Spain, Mussolini's Italy, Hitler's Germany and Stalin's Russia.

116   Rorty's interpretative assumption that (at the least the first two-thirds of) the novel is primarily concerned to offer a description of Soviet Russia chimes with the reading of the novel put forward in American right wing circles at the inception of the Cold War. (It is a reading which Orwell found extremely disheartening and went out of his way to disown in interviews, letters, and press-releases; all reprinted in *CEJL*, IV; see also Crick, *op. cit.*, pp. 393–398.) Rorty's interpretative assumption finds its mirror-image in the equally valid and equally partial reading of the novel championed by the Soviet press in the 1980s: "George Orwell with his prophetic gift diagnosed the syndrome of present-day capitalism with which we must co-exist today for lack of something better" (quoted by John Rodden in *The Politics of Literary Reputation*; Oxford: Oxford University Press, 1989; p. 208). As we shall see, when we turn to Orwell's writings on the Spanish Civil War, Judith Shklar comes much closer to the truth (than either Rorty or the Soviet press) when she writes: "[A]buses of language were in Orwell's view the way in which dishonesty worked. No one, moreover, was in his view more reprehensible in this respect than the English fellow-traveling intellectual establishment . . . The intellectual who cannot abide intellectuals is not an uncommon type, of course, but what sets Orwell apart is that he translated this contempt into a vision of a society governed by the objects of his scorn. The totalitarian state he projected was neither Stalin's nor Hitler's entirely. The Inner Party that dispenses Ingsoc and rules Airstrip One in *1984* is made up of radical Anglo-American intellectuals" (*op. cit.*, pp. 342–3).

117   *CEJL*, III; p. 88.

118   In *Homage to Catalonia*, for example, Orwell discusses in this connection "the seemingly trivial matter" of the sorts of "habits of mind" which render certain sorts of libels and press-campaigns possible with their resulting capacity to do "the most deadly damage" (*Homage to Catalonia*, New York, Harcourt Brace Jovanovich, 1952; pp. 177–8).

119   "To be corrupted by totalitarianism one does not have to live in a totalitarian country. The mere prevalence of certain ideas can spread a kind of poison" (*CEJL*, IV, p. 67).

120   Aside from the obvious fact that it is set in Britain, numerous aspects of the world depicted in *Nineteen Eighty-Four* clearly indicate that it is envisioned as a future development of Capitalist Britain (as Orwell portrays it in his non-fiction of the 1930s and 1940s) and not as a future development of Stalinist Russia. To mention just one such example, in Stalinist Russia, the primary target of indoctrination and consumer of propaganda was "the Russian worker." This is not the state of affairs depicted in Orwell's novel. In the world of *Nineteen Eighty-Four*, though the proles make up eighty-five percent of the population, nobody much cares what the proles do or say or think as long as they show up at the factory:

Heavy physical work, the care of home and children, petty quarrels with neighbours, films, football, beer, and above all, gambling filled up the horizon of the minds [of the proles] . . . There was a vast amount of criminality in London, a whole world-within-a-world of thieves, bandits, prostitutes, drug-peddlers and racketeers of every description; but since it all happened among the proles themselves, it was of no importance . . . The sexual puritanism of the Party was not imposed upon them. Promiscuity went unpunished, divorce was permitted. For that matter, even religious worship would have been permitted if the proles had shown any sign of needing or wanting it. (N, pp. 71–2)

In the world of *Nineteen Eighty-Four*, the life of the English prole still in many respects closely resembles the life of the "English common people" of 1944 (at least as characterized by Orwell in *The Lion and the Unicorn*, *CEJL*, II, pp. 56–108). The prole is more or less free to do as he likes as long as he remains politically apathetic, serves as a cogwheel in the economy, and is imbued with enough patriotic fervor to serve effectively as fodder for the war-machine. The primary targets of intellectual enslavement in the world of *Nineteen Eighty-Four* are the members of the Party, a minority of the population. As we shall see, the tendencies which are depicted in the novel (as having evolved into the practices of "reality control" and the monitoring of "thoughtcrime") are ones which Orwell saw as underway already in the 1930s within (both the left and right wing of) the English intellectual elite class.

121   *CEJL*, IV, p. 502.
122   Orwell repeatedly emphasizes that "if one . . . doesn't point to the sinister symptoms" then one is oneself "merely helping to bring totalitarianism nearer" (*CEJL*, III, p. 150).
123   Thus Orwell summarizes "the moral" of the novel as follows: "The moral to be drawn from this dangerous nightmare situation is a simple one: *Don't let it happen. It depends on you*" (quoted by Crick, *op. cit.*, p. 395).
124   "[O]rthodoxy in the full sense demands a control over one's mental processes as complete as that of a contortionist over his body" (N, p. 213).
125   *CEJL*, III; p. 88. This passage echoes countless passages in *Nineteen Eighty-Four* (which detail the ways in which the Party "shuts you up in an artificial universe in which you have no standards of comparison") such as the following: "[T]he claim of the Party to have improved the conditions of human life had got to be accepted, because there did not exist, and never again could exist, any standard against which it could be tested" (*N*, p. 93).
126   *CEJL*, II, p. 258.
127   See, for instance, *CEJL*, IV, p. 64.
128   See *CEJL*, IV, p. 64, see also *CEJL*, III, p. 149.
129   The proliferation of atrocities constitutes, for Orwell, one of the many genuinely deplorable consequences of totalitarianism. It is, however, as Orwell sees the problem, itself a consequence of (what he calls) "the denial of the existence of objective truth." If your only standard for assessing whether acts of cruelty have been committed is whether your comrades say they have been committed, then you are unable to identify and prevent acts which your comrades refuse to countenance as ones of cruelty. This leads to a set of conditions under which atrocities become commonplace and undetectable.
130   Thus Rorty is certainly right (a) that Orwell abhors cruelty, (b) that he cherishes freedom, and (c) that he associates the proliferation of the one and the eradication of the other with totalitarianism. But Rorty is mistaken to suppose that (a)–(c) suffice to warrant the attribution of the distinctive doctrines of Rortian liberal ironism to Orwell.
131   *CEJL*, III; p. 88.
132   *CEJL*, II, p. 252.
133   We are now in a position to see why readers of Orwell such as Trilling might want to say things such as the following in characterizing the themes of the novel:

• There is such a thing as reminding someone of some plain truths (whose obviousness is on a par with "two plus two is four").

- In certain extraordinary (i.e. totalitarian) contexts, the furnishing of such reminders can be an act of moral and political courage.

- *Nineteen Eighty-Four* is an attempt to depict a world in which such acts of courage are (or shall soon be) no longer possible.

Rorty is certainly right when he says: "To admirers like Trilling, Orwell provided a fresh glimpse of obvious moral realities" (*CIS*, p. 174). So what? Some moral cases are not hard cases. As Orwell repeatedly says: it is possible to see the unspeakable wrongness of an act. (See, e.g., *CEJL*, I, p. 45.) I don't see how Rorty, without reneging on his ethnocentrism, can deny that, judging by the lights of our community, certain acts count as plainly wrong. I also don't see how Rorty, without again reneging on his ethnocentrism, can deny that, judging by the lights of our community, it is sometimes a plain fact that an act of this sort has been committed – that, e.g., the deniers of the Holocaust have got the facts wrong. One doesn't need to be a Realist to think that it is sometimes worth reminding people (e.g., whose view of the facts are clouded by totalitarian ideas) of such facts. Rorty, in his eagerness to convict readers such as Trilling of Realism, fails to locate wherein the pertinence of furnishing such reminders lies in their view. What Rorty claims is that such readers think that the descriptions offered in *Animal Farm* and *Nineteen Eighty-Four* are accomplished simply by doing something akin to asserting "two plus two is four." (Surely, no one who is not a lunatic would attempt to summarize the literary means employed in these tremendously imaginative works of fiction in this way.) Eager to oppose this (lunatic) view of Orwell's novels, Rorty moves from the unobjectionable observation that these novels are *novels* (i.e., employ imaginative literary resources) to the objectionable conclusion that Orwell understands himself to be doing the same kind of thing as his opponents (*CIS*, pp. 173–4).

134 Along the lines, e.g., of the account Thomas Kuhn gives for the abandonment of certain scientific concepts in *The Structure of Scientific Revolutions* (Chicago, IL: University of Chicago Press, 1962).

135 Along the lines, e.g., of the account Kierkegaard gives of our present use of the term 'Christian'; see my "Nietzsche, Kierkegaard and Anscombe on Moral Unintelligibility" (in *Morality and Religion*, edited by D.Z. Phillips, St. Martins Press, NY: 1996).

136 Compare: "[A]ctually, [Winston] thought as he readjusted the Ministry of Plenty's figures, it was not even forgery ... Most of the material that you were dealing with had no connection with anything in the real world, not even the kind of connection that is contained in a direct lie" (N, p. 41).

137 *CEJL*, II, pp. 256–258. Caleb Thompson, in his article "Philosophy and Corruption of Language" (*Philosophy*, January 1992), adduces this passage in the context of an illuminating discussion of the importance to Orwell of the contrast between telling lies and those uses of language which impede or erode our attaining the sort of relation to truth implicit even in a direct lie.

138 Winston, early in *Nineteen Eighty-Four*, reflects: "The past ... had not merely been altered, it had been actually destroyed. For how could you establish even the most obvious fact when there existed no record outside your own memory?" (N, p. 36). The Party's aim in *Nineteen Eighty-Four*, in promulgating the doctrine of the mutability of the past and in destroying all reliable records, is to achieve with respect to the entire history of the past what Orwell claimed would in all likelihood turn out to have been achieved in fact in the case of the history of the Spanish Civil War:

> [T]he chances are that those lies, or at any rate similar lies, will pass into history ... [A]fter all, *some* kind of history will be written, and after those who actually remember the war are dead, it will be universally accepted. So for all practical purposes the lie will have become truth. (*CEJL*, II, p. 258)

In *Nineteen Eighty-Four*, Winston concludes: "The past was erased, the erasure was forgotten, the lie became truth" (*N*, p. 75).

139   As I use the term, a 'totalitarian scenario' is always relative to a set of beliefs and the subject-matter of those beliefs. The British intellectuals discussed by Orwell inhabited a totalitarian scenario with regard to the formation of their beliefs about the Spanish Civil War (and no doubt certain other matters); but there is no reason to suppose that the formation of their beliefs about what was happening at any given time, say, in their vegetable gardens was equally insensitive to the subject-matter of those beliefs. Thus by a "totalitarian scenario" I always mean only to refer to a *locally* totalitarian scenario. I don't think any sense is to be made of a *fully global* totalitarian scenario – though *Nineteen Eighty-Four* offers what I take to be a depiction of as global a totalitarian scenario as one can form an at least minimally coherent conception of. (This is perfectly compatible with its being, along a different dimension, quite local in a quite different sense of "local" – i.e., not with respect to the range of beliefs, but rather with respect to the range of the population of believers; so in *Nineteen Eighty-Four* the beliefs of only 15% of the population of Oceania fall within the maximally global totalitarian scenario the novel depicts.) Conversely, when I use the term 'non-totalitarian scenario,' I mean to refer to a scenario which is not even locally totalitarian. Notice: there is nothing about the concept *totalitarian*, so defined, that specifies the sorts of beliefs which are at issue (e.g., only beliefs of an overtly *political* nature) or the source of the totalitarian pressure on their formation (e.g., a political party or a government). Thus, in Orwell's sense of the word, George Cukor's (depiction of the marriage of Gregory and Paula Anton in the film) *Gaslight* is no less in-depth a study of totalitarianism than Arthur Koestler's (depiction of the Moscow Trials in) *Darkness at Noon*.

140   "The process of continuous alteration was applied not only to newspapers, but to books, periodicals, pamphlets, posters, leaflets, films, sound tracks, cartoons, photographs – to every kind of literature or documentation which might conceivably hold any political or ideological significance ... [E]very prediction made by the Party could be shown by documentary evidence to have been correct; nor was any item of news, or any expression of opinion, which conflicted with the needs of the moment, ever allowed to remain on record. All history was a palimpsest, scraped clean and reinscribed exactly as often as was necessary. In no case would it have been possible, once the deed was done, to prove that any falsification had taken place ... It might very well be that every word in the history books, even things that one accepted without question, was pure fantasy ... [T]he claim of the Party ... had got to be accepted, because there did not exist, and never again could exist any standard against which it could be tested ... [Members of the Party] could be made to accept the most flagrant violations of reality" (*N*, pp. 40–41, 74, 93, 157).

141   For reasons that we will come to, this is not to say that the concept of objective truth has altogether faded out of the world of a Party member. When I say here it "has faded as far out of someone's world as it conceivably can" that means as far out of someone's world as it conceivably can without that person losing her mindedness – her ability to direct her thought at reality – altogether.

142   *N*, pp. 35–36.
143   See, e.g., *N*, pp. 80, 157, 198, 200, 216, 252. See also *CEJL*, p. 149.
144   *CIS*, p. 182.
145   *N*, p. 35.
146   *CEJL*, II, pp. 258–259.
147   *N*, p. 80. I have omitted from this passage the following sentence: "The heresy of heresies was common sense." The sentence raises an important topic (which this paper largely neglects): Rortian Ironism and the Party have a common enemy. Both are *opposed to common sense* (and the ways of employing the vocabulary of 'reality', 'truth', 'fact', etc. that common sense licenses).

148 In connection with the photograph of Rutherford (which contradicted the Party's official version of Rutherford's biography), Winston reflects: "[The photograph] was concrete evidence; it was like a fragment of the abolished past . . . [T]he fact of having held [the photograph] in his fingers seemed to him to make a difference even now, when the photograph itself, as well as the event it recorded, was only memory" (pp. 78–79).

149 Rorty's reading of the novel leaves it generally mysterious why words such as 'truth' and 'objective reality' should figure in the manner in which they do throughout the discussions between O'Brien and Winston, but especially so with respect to that moment of the novel for which one would have expected Rorty to be most concerned to have a textually plausible reading: namely, the moment in the pivotal torture scene in which O'Brien refers back to the convictions to which Winston gives voice in the focal passage and begins to undertake to strip him of those convictions:

> "Winston, you believe that reality is something objective, external, existing in its own right . . . But I tell you, Winston, reality is not external. Reality exists in the human mind, and nowhere else. Not in the individual mind, which can make mistakes, and in any case soon perishes; only in the mind of the Party, which is collective and immortal. Whatever the Party holds to be the truth *is* the truth. It is impossible to see reality except by looking through the eyes of the Party. That is the fact that you have got to relearn, Winston. It needs an act of self-destruction, an effort of the will. You must humble yourself before you can become sane."
> [O'Brien] paused for a few moments, as though to allow what he had been saying to sink in.
> "Do you remember", he went on, "writing in your diary, 'Freedom is the freedom to say that two plus two make four'?"
> "Yes", said Winston.
> O''Brien held up his left hand, its back toward Winston, with the thumb hidden and the four fingers extended.
> "How many fingers am I holding up, Winston?"
> "Four."
> "And if the Party says that it is not four but five – then how many?" (*N*, p. 252)

Notice: O'Brien undertakes to destroy Winston's conviction that "2+2=4" only (and immediately) after charging him with clinging to the belief that "reality is something objective, external, existing in its own right" and failing to acquiesce in the belief that "whatever the Party holds to be the truth *is* the truth." Before going on to remind Winston of what he wrote in his diary and undertaking to make him believe otherwise, O'Brien *pauses* for a few moments, in order to allow what he here says to sink in (so that Winston will keep in view why he is being tortured while he is being tortured). Rorty does not pause; he skips over O'Brien's remarks, moves straight to the topic of what Winston wrote in his diary, and then fixates on the word 'freedom,' thus ignoring the entire context of the novel's exploration of the question of what is involved in the "freedom to say that two plus two make four," and thus missing the internal relation (which the novel seeks to highlight) between appreciating that "reality is something objective, external, existing in its own right" and having the "freedom to say that two plus two make four."

150 This may seem less obvious with respect to arithmetical claims. It is for just this reason that Orwell goes out of his way to include scenes such as the scene in which Winston is asked to alter the figures of the Ministry of Plenty, the scene in which the quantity of the chocolate ration is altered, etc. These scenes require a certain plasticity in a Party member's conviction in the need for arithmetical results to tally: in all of these scenes alterations of quantitative fact are made by the Party, but Party members are required to believe both that no alteration of quantity has taken place and that the figures tally.

151 *CEJL*, II, p. 259.

152 I take a *conception* of *X* to be a proposal for how to flesh out our pre-theoretical intuitions about (our concept of) *X*. If the arbiter of truth appealed to in (b) is fallible, then (i) is

incoherent. The only way to interpret the conjunction of (a), (b) & (c) as forming a coherent proposal about anything is if they are interpreted – in accordance with (ii) – as a bizarre set of norms for how to use a piece of vocabulary (i.e.,'true'). The recipe can be interpreted in accordance with (i) only on the supposition that the Party is infallible – so that (a) and (b) will never conflict – thus rendering (c) idle. (Admittedly, with the exception of Winston and Julia and a few other heretics, every member of the Party does take the Party to be infallible. But if there were ever a case in which a Rortian will want to shrink from regarding community consensus as a reliable measure of truth, this is it! Rortianism, with its relentless emphasis on human finitude must reject the supposition that the Party is *actually* infallible.) If one allows that the Party is fallible, then one must also allow that there will be cases in which (b) conflicts with (a). But that is to concede that (i) leaves us with a set of criteria which, whatever else they might be taken to articulate, do not articulate a coherent conception of truth. In "Pragmatism, Davidson, and Truth" (see, especially *ORT*, p. 128), Rorty distinguishes between an endorsing use of 'true' and a disquotational use (as well as a third, cautionary, use which need not concern us here) and asserts that these two uses are equally legitimate but completely *distinct* ways of using the word. This is just what *Nineteen Eighty-Four* goes to great lengths to contest. According to Rorty, of course, – see (1') above – community-wide consensus is the ultimate arbiter of warrant and hence of which propositions one should endorse. But the supposition that such a criterion of "truth" will not conflict with the norm constituted by the disquotational principle only makes sense on the supposition that the community is infallible on matters on which community-wide consensus has been attained. (It might appear that there is wiggle-room for Rorty on this issue because he can claim that the appropriate criterion of "truth" is not *de facto* consensus but what we *at our best* would agree to. On this, see note 172.) As I will suggest in section VIII, it only makes sense to suppose that community-wide consensus is a reliable touchstone of truth if one assumes that the norms of inquiry which guide the community are internally related to the norm constituted by the disquotational principle. Pace Rorty, the endorsing and disquotational uses of 'true' are not two distinct uses of a homonymous term.

153   *CEJL*, II, p. 259.

154   This way of putting the objection presupposes that Rorty, if faced with the texts, would be prepared to acknowledge what his essay on Orwell implicitly denies: namely, that Orwell does indeed want to call upon the word 'truth' in this and similar ways.

155   "A Party member is required to have not only the right opinions, but the right instincts. Many of the belief and attitudes demanded of him are never plainly stated, and could not be stated without laying bare the contradictions inherent in Ingsoc" (*N*, p. 212).

156   "[T]he essential act of the Party is to use conscious deception while retaining the firmness of purpose that goes with complete honesty. To tell deliberate lies while genuinely believing in them" (*N*, p. 215).

157   "To make sure that all written records agree with the orthodoxy of the moment is a merely mechanical act. But it is also necessary to *remember* that events happened in the desired manner. And if it is necessary to rearrange one's memories or to tamper with written records, then it is necessary to *forget* that one has done so" (*N*, p. 215).

158   *N*, p. 216.

159   "[T]he labyrinthine world of doublethink. To know and not to know, to be conscious of complete truthfulness while telling carefully constructed lies, to hold simultaneously two opinions which cancel out, knowing them to be contradictory and believing in both of them, to use logic against logic, . . . to forget whatever it was necessary to forget, then to draw it back into memory again at the moment it was needed, and then promptly to forget it again, and above all, to apply the same process to the process itself – that was the ultimate subtlety: consciously to induce unconsciousness, and then, once again, to become unconscious of the act of hypnosis you had just performed. Even to understand the word 'doublethink' involved the use of doublethink" (*N*, p. 36).

160   I place "practices" here (and in the next two sentences) in scarequotes to signal that the
      expression when it so occurs – in contrast to when it occurs without scarequotes – does
      not refer to an alternative coherent set of norms for making claims. In charging Rorty with
      mistaking (what he calls) "practices" for practices, I am, of course, raising questions which
      I cannot afford to address here – questions such as: what is a practice?, and: how does one
      individuate practices? Rorty often talks as if these belonged to a kind of question that
      philosophy can afford to pass on to the social sciences without risk of confusion. This
      social-scientistic strain in Rorty's thinking is in tension with his enthusiasm for the work
      of Putnam and Davidson (in particular, with their theories of meaning and their insistence
      on the role of the constitutive ideal of rationality in licensing attributions of meaning).
      Rorty would readily assent that Putnam, in "The Meaning of Meaning" (in *Mind, Language
      and Reality: Philosophical Papers, Volume II*, Cambridge University Press, 1975;
      pp. 215–271,) shows that what a speaker must mean by, e.g., "gold" is constituted at least
      in part by her physical and social environment. But how should we understand the qualifier
      'social' in "social environment" here? Many of Rorty's remarks presuppose a very *thin* –
      essentially non-normative – understanding of the environing social "practices" (which are
      putatively partially constitutive of what a speaker can mean by her words). If all it takes to
      distinguish two different "practices" is that there is some systematic difference in the
      noises that members of two respective communities make (e.g., the members of one make
      a noise that sounds like our word 'gold' when confronted with fool's gold, the members of
      the other do not), then differences in "practices" come cheap. But such an understanding
      of "practice" is too thin to enable one to get into view what it would be to *misuse* a
      linguistic expression, and thus what it could mean to be using an expression *in accord* with
      a practice. What Putnam teaches (see especially "Dreaming and 'Depth Grammar'", *ibid*,
      pp. 304–321) is that it is the beginning of wisdom, when individuating meanings, not to
      conclude that a linguistic expression (e.g., one which is pronounced as our word "gold" is)
      has a different meaning when used by each of two distinct communities, if one's only
      ground for so concluding is that, alongside significant overlap in circumstances of use in
      the same physical environment (e.g., in nine out of ten cases both communities call what
      we call gold "gold"), the communities happen to differ with respect to a limited range of
      circumstances of use (e.g., one of them refers to fool's gold as "gold" and the other
      doesn't). In order to make its bearing on the present context of discussion explicit,
      Putnam's conclusion about what is going on in the sorts of examples he discusses could be
      reformulated as follows: the right thing to say is that the two (allegedly alien) linguistic
      communities have *the same practice* of employing the relevant word (e.g., they both have
      the same practice of employing the word "gold", but one of the communities is far better
      than the other at discriminating fake gold from genuine gold). The same holds, with regard
      to their respective employments of Oldspeak vocabulary, for the two linguistic communities
      constituted by members of the Party and present-day speakers of English: between the two
      communities, there is *only one set of linguistic practices* for employing expressions such as
      "five," "fingers," "photograph," etc. The evidence of frequent and flagrant disregard on
      the part of Party members of our present-day norms for employing Oldspeak expressions
      is not sufficient to license the attribution to them of an alternative set of linguistic practices.
      For the only coherent norms for employing such expressions Party members have are the
      ones which *we* have. Admittedly, under the pressure of the totalitarian demands of the
      Party, a pervasive incoherence is introduced into their employment of such expressions;
      and, to that extent, their linguistic behavior involves an overall pattern of use which is no
      longer characterized by the sort of *unity* which is constitutive of a practice. However, such
      apparent departures from our practice do not in and of themselves suffice to constitute an
      alternative practice (any more than two chess players who each try to get away with
      cheating as much as possible can be said to be "playing chess according to different rules");
      they merely represent a highly degenerate form of our practice. (For a searching discussion
      of the sort of "unity" at issue here, see Michael Thompson's *Practice and Disposition*; in

Preferences, Principles, and Practices, A. Ripstein and C. Morris, eds., Cambridge University Press, forthcoming.)

161   "A totalitarian society which succeeded in perpetuating itself would set up a schizophrenic system of thought" (*CEJL*, IV, p. 64).

162   Orwell's use of the term "schizophrenic" here is not merely a literary flourish. Totalitarian modes of thought, such as those enjoined by "The principles of Ingsoc," can usefully be thought of as literally inducing schizophrenia. Consider the following description of one of the characteristic features of clinically schizophrenic patients:

> A [characteristic] feature of schizophrenic patients is what has been called their "double bookkeeping." It is remarkable to what extent even the most disturbed schizophrenics may retain, even at the height of their psychotic periods, a quite accurate sense of what would generally be considered to be their objective or actual circumstances. Rather than mistaking the imaginary for the real, they often seem to live in two parallel but separate worlds: consensual reality and the realm of their hallucinations and delusions. A patient who claims that the doctors and nurses are trying to torture and poison her may nevertheless happily consume the food they give her; a patient who asserts that the people around him are phantoms or automatons still interacts with them as if they were real. (Louis A. Sass, *The Paradoxes of Delusion*, Cornell University Press: Ithaca, NY, 1994)

In matters of vital importance, which require the acknowledgment of such things as the nutritive value of food and the reality of other people, schizophrenics act with "a quite accurate sense" of what a non-schizophrenic would "consider to be their objective or actual circumstances." Such "double bookkeeping" is an equally characteristic feature of the lives of Party members. Methods of thought to which we non-Party members explicitly adhere, and which are opposed to the most fundamental avowed principles of the Party, tacitly inform the lives of Party members. Through his actions, a Party member continuously tacitly acknowledges the reality of that which he officially repudiates.

One might, however, think that at least those who belong to the higher echelons of the Party are quite unlike schizophrenics in at least the following respect: someone like O'Brien is able to attain a certain degree of self-consciousness with respect to his practice of double bookkeeping, so that he is able to know of himself that he is continually unconsciously engaged in double bookkeeping and such double bookkeeping and can even, on occasion, become fully self-conscious. Thus temporary local suspensions of the principles of Ingsoc are condoned whenever such a suspension conduces to the ends of the Party with regard to certain matters of vital importance: "The empirical method of thought, on which all the scientific achievements of the past were founded, is opposed to the most fundamental principles of Ingsoc . . . But in matters of vital importance . . . the empirical approach is still encouraged or at least tolerated . . . [B]ut once that minimum is achieved, [members of the Party] can twist reality into whatever shape they choose" (*N*, pp. 194, 200). But the capacity intermittently to indulge in doublethink self-consciously – and the sort of self-knowledge involved in knowing that one otherwise practices it unconsciously – hardly distinguishes Party members from schizophrenics. What Orwell has Emmanuel Goldstein say about members of the Inner Party, in the above extract from *The Theory and Practice of Oligarchical Collectivism*, strikingly resembles much of what Schreber has to say, in his more self-conscious moments, about his own relation to reality (Daniel Paul Schreber, *Memoirs of My Nervous Illness*, trans. Ida Macalpine and Richard Hunter (Harvard University Press: Cambridge, 1988)).

163   *CIS*, p. 182.

164   "Honesty" here refers to a *virtue* not an occurrent psychological state. An individual's honesty is not measured by the degree to which she is capable of remaining unconscious of lying while lying. If the cultivation of such forms of unconsciousness is itself consciously practiced – as the principles of doublethink enjoin – then what is cultivated is the vice of

dishonesty. *Nineteen Eighty-Four* is an attempt to envision a world in which the variety of dishonesty which the principles of doublethink enjoin has become second nature. It is because Judith Shklar sees this – and Rorty misses this – that she is able to offer a summary of the point of the novel which is almost a precise inverse of Rorty's summary: "In *1984* the possibility of saying 2 + 2 = 4 because one knows it to be true is lost. The plot is largely the story of how this last impulse to speak the truth is destroyed . . . *1984* is . . . a cognitive nightmare" (*op. cit.*, pp. 344–5).

165   I can imagine Rorty responding at this point: "OK, so it turns out that Orwell does talk a lot about 'objective truth' and 'objective reality' and does think that he is saying something worth saying when he talks that way. But I want to distinguish between the good Orwell (who cares about freedom and cruelty) and the bad Orwell (who cares about objective truth and objective reality). Orwell is split between a de-divinizing and a divinizing self. I admit that both these Orwells exist, but I am only interested in the former. In my reading of Orwell, I am trying to make Orwell more faithful to his own better self." (One often finds Rorty thus carving philosophers up into their "good" and "bad" sides when confronted with aspects of their thought that don't fit into his reading of them. His writings on Cavell, Dewey, Heidegger, Putnam and Wittgenstein all furnish cases in point.) But such a separation of a writer's thought into distinct components can only be effected if the (purportedly) "good" region of his thought can be partitioned off from the "bad" and still remain the region of his thought that it is. If the relevant regions of a writer's thought are internally related to one another, then one will misunderstand both in so far as one takes each to raise a set of concerns that can be formulated and grasped in complete independence from the other. In the case of Orwell, this boils down to the question whether Orwell's views on prevention of cruelty, preservation of freedom and regard for truth are only externally related to one another. It is the burden of the final section of this paper to argue that these three regions of Orwell's thought are internally related. (I have already touched a bit – see, e.g., notes 129 & 133 – on Orwell's view that a totalitarian disregard for truth leads to the proliferation of cruelty.) Orwell is every bit as much of a de-divinizer as Rorty claims he is; but Rorty's equation of the idea of the answerability of empirical claims to empirical reality with the idea of the answerability of mere mortals to a Deity would constitute, for Orwell, a step backwards in the project of de-divinization. It is just such a step (in which the very idea of the answerability of empirical claims to empirical reality comes to be viewed as a bit of antiquated superstition) which is required in order to effect the "total" enslavement of the mind of a Party member which is the *conditio sine qua non* of the possibility of the sort of divinization (of Big Brother) depicted in Orwell's novel.

166   *N*, p. 219

167   *N*, pp. 28–9.

168   Hilary Putnam, *Realism With a Human Face* (Cambridge, MA: Harvard University Press, 1990), p. 21.

169   *PRM*, p. 450.

170   The norms that Winston follows in making his claims are internal to a world view, just as Putnam urges norms must be. If we plug "Winston" in for S in Rorty's schema, it should be easy to see that there is no tension – as Rorty claims – between Putnam's rejection of Realism and his willingness to endorse the claim that S can be completely out of step with the beliefs of other members of his community and yet be warranted in asserting *p*.

171   I do not mean to suggest that Orwell thinks that one finds oneself in the situation in which Winston here finds himself – i.e. in which, e.g., one believes a statement to be unwarranted even though the majority of one's cultural peers believe it to be true – only if one inhabits a totalitarian scenario. Orwell is perfectly happy to say about this or that belief of his contemporaries: "I am not saying that it is a true belief, merely that it is a belief which all modern men do actually hold" (*CEJL*, II, p. 185).

172   *PRM*, p. 453. Rorty invokes the notion of "us, at our best" here. I agree that "us, at our best," appropriately understood, could do the work that Rorty wants it to do, but that

would require unpacking what is involved in "us, at our best" in a very unRortian way. The relevant notion of our *best* is a normative one (not a merely sociological one). Rorty in his subsequent gloss on the notion in this very passage already begins to drain it of the relevant normative content. A robustly normative conception of what "we, at our best" *ought* to say about X could fund the very distinction which Rorty, in the passages surrounding this quotation, insists he wants – and is able – to do without: namely, the distinction (which Putnam insists upon) between what everyone agrees to be the case with regard to X and what is in fact the case with regard to X. But in order to be entitled to invoke such a robustly normative notion of "us, at our best," one must respect the internal relation, which Rorty seeks to sever, between the endorsing and disquotational uses of 'true' – that is, one must take what we ought to say about X to be constrained not merely by what others in fact let us get away with saying about X, but by what they ought to let us get away with saying about X in the light of how things manifestly are with regard to X. This is just what the Party seeks to prevent. The Party wants you to disregard how things manifestly are with regard to X, if how things manifestly are with regard to X conflicts with what the Party wants to let you get away with saying about X.

173 *N*, p. 37.

174 "[Winston] had committed – would still have committed, even if he never set pen to paper – the essential crime that contained all others in itself. Thoughtcrime, they called it. Thoughtcrime was not a thing that could be concealed forever. You might dodge successfully for a while, even for years, but sooner or later they were bound to get you." (*N*, p. 20)

175 "*Crimestop* means the faculty of stopping short, as though by instinct, at the threshold of any dangerous thought. It includes the power of not grasping analogies, of failing to perceive logical errors, of misunderstanding the simplest arguments if they are inimical to Ingsoc, and of being bored and repelled by any train of thought which is capable of leading in a heretical direction" (*N*, p. 213).

176 "For whom, it suddenly occurred to [Winston] to wonder, was he writing his diary? For the future, for the unborn" (*N*, p. 9).

177 I say this is "*as close as we can come* to contemplating in imagination the implications of the adoption of a resolutely Rortian conception of objectivity" because I do not think that Rorty's conception is sufficiently coherent actually to permit of such contemplation. Even the inhabitants of a totalitarian scenario are still able to make claims. Rorty's conception, I would argue, deprives us of the resources for being able to understand those who engage in the practices Rorty describes as even so much as making claims. Since such an argument is out of place in this section of the paper – which is concerned with how Rorty would look to Orwell – I leave it for another occasion.

178 *ORT*, p. 129.

179 Rorty himself takes some time over the question whether O'Brien should be counted as an ironist – i.e., a proponent of (8') – and expresses only one reservation about declaring O'Brien to be one: O'Brien has mastered doublethink, and therefore is not troubled by doubts about himself or the Party. Rorty concludes "[O'Brien] still has the *gifts* which, in a time when doublethink had not yet been invented, would have made him an ironist . . . In this qualified sense, we can think of O'Brien as the last ironist in Europe" (*CIS*, p. 187). What Rorty misses is that, on Orwell's view, O'Brien's ironist "denial of objective reality" can – as we saw in the section on Orwell and Totalitarianism – only be put into practice by someone who has perfected the art of doublethink.

180 *N*, pp. 251–2.

181 See also *N*, p. 269: "'I told you Winston', [O'Brien] said, 'that metaphysics is not your strong point. The word you are trying to think of is solipsism. But you are mistaken. This is not solipsism. Collective solipsism, if you like. But that is a different thing; in fact, the opposite thing.'" And *N*, p. 281: "What knowledge have we of anything, save through our own minds? . . . Whatever happens in all minds, truly happens."

182 *CIS*, p. 176.

183 Sartre, as quoted by Rorty, *Consequences of Pragmatism* (Minneapolis, MI: University of Minnesota Press, 1982, p. xlii). The passage is from Sartre's essay *Is Existentialism a Humanism?*, reprinted in *Essays in Existentialism* (New York, NY: Citadel, 1993), p. 47. I feel obliged to remark that I think Rorty misreads this passage. In saying that fascism may become the human reality, Sartre is not urging that an inhabitant of such a future fascist community would have no criteria available from within that community for rejecting fascism. Sartre, admittedly, does make things difficult for himself in this essay by paring his normative ethics down to a single austere norm: authenticity. Nevertheless, it is clear that Sartre thinks that this norm can be shown, by the end of the day, to have considerable clout built into it. The essay is meant to be a prolegomena to a treatise on ethics. In Sartre's ethics, an "authentic fascist" is to be revealed as a contradictory description on grounds (i.e., fascism presupposes bad faith) not unlike those Orwell's novel adduces for why there is no such thing as an "honest Party member" (i.e., the triumph of totalitarianism presupposes the cultivation of doublethink).

184 *Consequences of Pragmatism*, p. xlii.

185 When Rorty says "there is nothing to be said" using words of this form, he is, as usual, concerned to reject a particular (Realist) understanding of what those words might mean. In particular, Rorty takes the bit about "there is something within you which you are betraying" to rest on an implicit appeal to thesis (7).

186 See, e.g., *N*, p. 80. For reasons reviewed above, the denial must remain tacit, if the Party is not to deprive its members of the capacity to judge altogether.

187 *CEJL*, III, pp. 88–89.

188 To wit: pertaining to a free man.

189 Virtually all of the established senses of the word bear some trace of the original Latin meaning of the word. A liberal person is one who is free in bestowing – i.e. generous. A liberal point of view is one that is free of prejudice and hence tolerant of dissenting opinions. A liberal construction of someone's meaning is one that is free – i.e. not literal. The liberal arts and sciences were originally so-called because they were considered worthy of a free man – i.e. becoming to a gentleman, unlike the servile occupations of a workman. And so on.

190 *CEJL*, I, p. 460.

191 *CIS*, pp. xiv–xv.

192 Specifically with thesis (6). See (6′) for a fuller specification of what Rorty thinks the rejection of (6) entails.

193 *N*, p. 29.

194 This is not quite right, in so far as it appears to assert that I if were to become stranded on an uninhabited island I would suddenly cease to be able to arrive at a free verdict concerning what transpires in my environment. To put the point more carefully: (a) initiation into a genuine community is a condition of the acquisition of the capacity to arrive at such verdicts, and (b) in so far as one continues to live in the society of one's fellow human beings, one can fully exercise freedom of judgment in their company only to the extent that they are not devoted to undermining one's capacity to do so (i.e., only to the extent that the "community" one forms with them is not a totalitarian one).

195 A central theme of all of Orwell's writing – especially his writings on the relative strengths and shortcomings of English versus other kinds of imperialism – is that once all forms of answerability are effaced except accountability to the demands of those who happen to have power, then the lives of those who are not in power are flooded with cruelty. Rorty, of course, might be perfectly willing to concede that the fact that the Party possesses virtually limitless power (a power "more absolute than had previously been imagined possible") over its members and the fact that the most apt image of the life of a Party member is an image of "a boot stamping on a human face" (*N*, p. 271) are not, for Orwell, externally related facts about the world of *Nineteen Eighty-Four*. But the fact that the Party

has such complete power over the minds of its members is, as we have seen, a function of the inability of its members to arrive at an independent verdict concerning how things are (of "the dislocation of their sense of reality"). Thus there obtains, for Orwell, an internal relation between the fact that the life of a Party member is "a boot stamping on a human face" and the fact that the world in which a Party member lives is one in which "the very concept of objective truth is on the verge of fading out."

196 Thus Orwell's notion of freedom is considerably weightier than Rorty's. Officially, there are no prohibitions on what a Party member is allowed to say, for there are no laws that prohibit anything in the world of *Nineteen Eighty-Four*. ("[N]othing was illegal, since there were no longer any laws"; *N*, p. 8) A Party member is simply expected to act, speak and think in the appropriate fashion. The average "well-adjusted" Party member – unlike Winston – is not conscious of any deprivation of freedom. According to Rorty's purely negative concept of freedom, he is free (he can say anything he likes and no one will hurt him); and Winston is comparatively lacking in freedom (there is much that he wants to say but cannot). But, on the positive concept of freedom central to the novel, the average Party member is, in comparison to Winston, utterly lacking in freedom. (He lacks what in Newspeak is called *ownlife*; see *N*, pp. 81–2) The following point is central to Orwell's concept of freedom: the more completely captive a mind is, the less conscious it is of its lack of freedom. If one identifies freedom with the freedom from juridical constraint accorded to the well-adjusted Party member, then there is a reading of the Party's slogan about freedom on which, in the world of the novel, it (like all of the Party's slogan's) is true: Freedom *is* slavery.

197 For reasons given in the previous note, it would be more precise to say: the aim of the Party is to bring about a state of affairs in which everyone is juridically free to say what they like. Hence O'Brien explains to Winston:

> We are not content with negative obedience, nor even the most abject submission. When finally you surrender to us, it must be of your own free will. We do not destroy the heretic because he resists us: so long as he resists us we never destroy him. We convert him, we capture his inner mind, we reshape him. We burn all evil and illusion out of him; we bring him over to our side, not in appearance, but genuinely, heart and soul. (*N*, p. 258).

The above remarks constitute O'Brien's answer to Winston's question (if "nothing will remain of me", not even "a name in a register" or "a memory in a living brain") "why bother to torture me?" (*N*, pp. 257–8). Rorty's answer to this question (O'Brien tortures people solely for the pleasure it affords him) obliges him to overlook O'Brien's own answer to the question.

198 Orwell takes one of the things Rorty claims really matter to Orwell – namely, a preservation of the sense of the coherence of one's own identity – to depend on the thing Rorty views as a red herring. The novel makes vivid how the answerability of your beliefs concerning how things are to how things are is a condition of maintaining your sense of self. Without such answerability – in the absence of any "external records that you can refer to" – even the "narrative outline of your own life loses its sharpness." You no longer fully have an identity – your identity is on the verge of "crumbling" – if, when you try to remember who you are and what you have done, "you remember huge events which [you have good reason to think] quite probably never happened to you" and most of your memory of the past is simply filled with "long blank periods to which you can assign nothing" (*N*, p. 33). Under such conditions, only someone who is a master of self-deception can retain the impression that she is able to "justify herself to herself."

199 Rorty's inability to construe talk of "humanity" in any terms other than the biological or the metaphysical are partially responsible for his inability to understand the views of Cavell, Conant, and Putnam discussed in *PRM*, pp. 445–446. For a discussion of Rorty's blindness to the relevant ethical notion of humanity, see Cora Diamond's "The Importance

of Being Human" (in *Human Beings*, edited by David Cockburn; Cambridge: Cambridge University Press, 1991).

200 *N*, p. 29.

201 *N*, 273. This theme – of what it is to be human, and of Winston being the last human – recurs throughout the novel, perhaps most poignantly in the following thoughts of Winston's:

> If you can *feel* that staying human is worth while, even when it can't have any result whatever, you've beaten them . . . One did not know what happened inside the Ministry of Love, but it was possible to guess: tortures, drugs, delicate instruments that registered your nervous reactions, gradual wearing down by sleeplessness and solitude and persistent questioning . . . But if the object was not to stay alive but to stay human, what difference did it ultimately make? (*N*, pp. 167–8)

The idea that staying human is worth while, *even when it can't have any result whatever*, and *even at the expense of enduring great cruelty* (tortures, drugs, etc.) is hardly the expression of a Rortian ideal. In this respect, it difficult to imagine two sensibilities more perfectly opposed than those of Orwell and Rorty.

202 Indeed, there are passages in Orwell's work that express Orwell's antipathy for the idea that there is such a thing as a timeless and indestructible "human nature" much more forcefully than any Rorty cites; such as, for example, the following:

> In the past every tyranny was sooner or later overthrown, or at least resisted, because of "human nature," which as a matter of course desired liberty. But we cannot be at all certain that "human nature" is constant. It may be just as possible to produce a breed of men who do not wish for liberty as it is to produce a breed of hornless cows. The Inquisition failed, but then the Inquisition had not the resources of the modern state. The radio, press-censorship, standardized education and the secret police have altered everything. Mass-suggestion is a science of the last twenty years, and we do not yet know how successful it will be. (*CEJL*, I, pp. 381–382)

203 "The whole of modern European literature – I am speaking of the literature of the past four hundred years – is built on the concept of intellectual honesty, or, if you like to put it that way, on Shakespeare's maxim, 'To thine own self be true'. The first thing that we ask of a writer is that he not tell lies, that he shall say what he really thinks, what he really feels. The worst thing we can say about a work of art is that it is insincere . . . Modern literature is essentially an individual thing. It is either the truthful expression of what one man thinks and feels, or it is nothing" (*CEJL*, II, p. 135).

204 *CEJL*, IV, pp. 61, 71.

205 Rorty's claim that Orwell understands himself to be doing the same kind of thing as his opponents fails to discriminate between the complex varieties of relation (or absence of relation) to truth – so important to Orwell – possessed by different varieties of (what Rorty likes to call) "persuasive redescription". In particular, it fails to distinguish between the sort of totalitarian "redescription" which characterizes (what Orwell calls) "propaganda" and the sort of imaginative "redescription" which characterizes (what, in the passage quoted in the last note but one, he calls) "literature."

206 *CEJL*, IV, p. 137. The centrality of the topic of the corruption of language in Orwell's work is a main theme of Caleb Thompson's "Philosophy and Corruption of Language," *op. cit.*

207 *CEJL*, IV, p. 128.

208 *CEJL*, IV, p. 136.

209 *CEJL*, IV, p. 135.

210 *N*, pp. 303–314.

211   I think that with respect to most philosophical problems the premise is false, but I shall
      not argue the point here.
212   N, p. 303. Thus in *The Principles of Newspeak* we find:

> Take for example the well-known passage from the Declaration of Independence: "We
> hold these truths to be self-evident, that all men are created equal, that they are endowed
> by their creator with certain inalienable rights, that among these are life, liberty and the
> pursuit of happiness. That to secure these rights, Governments are instituted among
> men, deriving their powers from the consent of the governed. That whenever any form
> of Government becomes destructive of those ends, it is the right of the people to alter or
> abolish it, and to institute new Government . . ." It would have been quite impossible to
> render this passage into Newspeak while keeping to the sense of the original. The nearest
> one could come to doing so would be to swallow the whole passage up into the single
> word *crimethink*. (*N*, pp. 313–314)

> If Rorty's brave new "post-philosophical culture" were ever to be realized and his proposals
> for a "replacement vocabulary" adopted, then – as far as I can see – the term 'Realism'
> would function just the way the term 'crimethink' is supposed to in Newspeak. It would
> serve as a linguistic device which simultaneously fulfills two purposes: (i) that of ostending
> a stretch of thought that cannot be rendered into the new vocabulary, and (ii) that of
> indicating that the stretch of thought in question is precisely of the sort that the new
> vocabulary has been adopted in order to render inexpressible.

213   *N*, pp. 51, 52, 53–54.
214   This paper is indebted to conversations about Rorty over the past decade with Stanley
      Cavell, John Haugeland and Hilary Putnam and to comments on drafts by David
      Finkelstein and Lisa Van Alstyne. Its two largest debts are to Cora Diamond and John
      McDowell: to Diamond's article "Truth: Defenders, Debunkers, Despisers" (in *Commit-
      ment in Reflection*, edited by Leona Toker; New York, NY: Garland, 1994), to McDowell's
      contribution to this volume, and to conversations with each of them about Rorty.

RESPONSE TO JAMES CONANT

James Conant says that "in non-totalitarian societies, the following two tasks generally
coincide: the task of seeking to justify a claim to the satisfaction of other people and
the task of seeking to establish that a claim is justified in the light of the facts" (p. 306).
Rather than distinguishing two tasks, I would say: in non-totalitarian societies, we take
the facts to be established when we have conciliated our opinion with those of others
whose opinions are relevant (our fellow-citizens, our fellow-jurypersons, our fellow-
experts, etc.). Conant goes on to say that these two tasks "diverge radically" in
totalitarian societies. I would say: in such societies it becomes very difficult, and often
impossible, for anyone to find out what the facts are, because agreement is no longer a
good sign of truth.

The difference between Conant and myself is that he thinks that someone like
Winston, trapped in such a society, can turn to the light of facts. I think that there is
nowhere for Winston to turn. People in such societies are in the same position as
people with real or purported psychotic delusions. They may never be able to reconcile
their memories with what the people around them are saying. They may never know
whether they are crazy or whether the people around them are liars or dupes. There is
no prodcedure called "turning to the facts" which will help them. The lack of such a
procedure is my reason for saying that all we can do to increase our chances of finding

truth is to keep the conditions of inquiry free. (This view – that if we take care of freedom, truth will take care of itself – is said by Conant to be "roughly the opposite of Orwell's view." I think that Conant here confuses truth with truthfulness – a point to which I return at the end of my response.)

In the case of Winston and the "patients" whom the KGB used to send to what it called "psychiatric clinics," their memories are right and the people around them are lying. In the case of other people in similar situations – for example, the person who has a clear, distinct, forceful, and vivacious memory of Elvis riding though Yosemite on the back of Godzilla, a memory which coheres beautifully with many of his other relevant beliefs – their memories are wrong. But neither Winston nor the Elvis-sighter is in a position to find out whether their memories are right or wrong. For neither can turn away from the effort to achieve coherence among their beliefs (for example, the belief that all these seemingly intelligent and decent people think they are crazy) and instead start comparing their memories with "the facts."

Conant speaks as if Winston's memories are the best evidence as to the facts. Orwell and we know that they are, but how is Winston supposed to know that? Conant treats these memories as somehow intrinsically veridical. But Winston's memories no more bear an intrinsic mark of veridicality than do the Elvis-sighter's. Winston's tragedy is that he is in a position in which he will probably be led away, either by force or persuasion, from what we know to be true. The Elvis-sighter's good fortune is that he may, with luck, gradually be led away, either by force or persuasion, from what we know to be false. But the difference between tragedy and good fortune is only recognizable from the outside – from where we are.

Conant believes that one can hold both that "there is no way of determining warrant *sub specie aeternitatis*" and that "there is a way of determining the warrant of *p* apart from S's ability to justify *p* to those around her" (p. 306). If "a way of determining" means "a way *for S* to determine," then I do not believe this. My tediously familiar strategy for defending my disbelief is to infer from an old coherentist chestnut – that you can only get at "the facts" by way of conciliating beliefs, memory-images, desires, and the like – to the view that there is no procedure of "justification in the light of the facts" which can be opposed to concilience of one's own opinion with those of others.

Conant says that "assuming that Winston's memory does not deceive him . . . then Winston's belief is warranted" (p. 306). If he means, tautologously, that if Winston trusts his memory his belief will be warranted in Winston's own eyes, he is of course quite right. But there remains the question O'Brien raises: why should Winston trust his memory? As O'Brien points out, we do not ordinarily trust memories that fail to cohere with everything everybody else believes. Why should Winston make an exception for himself? Well, perhaps because he finds himself to be living in a totalitarian society? But this just postpones the question. For his evidence that he is living in such a society consists in the memories which O'Brien disputes.

I should have thought that only someone who holds the views which Conant calls "Realist," and disavows, would want to oppose ordinary intersubjective justification to "justification in the light of the facts." So my problem with Conant is to figure out how he differs from van Inwagen – a straightforward, self-confessed Realist. Early in his paper, Conant says that he will not be criticizing me "on the grounds on which his Realist critics do." But I have trouble seeing how the grounds have been changed.

Presumably Conant would see my difficulty here as a result of what he calls my "blindness to intellectual options that occupy the intervening space between the rejection of Realist theses and the affirmation of their Rortian counterparts." I do not think I am as blind as all that; I have spent a lot of time arguing against various such options (for instance, Putnam's, Wright's, Haack's). It would have helped if Conant had said more about the position he himself occupies in this intervening space, and in particular of how he has managed to avoid the fixations and obsessions to which he believes me to have fallen victim.

****

Turning now to questions of Orwell-exegesis, I do not see much justification for Conant's[1] claim that my "discussion of Orwell is structured around the assumption that there are two natural ways to read Orwell: either as a Realist or as a Rortian." Reading Orwell as a Rortian would obviously be very unnatural indeed. My reading of him was not intended to claim him as fellow pragmatist, but to explain why one could be a non-Realist and still have one's moral horizon expanded by *1984*, why one could agree with O'Brien's coherentism and still be intrigued, fascinated and appalled by O'Brien's way of coming to terms with the absence of freedom. That is why I spend much of my Orwell chapter arguing that what matters is freedom rather than truth, and that the truth of Winston's beliefs is irrelevant to the relation between himself and O'Brien. The idea was to say how the book looks when seen through non-Realist eyes.

As an analogy: I might have written an account of how even atheists like myself are impressed, improved and morally instructed by *Pilgrim's Progress*, but it would not have occurred to me to argue that Bunyan had latent atheistical tendencies.[2] I do not see that Conant has much textual basis for the claim that I read Orwell "as centrally concerned with defending theses whose motivation depends on the desire to distance oneself as far as possible from Realism" (p. 283). I certainly cite passages in Orwell's writings which I then read in a non-Realist sense, but I could also cite passages in Bunyan that I would proceed to read in an atheist sense. I would do so without imagining that Bunyan himself would have appreciated my efforts. As I said in my book, my reading of *1984* was "not a matter of wanting to have him [Orwell] on my side in a philosophical argument"[3] (*CIS*, p. 173). Had Orwell taken an interest in such arguments, I imagine, he would have sided with the Realists.

Conant sees van Inwagen and myself as sharing a set of obsessions (see p. 283), and Putnam, Cavell, Diamond and himself as relatively free from those obsessions. He believes himself to be reading Orwell's book not just through non-Realist eyes, but through eyes unclouded by the "metaphysical," militantly anti-Realist, beliefs which I hold. However, just as Conant predicts, I resist his description of my views as "metaphysical."

I think of all the "Rortian" theses he lists as suggestions about how to redescribe familiar situations in order to achieve various practical goals. I think of both archetypal metaphysicians like Plato, Spinoza and Hegel and archetypal anti-metaphysicians like Dewey, Wittgenstein and Heidegger as having made similar suggestions.[4] I see the difference between the metaphysicians and the anti-metaphysicians as consisting mainly in the anti-Realism of the latter. In my jargon, "metaphysical" and "Realist" are pretty well co-extensive terms.

Conant obviously attaches a very different meaning to the term "metaphysical" than I do, and I wish that he had explained his use of the term in more detail. Is a view metaphysical insofar as it is contentious, or just insofar as philosophy professors are likely to contend about it? Is all such contention between philosophers pointless? Well, presumably the present contention between Conant and myself is not. To grasp his sense of "metaphysical" I should have to have a better sense than I do of which philosophical contentions he takes to be the result of obsessions and which not.

Conant says that the obsessed – van Inwagen and I – are not "able to envisage the possibility that what is at stake in Winston's remarks – remarks such as 'The obvious, the silly, and the true have got to be defended' or 'The solid world exists, its laws do not change' – is not the truth or falsity of a metaphysical thesis." (p. 283) This possibility seems to me easily envisagable, and obviously actual. Conant's charge seems to me as odd as would be a suggestion that "obsessed" seventeenth-century Copernicans were unable to recognize what is at stake in the remark "the sun is about to rise above the horizon" is not the truth or falsity of an astrophysical thesis.

Commonsensical remarks or platitudes can be used as objections to proposals for conceptual revision, but they should not be.[5] Appeals to ordinary language are of no philosophical interest. Revisionist philosophers like myself (and like Austin's chief target, Ayer) do not wish to stop people making commonsensical assertions. We wish rather to change the inferential connections currently holding between those assertions and more controversial assertions. Thus Galileo wanted to stop people inferring from "The sun is rising" to "The sun goes round the earth." I want to stop people inferring from protests such as Winston's to Realist philosophical views. Pragmatists want, for example, to block the inference from "'P' is true iff p" to "There is a way the world is, independent of such human needs and interests as O'Brien's or Winston's" or to "When we begin to suspect that we live in a totalitarian society, we can turn to the facts for help."

****

Let me now drop questions about the exegesis of Orwell and turn to Conant's attempt to "demonstrate" to me that my "way of rejecting philosophical problems does not enable us to care about the very sorts of goods that he thinks we should care about instead" (p. 269).

My first reaction to this formulation of Conant's strategy was that predictions of what will happen if certain revisions in belief or vocabulary are made are not suitable candidates for *demonstration*. Such predictions may be confirmed or disconfirmed as the result of experiment or past experience, but how could one give them *a priori* backup? The notion of "demonstration" seems out of place when the question is whether a new tool can replace an old tool without untoward side-effects.

Yet Conant offers *a priori*, "conceptual analysis" arguments to show that we cannot adopt the theses he cites as "Rortian" and still achieve certain practical goals (for instance, the defense of freedom against totalitarianism). He is not arguing, on the basis of past experience, that the risks of making the suggested changes are so great that it would be foolish to perform the relevant social experiment.[6] Rather, if I understand him, he is claiming that the changes in belief and vocabulary I suggest would lead to the unraveling of the only vocabulary in which we state the goals which it is hoped such changes would facilitate.

His argument thus comes down to claiming that there is a presuppositional relation between certain old, familiar, beliefs and vocabularies and the ability to formulate (or perhaps the will to achieve) certain goals – the political goals which Orwell, Conant and I share. For this argument to succeed, he must show that, as he says, "the ways in which the Party wants its members to think and judge cannot be captured in terms of a coherent set of ground-rules for the application of concepts." He must show that "Party members are supposed simultaneously to abide by our ordinary norms for making claims and not to abide by these norms" (p. 302).

At pp. 309–10 Conant says that when Orwell asserts what he takes O'Brien to deny – the "very existence of external reality" – he is not presupposing "any commmitment to Realist theses," but only "norms internal to our practices of making claims." So one expects him to tell us what these norms are, and how the Party stabs itself in the back by trying to evade them.

But the *only* relevant norm Conant cites is the one that says it's always OK, for any proposition p, to assert both "Everybody always has and always will believe that p" and "P is false." Presumably he thinks that the Party asks us both to abide by this norm and not to abide by it. But I do not see why the Party has to do this.

I not only agree that this is one of our norms, I agree with Conant that no society is imaginable in which this norm does not hold. If "denying the very existence of external reality" means suggesting that we drop this norm, then I make no such denial. Nor need the Party do so to bring about the universal consensus it requires. I cannot imagine a society in which this norm would not hold, either when "p" is replaced by is "two and two is four," or by "the Holocaust was a moral abomination" or by "Party invented the airplane." I can, however, imagine societies in which it would seem as absurd to doubt one or another of the latter two claims as to doubt the former.

Conant sometimes says that the Party wants people to violate this norm and sometimes (as at p. 307) that I want to "outdo the Party" by arranging for it to be impossible to "distinguish at least in principle" between the questions "Who invented the airplane?" and "Who does everybody say invented the airplane?" But nobody could make such an arrangement, and the Party can settle for something much easier: namely the absence of doubts about who invented the airplane. In-principle-distinguishability guarantees at most what Peirce called "make-believe doubt." To get real doubt one needs something more than the norm which Conant rightly says every use of language presupposes. All the Party wants or needs to do is to make all doubt of the relevant sort seem absurd, crazy, comparable to the doubts of the Elvis-sighter about Elvis' death.

Conant goes on to say that I am wrong to assert that there is no answer to be given to people like O'Brien who are carrying out this aim. He proposes an answer which I explicitly reject, viz, "Though you embody the practices of a totalitarian society which will endure forever, there is something beyond those practices which condemns you." My problem with this answer is that saying "reality condemns you" seems too much like saying "God condemns you" – it is equally unverifiable, and equally ineffective, given the totalitarian set-up. One can picture the last Christian in an atheist society saying "God condemns your practices," but would that be an *answer* to her atheist audience?

To Christians like Bunyan or C. S. Lewis, non-Christians appear (and here I paraphrase Conant's description of totalitarianism at p. 307) to spend an enormous amount of energy hiding God's existence, and His condemnation, from themselves. O'Brien and his colleagues have created a situation in which the assertion "there is an external reality which you have hidden from yourself which condemns you" has no familiar inferential relations to any statements believed by anybody other than Winston, just as the assertion "God condemns you" has no famliar inferential relations to any statements believed by anybody in the audience addressed by the last Christian.

For Conant to accomplish the sort of "demonstration" he wants he would have to show the relevance of the in-principle-distinguishability of the agreed-upon from the true to some imagined argument between Winston and O'Brien. He would have to find some disanalogy between the Christian's invocation of God and his suggested answer to O'Brien – a disanalogy which rests upon the difference between practices as optional as Christianity's and non-optional practices, practices underwritten by some sort of transcendental guarantee. I do not see what such a disanalogy would be, because – back to the old coherentist chestnut – I cannot see how you break out of the social practices around you into a realm that transcends those practices.

Conant agrees with me that we should not make a tacit appeal "to the idea that there is something deep inside each of us, some indestructible common human nature, some built-in guarantee of human solidarity that will last forever" (p. 313) But without something like that, how can he "demonstrate" that my "way of rejecting philosophical problems does not enable us to care about the very sorts of goods he thinks we should care about instead"? How can he "demonstrate" that to accept my claim – the claim that if we promote freedom, then truth will take care of itself – will prevent us from formulating or defending the political goals we both share?

I entirely agree with Conant that vocabulary replacement of the sort I propose "cuts both ways" and can "deprive us of the ability to talk about some things we might still want to talk about" (p. 314). But the second of the demonstrations he proposes in the initial section of his paper would require him to spell out in detail just why, if our descendants adopt the views he labels "Rortian," they will be unable to talk about the desirability of freedom and human solidarity, the undesirability of lying, the need for reciprocal trust, and the like.

I do not see that Conant has met this obligation. His criticisms require him to switch back and forth between the transcendental and uncontroversial necessity of the in-principle-distinguishability of the agreed and the true, on the one hand, and crypto-Realist restatements of this necessity on the other.

****

Much of Conant's criticism of me, as well as many other philosophers' criticisms of pragmatism, run together truthfulness and truth. Pragmatists are often said not to recognize the political and moral importance of truth-telling.

I do not think this charge is even remotely plausible. Truthfulness, in the relevant sense, is saying publicly what you believe, even when it is disadvantageous to do so. This is a moral virtue whose exercise is punished by totalitarian societies. This virtue has nothing to do with any controversy between Realists and non-Realists, both of whom pay it equal honor. My claim that if we take care of freedom truth will take care of itself implies that if people can say what they believe without fear, then, just as Conant says, the task of justifying themselves to others and the task of getting things right will coincide. My argument is that since we can test whether we have performed the first task, and have no further test to apply to determine whether we have performed the second, Truth as end-in-itself drops out.

Conant cites approvingly an article by Cora Diamond called "Truth: Defenders, Debunkers, Despisers" which defends the idea that truth *is* an end-in-itself. But that article constantly runs that idea together with the claim that a world in which human beings can trust each other is as precious as anything can be. Who doubts the latter claim? Certainly not Jane Heal or myself, who are the targets of Diamond's article. Both of us would heartily agree with Diamond that

> We need that world of truth within which a lie is merely a lie, within which there are records, within which the reality of each of us is entrusted to the rest, within which the destruction of human lives is not erasable.[7]

We can also agree with Diamond that writers such as Primo Levi, Zbigniew Herbert, and Orwell

> together with the anonymous author of the Polish slogan 'We fight for Truth and Freedom' are not writing about truth conceived simply as something sentences or beliefs or propositions exemplify, they are calling on words to help them understand and respond to evil, to help them articulate the kind of evil they take their world, our world, to be threatened by. They call on the word "truth" in that context . . .

So they do, but we philosophers still retain the right to say that this is not the right word to call on, and that they should talk instead (as, indeed, they often do) of truthfulness. (Would the banners of the Polish dissidents have been less inspiring had they read "Honesty and Freedom?") Some of the same people who describe Truth as an end-in-itself identify God and Truth. Philosophers retain the right to say that both words ought to be replaced with others ("Democracy" and "Humanity," for example).

It is no objection to Heal or to me to point out that lots of people use the word "truth" as the name of an end-in-itself, any more than it is a rebuke to the atheist to point out that the word "God" is so used. Atheists are not against loving certain things (for instance, Human Solidarity, Freedom, Democracy) with all one's heart and soul and mind, but they do not want an Omnipotent Creator and Law-Giver to be so loved. Pragmatists do not want Correspondence to the Intrinsic Nature of Reality to be so loved.

Atheists can grant that lots of people use the word "God" for admirable purposes without having any theological views, and pragmatists can grant that lots of people use the word "Truth" for such purposes without having any philosophical views. But neither admission gives them reason to stop their campaigns to change our linguistic habits. Conant seems to want a world in which no philosopher ever recommends any change in our linguistic habits. Philosophers should, he seems to think, "devote themselves to the task of *reclaiming our present vocabulary*". (See p. 313). This is not a project in which I can take any interest. I do not see what Conant thinks is wrong with sifting through our present vocabulary and suggesting that we revise the inferential relationships between our uses of the words it contains – thereby, perhaps, increasing the chance of reaching such goals as Freedom and Human Solidarity.

Somebody sometimes needs to suggest such revisions, or intellectual progress would come to a halt. The metaphilosophical difference between Conant and myself can be summed up by saying that he sympathizes with Putnam's and McDowell's attempts to prevent us philosophers from, as Putnam nicely puts it, "leaping from frying pan to fire, from fire to a different frying pan, from different frying pan to a different fire, and so on apparently without end." I do not share this wholesale quietistic impulse. I am anxious to give the peace of the grave to lots of worn-out old philosophical problems (for instance, those taken up by G. E. Moore), but I have no doubt that every attempt to get rid of old problems by revisionary attempts to break old inferential connections will itself generate unexpected new inferential connections, new paradoxes, and (eventually) new "problems of philosophy" for the textbooks to mummify.

Where Putnam and Conant see leaps from fires to frying-pans, I see the dialectical progress of the World-Spirit, correctly described by Hegel as the discovery of incoherence in any given way of making things hang together, followed by the formulation of an alternative way, the incoherence of which will be revealed a little later. I do not believe that there is, in addition to the so-called fixations and obsessions of us philosophical revisionists, a peaceful, non-obsessed, vision of how things deeply, truly, unproblematically are. If there were – if there were something like what Cavell calls "the Ordinary" – I doubt that I should have any interest in dwelling within it. I see the desire for ever-new, revisionary, extraordinary, paradoxical languages and problems as the manic eros which gave us the Platonic dialogues, *The Phenomenology of Spirit*, *Concluding Unscientific Postscript*, "Empiricism and the Philosophy of Mind," "A Nice Derangement of Epitaphs," and *The Postcard*.

If you want genuinely and permanently unproblematic peace, you should stay out of philosophy. You might try, for example, becoming a gardener in a monastery, or a hermit on a desolate shore. Wittgenstein's importance lies not in his intermittent escapism, but in the intensity of his revisionary obsessions – in the fires he stoked, and the energy with which he hammered out a frying-pan of a kind never seen before.

Notes

1   There are a couple of other places at which Conant attributes strange views to me without adequate evidence. He says, for example, that I advocate political quietism as well as philosophical quietism, and therefore interpret Orwell as agreeing with me that "the future outcome of history is essentially *out of our hands*" (p. 287). He also says that I regard "the concerns of literature as incommensurable with those of politics." The only evidence Conant offers for the latter claim is a passage in which I say that the demands of self-creation and of human solidarity are incommensurable. But why should he attribute to me the belief that novels and poems never speak to the latter demands? At p. 145 of *CIS* I say that "The pursuit of private perfection is a perfectly reasonable aim for some writers – writers like Plato, Heidegger, Proust, and Nabokov, who have certain talents. Serving human liberty is a perfectly reasonable aim for other writers – people like Dickens, Mill, Dewey, Orwell, Habermas, and Rawls, who share others."

2   If my Orwell chapter contributes anything to our appreciation of *1984*, it is by suggesting that we read the book as illustrating, among other things, how "intellectual gifts are as malleable as the sexual instinct" (*CIS*, p. 187), and how, when the hope of freedom is gone, torture can replace intersubjective agreement as a goal. Though, in a trivial sense, non-Realist, this reading has nothing to do with anti-Realism. It amounts to an attempt to change the subject, to suggest that the reader attend to O'Brien's pleasure rather than to Winston's pain.

3   On the other hand, Conant is right that there are passages in my Orwell chapter in which I do seem to be claiming that Orwell had Rortian tendencies. The most regrettable of these is one that he quotes: "In his better moments, Orwell himself dropped the rhetoric of transparency to plain fact and recognized that he was doing the same *kind* of thing that his opponents, the apologists for Stalin, were doing." (*CIS*, p. 174) "In his better moments" suggests that the rhetoric of transparency was a mere lapse on Orwell's part, and "recognized" suggests a conscious realization on Orwell's part. Both suggestions are wrong. I should have argued that *Animal Farm* was a good example of what Orwell called "using words in a tricky, roundabout way" without suggesting that Orwell ever came close to abandoning the Realist "rhetoric of transparency."

4   I realize that Conant does not wish Wittgenstein to be read as having anti-Realist views, or as attached to any philosophical theses. I cannot help reading him as being attached to many such theses. One difference between us may be that I should like to give philosophy peace by setting aside a lot of familiar old philosophical topics in the quiet confidence that lots of new

philosophical topics will present themselves. Conant may hope (and presumably reads Wittgenstein as hoping) to give philosophy a deeper and more lasting sort of peace.

5   Conant lists eight things that "Orwell has it at heart to say" (p. 279) and goes on to say that I "manage to read Orwell without ever realizing that such remarks occur throughout his corpus" – or, in the rare instances in which I do realize this, I "view them as unfortunate and dangerously misleading rhetorical flourishes" (p. 280). I think they are unfortunate and dangerously misleading only when taken out of context and used as premises in philosophical arguments, as they are by van Inwagen – and, it seems to me, by Conant as well.

6   Many people have argued in this way, Such people typically say that "the only trouble with pragmatism is that it won't work." My response is that we shan't find out till we try.

7   Diamond, when citing some lies told by a President of Uruguay, says that this President "took a Rortyan view" (Cora Diamond, "Truth: Defenders, Debunkers, Despisers", in Toker, Leoua (ed.) *Commitment in Reflection* (Garland Press, Hamden; 1993) p. 210). I cannot follow Diamond's inference from my views to tolerance for lies. This passage (from Putnam's Dewey Lectures) is quoted approvingly in Conant's introduction to Putnam's *Words and Life* (p. xiii).

13
Post-ontological Philosophy of Mind: Rorty versus Davidson

BJØRN RAMBERG

1. Davidson in Rorty's dialectic

For thirty years or more, Rorty has worked to break the grip on analytic philosophy of two problem-defining assumptions. The first is the Kantian idea that knowledge, or thinking generally, must be understood in terms of some relation between what the world offers up to the thinker, on one side, and on the other the active subjective capacities by which the thinker structures for cognitive use what the world thus provides. The second is the Platonic conviction that there must be some particular form of description of things, which, by virtue of its ability to accurately map, reflect, or otherwise latch on to just those kinds through which the world presents itself to would-be knowers, is the form in which any literally true – or cognitively significant, or ontologically ingenuous – statement must be couched. Together, these comprise what Rorty calls representationalism. As Rorty exhibits it in his large-scale frontal assault on representationalist epistemology and metaphysics, *Philosophy and the Mirror of Nature* (1979), the key pivots in the dialectical self-immolation of the representationalist paradigm in analytic philosophy are, naturally enough, Quine's "Two Dogmas of Empiricism" and Sellars' "Empiricism and the Philosophy of Mind." But in this book, and indeed in a paper published already in 1972, Rorty also makes use of Davidson's work in his effort to circumvent the intuitions that entrench the representationalist framework.[1] And where Sellars and Quine in Rorty's hands are subject to dialectical critiques, each providing the anti-representationalist corrective to the other's still-unliberated thought, Davidson appears finally to set analytic philosophy free. Once we give up the attempt to demonstrate to ourselves why (some eminent subset of) our strategies for framing descriptions of the world really are the ones we ought, because of how the world actually is, to be using, then, says Rorty in *The Mirror of Nature*, "philosophy of language is simply 'pure' Davidsonian semantics, a semantics which does not depend upon mirror-imagery, but which, on the contrary, makes it as difficult as possible to raise philosophically interesting questions about meaning and reference." (1979, p. 299) For Rorty, the Davidsonian account of meaning and thinking is the thing of beauty it is exactly because it makes it seem pointless to raise the sorts of questions about our thinking and its relation to the world that philosophers of the representationalist variety wish to pursue.

Through the 1980s Davidson remains a focal point of Rorty's attention. Of four central chapters in his *Objectivity, Relativism, and Truth* (1991a), Rorty says, "I have been . . . trying to clarify [Davidson's] views to myself, to defend them against actual and possible objections, and to extend them into areas which Davidson himself has not yet explored." (1991a, p. 1) Rorty's hermeneutic efforts are not without critical edge toward Davidson, but the disagreements with him that Rorty expresses, largely in "Pragmatism, Davidson, and Truth" (1986), concern how best to characterize, from a metaphilosophical perspective, the positions Davidson takes and the strategies he employs to develop them.[2] Such issues are far from incidental to Rorty's project, of course. Still it is clear that at this stage in his articulation of his view of philosophy, Rorty finds that Davidson's conception of the capacities that make us thinking, speaking creatures is made to the pragmatist's measure. As he says in "Non-reductive Physicalism" (1987):

> Davidson's views . . . help us work out a picture of the relations between the human self and the world which, though 'naturalized' through and through, excludes nothing. Davidson's works seems to me the culmination of a line of thought in American philosophy which aims at being naturalistic without being reductionistic . . . Davidson's philosophy of mind and language enables us to treat both physics and poetry evenhandedly. (p. 113)

The pragmatic naturalism Rorty finds expressed in Davidson permeates all his work from this period. Of the remaining ten essays of *Objectivity, Relativism, and Truth*, the first six work out what it means to "treat physics and poetry evenhandedly," providing an interpretation of objectivity which does not trade on the idea that the way the world is can be invoked to under-pin an order of rank of our various disciplines or discursive practices. The final four essays suggest a way to think about the relation between philosophical theory and political commitment once we give up on the representationalist idea that latter is rationally vindicated only once the former delivers the appropriate metaphysical or ontological foundations. In *Essays on Heidegger and Others* (1991b), Rorty frequently uses Davidson's holistic view of intentional ascriptions and his causal account of metaphor as reference points to situate the post-Nietzschean European theorists he discusses. Finally, when Rorty develops his vocabularies-as-tools view in chapter one of *Contingency, Irony and Solidarity* (1989), he makes essential use of Davidson. The result, "The Contingency of Language," is the critical pivot in what has come to constitute something of an existentialist manifesto for pragmatists (1989, chapters 1–4).

Recently, however, this enthusiastic endorsement has become qualified, as Rorty has criticized Davidson on two substantive scores. The first of these concerns Davidson's claims about the significance of the concept of truth, while the second turns on Davidson's account of the relation between the mental and the physical. Both seem to faithful Davidsonians to be matters of essential doctrine, so when he distances himself from Davidson along these lines, it appears that Rorty is reassessing Davidson's dialectical position in the narrative of the dedivinization of philosophy.

The first issue, in a nutshell, is this. For Davidson, the notion of truth has great philosophical import. The notion of truth, and our understanding of it, is in his presentation (for instance, 1990a, 1996) the cornerstone of the very account of thought, language, and agency that Rorty praises. For Rorty, by contrast, it seems specious to accord special philosophical significance to this concept once you take a theory of truth to be "an empirical theory about the truth-conditions of each sentence in some corpus of sentences." (Davidson 1990a, p. 309, quoted in Rorty 1995b, p. 284) Such a theory,

Rorty thinks, "could as well be called a 'theory of complex behavior' as a 'theory of truth'." (1995b, p. 286)

In what follows I am going to pass over the exchange on truth, and focus instead on Rorty's second critical point. The two are not unrelated, however, and along the way I will suggest a reason for describing the particular kind of theory of complex behavior that the radical interpreter offers as a theory of truth.

The second issue is the topic of two recent papers (in press *a*, in press *b*), where Rorty doubts that there is a "philosophically interesting" distinction to be drawn between the mental and the physical, and criticizes Davidson for thinking that there is. "As I read the history of philosophy," Rorty says in "McDowell, Davidson and Spontaneity," "Brentano distilled the essence of Kant's grandiose scheme–content distinction into his criterion of the psychical, and Quine and Davidson swallowed the resulting poisoned pill." (In press *b*, p. 10)

As I examine Rorty's dissatisfaction with Davidson's conception of the mental–physical distinction, it will not be my principal concern to defend Davidson against Rorty's diagnosis. Indeed, with regard to the original statement of anomalous monism (Davidson, 1970), I find Rorty's critical points quite plausible – as indeed might Davidson himself, looking back at "Mental Events." The point I care about is that it is possible to give Davidson's distinction between the vocabulary of propositional-attitude ascription – what I call the vocabulary of agency – and vocabularies of scientific explanation a reading, and a metaphilosophical context, that renders it impervious to Rorty's criticisms. I will suggest, moreover, that the direction in which my use of Davidson's distinction points is best pursued in what are distinctively Rortyan terms. Unlike Rorty, I believe that as naturalistic pragmatists we ought not only to recognize the distinctiveness of agency (as I will refer to the claim at issue), but also do our bit to entrench it in philosophy. While Rorty in effect criticizes Davidson for being insufficiently Davidsonian in hanging on to the idea of the philosophical distinctiveness of agency, I criticize Rorty for being insufficiently Rortyan in his negative assessment of the motivations for drawing a philosophical distinction between the vocabulary of agency and vocabularies of scientific explanation. I suggest to Rorty that his negative assessment turns on a narrow conception of philosophical interest, which induces in him a general skepticism toward the very idea of philosophically interesting differences between vocabularies. This conception of philosophical interest is a negative, reactive one; it chains Rorty to an understanding of what philosophical theory is that he has spent most of his professional life trying to undermine, and it underwrites the suspicion that in some of his writings Rorty is not untouched by that streak of self-loathing to which anti-metaphysical – "therapeutic" is Rorty's term – philosophizing is vulnerable. This conception – and the streak – goes against the grain, however, of the assertive, constructive account of the motivations for and resources of philosophical thinking which we also find in some of Rorty's recent writings. It is to the latter that a Rortyan, post-ontological case for the philosophical distinctiveness of agency appeals.

2. Rorty's Complaint

The thrust of the criticism that I want to dwell on here is that Davidson fails to take full account of the extent to which his anti-representationalist views undermine the Quinean contrast between indeterminacy and underdetermination. It is his inability to shake loose from this contrast, Rorty suggests, which leads Davidson to see the distinction between the intentional and the non-intentional as marking a philosophically significant divide, importantly different from the divisions marked by the distinctions we might draw between vocabularies that do not involve psychological ascription. "Quine's invidious distinction," says Rorty,

> between the "baselessness of intentional idioms" and the better "based" idiom of physical science strikes pragmatists like me as a residue of the unfortunate positivist idea that we can divide culture into the part in which there is an attempt to correspond to reality and the part in which there is not. If you drop the idea that some of our sentences are distinguished by such correspondence, as Davidson has, it seems natural to say, as Dewey did, that all our idioms are tools for coping with the world. This means that there can be no philosophical interest in reducing one idiom to another . . . (In press *a*, p. 3)

Perhaps we can think of "parts" or segments of culture as characterized in terms of commitments to different vocabularies, and of vocabularies as linguistic practices distinguished by the particular ends and standards of appropriateness that they embody. Rorty's pragmatist point then is that while sentences in context of course may be true or false, there is no merit in the thought that some vocabularies, by virtue of their relation to reality – to that to which all our talk must ultimately be related – are particularly well-suited for the production of first-rate, literal, truths.[3] For pragmatists, therefore, whether or not we are able to reduce one way of talking about things to another way of talking about things just has no bearing on how seriously we ought to be taking claims to truth made in the one way or the other. In Rorty's picture, no room is left for the kind of contrast Quine draws:

> The only invidious distinctions which pragmatists allow themselves to draw are those between the purposes various disciplines fulfill, and between the amounts of good done by fulfilling these various purposes . . . So pragmatists are baffled by the claim that the gap between psychology and biology is somehow deeper than that between biology and chemistry – a claim Davidson and Quine both make. (In press *a*, pp. 4, 5)

If we abandon the idea that "adequacy to the world" is a concept that may be invoked in explanation of the relative success or failure of various descriptive practices, then we also give up any notion of "the physical" or of "facts of the matter" with the requisite contrastive force available to support the opposition between what is indeterminate and what merely underdetermined. Without this opposition in place, Rorty claims, we have no reason to think of the vocabulary of psychological ascription as falling into a distinct philosophical class – or more precisely: we have no reason to think of the difference between this vocabulary and other (in various ways distinguishable) vocabularies as being a difference of particular philosophical import.

3.   Davidson on Indeterminacy and Underdetermination

Rorty has a point when he chides Davidson for accommodating Quine's distinction. I think he is right about the commitment to ontology as a ranking of vocabularies that this distinction, as Quine wields it, carries in its trail. For that reason, it may be a misleading terminological allegiance on Davidson's part. It is not clear, however, that in the form that Davidson actually endorses the idea of the indeterminacy of interpretation the Quinean commitment to ontology is retained. Let me try to show why.

The contrast between indeterminacy and underdetermination purportedly sorts into two philosophical kinds predicaments where we cannot form a rationally grounded preference between two (or more) theories which appear to embed incompatible claims about some subject matter. The difference between these kinds of predicament turns on the nature of the subject matter to be described. Underdetermination obtains between alternative descriptions of the world in physical terms – it is a logico-epistemic predicament, an expression of the fact that there will always be more than one way of systematically accounting for any body of observations, no matter how large. Relative to any such body, there will be alternative theories with equal logical warrant (though perhaps not with equal epistemic warrant, if we take the latter to involve criteria beyond logical compatibility with a set of observation statements). Indeterminacy, by contrast, characterizes the relation between alternative descriptions framed in a vocabulary which is so constituted that undecidabilities will remain even where a scheme of physical description is settled. Having made our choice of physical theory, we find that alternative descriptions of people's sayings and intentional doings remain logically available. Choice between such alternative interpretation schemes is impervious to questions of fact, since the facts are, by physicalist hypothesis, settled – which is to say, such choice does not concern what is the case.

It is important to note that if we want to rest a philosophically interesting contrast between intentional vocabulary and non-intentional vocabulary on the opposition between indeterminacy and under-determination, it will not suffice to point out that agency-descriptions may not be determined by our observations even where choice of physical theory is fixed. You also need the idea that the latter mode of description is the fact-expressing one. However, when Davidson affirms the Quinean distinction, he does so in a way which commits him only to the former claim. Here is a relatively recent statement of the point, one which Rorty also quotes (cf., Rorty, In press *a*, p. 9):

> Because there are many different but equally acceptable ways of interpreting an agent, we may say, if we please, that interpretation or translation is indeterminate, or that there is no fact of the matter as to what someone means by his or her words. In the same vein, we could speak of the indeterminacy of weight or temperature. (Davidson 1991, p. 161)

To this Rorty, is, as he says,

> inclined to reply: we *could* speak of the indeterminacy of weight or temperature, and [decide] to say that there is no fact of the matter about what temperature somebody has, but we do not. We do not because the possibility of using another scale of measurement seems to have nothing to do with factuality. Temperature seems as factual as ever, even after somebody points out that you could replace Fahrenheit with Centigrade. (In press *a*, p. 9)

In what sense, however, could this reply be said to press an objection against Davidson? The quoted passage from Davidson continues thus:

> But we normally accentuate the positive by being clear about what is invariant from one assignment of numbers to the next, for it is what is invariant that is empirically significant. The invariant *is* the fact of the matter. We can afford to look at translation and the content of mental states in the same light.

It seems to me that Davidson here is making just the point that Rorty wants; the ineliminable possibility of alternative ways of stating the facts does nothing to threaten the factuality of our statements. "Facts," evidently, does not refer to the truths captured by the vocabulary of some basic science, since those truths are not stated in the vocabulary of psychological ascription; facts, for Davidson, are just what true statements express, and the truths expressed by psychological and semantic ascriptions cannot, according to anomalous monism, be restated in terms of non-intentional theory.

Twenty five years ago, Rorty made the point against Quine that without the physicalist ontology, what Quine called indeterminacy was just another instance of underdetermination (Rorty 1972b). For Rorty, to persist in using the terminology to make a distinction indicates some form of allegiance to this ontology. However, Davidson may be using Quine's terminology to make a point that is independent of Quine's commitment to physics as ontology, as fixing the first-rate kinds. It is *simply* the point that making a physical-theory choice will not settle agency-description. To accept this point is to recognize that even when the rational undecidability of alternative physical theories is resolved, alternative ways of stating semantic and psychological facts remain open. Now, the important point to notice here is that this suggestion carries no hint of the implication that psychological and semantic facts are *really* dimly glimpsed facts of a different, that is, physical, order. So this alleged fact about the relation between theory-options in two (classes of) vocabularies does not have as a consequence an invidious philosophical distinction between the vocabularies. Indeed, the abstract relation here recognized is symmetrical, ontologically unbiased. To see this, we need only recall that on Davidson's conception, the application-conditions of the predicates that figure in the intentional vocabulary are governed by different kinds of evidential considerations from those in non-intentional vocabularies. What this means is that the observation statements that serve as evidence for psychological ascriptions may all be available to some ideal interpreter, and that interpreter may have opted for specific ascriptive and semantic theories of all interlocutors, and still, when reflecting upon the nature of the physical world, find herself in the predicament that Quine calls the empirical underdetermination of theory.[4]

I thus take Davidson to be endorsing Quine's distinction as an instance of a general point: First, there is the claim that, within some vocabulary, two theories may comport equally well with the statements that capture some body of what we regard as relevant evidence. Secondly, there is the claim that when we settle on a theory within one vocabulary, this will not necessarily mandate a choice of theory in another, even though we want to say that we are, in the two vocabularies, in some sense talking about the same things or events. When will it not? Precisely when the two vocabularies stand in the sort of relation to each other that anomalous monism expresses; that is, when vocabularies by which we frame descriptions of the same causal relations are not reducible, definitionally or nomologically, one to the other.

It is, then, as Quine says, and as Davidson affirms; Brentano's irreducibility of intentionality and the indeterminacy of translation are of a piece. But while this suggests to Quine that intentional ascriptions are second-rate forms of description, it is in Davidson's deontologized version *simply* a way of putting the point that one vocabulary is not reducible to the other.[5] Once we give up the idea, as Davidson has done, that one vocabulary is especially suited to express the facts, to shape itself after the way things intrinsically are, the independence of theory-decisions across vocabularies becomes an ontologically insignificant fact. Not all truths are expressible in terms of the same vocabulary, because vocabularies are tailored to suit different needs and interests – that, indeed, is what makes them distinct vocabularies.

My point here has been that we can make sense of Davidson's use of Quine's indeterminacy-underdetermination distinction without saddling the former with the latter's "adventitious ontological puritanism" – indeed without seeing him as pursuing *ontology* at all, but simply as discussing the relations between different descriptive strategies. The indeterminacy–underdetermination contrast, on my reconstruction, need not be backed by anything more philosophically potent than a distinction between vocabularies. But does this recasting of terminology answer Rorty's worry?

We can quickly see that it does not. Quine's physicalism provides a principle of rank which gives clear content to the idea of a philosophically interesting difference between vocabularies. It is a ranking relative to which the undecidability prevailing between intra-vocabularic theory-alternatives is, as we might say, deemed fact-insensitive just in so far as it remains unsettled by our opting for a particular theory in the privileged vocabulary of physics. This, I have suggested, is just the aspect of Quine's doctrine that Davidson dispenses with; he precisely does not identify the truths expressed by the vocabulary of physics with "the facts." But even if I am right that this still leaves room for a distinction between underdetermination and indeterminacy, once this distinction is deontologized it is hard to see what reason indeterminacy-considerations might give us for insisting that there is something philosophically distinctive about the character of the vocabulary of the mental. What we are left with, once we accept Rorty's picture of vocabularies as tools, is just the bland claim that different vocabularies are different – the lesson that pragmatists take from the argument of "Mental Events" is that we should just stop worrying about the "ontological status" of various descriptive strategies. When we reconstruct the Quinean distinction in a manner that comports with this Rortyan moral, as I have tried to do, we thereby give up Quine's implicit understanding of what made the distinction a "philosophically interesting" one in the first place. The effect is simply to leave it mysterious what the basis could possibly be for claiming that the vocabulary of agency is philosophically distinctive, rather than – like the vocabularies of biology, political geography, or economics, or of public administration or of Talmudic midrash, or advertising, or Tantric yoga – just different.

4. Norms and the Distinctiveness of Agency

In fact, already in "Belief and the Basis of Meaning" Davidson explicitly drops the idea, advanced in "Mental Events," that indeterminacy is a key to understanding what makes the vocabulary of agency distinctive. The irreducibility of this vocabulary, says Davidson,

> is not due ... to the indeterminacy of meaning or translation, for if I am right, indeterminacy is important only for calling attention to how the interpretation of speech must go hand in hand with the interpretation of action generally, and so with the attributions of desires and beliefs. It is rather the methods we invoke in constructing theories of belief and meaning that ensures the irreducibility of the concepts essential to those theories. (1984, p. 154).

Such theories, Davidson concludes, "are necessarily governed by concern for consistency and general coherence with the truth, and it is this that sets these theories forever apart form those that describe mindless objects, or describe objects as mindless."

The idea that the distinctiveness of agency depends on the kinds of norms that govern the application of the relevant predicates, and specifically on the way that those norms are supported and held in place by a community of interpreters, surfaces again in "Three Varieties of Knowledge" (1991) and in "Could There Be a Science of Rationality?" (1995) Regarding the considerations put forward in these papers, however, Rorty finds no grounds for a compelling response to his criticism.

> I do not see that the notions of normativity and of rationality add anything to that of complexity of criteria of application of intentional predicates, any more than the notion of "causal concept" does. One can speak normatively – talk about conforming to rules and standards instead of talking about exhibiting regularities and similarities – whenever one wants to. But I do not see anything which distinguishes psychological from biological descriptions that makes it important to do so (In press *a*, p. 23).

As a way into a discussion of the role of normativity in Davidson's conception of the mental, let us note the significance of Rorty's reference to biological description in this passage. This points to an important question about Davidson's notion of a physical vocabulary, that with which the vocabulary of agency is supposed to contrast. "My suggestion," says Rorty, pressing just this question,

> that biology and psychology are on a par in their relation to the laws of physics can be reinforced by noting that Davidson sometimes uses "physics" in a narrow sense to mean what the physicist, as opposed to the chemist and the biologist, does. Sometimes he uses it in larger sense, synonymous with "natural science", in which physics extends all the way up through biology, though stopping short of psychology (In press *a*, p. 24).

As Rorty notes (fn 18), Davidson is explicit about these shifts in the scope of "the physical." Furthermore, as Rorty also observes, Davidson is quite clear that neither the causal character of the predicates employed nor the bare invocation of normativity will allow him to draw a sharp line between agency-talk and the vocabularies that are physical when this term is taken in the larger sense:

> Much of what I have said about what distinguishes mental concepts from the concepts of a developed physics could also be said to distinguish the concepts of many of the special sciences such as biology, geology, and meteorology. So even if I am right that the normative and causal character of mental concepts divide them definitionally and nomologically from the concepts of a developed physics, it may seem that there must be something more basic or foundational that accounts for this division. I think there is (Davidson, 1991, p. 163).

Now it seems to me that Davidson here moves to a position which revises, or resituates, the classic articulation of anomalous monism (1970) in a significant way – in the direction of Rortyan pragmatism. Let us take it that the distinction Davidson wants to draw is between the vocabulary of intentional ascription and vocabularies which do not rely on intentional predicates. In the quotation just offered, Davidson is quite clear that in drawing *this* distinction, rather than that between physics and everything else, we cannot rest on the observation that the predicates of the vocabulary of agency are nomologically and definitionally irreducible to those which figure in articulation of strict physical law. For that feature is one intentional predicates *share* with vocabularies which qualify for Davidson's purposes as physical. What Davidson must claim, to draw his line between the vocabulary of agency and non-intentional descriptive strategies of various heterogenous sorts, is that the irreducibility of the vocabulary of agency is due to features of that vocabulary which are unique to it. Following Davidson, we must propose to view those features as the very ones by which the vocabulary of agency may serve the purposes that make it the vocabulary that it is. In doing so, we are, of course, at the same time urging a certain conception of those purposes. Let us compare this with the line of thought in "Mental Events." There Davidson says,

> If the case of supposed laws linking the mental and the physical is different [from laws of empirical sciences], it can only be because to allow the possibility of such laws would amount to changing the subject. By changing the subject I mean here: deciding not to accept the criterion of the mental in terms of the vocabulary of the propositional attitudes (1970, p. 216).

This suggests that it is the presence or absence of the possibility of strict law linking their respective predicates which settles whether a shift from one vocabulary to another constitutes a change in subject. But in "Three Varieties of Knowledge," as we have just seen, Davidson grants that the relevant kind of law – that is, the strict kind – is no more likely to link special sciences to physics than it is to link psychology to physics. Yet Davidson still holds on to the claim he makes in this passage from "Mental Events;" to switch from the vocabulary of agency to the vocabularies of the natural sciences (the broad-sense physical) is to change the subject.[6] To state the implied revision in the language of "Mental Events;" it is not simply the fact that generalizations linking intentional predicates and predicates of physics are heteronomous generalizations that accounts for the distinctive character of the former.

This is to say that Davidson has come to give up on the idea, implicit in "Mental Events," that "the subject" can be identified by invoking the possibility of nomological reduction. For Davidson continues to want to say that there is something significant about the difference between the psychological and the special sciences, which is not reflected in the difference between these and physics. And while acknowledging that special-science predicates may be no less irreducible to physics than are predicates of agency, Davidson still expresses the distinctiveness of agency by suggesting that a switch from predicates of agency to those of the natural sciences represents a change in subject, while movements from the latter to the predicates of physics do not. But then, subjects may in some sense remain the same even when we substitute for one set of predicates another set to which the first is irreducible. Irreducibility itself is not what supports Davidson's claim to present an account of a philosophically distinctive vocabulary, one with a unique subject matter. Clearly, the critical question becomes; what are the considerations that warrant claims about sameness and difference of subject? It is this question which Davidson goes on to address after the passage from "Three Varieties of Knowledge" that I quoted above.

His answer, as I have suggested, is not simply the claim that agency-talk involves the application of norms, but concerns the particular way in which the normative element gives structure to the vocabulary. Rorty sees little promise in this direction.[7] After quoting Davidson (1995) to the effect that the application of predicates of agency requires us to apply standards of rationality, Rorty says,

> I would rejoin that there is nothing especially normative about my effort to translate, since all I am doing is trying to find a pattern of resemblances between my linguistic behaviour and the native's. I am trying to mesh her behaviour with mine by finding descriptions of what she is doing that also describe what I sometimes do. I cannot see that this attempt

differs from my attempt to find, for example, resemblances between the structure and behavior of an unfamiliar insect and those of familiar insects – resemblances which will permit me to assign the newcomer its proper place in the entomological scheme of things. Attributing species-membership to a new, strange, and ambiguous object is a matter of playing off a lot of considerations against a lot of other considerations, and so is figuring out how to translate a string of native noises (In press *a*, p. 22).

Rorty isn't suggesting that Davidson's normatively-laden model of radical interpretation is misguided, exactly. He adds, "I *can* of course describe myself as asking whether the native meets the norms of rationality, but all it will take for her to do so is to exhibit linguistic behavior that sufficiently parallels my own" (In press *a*, p. 22).

There is something right about this – at a high level of abstraction. Certainly Rorty is right that holism is a matter of degree, and if he were also right that the only thing distinctive of the intentional is that it is very, very holistic (In press *a*, p. 7), my Davidsonian game would be up. The distinction Davidson is drawing, however, trades on a suggestion about the particular way in which the application-conditions of predicates of agency are holistically constrained; Davidson invokes the norms embodied in the principle of charity to venture a proposal about the *kinds* of similarities that we seek when we describe creatures as agents. The distinctiveness of agency lies not in the holism that characterizes the vocabulary, but in the fact that the predicates thus applied take their point from a normativity we invoke when we try to explain to ourselves what it is that makes communication possible.

So far though, this is just an assertion. To begin to see if we can back it up, let us consider Rorty's deflationary parallel, entomological species classification. Is this in relevant respects a good parallel to the process of fixing of a theory of belief and meaning? *Any* classification of unfamiliar objects, it seems to me, is like any other in being a matter of "playing off a lot of considerations against a lot of other considerations." However, to give an *entomological* classification will involve a commitment to seek similarities and differences between the objects under consideration along certain general axes – axes that give empirical application to terms we rely on when considering insectish things, terms, indeed, the successful application of which is what makes us take ourselves to be dealing with *insects* in the first place. Though a lot of considerations will be relevant to our classification project, once we take it to be an entomological one, not any old property of our little critter will be a relevant consideration. Can we say something quite general about the kinds that matter? Sure we can – if we can say what entomology is about.[8] Similarly, for an interpreter, not *any* complex pattern of resemblance traced in behavior will be identifiable as a pattern of *linguistic* behavior, just as not any detectable complex pattern of movement will be recognized as action, as embodying thought. Davidson, invoking charity, is making a claim about just what *sort* of similarities count.

A little more specifically, the claim is that the concepts we apply when we trace the relevant patterns function in a way which is distinct not only form those predicates whose function is to allow formulation of the strictest possible law, but also, as we have seen, from the causal and even normative predicates of natural sciences in general. "The fundamental difference," Davidson says,

> between my knowledge of another mind and my knowledge of the shared physical world has a different source [than of the difference between my knowledge of my own mind and my knowledge of the minds of others]. Communication, and the knowledge of other minds that it presupposes, is the basis of our concept of objectivity, our recognition of the

distinction between true and false belief. There is no going outside this standard to check whether we have things right . . . (1991, p. 164).

Rorty quotes this remark, putting it together with what Davidson says two short paragraphs later: "It is here, I suggest, that we come to the ultimate springs of the difference between understanding minds and understanding the world as physical. A community of minds is the basis of knowledge; it provides the measure of all things." Rorty then comments,

> I can only think of one construal which would make this passage relevant to the question of why the psychology-biology gap is different from the biology-chemistry gap. This is to read it as saying: because we can test our views of physics and biology against the standard provided by "a community of minds," but cannot test our knowledge of psychology against our knowledge of physics and biology, there is a gap between knowledge of mental states and knowledge of everything else. (In press a, p. 27).

Rorty points out that this asymmetry is hard to square with Davidson's doctrine of triangulation, which makes intentional ascriptions out to be characterizations of patterns of causal interaction between interpreters in a world. Moreover, Rorty thinks, this construal is difficult to reconcile with the punch line of "A Nice Derangement of Epitaphs," that "we have erased the boundary between knowing a language and knowing our way around in the world generally." (Davidson, 1986b, pp. 445–6, quoted in Rorty In press a, p. 28).

I think we can understand Davidson's point in "Three Varieties of Knowledge" in a different way, one which is not in tension with the Davidsonian doctrines Rorty mentions and that he and I both admire, and which, moreover, helps us understand the particular way in which normativity is invoked to underwrite the distinctiveness of agency. Let me approach this by filling in some surrounding text. Between the passages that Rorty's quotation links, Davidson brings out a disanalogy between measurement of temperature and interpretation. He says,

> the nature of the scaling device differs in the two cases. We depend on our linguistic interpretations with others to yield agreement on the properties of numbers and the sort of structures in nature that allow us to represent those structures in numbers. We cannot in the same way agree on the structure of sentences or thoughts we use to chart the thoughts and meanings of others, for the attempt to reach such an agreement simply sends us back to the very process of interpretation on which all agreement depends. (1991, p. 164)

This paragraph suggests to me that Rorty gets the emphasis wrong when he glosses Davidson's point that a "community of minds is the basis of knowledge" as the claim that "knowing our way around the community of beliefs is the *basis* of the rest of our knowledge." (In press a, p. 28) And it is because he gets the emphasis wrong in this way that he ends up with a construal of Davidson's key point in "Three Varieties of Knowledge" that is in tension with other pragmatic Davidsonian theses. In fact, Davidson is not holding one particular kind of knowledge up as the basis for other kinds; as Rorty sees and argues, the thought that any kind of knowledge is in that sense *basic* is quite at odds with the general thrust of Davidson's paper – indeed with his antirepresentationalism in general. The basis of knowledge, any form of knowledge, whether of self, others, or the shared world, is not a community of *minds*, in the sense of mutual knowledge of neighboring belief-systems, as Rorty here takes it to be. Rather, it is a *community* of minds; that is, a plurality of creatures engaged in the project of describing their world and interpreting each other's descriptions of it. This suggestion entails no priority of one kind of knowledge of the sort that Rorty's reading suggests, but emphasizes the intersubjective nature of *all* knowledge.

It is in this intersubjectivity that we must locate the sense in which the normativity of the predicates of agency underwrites the claim that this vocabulary constitutes a distinctive subject matter. We can agree with Rorty that we typically have a choice whether to describe patterns normatively, as conforming to rules, or descriptively, as manifesting regularities. Typically, but not, on Davidson's picture, unconditionally. *Describing* anything, if Davidson is right, is an ability we have only because it is possible for others to see us as in general conforming to the norms that the predicates of agency embody. We do not stand over against the normative demands embodied in the principle of charity as subjects of reflective choice. This is a point that Rorty ought to accept, because it supports his claim, against the project of normative epistemology, that we do not in general "have any choice about how to form beliefs" (1995c, p. 152). We are made the believers we are by the communicative interactions constituted by complex patterns of causal interaction with others in a shared world. This point really is a reflection of Davidson's doctrine of triangulation, transposed from meaning to belief. The norms of agency, those expressed by the charity of the ideal interpreter, are not norms that we can hold up before ourselves or others as directives or guides to behavior. *That* we generally conform to them is what makes us language-users, and so thinkers and knowers. *Whether* in general to conform to them is not a question of subjective choice at all; in just the same way, and indeed for the same reason, that what to mean by our noises cannot, in general, be a matter of subjective, deliberative choice. It is just on this point that the normativity of agency differs distinctively from the normativity of some of the functional concepts we use for the purposes of prediction and explanation in domains where we are not concerned to describe the objects or creatures as thinking beings. Of course we sometimes find it convenient to describe patterns in our own behavior or that of others in purely descriptive terms, even patterns which are also describably, and commonly are described, in the terms of the vocabulary of agency. However, in such cases, too, norms are involved; the descriptions emerge as descriptions of any sort at all only against a taken-for-granted background of purposive – and hence normatively describable – behavior on the part of the communicators involved. The point of the principle of charity in Davidson's account is that this background is *inescapable* for language users, whether we for some particular purpose are using purely descriptive predicates.

This, I think, gives us a reason for insisting that a theory of behavior of the sort that the ideal interpreter produces is a theory of truth – or perhaps of error. Perhaps this point would appear more congenial to Rorty, if we make it by taking off from the kind of Darwinian naturalism that he recommends.

Rorty tries to get us into a philosophical position from which it is clear that when we have explained the ability to use language as a gift of evolution, we have dissipated any metaphysical puzzle about the relation between thought and reality. The idea of the world being a certain way *in itself* loses its contrastive force, Rorty urges, when we conceive of language in such Darwinian terms, as a (very interesting) feature of the world. I think he is right about this; we should drop the representationalist idea of a world in itself that we cognizers confront. However, even on Rorty's pragmatic, Darwinian picture of language, a good way to conceive of what we language-users are able, as such, to do for ourselves, will invoke the truth–error contrast.

Rorty, we know, often speaks of redescription as a way of achieving certain kinds of changes. Some critics see this as a kind of idealism, but that is a misguided response. Rather, different strategies of description, on this view, are ways of bringing salience to different causal patterns in the world, patterns with which we engage. And that is just the great ability that language brings, this ability to reprogram our causal dispositions through salience-alteration. We are organisms causally engaged with the rest of the world in ways that we have developed this very nifty means – language – of modifying. By changing our causal dispositions, redistributing significance across kinds, we affect how we engage with the world, and thus also the world. Indeed, if changing descriptive strategies – vocabularies – didn't have a causal impact on how things are, it would be hard to see how language could have evolved as a useful tool. On the pragmatist view I impute to Rorty, changing descriptions matters, just because it makes a causal difference in the world. This it does because it changes *us*, our dispositions.

But how does it do this? It is as an answer to this question that the concept of error, or the truth–error contrast, becomes useful. To be linguistically reprogrammable in the way I have sketched must involve a capacity to register a difference between different descriptions of the same salient object or event. Such awareness depends on a certain rigidity of language, preventing the conversational payload of particular utterances from simply collapsing into their particular salient causes: it depends on what we often call meaning, or sense. A descriptive utterance is descriptive in so far as it presents something as a *kind* of thing. But this is just to say that any linguistic utterance, as opposed to a mere noise, will have appropriateness-conditions. The possibility of *error*, generalized in the notion of inappropriateness with respect to purpose, goal, or end, takes the form in (assertively-used) language of the possibility of a failure of a claim to be in accord with what it says something about. That possibility is inseparable from the capacity of redescription to affect our *dispositions*, because it reflects the fact that utterances are utterances – uses of language – just in so far as they link particular occasions of utterance with other possible or actual occasions or situations. Thus the concept of error marks our ability to get our noises and (the rest of the) world prized locally apart to a sufficient extent to allow for intentionality, for there *being* meaning and mind, that is to say, for there being a point to treating some things as thinkers, with a point of view on the world. In a sense, this picture inverts the framing assumptions of traditional normative epistemology since Descartes. For the mystery really cannot be, for the Darwinian naturalist, how mind and meaning could possibly connect with, relate to, or correspond with the world. The mystery, a scientific one, is how we have been able to develop this amazing system of behavior that allows us to stand, locally and for particular purposes, at a distance from some aspect of the world, and then exploit that distance to modify our dispositions in systematic ways.

That we have this capacity, however, is what we make clear when we call the radical interpreter's theory of behavior a theory of truth – or, what is the same point, a theory of *action*. To be sure, if we are committed to Darwinian naturalism we are required to explain – in, as Rorty says (borrowing from Dennett), "reverse engineering terms" – the genesis of this ability to reprogram the pattern of our dispositions. But that project certainly does not require us to describe the "very good trick" that is the explanandum, to articulate the capacities that language-use confers on us, without invoking normative notions. And indeed, if the picture I just sketched has any plausibility, this cannot be done – at least it cannot be done if we also want to highlight the manner in which the ability to communicate linguistically distinguishes agents from other sorts of things.

That is how I take Davidson's project, and it gives us a reason to find a point in describing theories of interpretation as theories, in particular, of *truth*.

5.   The Interests of Philosophy

To say what it is a language user does, we invoke normative notions. Moreover, these notions, as wielded in the vocabulary of agency, have the unique feature that they do not perform their function by constraining our subjective choices in the way, say, that what we might take to be the norms of good behavior might do. They perform their function by depicting us generally as error-makers, and thus also knowers of some truths, and hence also capable, by producing new descriptions, of modifying our causal dispositions. It may be, however, that Rorty would be quite willing to grant all this. Still he might ask, "why should any of this make us inclined to say that the psychological is *philosophically* special?" It may be that Rorty's issue is not with claims about the nature of the vocabulary of agency of the sort I have been making, but with the idea that these claims confer on this vocabulary special philosophical status. That claim, to Rorty's ears, is regressive. This brings me to my final topic – the nature of philosophical interest.

Rorty certainly has sympathy for Davidson's attempt to stifle the reductive (or eliminative) impulse that dominates in quarters where natural science is cast in the role of what used to be called ontology. Casting science in the role of ontology is not simply to assert that only what scientific theories quantify over is real – this is a fairly innocuous (though not obviously true) claim, until it is coupled with the attempt to formulate a *criterion* of the scientific. Science as ontology is what we get when we make the innocuous assertion, pick an ideal science, fix its essence, and anoint it Science (physics is the only serious candidate), and then seek to specify ways of being related to the predicates of Science that confer ontological legitimacy. This line of thought, which Rorty calls scientism, is certainly one of Davidson's targets. However, Rorty suspects, by grounding his enduring commitment to the philosophical distinctiveness of the mental in an antireductivist account of the vocabulary of agency, Davidson affirms the ontological significance of the possibility of vocabulary reduction. The thought that questions of ontology must turn on the possibility of reduction is a widely shared assumption, a premise of those who seek to account for the content of intentional ascription in non-intentional terms, as well as of those who predict – or desire – the elimination of intentional idiom precisely because they are skeptical about the prospects of bringing folk-psychological predicates into systematic nomological relations with predicates of natural science. Rorty rejects this thought. This is not, of course, because he is hawking an alternative ontological method. Rorty rejects the very idea of ontology, understood as a search for principles yielding orders of rank of reality-responsiveness for our various vocabularies or descriptive practices. His naturalism is such that he sees any attempt to work up general adequacy-conditions on vocabularies as regressive, as harking back to a time when getting things right and responding differentially to environmental stimuli were construed as categories of different order, with the former a candidate for (philosophical) explanation of the striking success of certain very sophisticated cases of the latter. In Rorty's view, however, neither truth and its cognates (with respect to beliefs) nor referential adequacy (with respect to vocabularies) has the sort of conceptual autonomy with respect to other desirable features or consequences of beliefs and linguistic habits that is required if we are to invoke these notions in *explanation* of occurrences of the features. Vocabularies can be evaluated, in so far as different vocabularies may serve different purposes and interests. But human purpose and interest provide both the framework for individuations of vocabularies, and the ultimate terms of any evaluation.

In Rorty's view, the right response to the scientistic impulse which poses a choice between elimination and reduction is to be *a*reductivist, rather than *anti*reductivist; it is to formulate a view of the point of linguistic behavior which deprives the success or failure of the reduction of one vocabulary to another of all ontological significance. Only on such a view, believes Rorty, can the connection between reduction and philosophical legitimation be completely severed. Davidson, Rorty thinks, has done more than anyone to help us articulate such a view. However, Davidson's insistence on the distinctiveness of the mental suggests to Rorty that Davidson is not yet willing to follow his own line of thought through to its post-ontological conclusions.

Rorty takes it that a full appreciation, or absorption, of the Deweyan tool-analogy will prevent us from seeing any virtue in the kind of proposal that Davidson makes. Rorty thinks, we recall, that once we accept this Deweyan stance, "there can be no philosophical interest in reducing one idiom to another . . ." But why should we think this must follow? What is the conception "philosophical interest" at work that makes Rorty think it does? Since "philosophically interesting things" do not constitute, in Rorty's view, a natural kind, then couldn't it happen that in some context reduction would actually be an interesting issue for philosophers to get engaged in? We could preclude this in general either if there is no such thing as a philosophically interesting thing, or if it is a priori that whatever is philosophically interesting cannot include the success or failures of reductive efforts. Neither seems obvious. I would suggest that it must be possible to criticize the idea that exploration of the possibility of conceptual or nomological reduction is a metaphysical tool, without having to claim that reductive efforts *cannot* be of philosophical interest. Thinking of idioms as tools, the right thing to say about this question would be, it seems to me, "that just depends – show me the context and the stakes."

The problem, I think, is that Rorty sometimes works with a conception of philosophical interest which makes the right thing to say be that there is *nothing* which would be of *philosophical* interest in particular; we should stop thinking that "of philosophical interest" is an informative way to pick out questions or topics at all. In this usage, "philosophically interesting issue" just means "topic where degree and nature of contact with what's really there is believed to be at issue." Taken that way, it is of course true that Davidson's account of agency does not point to a philosophically interesting distinction. Indeed, taken this way, peace will only come when no-one any longer finds philosophical interest in anything.

But for those of us who have had our thinking about philosophy shaped by Rorty, this understanding of philosophical theory as inherently ontological seems unnecessarily restrictive. If we take on board Rorty's tool-metaphor, and accept, as I try to do, the vocabulary-vocabulary, it seems we clearly do have a much more positive understanding of "philosophical interest" available to us.[9] The vocabulary-vocabulary is itself a tool, a tool of philosophy, whereby we precisely reflect on the nature of our tools and the purposes they serve. As Rorty says, we evaluate tools comparatively, in terms of purposes. And one thing certainly true of tools is that using one kind of tool to solve a particular kind of problem may interfere with, or preclude, or facilitate, the use of another, or force one to go a certain way, with a certain tool, later in the project; "the wrench may get the screw, but now the cylinder will be stripped – better to use the screwdriver and the rust-remover, since tomorrow we just might want to be able to reinsert a screw there." Why could vocabularies or idioms not be suspected of standing in similar sorts of relation, and therefore be subject to analogous treatment?

Indeed it is clear that Rorty thinks they can. It well fits the mandate of philosophy that Rorty appropriates from Dewey:

> Dewey construed Hegel's insistence on historicity as the claim that philosophers should not try to be the avantgarde of society and culture, but should be content to mediate between the past and the future. Their job is to weave together old beliefs and new beliefs, so that these beliefs can cooperate rather than interfere with one another. Like the engineer and the lawyer, the philosopher is useful in solving particular problems that arise in particular situations – situations in which the language of the past is in conflict with the needs of the future. (1995a, p. 199)

Now I take this be not primarily a directive as to how to do philosophy, but a directive for thinking about what philosophers actually do. My interpretation of Davidson arises out of an application of that directive to his account of agency. The upshot of that interpretation is that the vocabulary of agency marks a distinctive subject because it is built to serve interests that we pick out not simply by reference to the kinds of things we want to predict (people, as opposed to electrons or super-novas), but also by virtue of features that are not merely predictive. What links special sciences together, if anything does, into a single contrastive entity with respect to the vocabulary of agency, is not an alleged reducibility of any bona fide natural science to a purely structural vocabulary (basic science, ideal physics, what have you). Rather it is a certain homogeneity of interest; that it can be characterized in terms of a purely predictive aspect. There is a sense in which we are not changing the subject by substituting one set of predicates for another in a science, or switching from one set to another, even if there's no reduction or prospect of reduction, as long as the switch is motivated by an attempt to better serve prediction of the phenomena in some domain, even a very loosely and tentatively characterized domain, where we change even our conception of the phenomena to be explained. With agency-vocabulary, by contrast, we are characterizing a domain of kinds of objects (language-users) with a vocabulary not *just* geared toward prediction of the behavior of that kind. Or perhaps we should rather say that the predictive interests that are expressed in the dynamics of agency-vocabulary are of a very peculiar sort – they turn on our revealing the kinds of traits that allow us to *recognize ourselves* in what we are talking about, and to bring to bear all those complicated considerations that we gesture at with the moral notion of a person. I would argue that charities and rationality-constraints, presented as a necessary methodological assumption of the ideal interpreter, really embody the very *point* of agency-talk, precisely because they are inextricably connected with this notion. If agency-vocabulary is shaped by the interests that turn on this kind of recognition, perhaps the effort to extend that recognition is served by our attempts to entrench the vocabulary, and by efforts to show that with it we articulate truths as first-rate as any.

I do not see that this depends on claims about gaps between ontological kinds, nor on claims about the ontological significance of reducibility, nor on claims about the greater factuality of structural, rather than functional, terms. Rather, thinking along these lines about Davidson's distinction, it appears as an attempt to provide us a way to distinguish the interests that intentional-language vocabulary serves from those interests that vocabularies of scientific explanation serve. If we do not so distinguish them, if we become content to think of what we are doing with intentional language *simply* in terms of vocabularies of prediction and control, then we may attenuate dangerously an aspect of our conception of ourselves that I think we ought instead to strengthen. In my metaphilosophical frame, Davidson's anomalous monism is a proposal for a characterization of what we are that is designed to keep us from trying to pursue the purposes for which we use it with vocabularies built for prediction and control of manipulable objects. By contrast, if we describe this tool – construe this vocabulary – as of a piece with natural science, we might make ourselves more likely to employ such vocabularies for purposes where, so I think, the vocabulary of agency leaves us better off, better in the sense of "politically more free." I see Davidson as providing a tool, a marginal tool, to be sure, since he is a theorist, in a struggle against the steady spread of dehumanizing, homogenizing management of human existence that is the real threat of scientism. Scientism is not bad, I am sure Rorty would agree, because it gets the world wrong, or even because it is a rehash of Kantian and Platonic ontology, but because it renders us subject to certain forms of oppression.

Of course, these last paragraphs are very speculative. But they suggest, I think, that nothing Rorty says *precludes* the idea that the philosophical distinctiveness of agency is worth entrenching, and it may give some reason for thinking that it is a good idea. At least I hope I have made plausible that we can think so without betraying Rorty's post-ontological picture of what philosophers are doing.

6.   Conclusion

Though Davidson has long since dropped the idea that indeterminacy-considerations underpin the specialness of the mental, Rorty dwells on it because for him only an attachment to the Quinean ontology embedded in the contrast between underdetermi-nation and indeterminacy can motivate a sense that the contrast between the vocabulary of agency and other descriptive strategies is philosophically special. Davidson's continu-ing declarations of allegiance to this Quineism strengthens Rorty's suspicion that Davidson's anti-reductivist argument is a hangover from the days of ontology. My essentially terminological point, explaining this allegiance and rendering it ontologically innocuous, does little to meet Rorty's worry; granting it simply leaves Davidson's doctrine of the distinctiveness of the mental unmotivated. Even if we accept my next point, that normativity, on Davidson's story, figures in a distinctive manner in the vocabulary of agency, it is hard for Rorty to see why we would want to say that this confers special philosophical status on the subject of that kind of talk. I then suggested that this is difficult only if we retain the idea that philosophical accounts of vocabularies are attempts to do ontology – that is to say, to distinguish and offer criticism of or warrant for descriptive strategies by appealing to the way the world is. But to give up on ontology is also to give up the idea that philosophical theory performs this function. We should instead take our cue from Rorty, and develop a conception of philosophy that fully integrates the vocabularies-as-tools metaphor. Once we do that, however, it is no longer true that vocabulary-reduction can have no philosophical interest. What is true is that reductive efforts as such have no *intrinsic* philosophical interest. But whether reductive or anti-reductive proposals matter to us as Rortyan philosophers depends entirely on what the particular vocabularies – the tools – in question are for. I suggest we construe a philosophical account of a vocabulary of the sort that Davidson offers as precisely an attempt to say what some vocabulary is *for*. Now any such specification is a redescriptive exercise of the sort that Rorty recommends, urging a particular way to conceive of ourselves, and thereby urging a particular way to structure our causal dispositions. What sort of warrant can we give for the particular proposal Davidson offers, that we cast the vocabulary of agency around norms of rationality? The point of the proposal, as I take it, is to foster a conception of what we are doing that preserves our sense of ourselves as creatures with purposes that are not exhausted by prediction and control. The point is to show that we have a way to talk about ourselves, that there are truths about us that matter, subjects of fundamental concern, that are not truths of explanatory theory. The point of this, in turn, is to strengthen those aspects of ourselves that make us less compliant in the face of steadily-expanding, homogenizing, technocratic, managerial forms of social organization.

Now, these kinds of considerations are just the sort that should matter to you if you take seriously the idea of the priority of democracy to philosophy. How do we decide whether they are convincing or not? Like all metaphilosophical argument, this one bottoms out in hunches about how pursuit of some descriptive strategy will effect how we live. I hope I have given Rorty some reasons to think again about the nature and point of the Davidsonian distinction he criticizes. But whether the proposal is a good one or not is a matter we can settle only by existentially experimenting with it; it is, as Rorty would insist, something that only experience will reveal.[10]

References

Brandom, Bob, 1998. "Vocabularies of Pragmatism: Synthesizing Naturalism and Historicism." This volume.

Davidson, Donald, 1970. "Mental Events." Reprinted in 1980a.

Davidson, Donald, 1974. "Belief and the Basis of Meaning." Reprinted in 1984.

Davidson, Donald, 1980. *Essays on Action and Events*. Oxford: Oxford University Press.

Davidson, Donald, 1984. *Enquiries into Truth and Interpretation*. Oxford: Oxford University Press.

Davidson, Donald, 1986. "A Coherence Theory of Truth and Knowledge." In Ernest LePore (ed.), *Truth and Interpretation*. Blackwell.

Davidson, Donald, 1986b. "A Nice Derangement of Epitaphs." In LePore.

Davidson, Donald, 1987. "Afterthoughts, 1987." Published with "A Coherence Theory of Truth and Knowledge," in Alan Malachowski (ed.), 1990. *Reading Rorty*. Blackwell.

Davidson, Donald, 1990. "The Structure and Content of Truth." *The Journal of Philosophy*, 87 (6).

Davidson, Donald, 1991. "Three Varieties of Knowledge." In Phillips Griffiths.

Davidson, Donald, 1995. "Could There Be a Science of Rationality?" *International Journal of Philosophical Studies*, 3 (1).

Davidson, Donald, 1996. "The Folly of Trying to Define Truth." *The Journal of Philosophy*, 93 (6).

Ramberg, Bjørn, forthcoming a. "What Davidson Said to the Sceptic." In *Interpreting Davidson: Proceedings of the fifth Karlovy Vary Symposium on Analytic Philosophy*.

Ramberg, Bjørn, forthcoming b. "Rorty and the Instruments of Philosophy." In *Proceedings of the 1997 Belo Horisonte Symposium on Analytic Philosophy and Pragmatism*.

Rorty, Richard, 1972a. "The World Well Lost." Reprinted in 1982.

Rorty, Richard, 1972b. "Indeterminacy of Translation and of Truth." *Synthese* 23.

Rorty, Richard, 1979. *Philosophy and the Mirror of Nature*. Princeton University Press.

Rorty, Richard, 1982. *Consequences of Pragmatism*. Minnesota University Press.

Rorty, Richard, 1986. "Pragmatism, Davidson, and Truth." Reprinted in 1991.

Rorty, Richard, 1987. "Non-reductive Physicalism." Reprinted in 1991.

Rorty, Richard, 1988. "Representation, Social Practice, and Truth." Reprinted in 1991.

Rorty, Richard, 1989. *Contingency, Irony, and Solidarity.* Cambridge University Press.

Rorty, Richard, 1991a. *Objectivity, Relativism, and Truth.* Cambridge University Press.

Rorty, Richard, 1991b. *Essays on Heidegger and Others.* Cambridge University Press.

Rorty, Richard, 1995a, "Philosophy and the Future." In Herman Saatkamp (ed.). *Rorty and Pragmatism.* Nashville, TE: Vanderbilt University Press.

Rorty, Richard, 1995b. "Is Truth a Goal of Enquiry?" *The Philosophical Quarterly*, 45 (180).

Rorty, Richard, 1995c. "Reply to Haack." In Herman Saatkamp (ed.). *Rorty and Pragmatism.* Nashville, TE: Vanderbilt University Press.

Rorty, Richard, In press *a*. "McDowell, Davidson, and Spontaneity." Forthcoming in *Philosophy and Phenomenological Research.* (Page references are to manuscript.)

Rorty, Richard, In press *b*. "Davidson's Mental-Physical Distinction." Forthcoming in *Donald Davidson*, Library of Living Philosophers, Lewis E. Hahn (ed.), Open Court. (Page references are to manuscript.)

Notes

1 See "The World Well Lost" (1972a), and Chapter IV of *Philosophy and the Mirror of Nature* (1979).

2 For example, Rorty thinks Davidson is misleading when he claims to have an *argument* against the skeptic (1986, pp. 134–6). For Davidson's accommodating response, see his "Afterthoughts, 1987" to "A Coherence Theory of Truth and Knowledge." I discuss Rorty's criticisms of Davidson on this score in "What Davidson Said to the Skeptic." Rorty's attitude to argument, and the significance of this attitude to critics of Rorty, is my topic in "Rorty and the Instruments of Philosophy."

3 In "Representation, Social Practice, and Truth" (1988), Rorty criticizes Sellars for retaining the idea of correspondence at the level of vocabulary.

4 The point is intended with respect to theories in physics, rather than with respect to the ordinary descriptions that we rely on in our daily traffic with common, middle-sized objects, since the former is what physicalistic ontological puritans wish to privilege. Opting for undetached rabbit-parts rather than instantiated Rabbithood will not help the theoretical physicist one bit. In a perverse mood, we might say, "With respect to the facts of meaning, empirical undecidabilities of theoretical physics are simply indeterminate!"

5 Consider a remark Davidson makes in "Three Varieties of Knowledge."

> I once thought the indeterminacy of translation supplied a reason for supposing there are no strict laws connecting mental and physical concepts, and so supported the claim that mental concepts are not even nomologically reducible to physical concepts. I was wrong: indeterminacy turns up in both domains. (1991, pp. 161–2)

This rather enigmatic, un-Quinean statement makes good sense on the reading I propose; if the indeterminacy-claim just is a way of making the irreducibility-claim, then it cannot serve as a reason to be adduced in support of it. As I make out the indeterminacy-relation, we get just the symmetry that Davidson here appears to acknowledge. It is this symmetry which makes it hard to see how indeterminacy can support claims about the distinctiveness of the mental.

6 Compare:

> For the case of causal properties like elasticity, slipperiness, malleability, or solubility we tend to think, rightly or wrongly, that what they leave unexplained can be (or already has been) explained by the advance of science. We should not be changing the subject if we

were to drop the concept of elasticity in favor of the microstructure of the materials in the airplane wing that cause it to return to its original shape when exposed to certain forces. Mental concepts are not like this. (Davidson 1991, p. 163)

7   In fact, as he makes explicit in the final section of "Davidson's Mental–Physical Distinction," Rorty sees promise for Davidson's distinction in *no* direction. Here Rorty traces the motivations for drawing a line between the mental and the physical to the urge to maintain a neat division between the made and the found, and suggests that "if one insists on drawing such a line . . . one would be better advised to follow [David] Lewis rather than Davidson." (In press *a*, p. 32) But then, if one draws the distinction where Lewis, and sometimes Quine, draws it, at the line "between the elementary particles and everything else . . . where pure structure stops and function begins – or, as I would put it, the line between the ideal and the actual – the insects and the birds turn out to be as much "made" as the meanings." (In press *a*, p. 31) Physics, rather than unified (non-intentional) science, is your best bet if you suffer from an impulse to mark ontological gaps. Rorty, of course, thinks that such "impulses should be firmly repressed, rather than sympathetically cultivated" (In press *a*, p. 36). I agree with Rorty about that. Yet I want to defend Davidson's distinction. Hence, I suggest to Rorty that we take the unsuitability of Davidson's mental–physical distinction to serve as a marker for such gaps as a reason for thinking its function is not to serve that purpose.

8   Usually we take a shortcut and say it is the branch of zoology dealing with insects. This doesn't say nothing, of course, but to get the kind of analogy I am after better into focus, we could imagine ourselves explaining "entomology" to someone who is unclear on exactly what zoology is, and wonders what inclines us to call some little buzzing thing an insect.

9   See Brandom, this volume, for development of the idea of the vocabulary vocabulary.

10   I want to thank Richard Rorty for illuminating and extensive comments on an essay of mine on topics related to that of the present paper. Much of what I say here develops points which were triggered by those comments. I am also very grateful to Martin Allen, Laney Doyle, Alan Engle, Heather Harrington, Thomas Hribek, Robert Sinclair, Nadine Syrjala, and Paul Thorne, who patiently endured my efforts to get the issues I discuss in this paper into clearer focus. Their contributions to our seminar at SFU during the spring of 1997 were a great help to me in that process.

RESPONSE TO BJØRN RAMBERG

Most of my responses in this volume are, at least to some extent, rebuttals. But in the case of Bjørn Ramberg's paper, I find myself not only agreeing with what he says, but very much enlightened by it. So I shall be trying to restate Ramberg's arguments rather than to rebut them – trying to strengthen them rather than weaken them.

Ramberg offers answers to two questions about Davidson's work which have troubled me for years. These are: (1) Why does it seem important to Davidson to think of a Tarski-type theory for a natural language as a *truth*-theory for that language rather than simply as a way of predicting regularities in the behavior of speakers of that language? Why, given our agreement on the indefinability of "true," does Davidson object to my saying that there is nothing much to be said about truth? (2) Why is Davidson so perversely loyal to Quine when it comes to the indeterminacy of translation? Why does he keep saying that the intentional stance is special, in a way that the biological stance, the chemical stance, etc., are not?

Ramberg answers both questions by suggesting that the famous Brentanian irreducibility of the intentional is an unfortunate distraction from the inescapability of the normative. By concentrating on the latter, he shows how Davidson offers what he nicely describes as a "post-ontological philosophy of mind."

"Ontological" philosophy of mind says that we have something that other creatures do not have, a mind, and that this extra added ingredient is mysterious. Much current criticism of this sort of philosophy, notably Dennett's, has said that mentalistic descriptions are no more mysterious than physical or biological descriptions. They are simply different. Once one stops asking how the two ingredients of the human beings are related, and instead asks how and why it is useful to have (at least) two descriptions of human behavior, the mystery vanishes. In this spirit I urged, in an article Ramberg cites, that the irreducibility of the intentional is no more philosophically interesting than the irreducibility of any descriptive vocabulary to any other.

But in that article, and in most of what I have written, I have turned a blind eye to the fact that the mind–body distinction is intertwined with the person–thing distinction. I have not tried to relate the two distinctions. Davidson, by combining a theory of action with a theory of truth and meaning, has. Ramberg helps bring Davidson's two lines of inquiry together when he says that an account of truth is automatically an account of agency, and conversely. He helps us see that Davidson, like Dewey, is trying to break down the distinction between the knowing, theorizing, spectatorial mind and the responsible participant in social practices.

Kant did his best to separate the mind–body distinction from the person–thing distinction by arguing that the former was within the realm of the understanding (or, as we should say, the descriptive) and the latter within the realm of practical reason (or, as we should say, the normative). Yet Kant's own use of the term "rational" (in such contexts as in "Treat all rational beings . . .") tempts us to run the two distinctions back together again. Davidson follows up this lead, and often uses "rationality," "normativity," "intentionality," and "agency" as if they were roughly co-extensive predicates.

We can, however, hold on to Kant's distinction between the normative concept "person" and the descriptive concept "mind," by making a distinction between two senses of "rationality." The obvious way to do this is identify the descriptive sense of rationality with the possession of beliefs and desires and the normative sense with being "one of us" – with being a member of our community, tied to us by reciprocal responsibilities. Most of the things which are rational in the first sense are also rational in the second, and conversely. But there are occasional exceptions. We may use an intentional vocabulary to get a grip on the pattern exhibited by a robot's behavior, even while continuing to regard the robot as a thing rather than a person. We regard infants and speechless paralytics as persons rather than things, even though their behavior can be readily predicted in a physiological vocabulary, without the help of an intentional one.[1]

Ramberg suggests that we see the ability to ascribe rights and responsibilities (along the lines of Brandom's "social practice" reconstruction of the vocabularies of logic and semantics) as (usually) a prerequisite for the ability to predict and describe. The key to understanding the relation between minds and bodies is not an understanding of the irreducibility of the intentional to the physical but the understanding of the inescapability of the normative.

By contrast, no merely descriptive vocabulary is inescapable, except perhaps (for Kantian/Strawsonian reasons) the commonsense vocabulary in which we describe the motions of middle-sized physical objects perceptible by human sense organs. We could have done a lot of predicting and controlling even if it had never occured to us go microstructural – even if science had remained Aristotelian. But we could not have spoken either commonsensical or Aristotelian or corpuscularian unless we were already treating each other as persons who had duties to respond to certain situations with certain words rather than others.

A normative vocabulary is presupposed by any descriptive vocabulary – not because of any inferential relations between sentences in the one vocabulary and those in the other, but pragmatically. We could not deploy the descriptive vocabulary unless we could also deploy the normative one, just as we could not employ a screwdriver if we did not have hands. As Ramberg says "*Describing* anything, if Davidson is right, is an ability we have only because it is possible for others to see us as in general conforming to the norms that the predicates of agency embody." Agency – the ability to offer descriptions rather than just to make noise – only appears if a normative vocabulary is already being used: "the descriptions emerge as descriptions of any sort at all only against a taken-for-granted background of purposive – hence normatively describable-behavior on the part of the communicators involved."

Why are we so tempted to run together the concepts of mind and of person, and to run together rationality-as-intentionality and rationality-as-having-responsibilities? Why was this temptation strong enough to make Kant slide back into metaphysics – to claim that freedom is possible only if there is a non-spatio-temporal kind of reality? The answer to both questions, I take Ramberg to be saying, is that there is considerable overlap between the beings we talk *about* using the intentional vocabulary and the beings whom we talk *to* using the normative vocabulary. This overlap is far from accidental, but neither is it complete.

It is not accidental because the behavior of language-users is very hard to predict without taking the intentional stance. Language-users are also the beings toward whom we are most likely to feel responsibilities, and from whom we are most likely to demand respect. That is because they can talk back to us, argue with us about is to be done (including what various things are to be called). But we cannot simply identify being a language-user, something rendered predictable by taking the intentional stance, with being a person. For the overlap is not complete. We cannot use any of the three as either a necessary or a sufficient condition for any of the others. We philosophers keep trying to lock these three concepts together more tightly. Yet there is no need for such tightness. It is enough to understand why we so often use them in dealing with the same beings.

We talk both to and about each other. We both criticize each others performances and describe them. We could not do the one unless we could do the other. There are many descriptive vocabularies (many "ways of bringing salience to different causal patterns in the world," as Ramberg puts it) and many different communities of language-users, but we must always both pick some such pattern and belong to some such community. We cannot stop prescribing, and *just* describe, because the describing counts *as* describing only if rule-governed, only if conducted by people who talk about each other in the vocabulary of agency. Ramberg puts the point as follows:

> With agency-vocabulary, by contrast, we are characterizing a domain of kinds of objects (language-users) with a vocabulary not *just* geared toward prediction of the behavior of that kind – or perhaps we should say that the predictive interests that are expressed in the dynamics of agency-vocabulary are of a very peculiar sort – they turn on revealing the kinds of traits that allow us *to recognize ourselves* in what we are talking about, and to bring to bear all those complicated considerations that we gesture at with the moral notion of a

person ... Davidson's distinction appears as a way to distinguish the interests that intentional-language vocabulary serves from those interests that vocabularies of scientific explanation serve. (p. 366)

The last sentence I have quoted implies that I was missing Davidson's point when I kept asking him the second of the two sets of questions I listed earlier: Why is the intentional not just one more useful descriptive vocabulary? Why is its irreducibility to other such vocabularies such a big deal? Why is the so-called "indeterminacy of translation" something different from the ordinary underdetermination of theory?

Ramberg is replying, on Davidson's behalf, that there is a vocabulary which is privileged, not by irreduciblity, but by inescapability. It is not, however, the descriptive vocabulary of intentionality but the prescriptive vocabulary of normativity. The latter tends be used *to* talk to the same beings as are talked *about* in the former. But the two are not the same.

I think Ramberg is right, and very acute, in his diagnosis of the impasse between myself and Davidson on the topic of indeterminacy of translation. Ramberg is suggesting that I should have read Davidson as telling us something Hegelian rather than something Brentanian: something about *Anerkennung*. Davidson, he rightly says, has understood better than I that recognizing some beings as fellow-obeyers of norms, acknowledging them as members of a community, is as much a requirement for using a language as is the ability to deploy a descriptive vocabulary. The recognition establishes, so to speak, a community of tool-users. The various descriptive vocabularies this community wields are the tools in its kit. No toolkit, no community – if we did not describe we would have no criticisms to offer of one another's descriptions. But no community, no toolkit – if we did not criticize each other's descriptions, they would not be descriptions. Ramberg makes the latter point as follows:

The basis of knowledge, any form of knowledge, whether of self, others, or the shared world, is not a community of *minds*, in the sense of mutual knowledge of neighboring belief-systems ... Rather, it is a *community* of minds, that is, a plurality of creatures engaged in the project of describing their world and interpreting each other's descriptions of it. (pp. 361–2)

I can epitomize what Ramberg has done for my understanding of Davidson by saying that he has helped me understand the point of a sentence of Davidson's which I had previously found utterly opaque. Ramberg quotes Davidson as saying

We depend on our linguistic interpretations with others to yield agreement on the properties of numbers and the sort of structures in nature that allow us to represent those structures in numbers. We cannot in the same way agree on the structure of sentences or thoughts we use to chart the thoughts and meanings of others, for the attempt to reach such agreement simply sends us back to the very process of interpetation on which all agreement depends.

I did not understand the second sentence in this passage until I read it in Ramberg's way. Read that way, it can be paraphrased as saying "Whereas you can, in the course of triangulation, criticize any given claim about anything you talk about, you cannot ask for agreement that others shall take part in a process of triangulation, for the attempt to reach such an agreement would just be more triangulation." The inescapability of norms is the inescapability, for both describers and agents, of triangulating.

****

So much for the question about Davidson's invocation of the doctrine of the indeterminacy of translation. What about the first of the questions I listed earlier – the question of why Davidson thinks that my dismissive attitude toward the concept of "truth" is misleading?

Ramberg sets me straight here too. He tells me, in effect, that it was a mistake on my part to go from criticism of attempts to define truth as accurate representation of the intrinsic nature of reality to a denial that true statements get things right. What I should have done, he makes me realize, is to grant Davidson's point that most of our beliefs about anything (snow, molecules, the moral law) must be true of that thing – must get that thing right.

For when Davidson argues that most of anybody's beliefs must be true, he is not just saying (as I have sometimes been tempted to construe him) that most of the beliefs of anybody whom we can treat as a language-user must accord with our own beliefs. He is saying that most of what anybody says about whatever they are talking about *gets that thing right*. Since I now want to agree with Davidson on this point, I am going to have to stop saying, in imitation of Sellars, that "true" and "refers" do not name word–world relations. Nor shall I any longer be able to say that *all* our relations to the world are causal relations. I shall instead have to say that there are certain word–world relations which are *neither causal nor representational* – for instance, the relation "true of" which holds between "Snow is white" and snow, and the relation "refers to" which holds between "snow" and snow. These relations, however, do not hold between that sentence and what philosophers like to call "reality as it is in itself," but only between those expressions and snow. No snow, no truth about snow, because nothing to get right.

I can epitomize up what I have been sayinig as follows: *What is true in pragmatism is that what you talk about depends not on what is real but on what it pays you to talk about. What is true in realism is that most of what you talk about you get right.*[2] Would there still be snow if nobody had ever talked about it? Sure. Why? Because according to the norms *we* invoke when we use "snow," we are supposed to answer this question affirmatively. (If you think that that glib and ethnocentric answer is not good enough, that is because you are still in the grip of the scheme–content distinction. You think you can escape the inescapable, cut off one corner of Davidson's triangle, and just ask about a relation called "correspondence" or "representation" between your beliefs and the world.)

How does this partial reconciliation of pragmatism and realism tie in with Ramberg's argument? Like this: for the same reason that most of our beliefs must be true, most of our norms must be obeyed. *Pacta sunt servanda*, as Brandom says. Snow would not be what it is if we were mostly wrong about it, and the norms for the use of "snow" would not be the norms they are if we did not, most of the time, obey them. That norms are mostly obeyed and objects mostly gotten right are two ways of making a single point: none of the three corners of his process of triangulation can be what they are in independence of the other two.

In the previous paragraphs I have been trying to draw the moral of the following passage in Ramberg's paper:

> A descriptive utterance is descriptive in so far as it presents something as a *kind* of thing. But this is just to say that any linguistic utterance, as opposed to a mere noise, will have

appropriateness-conditions. The possiblity of error, generalized in the notion of inappropriateness with respect to purpose, goal, or end, takes the form in (assertively used) language of the possibility of failure of a claim to be in accord with what it says about something. (p. 363)

Ramberg is right to suggest that Davidson's point is clearer if we call a Tarski-type theory a theory of error rather than a theory of truth. Because norms are not regularities, you can only get right what you can get wrong. So a being who could not be wrong about snow would not be a describer of snow, because she would not be a member of a norm-governed community of snow-describers. We cannot make sense of the notion of omniscience, for we cannot make sense of an uncriticizable describer, a describer related only to one of the other corners of the triangle (the corner where the snow is, but not the corner where the other snow-describers are).[3] The idea of omniscience goes when the idea of total skepticism goes: we could no more get something all right – indisputably, uncriticizably, right – any more than we could get it all wrong. Only *most* of our beliefs about something must be true. Belief is as intrinsically disputable as it is intrinsically veridical.

****

Some readers may have noticed that Ramberg has persuaded me to abandon two doctrines which I have been preaching for years: that the notion of "getting things right" must be abandoned, and that "true of" and "refers to" are not word–world relations. These readers may wish to know about the ramifications of these concessions to my "realist" opponents. How many of my previous positions – positions criticized by McDowell, Dennett and others in this volume – am I now forced to give up? Not many. Here are some doctrines which remain unaffected:

1   No area of culture, and no period of history, gets Reality more right than any other. The differences betewen areas and epochs is their relative efficiency at accomplishing various purposes. There is no such thing as Reality to be gotten right – only snow, fog, Olympian deities, relative aesthetic worth, the elementary particles, human rights, the divine right of kings, the Trinity, and the like. (Can you get right something that does not exist? Sure. Thanks to advances in archaeology and epigraphy, for example, we know a lot more about Zeus than was known in the Renaissance. The Fathers who met at Nicea knew a lot more about the Trinity than did the Apostles.)

Why cannot we get Reality (aka How the World Really Is In Itself) right? Because there are no norms for talking about it. *Quot homines, tot sententiae*: you can say anything you like about the deep underlying nature of reality and get away with it. There are norms for snow-talk and Zeus-talk, but not for Reality-talk. That is because the purposes served by the former, but not those served by the latter, are reasonably clear.

There is an analogy here with Michael Williams' treatment of skepticism. Williams has pointed out that epistemology, the idea of a philosophical account of something called "human knowledge," and skepticism, the idea that human beings are incapable of knowledge, go hand-in-hand. As long as you talk about knowledge of snow, or the Trinity, or positrons, it is hard to be either an epistemologist nor a skeptic, for you have to respect the norms built into discourse about these various things. Only when you start talking about Our Knowledge of Reality as such, a topic concerning which their are *no* norms, can you become either. "Reality" and "Our Knowledge of Reality" are alternative names for the normless. That is why metaphysics and epistemology go together like ham and eggs.

2   Pace McDowell, there is no second norm given us by the facts, in addition to the norms given us by our peers. Still, McDowell would be right to point out that I should not speak of "norms set by our peers." It was a mistake to locate the norms at one corner of the triangle – where my peers are – rather than seeing them as, so to speak, hovering over the whole process of triangulation. (Brandom's slogan "We have met the norms, and they are us" is acceptable only if "us" means "us as engaged in the process of triangulation.") It is not that my peers have more to do with my obligation to say that snow is white than the snow does, or than I do.

3   To say that we get snow mostly right is not to say that we represent snow with reasonable accuracy. Talk of representing goes along with talk about sentences being made true by facts, and with talk of "structural isomorphism" between mind and world (such as Dennett's "real patterns"). The holism of intentional ascription forbids any such talk. As Davidson says, "If we give up facts as entities that make sentences true, we ought to give up representations at the same time, for the legitimacy of each depends on legitimacy of the other."[4]

4   My militant anti-authoritarianism, exhibited in my response to Williams and critically discussed by McDowell, remains unchanged. For I can still maintain that there is no such thing as the search for truth, as distinct from the search for happiness. There is no authority called Reality before whom we need bow down.

     "Happiness," in the relevant sense, means "getting more of the things we keep developing new descriptive vocabularies in order to get." Getting snow right – getting still more truth about snow – is not an end in itself but a means to the purposes for which we invented the term "snow." Intellectual progress is not progress toward better and better representations of what is out there. It is not a matter of separating apparent patterns from real patterns. It is, in Ramberg's terms, finding more and more useful ways of "bringing salience to different causal patterns in the world." No such pattern (for instance, the pattern made salient by positron-talk as opposed to the pattern made salient by Zeus-talk) is more "real" than any other such pattern. Utility for human happiness is all that distinguishes them.[5]

Notes

1   Infants and speechless paralytics are not exactly full-fledged members of our moral community, since they have rights but no responsibilities. But they are certainly persons. We are less certain whether robots and slaves (who have responsibilities but no rights) are persons.
2   This compromise between the realist and the pragmatist may be something like what Putnam had in mind when he described himself as an "internal realist."
3   The Absolute Idealists said that Reality is defined by perfect knowledge, and thereby tried to give sense to the claim, common to Aristotle and Hegel, that perfect knowledge is self-knowledge. If there could be knowledge, meaning, and truth without triangulation, they would have been right. Indeed, one might say, Pickwickianly, that the idea of Absolute

Reality is precisely the idea of Reality as it would be if triangulation were not required to know it. But since triangulation *is* required, we cannot identify perfect knowledge with self-spectatorship, or with anything else. Nor can we make sense of the notion of Absolute Reality – reality under no particular description, in no particular language.

4   "The Structure and Content of Truth," p. 304. See also Ramberg, "What Davidson Said to the Sceptic": "Similarly with regard to the correspondence locution: true beliefs do correspond to reality – true beliefs are true because the world is the way it is. What we cannot say, if we are with Davidson, is that this adds anything to the claim that a belief is true; we must resist the idea that the nature of true beliefs can be illuminated by some relation which obtains differentially between truth-vehicles and particular ontological structures."

5   Portions of this "Response" have appeared previously in "Davidson between Wittgenstein and Tarski", *Critica* vol. 30, no. 88 (April, 1998), pp. 49–71.

Richard Rorty: Selected Publications

Books

Note: Bold type indicates that a translation in that language has appeared. Regular type indicates that a translation is in preparation, but has not yet been published.

The Linguistic Turn (ed.), University of Chicago Press, Chicago, 1967 (second, enlarged, edition, 1992).

Exegesis and Argument: Essays in Greek Philosophy presented to Gregory Vlastos (co-editor with Edward Lee and Alexander Mourelatos), Van Gorcum, Amsterdam, 1973.

Philosophy and the Mirror of Nature, University of Princeton Press, Princeton, 1979 (translations: **Chinese, German, Italian, Spanish, Portuguese, French, Serbo-Croat, Japanese, Polish, Russian, Korean,** Greek, Bulgarian, Slovak, Turkish, Hebrew).

Consequences of Pragmatism, University of Minnesota Press, Minneapolis, 1982 (translations: **Italian, Japanese, Serbo-Croat, French, Spanish, Korean**).

Philosophy in History (co-editor with J. B. Schneewind and Quentin Skinner), Cambridge University Press, Cambridge, 1985 (partial translation: **Spanish**).

Contingency, Irony, and Solidarity, Cambridge University Press, Cambridge, 1988 (translations: **German, Italian, Spanish, Dutch, Danish, French, Portuguese, Hungarian, Serbo-Croat, Turkish, Korean, Polish, Russian, Bulgarian, Chinese, Swedish, Romanian,** Greek, Czech, Estonian, Latvian, Japanese).

Objectivity, Relativism and Truth: Philosophical Papers I, Cambridge University Press, Cambridge, 1991 (translations: **Italian, French, Spanish, Korean, Romanian**).

Essays on Heidegger and Others: Philosophical Papers II, Cambridge University Press, Cambridge, 1991 (translations: **Italian, Spanish, French, Hungarian, Korean**).

Hoffnung statt Erkenntnis: Einleitung in die pragmatische Philosophie, Passagen Verlag, Vienna, 1994. (This volume contains three lectures delivered in Vienna and Paris in 1993. The French version appeared as *L'Espoir au lieu de savoir: introduction au pragmatisme*, Albin Michel, Paris, 1995. A Spanish translation has appeared, and Hungarian and Russian translations are in preparation. The original English text of these lectures, slightly revised, is included in *Philosophy and Social Hope*, listed below.)

Achieving Our Country: Leftist Thought in Twentieth-Century America, Harvard University Press, Cambridge, MA, 1998 (translations: **German, Italian, Russian, Dutch, Portuguese, Spanish,** French, Korean, Chinese, Japanese, Romanian, Greek).

Truth and Progress: Philosophical Papers III, Cambridge University Press, Cambridge, 1998 (translations: German, Spanish, Romanian).

Philosophy and Social Hope, Penguin, London, 2000 (a collection of non-technical essays, as opposed to philosophical papers; it contains the English original of *Hoffnung statt Erkenntnis*).

Collections of Articles in Foreign Translation

Solidarität oder Objectivität?, Reclam Verlag, Ditzingen, 1988 (contains: 1. Solidarity or objectivity; 2. The priority of democracy to philosophy; 3. Freud and moral reflection).

Solidariteit of Objectiviteit: Drie filosofische essays, Uitgeverij Boom, Meppel, 1990 (Dutch translation of the three essays included in *Solidarität oder Objectivität?*).

Rentaito Jiyuno Tetsugaku: Nigenronno Gensoo Koete (*Philosophy of/for Solidarity and Freedom: Beyond the Illusions of Dualisms*), Iwanami Shoten, Tokyo, 1988 (contains: 1. Science as solidarity; 2. Texts and lumps; 3. Pragmatism without method; 4. The historiography of philosophy: four genres; 5. The priority of democracy to philosophy; 6. Pragmatism, Davidson, and truth).

Vérité sans pouvoir: la philosophie sans authorité, Editions de l'Eclat, Paris, 1990 (contains: 1. Pragmatism, Davidson, and truth; 2. Science as solidarity; 3. Is natural science a natural kind?; 4. Deconstruction and circumvention).

Heidegger, Wittgenstein en Pragmatisme, Uitgeverij Kok Agora, Amsterdam, 1992 (contains: 1. Pragmatism without method; 2. Texts and lumps; 3. Inquiry as recontextualization; 4. Philosophy as science, as metaphor, and as politics; 5. Heidegger, contingency, and pragmatism; 6. Wittgenstein, Heidegger, and the reification of language).

Eine Kultur ohne Zentrum: Vier philosophische Essays, Reclam, Stuttgart, 1993 (contains: 1. Is natural science a natural kind?; 2. Non-reductive physicalism; 3. Heidegger, Kundera, and Dickens; 4. Deconstruction and circumvention).

Chung Wei Literary Monthly, 22/7 (December 1993) (a Rorty issue containing Chinese translations of: 1. Trotsky and the wild orchids; 2. A pragmatist view of rationality and cultural difference; 3. Feminism and pragmatism; 4. Deconstruction; 5. Comments on Eco).

Hou Zhe Xue Wen Hua (*Towards a Post-Philosophical Culture*), Shang Hai Yi Wen Chu Ban She, Shanghai, 1991 (contains Chinese translations of: 1. Introduction to *Consequences of Pragmatism*; 2. Philosophy as science, as metaphor, and as politics; 3. Is natural science a natural kind?; 4. Deconstruction; 5. Anti-essentialism and the literary left; 6. The priority of democracy to philosophy; 7. Postmodernist bourgeois liberalism; 8. Pragmatism, Davidson, and truth; 9. Pragmatism, relativism, and irrationalism; 10. Science as solidarity).

La Svolta Linguistica, Garzanti, Milan, 1994 (contains Italian translations of: 1. Metaphysical difficulties of linguistic philosophy; 2. Why does language matter to philosophy? – ten years later; 3. Twenty-five years later).

Scritti sull'educazione, a cura di Flavia Santoianni, La Nuova Italia Editrice, Florence, 1996 (contains a new preface as well as: 1. Hermeneutics, general education and teaching; 2. Education, socialization, and individuation).

Articles and Reviews

Note: Initials of book titles in parentheses indicate that the piece was reprinted in *Consequences of Pragmatism* (CP) or *Objectivity, Relativism, and Truth* (ORT) or *Essays on Heidegger and Others* (EHO).

1959

a. "Review of Alan Pasch's *Experience and the Analytic: A Reconsideration of Empiricism,*" *International Journal of Ethics* (October 1959), 70, pp. 75–7.

1960

a. "Review of John Blewett's (ed.) *John Dewey: His Thought and Influence,*" *Teacher's College Record* (October 1960), 62, pp. 88–9.
b. "Review of David L. Miller's *Modern Science and Human Freedom,*" *International Journal of Ethics* (April 1960), 70, pp. 248–9.

1961

a. "Pragmatism, categories, and language," *Philosophical Review* (April 1961), 70, pp. 197–223.
b. "Recent metaphilosophy," *Review of Metaphysics* (December 1961), 15, pp. 299–318.
c. "The limits of reductionism," in I. C. Lieb (ed.), *Experience, Existence, and the Good,* Southern Illinois University Press, 1961, pp. 100–16.
d. "Review of Raymond Aron's *Introduction to the Philosophy of History,*" *The New Leader* (December 25, 1961), pp. 18–19.

1962

a. "Review of Edward C. Moore's *American Pragmatism: Peirce, James, and Dewey,*" *International Journal of Ethics (Ethics)* (January 1962), 72, pp. 146–7.
b. "Review of W. D. Lamont's *The Value Judgment,*" *Journal for the Scientific Study of Religion* (Fall 1962), 2, pp. 139–40.
c. "Realism, categories, and the 'linguistic turn'," *International Philosophical Quarterly* (May 1962), 2, pp. 307–22.
d. "Second thoughts on teaching communism," *Teacher's College Record* (April 1962), 63.

1963

a. "Review of Paul Goodman's *Utopian Essays and Practical Proposals,*" *Teacher's College Record* (May 1963), 64, pp. 743–4.
b. "The subjectivist principle and the linguistic turn," in George L. Kline (ed.), *Alfred North Whitehead: Essays on His Philosophy*, Prentice-Hall, New Jersey, 1963, pp. 134–57.
c. "Matter and event," in Ernan McMullin (ed.), *The Concept of Matter*, Notre Dame University Press, 1963, pp. 497–524. (A revised version appears in L. Ford and G. Kline (eds.), *Explorations in Whitehead's Philosophy*, Fordham University Press, New York, 1983, pp. 68–103.)
d. "Empiricism, extensionalism, and reductionism," *Mind* (April 1963), 72, pp. 176–86.
e. "Review of Victor Lowe's *Understanding Whitehead,*" *Journal of Philosophy* (April 25, 1963), 60, pp. 246–51.
f. "Review of Brand Blanshard's *Reason and Analysis,*" *Journal of Philosophy* (September 12, 1963), 60, pp. 551–7.
g. "Comments on Professor Hartshorne's paper," *Journal of Philosophy* (October 10, 1963), 60, pp. 606–8.

1964

a. "Review of Edward H. Madden's *Chauncy Wright and the Foundations of Pragmatism,*" *Philosophical Review* (April 1964), 73, pp. 287–9.

b. "Questions to Weiss and Tillich," in Beatrice and Sidney Rome (eds.), *Philosophical Interrogations*, Holt, Rinehart and Winston, 1964, pp. 266–7, 369–70, 392–3.

c. "Review of H. D. Lewis's *Clarity is not enough: Essays in Criticism of Linguistic Philosophy*," *International Philosophical Quarterly* (1964), 4, pp. 623–4.

1965

a. "Mind–body identity, privacy, and categories," *Review of Metaphysics* (September 1965), 19, pp. 24–54. (Also in S. Hampshire (ed.), *Philosophy of Mind*, Harper & Row, New York, 1966, pp. 30–62; and in David M. Rosenthal (ed.), *Materialism and the Mind–Body Problem*, Prentice-Hall, New Jersey, 1971, pp. 174–99; and in John O'Connor (ed.), *Modern Materialism: Readings on Mind–Body Identity*, Harcourt, Brace & World, New York, 1969, pp. 145–74.)

1966

a. "Aristotle," in Walter D. Scott (ed.), *The American Peoples' Encyclopedia, vol. 2*, Spencer Press, 1966, pp. 399–400.

b. "Review of John F. Boler's *Charles Peirce and Scholastic Realism: A Study of Peirce's Relation to John Duns Scotus*," *Philosophical Review* (January 1966), 75, pp. 116–19.

1967

a. "Introduction," in Richard Rorty (ed.), *The Linguistic Turn*, University of Chicago Press, Chicago, 1967, pp. 1–39.

b. "Intuition," in Paul Edwards (ed.), *The Encyclopedia of Philosophy, vol. 4*, Macmillan and Free Press, 1967, pp. 204–12.

c. "Relations, internal, and external," in Paul Edwards (ed.), *The Encyclopedia of Philosophy, vol. 7*, Macmillan and Free Press, 1967, pp. 125–33.

d. "Review of James W. Cornman's *Metaphysics, Reference, and Language*," *Journal of Philosophy* (November 23, 1967), 64, pp. 770–4.

e. "Do analysts and metaphysicians disagree?" *Proceedings of the Catholic Philosophical Association* (1967), 41, pp. 39–53.

1970

a. "Review of Wilfrid Sellars' *Science and Metaphysics: Variations on Kantian Themes*," *Philosophy* (March 1970), 45, pp. 66–70.

b. "In defense of eliminative materialism," *Review of Metaphysics* (September 1970), 24, pp. 112–21. (Also in David M. Rosenthal (ed.), *Materialism and the Mind–Body Problem*, Prentice-Hall, New Jersey, 1971, pp. 223–31.)

c. "Strawson's objectivity argument," *Review of Metaphysics* (December 1970), 24, pp. 207–44.

d. "Cartesian epistemology and changes in ontology," in John E. Smith (ed.), *Contemporary American Philosophy*, Humanities Press, New York, 1970, pp. 273–92.

e. "Incorrigibility as the mark of the mental," *Journal of Philosophy* (June 25, 1970), 67, pp. 399–429.

f. "Wittgenstein, privileged access, and incommunicability," *American Philosophical Quarterly* (July 1970), 7, pp. 192–205.

1971

a. "Verificationism and transcendental arguments," *Nous* (Fall 1971), 5, pp. 3–14.

b. "Review of A. J. Ayer's *The Origins of Pragmatism: Studies in the Philosophy of Charles Sanders Peirce and William James*," *Philosophical Review* (January 1971), 80, pp. 96–100.

1972

a. "Functionalism, machines, and incorrigibility," *Journal of Philosophy* (April 20, 1972), 69, pp. 203–20.
b. "Dennett on awareness," *Philosophical Studies* (April 1972), 23, pp. 153–62.
c. "The world well lost," *Journal of Philosophy* (October 26, 1972), 69, pp. 649–65 (CP).
d. "Review of Stanley Rosen's *Nihilism*," *The Philosophy Forum* (1972), 11, pp. 102–8.
e. "Indeterminacy of translation and of truth," *Synthese* (March 1972), 23, pp. 443–62.

1973

a. "Criteria and necessity," *Nous* (November 1973), 7, pp. 313–29.
b. "Genus as matter: a reading of metaphysics Z-H," in R. Rorty, E. N. Lee, and A. P. O. Mourelatos (eds.), *Exegesis and Argument: Essays in Greek Philosophy Presented to Gregory Vlastos*, Van Gorcum, Assen, 1973, pp. 393–420.

1974

a. "More on incorrigibility," *Canadian Journal of Philosophy* (September 1974), 4, pp. 195–7.
b. "Matter as goo: comments on Grene's paper," *Synthese* (September 1974), 25, pp. 71–7.

1976

a. "Keeping philosophy pure," *The Yale Review* (Spring 1976), 65, pp. 336–56 (CP, chapter 2).
b. "Realism and reference," *The Monist* (July 1976), 59, pp. 321–40.
c. "Realism and necessity: Milton Fisk's *Nature and Necessity*," *Nous* (September 1976), 10, pp. 345–54.
d. "Overcoming the tradition: Heidegger and Dewey," *Review of Metaphysics* (December 1976), 30, pp. 280–305 (CP, chapter 3).
e. "Professionalized philosophy and transcendalist culture," *The Georgia Review* (1976), 30, pp. 757–69 (CP, chapter 4).
f. "Review of Michael Oakeshott's *On Human Conduct* and Roberto Mangabiera Unger's *Knowledge and Politics*," *Social Theory and Practice* (Fall 1976), 4, pp. 107–16.

1977

a. "Wittgensteinian philosophy and empirical psychology," *Philosophical Studies* (March 1977), 31, pp. 151–72.
b. "Dewey's metaphysics," in Steven Cahn (ed.), *New Studies in the Philosophy of John Dewey*, University of New England Press, 1977, pp. 45–74 (CP).
c. "Review of Ian Hacking's *Why does Language Matter to Philosophy?*" *Journal of Philosophy* (July 1977), 74, pp. 416–32.
d. "Derrida on language, being, and abnormal philosophy," *Journal of Philosophy* (November 1977), 74, pp. 673–81.

1978

a. "Epistemological behaviorism and the de-transcendentalization of analytic philosophy," *Neue Hefte fur Philosophie* (1978), 14, pp. 117–42. (Also in Robert Hollinger (ed.), *Hermeneutics and Praxis*, University of Notre Dame Press, 1985, pp. 89–121.)
b. "A middle ground between neurons and holograms?" *The Behavioral and Brain Sciences* (1978), 2, p. 248.

c. "Philosophy as a kind of writing: an essay on Derrida," *New Literary History* (Fall 1978), 10, pp. 141–60 (CP).

d. "From epistemology to hermeneutics," *Acta Philosophica Fennica* (1978), 30, pp. 11–30 (chapter 7 of *Philosophy and the Mirror of Nature*).

1979

a. "Transcendental argument, self-reference, and pragmatism," in Peter Bieri, Rolf-P. Horts-man, and Lorenz Kruger (eds.), *Transcendental Arguments and Science*, D. Reidel, Dordrecht, 1979, pp. 77–103.

b. "The unnaturalness of epistemology," in Donald Gustafson and Bangs Tapscott (eds.), *Body, Mind, and Method: Essays in Honor of Virgil C. Aldrich*, D. Reidel, Dordrecht, 1979, pp. 77–92.

1980

a. "Pragmatism, relativism, and irrationalism," *Proceedings and Addresses of The American Philosophical Association* (August 1980), 53, pp. 719–38 (CP).

b. "Idealism, holism, and the 'paradox of knowledge'," in P. A. Schilpp (ed.), *The Philosophy of Brand Blanshard*, Open Court, La Salle, IL, 1980, pp. 719–38.

c. "Kripke vs. Kant" (review of Saul Kripke's *Naming and Necessity*), *London Review of Books* (September 4, 1980), pp. 4–5.

d. "On worldmaking" (review of Nelson Goodman's *Ways of Worldmaking*), *The Yale Review* (1980), 69, pp. 276–9.

e. "Reply to Dreyfus and Taylor," *Review of Metaphysics* (September 1980), 34, pp. 39–46.

f. "A discussion" (with Dreyfus and Taylor), *Review of Metaphysics* (September 1980), 34, pp. 47–55.

g. "Searle and the secret powers of the brain," *The Behavioral and Brain Sciences* (1980), 3, pp. 445–6.

h. "Freud, morality, and hermeneutics," *New Literary History* (Fall 1980), 12, pp. 177–85.

1981

a. "Is there a problem about fictional discourse?" *Funktionen Des Fictiven: Poetic und Hermeneu-tik* (1981), Fink Verlag, Munich (CP).

b. "Review of J. D. Lewis and R. L. Smith's *American Sociology and Pragmatism*," *Review of Metaphysics* (1981), 35, p. 147.

c. "Reply to Professor Yolton," *Philosophical Books* (1981), 22, pp. 134–5.

d. "Nineteenth-century idealism and twentieth-century textualism," *The Monist* (1981), 64, pp. 155–74 (CP).

e. "From epistemology to romance: Cavell on skepticism," *Review of Metaphysics* (1981), 34, pp. 759–74 (CP).

f. "Beyond Nietzsche and Marx" (review of three books by or about Foucault), *London Review of Books* (February 19, 1981), pp. 5–6.

g. "Method, social science, and social hope," *The Canadian Journal of Philosophy* (1981), 11, pp. 569–88 (CP).

h. "Being business" (review of Roger Waterhouse's *A Heidegger Critique*), *Times Literary Supplement* (July 3, 1981), p. 760.

i. "Review of Edward Shils' *The Calling of Sociology and Other Essays*," *Review of Metaphysics* (1981), 35, pp. 167–8.

1982

a. "Philosophy in America today," *The American Scholar* (1982), 51, pp. 183–200 (CP).

b. "From philosophy to post-philosophy" (interview), *Radical Philosophy* (Fall 1982), pp. 10–11.

c. "Persuasive philosophy" (review of Robert Nozick's *Philosophical Explanations*), *London Review of Books* (May 20, 1982), pp. 10–11.

d. "Introduction," *Consequences of Pragmatism*, University of Minnesota Press, 1982, pp. xiii–xlvii. (Reprinted as "Pragmatism and philosophy" in K. Bayles, J. Bohman, and T. McCarthy (eds.), *After Philosophy*, 1987, pp. 26–66. Abridged version appeared as 'The fate of philosophy', *The New Republic* (October 18, 1982), pp. 28–34.)

e. "Contemporary philosophy of mind," *Synthese* (November 1982), 53, pp. 323–48. (Reprinted as "Mind as ineffable" in Richard Elvee (ed.), *Mind in Nature* (Nobel Conference 17, 1982), pp. 60–95.)

f. "Comments on Dennett," *Synthese* (November 1982), 53, pp. 181–7.

g. "Brute and raw experience" (review of A. J. Ayer's *Philosophy in the Twentieth Century*), *The New Republic* (December 6, 1982), pp. 33–6.

h. "Hermeneutics, general studies, and teaching," *Synergos* (1982), 2, pp. 1–15.

1983

a. "Unsoundness in perspective," (review of R. Schacht's *Nietzsche* and G. DeLeuze's *Nietzsche and Philosophy*), *Times Literary Supplement* (June 17, 1983), pp. 619–20.

b. "Against belatedness" (review of Hans Blumenberg's *The Legitimacy of the Modern Age*), *London Review of Books* (June 16, 1983), pp. 3–5.

c. "What are philosophers for?" *The Center Magazine* (September/October 1983), pp. 40–4.

d. "Pragmatism without method," in Paul Kurtz (ed.), *Sidney Hook: Philosopher of Democracy and Humanism*, Prometheus Books, Buffalo, 1983, pp. 259–73 (ORT).

e. "Postmodernist bourgeois liberalism," *Journal of Philosophy* (October 1983), 80, pp. 583–9 (ORT).

f. "The pragmatist" (review of Jacques Barzun's *A Stroll with William James*), *The New Republic* (May 9, 1983), pp. 32–4.

1984

a. "A reply to six critics," *Analyse & Kritik* (June 1984), 6, pp. 78–98.

b. "Habermas and Lyotard on post-modernity," *Praxis International* (April 1984), 4, pp. 32–44. (Also in R. J. Bernstein (ed.), *Habermas and Post-Modernity*, Polity Press, Cambridge, 1985, pp. 161–76 (EHO).)

c. "Heidegger Wider den Pragmatisten," *Neue Hefte fur Philosophie* (1984), 223, pp. 1–22 (EHO).

d. "Deconstruction and circumvention," *Critical Inquiry* (September 1984), 11, pp. 1–23 (EHO).

e. "Solidarity or objectivity," *Nanzan Review of American Studies* (1984), 6, pp. 1–19. (Also in John Rajchman and Cornel West (eds.), *Post-Analytic Philosophy*, Columbia University Press, New York, 1985, pp. 3–19. Presented as "Relativism," the Howison Lecture at UC Berkeley, January 31, 1983 (ORT).)

f. "Signposts along the way that reason went" (review of Jacques Derrida's *Margins of Philosophy*), *London Review of Books* (February 16, 1984), pp. 5–6.

g. "Introduction" (with Schneewind and Skinner), in R. Rorty, J. B. Schneewind, and Q. Skinner (eds.), *Philosophy in History*, Cambridge University Press, Cambridge, 1984, pp. 1–14.

h. "The historiography of philosophy: four genres," in R. Rorty, J. B. Schneewind, and

Q. Skinner (eds.), *Philosophy in History*, Cambridge University Press, Cambridge, 1984, pp. 49–75.

i. "What's it all about?" (review of John Searle's *Intentionality*), *London Review of Books* (May 17, 1984), pp. 3–4.

j. "Life at the end of inquiry" (review of Hilary Putnam's *Realism and Reason: Philosophical Papers III*), *London Review of Books* (August 2, 1984), pp. 6–7.

1985

a. "Feeling his way" (review of *The War Diaries of Jean-Paul Sartre November 1939–March 1940*), *The New Republic* (April 15, 1985), pp. 32–4.

b. "The humanities: asking better questions, doing more things" (interview), *Federation Review* (March/April 1985), 8, pp. 15–19.

c. "Comments on Sleeper and Edel," *Transactions of The Charles S. Peirce Society* (Winter 1985), 21, pp. 40–8.

d. "Le Cosmopolitanisme sans emancipation: réponse à Jean-François Lyotard," *Critique* (May 1985), pp. 569–80; 584 (ORT).

e. "Review of Ernst Tugendhat's *Traditional and Analytical Philosophy: Lectures on the Philosophy of Language*," *Journal of Philosophy* (1985), 82, pp. 720–9.

f. "Philosophy without principles," *Critical Inquiry* (March 1985), 11, pp. 132–8. (Also in W. J. T. Mitchell (ed.), *Against Theory*, University of Chicago Press, Chicago, 1985, pp. 132–8.)

g. "Texts and lumps," *New Literary History* (1985), 17, pp. 1–15 (ORT).

h. "Absolutely non-absolute" (review of Charles Taylor's *Philosophical Papers*), *Times Literary Supplement* (December 6, 1985), pp. 1379–80.

1986

a. "The contingency of language," *London Review of Books* (April 17, 1986), pp. 3–6 (chapter 1 of *Contingency, Irony, and Solidarity*).

b. "The contingency of selfhood," *London Review of Books* (May 8, 1986), pp. 11–14 (chapter 2 of *Contingency, Irony, and Solidarity*).

c. "The contingency of community," *London Review of Books* (July 24, 1986), pp. 10–14 (chapter 3 of *Contingency, Irony, and Solidarity*).

d. "Freud and moral reflection," in Joseph H. Smith and William Kerrigan (eds.), *Pragmatism's Freud: The Moral Disposition of Psychoanalysis*, Johns Hopkins University Press, Baltimore, 1986, pp. 1–27 (EHO).

e. "Should Hume be answered or bypassed?" in A. Donegan (ed.), *Human Nature and Natural Knowledge: Essays Presented to Marjorie Grene*, D. Reidel, Dordrecht, 1986, pp. 341–52.

f. "From logic to language to play," *Proceedings and Addresses of The American Philosophical Association* (1986), 59, pp. 747–53.

g. "The higher nominalism in a nutshell, a reply to Henry Staten," *Critical Inquiry* (1986), 12, pp. 462–66.

h. "On ethnocentrism: a reply to Clifford Geertz," *Michigan Quarterly Review* (1986), 25, pp. 525–34 (ORT).

i. "Sex and the single thinker" (review of Roger Scruton's *Sexual Desire: A Moral Philosophy of the Erotic*), *The New Republic* (June 2, 1986), pp. 34–7.

j. "Pragmatism, Davidson, and truth," in E. LePore (ed.), *Truth and Interpretation: Perspectives on the Philosophy of Donald Davidson*, Blackwell, Oxford, 1986, pp. 333–68 (ORT).

k. "Foucault and epistemology," in D. C. Hoy (ed.), *Foucault: A Critical Reader*, Blackwell, Oxford, 1986, pp. 41–9.

l. "Comments on Toulmin's 'Conceptual Communities and Rational Conversation'," *Archivio di Filosofia* (1986), pp. 189–93.

m. "Freedom as higher than being," in Robert Langbaum (ed.), *Working Papers: Critique of Modernity* (April 1986), 1, pp. 16–26.

n. "Beyond realism and anti-realism," in Ludwig Nagl and Richard Heinrich (eds.), *Wo steht die Analytische Philosophie heute?*, R. Oldenbourg Verlag, Munich, 1986, pp. 103–15 (EHO).

o. "Introduction", in Jo Ann Boydston (ed.), *John Dewey: The Later Works, vol. 8: 1933*, Southern Illinois University Press, Carbondale, 1986, pp. ix–xviii.

p. "Interview with Richard Rorty," *Journal of Literary Studies / Tydskrif Vir Literatuurwetenskap* (November 1986), 2, pp. 9–13.

q. "Philosophie als Wissenschaft, als Metapher, und als Politik," in Michael Benedikt and Rudolf Burger (eds.), *Die Krise der Phänomenologie und die Pragmatik des Wissenschaftsfort-schritt*, Verlag der Österreichischen Staatsdruckeri, Vienna, 1986, pp. 138–49.

1987

a. "Non-reductive physicalism," in Konrad Cramer et al. (eds.), *Theorie der Subjektivität*, Suhrkamp, Frankfurt, 1987, pp. 278–96 (ORT).

b. "Thugs and theorists: a reply to Bernstein," *Political Theory* (November 1987), 15, pp. 564–80.

c. "Unfamiliar noises: Hesse and Davidson on metaphor," *Proceedings of the Aristotelian Society* (1987), suppl. vol. 61, pp. 283–96 (ORT).

d. "Posties" (review of Jürgen Habermas' *Der Philosophische Diskurs der Moderne*), *London Review of Books* (September 3, 1987), pp. 11–12.

e. "Waren die Gesetze Newtons schon vor Newton Wahr?" *Jahrbuch des Wissenschaftkollegs zu Berlin* (1987), pp. 247–63.

f. "Nominalismo e Contestualismo," *Alfabeta* (September 1987), 9, pp. 11–12.

g. "Science as solidarity," in John S. Nelson, A. Megill, and D. N. McCloskey (eds.), *The Rhetoric of the Human Sciences*, University of Wisconsin Press, Madison, 1987, pp. 38–52 (ORT).

1988

a. "The priority of democracy to philosophy," in Merill Peterson and Robert Vaughan (eds.), *The Virginia Statue of Religious Freedom*, Cambridge University Press, Cambridge, 1988, pp. 257–88 (ORT).

b. "Is natural science a natural kind?" in E. McMullin (ed.), *Construction and Constraint: The Shaping of Scientific Rationality*, Notre Dame University Press, 1988, pp. 49–74 (ORT).

c. "Unger, Castoriadis, and the romance of a national future," *Northwestern University Law Review* (Winter 1988), 82, pp. 335–51 (EHO).

d. "Representation, social practice, and truth," *Philosophical Studies* (1988), 54, pp. 215–28 (ORT).

e. "I Professori Sono Meglio dci Torturatori" (interview), *Alpfabeta* (March 1988), 10, p. 5.

f. "That old-time philosophy," *The New Republic* (April 4, 1988), pp. 28–33.

g. "Taking philosophy seriously" (review of Victor Farias' *Heidegger et le Nazisme*), *The New Republic* (April 11, 1988), pp. 31–4.

h. "Review of Stanley Rosen's *The Limits of Analysis*," *Independent Journal of Philosophy* (1988), vols. 5/6, pp. 153–4.

1989

a. "Two meanings of 'logocentrism': a reply to Norris," in Reed Way Dasenbrock (ed.), *Redrawing the Lines: Analytic Philosophy, Deconstruction, and Literary Theory*, University of Minnesota Press, Minneapolis, 1989, pp. 204–16 (EHO).

b. "Is Derrida a transcendental philosopher?" *Yale Journal of Criticism* (April 1989), (EHO).

c. "Identité morale et autonomie privée," *Michel Foucault Philosophe: Rencontre Internationale*, Paris, Editions du Seuil, 1989, pp. 385–94 (EHO).

d. "Review of *Interpreting Across Boundaries*, Eliot Deutsch (ed.)", *Philosophy East and West* (July 1989), pp. 332–7.

e. "Review of Arthur C. Danto's *Connections to the World: the Basic Concepts of Philosophy*," *New York Newsday Books* (March 19, 1989).

f. "Education without dogma," *Dissent* (Spring 1989), pp. 198–204. (Also as "Education, socialization, and individuation" and accompanied by "Replies to commentators", *Liberal Education* (October 1989); also in shortened form as "Truth and freedom in education," *Harper's* (June 1989).)

g. "Social construction and composition theory: a conversation with Richard Rorty," *Journal of Advanced Composition* (1989), 9, pp. 1–9.

h. "Philosophy and post-modernism," *The Cambridge Review* (June 1989), 110, pp. 51–3.

i. "Comments on Castoriadis' 'The End of Philosophy'," *Salmagundi* (Spring–Summer 1989), no. 82–3, pp. 24–30.

j. "Wittgenstein e Heidegger: due percorsi incrociati," *Lettere Intenazionale* (October–December, 1989), 22, pp. 21–6. (In English in Charles Guignon (ed.), *The Cambridge Guide to Heidegger*, Cambridge University Press, 1993 (EHO).)

k. "The humanistic intellectual: eleven theses," *ACLS Occasional Papers* (November, 1989), no. 11.

l. "Philosophy as science, as metaphor, and as politics," in Avner Cohen and Marcello Dascal (eds.), *The Institution of Philosophy*, Open Court, 1989, pp. 13–33 (EHO).

m. "Philosophers, novelists, and intercultural comparisons," to appear in the *Proceedings of the 6th East–West Philosophers Conference* (EHO).

1990

a. "The dangers of over-philosophication – reply to Arcilla and Nicholson," *Educational Theory* (1990), 40, pp. 41–4.

b. "Two cheers for the cultural left," *South Atlantic Quarterly* (1990), 89, pp. 227–34.

c. "Another possible world" (on Heidegger's Nazism), *London Review of Books* (February 8, 1990), p. 21. (Reprinted in Christoph Jamme and Karsten Harries (eds.), *Martin Heidegger: Politics, Art, and Technology*, Holmes and Meier, New York and London, 1994, pp. 34–40, and in translation in the German edition of that book.)

d. "Truth and freedom: a reply to Thomas McCarthy," *Critical Inquiry* (Spring 1990), 16, pp. 633–43.

e. "Twenty–five years after" (a postscript to 1967a, published (in Spanish translation) along with 1967a and 1977c), in G. Bello (tr.), *El Giro Linguistico*, Ediciones Paidos, Barcelona, 1990; subsequently published in English in the second edition of *The Linguistic Turn*.)

f. "Foucault/Dewey/Nietzsche," *Raritan* (Spring 1990), vol. IX, no. 4, pp. 1–8.

g. "Consciousness, intentionality, and pragmatism," in Jose Quiros (ed.), *Modelos de la Mente*, Madrid, 1990.

1991

a. "Feminism and pragmatism," *Michigan Quarterly Review* (Spring 1991).

b. "The philosopher and the prophet" (review of Cornel West's *The Genealogy of Pragmatism*), *Transition* (1991), no. 52, pp. 70–8.

c. "The guru of Prague" (review of three books by January Patocka), *The New Republic* (July 1, 1991), pp. 35–40.

d. "Just one more species doing its best" (review of four books about John Dewey), *London Review of Books* (1991).

e. "Pragmatismo" in Manuel Marchia Carrilho (ed.), *Dicionario do Pensiamento Contemporanaio*, Publicacoes Dom Quixote, Lisbon, 1991, pp. 265–78.
f. "Intellectuals in politics," *Dissent* (Fall 1991).
g. "Comments on Taylor's 'Paralectics'," in R. P. Scharlemann (ed.), *On the Other: Dialogue and/or Dialectics* (1991), Working paper # 5 of the UVa Commitee on the Comparative Study of the Individual and Society, pp. 71–8.
h. "Nietzsche, Socrates and pragmatism," *South African Journal of Philosophy* (August 1991), vol. 10, pp. 61–3.
i. "Blunder around for a while" (review of Daniel Dennett's *Consciousness Explained*), *London Review of Books* (November 21, 1991), pp. 3–6.
j. "The banality of pragmatism and the poetry of justice," in Michael Brint and William Weaver (eds.), *Pragmatism in Law and Society*, Westview Press, Boulder, CO, 1991, pp. 89–97. (This article had previously appeared in *Southern California Law Review*.)

1992

a. "The politicization of the humanities," *UVa Alumni Journal* (Winter 1992).
b. "Nietzsche: un philosophe pragmatique," *Magazine Littéraire* (April 1992), pp. 28–32 (translation of "Bloom's Nietzsche," a piece not yet published in English).
c. "The intellectuals at the end of socialism," *The Yale Review* (April, 1992), vol. 80, nos. 1 & 2, pp. 1–16. (An abbreviated version of this article appeared under the title "For a more banal politics," *Harper's* (May 1992), pp. 16–21. A longer version appeared as 1995e.)
d. "Introduction," in Vladimir Nabokov's *Pale Fire*, Everyman's Library, London and New York, 1992, pp. v–xxiii.
e. "The pragmatist's progress," in Umberto Eco et al., *Interpretation and Overinterpretation*, Cambridge University Press, Cambridge, 1992, pp. 89–108.
f. "Reply to Andrew Ross," *Dissent* (Spring 1992), pp. 265–7.
g. "What can you expect from anti-foundationalist philosophers? A reply to Lynn Baker," *Virginia Law Review* (April 1992), 78 pp. 719–27.
h. "Love and money," *Common Knowledge* (Spring 1992), vol. 1, no. 1, pp. 12–16.
i. "A pragmatist view of rationality and cultural differences," *Philosophy East and West* (October 1992), vol. 42, no. 4, pp. 581–96.
j. "Robustness: a reply to Jean Bethke Elshtain," in David W. Conway and John E. Seery (eds.), *The Politics of Irony*, St. Martin's Press, New York, 1992, pp. 219–23.
k. "The feminist saving remnant" (review of John Patrick Diggins' *The Rise and Fall of the American Left*), *The New Leader* (June 1–15, 1992), pp. 9–10.
l. "Trotsky and the Wild Orchids," *Common Knowledge* (1992), vol. 1, no. 3, pp. 140–53. (Previously appeared in French translation in *Lire Rorty* (see 1992m below); also in Mark Edmundson (ed.), *Wild Orchids and Trotsky: Messages from American Universities*, Viking, New York, 1993).
m. "Reponses de Richard Rorty" (to Jacques Bouveresse, Vincent Descombes, Thomas Mac-Carthy, Alexander Nehamas, and Hilary Putnam) in Jean-Pierre Cometti (ed.), *Lire Rorty*, Editions de l'Eclat, Paris, 1992, pp. 147–250.
n. "Dewey entre Hegel et Darwin," *Rue Descartes* (November 1992), nos. 5–6, pp. 53–71.
o. "We anti-representationalists" (review of Terry Eagleton's *Ideology: An Introduction*), *Radical Philosophy* (Spring, 1992), 60, pp. 40–2.

1993

a. "Centers of moral gravity: comments on Donald Spence's 'The Hermeneutic Turn'," *Psychoanalytic Dialogues* (1993), vol. 3, no. 1, pp. 21–8.
b. "Paroxysms and politics" (review of James Miller's *The Passion of Michel Foucault*), *Salmagundi* (Winter 1993), no. 97, pp. 61–8.

c. "Holism, intentionality, and the ambition of transcendence," in Bo Dahlbom (ed.), *Dennett and His Critics: Demystifying Mind*, Blackwell, Oxford, 1993, pp. 184–202.

d. "Feminism, ideology, and deconstruction: a pragmatist view," *Hypatia* (Spring 1993), 8, pp. 96–103.

e. "An anti-representationalist view: comments on Richard Miller, van Fraassen/Sigman, and Churchland" and "A Comment on Robert Scholes' 'Tlon and Truth'," in George Levine (ed.), *Realism and Representation*, University of Wisconsin Press, Madison, 1993, pp. 125–33; 186–9.

f. "On democracy, liberalism, and the post-communist challenge" (interview), *Mesotes: Zeitschrift für philosophischen Ost–West Dialog* (1992), 4 pp. 491–500.

g. "Review of Thomas McCarthy's *Ideals and Illusions: On Reconstruction and Deconstruction in Contemporary Critical Theory*," *Journal of Philosophy* (July 1993), XC, pp. 370–3.

h. "Putnam and the relativist menace," *Journal of Philosophy* (September 1993), XC, pp. 443–61 (previously published in French: see 1992m).

i. "Du pragmatisme en politique" (interview), *Le Banquet* (2eme Semestre 1993), no. 3, pp. 135–47.

j. "Intersubjectividad y libertad" (interview), *Theoria: Revista de Filosofia* (July 1993), vol. 1, no. 1, pp. 113–22.

k. "Human rights, rationality, and sentimentality," in Susan Hurley and Stephen Shute (eds.), *On Human Rights: The 1993 Oxford Amnesty Lectures*, Basic Books, New York, 1993, pp. 112–34. (A shortened version, without the footnotes, appeared in *The Yale Review* (October 1993), vol. 81, no. 4, pp. 1–20.)

1994

a. "Replies" (to Burzta and Buchowski, Dziemidok, Gierszewski, Kmita, Kwiek, Morawski, Szahaj, Zeidler, and Zeidler-Janiszewska), *Ruch Filozoficzny* (1994), vol. 50, no. 2 , pp. 178–9, 183–4, 188–9, 194–5, 198–200, 205–7, 209–10, 214–16, 218.

b. "Review of Richard Flathman's *Willful Liberalism: Voluntarism and Individuality in Political Theory and Practice*," *Political Theory* (February 1994), vol. 22, no. 1, pp. 190–4.

c. "The unpatriotic academy," *New York Times* (February 13, 1994), op-ed page.

d. "Why can't a man be more like a woman, and other problems in moral philosophy" (review of Annette Baier's *Moral Prejudices: Essays in Ethics*), *London Review of Books* (February 24, 1994), vol. 16, no. 4, pp. 3–6.

e. "Taylor on self-celebration and gratitude," *Philosophy and Phenomenological Research* (March 1994), vol. LIV, no. 1, pp. 197–201.

f. "Does democracy need foundations?" *Politisches Denken: Jahrbuch 1993*, Metzler Verlag, Stuttgart & Weimar, 1994, pp. 21–3.

g. "Review of Agnes Heller and Ferenc Feher's *The Grandeur and Twilight of Radical Universalism*," *Thesis Eleven* (1994), no. 37, pp. 119–26.

h. "Religion as conversation-stopper," *Common Knowledge*, (Spring 1994), vol. 3, no. 1, pp. 1–6.

i. "Tales of two disciplines," *Callaloo* (1994), vol. 17, no. 2 , pp. 575–607.

j. "Dewey between Hegel and Darwin," in Dorothy Ross (ed.), *Modernist Impulses in the Human Sciences*, Johns Hopkins University Press, Baltimore, 1994 (previously published in French; see 1992n).

k. "Sex, lies, and Virginia's voters," *New York Times* (October 13, 1994), op-ed page.

l. "A leg-up for Oliver North" (review of Richard Bernstein's *Dictatorship of Virtue: Multiculturalism and the Battle for America's Future*), *London Review of Books* (October 20, 1994), pp. 13–14. (A revised version appeared in *Harper's* for January, 1995, under the title "Demonizing the academy.")

m. "Taylor on truth," in James Tully (ed.), *Philosophy in an Age of Pluralism: The Philosophy of Charles Taylor in Question*, Cambridge University Press, Cambridge, 1994, pp. 20–36.

n. "Does academic freedom have philosophical presuppositions?" *Academe* (November/December 1994), vol. 80, no. 6, pp. 52–63. (Also in Louis Menand (ed.), *The Future of Academic Freedom*, University of Chicago Press, Chicago, 1996, pp. 21–42.)

o. "Sind Aussagen universelle Geltungsanspröche?" *Deutsche Zeitschrift für Philosophie* (1994), vol. 42, no. 6, pp. 975–88.

1995

a. "Campaigns and movements," *Dissent* (Winter, 1995), pp. 55–60.

b. "Two cheers for elitism" (a review of Christopher Lasch's *The Revolt of the Elites and the Betrayal of Democracy*), *The New Yorker* (January 30, 1995), pp. 86–9.

c. "Is Derrida a *quasi*-transcendental philosopher?" (review of Geoffrey Bennington and Jacques Derrida's *Jacques Derrida*), *Contemporary Literature* (Spring 1995), 36, pp. 173–200.

d. "Response to Steven Lukes," *Dissent* (Spring 1995), pp. 264–5.

e. "The end of Leninism and history as comic frame," in Arthur M. Melzer et al. (eds.), *History and the Idea of Progress*, Cornell University Press, Ithaca, NY, 1995, pp. 211–26 (a shortened version of this paper appeared as 1992c).

f. "Untruth and consequences" (a review of Paul Feyerabend's *Killing Time*), *The New Republic*, (July 31, 1995), pp. 32–6.

g. "Response to Hartshorne," pp. 29–36; "Response to Lavine," pp. 50–3; "Response to Bernstein," pp. 68–71; "Response to Gouinlock," pp. 91–9; "Response to Hance," p. 122–5; "Response to Haack," pp. 148–53; "Response to Farrell," pp. 189–96; "Philosophy and the future," pp. 197–205, in Herman Saatkamp (ed.), *Rorty and Pragmatism*, Vanderbilt University Press, Nashville, Tennessee, 1995. (This volume also includes "Dewey Between Hegel and Darwin," previously published as 1994j.)

h. "Is truth a goal of inquiry? Davidson vs. Wright," *Philosophical Quarterly* (July 1995), vol. 45, no. 180, pp. 281–300.

i. "Cranes and Skyhooks" (review of Daniel Dennett's *Darwin's Dangerous Idea: Evolution and the Meanings of Life*), *Lingua Franca* (August 1995), pp. 62–6.

j. "Introduction," in reprint of Sidney Hook's *John Dewey: An Intellectual Portrait*, Promotheus, Buffalo, 1995, pp. xi–xviii.

k. "Deconstruction," in Raman Selden (ed.), *The Cambridge History of Literary Criticism: volume 8, From Formalism to Poststructuralism*, Cambridge University Press, Cambridge, 1995, pp. 166–96.

l. "Toward a post-metaphysical culture" (interview), *The Harvard Journal of Philosophy* (Spring 1995), pp. 58–66.

m. "Color-blind in the marketplace" (review of Dinesh d'Souza's *The End of Racism: Principles for a Multicultural Society*), *New York Times Book Review* (September 24, 1995), p. 9.

n. "Consolation prize" (review of Kazugo Ishiguro's *The Unconsoled*), *Village Voice Literary Supplement* (October, 1995), no. 139, p. 13.

o. "A spectre is haunting the intellectuals" (review of Jacques Derrida's *Spectres of Marx*), *European Journal of Philosophy* (December 1995), vol. 3, no. 3, pp. 289–98.

p. "Habermas, Derrida, and the functions of philosophy," *Revue Internationale de Philosophie* (1995), no. 4, pp. 437–60.

1996

a. "The inspirational value of great works of literature," *Raritan* (Summer 1996), vol. 16, no. 1, pp. 8–17.

b. "Half a million blue helmets?" *Common Knowledge* (Winter 1996), pp. 10–13.

c. "Universalisme moral et tri économique," *Diogène*, (1996), no. 173, pp. 3–15. (To be published also in *Qui Sommes-Nous?: les deuxièmes rencontres philosophiques de UNESCO*.)

d. "The sins of the overclass" (review of Michael Lind, *The Next American Nation*), *Dissent* (Spring 1996), pp. 109–12.

e. "The ambiguity of 'rationality'," *Constellations* (April 1996), vol. 3, no. 1, pp. 73–82.

f. "What's wrong with 'rights'?" *Harper's* (June 1996), vol. 292, no. 1733, pp. 15–18.

g. "Something to steer by" (review of Alan Ryan's *John Dewey and the High Tide of American Liberalism*), *London Review of Books* (June 1996).

h. "Sigmund on the couch" (review of Jacques Bouveresse's *Wittgenstein reads Freud*), *New York Times Book Review* (September 22, 1996), p. 42.

i. "Fraternity reigns," *New York Times Magazine* (September 28, 1996), pp. 155–8.

j. "Duties to the self and others: comments on a paper by Alexander Nehamas," *Salmagundi* (Summer 1996), no. 111, pp. 59–67.

k. "Knowledge and acquaintance" (review of Ray Monk's *Bertrand Russell: The Spirit of Solitude, 1872–1921*), *The New Republic* (December 2, 1996), pp. 46–52.

l. "Emancipating our culture: a response to Habermas," pp. 24–30; "Relativism: finding and making," pp. 31–47; "On moral obligation, truth, and common sense," pp. 48–52; "Response to Kolakowski," pp. 58–66; "The notion of rationality," pp. 84–8, in Jozef Niznik and John T. Sanders (eds.), *Debating the State of Philosophy: Habermas, Rorty, and Kolakowski*, Praeger Publishers, Westport, 1996.

m. "Remarks on deconstruction and pragmatism," pp. 13–18; "Response to Simon Critchley," pp. 41–6; "Response to Ernesto Laclau," pp. 69–76, in Chantal Mouffe (ed.), *Deconstruction and Pragmatism*, Routledge, London and New York, 1996.

1997

a. "Back to class politics," *Dissent* (Winter 1997), pp. 31–4.

b. "Intellectuals and the millennium," *The New Leader* (February 24, 1997), pp. 10–11.

c. "Realism, antirealism, and pragmatism: comments on Alston, Chisholm, Davidson, Harman, and Searle," in Christopher Kulp (ed.), *Realism/Antirealism and Epistemology*, Rowman and Littlefield, London, 1997, pp. 149–71.

d. "Justice as a larger loyalty," in Ron Bontekoe and Marietta Stepaniants (eds.), *Justice and Democracy: Cross-Cultural Perspectives*, University of Hawaii Press, Honolulu, 1997, pp. 9–22. (Also in Luiz Soares (ed.), *Cultural Pluralism, Identity, and Globalization*, UNESCO/ISSC/EDUCAM, Rio de Janeiro, 1997.)

e. "Religious faith, intellectual responsibility, and romance" in Ruth-Anna Putnam (ed.), *The Cambridge Companion to William James*, Cambridge University Press, Cambridge, 1997, pp. 84–102.

f. "Introduction" in Wilfrid Sellars, *Empiricism and the Philosophy of Mind*, Harvard University Press, Cambridge, MA, 1997, pp. 1–12. (A slightly enlarged version of introductions previously published to French and Italian translations of the same book.)

g. "Review of Hilary Putnam, *Pragmatism: An Open Question*," *The Philosophical Review* (October 1996), vol. 105, no. 4, pp. 560–1.

h. "First projects, then principles," *The Nation* (December 22, 1997), pp. 18–21.

i. "Global utopias, history, and philosophy" in Luiz Soares (ed.), *Cultural Pluralism, Identity, and Globalization*, UNESCO/ISSC/EDUCAM, Rio de Janeiro, 1997, pp. 457–69.

j. "Review of W. J. Wilson, *When Work Disappears*," *Dissent* (1997).

1998

a. "A defense of minimalist liberalism," in Anita L. Allen and Milton C. Regan, Jr. (eds.), *Debating Democracy's Discontent: Essays on American Politics, Law, and Public Philosophy*, Oxford University Press, New York, 1998, pp. 117–25.

b. "Pragmatism as romantic polytheism," in Morris Dickstein (ed.), *The Revival of Pragmatism*, Duke University Press, Durham, N.C., 1998, pp. 21–36.

c. "Against unity" (a review article about E. O. Wilson's *Consilience*), *Woodrow Wilson Quarterly* (Winter 1998), vol. 22, no. 1, pp. 28–38.

d. "Endlich sieht man Freudenthal," *Frankfurter Allgemeine Zeitung* (February 20, 1998), p. 40. Also published as *Das Kommunistische Manifest 150 Jahre danach: Gescheiterte Prophezeiungen, glorreiche Hoffnungen*, Frankfurt, 1998.

e. "Überreden ist gut: Werkgespräch mit Richard Rorty" (interview with Wolfgang Ullrich and Helmut Meyer), *Neue Rundschau* (1998), no. 109, pp. 87–112.

f. "McDowell, Davidson, and spontaneity," *Philosophy and Phenomenological Research*, (June 1998), 58, pp. 389–94.

g. "Marxists, Straussians, pragmatists," *Raritan* (Winter 1998), pp. 128–36.

h. "Review of Rudiger Safranski's *Martin Heidegger between Good and Evil*," *New York Times* (May 3, 1998), pp. 12–13.

i. "Davidson between Wittgenstein and Tarski," *Critica: Revista hispanoamericana de Filosofia* (April 1998), vol. 30, no. 88, pp. 49–71.

j. "Pragmatism," *Routledge International Encyclopedia of Philosophy* (1998), vol. 7, pp. 632–40.

k. "Response to Stuart Rennie's 'Elegant Variations'," *South African Journal of Philosophy* (November 1998), vol. 17, no. 4, pp. 343–5.

l. "Pragmatism and law: response to David Luban," in Morris Dickstein (ed.), *The Revival of Pragmatism*, Duke University Press, Durham, N.C., 1998, pp. 304–11.

1999

a. "Pragmatism as anti-authoritarianism," *Revue Internationale de Philosophie* (1999), no. 1, pp. 7–20.

b. "Saved from hypocrisy," *Dissent* (Spring 1999), pp. 16–17.

c. "Mein Jahrhundertbuch: Freud's *Vorlesungen zur Einführung in die Psychoanalyse*," *Die Zeit* (May 20, 1999), p. 61.

d. "The communitarian impulse," *Colorado College Studies* (1999), no. 32, pp. 55–61.

e. "Not all *that* strange: a response to Dreyfus and Spinosa," *Inquiry* (March 1999), vol. 42, no. 1, pp. 125–8.

f. "Comment on Robert Pippin's 'Naturalness and mindedness: Hegel's compatibilism'," *European Journal of Philosophy* (August 1999), vol. 7, no. 2, pp. 213–16.

g. "Can American egalitarianism survive a globalized economy?" *Journal of the Society for Business Ethics* (1999), Ruffin Series, special issue no. 1, pp. 1–6.

h. "Rorty v. Searle, at last: a debate" (with John Searle), *Logos* (Summer 1999), vol. 2, no. 3, pp. 20–67.

i. "I hear America sighing" (review of Andrew Delbanco's *The Real American Dream*), *New York Times Book Review* (November 7, 1999), p. 16.

j. "Davidson's mental–physical distinctions," in Lewis Hahn (ed.), *The Philosophy of Donald Davidson*, Open Court, 1999.

k. "Aristotle had it right" (review of Stanley Fish, *The Trouble with Principle*), *The New Leader* (December 13–27, 1999), pp. 5–6.

2000

a. "Response to Randall Peerenboom," *Philosophy East and West*, vol. 50, no. 1 (2000), pp. 90–1.

Index